PAT ROBERTSON

Pat Robertson

A LIFE AND LEGACY

David Edwin Harrell Jr.

WILLIAM B. EERDMANS PUBLISHING COMPANY
GRAND RAPIDS, MICHIGAN / CAMBRIDGE, U.K.

Published 2010 by

Wm. B. Eerdmans Publishing Co.

2140 Oak Industrial Drive N.E., Grand Rapids, Michigan 49505 /

P.O. Box 163, Cambridge CB3 9PU U.K.

Printed in the United States of America

14 13 12 11 10   7 6 5 4 3 2 1

Library of Congress Cataloging-in-Publication Data

Harrell, David Edwin.

Pat Robertson: a life and legacy / David Edwin Harrell, Jr.

p.   cm.

Includes bibliographical references (p.   ).

ISBN 978-0-8028-6384-3 (cloth: alk. paper)

1. Robertson, Pat.   I. Title.

BX6495.R653H365   2010

269′.2092 — dc22

[B]

2010006417

www.eerdmans.com

Contents

—⟨øⁿ⟩—

Contents

Preface

—✦✦✦—

From one perspective, this is an "insider" book. In 2007, after the release of an American history textbook I co-authored, *Unto a Good Land,* Pat Robertson interviewed me on *The 700 Club.* Afterward, the two of us talked about his life and legacy. I told him that I would be interested in writing a definitive book about him and his ministries, but only if I were given access to his extensive personal and ministries files. After that conversation we walked through a room filled with file cabinets containing his personal correspondence and CBN records and, with a wave, he invited me to read. It was a stunning decision on his part — an extraordinary act of trust. Of course, I was not a total unknown to Robertson, having written widely, and respectfully, about America's leading evangelists for many years. Nonetheless, it was an act of confidence that surprised me and many of those closest to Robertson. After reading an early draft of several chapters, one of the senior executives at CBN quizzed me about my access to the array of sources I had cited. When I told him that I had been given free access to the files in Pat Robertson's office, he responded: "It's a miracle."

This densely documented book is the product of months of plowing through those files as well as the large body of academic and journalistic literature about Robertson. In addition, I interviewed Pat Robertson for many hours and talked extensively with members of his family and scores of people who have worked with him in the past or present. I also visited Christian Broadcasting Network regional centers on four continents, talking with scores of WorldReach and Operation Blessing workers. My access to Robertson's personal and ministries files may sometimes seem to skew the content of the book toward the thinking and explanations of Robertson and his supporters. While at times the ministry reporting was carefully crafted "spin," it represented a point of view that was shared by millions of people, offering explanations that found little voice in the media. Given this broad access to ministry sources, this could be seen as an "insider" book.

On the other hand, I have also listened to, and cited, an array of Robertson's critics, particularly his most dogged and perceptive opponents at Americans United for Separation of Church and State, People for the American Way, and Media Matters. The endnotes reflect the extent of my debt to the scores of journalists who have carefully scrutinized and criticized Robertson through the years. I have not avoided any of the controversies sparked by Robertson's often controversial writings, his highly publicized "gaffes" on *The 700 Club,* his speculative business ventures, or his most controversial political and religious views. I have tried to view both his accomplishments and failures honestly, viewing the highs and lows in his long life from the perspectives of both his friends and foes.

Personally, I am not an "insider." I am not a charismatic Christian, though after many years of studying that community, I do speak its language and understand its mindset. I also have strong sympathies with many of Robertson's political views, though I disagree with some of his most strident positions.

So this is not an "authorized" biography, or an "official" history; it is my book. Authorized books can be useful and respectable, but I have never been comfortable writing anything that gave editorial control to another party. The views expressed here are mine; no one at CBN suggested the inclusion or omission of any topic. I found it a fascinating tale of an extraordinary life and legacy.

In the "Preface" to my small campaign book, *Pat Robertson: A Personal, Political and Religious Portrait,* written in 1987, I described myself as "an old-fashioned historian with a rigid commitment to an objective study of the past": "There are no eternal verities in historical stories, but good historians write as truthfully as possible. A story well told can instruct a wide variety of people.... Telling stories objectively does not imply the absence of interpretation. This book is filled with my interpretations of Pat Robertson's motives, his meanings, and the forces that influenced him.... The validity of those interpretations depends on how logically I have used the evidence. What I have not done is offer overt judgments about the morality or the sanity of the story. That, it seems to me, is what a good historian leaves to readers."

I have studied and written about the charismatic movement of which Pat Robertson has been an important part for forty years, and I have come to know well many of his good friends who were leaders in that movement. I have always been struck by the juxtaposition of the gracious, professional atmosphere at the lovely campus of CBN and Regent University in Virginia Beach and the popular perception that the organizations founded by Robertson are sinister to the core, led by "the most dangerous man in America," a "wacko," "fascist" extremist. This seemed to me to be an irony worth exploring. How could a man so respected, indeed revered, by seemingly bright and reasonable people around the world who know him well be perceived by so many critics as an inconsequential buffoon?

In the more than two years spent researching and writing this book, nothing impressed me more than Pat Robertson's magnanimity in discussing and reading about his own life. At my request, he read early drafts of the manuscript, offering minor corrections here and there, and providing some interesting personal vignettes I had never heard before, but only half-a-dozen times did his sensibilities lead him to ask for a rewording of the text. His editorial suggestions were interesting, generally revealing old personal wounds not completely healed, but they never seemed to me to be efforts to skew the story. Mostly, he read every account of his miscues and failures, as well as his substantial successes, without comment.

Pat Robertson is neither "wacko" nor inconsequential. That has long been clear to those acquainted with the worldwide charismatic revival; Pat Robertson and the Christian Broadcasting Network carved out an important niche in that consequential story. A symbol of respectability and pedigree in the charismatic movement from the time of his tongues-speaking experience in 1956, Robertson has made important contributions to its expansion through the Christian Broadcasting Network's WorldReach, Operation Blessing, and Regent University. His innovative concept of producing high-quality, culturally sensitive Christian programming in centers around the globe has had a visible impact on the religious demography of the modern world. This mission concept, nurtured and sharpened by his son Gordon, has proven to be one of the most effective tools in the distinctively non-colonialist promotion of indigenous Christian movements in the developing world.

As this book bountifully documents, the Pat Robertson legacy is defined not by one singularly important contribution, but by the breadth of his interests. His contributions to the formation of American political thought and action in the years from 1985 to 2000 have been chronicled by friends and foes. That political persona has been the source of most of the public attacks on him. But Robertson's reach has extended far beyond politics. He was a pioneer in the development of the cable television industry, a relentless innovator in religious programming, the founder of a significant humanitarian organization, a major player in the worldwide Pentecostal/charismatic revival in the developing world, the founder and molder of a respected and well-endowed university, and the founder and patron of one of the most successful conservative legal advocacy organizations in the country. This book is the story of the stunning reach of Pat Robertson's restless mind and his dogged persistence in bringing his dreams to fruition.

The interpretative framework of this work that is likely to rouse the most controversy is my portrayal of Pat Robertson as a "centrist" rather than an extremist or radical. For those who consider all of Robertson's views, both religious and political, as fringe aberrations, the "centrist" label will no doubt raise eyebrows. However, if one accepts Pentecostal/charismatic religion as a legitimate part of the Christian tradition, as it has increasingly been perceived in the past three decades, and if one accepts the conservative Republican agenda as a part of mainstream American politics, it is important to recognize that Robertson's posture within those communities is basically centrist. That conclusion seemed more and more inevitable to me as I read through the hundreds of letters and memos in Robertson's files.

During his presidential campaign and his high-profile leadership of the Christian Coalition, Robertson exhibited a willingness to accept compromises that more rigid leaders of the religious right found objectionable. He was a pragmatic politician, seeking along with Ralph Reed a place at the table. Robertson's political compromises sparked some testy exchanges with more brittle single-issue reformers.

Religiously, Robertson has clearly been a centrist within the charismatic movement. Throughout his life he has associated with and defended some of the most radical independent Pentecostal evangelists; at the same time, he opposed a number of teachings that he considered extreme and fearlessly resisted efforts to restrict freedom of thought within the movement. Robertson embraced the broad ecumenism of the early charismatic movement and vigorously built bridges to Roman Catholics and Jews. Disenchanted by some of the radical ideas in the charismatic movement in the 1960s, for two decades Robertson insisted that he and his ministries be called "evangelical." Not until a younger collection of evangelical intellectuals at the turn of the century set out to rescue the name "evangelical" from the likes of Pat Robertson did he once again embrace the term "charismatic."

Preface

Pat Robertson is the intellectual architect of the entire array of religious, political, educational, humanitarian, and business enterprises described here, and he retains a remarkably detailed interest in them, but increasingly his legacy is in the hands of an array of lieutenants. The most conspicuous of this next generation of leaders is Gordon Robertson, Pat and Dede's youngest son. His contributions, and those of other talented leaders of the organizations envisioned by Pat Robertson, including Ralph Reed and Jay Sekulow, are duly noted in this book. But Pat Robertson is the glue that holds the story together. The other important actors in this drama have served Robertson well because they instinctively grasped and believed in his vision. That vision is a legacy that is likely to influence Christianity around the world and American politics for many years.

DAVID EDWIN HARRELL JR.
Daniel Breeden Eminent Scholar
  in the Humanities Emeritus
Auburn University

Acknowledgments

—⚜—

This book would not have been possible without the cooperation of scores of people around the world who talked openly and candidly about their experiences with Pat Robertson and the Christian Broadcasting Network. That debt will become apparent to anyone browsing through the endnotes. Most of all, I want to thank Pat Robertson and others in his family who were ever ready to make time in their busy schedules to answer questions with admirable openness.

Several people were indispensable in scheduling my time and access at CBN. G.G. Conklin, Personal Assistant to Dr. Robertson, and Barbara Johnson, Executive Assistant to Dr. Robertson, head that list of facilitators. G.G. scheduled my frequent stays in Virginia Beach with incredible efficiency; in addition, she often pointed me toward facets of this story that I might otherwise have missed. Barbara Johnson is the guardian of the gate in Pat Robertson's office. She was an invaluable guide as I made my way through the labyrinth of file cabinets in Robertson's office. No one in Virginia Beach knows more about Pat Robertson, or is more loyal to him, than these two women. Readers will find them cited frequently in the pages that follow, explaining to inquirers Pat Robertson's actions and motives. I am fortunate to have become their friend.

Other executives within the ministry were extremely helpful in guiding me to sources and acquainting me with the complex organizational structure of the Christian Broadcasting Network and its affiliated organizations. Gordon Robertson was unswervingly honest and forthcoming in his interviews and comments, and he was always ready to open doors for me within the organization. CBN President Michael Little offered valuable guidance, especially during my early weeks of research. Among Michael's suggestions when I began searching for documentary records was that I look at the personal collection of Jay Comisky, CBN Vice-President of Support Operations. Not only did Jay share his extensive collection of ministry publications with me, he also befriended me and made me feel welcome when we met at various ministry programs. Jay, along with two other vice-presidents, Joel Palser and John Turver, not only supplied me with information, but also became conversational friends.

I owe a particular debt to Gordon Robertson and the staff of WorldReach for making arrangements for me to visit the CBN regional centers in Beijing, Manila, Jakarta, New Delhi, Hyderabad, Kiev, and Abuja. This research jaunt, funded by an advance from Eerdmans, contributed much to my understanding of the impact of the Christian Broadcasting Network around the world. It would have been impossible to schedule this round-the-world venture without the assistance of WorldReach Vice-President Ben Edwards. Kim Mitchell, WorldReach Director of International Operations, met me in Abuja and was a good companion and guide.

From the very beginning of this venture, one of the most important backers of the project within the CBN organization was my old friend Vinson Synan, who is currently Professor of Church History and Dean Emeritus of the Divinity School at Regent University. I have known Vinson since I read his dissertation while teaching at the University of Georgia, where he had recently received his Ph.D. in history. Our mutual interest in Pentecostal history led to a lifetime friendship. Vinson has been a vocal supporter of the book, and he generously shared his research and thoughts with me during my months in Virginia Beach.

I am also indebted to the helpful staffs in the Special Collections divisions of the Early Gregg Swem Library on the campus of William and Mary University, where the Willis Robertson Papers are housed, and at the University Library at Washington and Lee University. I spent many hours working in the Regent University Library, where my work was facilitated by Administrative Coordinator Ellen Cox. Always ready to accommodate my requests for access to materials in the Regent University Archives were Special Collections Coordinator Robert Sivigny and Special Collections Assistant Donald Gantz.

Finally, I give my hearty thanks to the many individuals listed in the bibliography of interviews which I conducted and taped. My interviewing technique is pretty conversational, and these personal exchanges were both enjoyable and fruitful. In some cases, we talked for hours; in every case, I was impressed by the forthrightness of the conversations.

This was an arduous research journey and a complicated writing experience. It demanded that I attain some degree of expertise in the diverse worlds lived in and influenced by Pat Robertson. Tim and Gordon Robertson were excellent guides into modern media technology; Ralph Reed, Jr., Jay Sekulow, and Barry Lynn were skillful tutors offering diverse views on the politics and constitutional platform of religious conservatives. Pat Robertson was often a good instructor when I knew the right questions to ask. I express my appreciation for all who tutored me, and I accept full responsibility for any errors that remain.

Finally, I want to thank the senior management of the William B. Eerdmans Publishing Company for their support, guidance, and encouragement. We all wanted a shorter book, but Editor-in-Chief Jon Pott and others at Eerdmans never flinched in their desire to present a balanced and definitive book about Pat Robertson. Especially, I am deeply indebted to David Bratt, who has edited this book from beginning to end, performing the tedious job of improving the citations and making numerous splendid suggestions for organizational changes. David initiated my discussions with Eerdmans about the publication of this book, and he has become a valued friend in the months since we embarked on this journey together.

CHAPTER 1

Origins

—《*e/e/e*》—

It has been a matter of pride and meaning in the thinking of Pat Robertson that the "first landing" of English-speaking settlers in the New World, planting the seeds that would grow into the most powerful nation in the world in the twentieth century, was in Virginia, not Plymouth or Massachusetts Bay. At Cape Henry, on April 29, 1607, a group of English settlers came ashore and planted a cross on the Atlantic coast in what is now Virginia Beach. Reverend Robert Hunt knelt in prayer and claimed "this nation for the glory of God and propagation of the gospel from these shores to the uttermost parts of the earth." That remembrance of beginnings has surfaced repeatedly in the thinking and rhetoric of Robertson; to him, it is a matter of great consequence.[1]

Home and Family

Robertson's childhood memories of Virginia are rooted in the village of Lexington, situated near the center of the Valley of Virginia in a setting rich in both beauty and history. In 1774 Thomas Jefferson was granted a land patent that included the nearby natural rock bridge, a site where as a young man George Washington had carved his name. In 1796 Washington endowed a college that had been established in Lexington forty-seven years earlier, whereupon grateful trustees renamed the school Washington College. In 1839 Virginia Military Institute joined Washington College in Lexington; it became the oldest state-supported military college in the nation.

Other names forever associated with Lexington made it a hallowed place in Southern history. Thomas J. Jackson became professor of natural philosophy at Virginia Military Institute in 1851 before becoming one of the martyred heroes of the Confederacy. After the Civil War, Washington College became the last home and final resting place for Robert E. Lee. He accepted the school's presidency in 1865, and after his death and interment on school grounds in 1870, trustees changed the college's name again, to Washington and Lee. Thereafter, the adjoining campuses of VMI and Washington and Lee stood sentinel over the memory of the Confederate cause for generations to come.

In the years that followed, change came slowly to Lexington, befitting its status as a repository of cherished regional memories. In the census of 1930, the population of Lexington was still less than 3,800. It took another twenty years for the town to install its first traffic light. Churches raised money to support Bible teachers in the local public schools. The *Lexington Gazette* featured generous helpings of Christian teaching along with a regular column on "The American Way."[2]

In spite of the deepening Depression around the world, on March 25, 1930, the weekly edition of the *Gazette* related mostly Lexington's local news. The weather had been unseasonably warm, Virginia Military Institute had begun its spring sports activities, and local merchants were disturbed by the recent invasion of "chain stores." Anticipating the coming Easter season, the weekly Sunday School lesson featured in the newspaper took its "Golden Text" from Isaiah 9:6: "For unto us a child is born, unto us a son is given: and the government shall be upon his shoulder. . . ." And a brief note in the "Personals" section reported that "Mr. and Mrs. A. W. Robertson are the proud parents of a son, who arrived Saturday, March 22nd."[3]

Senator Absalom Willis Robertson, Pat Robertson's father, was born in Berkeley County, West Virginia, in 1887 and moved to Lynchburg, Virginia, at age three. From the beginning, Absalom Willis Robertson was a larger-than-life figure. Physically, he was an extraordinary specimen — tall and muscular, a college athlete who in later years was often seen in the United States Senate gymnasium. He was a lifelong outdoorsman who loved hunting and fishing. His affection for the outdoors extended to his political life; he introduced legislation establishing the Commission of Game and Inland Fisheries in his first year in the Virginia Senate, where he served from 1916 to 1922, and ten years later he was appointed chairman of the commission. He was formal but warm and charming, known to close associates as a captivating storyteller and to audiences around Virginia as a spellbinding orator. It was his personal charm in such settings that accounted for what would prove to be a long career in politics; one local journalist commented that by the end of his career Robertson had "hunted and prayed with everyone in the state." Never part of the Virginia Democratic Party machine, he nonetheless managed to serve six consecutive terms in the United States House of Representatives and three in the U.S. Senate, winning his final term with an unprecedented 81 percent of the vote.[4]

Senator Robertson's political career followed the arc of Southern regional politics. An early supporter of the New Deal, by 1935 he became deeply suspicious of the deficit spending the program required, and thereafter he kept a careful eye on government expenditures. Over the course of his career he claimed credit for removing billions of dollars from the federal budget, and his staff annually notified his constituents of just how much money he had saved taxpayers that year. Still, in the years immediately following World War II, he supported the Truman Doctrine granting aid to Greece and Turkey and the Marshall Plan for rebuilding Europe. Writing to his close friend Douglas Southall Freeman, editor of the Richmond *News Leader,* Robertson revealed the deeply moral context of his support for postwar economic aid for Europe:

> Like yourself, I am an Internationalist, believing that it is our manifest destiny to assume world leadership. Like yourself, I believe that a Christian nation should be influenced by humanitarian principles, as well as an enlightened self-interest, to give support and encouragement to Democratic institutions elsewhere in the world when threatened by economic distress or financial chaos as in Greece.... Naturally, I had hoped that after the end of the most destructive war of history . . . we as the greatest and most powerful Christian nation on earth would attempt to lead the world in a practical application of the principles of Christianity.[5]

Willis Robertson was a lifelong conservative. He opposed the repeal of right-to-work laws and proposed antitrust legislation to control labor unions. He opposed the 1954 Supreme Court decision outlawing public school segregation, signed the 1956 Southern Manifesto (along with more than 100 other Southern congressmen) which denounced the decision, and remained a staunch opponent of civil rights legislation during the Kennedy and Johnson administrations, though he always couched his opposition to such legislation in constitutional language. He considered himself a constitutional watchdog as well as a fiscal one. He shared with his

Southern colleagues deep-seated resentment of the federal government's encroachment on the cherished ideals of states' rights. When the Supreme Court ruled against prayer in public schools in 1962, Robertson introduced a Senate resolution challenging the ruling.

Senator Robertson was as frugal in his personal life as he was with the taxpayers' money. Throughout much of his Senate career he lived alone in a basement room in a Washington hotel while his wife kept the children in the family home in Lexington. He kept careful check on the gasoline mileage of his automobile and regularly passed down clothing to his sons. He once reminded Pat that his collect telephone calls to his mother cost about fifteen dollars each, and that four calls a month resulted in an average of two dollars a day. When the senator thoughtfully arranged a vacation for his floundering son in 1958, he considered the expense justified only because he feared Pat might suffer a breakdown that would lead to medical expenses and a loss of time from his work. All in all, he was a "formal father," recalled his grandson Timothy Robertson, a product of the "old school. . . . Women waited on him. The children were there when he wanted to see them." The Robertson family dynamics were probably somewhat dictated by age separations: the senator was married at age thirty-three and was ten years older than his wife; his first son was born when the senator was thirty-six; his younger son, Marion Gordon (Pat), was born when he was forty-three.[6]

In 1920, Willis Robertson married his cousin, Gladys Churchill Willis. She was reared in Alabama, but her father died when she was a young girl and she moved to Roanoke, Virginia, to live in the home of her brother, Holman Willis. She graduated from Hollins College with a major in music. Mrs. Robertson had a lifelong interest in genealogy, carefully documenting her ties to such colonial luminaries as James Gordon of Orange County, the wealthy and politically powerful Robert "King" Carter, and Winston Churchill. She was a member of the Colonial Dames of America, the Jamestown Society, and the Daughters of the American Revolution. In later years, her son Pat recalled that his mother "would always be talking to me about such-and-such nobleman or king who was a part of my ancestry."[7]

Gladys Robertson proved to be a charming Washington hostess, but she was always most comfortable in the large ten-room home the senator had built in an apple orchard on the outskirts of Lexington. The outbreak of World War II turned her preference for living in Lexington into a necessity. Up to that time, Washington had been the family's primary residence, but the outbreak of the war made it almost impossible to find adequate housing for the family in the city, so Mrs. Robertson and her two sons returned to Lexington. Thereafter Senator Robertson became a solitary figure in Washington, returning to Lexington and his family on weekends and when Congress was not in session. In a rare public interview, Mrs. Robertson insisted that she could best help the senator by staying close to his constituents in his home town. But in fact by that time she had become quite reclusive; as early as 1958 the senator expressed concern to his son about her health and almost total confinement to their home in Lexington.[8]

She remained in close contact with her husband and often read his speeches before they were delivered, but her change in residence signaled deeper changes in her personality and religious outlook. "After she found the Lord," recalled Pat, "the lure of glamorous parties and travel and the social scene just didn't terribly appeal to her anymore. She loved her home." In her later years Mrs. Robertson declined invitations to the White House and refused an invitation to christen the submarine James Madison. Increasingly, religion came to dominate her mind. She embraced conservative evangelical thinking and grew increasingly disgusted with the minister of the Baptist church in Lexington where she and the senator were members. In 1949, she wrote to her friend Louise Lumpkin, "He looks at most things thru the eyes of logic. If Reinhold Niebuhr puts his seal of approval on a thing . . . nothing more need be said. . . . Putting God on an entirely intellectual basis restricts me completely and smothers the free beautiful joy of sharing God." In a 1966 interview a Richmond reporter found her "outspoken about her religion," which she candidly described as "fundamentalist." She distributed tracts to the students in Lexington's colleges and befriended an array of local fundamentalist ministers, often calling them on the telephone to engage in marathon discussions on theological issues and to discuss her spiritual concerns for her husband and sons.[9]

A Privileged Upbringing

While growing up, the two Robertson sons, A. Willis Jr., called Taddy, and Marion Gordon, nicknamed Pat because of his older brother's penchant to "pat, pat, pat" the new baby boy's chubby cheeks, thought little about the inner dynamics of the family relationships. More than six years apart in age, the two sons had considerably different family experiences. Taddy was nearly grown by the time the family moved from Washington; he became a successful investment banker in Atlanta, where he gained a reputation as one of the city's most eligible bachelors before marrying late in life. He never identified closely with Lexington, and to local residents he seemed "quite reserved" compared to his ebullient younger brother. He remained close to his father, often hunting with him and offering financial advice.[10]

On the other hand, Pat's home was Lexington. He was young during the family's Washington years, and even then he spent summers in Lexington. Later he remembered fondly the "gorgeous views of nearby mountains and the fragrance of apple blossoms in the Spring, and a profusion of apples in the Fall." "[B]eing a youngster in that beautiful little town" was uniformly "pleasant." It was an ideal setting for his family's traditional values to take root. When Robertson received a letter in 1995 from Miss Marguerite Hall, one of his Sunday School teachers, he replied: "Thank you so much for the great work you did in bringing the good news of Jesus Christ and the teachings of the Bible to so many of us who were growing up at that time."[11]

During his early years, Pat Robertson had a respectful, if somewhat formal, relationship with his father, but he was the darling of his mother's eye. As a little boy, recalled his friend Matt Paxton, his mother dressed him so well and kept his childhood tresses so long that Pat needed to become a "little pugnacious" in self-defense. Always big for his age, he played with older boys; Paxton considered him "popular," "a rounder," "mischievous," and a "real social animal." Even as his mother increasingly eschewed social activities, she always created a welcoming environment for Pat's friends.[12]

In school, Pat was a precocious student; he skipped the seventh grade and seemed to revel in competing with older schoolmates. He completed the last two years of high school, from 1944 to 1946, at the McCallie School in Chattanooga, Tennessee, a respected prep school attended by generations of male heirs of the South's finest families, where he proved to be an excellent student. At McCallie Pat roomed with his Lexington friend Edwin Gaines, whose father was president of Washington and Lee. During his years at McCallie, Robertson played on the school's football team and boxed in the Golden Gloves competition. Robertson was never the outstanding athlete his father had been, but he persisted with characteristic tenacity; years later, he recalled that after losing in the finals of the novice division of the Golden Gloves, he "was given a tiny silver glove to memorialize my final moment of glory." Senator Robertson was proud of his younger son. Writing to a friend in 1945, the senator boasted that his son had lettered in boxing at McCallie and was precociously mature for his age. He also boasted that Pat had the highest average of anyone in his class even though he was the youngest student.[13]

In 1946, at age sixteen, Pat returned to Lexington to attend Washington and Lee. During his time there, the university had an enrollment of around 1,250 students. Favored by the best families of Virginia to train their sons, W & L was described by a female student who had visited the campus as "a league of fraternities, bounded by classes and surrounded by women's colleges." Her description of the typical student pretty well captured young Pat Robertson: "Washington and Lee men are very charming, well-mannered, well-dressed, slightly suave and sophisticated, and, we are told, sometimes *just too* juvenile. . . . They often carry their own cigarettes and always carry a bottle — both are very carefully guarded. They are fun, witty, fairly good dancers, and very confident of their own charm."[14]

Pat Robertson found Washington and Lee to be a perfect fit; both social success and academic success came easily. Like most of the local boys, he lived at home rather than in a fraternity house, but that did not stop his fraternity brothers from giving him a crash "post-graduate course in wild partying." He was also a member of the Gauley Bridge Hunt Club, which, contrary to its name, was "a good old boy drinking club" which inducted "all of the characters on campus." He was a steady participant in excursions to Sweet Briar and other nearby women's colleges, though he never developed any serious relationships. Yet he continued to excel as a student, earning a Phi Beta Kappa key as a junior and graduating magna cum laude in 1950 at the age of twenty.[15]

On one of these weekend excursions Robertson was a character in a story that has become part of the university's lore. The fact that Pat was a senator's son could hardly have escaped the notice of his friends and acquaintances, but such connections were not extraordinary at Washington and Lee. On their way to Sweet Briar to pick up dates, Robertson and two of his friends were pulled over by a patrolman. One friend was Fred Vinson, son of the chief justice of the United States, and the other was Robert E. Lee IV, known as Bobby.

> The state trooper said, "All right, show me your identification cards."
>
> So Pat Robertson pulled his out, and [the trooper said,] "From Lexington? Is Senator Robertson kin to you?"
>
> Pat said, "That's my father."
>
> Then to Fred Vinson, "Young man, what is your name?"
>
> "I'm Fred Vinson."
>
> He said, "That's the name of the chief justice of the Supreme Court."

Fred said, "He's my father."

And he looked in the backseat at Bobby Lee. "Well, I suppose you're going to tell me you're Robert E. Lee."[16]

Senator Robertson had promised his younger son that he would finance a summer of study in Europe if Pat earned a Phi Beta Kappa key, so immediately after graduation in June 1950 Pat departed for London, where he enrolled in a course called "The Arts in Britain Today" at the University of London. He heard T. S. Eliot read poems, watched Dame Margot Fonteyn dance at Covent Garden, and studied the paintings at the Royal Gallery. He also traveled in France and Italy, drinking in culture and good times, a carefree, high-spirited young man.[17]

It was while sitting at a sidewalk café in Paris that Pat learned that Marine reserve units were being activated because of the Korean War. Upon his graduation, Robertson and his friend Edwin Gaines had been commissioned Second Lieutenants in the Marine Corps; the two had been in a special training program during their college years, spending two summers at Marine boot camp in Quantico, Virginia. Shortly after his return to the United States, on October 2, 1950, Robertson was ordered to report for duty, and the following January Robertson found himself aboard a transport along with about ninety other young officers headed for Japan.[18]

While most of the young men, including Gaines, eventually saw combat duty in Korea, Robertson was assigned to a replacement-training command in Japan. He later was sent to Korea as assistant adjutant in division headquarters and served in a forward command post near the battle lines. Though he never was at the front, his service in a combat zone qualified him for a unit citation for combat duty, and, as he recalled, "three battle stars for 'action against the enemy.'" Robertson's career in the Marines remained a source of pride to him throughout his life; he often called on the experience for moral lessons. By the spring of 1952 he was back at Quantico, Virginia, where he received a promotion to First Lieutenant in April shortly before his discharge.[19]

Pat Robertson was admitted to Yale Law School beginning in the fall of 1952. All seemed well. Senator Robertson was thrilled to have his son home from the war and ready to face the next challenge. The senator secured a choice seat for Pat at the Democratic National Convention in Chicago in July; he commissioned a portrait of Pat in his Marine uniform, meticulously reminding his son to be sure the ribbons were colored correctly; he forwarded to Pat queries from several friends who had asked for information on behalf of their daughters. Money should not be the determining factor in a marriage, the senator wrote to his son, but the beautiful daughter of one of the nation's leading lawyers should be given serious consideration. Concerned about his son's hedonistic habits and his inability to live within his means, the senator reminded him of a family adage attributed to Pat's great-grandfather: "The tendency of everything is to be more so."[20]

From Yale to Christ

Senator Robertson was well aware of his son's appetites as Pat was poised to enter law school at Yale in 1952. He urged Pat to put behind him the frivolities of fraternity parties and get down to business in his classes. When his fall semester grades were disappointing, the senator surmised that he was spending far too much time indulging in the temptations of nearby New York and warned him that the hard-nosed faculty at Yale would oust a senator's son as quickly as they would a janitor's son.[21]

At Yale, for the first time in his life, Pat Robertson proved to be a mediocre student. His parents were disappointed, and he became disillusioned. In his first year he complained that the students trained in Northern schools were better prepared than those from the South. He suddenly found himself competing with bright young people whose approach to education had been much more serious than his own.[22]

But on the surface, through most of his three years in law school, Pat Robertson's life seemed remarkably similar to his time at Washington and Lee. He continued to be what Paxton had called him earlier: a "real social animal." He intended to make a fortune, and make it quickly. He spent the summer of 1953 working for the Senate Appropriations Committee, where he whiled away many pleasant hours chatting in his father's office, getting to know the senator better than ever before. The next summer he worked as an assistant to the tax counsel of W. R. Grace & Company in New York, a large conglomerate with worldwide interests in banking, shipping, and chemical production — an appointment for which J. Peter Grace Jr. received a note of thanks from Senator Robertson.[23]

Years later Pat Robertson recalled that he went to Yale looking for a "noble cause," only to be disillusioned by the "Legal Realists" who dominated the faculty in the early 1950s. His instructors were "skeptics who believed with Justice Holmes that the law is not a great omnipresence in the sky, but can be explained by politics, economic interests, and 'what the judge had for breakfast.'" At the time, however, these intellectual misgivings were not apparent; indeed, other problems seemed far more pressing.

Shortly after his graduation in 1955, he failed the New York bar examination — a prospect his worried father had seen coming for several months. But Pat had still more to contend with: by the time he failed the bar, he was a married young father.[24]

Pat Robertson's marriage on August 27, 1954, to Adelia (Dede) Elmer, a nursing student at Yale, was sudden and secret. Ten weeks later, their first child, Timothy, was born. When Pat's parents learned of this, they were shocked and embarrassed — especially his mother. It was hardly the prestigious union they had envisioned. The Robertsons did not meet Dede and Timothy until July 1955, when Pat brought his new family to Washington, and more months passed before the shock subsided. The senator quickly became supportive and helpful, but Dede felt that her mother-in-law never accepted her.[25]

The union had obviously been the product of strong physical attraction. Dede was working on a master's degree in nursing and encountered Pat when the law students were invited to the nursing dorm one evening for a party. He was charming and adventuresome, and she was strikingly beautiful. Dede had been a fashion model and runner-up in the Miss Ohio State contest as an undergraduate. Some family friends said she looked a great deal like Pat's mother. She was from a conservative, well-to-do family, with a grandfather who had served as a state senator in Ohio. Her family was Roman Catholic; most of them were nominal church members, but her mother was devout. Pat recalled that his mother-in-law "never liked me, having felt that Dede should have married a Catholic — a wealthy one." Instead, she ended up being married to a "selfish brute who was more interested in [himself] than in her precious daughter."[26]

Dede was, by her own admission, "a party girl" who "liked to have a good time." She was a perfect match for Pat at a party, but their hastily consummated relationship had to survive some profound strains before becoming a strong marriage. "I guess," Pat later said of their union, "it was just the appropriate time." He eventually saw his marriage to Dede as one of the best things ever to happen to him. But that insight would not come quickly or easily.[27]

The circumstances of Robertson's marriage did not become public knowledge until his presidential race in 1988. He was "hurt . . . when the date of my marriage was revealed by the media," he wrote to inquirers in later years, but he had never tried to hide his misguided conduct as a young man: "Neither Dede or I knew the Lord when we were married in August, 1954. However, we loved each other then, and have been happily married for over forty years, and have four grown children and ten grandchildren." But at the time, the decision to marry was excruciating. Before the marriage, which came in the seventh month of Dede's pregnancy, Dede and her family, whose Roman Catholic convictions eliminated abortion as an option, tried to make the best of it. She was in the middle of her second year as a graduate nursing student, so her parents kept young Timothy for nine months to allow her to graduate. Pat continued to room with three fellow students, never telling his roommates that he was married. Not until the spring of 1955 did the two begin to live together as a couple. But the string of challenges was not yet at an end. By the end of 1955, Dede discovered that she was carrying a second child.[28]

For all the turmoil, though, there was no outward sign of change in Pat Robertson's demeanor or goals. Immediately after his graduation, Robertson took a job as a management trainee with W. R. Grace & Company in New York. Assigned to the company's foreign service school to study economic conditions in South America, Robertson received assurances from Peter Grace that he had a bright future with the company.

After about nine months with Grace, Robertson left his position — and the regular salary that went with it. He later surmised that he had learned much about financial analysis during his months at Grace, but he wanted a faster climb up the ladder of success. Robertson resigned to become co-founder, co-owner, and executive of the Curry Sound Corporation, the first of many failed ventures he would begin in his lifetime. Robertson and two of his Yale law school friends launched the venture to market an electrostatic loudspeaker invented "by an overweight, eccentric, genius named Curry." The invention, Robertson later recalled, "was a marvel of high-end sound reproduction," which the group hoped to patent, but they encountered technical difficulties that doomed their effort to failure. For several months the partners rode a psychological rollercoaster as prospects rose and fell. As always, Senator Robertson offered as much support as possible. He helped expedite their quest for a patent and gave guarded advice about potential investors, but he consistently predicted that the venture was destined for failure. When the enterprise ultimately collapsed, the lesson he learned, Pat Robertson later recalled, was that "the greatest concepts can fail because of failure to recognize significant impediments to success." A penchant for high-risk business ventures would prove to be an incurable, and often costly, Robertson personality trait.[29]

Increasingly, Pat Robertson's life was not going according to plan, but he was now experiencing a stirring that would change the direction of his life once and for all. At this low point, "a longing in his heart led him to the study of the Bible and the truths of Christianity." Suddenly, surprisingly, Pat was beginning to feel a calling to become a minister.[30]

As implausible as it might have seemed at the time, given the direction his life had taken, his turn to religion was in some respects a natural one. Pat had spent his early years in the Manly Memorial Baptist Church in Lexington, attending Sunday School regularly and enjoying the church socials along with the other youngsters. Pat and his fellow young churchgoers were "good kids," recalled George Lauderdale, though "none of us were strong Christians — if Christians." His decision to enter the ministry, reported to his parents in April, pleased his father, who had idolized his own minister father, and who believed that his son could go far in any career he chose.[31]

Pat paid a visit to Lexington to discuss his decision to enter the ministry with his mother, who had been speaking with him frequently on the telephone, telling him that she was praying for his conversion. Pat's mother was delighted that he had decided to enter the ministry, but Pat was surprised to find that she "questioned his commitment to Jesus Christ." "The pulpits of America are filled with men just like you," she told her son. "There's no use going into the ministry, Pat, unless you've first surrendered your life to Him." Pat didn't need Christianity, Gladys Robertson insisted; he needed Christ.[32]

His mother touched a nerve. Robertson's dramatic career change, he later recalled, was a choice made by a troubled soul in search of peace: "It was in that period that there was just this incredible emptiness in my heart and I was looking for something better. I tried it all. I had pleasure. I had philosophy. I had made good grades. I had traveled all around the world. It looked like I was going to be able to make a lot of money. And what I wanted was just not in any of those things. And I didn't know what it was." In his confusion and depression, he even considered suicide. He was looking desperately for a dramatic change: his life needed meaning. He turned to Christianity with the same voracious appetite that had characterized his social life and his pursuit of success.[33]

Pat's mother was eager to offer him guidance. Though still a member of the Southern Baptist church in Lexington, Mrs. Robertson was already well down the fundamentalist path that would characterize her later years. She regularly gave money to a number of fundamentalist ministers and circulated their literature among Lexington university students. Among those whom she supported was an ex-Marine evangelist, Cornelius Vanderbreggen, whose tract ministry was called the Bible Truth Depot. She recommended that her son contact him for a discussion.

In May 1956, Pat met Vanderbreggen for dinner in a Philadelphia restaurant. Robertson's future contacts with Vanderbreggen were few, but he later traced his experience of being "born again" to this initial encounter. It was more Vanderbreggen's demeanor than his message that moved the troubled young Robertson. The evangelist was a staunch fundamentalist, a militant branch of evangelicalism that Robertson explored but never embraced. But he thought that the evangelist was transparently a "very fine person." Most of all, he was a classic, unabashed, born-again Christian, opening his Bible in the midst of the elegant restaurant, guilelessly probing those private innermost feelings that genteel Christians did not discuss with strangers. Robertson later recounted the conversation: "I poured my soul out to him, but when I finished, he said quietly, 'Isn't there something more? A Mohammedan could have told me what you did.'... In a moment I blurted out, 'Yes, I believe that Jesus Christ died for the sins of the world — and for my sins, too!'... I accepted Jesus as Savior. I had given my life to God earlier, but I hadn't met His Son."[34]

Perhaps the most objective quality in the subjective Christian experience of being "born again" is the personal peace that comes, the sense of beatitude, the appearance of a serene confidence in one's relationship with God. Before his meeting in Philadelphia, Robertson felt that he had known only a compartmentalized religion, an intellectual belief that was kept in its place and never allowed to surface in ways that might cause embarrassment or ridicule. What he saw in Vanderbreggen was a born-again commitment — a manner that sometimes seems rude and presumptuous to outsiders but is a living testimony of salvation to the believer. The next day, Robertson reviewed the events of the evening and embraced the evangelical meaning of what had happened. He began laughing, rejoicing that he had been saved. At the time, Dede was baffled by his behavior. But Robertson had found something that would forever change their lives.

Wanting More

Born-again Christians, as Robertson's friend Bob Slosser put it, "don't talk a lot about their private life before Christ." It is less a matter of remorse or embarrassment, and more a matter of reorientation. When an individual has experienced a rebirth, evangelical Christians believe, he or she really becomes a new person.[35]

Everyone around him saw evidence of this change in Pat Robertson.

Gladys Robertson, for one, was thrilled; this was an answer to long and fervent prayer. The senator, meanwhile, was accepting and supportive. He wrote to his son in April 1956: "If, in losing some of the material things of life to which you previously aspired, you have saved your soul, it will be an occasion for rejoicing for us all." He was pleased that Pat had plans to attend a Bible conference in Canada in July and that he was exploring enrollment at Fuller Theological Seminary in the fall.[36]

Dede, for her part, didn't know what to make of it all. The man she had fallen for as an accomplished partier seemed to disappear overnight, and when her husband poured a bottle of scotch down the drain, Dede protested, "Have you completely lost your mind?" She was pregnant, and now she felt abandoned.[37]

Meanwhile, for Pat, it wasn't enough simply to be saved while going about business as usual. With his convert's zeal, he craved to learn more. He began to explore a network of conservative evangelical organizations that took him deeper into his quest for God. Vanderbreggen recommended that he spend July at Campus in the Woods, a camp sponsored by the Canadian Inter-Varsity Fellowship at Lake of Bays, Canada, a kind of Christian boot camp designed to "train college and university students in discipling." Although Inter-Varsity was not strictly associated with the militant fundamentalist wing of evangelicalism, it did bear at least one mark of its Plymouth Brethren founders: during the summer Robertson was introduced for the first time to dispensational premillennialism, the doctrine that the world was at the end of the fifth dispensation, or age, awaiting the sixth and seventh, the biblical millennium and final judgment.

The coming year brought a variety of activities that continued to expand Robertson's horizons as a born-again Christian. Upon his return from Canada, he spent several months as a volunteer working on *The Evangel* magazine, a publication of the Faith and Work ministry established by noted evangelical Episcopalian Sam Shoemaker. The next summer he was a volunteer worker in the Billy Graham crusade in New York City, and he and Dede attended a summer camp sponsored by the Word of Life Fellowship. Headed by Jack Wyrtzen, the camp was another of those evangelical parachurch organizations designed to train young people in Christian living. During these months, he met many of the foremost evangelical leaders in the nation. While attending a presidential prayer breakfast at which his father spoke, Robertson encountered Robert Walker, editor of a widely circulated evangelical magazine, *Christian Life*. Their conversation left the eager young convert certain that he had only begun exploring the depths of God's will for his life. He remembered that his mother had urged him to seek to "be filled with the Holy Spirit."[38]

In the fall of 1956, Robertson enrolled in seminary. He had considered Fuller Theological Seminary in California, as he had mentioned to his father, and Gordon Divinity School in Massachusetts. Either institution would have placed him squarely in the burgeoning and newly respectable wing of conservative American religion coming to be called "neo-evangelicalism" (and later simply "evangelicalism"). But instead he decided to enter The Biblical Seminary of New York (which would be renamed New York Theological Seminary in 1965). New York City was a place he and Dede were already comfortable, and it offered a bracing environment in which to win souls to Christ during his years as a student.

At this seminary Robertson would encounter a distinctive version of a fundamentalist approach to the Bible. The Biblical Seminary of New York was one of the spate of more conservative schools founded around the turn of the twentieth century in response to what their founders saw as the leftward theological drift of a number of older seminaries, but The Biblical Seminary had a distinctive history and theological emphasis that set it apart from other such traditionalist schools. Founded by Wilbert Webster White, the school emphasized White's theory "that Scripture should be studied inductively and that it should occupy the central position in a theological curriculum." "Inductive Bible study," sometimes called "charting," insisted that all theological truth could be ascertained through a disciplined reading of the Scriptures. "I couldn't have found a better place," observed Robertson in later years. "It was exactly what I needed."[39]

During his three years at The Biblical Seminary, Robertson studied the Bible relentlessly, later recalling: "I just wanted more. . . . I just wanted the experiences of the New Testament church. . . . If they had miracles and they had a very close personal walk with Jesus, I wanted it too." He once again became an exemplary student, as he had been earlier in life. And he fell in with a coterie of zealous and spiritually hungry students at the seminary. The group included Dick Simmons, a Presbyterian who had already graduated from a seminary in San Francisco but had come to New York after a disappointing pastorate; his wife, Barbara; Gene Peterson, the president of the student body, who had been reared as a Pentecostal but was a Presbyterian by the time he came to the seminary; and Dick White, who had worked for Inter-Varsity at Columbia University before enrolling at the seminary. A variety of other students attended irregularly, including Su Nae Chu, the widow of a Presbyterian minister who had been "martyred" during the Korean War. What united the students, recalled Robertson, was

an "intense hunger for God." As the months passed, their meetings sometimes stretched into the afternoon, and sometimes into the evening. It
was, Robertson believed, "one of the most intense spiritual quests I have
ever seen."[40]

By the summer of 1957, the students' intense spiritual quest pointed
them toward a quest for the miraculous power of the Holy Spirit.
Pentecostalism in America traces its beginnings to the hunger of evangelicals like John Wesley and Charles Finney for the baptism of the Holy Spirit.
When it emerged as a distinct movement in the early twentieth century,
the hallmark of Pentecostalism was its identification of the baptism of the
Holy Spirit with speaking in tongues (that gift was the "initial evidence"
that one had received the experience). Pentecostals also embraced the
other New Testament gifts of the Holy Spirit, such as prophecy and divine
healing. Such radical practices, as well as the poverty and cultural isola-
tion of most early-twentieth-century Pentecostals, separated them from
other evangelical Christians throughout most of the twentieth century.

In the spring and summer of 1957, Robertson and his student friends
roamed all over the city of New York, visiting numerous Pentecostal outposts and rescue missions in storefronts and dilapidated buildings. Robertson marveled at the spiritual ecstasy that enlivened weary audiences
late into the hot evenings. He watched them vanish rejoicing into the sub-
ways after experiencing the embraces of the Holy Spirit. He believed he
was seeing raw, personal, experiential religion. Robertson and his friends
wanted what they saw.

This hunger coincided — Robertson believed providentially — with a
number of interactions that shaped his spiritual quest. When Pat Robertson met Robert Walker at the presidential prayer breakfast in early 1957, he
discovered an evangelical-charismatic pioneer, one who had opened himself to the Pentecostal baptism of the Holy Spirit long before the modern
charismatic movement began. In the 1950s, Walker was a lone, quiet voice
defending the charismatic experience within evangelicalism, correctly believing that it would eventually find acceptance outside the traditional
Pentecostal denominations. In 1954, he published a trailblazing article in
Christian Life entitled "Are We Missing Something?" The article urged
evangelicals to investigate the Holy Spirit, though it did so without the use
of Pentecostal phraseology. Walker and others felt that he paid a price for
his heterodoxy, both financially and in the diminishing influence of his
magazine.[41]

A few days after his initial conversation with Robertson in Washington, Walker made a business trip to New York. Late one night he was awak-

ened by the phone in his hotel room. On the other end was Pat Robertson, asking if he could arrange an appointment to pursue further the discussion they had begun. Walker asked when he would like to meet; Robertson, as it turned out, was downstairs in the lobby. Walker invited him up, and they were soon deep in spiritual conversation. Robertson recited to Walker the "astonishing things" that had been happening in his life, and the two spent the rest of the night discussing the baptism of the Holy Spirit and the other miracles they believed they had witnessed.

Soon afterward, Robertson met Harald Bredesen, who would have an even greater impact on Pat Robertson at this impressionable moment. Bredesen had always been attracted to celebrity, frequently dropping the names of movie stars, politicians, and other wealthy and powerful people he had met. When he saw Robertson at an annual banquet sponsored by Christian Soldiers, Inc., an inner-city mission that had appointed Robertson to its board, he was intrigued by this energetic senator's son, and when the speeches were over, he rushed to meet him.[42]

Before meeting Robertson, Bredesen's life had been a mix of high hopes and floundering realities. Born into a family of Lutheran ministers, he graduated from seminary but never accepted a Lutheran pastorate. From there his life became a bizarre and mostly downward spiritual spiral. He set out to make a fortune and failed; he wandered as a religious vagabond in Florida ministering to the Jesus people and flower children; he lived alone in a boardinghouse in Pine Bluff, Arkansas, where he was threatened by the Ku Klux Klan after being accused of harboring prostitutes; and he finally returned to New York City, accepting a job in public relations shortly before meeting Robertson. Bredesen was bright and literate (Senator Robertson later introduced one of his papers into the *Congressional Record* as "a timely sermon by a brilliant young pastor of Mount Vernon, N.Y."), but there was an engaging, childlike simplicity about his faith. When Pat Robertson met him, Bredesen had fought more spiritual battles than most Christians fight in a lifetime.[43]

Like Walker, Bredesen had sought the baptism of the Holy Spirit before it gained wider acceptance. He initially encountered Pentecostalism while a student assistant pastor in a Lutheran church in North Dakota, and he was struck by the difference between the cold and dying denominationalism in the church he pastored and a live, experiential religion he had glimpsed in the homes of Pentecostal friends. In 1946 — long before the emergence of the modern charismatic movement — he attended a Pentecostal camp meeting, and shortly thereafter spoke in tongues. He later wrote that in 1946 "not one pastor of the historical

churches had ever received the baptism with the Holy Spirit . . . and survived in the historic church." Bredesen did not lose his ordination, partly
because he had friends in the church's administrative offices and partly because he was not actively employed by a church. But for many years he remained a charismatic oddity submerged in a historic denomination. He
found fellowship mostly in independent Pentecostal circles, but he was
constantly looking for adventuresome evangelicals who might be willing
to listen to his testimony about his experience with the Holy Spirit.[44]

Bredesen and Robertson discovered that they were taking the same
subway home after the banquet, and on the journey home they began to talk
about the religious quest they had in common. It turned out the two men
had in common a connection with Robert Walker; Bredesen and Walker had
been friends for some time, having met at a convention of the National Association of Evangelicals and compared notes on the baptism with the Holy
Spirit. Bredesen shared their conversation with Robertson. The next morning, Bredesen appeared unexpectedly at Robertson's apartment, having rid-
den his bike across town to continue the visit. He left behind a copy of a book
by Pentecostal minister J. B. Stiles on the gifts of the Holy Spirit, and Robertson invited Bredesen to meet with the student group at the seminary.

As the seminary students' quest intensified, Bredesen began to supply
knowledge and enthusiasm. He introduced the group to Paul Morris, the
minister of the Hillside Avenue Presbyterian Church in Jamaica, who had
himself experienced the baptism of the Holy Spirit. They began holding
regular meetings at the Hillside Church. One by one, the students spoke in
tongues; by the time Robertson graduated in the spring of 1959 sixteen of
the seminary students had claimed the baptism of the Holy Spirit.
Bredesen was ever present, instructing and encouraging.

In the charged environment of this religious pursuit, Robertson began
to doubt the validity of his boyhood baptism. He sought a rebaptism from
Bredesen, who was so overcome by the experience that, as he later said,
"the glory of the Lord came down on me," and he gushed forth in tongues.
Robertson's first experience of speaking in tongues happened privately. He
returned home from school one day to find his son Tim sick with a high fe-
ver. Unable to contact a doctor, he prayed. In the midst of the prayer, he
suddenly became conscious that he was "speaking in another language," a
language he later believed to be an "African dialect." This was the experience that Robertson had been pursuing for months. It defined him in the
years ahead as a "charismatic," though no one used that term at the time.[45]

In the fall of 1957 Harald Bredesen received an invitation to become
the pastor of the Dutch Reformed Church in Mount Vernon, one of New

York City's struggling mainstream churches in a decaying urban neighborhood. He immediately asked Robertson to be his assistant. Bredesen's church now became the center for the activities of the students. They spent hours together praying and fasting, exploring their newfound gifts of the Spirit. Bredesen said nothing about his charismatic beliefs and gifts when he accepted the pastorate; he and his young friends were careful not to alienate the members of the congregation who knew nothing of their spiritual explorations. Robertson later believed that these tentative months taught him spiritual restraint; he learned not to push his experience on others who did not understand it or want it. For nearly two years the group of young people met clandestinely, behind the massive stone walls and double-locked doors of the Mount Vernon church. Their meetings, joked the young Robertson, were reminiscent of those of "the disciples who locked the doors" for fear of persecution. Not only did they speak in tongues, but they experimented with the whole range of "Spirit-led worship." Quaker-like, they would "wait on God" until someone received an impulse to lead a song, or pray, or read a passage of Scripture, or prophesy. In these early meetings, Robertson often exercised a gift of prophecy that was to mark his later career.

As graduation drew nearer, the students' search for deeper spirituality became more frenetic. On March 22, 1959, they met to celebrate Pat's twenty-ninth birthday. Harald Bredesen began to speak in tongues and then interpreted the message. It was, he said, a divine directive to share their knowledge of the gifts of the Spirit with Ruth Stafford Peale, the wife of Norman Vincent Peale, the Dutch Reformed Church's most famous minister. It was a bold idea; Bredesen had never had any association with the Peales. Nonetheless, he called Mrs. Peale, told her that he needed to discuss some church business with her, and then announced that he wanted to explain to her the baptism of the Holy Spirit. She replied that she could not help with his church business, but that she was interested in hearing what he had to say about speaking in tongues.

After dinner with Mrs. Peale in her Fifth Avenue apartment, Bredesen, Robertson, and Dick Simmons gave an exhibition of speaking in tongues and told of their personal spiritual experiences, and Robertson gave a prophecy. Mrs. Peale was impressed, if not convinced; she pondered the discussion after she left to attend an editorial meeting of *Guideposts* magazine, one of the most widely circulated religious magazines in the world. At that meeting she urged John Sherrill, senior editor of *Guideposts,* to write a story about speaking in tongues. Sherrill contacted Bredesen and thus began a career that made Sherrill the most important publicist in introducing the early charismatic Christian movement to broader audiences. His two books, *They Speak with Other Tongues,* written after his initial encounter with the New York group, and *The Cross and the Switchblade,* written after Bredesen and Simmons introduced him to the inner-city rescue work of Assembly of God minister David Wilkerson, sold millions of copies and awakened many mainstream Protestants and Roman Catholics to the charismatic experience. "We were just students," recalled Robertson, "and we wanted God," but they were present at the beginning of a momentous modern religious movement. Looking back on the evening with Ruth Stafford Peale, Bredesen came to believe, along with many others, that "The charismatic renewal may have begun that night."[46]

On the Sunday that Pat Robertson preached his final sermon as assistant minister at Mount Vernon, Bredesen made public the student group's charismatic beliefs. In one of their evening meetings, Bredesen had begun "twirling around like a dervish," shouting that God wanted him to reveal their secret before his congregation on Pentecost Sunday. The students were ready; they were excited and "gung-ho," Bredesen later recalled, but he was "scared stiff" that he would be fired on the spot. The promised revelation came immediately after Robertson finished his lesson. Bredesen rose and began to speak in tongues and to interpret. The congregation was stunned. But Bredesen's public acknowledgment did not end in disaster. In fact, in the next few years, the Mount Vernon church became a center of the charismatic movement.[47]

Bedford-Stuyvesant

Robertson graduated from The Biblical Seminary in May 1959 unsure of what to do next. He was offered several pastorates, including one Methodist church in New York City that offered an attractive salary, but he did not "feel led" to accept a job. Among the churches Robertson considered was the Classan Avenue Presbyterian Church in the Bedford-Stuyvesant section of Brooklyn. The old church auditorium seated 1400 people, but on a typical Sunday fewer than fifty people attended services. He turned down an offer to become pastor of the church, but recommended his friend Dick Simmons. Simmons accepted and moved his family into the decaying old church manse, which was located next to a house of prostitution.[48]

Robertson explored several different options that summer, but with no success. He was turned down in his bid to serve as a missionary of the Dutch Reformed Church. He visited Norman Grubb, head of Worldwide

Evangelization Crusade, hoping to join that ministry, but to no avail. Then, while Dede was away visiting her family in Ohio, Pat sold their furniture, gave a portion of the money to needy people in Bedford-Stuyvesant, and moved in with the Simmons family. This impulsive act of charity was triggered by his reading of a passage in Isaiah: "Sell all you have and give alms." When he told Dede what he had done, she was frantic, wondering how they would live. The entire family, now including three children, took up residence in one room in the Simmons manse, which also housed fellow student Dick White and an assortment of vagabonds.[49]

It was a difficult time, but Dede did not become embittered about her husband's spiritual choices; indeed, she now began to share them. She received the baptism of the Holy Spirit while attending a Bible study at Paul Morris's church. Yet in spite of her spiritual transformation, she did not feel at home in the physical surroundings her husband had chosen. "I wasn't meant to live in a commune," she later remembered. "I don't like sharing my husband and children with anyone else. I had to live with rats, mice, roaches, and even bedbugs." She wanted to leave, but the more she prayed about it, the more she realized that "if I left Pat I would never be happy because I'd be going against Jesus. At that point I gave up and let Jesus take over." Still, when her mother came to visit, she was horrified, and she tried to persuade her daughter and grandchildren to leave with her.[50]

While Dede suffered, Pat gamely joined Simmons in trying to minister to the poor, racially-mixed neighborhood. The senator's son invested himself as best he could in the mission, which he believed in wholeheartedly, but he was an odd fit in this setting. Nonetheless, when the brothel next door went up for sale, Robertson considered buying it and turning it into a mission.

Dede became more and more restive in this environment, and Pat's father was growing increasingly horrified at what was going on as well. Pat's migration from hedonistic Yale student to forced marriage to failed businessman to religious zealot had strained his relations with his father, who was always fearful it would kick back on him to pay the clean-up costs. He constantly reminded his son that he was not a wealthy man and that he could ill afford to take on obligations of failed businesses. Nonetheless, even when most chagrined by his son's conduct, the senator gave loving encouragement, along with practical advice based on careful research. He never accepted charismatic theology, but he tried to understand it; he requested a copy of famed evangelical radio minister Donald Grey Barnhouse's series on "Signs and Wonders," boning up on a skeptical evangelical perspective on the question.[51]

Senator Robertson explored a variety of options to try to get his son suitably settled. Because Harald Bredesen was an ordained minister in a mainstream church, the senator saw him as a potential ally in giving sound guidance to his son, and he frequently talked with him on the telephone seeking help. He queried his friend Dr. L. Nelson Bell, Billy Graham's father-in-law, about the background of the Dutch Reformed Church and whether ordination in that denomination would allow Pat's appointment to a position in Presbyterian churches. As graduation approached, the senator fervently advised his son to seek ordination and secure a preaching position that would allow him to establish a normal life for his family. In April, his father talked with the chief of naval chaplains and assured Pat that he was a prime candidate for a well-paying job as a Marine chaplain. By June, he urged Pat not to rush into anything just to relieve himself of the financial burden he was carrying, but he also sent a notice about the need for rural ministers in Virginia.[52]

Back to Virginia

In August, Pat and his family visited his mother in Lexington, still without a job and without ordination, but with an invitation to speak to a Bible Presbyterian church and on a local radio station. The senator wrote that he did not know what he was doing in Lexington, or what he planned to do, but suggested that at least he should help his mother with the dishes. His mother, who had no doubt been instrumental in arranging the preaching appointment, was overjoyed. She wrote to a friend, "You cannot imagine what it has meant to me seeing my own dear boy so often these past four weeks, and hearing him on radio each day."[53]

The visit to Lexington was a welcome respite for Pat, Dede, and the children from the challenges of Bedford-Stuyvesant. But it was not a triumphant return for the promising youngster who had left Washington and Lee with a Phi Beta Kappa key in 1950. He came home subdued, his future unresolved. To his former friends he seemed "serious and solemn." He had ample reason to be seriously depressed, but from all appearances, he was not. Internally he was resolute, even though his life was filled with doubt and tension. He was at peace with himself and with God, and he was waiting for God's direction, as he had learned to do in those meetings with his fellow students. Mrs. Robertson seemed to understand. That summer, she told friends, her son "walked softly before the Lord."[54]

Her patience, along with her son's, paid off; what happened next would lead the Robertson family into a dramatic new chapter of their lives. Gladys Robertson's contacts with the conservative Presbyterian churches of Rockbridge County in the 1950s had renewed her acquaintance with George Lauderdale, a former high school classmate of Pat's who was pastoring a rural church in Norfolk, Virginia. Lauderdale became one of the targets of Mrs. Robertson's marathon telephone calls; he listened sympathetically as she told in great detail of Pat's "zeal for the Lord," as well as her concerns about the spiritual welfare of the senator. That contact proved to be monumentally important.

A year earlier, while preaching a series of mission sermons in Portsmouth, Virginia, Lauderdale had heard about a local UHF television station that offered free time to preachers. He sought out the rickety station located on Spratley Street in Portsmouth and was offered free time if his program included a gospel music segment. It was an unpromising beginning, but Lauderdale resigned his pastorate and moved his family to Portsmouth. Lauderdale worked to support himself and preached in the evenings, but by the summer of 1959 it was clear that his future on television was not going to work out. On August 2, 1959, the television station closed without warning. It had been a fly-by-night operation that, Lauderdale thought, the owner had used as a tax deduction to balance his profitable automobile business. The owner, Tim Bright, asked Lauderdale if he would be interested in buying the station. The impoverished Lauderdale frankly admitted that he could not entertain such an idea, but he immediately thought of his conversations with Mrs. Robertson and about his old friend Pat. He told Bright he had a friend who might be interested, assuming that the senator's son would have no problem raising the needed financial backing. In a letter to Mrs. Robertson, Lauderdale included a casual but portentous inquiry, remembered later by both parties as a postscript, asking if Pat might be interested in buying a television station that was for sale. Mrs. Robertson informed her son. He seemed uninterested, but the idea lingered in the back of his mind during the summer of 1959.[55]

During his summer visit to Lexington, Robertson crossed paths with Lauderdale. It was one of those coincidental meetings that born-again Christians attribute to providence. Lauderdale had reluctantly driven to Lexington from Norfolk to be executor of the estate of one of his former parishioners. He was also responding to a dream he had a few days earlier instructing him that his work in the Lexington area was not finished. Robertson later labeled his friend's experience a "vision," though Lauderdale believed it was "just a dream." The two met each other outside the Lexington post office and greeted one another as old friends. Robertson was on his way to the local radio station, WREL (named for Robert E. Lee), where two Christian businessmen had arranged for Pat to preach each day. Lauderdale accompanied him and led a prayer during the broadcast, and then the two old friends talked about the television station that had just been closed. Lauderdale thought that Pat seemed only mildly interested; he had no idea that his old classmate had not a penny of his own to invest in such a venture.[56]

After they returned to New York City, Pat and Dede occasionally discussed the television idea. Pat showed signs of anxiety about the future, no doubt heightened by his wife's misery and his father's concern over their situation. In October he took seven cans of fruit juice and a sleeping bag into the Classen Avenue Presbyterian Church and began a seven-day "prayer vigil seeking God's guidance." In his autobiography he wrote: "That week, fasting and praying alone in the gloom and murkiness of that old church, I learned as much about the depths of Scripture as I had learned in three years in the seminary." In the midst of his prayer, "God led me to a verse in the Bible that said, 'Thou shalt not take a wife or have children in this place.'" Jeremiah 16:2, Robertson has frequently told audiences, "was one of the most beautiful verses I'd ever seen because it enabled me to leave that part of the world." He later recalled: "I met with the Lord during that extraordinary time. He gave me my ministry office in the church; He told me that I should go and claim the airwaves.... He told me that I would be an 'intercessor.'"[57]

The time had come to leave Bedford-Stuyvesant. In a few weeks, he and his family were on their way to Virginia for good. He and Dede packed the three children into their 1953 DeSoto and their few possessions in a U-Haul trailer, and their friends gathered around to pray and send them off. Harald Bredesen telephoned to tell him that God had given him a prophetic verse: "The Lord, before whom I walk, will send his angel with thee, and prosper thy way." Surrounded by Dick and Barbara Simmons, "who had been used by God to succor us in a time of need," and an array of friends "who had sat with me on the ash heap of despair and discouragement while we waited for God to speak," the Robertsons headed into the future. It was a happy journey. Pat had been delivered from "the fear that one day [God] might send me to minister in a slum," and "God had brought Dede to a point of yieldedness" so that she could stand beside Pat "as a true partner in the ministry." Enduring the trials, Dede later recalled, she grew from being "Daddy's little girl to being a woman."[58]

The family arrived in Portsmouth with seventy dollars in cash (thanks to Pat's mother) and no visible means of support. They rented an unfurnished apartment, splurged to buy a turkey for Thanksgiving, and invited George Lauderdale and his family for dinner, passing out placemats to sit on in the absence of dining room furniture. As he neared thirty years of age, Pat Robertson believed — correctly, as it turned out — that he had reached the end of his tortuous search for deeper meaning.[59]

CHAPTER 2

Christian Broadcaster

—◦◦◦—

Improbable Triumph, 1960-68

To someone with less faith and better judgment, the Robertsons' journey from New York to Portsmouth to acquire a television station would have seemed sheer folly. The first ominous sign came when Robertson immediately tried to contact Tim Bright, the owner of the defunct television station; Bright was out of town and would not return until January. In the meantime, family funds dwindled. Dede got a weekend job nursing at the local hospital, and George Lauderdale arranged some preaching appointments at several small churches in the Tidewater area for Pat that offered meager, but welcome, pay. One church paid him a seventy-five-pound bag of soybeans. For the Robertson family, soybeans became the "staff of life."[1]

The gloomy prospects did not abate when Pat and Dede investigated matters further. Shortly after arriving in Portsmouth, Pat and Dede found the building where the station had been; it was dilapidated on the outside, windows had been broken out, and the inside had been vandalized. But Robertson did not lose heart. He finally met the owner, Tim Bright, at the station on January 3, 1960. He informed Bright that God had sent him to buy the station; Bright, whom Robertson described as "a middle-aged country boy from the coal-mining section of Virginia," dryly asked how much God was willing to pay for it. His asking price for the television station was $50,000. Robertson offered $37,000, with no cash down, for a six-month option on the station. Knowing Robertson's family background, Bright assumed that there was a safety net behind the offer.[2]

But the safety net Bright had in mind was deeply skeptical. Senator Robertson saw only folly in the venture; he wrote sternly to his son that making the trip to Portsmouth would be a waste of time, since he had no money to invest. He researched with experts the potential of UHF television and of Pat's scheme to finance the station with contributions, and everyone he consulted agreed that it was totally unworkable. Senator Robertson implored Harald Bredesen to "talk some sense into my boy," and he wrote to his son asking him to consult Bredesen before making any commitments, but for all the respect Senator Robertson had for Bredesen, he had chosen the wrong person to persuade his son to be practical and responsible. His disappointing son seemed bent on yet another reckless act.[3]

Relations between father and son were further strained by Senator Robertson's misgivings about Pat's new charismatic beliefs. "Don't tell me you can do this through prayer," the senator replied to his son when told that the venture would succeed by faith. When he reluctantly accepted the fact that the business was going to be launched, he urged Pat and Lauderdale to try to get the support of the "leading ministers of Norfolk," only to be politely told by his son that they might disagree about the identity of the "leading ministers." The senator was repelled by his son's new charismatic vocabulary and his claims of divine leading. Things would get better later, but not before father and son had some barbed exchanges that betrayed the unwavering common sense of the senator and the unquenchable charismatic faith of his son.[4]

Robertson's charismatic faith made relations difficult with others as well. When he arrived in the area, he visited a number of the churches seeking help for the new television station, but was rebuffed by several congregations because of his charismatic beliefs. In the 1960s, nearly all mainstream denominations still looked upon the gifts of the Holy Spirit as dangerous extremism.

But Robertson found support when he visited the Freemason Street Baptist Church, a prestigious old Southern Baptist congregation in downtown Norfolk. There Robertson was hired as the minister of education at a salary of $100 a week. The pastor of the church was Dr. William L. Lumpkin, former pastor of the Manly Memorial Church in Lexington, track coach at Lexington High School, and a close and respected friend of Senator and Mrs. Robertson. A few weeks after he was hired, in a ceremony attended by his father and mother and other political dignitaries, Pat was ordained by Dr. Lumpkin and two other Baptist ministers. Pat's father was understandably relieved that his son had finally become ordained in a respectable church — and gainfully employed. Robertson proved to be popular with the young people of the church; he did his work well, recalled Lumpkin in later years, although he was "a little overzealous" in his efforts to "convert the church members." But the job was far more important to Robertson than to the church. It provided an opportunity to repair his relationship with his father, it provided for his family's necessities, and it gave him time to get his television station on the air.[5]

The Christian Broadcasting Network (CBN) was formally chartered on January 11, 1960. Robertson did the necessary legal work, but he made it clear to his friend George Lauderdale "that the Lord Jesus Christ is the head of this thing." The new organization's by-laws included a "Statement of Faith" that was conventionally fundamentalist in its belief that "the Holy Bible is the inspired, infallible, and authoritative source of Christian doctrine and precept," conspicuously charismatic in its belief that "the Holy Spirit indwells those who have received Christ for the purpose of enabling them to live righteous and godly lives," and evangelical in its belief that "the mission of the church is worldwide evangelization on the one hand and the nurture and discipline of Christians on the other." Jigger Jackson, an old friend of Lauderdale's, sent three one-dollar bills to support the enterprise, the first contribution received by CBN, and Robertson opened a bank account with the donation. It was all "absolutely insane talk," recalled Lauderdale years later, "unless he was sure enough speaking the word of faith. And he was."[6]

Robertson assembled a five-person board composed of Dede, Bredesen, Lauderdale, Robert Walker, and himself. Bredesen and Lauderdale were obvious choices because they had been privy to the venture from the beginning. When Pat contacted Walker, the aspiring broadcaster confessed that his plans were so grandiose and nebulous that he needed some "way-out guys" to help him. The four men on the board met for the first time in January 1960 during a Full Gospel Business Men's Convention in Washington, D.C. Late in the evening, in a hotel storage room, the new board approved the constitution and signed the articles of incorporation for the Christian Broadcasting Network. Demos Shakarian, the founder and president of the Full Gospel Business Men's Fellowship, came by to encourage the venture — but only spiritually, not financially.[7]

When Robertson received his permit from the FCC for UHF television broadcasting, he announced that his television station would use the call letters WTFC (Television For Christ) and that the station would open by December 1960. But the call letters Robertson had selected had already been assigned to another station, and the station was still far from opening at the end of 1960. The second choice for call letters for the station, WYAH, was no less symbolic: these were the first three letters in *Yahweh,* the Hebrew name for God.

Even though the venture now had a name, it was still a far-fetched dream, at least in financial terms. In February 1960, Robertson's friend from New York who had mentored him in charismatic theology, Paul Morris, paid him a visit and brought an $8,000 check for the network from his personal funds — becoming, in Harald Bredesen's words, "the unsung hero" in the founding of CBN. Robertson received his permit to broadcast from the FCC on November 2, 1960, but his hope of opening the station before Christmas was crushed when a donor withdrew a $31,000 pledge he had been counting on. The situation became dire enough in early 1961, when Robertson met with the CBN board, that he was seriously considering selling the network to the Tidewater school board. He had received an offer that would pay all his debts and net a $30,000 profit. But bolstered by the faith of his board and by a $500 pledge forwarded to him in Washington by a donor who called himself "A Repentant Procrastinator," he returned to Virginia and printed 30,000 copies of a newspaper he called *The Christian Viewer* with the headline, "God's Decision: No Sale!" In an editorial he wrote, "We should all be grateful that the Board of Directors have sensed that it still remains the will of the Lord to put station WYAH-TV on the air." Gifts trickled in, and Robertson made the decision to lease the television tower at a rental rate that would repay his total investment within eight years.[8]

As the new announced opening date of October 1, 1961, drew close, it appeared the station would have to postpone once again because a $10,000 debt to RCA had not been paid. But Robertson insisted they must open as promised. On Labor Day 1961, the staff met for a time of prayer — in later years Labor Day became a compulsory time for employees of CBN to come together for a "time of fasting, prayer, and communion," "a time to rejoice at what God has done, and a time to get His direction for a new season of broadcasting and ministry." On the Friday before the air date, Robertson sold for $5,000 a radio station he had bought the year before, and at 12:45 Sunday, fifteen minutes before airtime, he received a $5,000 loan. "We were late getting on the air," Robertson recalled, "but we finally made it." "My name is Pat Robertson," said the smiling host in front of the camera. "Welcome to the Christian Broadcasting Network."[9]

The beginnings of the Christian Broadcasting Network were modest indeed. The television station consisted of one studio on Spratley Street, one camera, and three offices. Robert Walker was a veteran observer of wild-eyed evangelical schemes, but the first time he visited the facilities of

WYAH he privately thought, "I have seen off-the-cuff operations, but this beats them all." Ben Armstrong of the National Religious Broadcasters visited the facility in 1962, and his impression was that it "looked like something put together with coat hangers." "I wondered," he later recalled, "how anyone could have the audacity to think he could have a real program under these conditions."[10]

But in the midst of this modest beginning, Robertson had bigger plans, even if the physical resources at his disposal were unprepossessing at best. By 1962, Robertson had managed to buy back the radio station he had sold, which was housed in a makeshift, refurbished garage and furnished with worn-out turntables. Its message was transmitted from an antenna described in the legal documents as "one creosote pole." CBN's first radio broadcast aired on August 3, 1962. WXRI-FM, whose call letters were the first three letters in the Greek word for Christ, sent out a weak signal that was received only in the immediate Tidewater area.[11]

For several years, Robertson scrambled to find employees who shared his vision and who had some expertise in the broadcasting business. The original heroes in the launching of the network, Neil Eskelin, a young man with a master's degree in radio and TV programming whom Robertson met on a trip to a Full Gospel Business Men's Fellowship meeting in early 1961, and Harvey Waff, a "first-class licensed engineer," were joined by a crew of earnest volunteers. There was considerable turnover in the original staff, but all in all, Robertson was able to assemble a gifted team in the first five years of CBN's existence.[12]

In the early years, finding suitable programs was almost as difficult as attracting a competent technical crew. In 1963 the station was on the air for just three hours each evening, Tuesday through Saturday, and five hours on Sunday afternoons. The station aired all of the religious films that were available, but there were never enough to fill the time. The employees and local volunteers improvised programming ranging from puppet shows to commentaries on Sunday School lessons. Robertson spent considerable time on the air himself, discovering and honing his skills as a communicator. Interviewed on the air by Robertson one day in the early 1960s, Robert Walker was amazed at Robertson's erudition as he nonchalantly lectured the single camera on a variety of exacting theological subjects. The station also aired non-religious films occasionally to fill the time; the programs frequently were not carefully screened, and early Christian viewers had to tolerate some mildly risqué scenes.[13]

Keeping enough money coming in was the perpetual challenge of the early years. "Two paid religious broadcasts" helped financially, but mostly

they depended on "the gifts of viewers and friends." Robertson was determined to operate the stations on a noncommercial basis, funding CBN
with gifts from viewers. By 1963, however, the budget of CBN had reached
$7,000 a month, and the network desperately needed a regular source of
income. Robertson discussed with a local minister friend, Jack White, a
scheme to hold a telethon, asking 700 viewers to pledge ten dollars a
month to guarantee the monthly budget. White suggested that these supporters be called "The 700 Club." In 1963 and 1964 telephones were installed in the studio during the telethons, and viewers were asked to call in
for prayer and to make pledges. The first telethon "failed miserably," Robertson later recalled; only 350 people signed up for *The 700 Club*. The next
year's telethon was slightly more successful, resulting in $40,000 in
pledges, but still, "finances were very tight and so were spiritual results."
Nonetheless, the telethons provided the first dependable base of financial
support in the organization's history, and CBN had discovered the fundraising technique that would provide its lifeblood.[14]

In 1963 Robertson purchased a 50,000-watt transmitter for radio station WXRI, vastly extending its potential audience, and by the fall of 1964
the station had become one of the most listened-to in the area. It was an
effective tool to advertise the television station, and by 1965 the viewing
audience of WYAH was expanding steadily. Buoyed by these successes, in
1965 Robertson made significant additions to CBN's staff. Jay Arlan, who
had worked with Billy Graham's radio station in North Carolina and had
also worked for ABC, moved to Virginia to be the station manager, and
John Carraway left a local station to join WXRI.

Most notably, Robertson hired Jim and Tammy Bakker, a young couple
who had been successful itinerant evangelists in the Assemblies of God.
The Bakkers' children's program, "Come on Over," was a smashing success,
drawing a large audience of viewers every afternoon. It was a "schmaltzy
show" that made the "critics cringe," but within two years a local reporter
dubbed it the "flagship of Channel 27." The twenty-five-year-old Bakker
and his twenty-three-year-old wife, described by a ministry press release
as "cute as a button," soon became local favorites. By 1967 Bakker had been
named "Vice-President and Production Manager." By this time Jim and
Tammy had become local celebrities. They toured local shopping centers
with their "family," which included the puppets "Allie the Alligator, Allie's
6-foot 'mother,' Mr. Clown, Susy Moppet, and Dum-Dum." Their show
would eventually be renamed the "Jim and Tammy Show."[15]

The 1965 telethon was a turning point in the history of CBN, when,
Robertson recalled, "God sovereignly intervened and gave the revival we

had prayed for the past three years." In 1965, for the first time, the telethon featured a celebrity guest, Tony Fontaine; at its close CBN had received $105,000 in pledges. "We have testimonials that show it must have been God's work," Robertson told a local reporter. "Some of those pledging told us they were awakened from a sound sleep with the compelling urge to donate to our cause."[16]

Jim Bakker had a different perspective on what happened in and after the 1965 telethon. In Bakker's mind, he was the central figure in the 1965 financial breakthrough. He would eventually prove to be one of the most gifted fundraisers in modern religious history. Some of the components in his formula for financial success — a childlike willingness to expose his feelings and his financial needs to the public, a seemingly genuine faith in God's personal presence, and an emotional personality that swung from flights of rapture to fits of despair and weeping — surfaced dramatically in the 1965 telethon. Late on the final evening of the event, with the telethon still far short of the financial goal, Bakker broke down while on camera. Weeping, he told the audience that all was lost because the goal had not been reached. The spontaneity of the occasion was electric, and the cameras kept rolling long past sign-off time. The telephone lines were jammed with calls. Unable to call in on the crowded lines, scores of viewers came to the station, many with money in their hands. By the time WYAH shut down in the morning, enough money had been pledged to pay off the debts of the network and to underwrite the budget for the coming year. It became known as "the telethon that wouldn't end"; for days after the close of the telethon, viewers continued to call making pledges and, in a new and important development, asking for prayer and guidance and reporting miracles that had taken place during the telethon. In later years, the 1965 telethon remained Robertson's "most exciting experience . . . as host of the '700 Club.'" For the first time, the human beings on the television screen had made a dynamic connection with the viewers, and upon that linkage hung the spiritual and financial future of CBN.[17]

The 1966 telethon was a similar success; viewers flooded the telephones with calls offering financial support and asking for prayer. The planned weekend fundraising event was extended to ten days and reported $150,000 in pledges. The telethons became a financial bonanza. In 1967 the telethon reached the targeted $250,000 in two and a half days; the 1968 telethon brought in more than $400,000, and the targeted amount in 1969 was $480,000. The telethons increasingly featured celebrity guests, including Mahalia Jackson, the Singing Rambos, and Dale Evans.[18]

Following the successful 1966 telethon, Jim Bakker and Bill Garthwaite approached Robertson about beginning an evening program that would combine the telethon's viewer call-in system with a talk-show format. Bakker had long been intrigued by *The Tonight Show,* and the telethon success convinced him that such a format would allow the Holy Spirit to move on television. Robertson was less sure that the spirituality of the telethons could be captured on a regular basis, but he agreed to air the program, and the decision was made to call it *The 700 Club.* Bakker hosted the program for several weeks, but in Robertson's estimation, "it was terrible." He insisted that the program become a "team ministry of prayer and praise." Robertson joined the program as co-host and brought in other members of the CBN team as occasional co-hosts.[19]

In later years, Robertson and Bakker harbored differences of opinion about who contributed most to the creation of the new program. "Jim took credit for all of it," recalled Tim Robertson, "credit for a lot of the ideas that came from my dad and John Gilman." But everyone soon knew that they had struck on a successful formula: a program of prayer and ministry linked with telephone response from viewers. Beginning at 10:15 each evening, *The 700 Club* usually continued until midnight, but sometimes the hosts extended the program far into the morning hours if viewer response was strong. The early programs avoided overt charismatic demonstrations such as speaking in tongues, as did the CBN network in general, but by the late 1960s *The 700 Club* became more and more an open laboratory for Spirit-filled worship and teaching. Jim Bakker recalled that the early programs stayed "discreetly quiet about the Baptism with the Holy Spirit and speaking in tongues," but during a show in late 1967, the "presence of the Holy Spirit began to intensify in the studio." Scott Ross, a talented young broadcaster who joined CBN in the late 1960s, described the environment:

> The TV cameras and radio station in that city belong to Jesus. If an artist is on the air and an anointing falls and the Lord starts moving, the program can run five or ten hours. In this kind of broadcasting, Jesus does what He wants to do. I have seen the power of God move in those TV studios many times. One time, when a phone call came from a listener prophesying that God was going to move, Pat felt he should simply start praising Jesus there in the studio and open up the ten telephone trunk lines. Well, that night we didn't go off the air. Some of us didn't even sleep or eat. . . . The power of God fell that night, there in the studio and in the homes of the listeners, and in a five-day period that followed, 400 people accepted Christ and others received the baptism in the Holy Spirit over the phone.

During these early programs the Pentecostal spirit was so strong, recalled historian Vinson Synan, that on occasion "the whole staff was slain in the spirit."[20]

A spat between Jim Bakker and the CBN program director nearly led to Bakker's departure in 1966, until Robertson resolved the tension. Bakker would continue to contribute to the growth of CBN, but the relationship could not last, and he finally left in 1972. Bakker later claimed that he felt spiritually depleted at CBN; Tammy Faye Bakker revealed that the Bakkers never agreed with Robertson's concept of broadcasting non-religious programming. In truth, both Bakker and Robertson were ready for Bakker's departure when the time came. One journalist concluded that the rift came as "Jim and Pat were beginning to claw each other to bits in competition for the limelight." After a short and tempestuous relationship with Paul Crouch ended in a reported dispute over control of the Trinity Broadcasting Network, Bakker created his own PTL (Praise the Lord) television empire in Charlotte, North Carolina. As PTL expanded in the 1970s, Robertson was sometimes understandably peeved by its success, but he told Jamie Buckingham that, contrary to public perception, "I am very happy Jim has finally found his ministry and place in God. He has a very appealing manner on television and has led many people to the Lord." Nevertheless, Robertson told Buckingham, during his seven years at CBN Bakker "was a source of simply unbelievable contention and strife. This tendency continued when he went to California and Paul Crouch told us that the year with Jim was 'one year of hell.'" Robertson seemed content that the "responsibilities of having his own operation have seemingly brought maturity to him." He explained to a supporter who inquired about his rift with Bakker: "Unfortunately everything that The Christian Broadcasting Network does, from the name of our television program called *The 700 Club*, to the format of the program, to the nature of the affiliation with other stations, to the building of a school, . . . to the launching of a satellite earth station, and any other conceivable thing, is copied with great fanfare by PTL in Charlotte — often to the accompaniment of claims that they are first." Such conduct made it extremely "difficult to work in harmony."[21]

Partly as a reaction to PTL, the exasperated Robertson revised *The 700 Club,* turning it more and more into a magazine format. "He has copied everything else," Robertson told his son Tim, "but he can't do news." In CBN's ministry publication, Robertson spoke more obliquely about his resentment: "*The 700 Club* is God's gift to His Body and to CBN, it is an enormously powerful means of ministry, and it utilizes mass communications to the maximum. Because of this, the concept can be misused for personal advantage, and I am concerned about this from time to time. I am more concerned that keen Christian broadcasters would focus all their efforts on copying a concept which is now 13 years old, instead of asking God for a revelation uniquely suited for them." Years later, in the wake of the collapse of PTL, Robertson wrote to one inquirer: "In the case of PTL, I knew some of the things that were going on, and wrote personally to Jim about them. I did not feel, however, that it would be received well by the PTL partners if I had gone on public television to tell the world."[22]

Relations between Robertson and Bakker remained strained, although Bakker was one of the religious dignitaries to attend the opening of the CBN International Headquarters Building in 1979, and Robertson visited with him in Charlotte in the early days of his political campaign. But after the collapse of PTL in scandal, the relationship dwindled to a sad end. In public comments after Bakker's trial and sentencing, some correspondents thought Robertson judged his former friend too harshly. On the other hand, Robertson publicly insisted that Bakker's sentence was "unusually hard for the crime" and urged that the sentence be "reviewed." Some people urged Robertson to visit Bakker while he served his prison term, as Billy and Franklin Graham did, but Robertson was noncommittal: "I appreciate your concern for him and we will pray that God will direct in this matter." God never gave Robertson the nod. Outwardly, neither Robertson nor Bakker seemed to hold any lasting animosity; when Larry King pressed Bakker to vent hidden resentments against Robertson, he expressed nothing but respect. Tammy Faye was less forgiving in an interview with Larry King; she insisted to the end of her life that Robertson had stolen the idea for *The 700 Club*. When a documentary about her life made that claim, the internal reaction of CBN was "Really, *The 700 Club* was started by a move of the Holy Spirit — not by any one person."[23]

But the relationship between Robertson and Bakker was still going strong in 1965, when the newfound financial stability of CBN ushered in two unbroken decades of expansion. By the fall of 1967, in its sixth season, the television station had increased its power with a new 175,000-watt transmitter, had installed color cameras, and was on the air from 6 p.m. until midnight Monday through Saturday and from 1 p.m. to 6 p.m. on Sundays. It advertised itself as "America's only religious television station" and regularly broadcast the programs of Billy Graham, Rex Humbard, Kathryn Kuhlman, and T. L. Osborn, as well as live "gospel music singing" from the studio. But the station was never entirely religious. The variety of programs offered included "beautiful color travel adventure films" and "hunting and fishing programs" that featured "breathtaking color shots from

Alaska, India, Africa, . . . and the American West," in addition to the popular *Jim and Tammy Show,* "appearances by local ministers and music shows," and *The 700 Club.* By 1967 CBN had initiated a regular newscast. The broadcast day was extended to begin at 5 p.m. in 1968, and "at 5:30 P.M. [the station] broadcast the earliest evening edition of the news in Tidewater, with newscaster Mike Little," who in 1987 became president of CBN.[24]

In 1966, Robertson borrowed $225,000 to finance the construction of a new building to house CBN's radio and television studios; the proposed "million watt" television station would be "the most powerful broadcasting unit in the Tidewater area." At a gala dinner in the Norfolk Arena, attended by 1,200 people, Robertson unveiled the plans. Senator Robertson proudly said to the gathering, "I am glad Pat is one of you, and may God richly bless his efforts." A groundbreaking ceremony followed, featuring the vice-mayor and the director of the Chamber of Commerce. Robertson's spirits soared as he explained his more and more realistic vision of becoming a worldwide media missionary. The new facility, he announced, would allow CBN to "direct and produce Christian film footage and video tapes for use all over the world." "This tremendous expansion is the direct answer to the prayers of thousands of people in Tidewater," he told the audience. "It represents the step which will open a vast audience for Christian Broadcasting not only in Tidewater, but across the United States as well." Ground was broken on June 5, 1967. Robertson attached symbolic meaning to the date, as he often did: this was the same day the Six-Day War began in Israel, a portentous day for Robertson and those who shared his beliefs about the importance of the return of Israel to the Jews in end-times prophecy.[25]

On May 5, 1968, more than 11,000 people attended the dedication of the new facilities. "A lovely Gothic prayer chapel" was dedicated as the Gladys Churchill Robertson Prayer Chapel, in honor of Robertson's mother, who had died in April at age 70. Summarizing the achievement, Robertson pointed out that the radio station was operating on a twenty-four-hour schedule, and that the television station was poised to expand its six-hour daily schedule, with plans to "increase its production for other stations." It seemed an incredible achievement in less than a decade.[26]

In the midst of the euphoria of moving into the new facilities, at a luncheon that preceded the dedication ceremonies, Harald Bredesen delivered a startling prophecy: "The days of your beginning seem small in your eyes in light of where I have taken you, but, yea, this day shall seem small in the light of where I am going to take you, for I have ordained you to usher in the coming of My Son." Robertson later wrote: "I was dumbfounded. . . .

CBN had started from nothing, but by 1968 God's blessings were evident and everything had changed. As we entered this new building, how could it be that something even greater would eclipse this accomplishment." In fact, grander thoughts were already whirling in his mind. While still distressed following the death of his mother, during a prayer meeting with the staff, "a great spirit of confession and weeping fell on the room." Robertson began to pray fervently for the $200,000 needed to pay the debt on the new building, but "the Holy Spirit checked me" and told him: "I want you to pray for the world." The journey was just beginning.[27]

Building a Network to Claim the World, 1968-79

The brochure announcing the open house to celebrate the opening of the new "million dollar color Radio Television Center" in 1968 boldly proclaimed the global ambitions of founder Pat Robertson. "Even his critics," noted one article, "must grudgingly admit that there may be some substance in the dream of Pat Robertson . . . that one day there will extend a microphone from Tidewater that will go around the world." CBN had already applied to the FCC for a license to operate a television station in Atlanta and had plans in place to acquire other stations around the country. Robertson was happy to have met and hired Scott Ross in 1967 because he was "a close friend of such pop singing groups as The Beatles, the Rolling Stones, and Peter, Paul and Mary" and planned productions featuring such groups that would give access to "prime time on commercial stations across the country." CBN was actively exploring the possibilities of distributing its products in South America, Africa, and Asia. And, "finally, the Christian Broadcasting Network is keeping abreast of developments of the Satellite communications system." In the mind of Pat Robertson, the vision of distributing quality programming throughout the world was well defined by 1968.[28]

Less well defined, but already present in 1968, was the desire to make CBN a major presence in humanitarian relief. In response to a caller who requested aid for Navajo and Hopi Indians in northern Arizona who were "suffering through the worst disaster in the tribes' history," CBN purchased and shipped 30,000 pounds of food and clothing to the reservation. It was the beginning of a humanitarian concept that would finally mature into Operation Blessing.[29]

By 1972, when Robertson's autobiographical *Shout It from the Housetops* was published, CBN had acquired ownership of an AM radio station in

Bogotá, Colombia, *Nuevo Continente,* which, Robertson predicted, "will be the spring board for a radio and television thrust throughout South America," providing "a toehold on the world." In addition, CBN had been given five radio stations in New York state, and had acquired a license to open a UHF television outlet in Atlanta. Robertson estimated that the combined stations of the network had a potential audience of 10 million people.[30]

During the next five years, the network expanded at breathtaking speed. A television station in Dallas was added to those in Portsmouth and Atlanta, providing desperately needed additional exposure for *The 700 Club.* In 1971 advertising executive Stan Ditchfield joined CBN, and he quickly came up with the idea of syndicating *The 700 Club* to UHF stations. Syndicating programming by telephone lines was too expensive, so they "bicycled" videotapes from city to city. The first syndication was at a struggling Ted Turner station in Charlotte, where Robertson secured a block of four hours of broadcast time in return for a share of the revenues raised in CBN's Charlotte telethon. CBN began buying time on commercial television channels, adding several cities in 1972 and 1973, tripling the number of potential viewers in 1974 and doubling that number again in 1975. In 1975, for the first time, *The 700 Club* was seen in New York City, Los Angeles, and San Francisco. In addition, CBN was able to take advantage of a new medium, cable television, in which struggling stations were desperate for programming. Many of them welcomed the free offerings of CBN, so that by 1975 its programs were being shown on 1,200 cable systems. Pat Robertson and *The 700 Club* team traveled around the country conducting telethons in cities where the program appeared. In one year in the 1970s, Robertson hosted telethons in twenty-three cities while maintaining his schedule of regular appearances on *The 700 Club.* "It was absolutely exhausting," he later recalled; "we kept one of the most incredible schedules to hold the thing together."[31]

CBN had reshaped itself in many other ways by 1975. *The 700 Club,* which underwent periodic revision in format throughout its long life, changed noticeably by 1975 under the supervision of producer John Gilman. Now the program featured more sophisticated sets, a live audience, and a live band. There was a "new emphasis on music that ministers to the soul and brings worship" and a growing emphasis on "issue-oriented interviews with nationally known guests." It was a format ideally designed to take advantage of the expertise of Pat Robertson. Predictably, early guests included such Christian figures as Anita Bryant, Pat Boone, and Charles Colson, but the show also had some notable coups, including an interview with President Jimmy Carter broadcast the day after his election and an exclusive interview with Israeli Prime Minister Yitzhak Rabin on Christmas 1975.[32]

The network increasingly diversified its offerings of programs in the 1970s. By the end of the decade, its stations were laden with reruns of family oriented shows such as *Father Knows Best, The Brady Bunch, The Partridge Family, The Andy Griffith Show,* and *The Lucy Show.* The programming did not represent a change, only an improvement. Robertson had always envisioned secular programming as a means of expanding the audience for the network's religious programs. In a 1973 interview, he explained the concept that had driven his thinking from the beginning: "We feel that to be a significant factor in the market place it is necessary to draw people to watch and we have also found that wholesome programs, family situation comedies and some of the better programs of past years on television are extremely suitable for family audiences, yet at the same time, they draw tens of thousands of viewers to the station."[33]

This emphasis on diversified family programming combined in Robertson's thinking with a commitment to produce high quality original programming that was to be the hallmark of CBN throughout its history. Robertson explained to a supporter in 1973: "The programs for the Lord we are producing are of good quality. You can only do so many of them at a time. In the meantime, with the threat of open pornography coming to our screens . . . don't you feel it would be better for the children of Tidewater to watch 'Lassie' and 'Leave It To Beaver' and such other programs as an alternative?" But he was always hungry to improve the quality of CBN's original offerings. Compared to other religious programming, Robertson told a reporter in 1977, CBN's productions were "certainly a higher cut than most. But in terms of what the world does, we have a lot to learn."[34]

CBN walked a tightrope with its programming throughout the decade. Only the most discerning journalists understood the middle path that Robertson was trying to blaze — including eschewing extreme charismatic manifestations. Edward E. Plowman of *Christianity Today* reported in 1972 that "Robertson soft-pedals Pentecostalism on the air" in comparison to CBN's new competitor, Trinity Broadcasting Network, which was totally religious and loudly Pentecostal. But there was never any overt effort to hide the charismatic roots of CBN. Plowman reported that "virtually all of CBN's staff members have had the charismatic experience, beginning with Robertson," and some of them, such as Jim Bakker and Robertson's long-time sidekick on *The 700 Club,* Henry Harrison, were never adept at quenching the Holy Spirit. A programming coordinator explained to a *New York Times* reporter in 1974: "We are within the new charismatic renewal movement." A front-page story in the *Wall Street Journal* noted that the network "stresses the fundamentalist beliefs of 'charismatic' Christianity, which is grounded in the belief that the power of the Holy Ghost needs to be reawakened," while at the same time being "ecumenical in its outlook." But if overt charismatic displays were discouraged on the program, Robertson insisted in 1977 "that supernatural works of God are constantly mentioned on the show." Indeed, the emphasis remained sufficiently strong for an Alabama pastor to complain that "Bible-believing people are sick to death of having the gift of tongues crammed down their throats." Robertson urged him to "step back and look at the grandeur of His plan instead of dwelling on the differences which arise over supposed divergences from church dogma."[35]

On the other hand, CBN's hard-core Pentecostal constituency was sometimes brittle about the network's religious openness. An interview with an eighty-year-old Catholic priest on *The 700 Club* elicited "many comments," leaving Robertson feeling that his appearance "must have been a mistake." Other viewers had narrow standards of modesty that were offended by some of the programming. Responding to a complaint about a "spirit filled" singing group that had appeared, Robertson wrote: "It's funny that you found them 'leud [*sic*] and sensuous,' and I saw none of that whatsoever in what they were doing — I trust I still have the normal male sense for that kind of thing — perhaps not." Yet in spite of the sporadic complaints, Robertson insisted that most viewers understood the mission: "I am amazed, frankly, at how well these programs are accepted because the people in the Christian community realize that it is necessary to have a balanced program day. None of us can sit in church all day long."[36]

In 1975 Robertson announced yet another series of eye-catching proposals for expansion. Early that year he began negotiating for a five-acre tract of land in Virginia Beach when "suddenly God spoke," telling him: "Don't just buy five acres. Buy the entire tract of land, and build a headquarters and school for My glory." By the end of the year the deal had been closed. The initial plans called for building a $20 million CBN Center that would house studios, offices, a "prayer center," facilities for translating CBN programs into French (and eventually other languages), and a satellite earth station for international television transmission.[37]

The purchase of the Virginia Beach property was soon surrounded with symbolic meanings. A CBN researcher discovered the "little-known fact of American history" that the "first recorded Protestant prayer meeting in the New World was held by about 100 colonists on a spit of ocean beach named that day as Cape Henry." They were led by the Anglican chaplain of the Jamestown settlement, Robert Hunt. Now a part of the city of Virginia Beach, Cape Henry was only about twelve miles from the new CBN property. Robertson envisioned CBN as the fulfillment of the early settlers' desire to claim the New World for Christianity. On September 25, 1976, at the beginning of a "Seven Days Ablaze" rally held by CBN employees on the new site, Pat Robertson delivered an extended prophecy: "Yea, My people, said the Lord, before the foundation of the earth I have planned this moment. Was it not My hand which led from England those settlers who came to these shores? Has it not been My ear that heard their prayer and My heart that remembered? Are you not walking in a fulfillment of the prayer that has been prayed years before you? Was not this land sanctified and held apart for you? Did you not marvel that there is nothing built here upon this land, this beautiful land? . . . But I, the Lord your God, have assembled it for you, and I have formed it and created it for you. . . . Do not be afraid of the places that I will take you, for I AM a mighty God. . . . I have called you for this moment."[38]

Ground was broken on June 5, 1976. Robertson noted that the day was the anniversary of the beginning of the Six-Day War, when "Jerusalem came to the Jews for the first time since 586 B.C." While others might deem these concurrences to be "coincidental," Robertson increasingly came to believe "that God in some fashion called us to build in order to be ready for His last-day thrust to the nations of the world."[39]

The dedication of the new facility on October 6, 1979, was an auspicious occasion. Billy Graham was the featured speaker, and among the guests were such religious celebrities as Bill Bright, Rex Humbard, Demos Shakarian, Jim Bakker, and Oral Roberts. CBN board member (and former assistant national editor of the *New York Times*) Bob Slosser noted that the event received little coverage in the press, and that the "news people" covering the events "failed to understand the significance of the harmony experienced during that weekend by evangelicals and charismatics, Pentecostals and mainline churchmen." But Robertson was fully attuned to the central position that he and CBN had carved out to bring together a broad spectrum of the Christian community.[40]

The International Headquarters Building was an impressive accomplishment. It was an elegant Georgian structure designed by architect Archie Royal Davis, one of the nation's leading authorities on colonial architecture. The James River-type bricks and Indiana limestone exterior were complemented by a rich interior design. The building reflected in every way the privileged Virginia background of Pat Robertson. Inevitably, Robertson had to offer occasional explanations to supporters in defense of the grandeur of the structure: "The building is actually not as extravagant as it may appear. When you get inside, you can especially see that everything has been planned to be efficient and practical. . . . The premium for pretty brick versus ugly brick is about $16,000. I believe that God wants something of worldwide significance and not a shack, but at the same time we endeavored to do everything possible to hold the cost down." He cautioned the CBN staff to keep in sight their mission in the midst of the new grand surroundings: "Our center will be the finest in the television industry — but God wants in it 'a lowly people who trust in the name of the Lord.'" Built at a cost of around $10 million, it housed corporate offices, a large prayer chapel, facilities for a counseling center, and "30,000 square feet of studio space that will house production for the nation's largest syndicator of religious programming." Fully furnished, the building housed two state-of-the-art television studios and other recording facilities valued at $22 million.[41]

The foremost achievement of the Christian Broadcasting Network during the 1980s was its emergence as an important network in the modern American television industry. That accomplishment resulted from a series of bold decisions made by Robertson and from technological developments that opened the industry to latecomers. Perhaps the most far-reaching of those choices was Robertson's decision in 1976 to "install the first satellite earth station in history to be devoted to the transmission and reception of the gospel message of the Lord Jesus Christ." It was that critical decision, Robertson recalled, that took CBN "into a whole new dimension." The first broadcast was "overwhelming and very moving for all of us." Robertson's fascination with the potential of satellites, which became the basis for the financial endowment for his entire empire, was based both on intense study and research and on a religious belief that they were like angels prepared to "proclaim Christ's return." In April 1977, after signing a contract with RCA Americom, CBN began satellite transmission on a limited basis, feeding the organization's dream of soon becoming "the fourth network." The satellite earth station made possible the transmission of CBN programs to cable outlets across the nation. Although the number of potential cable viewers was still quite small in 1977, CBN quickly became a major player in the expanding industry.[42]

Satellite transmission unlocked a variety of new opportunities for CBN. In April 1977 the annual telethon was broadcast simultaneously in eighteen cities, greatly streamlining the organization's most important fundraising event. This first use of the earth station, Robertson boasted, brought "1993 souls to Christ" during the telethon. In 1977 Robertson signed a contract to begin delivering twenty-four-hour programming to cable networks over RCA SATCOM II. CBN was "the first basic cable network ever," according to Pat's son Tim, although HBO and WTBS did begin to broadcast satellite transmissions before CBN. Cable broadcasting did not dramatically expand until the 1980s, and in 1978 CBN programs were seen on cable in only about 1.5 million homes, but by 1979 that number jumped to more than 5 million households and the network claimed to be "the largest cable/satellite service in the world."[43]

From Network Builder to Christian Media Mogul, 1979-87

Pat Robertson's grandiose plans for the future reached far beyond constructing a new international headquarters building and satellite earth station. His vision of the future included plans for a CBN Institute to train workers in the radio and television industry, a CBN School of Theology, and a CBN Conference Center and Auditorium. The expansion of the cable network transformed CBN and vaulted Pat Robertson into leadership of the booming Christian charismatic movement in America.[44]

In 1978, in a move loaded with future consequences, CBN spun off its television stations and cable system into a for-profit corporation called the Continental Broadcasting Network. All of the initial stock in Continental was owned by CBN, but the independence of the network allowed more flexibility in programming and the potential to move full speed ahead into the booming cable television industry. In the future, CBN would simply buy time from Continental for its programming, as it had bought time from other outlets to air its programs. In return, the network would become a major source of income for the ministry. From the beginning, there was "some discussion about a public offering," but insiders agreed that "this would come at a later point perhaps several years down the road."[45]

By 1982 the CBN cable network had become a financially self-sufficient wing within the Robertson organization. While the religious image of CBN caused some early difficulties in selling advertising, the network's success in producing a "high quality mixture of family-oriented entertainment" became increasingly marketable. In 1987 CBN began charging cable systems that received the broadcasts. By that time, observed Tim Robertson, CBN leaders felt certain that the "cable network is going to . . . make a lot of money that can be used in the Lord's work."[46]

The success of the network was accompanied by more dramatic changes in programming: in 1981 CBN eliminated weekly religious broadcasts with the sole exception of *The 700 Club.* CBN's decision to continue distancing itself from religious "narrowcasting" was both a pragmatic and a philosophical decision. Partly, it had to do with ratings. In the late 1970s and early 1980s, the explosion of religious programming attracted increased attention from scholars, who often expressed skepticism about bloated audience claims made by the rising generation of televangelists. Sociologist William Martin asserted, "The weekly audience for syndicated television preachers is small." A spate of scholarly studies concluded that the electronic preachers were talking mostly to a shrinking body of people who already shared their beliefs. (By 1986 Jeffrey K. Hadden, one of the prominent skeptics of televangelist audience share, acknowledged that Nielsen ratings showed a "much larger" audience than he had earlier thought.) The ratings debate caught the attention of the leadership of CBN. In 1983 Robertson explained the programming changes in a letter to ministry partners: "Several years ago we tried the 'all-religious' program schedule, and found that we were reaching a very limited audience. . . . Since we changed the format to include family entertainment with a major religious emphasis, the audience increased dramatically. Instead of a few million, we are now reaching 17 million households. I feel it would be better to have a 60-second religious spot in the Super Bowl than to have 10 hours on a UHF station that nobody watches. It's a strategy, but it seems to be working."[47]

Most indicators confirmed the success of the strategy. The secularization of the network, along with changes in the format of *The 700 Club,* moved CBN outside television's religious ghetto and greatly expanded its body of viewers. In an extraordinary manifestation of the reach for a wider audience, in 1978 CBN purchased an advertisement in the *National Enquirer,* urging its readers to "Watch the TV Show that Changes Lives." The network's success was "gloriously vindicated" in October 1986, when "during just two weeks we saw 12,000 people give their hearts to Jesus Christ." "We are aware of some of the problems you raised and have been in active discussion about them in meetings," Robertson conceded to concerned partners, but "to reach those people we have to put on some entertainers with whom they identify so that first they will watch our program, and then we can bring them to the Lord."[48]

The changes at CBN in the 1980s also reflected the growing artistic sophistication of the production staff. CBN both contributed to and was fed by a new evangelical interest in the arts. The new generation of evangelical media experts called not for a rejection of the world, but instead for a Christian permeation of society. Christian culture demanded Christian journalism, Christian painting, and Christian drama, and to bring these things about, evangelicals began in ever larger numbers to view the arts as allies rather than enemies. Christians, they believed, needed to regain the artistic skills needed to reassert themselves, not by preaching or bullying, but by permeating the society with the leaven of good values embodied in good art forms.

With ratings and artistic excellence in their sights, "The thing that is really driving the business," observed Tim Robertson in 1987, "is programming." In 1978 Pat Robertson announced that within three years CBN would be "producing up to 32 hours a week of 'morally uplifting' TV movies, serial dramas, and variety programs." In the decade that followed, the network tried to develop a slate of marketable original programming, conceived and performed by a new generation of Christian artists. Most of the network's creations were short-lived; in *Charisma* magazine, Robertson's biographer Jamie Buckingham observed that "CBN is a junkyard of programs which have started with great flourish — and just as quickly fallen by the wayside." But the program experimentation of the 1980s was not uniformly unsuccessful; some original programs caught on, at least to a limited extent. Two of the more popular offerings were "an upbeat, early morning show" called *USam* and a "positive, godly soap opera" called *Another Life.* The "soap" aired 875 segments from June 1, 1981, until October 5, 1984. But original production was expensive, and the show could not attract adequate sponsorship to cover the production expenses.[49]

As early as 1978, CBN attempted to "make its entrance into hard news" on 400 cable stations, but that effort also proved to be expensive and was short-lived. In the early 1980s *The 700 Club* began to fill the need for news by featuring more and more news documentaries. The ratings of the show had been either flat or declining for several years, Robertson explained to a disgruntled supporter, and their polls showed that a majority of "the adults in the country said they wanted news." An attempt to begin a full-scale news broadcast in 1986 lasted only a few weeks because of the inability to attract commercial sponsors. The network retained news bureaus in Washington, D.C., and the Middle East, however, as well as remote crews capable of worldwide coverage that furnished news briefs and contributed reports to *The 700 Club.* Robertson remained as certain as ever that news was critical to audience expansion.[50]

Probably the most successful original programming produced by CBN during these years was a series of specials. The first of the specials, *It's Time to Pray, America,* was aired in the summer of 1976 on 228 television stations and 300 radio stations; at the time it was advertised as "the largest simultaneously released production from a Christian organization." Often combining religious and patriotic themes, the specials frequently had good ratings. The 1984 special *Don't Ask Me, Ask God* was the "most-watched TV religious special" of the year, and a 1987 special, *Terrible Things My Mother Told Me,* "an afterschool special produced for ABC . . . has been recognized as the highest rated dramatic special of its kind run by ABC during the 1987/88 viewing season."[51]

Yet throughout this period of transition, and indeed throughout the history of CBN, *The 700 Club* remained the centerpiece of the ministry. Constantly revised in format over its first two decades of existence, during the 1980s the program varied from an hour to ninety minutes in length and was generally broadcast live in the morning and rerun in the evening over the CBN cable network. In addition, by 1987 *The 700 Club* was being aired on about 190 stations in the United States and overseas in time slots purchased by CBN.

The drift of *The 700 Club* from a predominately religious format toward a news, information, and inspirational program was gradual, steady, and a reflection of the maturing of Pat Robertson's broadcast vision. Partly, the direction of the program was dictated by ministry polling data that showed that an increase in news content expanded the number of young and male viewers. The program continued to highlight "people experiencing spiritual phenomena" and never wavered in its unabashed support of the miraculous. Still, viewers were treated to experts discussing topics ranging from unemployment and the budget to religious liberty and church-state issues. Under the heading "world affairs," experts spoke on such diverse topics as international terrorism, world hunger, famine in Ethiopia, and anti-Semitism. The program also explored health and medicine, science, the economy, education, diet, the arts, and personal and family living, and it featured a steady stream of celebrities and political figures. No other religious television personality and few religious leaders in the nation could have orchestrated a program with the breadth of *The 700 Club.*[52]

In spite of prompt apologies for inappropriate views expressed by non-Christian celebrity guests on *The 700 Club,* CBN constantly engaged in damage control both within the organization and with partners. Robertson was clearly miffed when he talked with the CBN staff at a prayer meeting on April 10, 1981. After being told that "there was a great deal of concern" among some CBN employees about *The 700 Club,* Robertson explained to them the religious significance of recent interviews with an expert on credit cards and a congressman about the gold standard. Such subjects explored "fiendish" practices that were infecting the "whole population." He warned: "Christians would rather say, 'Well, hey, you're not praying enough. You ought to pray for people to get healed.' What about the whole population coming under the antichrist?" The diversification of the program was working, Robertson insisted: "People in all walks of life — business people, Jewish people, Catholic people, Protestant people, people in government, and others are watching *The 700 Club* and it's starting to make an impact on them which is what we wanted to do." In 1985 Senior Producer Terry L. Heaton acknowledged that "our use of celebrities . . . must rate as the most confusing element of our show." "One of our guidelines," he wrote, "is that we try to be 'all things to all men that by all means we might save some.' . . . Nevertheless, . . . one often runs afoul of those who see only the act and not the other dynamics involved." "Non-Christian celebrities" were on the program because "they are promotable to a secular audience. We have a saying around here, 'You can't shoot any ducks until they are within range of your guns.'" Replying to a "disappointed" Baptist minister after airing a controversial segment on a "Las Vegas comedy team," producer Michael Little wrote: "I have today directed changes to be made to try to correct future such presentations. . . . We need your prayers daily to present the highest caliber of Christian programming and do battle in the intense war for man's soul."[53]

But Robertson did receive encouragement from some friends who understood the pioneering trail CBN was trying to blaze. Rex Humbard Jr., son of the famed evangelist, wrote in 1983: "I would also like to make a personal comment on your new program format, and tell you how much I appreciate what you are trying to do with it. I'm sure you have come under some steam from our old time religious viewers who don't understand some of the things you are doing, but as a young man . . . I can tell you from my own experience that your program reaches me . . . and I appreciate so very much what you are doing."[54]

The 700 Club continued to evolve with the addition of new co-hosts, most notably Ben Kinchlow. Kinchlow was hired by CBN in 1974 as director of the counseling center in Dallas; in 1977 he became a regular co-host of *The 700 Club*. The son of a black Methodist minister in Uvalde, Texas, Kinchlow had come through a period of black militancy before establishing a charismatic ministry working in drug rehabilitation. Kinchlow first appeared on *The 700 Club* as a guest; invited back a few months later, Kinchlow assumed that he would once again be interviewed by Robertson, but minutes before the program began he was told that Robertson was out of town and that he would be hosting the program. Tall, graying, and dignified, Kinchlow was a natural — he radiated a warmth, humor, and sincerity that endeared him to listeners. Shortly after his second appearance, he was asked to become Robertson's co-host.[55]

Ben Kinchlow in later years thought that Robertson had taken a "risk by putting an African American on the program," but the addition of a black co-host to the program was a touch that had many practical benefits, including reaching out to the growing black evangelical and charismatic community and cutting short any lingering doubts about Robertson's genuine commitment to racial equality. Through the years Kinchlow remained an unflinching friend and admirer of Robertson. Kinchlow defused racial tensions with solutions that "endeared [him] to so many people of all different ages, skin colors, and occupations: If you treat someone the same as you treat your own family, with firmness in love, then we all become equals."[56]

In March 1983 Robertson and Kinchlow were joined by Danuta Rylko Soderman. An experienced talk show hostess in San Diego, Soderman fell into the spiritual orbit of Harald Bredesen and, at Bredesen's suggestion, she contacted CBN. Soderman added zest, humor, and spontaneity to the program.[57]

But Pat Robertson was always the focus of the show; it was his vehicle of expression. Robertson crafted the program to be "advocacy journalism." More than any modern religious figure, Robertson was determined to use television as a teaching tool, not allowing the message to be overshadowed by the medium. He took Ben and the viewers through extensive technical discussions of current events and theoretical topics ranging from supply-side economics to nuclear fusion. In the decade of the 1980s Robertson became an instructor for millions of Americans who shared his religious commitment, if not his education or naturally wide range of interests.

Pat Robertson's run for the presidency led to the most far-reaching changes in the history of *The 700 Club*. Robertson hosted the show only sporadically in 1987; he made his last live appearance on the program at the end of September. Even before Robertson's departure, Danuta Soderman left the program. CBN officials explained that Soderman had been assigned to new duties as a correspondent, but her sudden departure remained something of a mystery. A ministry letter crafted to explain her departure to hundreds of inquiring viewers explained that she had accepted an offer "to do a nationally syndicated talk show in California"; but in later years she admitted she had had difficulty with Robertson's political agenda. By the end of the summer of 1987, with Robertson off on the campaign trail, Ben Kinchlow was the only familiar face on *The 700 Club*.[58]

A Sprawling Empire

By 1977, CBN had a $20 million annual budget. The budget jumped dramatically year after year. By 1980 CBN's income passed $50 million, and in the early 1980s it boomed in cadence with the expansion of the "electronic church," reaching $182.8 million by 1987. Of that amount, 74 percent came from gifts, mostly from individual donors.[59]

From a financial point of view, the most important television events at CBN were the telethons. As the telethons increased in number, Robertson sometimes had to explain to donors that they served multiple purposes: "I certainly do not enjoy taking up valuable time asking for money. However, when I asked the Lord to meet the need in another way, He reminded me that He wanted to bless thousands, not just a few. Telethons have always been the most fruitful spiritually. (During the recent telethon, there were over 18,000 people who met Jesus Christ as their Saviour, plus hundreds who were healed, and hundreds of marriages helped.)" The structure of the telethons evolved much like *The 700 Club*. The programs continued to feature banks of telephones that reported prayer requests, miracles, and pledges from new and old partners, but they increasingly focused on topics such as "Battle for the Family" and "Lives in Crisis" and featured news reports and commentary. Vignettes of changed lives became more and more sophisticated.[60]

The financial potency of the telethons paved the way for the huge growth of CBN in the decade after 1975; at the same time, that growth expanded the reach of the telethons. The 1978 telethon was four times larger than any previous effort. After the 1983 telethon, Robertson informed his staff that "the numbers were staggering." He wrote: "God gave me a verse from the 81st Psalm. 'Open your mouth wide, and I will fill it.' . . . Our goal for 1983 was $12 million. As we opened our mouth wide, God gave us $20,222,544. PRAISE HIS NAME!"[61]

To a very large degree the financial success of CBN was built on a huge base of small donors. Political expert Paul Weyrich was amazed to learn that the CBN "big donor" list included those who had given as little as $10,000. Pat Robertson's friend Tucker Yates concluded that Robertson always felt more comfortable with small donors than with "fat cats." In his autobiography, Robertson described at length a bizarre tale of his gullible entrapment in a hoax that promised to net CBN millions of dollars. Shaken by the experience, Robertson resolved never to become dependent on the beneficence of large donors. It was a stunning lesson that taught him that he was called to minister to God's "little ones." He wrote to a partner in

1977, "We don't have wealthy donors helping us — God told me it would be the 'little people' who would help build [CBN]."[62]

Robertson bristled when critics challenged the ethics of the fundraising tactics used to support the huge operating budget at CBN. He was infuriated when a young local reporter wrote a long and derogatory article suggesting that CBN was "on the air asking for your money so we can stay on the air and ask for your money." Robertson wrote to the author, whose name was Hatchett: "The moral of the story is that a person shouldn't trust himself to a 'Hatchett man' working for a competitor who is being beaten in the ratings by our cartoon show." More foreboding, in 1975, *TV Guide* published a snidely critical article of the electronic church in general, arguing that "the massive cash flow is disquieting to both the FCC and the major faiths." Robertson was outraged and warned his staff that this was just the opening salvo in "an attack by Satan against God's people. . . . You might make it a matter of prayer as to whether this should be answered." Robertson did answer; he angrily replied that it "reflected the mentality of a 22-year-old reporter with no comprehension of economic reality, because he ignored the sale by Walter Annenberg, owner of *TV Guide,* of his own broadcast properties for 110 million dollars more than the magazine article charges was spent on television programs by so-called 'big-time religion' during 1974." William Willoughby, a longtime friend and reporter for the *Washington Star,* wrote a supportive rebuttal to the article: "People get their distortion glasses on whenever the subject [of old-fashioned religion] comes up."[63]

During these years of growth, Robertson insisted that "I personally believe in the tightest standards of financial control. In our organization we have precise and detailed budgets which are approved by our Board of Directors and amended quarterly . . . to bring our spending into conformity to our income." At the same time, his distrust of the press ran deep: "In every instance that we have made revelation of financial data to the press it has been used by the press to injure us. . . . It has been used incorrectly to point out the 'huge' revenues coming to the 'enormous electronic church,' and has served as a springboard for vicious attacks by liberal churches, etc." Of course, Robertson pointed out, the organization was regularly audited and submitted filings with several government agencies, including the IRS, the FCC, and the SEC. Nonetheless, with the growth of the "electronic church," the scrutiny of CBN's finances was a popular topic. A 1986 article in *Time* noted that "even in CBN's flourishing state today, fundraising is pervasive, as it is on all Gospel TV."[64]

Actually, fundraising at CBN reached levels of sophistication and decorum uncommon in most religious ministries. But at the same time, CBN overlooked none of the tried and tested fundraising techniques used by other religious organizations — and nonreligious organizations as well. In the 1970s the ministry developed a sophisticated Development Department that offered "partners" expert advice on estate planning. The financial flow was dependent on mail contacts with partners, both through an ever-changing variety of ministry publications and through personalized mass mail. The fundraising potential of mass mail was first exploited by evangelist Oral Roberts in the 1960s; by the 1970s and 1980s, the strategy was used not only by religious organizations but by political and social action groups of every sort. Few organizations had more sophisticated tactics for collecting names and sorting potential contributors than CBN. Members of *The 700 Club* and other potential donors were constantly apprised of Robertson's latest "leading" — the challenge to build a fourth major network, the airing of a new special, an opportunity to broadcast in Japan or Brazil, the demands of Operation Blessing, retiring the debt on CBN Center — and were furnished with cards that could be marked for gifts of $1,000, or $100, or $25.

CBN did sometimes resort to the kinds of gimmickry many ministries used effectively in courting supporters. Donors' names were listed on microfilm and encased in a cross; members of *The 700 Club* received membership cards, bumper stickers, and "gold-tone lapel/collar pins"; other givers received special mailings of cassette tapes and ministry publications. Such gifts cost very little, Robertson told a regular donor, and it was the least CBN could do for "those who show such love."[65]

Expanding the Vision: Counseling, Operation Blessing, and CBN University

The diversity of activities funded by CBN and directed by Pat Robertson expanded at a dizzying pace during these flush financial times. Among the changes, none was more important to the internal functioning of CBN than the growing sophistication of the around-the-clock counseling centers. CBN launched its humanitarian subsidiary, Operation Blessing, in 1978, and CBN University was chartered under an independent board the same year. CBN also funded several other educational and legal organizations, including the Freedom Council, a nonprofit organization aimed at political education, and the National Legal Foundation, founded to offer legal assistance to Christian causes.

The counseling centers evolved out of Pat Robertson's passion to establish a real-time link with television viewers, both to raise financial support and to offer ministry. The counseling center concept evolved naturally out of the telephone response banks used during the early telethons. By 1979 eighty-two counseling centers were operating in the United States and "many countries overseas," "staffed with more than 7,500 trained volunteers" and receiving more than one million calls annually "from people with marital, alcoholism, drug addiction, financial, physical, spiritual and other problems." The volunteers were trained by full-time staff members from Virginia Beach and armed with a counselor's handbook that represented years of accumulated wisdom. Trained experts were always available for crisis cases, such as potential suicides. In 1987, the ministry developed a "call-back system," in which counselors were trained to make follow-up calls to the most promising or neediest contacts.[66]

By 1983, the number of calls received by the centers reached three million, and at one point in 1985, CBN surpassed American Airlines as the nation's largest user of toll-free telephone numbers. CBN partners were given scoreboard-like reports on the achievements of the centers, including the number of calls, the number of "salvations," and the number of reported "answers to prayer." During these years, the counseling centers were tied closely to local churches. Churches generally supplied volunteers to answer the telephones, and counselors were urged to make "referrals to local, Bible-believing churches." This arrangement gave the ministry ammunition to counter the growing criticism that the "electronic church" was undermining its local counterparts. Thousands of churches cooperated with the centers, and many pastors praised the referral system as a means of building local congregations. In 1987 Ben Kinchlow estimated that 600,000 people had been added to local church rolls through the efforts of CBN.[67]

Millions more were touched by CBN's humanitarian wing, Operation Blessing. Pat Robertson often invoked memories of his personal experience in Bedford-Stuyvesant. In 1978, while reading Isaiah 58, Robertson felt compelled to establish a humanitarian organization. In its early years, Operation Blessing, headed by Ben Kinchlow, was small and worked mostly through linkages between the counseling centers and local churches. Its earliest projects were carried out by local groups, with Operation Blessing contributing supplementary funds. In 1982, Operation Blessing reported donations of $184,717, which were used to help more than 16,000 families. The organization grew rapidly in the early 1980s; by 1987, the ministry had cooperated with nearly 15,000 local churches and hundreds of other relief agencies in a variety of projects, ranging from supplying food, clothing, and blankets to victims of natural disasters to providing vegetable seed for self-help gardens. Operation Blessing also funded famine relief in places such as Cambodia, Ethiopia, and Sudan (prompting Vice-President Bush to invite Robertson to accompany him on a trip to Sudan) and provided relief for refugees in Central America. By 1985, CBN estimated that it had contributed to programs helping nearly 9 million people. The total cost of its benevolence schemes reached $50 million, though much of that came in the form of matching funds, and Operation Blessing contributed only a fraction of that amount. In 1985, in cooperation with CBN University, Operation Blessing launched Heads Up, a program to combat illiteracy in the inner city featuring an "innovative phonetic reading program, Sing, Spell, Read and Write." Heads Up claimed to have enlisted 25,000 teachers by 1987 and had enrolled 100,000 students in cooperation with local churches. Robertson took great personal pride in the accomplishments of Heads Up. He wrote to a supporter in 1990: "Through a literacy program CBN sponsors, called SING, SPELL, READ AND WRITE, we have taught *thousands* to read and write. Most of these have been in the inner cities among blacks and Hispanics. It is because we are concerned and want to help them that CBN has given hundreds of thousands of dollars for these programs." By the time the program closed, Robertson estimated that 300,000 students had been enrolled and that he himself had "traveled to almost every inner city in America to teach literacy."[68]

By far the most ambitious expansion of the CBN family was the founding of CBN University in 1978. Robertson first revealed his desire to build a school in 1975, when he acquired the property for the CBN Center. Initially, he explored establishing a training school for Christians from Third World nations, but by 1977 he had decided to build a graduate university. In 1978 Pat Robertson was appointed acting president. David Clark, the school's dean and acting provost, drafted a plan to be submitted to the Southern Association of Schools and Colleges that set moderately high entrance requirements for students because the intent was "to educate young men and women with leadership capabilities." Clark wrote that "We visualize these programs as remaining relatively small and rigorous in their demands on students and faculty alike." "The key difference in this school," he added, "will be that our ideology is not guided by secular humanism but rather by a desire to exalt Christ." Clark projected that CBN University "may never be a large institution," but that it would provide "academic excellence in a spiritually enriched environment." Pat

Robertson explained to a supporter in 1979 his understanding of how the university's communications school would be a tool for evangelism: "There are many ways to bring Christ to the unbeliever. One way is through Christians being salt and light in secular places such as the existing networks, as writers, producers, actors, and so forth. Another is through a God-honoring network such as we envision our Continental Broadcasting Network to be. The Holy Spirit can work through Spirit-filled actors and actresses just as surely as He can through preachers. Some people will watch drama who will not listen to sermons!" The students in the communication program, CBN announced, "will have access to some of the finest production studios in the world in CBN's International Headquarters Building." Clark reported that more than 4,000 inquiries had been received before the school opened; the initial class enrolled seventy-seven students working in the area of communications.[69]

The School for Communications and the Arts began classes in September 1978, and the first class graduated in 1980. "You've been given a superb education," President Robertson told the graduates. "You are an elite group . . . dedicated ambassadors of the Lord Jesus Christ." In 1980 the university opened a school of education, in 1982 schools of business and divinity, in 1983 a school of public policy (later called the Robertson School of Government), in 1984 an institute of journalism, and in 1986 a school of law. An administration and classroom building was completed in 1979, a library building was dedicated in 1984, and a classroom building was completed in 1986. In 1987 CBNU reported an enrollment of 950 students from all 50 states and 15 foreign countries. In the spring, the university granted 240 M.A. degrees in "communication, biblical studies, divinity, public policy, journalism, business administration, counseling and education. In addition, 13 students were awarded doctoral degrees in law."[70]

CBN University observed a special dedication ceremony on October 1, 1980, installing Robertson as chancellor and Richard Gottier as the school's president. Gottier was president of Western New England College, and he had been one of a small coterie of charismatic advisors Robertson convened to offer advice about launching CBNU. Gottier seemed a perfect fit; he was the rare academic administrator in a state university in the 1970s who identified openly with the charismatic movement. He came to CBNU convinced that God had "been preparing me, since that day I was born, for this position. . . . I believe that through CBN and the university we will play a major role in the return of our Lord Jesus." In close cooperation with Robertson, Gottier recruited a faculty of Christian professors. The seminary was staffed entirely with professors who had "been Baptized in the Spirit," many of them former instructors at the Melodyland School of Theology in California, a pioneering effort to begin theological education in the charismatic movement. Although the School of Divinity "was advertised as an Evangelical institution, most of the students over the years came from classical Pentecostal, independent Pentecostal, and Charismatic backgrounds." Vinson Synan reported that about 95 percent of the student body came from charismatic and Pentecostal backgrounds, while 100 percent of the faculty members testified to being "baptized in the Holy Spirit."[71]

Gottier abruptly resigned in 1984 "for personal reasons"; CBN refused to "make public confidential personnel matters." He was replaced as president by Robertson's trusted friend Bob Slosser, who had been serving as executive vice-president of CBN and had been a member of the CBN board for fourteen years. Slosser's leadership brought a period of stability to the expanding institution. In 1984, CBNU was granted full accreditation by the Southern Association of Colleges and Schools. It was a notable achievement, remarked President Slosser, in view of the fact that "CBN University remains a Christian graduate university which insists that the Lordship of Jesus Christ be at the center of all aspects of university life," and the accrediting visitors knew "right where we stand."[72]

The addition of the law school in 1986 was another important step forward. Sparked by Oral Roberts's donation of the Oral Roberts University law library, valued at around $10 million, the School of Law's first star faculty addition was Herbert Titus, a brilliant Harvard Law School graduate who had taught at the O. W. Coburn School of Law at Oral Roberts University and migrated to CBNU along with the library. A student of Christian philosopher Francis Schaeffer, Titus believed strongly that "if a nation's legal and political structure does not reflect the law of God, it is bound to fail." The American Bar Association's Accreditation Committee denied "provisional accreditation" to the law school in 1987, and Titus irately charged "that CBN University's School of Law has been treated in a very prejudicial way." In the years ahead the law school and CBNU would discover that the road to building a university would be filled with roadblocks and detours.[73]

Evangelizing the World

In the 1990s, Operation Blessing and CBNU became independent entities; CBN, meanwhile, turned its attention to its burgeoning investment in international evangelization that would remain at the heart of the organization. In 1973, CBN's board voted to tithe, donating one-tenth of the network's gross income to other ministries. In 1974, the ministry spent $169,000 on "missions and the relief of human need at home and abroad." In the following thirty-five years, CBN sent funds to more than 2,000 individuals and ministries; the cumulative amount of these donations exceeded $100 million. Some of the recipients were traditional charities such as the American Heart Association, the American Bible Society, and the Southern Christian Leadership Conference; others, such as the Albemarle Food Bank in North Carolina and the Bowery Ministry, reflected Robertson's lifelong concern for the inner-city poor. A wide array of local churches and denominational organizations received donations, including the conservative magazine *Southern Baptist Advocate,* and local churches such as the Delray Beach Primitive Baptist Church and the Adirondack Church of the Nazarene. The extensive list of churches, parachurch organizations, and individuals from the Pentecostal/charismatic world included the Assemblies of God, the Church of God in Christ, Aglow International, Acts 29, David DuPlessis, Marilyn Hickey, and Oral Roberts. Pat Robertson's influence on the list was clear; while charismatics were the most favored ministries, the breadth of the distributions reflected Robertson's broad ecumenical interests. In 1984 and 1985 CBN sent $50,000 in contributions to "aid the poor and needy of the Archdiocese of Boston." Robertson's lifelong commitment to Israel resulted in millions of dollars in gifts being sent to a variety of agencies supporting Israel. Explaining the investments in Israel to a disgruntled contributor, Robertson wrote: "Reaching God's chosen people with the Gospel of our Lord is part of His commission. As a point of fact, the Bible tells us that God said 'I will bless them that bless thee, and curse him that curseth thee.' . . . Personally, I would rather be among those that God blesses rather than those whom God curses, wouldn't you?"[74]

Few things excited Robertson more than CBN's potential role in the booming worldwide Pentecostal/charismatic revival. In the midst of the campaign to build a new headquarters building in 1975, Robertson wrote: "I believe that God has told us to get our building programs out of the way in 1975 because from this year on it will be God's time to reach the world." CBN contributed a trickle of funds to foreign evangelists in the 1970s, but in the 1980s the organization poured millions of dollars into favored foreign mission agencies and ministries. Among the ministry's favorites were Alberto Mottesi, one of the most widely known evangelists in Latin America; Indian evangelist and healing minister D. G. S. Dhinakaran of Chennai; and German evangelist Reinhard Bonnke, who conducted massive and highly publicized healing crusades in Africa. In 1987, in the foreword to Bonnke's biography, Robertson dubbed him "one of the most outstanding missionaries in our world today," adding, "It has been our pleasure at CBN to give wholehearted support both spiritually and financially to Reinhard Bonnke's work."[75]

CBN's actual presence overseas began with the acquisition of a Bogotá radio station in 1968. Joined by his Virginia Beach friend, John Gimenez, Robertson led a tour group to visit the station in October 1967, proudly announcing that CBN had installed new equipment and begun a program, "Joy and Praise," that was "similar to WYAH's 700 Club." The next year CBN purchased the station. But the big expansion of the ministry overseas came after the building of the new headquarters in 1975. Robertson announced that 1976 would be "the year CBN shifted its focus to a world vision." During the telethon in March 1976 a CBN staff member gave a "message in tongues" which Robertson interpreted: "Yea, the miracles that you thought great will become commonplace in your sight. . . . For I would show the world that I Am God Almighty. I have called you to show the world, and I will give you the tools that you need, and I will give you the skills." In 1983, Robertson was rhapsodic about Christianity's spread around the world when speaking at the Conference of Itinerant Evangelists in Amsterdam, sponsored by the Billy Graham Evangelistic Association: "God is getting ready to send the greatest harvest of souls to the Church that . . . has ever been known."[76]

During the 1980s Robertson traveled extensively around the world seeking outlets for CBN programming. By 1978 the ministry's "global family" included more than 130 stations broadcasting *The 700 Club* in the United States and Canada. The program was also being aired in both English and Cantonese from Hong Kong, and in edited versions in Taiwan, Japan, the Philippines, Puerto Rico, and "almost every country in Central and South America." In the 1980s CBN experimented relentlessly to expand the reach of its radio and television programming. The network dubbed programs in several foreign languages and provided subtitles in other languages; in 1983 a surprisingly popular version of *The 700 Club* was produced with a Japanese host. CBN's Bible animation productions, *Superbook* and *The Flying House,* proved to be popular throughout the world. In 1986, Robertson proudly announced that a specially edited production of *The 700 Club* had been shown on government-owned television in China. In 1987, CBN television programs, mostly the international version of *The 700 Club,* were aired in over sixty foreign nations, including almost all the nations of Latin America. "700 Club Centers" in Latin America represented early attempts to provide the same sort of counseling service carried on in the United States.[77]

The CBN overseas venture closest to Pat Robertson's heart was the one beaming programming into the Middle East. Robertson's prophetic worldview whetted his appetite to begin sending his messages into the area. On board a flight on his first trip to Israel in 1968, Robertson believed that "God spoke to me." The message exhorted him to get it right in the Middle East: "You are entering Israel, the land of the Bible. You made mistakes in Portsmouth. You made mistakes in New York. You made mistakes in South America. You are not to make any mistakes here." In 1973 Robertson attempted to secure a radio station in Cyprus that would reach the Middle East. In another stopgap measure, in 1978 and 1979 the CBN aired *The 700 Club* and other programs to "the majority of four and five star hotels throughout Israel" through a cable television supplier in Jerusalem and Amman. Then in November 1981 Robertson's old friend, George Otis, during a lunch with Pat, Dede, Bob Slosser, and Tucker Yates, surprised Robertson by offering to give CBN a TV station he had recently built in southern Lebanon that he did not have adequate funds to operate. Robertson had been interested in buying the station, but he and his fellow diners were stunned by the offer. Robertson regarded it as "the greatest day in CBN history," opening the way to "prepare Israel and the entire Middle East for the very return of Jesus Christ." "Pat had believed for 15 years that CBN would be used by God to minister to millions of people in the Middle East," reported the ministry paper, "but had seen every effort frustrated." On April 10, 1982, with the approval and protection of Christian militia leader Major Saad Hadaad, CBN took over the television station in southern Lebanon that had been established by High Adventure Ministries. The station began airing *The 700 Club, Superbook,* and the soap opera *Another Life.* Robertson named the station METV (Middle East Television) and managed to keep it on the air despite two bombings in 1983 that caused several hundred thousand dollars in damages. By 1987 CBN had opened a counseling center in Cyprus to handle hundreds of monthly letters from the Middle East and employed several Arabic-speaking translators in Virginia Beach to prepare programs for METV. By 1983, CBN had news bureaus in Jerusalem and Beirut and regularly broadcast news updates from the region. "The truthfulness and impartiality of our news shows has made us the primary source of non-government generated television news in Jordan and Israel," Robertson boasted in 1987. "Even international news services quote us regularly." By 1987 the station also broadcast *Good News,* an Arabic language program modeled on *The 700 Club.*[78]

The Christian Broadcasting Network at Midlife

By the 1980s, CBN had become a huge and complex organization; scores of individuals had contributed to its growth. Most outsiders were impressed by the quality of the CBN employees. "For all the vibrant positivity and relentless goodwill, make no mistake," wrote journalist Kenneth R. Clark in 1985, "the 4,000 people who labor in his vineyard are neither blessed-out 'Jesus Freaks' from the 1960s nor Moonies hawking flowers at the airport. Credentials at CBN, professionally and scholastically, are awesome, and business is taken just as seriously as if it were being conducted on Wall Street."[79]

In 1986, Pat Robertson was listed as president and CEO of CBN and chancellor of CBN University. Bob Slosser remained Robertson's most trusted friend and aide. He left his position as executive vice-president in 1984 to complete some writing projects, but continued, Robertson wrote, "to stand by as a member of the Board of Directors, friend, confidant and counselor." Robertson persuaded Slosser to return to become president of CBN University in 1986 after the abrupt departure of President Gottier. Ben Kinchlow was vice-president of ministry and development, overseeing the counseling centers, Operation Blessing, and all ministry fundraising.[80]

CBN functioned much like any large business. The various subdivisions of the ministry competed for available funding; when contributions lagged, the competition naturally became more difficult. But a ministry such as CBN posed some unique administrative problems. One of the weaknesses of a Christian organization, observed Tim Robertson, was that people were not willing to "fight it out." Meekness was a Christian virtue, as was personal kindness, but they were traits that could dampen the needed give-and-take in high-level meetings.[81]

Compounding the tendency toward corporate conformity was the singular vision and constant presence of Pat Robertson. He had shaped the ministry, and he brought a forceful personality to the day-to-day operations. Tim Robertson believed that the biggest problem his father faced was getting good advice. Former black militant Ben Kinchlow confessed that he had long been intimidated by Robertson's intellectual presence. He recalled an evening in a Burbank, California, hotel when he blurted out to his friend, "Pat, I'm afraid of you." "When you couple the force of his arguments and his undying conviction . . . with the fact that he has been trained at Yale Law School," said Tim Robertson, "it is a very devastating array. You better be darn sure that you are absolutely right and that you've got the facts to back [you] when you tangle with him." Dede and Tim, Pat's wife and son, were probably the most willing to tangle, but CBN's founder also had great respect for his old friends Bredesen, Slosser, and Yates.[82]

In 1987 control of CBN was still vested in a five-person board. Three members remained from the original board: Pat and Dede Robertson and Harald Bredesen. George Lauderdale resigned in the mid-1960s because he objected to Robertson's cooperation with non-fundamentalist ministers and churches, though he remained a loyal friend, and Robert Walker left the board because of other commitments. They were replaced by Bob Slosser and Tucker Yates, a member of a wealthy North Carolina merchant family who was appointed to the board in 1972. Both Slosser and Yates became charismatics under the influence of Harald Bredesen, marking the continuing influence of Bredesen in the life of Robertson and the ministry.[83]

Bredesen, who first latched on to Robertson in New York, never let go. Though Bredesen was never an employee at CBN, the ministry became, in his words, "the biggest thing in my life." But his influence on Robertson and CBN always remained spiritual in nature. On practical and financial matters, Robertson regarded his old friend as one of the world's worst guides; if you took him on a trip, Robertson said playfully, you would probably end up paying the bills. But in spiritual matters, Robertson believed that more than anyone else he had ever met, Bredesen did "hear from God." "I would say that on spiritual matters," judged Bob Slosser, "Pat pays more attention to Harald than anybody else. Harald doesn't abuse that, but at board meetings or on social occasions, when Harald speaks . . . Pat listens." Though they were "complete opposites," Slosser observed, "there is a relationship there that is very deep and very profound and rich and good."[84]

The small, Robertson-dominated board might give the appearance of making CBN Pat Robertson's private property. However, board members insisted that their meetings were neither autocratic nor dominated by Robertson. "It is an independent board," insisted Bredesen; Dede fearlessly spoke her mind and the others "are strong men." Robert Walker looked on their gatherings as "spiritual meetings" of "men and women of great faith." George Lauderdale recalled that their meetings always reached a point in which they sought "to find out what God wants in this situation." When a question was on the floor for discussion, Pat would inquire whether anyone in the group had a "leading" about what to do. Sometimes, individual prayer would lead to Bredesen or Robertson delivering a "word of knowledge." Robertson told a reporter in 1983 that he reviewed "all major decisions" with his wife, whom he considered "a good advisor." Dede believed that her husband did "not take suggestions from me well," but "if I can say that I have a word from the Lord, he listens." While all of the early board members remembered that Pat was hard to budge when he had made up his mind, each could remember occasions when he was persuaded to change his mind. Tucker Yates "never felt less than a total peer in a board meeting."[85]

Still, no one would deny that the intellect and personality of Pat Robertson was the soul of the ministry. "I always felt," recalled Robert Walker, "that Pat was better alone than he was with a group of people." Gifted as a communicator, a television personality, and a public speaker, Pat Robertson was most persuasive in a small room, speaking softly, face to face. He also listened, and that added to the power of his personal presence. He has often demonstrated the gift of being able to work his will not by intimidation, but by argument and fervor.[86]

The first major reshuffling in CBN's organization came in the months leading up to Pat Robertson's run for the Republican nomination for the presidency. In December 1986, Tim Robertson was appointed president of CBN, and in October 1987, following Robertson's resignation to begin his political campaign, Bob Slosser was named CEO and chairman of the board of CBN. The transition was a challenge, but it was also remarkably smooth. Slosser and Ben Kinchlow had years of service under their belts and were devoted to Robertson and his goals, and the emergence of Tim Robertson as a ministry leader brought additional stability. Vivacious and intelligent, Tim brought much more than the Robertson name to his new position. He had worked his way up through the CBN television ranks, learning as he went. He was widely respected within the organization, and, although he would almost immediately be caught in a storm of financial troubles over which he had no control, in 1986 all seemed well in Virginia Beach. Pat Robertson had a team in place that he could trust, and that enabled him to depart with an air of confidence for a dizzying jaunt on the campaign trail.[87]

CHAPTER 3

Personal Life:
Family, Fame, and Religious Identity

—◁๛๛▷—

After 1960, the personal life of Pat Robertson was almost inseparable from the unfolding drama of building a multimillion-dollar business. In the early years of CBN, he worked a long and exhausting schedule, sometimes twenty hours a day, trying to master every facet of the new business. In later years, *The 700 Club* forced him into the confining routine of daily live appearances. But there were benefits to the routine, chief among them that, unlike conventional evangelists who often spent large blocks of time on the road, Robertson was able to stay close to home and family.

Family

In 1962, as Robertson was devoting more and more time to getting his television station on the air, it became obvious that he could no longer do justice to his job as a local Baptist minister. At the same time, CBN was not financially solvent enough to support him and his family. At this crucial juncture, a local philanthropist, Fred Beasley, offered to pay Pat $100 a week from the Beasley Foundation and provide a rent-free home for the family. The regular salary was the backbone of Robertson's support for a decade, but the house in a run-down neighborhood in Portsmouth subjected Dede and the children to two more years of slum living. In 1963 the fourth Robertson child, Anne, was born, and Dede became more insistent that the family move to a safer neighborhood, so Beasley offered the use of a lovely country mansion on the campus of Frederick College. It was a gracious and beautiful home, surrounded by woods and marshes where Pat could indulge his passion for riding horses. Settling into their new home, the family acquired a Doberman pinscher named Doby and two horses — a show jumper and a pony. For the next nineteen years the country mansion was the Robertson family home, the house remembered by the children.[1]

By the time the family moved to the country, the Robertsons had a regular routine. Pat arose early to study the Bible and pray. By 6:30 he was working on the format of the day's program. He then jogged before leaving to get ready for the 10 a.m. live broadcast. After that, he conducted ministry business before returning home, usually around 7 p.m. When he was home, Pat played with the children. They thought he provided plenty of discipline. He was "pretty rigid," recalled his son Tim, but "when he was home we all had a great time playing together as a family. I never sensed any kind of absence."

While Pat's routine provided some structure, Dede was the rock of the family. She began teaching nursing at a local college, but her schedule was arranged around the needs of the children. Neither Pat nor Dede had much time for socializing. The Robertsons were good friends with the Slossers and Harald and Gen Bredesen, but they generally kept to themselves.[2]

Robertson's relations with his father slowly improved as his family life and his business became more stable. Despite misunderstandings, both parents had been remarkably supportive during the trying years between Pat's conversion experience and the success of CBN. Mrs. Robertson had offered spiritual encouragement, and the senator had supported his son's turn to religion. Both parents were sources of clothes and other gifts. Once the family settled and Pat had a job, the senator sent them $1,600 to buy a Rambler station wagon. If his financial assistance usually came with advice — and sometimes rather direct remonstrance — it was never mean-spirited, and it was almost always correct. But the senator solicited advice from his son as well, partly to tap Pat's intellect and partly to boost his confidence. One such instance came in early 1959, at a time when their relations were fairly testy: the senator asked his son to provide him with biblical texts justifying an aggressive defensive posture against the Soviet Union. Senator Robertson did as much as he could behind the scenes for his son, helping to arrange a session of the Richmond Daughters of the American Revolution honoring Pat's service in Korea, taking him as a guest on a trip to the Interparliamentary Union in Sweden, and using his influence in securing Pat's employment and ordination at Freemason Street Baptist Church.[3]

Toward the end of the senator's life, father and son experienced full reconciliation. The senator spoke at the groundbreaking ceremonies for a new building at CBN in 1966, when he was running for reelection to the Senate, receiving "standing ovations" from the assembled crowd. Completely engrossed in his spiritual mission during his father's 1966 campaign defeat, Robertson later observed that he "was not able to actively campaign" in the senator's unsuccessful bid for reelection, though he "did write one speech which a local reporter declared to be 'The hardest hitting of the campaign.'" He was stunned and heartbroken by his father's defeat. When his distraught son called to speak to him, the senator "said a few words to cheer Pat up" in a "fine resonant voice." Dede Robertson remembered her father-in-law as "a very dear man." The senator's visit for the groundbreaking of CBN was one of her fondest memories: "The tremendous ovation the people gave him just thrilled my heart, and it thrilled him, too." "I know that my grandfather ended up having a lot of respect for my dad after he saw what he had done," observed Tim Robertson. And Pat was proud to be his father's son. In 1993, when one of his supporters wrote to Pat Robertson describing a kindness the senator had extended to him, Pat wrote back: "I can't tell you how much it means to me to know that my father helped you as a young man. . . . He was indeed a kind and gracious man, and has been an inspiration to me over the years."[4]

Family life changed for Pat and Dede Robertson in the 1970s as the demands of CBN became greater and the children began to leave home. Pat was increasingly busy speaking all over the country, building the image of CBN and "ministering to hungry-hearted people." In the summer of 1975, rather typically, Robertson spoke at regional meetings of the Full Gospel Businessman's Fellowship International in Winston-Salem, Willow Grove, Toledo, Charlotte, Annapolis, and Atlanta, the Greater Chicago Full Gospel Ministerial Association, "Fishnet '75" in Front Royal, "Summer Impact '75" at the Christian Centre Church, the Faith Evangelistic Church in Temperance, Michigan, the ninth anniversary banquet of WPOS-FM radio, and the Northern Virginia Teaching Conference at Marymount College of Virginia. As CBN grew, he received invitations to speak at more prestigious conferences. By the 1980s, many of his speeches had a political motif and were delivered before non-religious audiences. Along with his growing fame came swarms of awards and honors great and small: the Harmony Award from the Downtown Norfolk Association in 1978; Distinguished Merit Citation by the National Conference of Christians and Jews in 1979; Man of the Year Award from The Committee for International Goodwill in 1981; Humanitarian of the Year from Food for the Hungry, Inc., and the

George Washington Honor Medal for Individual Achievement from the Freedom Foundation at Valley Forge in 1982; the Philip Award for Distinguished Service in Evangelism from the National Association of United Methodist Evangelicals in 1985. Robertson also became a bestselling author during these years. His autobiography, *Shout It from the Housetops,* written in collaboration with popular religion writer Jamie Buckingham, was published in 1972 and remained in print for many years.[5]

Dede built her early years in Virginia around the children, but as they grew she found opportunities to work outside the home as well. In 1970, when Anne was in the second grade, Dede accepted a job as an assistant professor of nursing at Tidewater Community College — "so we could eat." She held that position until 1978. From 1961 to 1964, in the infancy of CBN, she hosted a "missionary TV program" called "Lifeline." As the fame of Pat and CBN spiraled after the mid-1970s, Dede also became increasingly in demand as a speaker at Christian schools and women's groups as a widely recognized figure in the booming charismatic movement in her own right. During the Reagan administration she was appointed a delegate to the Inter-American Commission of Women and represented the United States at meetings in South and Central America. In 1979 she collaborated with John Sherrill in writing a popular autobiography, *My God Will Supply,* and in 1984 she authored a book entitled *The New You.* She also wrote a monthly column for *Christian Life* magazine. In spite of such accomplishments, "early on" she accepted the conclusion that "we couldn't have two stars in the family."[6]

As time went on, Dede also devoted considerable time and attention to CBN. She had been an active member of the board of directors from the beginning. "She has great instincts," observed Bob Slosser; in the CBN board meetings, "many of the times that Pat has been challenged on something that he wanted to do, [the challenge] has come out of Dede's mouth." Though she had no training in decorating, she demonstrated her gifts by decorating the interior of all of the major buildings at CBN and Regent University. As a tribute to her public accomplishments, in 1986 Dede was named Christian Woman of the Year in a poll of leading evangelicals.[7]

The Robertson children who came of age during these busy years turned out to be capable, loyal, and independent adults. While they had somewhat formal relationships with their father, as he had with his father, none of the children ever doubted his clear devotion to God; each one remembered observing him beginning his day with "prayer and in the word." They matured in a home where they had to fight for their positions on a range of issues against a father who "would tear us apart" and a mother who was "tougher than everybody." "Throughout my whole family experience," recalled Tim Robertson, "ideas were constantly tested and hammered out and argued about, and we would yell at each other." With a family full of Type A personalities, they occasionally "blew the roof off the house," but there was never any doubt about the bond of "loyalty and love" that held the family together. Although the two younger children experienced adolescent rebellions, sometimes becoming a potential embarrassment to their father, friends of the Robertson family agreed that the children reflected well on their parents. By 1987, when Pat had entered the presidential race, Tim had risen to the head of the CBN ministry, and he and his wife had brought Pat and Dede three grandchildren; Elizabeth and her husband, Charlie, a mortgage banker, lived in Dallas and had one child; Gordon was a young lawyer in Norfolk with all the charms of his father thirty years earlier; and Anne was working for CBN while contemplating the values of a college education.[8]

Fame

Pat Robertson's personal life in the 1970s and 1980s was inseparably joined with the spread of charismatic Christianity, a movement in which CBN became one of the brightest achievements and he the foremost celebrity. When *Charisma* magazine named Pat Robertson the "most influential" individual in "the charismatic renewal" in 1985, surpassing in influence such luminaries as Oral Roberts and Jimmy Swaggart, the recognition rested both on the success of CBN and on Robertson's privileged pedigree in a movement led mostly by talented preachers who had arisen from working-class backgrounds. In February 1986, before his foray into politics made him a subject of rancorous public debate, he was the subject of mostly favorable attention and curiosity. In that year he was inducted into the "Religious Broadcasting Hall of Fame" at the convention of National Religious Broadcasters attended by approximately 9,000 luminaries from around the world and was featured on the cover of *Time* magazine. Perhaps the most unexpected recognition of his meteoric rise as an American religious icon was his selection by the *Christian Century*, never a fan of the electronic church or Pat Robertson, as the "Religious Newsmaker of the Year" in 1987. Editor James M. Wall candidly wrote: "Admire him, fear him, trust him or find in him a threat of theocracy — Pat Robertson was 1987's most significant figure in religion."[9]

Robertson's rise to fame and notoriety was very much a part of the spectacular worldwide charismatic revival that had been ablaze for decades but had only begun to gain public attention in the 1980s. The movement had begun as a more or less parallel movement to the Billy Graham evangelical revival in the years immediately after World War II. Led by a group of independent revivalists, the most acclaimed and enduring being Oral Roberts, the revival featured huge healing campaigns in the United States and abroad in the 1950s; by the 1960s its leaders were restlessly exploring the use of television as a medium to reach the masses. Aside from the independent ministries of the healing evangelists, the most influential parachurch organization to emerge in the 1950s was the Full Gospel Business Men's Fellowship International (FGBMFI), founded by California dairyman Demos Shakarian with the backing of Oral Roberts and other leading evangelists. The FGBMFI became a powerful vehicle for spreading the Pentecostal message to broader audiences. *Charisma* magazine was in the 1980s the most widely read herald of the movement; its circulation surpassed 100,000 by the middle of the decade. The magazine both fostered and advertised the independent "megachurches" that sprung up all over the country in the 1970s and 1980s. "It's likely that the one coming to your city will be Charismatic," boasted the editor of *Charisma* in 1985.[10]

By the 1980s the American charismatic community was fully attuned to the worldwide impact of the movement. Vinson Synan, the leading historian of the movement and a central figure in fostering charismatic unity, wrote in 1985: "The Spirit-fanned Charismatic revival flame is spreading throughout the planet, and soon it will engulf the Southern Hemisphere." Like other charismatic leaders, Robertson was euphoric about the soaring growth of the movement. Speaking to the National Religious Broadcasters Convention in 1986, Robertson told the audience that the United States had 60 to 70 million evangelical Christians and "the numbers are rolling like a great flood and a great tide."[11]

In a 1985 special issue probing the reasons for the charismatic movement's success, *Charisma* pinpointed several developments that had changed the face of American religion in general and evangelicalism in particular. By the 1980s, all churches, both Protestant and Catholic, were more open to charismatic theology and worship styles, including the "simple spontaneity" of Pentecostal services and the presence of women in the ministry. More and more, evangelical leaders welcomed charismatics into the fold. Presbyterian Richard Lovelace, a professor at Gordon-Conwell Theological Seminary, wrote: "After some 75 years of rejection and distrust, evangelical churchmen and Spirit-baptized preachers have been brought together by moral and political issues and have discarded negative stereotypes."[12]

The second reason for the growth of the charismatic movement in the 1960s and 1970s was its extraordinary adaptability to television. The potential for the religious use of television was clear to insiders by the early 1970s. In 1972, Edward E. Plowman wrote in *Christianity Today,* "There are signs that Christian television may be emerging from its long infancy." By the end of the 1970s, the secular press was awakening to the fact that "the growth in religious broadcasting has been startling, greater than anyone lacking prophetic powers could have imagined a decade ago." In the development of "the electronic media . . . in the past decade," wrote Ben Armstrong, "the Charismatics have led the way being creative, innovative and imaginative." That revolution began in 1961, Armstrong believed, with the launching of CBN.[13]

By the early 1980s the public was well aware of the phenomenon labeled the "electronic church." While early studies indicated that the audience of the electronic church was still small, by 1985 ratings were increasing, led by CBN. At the peak of the electronic church in 1986, the only non-charismatic broadcaster whose ratings ranked in the top six in a poll published by *Time* magazine was Jerry Falwell. The success of religious programmers caught the attention of secularists; *The Humanist* magazine warned that "Cable TV and satellite transmission threaten a massive evangelical transformation of society, with implications transcending politics."[14]

Pat Robertson was the right man in the right place at the right time. He rode the rising tide of the charismatic revival and of religious television to his extraordinary place of leadership in the mid-1980s. The emergence of what came to be called the electronic church was made possible by the technological breakthroughs in cable and satellite television, but the adaptability of the charismatic religious experience ignited the explosive growth of the electronic church. No one contributed more to that molding of a religious message to the medium of television than Robertson.

A third powerful force driving the conservative Christian revival in the 1960s and 1970s was the growing political angst felt by many fundamentalists and evangelicals. Beginning with the Supreme Court decision removing prayer from public schools through the *Roe v. Wade* decision in 1973 legalizing abortion, conservative Christians had been shocked and angered by the cultural changes in the country. "During the past decade," noted *Charisma* in 1985, "we Christians have discovered that not only can we voice our opinions, but by actually getting involved in the political process we can have great influence." "Give credit where it's due," reported *Washingtonian* magazine in 1986: the religious right had found a series of issues that resonated with Americans, including its emphasis on "family values."[15] The political awakening among conservative Christians both fed and was fed by the booming electronic church. Pat Robertson's profile in that movement rose in the national press and in a spate of academic studies. No other person was better equipped by background, temperament, and spiritual orientation to take advantage of the sweeping religious, technological, and political changes afoot.

The Shepherding Controversy and Pat Robertson's Religious Identity

The euphoria surrounding the explosion of the charismatic renewal in mainstream Protestant denominations and the Roman Catholic Church in the 1970s raised hopes of unity among charismatics, which climaxed in a 1977 charismatic conference in Kansas City. The conference drew around 50,000 Christians from scores of denominations to a convocation in Arrowhead Stadium. But the naïve ecumenical hopes of the 1970s soon settled into an icier retreat into denominationalism and efforts by individuals and parachurch groups to protect their own turf. "Is there a change in the Spirit's direction?" asked *Charisma* magazine in 1985. It was clear that "the impetus toward unity seems stalled." But the most serious schismatic episode in the history of the celebratory movement had begun to unfold much earlier, in 1974. Pat Robertson was a major combatant, and he, like the movement, left the battle with scars that healed slowly. The whole episode had a profound impact on where he positioned himself on the spectrum of charismatic Christianity.[16]

In what came to be known as the "shepherding" or "discipling" controversy, Pat Robertson saw himself as the defender of reason and evangelical orthodoxy against dangerous heresy. Throughout its history, the free-flowing Pentecostal/charismatic movement was plagued by extremists boasting private revelations from God. At one level, the shepherding movement was a quasi-denominational effort to impose a degree of order on the loose movement; at the same time, it was a far-reaching claim to extra-Biblical authority. Born out of an association of five influential teachers within the independent charismatic movement — Bob Mumford, Derek Prince, Don Basham, Charles Simpson, and Ern Baxter — working together in the Christian Growth Ministry, the controversy "focused on the movement's emphasis that believers needed to have a personal, submitted relationship to a shepherd/pastor to help them develop Christian maturity." The movement gained great respect in the 1970s and its monthly magazine, *New Wine,* quickly became the most widely circulated publication within the charismatic movement.[17]

As millions of mainstream Protestants and Roman Catholics embraced the charismatic renewal, they created a community open to the leading of the Holy Spirit but uncomfortable with the rampant disorder rife with an ever-increasing proliferation of new ministries and new voices claiming heavenly authority. Catholic charismatic Keith Fournier believed that in the discipling movement many participants "rediscovered authority with a vengeance." Many who had entered the movement from traditional backgrounds embraced the move to restore order and liturgy. The writings of Derek Prince were particularly influential. His 1976 book, *Discipleship, Shepherding, and Commitment,* seemed to add depth to the whole charismatic experience.[18]

Critics of the discipling/shepherding movement traced its origins to the teachings of Juan Carlos Ortiz of Argentina, whose book, *Call to Discipleship,* was published in English in June 1975. The book was written in collaboration with Jamie Buckingham, the widely respected charismatic author who had co-written *Shout It from the Housetops* with Pat Robertson. Ortiz's controversial concept gave pastors the authority to create what seemed to be a discipling pyramid organization: "The Word and the will of God for our lives today should come first to the group of pastors that get together in a certain city. When the pastors meet together and minister to the Lord . . . God reveals to them His purpose for the city and His purpose for the disciples. The Bible will help in discipleship. But the living Word of God, the will of God for today, is what really makes disciples." Ortiz in later years affirmed his belief that "Christ never intended to start a religion based on a book. . . . What really makes Christianity unique among religions is that our Founder is alive. . . . I believe in continuing revelation."[19]

The controversy began to simmer the year before the English publication of Ortiz's book. Traditional Pentecostal denominational leaders were wary of the shepherding concept, seeing it as baggage brought to the revival by mainstream Protestants and Roman Catholics, and most of the leading independent ministers such as Oral Roberts and Kathryn Kuhlman viewed the movement as a clear power grab. Bob Mumford and Derek Prince had been among the most popular teachers in the charismatic renewal, and the new teaching on shepherding endangered their relationship with several of the power centers within the loose movement. In 1974, the Full Gospel Business Men's Fellowship International, the most important platform for the charismatic teachers, began canceling the speaking engagements of Bob Mumford. Equally ominous, Pat Robertson, who had featured the teaching of Mumford and Prince on CBN, became increasingly skeptical. Speaking at Oral Roberts University in October 1974, Robertson warned that "there's a great deal of wild fire, there's a great deal of what passes for prophecy which is just foolishness" that was being taught in the charismatic movement that needed to be "proved." Asked about shepherding, or "submission," he replied, "This doctrine of submission has been carried to ridiculous extremes."[20]

The controversy became open and increasingly uncivil in 1975, drawing attention in the secular press. Pat Robertson was the center of the controversy. In a series of memos to the CBN staff, he denounced the doctrine and moved quickly to contain it. In a memo addressed to "all staff" on May 20, 1975, Robertson wrote: "In the move of God across America it often happens . . . that teachers will teach upon a truth and then will push it to such a degree that it becomes unbalanced, and, in some cases, heretical. This is the case of the teaching of so-called 'submission' and 'eldership.'" As a result, he continued, "Our Board of Directors and all of the officials at CBN feel that we cannot further endorse this particular teaching in any way." He still "loved" and "appreciated" these talented teachers, but he was determined to "stand with Scripture against error."[21]

Things moved quickly at CBN in May. On May 22, after a discussion with "two reliable witnesses in Fort Lauderdale" about the "complete control of finances" embedded in the shepherding pyramid, their interference in marriages, and other abuses, Robertson sent a series of memos to CBN administrators. To the director of counseling centers, he wrote: "Absolutely in Miami, Louisville, and these other cities I want the 'discipleship' cult off our staff before the end of this week. Spare no one to get it accomplished." He would give the "so-called 'apostles'" an opportunity to refute the things if they desire," but he was convinced that Christians were confronting "one of the worst heresies we have encountered in the modern day charismatic movement." Regarding programming, he instructed the staff: "I do not want anyone under any circumstances to be on THE 700 CLUB or to be in any way associated with it who is involved in 'shepherding.' . . . Particularly, I do not want Bob Mumford, Derek Prince, Don Basham, Charles Simpson, John Poole, Ern Baxter, or Ken Sumrall." On the same day, he instructed John Gilman even more directly: "Under no circumstances, at the risk of receiving serious consequences, are we to put on our radio or television tapes which feature Bob Mumford . . . or any of the lesser lights of the discipleship movement. . . . In the meantime I want all the tapes erased immediately which feature any of these people. . . . Do not delay in getting this memo implemented."[22]

In June, Robertson wrote a long letter to Bob Mumford detailing his concerns about the movement, "because of my personal regard for you" and because CBN had aired "various teaching programs" which had been produced for him, Prince, and Basham. He asked: "Bob, why do charismatics always have to take simple Bible truths and push them to such ridiculous extremes that they become unbalanced and heretical?" He then offered a detailed seven-page critique of the "Watchman Nee – Juan Carlos Ortiz 'submission' teachings as expanded and put into practice by you and your fellow teachers." He objected strenuously to the teachings of Ortiz on "revelation," charging that it was a rejection of classic Christian respect for the Bible. The doctrine of "submission" by every Christian to a "shepherd" was a fundamental violation of every Christian's "liberty" and was fraught with pitfalls — not the least being the financial pyramid that it established: "Subtle and overt pressure is exerted on the sheep to pay tithes to their shepherd. Then like a spiritual chain letter the shepherds submit (and pay tithes) up to the top shepherds, who in the United States finally submit to Bob Mumford." He suggested that a "counsel of wise brethren composed of David DuPlessis; Demos Shakarin [sic]; Dan Malachuk; Harald Bredesen; Howard Conatser; Dennis Bennett; Judson Cornwall" should meet to review the charges against him and give Mumford an opportunity to answer.[23]

A series of meetings ensued between representatives from both sides, and tempers flared. Robertson was angered that his May 22 memo to ministry executives had been leaked and "distributed in Fort Lauderdale and other parts of the United States one week after it had been received by [CBN's executives]." He wrote to his staff: "Either one of the people on this memo or a member of your staff has (a) been very foolish, (b) been disloyal to CBN, and (c) should either make things right, or I suspect should seek employment elsewhere."[24]

In this heated environment, a meeting of charismatic leaders was called on August 9-10, 1975, at the Curtis Hotel in Minneapolis. Robertson was peeved by the arrangements for the "hastily called meeting"; he wrote to Brick Bradford, General Secretary of the Presbyterian Charismatic Communion, who was chosen to moderate the Saturday session: "I noted from Derek's letter that he included twelve people who were either direct submission teachers or who were associated with the Shepherd's Conference in Kansas City. I noted that he included two people who would be considered neutral, and four people who would be opposed to the submission teaching. This seems in my humble opinion a stacked deck and I was not too much in favor." Furthermore, the planners had provided "no moderator, . . . no agenda, and there is no orderly procedure for arriving at the facts." Robertson wanted to bring "witnesses about the Fort Lauderdale heresy," but the others would not agree. "Unless there is a clear agenda, . . . and a list of participants which will include Harald Bredesen, Hobart Freeman, David Ebaugh, Gerald Derstine, plus several eye witnesses to the practices in Fort Lauderdale, I am not going to Minneapolis."[25]

Robertson's conditions were not met, but the "Shoot Out at the Curtis Hotel" convened after some delay to give time for an *ad hoc* committee to select twenty-nine men from the crowd of invited and uninvited charismatic leaders who had come to Minneapolis. The meeting lasted from two o'clock in the afternoon until midnight. Charles Simpson later recalled, "Blood pressures were high, affidavits, tape recordings, and accusations were everywhere." Mumford and Simpson later recalled that "the tone caught them off guard because they thought the meeting was intended for dialogue and reconciliation among trusted leaders." It instead appeared to be a court trial with Robertson the chief prosecutor, supported strongly by Dennis Bennett, a respected leader of the charismatic renewal in the Episcopal church, and by Harald Bredesen. The next day the participants informally asked Robertson to seek forgiveness for attacking Mumford without first personally discussing his accusations with him, and called on the Fort Lauderdale ministers to "temper teaching in regard to controversial doctrine." Brick Bradford reported: "What was accomplished? . . . Very little reconciliation arose between the strongest advocates for shepherding and those most visibly upset by the way in which shepherding and discipleship is being taught and applied. . . . No general conclusions were drawn. No joint statements were issued." The group appointed a committee to plan continued discussions, but that seemed highly unlikely.[26]

Robertson was outraged by the whole affair. He angrily stomped out of the room and washed his hands of the movement. "Brother, it is heresy," he told his young friend Scott Ross, who had submitted to Mumford as his pastor. In the months ahead, his assessment was that "the meeting in Minneapolis was the worst thing that has happened in my entire ministry, and scared me off from any further meetings."[27]

Meanwhile, Bob Mumford laid down the gauntlet in a September letter to Robertson, sent to a variety of charismatic leaders throughout the world. His seven-page letter rebutted Robertson's charges point by point. While Mumford was willing to admit excesses by some novices in the discipling movement, he felt vindicated, he wrote to Robertson, because the "thirty brothers included in the Minneapolis meeting agreed that you acted unscripturally toward me" by publicly upbraiding Mumford. He "welcomed the challenge, correction and adjustment that" was suggested during the meeting, but was "appalled" by the "exaggerations, misstatements and hostile attitudes which I experienced in the meeting and which have continued since." He insisted that there was no financial misconduct in the group and vociferously denied that he, or anyone else associated with the shepherding movement, "has *ever* taught or 'tended' to place rhema [utterances in tongues] or corporate decision above the infallible, inspired written Word of God." Clearly, the leaders of the shepherding movement were willing to take a slap on the wrist that would pacify their critics, but they had no intention of recanting.[28]

Robertson and CBN became much more aggressive adversaries of the "submission" teaching after the Minneapolis meeting. In response to a rather conciliatory letter from Charles Simpson expressing a desire for further dialog and reconciliation, Robertson urged Simpson to abandon the "utter madness" of the discipling movement. "Because of it," he wrote, "your great effectiveness as a Bible teacher has been destroyed, the unity of spirit filled brethren is being destroyed; and the faith of thousands will be destroyed." In response to Mumford, he denied that he had made a "personal" attack on him: "I love you as a brother in Christ, but I hate the doctrine which you are currently espousing." He washed his hands of further discussion, insisting that he did not "intend to spend my time fighting this teaching; but in like token I do not intend to spend my time in dialogue concerning it." Even though he repeatedly replied to questioners that "God has shown me that my ministry and call is not to fight anybody," Robertson continued to mince no words in answer to inquiries. "Do not be entangled in this yoke of bondage," he told one correspondent.[29]

The opposition of Robertson, the FGBMFI, and other independent ministries took a toll on the shepherding ministers. In 1977, Robertson wrote to an inquirer: "It is my understanding that excepting a few places, the discipleship movement has been thoroughly repudiated. I am not one who enjoys controversy, and I would be very reluctant to dig up the old controversy for a fresh go round at this time. It is my understanding that the principals of Christian Growth Ministries have been dispersed from Fort Lauderdale."[30]

Yet in spite of its powerful opponents, the shepherding movement flourished into the 1980s. Particularly important was the support they received from Stephen Strang, the editor of *Charisma* magazine. In "An Open Letter to Derek Prince, Bob Mumford, Don Basham, Charles Simpson, and Ern Baxter" in 1978, Strang wrote, "So from one who has benefited from your ministry, thank you for sticking to what you believed was right. Even though there have been abuses by some, you are speaking truth that the Body of Christ needs to hear." To Strang, the shepherding teachers offered something deeper than the "shallow emotional type of experience" of first-generation Pentecostals and most independent evangelists. Other influential leaders tried to encourage a rapprochement between the parties. In 1980, widely respected Pentecostal David DuPlessis, known as "Mr. Pentecost," made a "noble and supreme effort at reconciliation of the charismatic and classical Pentecostals with the Ft. Lauderdale group." DuPlessis rejected the shepherding doctrine, but he reached a personal reconciliation with Mumford.[31]

By 1985, however, the movement was in serious trouble. Many Roman Catholic charismatics had already distanced themselves from the Fort Lauderdale group. The chairman of the National Service Committee for Catholic Charismatic Renewal in Ann Arbor, Most Reverend Joseph C. McKinney, assured Pat Robertson in 1980 that the group in Ann Arbor had its own Catholic adaptation of the Ft. Lauderdale teachings on discipling. Derek Prince withdrew from the group in 1984, stating in a widely circulated letter that "there are doctrines and practices central to the churches associated with my brothers which do not seem to me to have an adequate scriptural basis: Specifically, that every Christian should have a personal human pastor, and the practice of a pastor overseeing another pastor translocally."[32]

For his part, Robertson never wavered. When Rev. Kilian P. McDonnell asked Robertson's permission in 1979 to include Robertson's letter to Mumford in a forthcoming two-volume collection entitled *Documents on the Charismatic Renewal,* noting that "your name is inextricably tied up with the origins of the controversy," Robertson's reply was as uncompromising as ever. He gave his consent and added: "I believe that the Jim Jones massacre was a perfect example of the shepherding concept carried out to its ultimate and terrible extreme." Like the Apostle Paul, he was "asked to compromise," but he refused to "give place to them . . . for one moment" regarding the "insidious teaching of shepherding." In 1987 he explained to a supporter why his reaction had been, and continued to be, so heated: "It was such a monumental evil that it had to be dealt with in severity. . . . Shepherding was and is a life-threatening illness to the Christian movement."[33]

The continuing influence of the discipling teachers, along with the excesses of some televangelists, were enough to cause Robertson to reassess his relationship to the charismatic movement. In a striking memo addressed to the leadership of Regent University and to the CBN Board of Directors, Robertson instructed the School of Biblical Studies to no longer identify itself as "charismatic." "I am very uncomfortable with the label 'charismatic,'" he wrote. "It carries with it baggage that my weak shoulders cannot carry — the shepherding of Ortiz and Mumford; the fund raising prayer cloths and holy handprints; the lies and deceit; the false tears and foolishness; the fiscal mismanagement; the poor scholarship; the ego trips. Ever since that horrible encounter in Minneapolis between so called 'Charismatic' leaders and Bob Mumford, Charles Simpson, Derek Prince, and Don Basham, I determined that never again would I be a 'Charismatic.' From that moment on I was an Evangelical."[34]

The shepherding movement unraveled in the late 1980s, beginning with the departure of Prince. *New Wine* steadily declined in circulation and was shut down in 1986. Finally, Bob Mumford made a series of stunning recantations. In 1989, Mumford issued a "Public Statement Concerning Discipleship" which did not reject any of the teachings of the movement but urged everyone to "reexamine how they are presently being applied." Mumford sent a copy of his public statement to Robertson along with a handwritten note asking "your forgiveness for my blindness and failure." Robertson's reply was personally gracious: "Thank you for your good letter . . . and the warm spirit that you have shown toward me over the last several years. Without question, you have a very valuable role to play in the Body of Christ. . . ." However, Robertson continued, his objections had never been to a "misapplication" but to the principles themselves. The "teaching of shepherding," he insisted, "can be made worse in the hands of tyrants, but the essential doctrine is flawed at its inception." Mumford came a step closer to reconciliation in an interview with his friend Jamie Buckingham, published in early 1990 along with a public apology. Finally, he confessed: "Discipleship was wrong. I repent. I ask forgiveness."[35]

For Robertson, the whole affair came to an end in a poignant exchange with Mumford in 1993. Mumford capitulated: "I have wanted to write you a letter of conciliation for some time now. It has been some years since we have communicated. This is the needed opportunity to thank both of you for the courage you exhibited, as well as the personal difficulty you experienced in your initial attempts to bring correction to the discipleship movement." Thoroughly penitent about the "extensive damage caused by Biblical principles wrongly applied," Mumford conceded that Robertson had played a "prophetic" role in warning about the damage the movement would cause. He had thought that Robertson's "initial alarm" had been exaggerated, and his tactics "given to theatrics and overkill," but time proved otherwise. "Please forgive me for being blind and stubborn," he wrote. "Of course, I forgive and understand your feelings," replied Robertson. "I know that we have talked before, but never before did I sense the true sincerity of your heart more than in this recent letter."[36]

Still, the controversy had left Robertson sufficiently wary of the charismatic movement that it changed the way he identified himself and his institutions. When Vinson Synan joined the university as dean of the divinity school in 1994, Pat Robertson gave him an extended lecture on the discipling heresy. He insisted that they continue to define themselves not as a charismatic institution, but as an evangelical institution.[37]

The first major theological battle within the booming charismatic movement had been bitter, long, and significant — and Pat Robertson, with his growing television empire and rising profile, had played a critical role in the outcome. But the battle changed him as much as he changed the young movement. Robertson had experienced a dramatic conversion into the charismatic movement many years before, fascinated by its spontaneity and freedom; now he had become disgusted by the extremes it had generated. He had always seen himself as a bridge between the charismatic movement and the mainstream evangelical world, but for a decade he came to doubt the possibility of accomplishing that feat. Healing came slowly, if surely, but it would be years before he re-embraced his charismatic roots and the word "charismatic" once again became respectable at CBN and on the campus of Regent University.

CHAPTER 4

From Television Entrepreneur
to Presidential Candidate

—◦◦◦—

Political Metamorphosis

At the end of the decade of the 1970s Pat Robertson was a successful television entrepreneur and an influential and honored leader in the worldwide
Christian charismatic movement. For two decades his personal attention
and resources had been focused almost entirely on business and religion.
In the midst of his giddy ascent, however, Robertson's restless mind frequently roamed across broader intellectual landscapes. He never turned
his back completely on his early educational and family training; always
hovering on the periphery of his mind was politics.

It could hardly have been otherwise. Reminiscing about his youth,
Robertson recalled: "We were at the center of Virginia politics. . . . Washington was a part of us." His childhood memories were filled with encounters with senators and other Washington celebrities in the company of his father. Until his father's departure from the Senate in 1966, he
occasionally critiqued speeches the senator was preparing, especially
when he spoke on religious topics. A reporter who interviewed Robertson in 1968 revealed that the broadcaster's "tiny office" gave hints of his
"political orientation." "On the walls," he noted, "are framed copies of the
Magna Charta, the Declaration of Independence, Washington's Farewell
Address, and the Gettysburg Address." At that early stage of his career as
a religious broadcaster, he told his interviewer, "I'm not political in
thinking, but spiritual." However, he acknowledged that all options remained open in the future: "I belong to the Lord. If He would be glorified

by putting me in the South Seas, the ghetto, the slums or some high office, I'd be willing."[1]

In the 1960s and 1970s, Robertson's political connections were almost uniformly within his father's Democratic Party. In a speech in June 1968, shortly after the assassination of Robert Kennedy, Robertson reminisced about a brief personal encounter with Kennedy and mourned his death: "In him was embodied the hopes and aspirations of many of the young people of America . . . many people of the minority groups . . . and other people in America who hope and dream for something better. They summed up their aspirations in him and they may have died with him!"[2]

Robertson's desire to air the news in the early days of CBN was a clear sign of his continued interest in politics. During state elections in 1967, the "public affairs department" of WXRI radio hosted a series of appearances by local candidates. Beginning in 1968, "newscaster Mike Little," later the president of CBN, began giving "the earliest evening edition of news" in the Tidewater region.[3]

During the 1970s Robertson expressed his political opinions and preferences more openly and more frequently in correspondence with supporters. He admired Richard Nixon because he was a "born again Christian." In 1972, Robertson commended the president because he had begun to resolve the "tragic mistake" of Vietnam, "without the reckless panic that others desired." While he still would make no public statement "in favor of any candidate," he believed that every Christian should support the president.[4]

Nonetheless, he told supporters, his primary mission remained unchanged: "Our basic ministry has to do with the proclamation of the Gospel of Jesus Christ. We just haven't been called to enter the arena of political dispute and debate however much we would like to do so. Therefore at the present time we do not make editorial comments concerning political activities." Responding to a request from a viewer to support a community relief effort, he wrote: "We are not political activists as such, but if you know of legitimate areas where another voice might do some good then please be sure to let me help."[5]

Robertson broke his public political neutrality in 1974. He was "shocked by the profanity, and the seeming lack of regard for the common good that the Watergate tapes showed." He reported, "I went on the 700 Club with fear and trembling and called upon our President to do what I had just done — namely to confess his sins before the Lord and to call upon the gracious forgiveness of our Saviour despite the personal cost." Robertson insisted that his criticism of Nixon was not partisan: "I'm not being Democrat or Republican. I couldn't care less about political parties one way or the other. I am not partisan one way or the other. I'm not conservative, liberal, or anything political. I belong to Jesus, and I'm a citizen of Heaven. But I belong to this nation, and I don't believe this has been anything but a cancer in our society." Robertson received "many letters criticizing me for saying anything about our President who they like so much," but he believed that his "very strong statement on the air" calling on the president to repent was fully justified.[6]

In the election of 1976 Robertson remained nonpartisan, urging a correspondent to support any "one of the three Christians which are now in the field — Gerald Ford, Ronald Reagan, or Jimmy Carter." He himself voted for Ford. But he was clearly excited by the emergence of the self-proclaimed "born-again Christian" Jimmy Carter, as were other evangelicals. In later years he believed that his support for Carter among steelworkers in Pennsylvania played an important role in his nomination.[7]

Like other evangelicals, Robertson was overjoyed at the election of Carter and soon disappointed by his appointments and policies. In 1991, Robertson revealed that he and pro-family activist Lou Sheldon of California spoke with the president-elect, suggesting that he might want to include "some evangelical Christians among his appointments." He recalled that Carter received the suggestion "with enthusiasm and agreed to receive a list if we could get it to him within two weeks." He and Sheldon carefully prepared a list of proposed appointees and flew to Plains to deliver the "booklet" to the president-elect. He later recalled: "We put together a list of potential appointees" and "Carter rejected all of them."[8]

Nonetheless, Robertson remained hopeful through the early months of Carter's presidency. In early 1977 in the personal newsletter sent to his core supporters, Robertson was upbeat, though he was "still unable to fully size up our new President." "President Carter is God's man," he wrote. "He is sincere, humble, frugal, and very bright." But by 1978 the good will was rapidly fading. "Consternation centers around the administration of President Carter," Robertson wrote in February. "Is he able; inept; Machiavellian; poorly advised; captured by Trilateralist bankers; liberal; conservative; blessed by God; some of these things; none of them?"[9]

By the end of the year, the verdict was in: Carter had "badly mismanaged" the country and offended his two core constituencies, organized labor and evangelical Christians. "Although Carter is personally devout," Robertson wrote, "his administration comes through as repugnant to many Christians." Like Ford, Carter had turned out to be "a decent, likeable guy who is regarded as not quite big enough for the Presidency."[10]

By 1979, as the Carter administration geared up for reelection, Robertson was thoroughly disgusted. Asked by a friend to submit to Carter's religion liaison, Reverend Robert Maddox, a list of influential charismatic leaders who might be willing to meet with the president for prayer, Robertson replied tartly: "I think Jimmy Carter has given the back of his hand to the evangelicals for the past three years. Now that he is in deep trouble with them, he has chosen Reverend Maddox to do a cosmetic job to make him look good before next November. . . . Maddox pressured Oral to join a campaign committee, and Oral turned him down flat." In later years, Robertson surmised that six million evangelicals switched from the Democratic to the Republican Party during the Carter years.[11]

The Carter disappointment focused the attention of Robertson and other evangelicals on a collection of political issues. By the mid-1970s, Robertson wrote, the catalog of evangelical grievances had been clarified by the Carter administration's policies on social issues: "His outspoken support of ERA, his lack of clarity against abortion, his openness to receive or be identified with gay liberation, rock musicians who advocate drug abuse, Bella Abzug as the representative woman, etc. have offended the very Christian groups who were his ardent champions." President Carter's only redeeming grace in Robertson's eyes was his effort to bring peace to the Middle East: "The Egyptian-Israeli Peace Treaty which Jimmy Carter forced through will go down as a personal triumph for him, regardless of other mistakes in domestic and foreign policy. It was fitting that a born-again Christian was the key in bringing together a religiously-inclined Jewish leader and religiously-inclined Muslim leader. Perhaps no other world leader could have been more uniquely used as an 'honest broker' than a born-again Christian President."[12]

In February 1975, *The 700 Club* focused on abortion. Robertson insisted that his opposition to abortion was religious, not political: "Abortion is not a legal matter. It is strictly a theological matter not subject to judicial interpretation." In 1977, Robertson began writing a wide-ranging newsletter called *Pat Robertson's Perspective*. The newsletter, which was mailed to CBN contributors, was loaded with outspoken religious and political commentary and provided a calendar of Robertson's awakening political conscience. Anita Bryant's "courageous crusade" to defeat a "Gay Rights Ordinance" in Miami opened Robertson's eyes to the potential of an "Evangelical-Catholic alliance for decency." He saw three lessons in the Miami victory: "First of all, it shows conclusively that concerned Protestants and Catholics united together have the political muscle to insist on higher standards of decency in America. Second, this lesson will not be lost on those politicians who have been catering to aberrant minorities. Third, it shows that the homosexual lifestyle is ... deeply repugnant to a majority of Americans."[13]

By the end of the 1970s Robertson's earlier political reticence had vanished. "Arguments raised against the candidacy for public office of 'born again' Christians are fatuous nonsense," he wrote in 1978. "The present thinking about the separation of church and state has no basis in United States history. . . . Christians across America are beginning to exercise their God-given rights to serve God in government." Robertson was conspicuously present at several rallies for conservative Republican hopefuls John Connally and Ronald Reagan leading up to the election of 1980, and a stream of candidates for office made appearances on *The 700 Club.*[14]

By 1976, as CBN was on the cusp of its satellite TV explosion, Robertson's attention increasingly drifted to the state of the nation. The theme of the summer telethon was *It's Time to Pray, America,* calling for a revival that "will make us 'one nation under God.'" "Without question," Robertson wrote, the call for the nation to pray would "be the most significant single ministry CBN has ever undertaken." For Pat Robertson, the call to prayer culminated in a life-changing experience at the "Washington for Jesus" rally.[15]

Washington for Jesus

A defining moment in the political awakening of Pat Robertson came on April 29, 1980. On that day, a huge crowd of Christians (estimated in various accounts from 200,000 to 500,000) rallied on the Mall in the "Washington for Jesus" rally. "Washington for Jesus" was the brainchild of John Gimenez, founder of the successful Rock Church in Virginia Beach. Gimenez was something of a protégé of Pat Robertson since the two had traveled together to South America. Robertson persuaded him to settle in Virginia Beach in 1965. The exuberant but sometimes unorganized Gimenez bore the brunt of organizing the rally, sometimes to the exasperation of Robertson. In February 1979 Robertson, who had agreed to serve on the board of directors, wrote to his energetic friend: "Just a word about the way boards of directors work as opposed to operating staff. The board of directors, or steering committee, is the policy board which approves budgets, the assignment of key staff, and sets the framework of an organization. . . . In my case in regard to the time in Washington, I can contribute influence and exposure, and a certain degree of wisdom. Unfortunately the amount of day to day work I can do is limited." In the end, Robertson's organizational contributions were many, particularly in the final scheduling of the events of the day.[16]

The original steering committee was composed of Robertson, Demos Shakarian, Margaret Moody, Vinson Synan, and Dr. Charles Stanley. Robertson became the critical member of the steering committee in the year preceding the rally, using his national influence to recruit participants. Perhaps his most significant organizational contribution was persuading Bill Bright to be co-chairman of the event with him. The original steering committee was almost entirely Pentecostal/charismatic; Bright's addition gave the organizers a legitimate claim to the name "evangelical." Robertson dispatched John Gilman, his close friend and longtime producer at CBN, to Arrowhead Springs to meet with Bright and assure him that the event "would not be a charismatic meeting *per se*." Gimenez and Robertson were delighted when Bright accepted, because he "brought a whole wing of the body of Christ that would otherwise not have come." "He joined us and said I am going to put my whole ministry on the line," recalled a grateful Gimenez years later. "Bill Bright may not speak in tongues, but he is a man of God."[17]

Another addition to the steering committee who was recruited by Robertson was Bishop J. O. Patterson of the Church of God in Christ, the largest black denomination in the country. Robertson wrote to Patterson, who was an old friend: "John Gimenez of our area has asked me to write to you concerning his vision of bringing God's people to the nation's capitol next Spring. We are very much concerned at some of the things that have been happening in Washington, and feel that a meeting to pray for our leadership would be especially effective in this most critical year. I have agreed to serve along with Demos Shakarian and others on the Steering Committee because I want to do what I can to see revival come to our land from the top down." Patterson accepted, believing that "this rally will have the endorsement of God."[18]

Jerry Falwell was a harder sell. Falwell was thoroughly politicized by 1980, but he and his core fundamentalist supporters were uneasy about mingling in a religious setting with charismatics and Pentecostals. "Mr. Falwell would not have anything to do with me spiritually," recalled Gimenez. A month before the rally, Robertson informed Falwell that "Washington for Jesus" had already registered more than 100,000 potential attendees, predicting that a final count of one million seemed "a very real possibility." He made a final appeal to his fundamentalist friend: "I know your concern for America and your desire, as you expressed it to me when we flew up to Washington, to have a broad coalition of people involved in a national revival. . . . The politicians are laughing at the evangelicals and fundamentalists because they believe we will never do anything in concert. If we can't pray together for God to spare our nation, how in the world are we going to work together for a better land. If the Moral Majority is going to have any creditability, you need to be involved in 'Washington for Jesus.' . . . I appreciate you personally, and want to invite you to participate in some way as a sign to the Lord, the devil, and God's enemies, that the church of Jesus Christ can work together in love for one another even though they may disagree on a few points of doctrine." At the last moment, Falwell participated.[19]

"Washington for Jesus" was touted as a non-political, patriotic religious event. But a document written by Robertson entitled "A Christian Declaration" stating the purpose of the rally bore a clear political imprint. It deplored in generic terms the moral decline in the nation, and specifically decried "the slaughter of unborn infants," the removal of "the truth of God" from public schools, the growth of a government "bureaucracy run wild," the weakening of the armed forces, and the tendency to make the poor "perpetual wards of the state." On foreign policy, the declaration warned: "Our government has aided our enemies and destroyed our friends. We have assisted the oppressors and weakened the victims. Government has encouraged atheistic enemies of God while often repressing the godly." A petition, which was presented to the president and Congress, warned that "the Federal Government has grown to such dangerous proportions it has become a serious threat to many of the most basic liberties of the American people," including "the conscience and religious rights of the people."[20]

The meticulously organized rally lasted for twelve hours and was broadcast throughout the country on the three major religious networks, CBN, PTL, and TBN, a "historic linkup" that made it the largest religious television event ever broadcast in the United States. More than twenty-five "well-known speakers" were allotted spots on the program ranging from three to ten minutes, interspersed with performances by musical groups and individual artists ranging from church choirs to popular recording artists. Predictably, witnesses disagreed about the size and impact of the rally. Liberal religious organizations, including the National Council of Churches, viewed it as an alarming sign of the growing political clout of the religious right. The *Washington Post* reported in March that a group of District of Columbia pastors had withdrawn support for the rally because of its political message. Afterward, major newspapers estimated the attendance at "more than 200,000," exceeding the number who had assembled a year earlier to greet Pope John Paul II. Supporters claimed from 500,000 to 750,000, and producer Lloyd Watson boasted that the broadcast was the "greatest Christian media event in history."[21]

According to press accounts, the rally was attended by sixteen members of Congress. None was more appreciative than Senator Jesse Helms, who wrote to Robertson afterward, "I thought the rally was a tremendous success. The Lord's hand surely was upon you and all the others who put it together." Robertson replied, "How sweet you were to write. It was a thrill to see you at the rally and I thank God for your stand for righteousness in our nation." The only politician who was invited to speak at the rally, Jimmy Carter, declined; he well understood the wide gulf that had developed between him and the collection of religious leaders sponsoring the rally. Robert Maddox, Carter's Special Assistant for Religious Liaison, received the leaders in the White House, and immediately after the event Robertson wrote a conciliatory note to him. "As I promised you," he wrote, "the 'Washington for Jesus' rally became the largest Protestant gathering in the nation's history and a time of prayer and intercession for our nation. Although many prayed for him, there was not one uncomplimentary word about the President." Noting that the hostage crisis in Iran seemed to be easing, Robertson added: "Tell Jimmy that good news is on the way, and that if, when it comes, he will give the credit to God in Heaven, he can expect a turning in his own personal situation as well as that of the nation." Maddox's reply was formal and icy: "Thank you for your letter. I was indeed encouraged by the high tone of the 'Washington for Jesus' rally. On behalf of the President, I thank you for the prayers. . . . I am sure that when the hostages are released, the President will give God the glory."[22]

After the rally, Gimenez "was prepared to close our One Nation Under God office" because of "financial obligations," but Robertson urged him "to keep [it] in operation with CBN's financial backing." The successor organization, renamed Americans for Jesus, held rallies around the country with varied success. Several subsequent "Washington for Jesus" rallies were staged, but nothing rivaled the impact of the original gathering.[23]

Perhaps the most significant lasting impact of the rally was its impact on Bill Bright and Pat Robertson. The two had been "good friends" before the rally; afterward they drew closer, bonded by a common belief that they had been involved in a momentous occasion. Immediately after his return home, Robertson wrote to Bright: "None of us had any conception of how far-reaching this event may be." Bright replied, "It was a special privilege to be associated with you in this project which I believe, under God, has the potential of helping turn our nation around." Both were overwhelmed by the "drawing together in the body of Christ"; the meeting had included Pentecostals, charismatics, fundamentalists (including Falwell), conservative evangelicals, a smattering of representatives of the Southern Baptist Church and other mainstream denominations, and Roman Catholics. Replying to a congratulatory letter from Senator William L. Armstrong, Robertson wrote: "Bill Bright feels it may be the most significant day in our nation's history. We all pray it will prove a turning point in these crisis days."[24]

Robertson never lowered his estimate of the importance of the rally. He wrote to one of the planners of a 1988 Robertson for President rally, "I believe that the first 'Washington for Jesus' Rally . . . was one of the greatest moments in the history of America. I believe that it sparked a revolution in our country." The momentum of that day set Pat Robertson on a steady journey toward a run for the presidency.[25]

The Road to Candidacy

Robertson was a peripheral participant in the spate of religious conferences and rallies preceding the election of 1980; to a large degree, he remained aloof from the cauldron of new organizations launched before and after Ronald Reagan's election. He accepted an invitation from James Robinson and Ed McAteer to speak at the highly publicized Dallas National Affairs Briefing in August 1980. That conference drew more than 10,000 religious leaders who heard calls to political action by leading conservative politicians, including Ronald Reagan. Like most of those in Dallas, Robertson was thrilled to be in the midst of such a spontaneous coming together of a "great army." In a major address before the gathering, Robertson exulted: "I would rather be alive at this time than any other time in history. . . . These are the greatest days that the Church of Jesus Christ will ever know in our history. Since the time of Pentecost there has never been such a coming together of God's people. . . . So, let's join together again as a mighty army — as a great crusade — to see the Lord Jesus exalted in America . . . and around the world." Robertson agreed to serve as a member of the "Council of 56" in the newly minted organization which had convened the briefing, called Providing Education & Direction for Leaders Concerned with National Moral Issues. That organization, made up mostly of Southern Baptist conservatives, was soon surpassed in influence by other groups.[26]

Like most of the religious leaders in Dallas, Robertson was captured by the personal charisma of Ronald Reagan. He sat next to Reagan at a banquet and was on the stage when Reagan spoke to the assembly. In April, he gave his partners a sweeping endorsement of Reagan's candidacy: "Ronald Reagan is a former Democrat, union leader, fiscal conservative and born-again Christian. He believes in free enterprise, limited government, public morality and strong national defense. He opposes abortion and ERA. He favors voluntary prayer in the schools. He is a strong anti-communist and entertains no illusions about Soviet intentions."[27]

Like most other conservatives, Robertson was captivated by Reagan's personal aura all during his presidency. When he failed to fulfill conservative hopes for measures such as a balanced budget, it was because of circumstances beyond his control, making him a ruler after the image of King Josiah of Judah: "Good King Josiah made all of the right moves to correct a system of evil that extended back fifty-five years before him. Yet, despite his most valiant attempts, he was unable to turn back the forces of deterioration which had gripped his people. . . . His reign merely postponed the inevitable."[28]

Robertson sustained an admiring, but not close, relationship with the president, unlike Jerry Falwell's insider status at the Reagan White House. Robertson was invited to the White House to attend several formal dinners, aired three interviews with the president on *The 700 Club*, including one taped in the Oval Office, and exchanged occasional personal notes with Reagan. He felt free to make suggestions and complain in his messages to the White House. Robertson biographer David John Marley writes: "Unlike Falwell, Robertson had no problem writing stern letters to the president. . . . The bulk of his letters after 1983 either asked for the president's time or complained about his policies." In 1982 Reagan named Robertson to an eight-member "President's Task Force on Victims of Crime"; when Robertson was honored by the city of Corona, California, during a visit there, President Reagan sent him a note of congratulations (framed in Robertson's office): "For many years you have worked diligently to bring a message of hope and faith to Americans across the land."[29]

In spite of his participation in the Dallas Briefing, and his overall admiration for Ronald Reagan, in the early 1980s Robertson backed away from direct political involvement and insisted he still had no party allegiance. In January 1980 he wrote: "I believe that God wants the church to be like Jesus. Obviously, individual Christians will enter politics; all of us owe Caesar informed and active citizenship. But, at least for the next couple of years, the church of Jesus Christ should concentrate on the salvation of the lost, rather than taking over temporal political power." "God isn't a right-winger or a left-winger," he told a *Newsweek* reporter in September, conspicuously separating himself from the growing religious right movement. He believed that "active partisan politics" was the "wrong path for true evangelicals."[30]

Partly, Robertson explained, he was still chafing from the perceived betrayal of Jimmy Carter: "There are good people in both parties, but most party professionals care nothing for the Kingdom of God. They will use religionists ... to gain votes. After the shouting dies down ... the evangelicals are left with what they now have under Carter — nothing." Only spiritual revival could save the country. "I have always been supportive of the Christians' rights to be citizens," he told a Catholic reporter, "but my focus is on the spiritual mission of reaching people for the Lord Jesus and helping to bring a spiritual-moral revival to America. We intend to avoid anything which could cause confusion in the accomplishment of that mission."[31]

At the practical level, Robertson backed away from the increasingly strident, and in his judgment politically naïve, leadership of the religious right in general, and in particular from Jerry Falwell and the Moral Majority. He publicly questioned what he regarded as the clumsy partisan approach of such groups as the Moral Majority: "We need justice and mercy and compassion without making the government God. Liberalism's fallacy is that government equals God. Conservatism is often dominated by fat cats who want to keep the world safe for Coca-Cola and General Motors." "I have nothing against how other ministries see their roles; each must do as it believes best," Robertson told a reporter, but he would do nothing to cause "confusion" about the mission of CBN. He told biographer David John Marley that as late as 1983 he still considered the idea of a presidential race "absurd."[32]

In retrospect, Robertson pictured the Moral Majority as the misguided "brain child" of conservative Washington activist Paul Weyrich; he believed it never exhibited the political savvy needed to have a lasting impact. Religiously, its reach was limited because Falwell's fundamentalist base was both small and brittle. Robertson respected Weyrich, and for several years was president of the Council of National Policy, a group set up by Weyrich to discuss "cogent conservative concepts," but he never liked being treated like a student. In spite of the early success of the Moral Majority, Robertson believed that "Christians as an interest group" would never coalesce under Falwell's leadership. "The Moral Majority wanted to be the Christian ACLU," acting as the public representative for Christians, observed Robertson advisor David West. Robertson never changed his mind about the political ineptness of the early religious right leaders, and he politely but firmly refused to identify with the influential but transient organizations of the early 1980s.[33]

On the other hand, Robertson's political retreat was far from neat; political issues became more and more central in his thought and in his public pronouncements. Speaking before a meeting of the National Council of Churches in February 1980, Robertson "coyly denied any interest in 'politics.'" "But it is a different Robertson who speaks daily on the '700 Club,'" commented *Christian Century* editor James M. Wall. On *The 700 Club* he daily exposed "millions of viewers to his interpretation of history, meshing millennialism with the most rigid kind of right-wing reactionary politics." Robertson shrugged off the *Christian Century*'s criticism, but he was "deeply grieved" when one of CBN's supporters complained about the political drift of *The 700 Club*. He explained that the main thrust of CBN continued to be winning people to Christ, but "at the same time, we both know that our nation is in desperate trouble. . . . I am sorry this seems political to you."[34]

In February 1981 Robertson established an overtly political organization under the CBN umbrella, the Freedom Council. By that time he was vigorously supporting a number of the initiatives of the religious right, including the passage of a prayer amendment supported by President Reagan. Testifying before the Senate Judiciary Committee in support of the amendment in 1982, Robertson appealed to his family history: "When my father, A. Willis Robertson, was a member of this distinguished body, he met with various colleagues every Wednesday morning in the Senate Dining Room to read the Bible and pray. This to him was the highlight of his week. . . . I want to assure this committee, that if the recent Supreme Court decisions are constitutionally sound, then the Senate prayer breakfasts are unconstitutional." Robertson assured the committee that the American people "overwhelmingly" supported "a reversal of the antireligious court rulings."[35]

When the amendment finally failed in 1984, Robertson denounced the result as a "blow against freedom in America." "The American people will not tolerate for long dominance by a minority of elitists who seek to strip them of treasured values," warned Robertson. Congressman Newt Gingrich praised Robertson for his help on the issue, asking him to "convert President Reagan's tape on school prayer into a 5 minute public service announcement," with a lead-in by Robertson and with "a crawler along the bottom asking people to contact their Senators and Congressman." Gingrich was "very optimistic about our chances for success."[36]

In the course of the long fight over the amendment, Robertson cultivated ties with many old and new friends in Washington. After the amendment failed to get the necessary two-thirds majority, Robertson sent letters of appreciation to the fifty-six senators who had voted for it: "The American people have lost one of their most cherished freedoms through court action over the past twenty years. Your voice was raised in support of freedom. I conveyed this fact to 11,000 American towns and cities today on our television network. I am sure that many others besides me will join in sending to you their thanks and appreciation as well." His friend Jesse Helms praised Robertson's efforts in behalf of the failed amendment: "The Lord has given you remarkable talent and intellect which, combined with your faith, have made you the conscience of America. I do thank you for all that you have meant to me personally." And again a few days later: "As I've told you so many times, just being on the same team with you has been a real blessing to me. You are a constant source of inspiration to me — and to millions of others." Senator Richard Lugar of Indiana informed Robertson that his constituents had indeed responded to Robertson's television appeals: "Your impact was considerable. My offices received hundreds of calls and letters from your viewers. Their support, and your continued support and encouragement are greatly appreciated."[37]

The early forays of the religious right, particularly Reagan's appearance at the Dallas briefing, drew increasing media interest in the emerging movement at the beginning of the 1980s; in the last half of the decade their curiosity turned into a feeding frenzy. By 1985, amid the growing speculation that Robertson would be a candidate for the presidency in 1988, the national press was focused on Robertson. In August 1985 he was a guest on *Face the Nation,* and in October he was interviewed by David Hartman on *Good Morning America* and spoke to the National Press Club. For months Robertson tried to explain to reporters how he differed from the earlier leaders of the religious right. It was difficult to shake stereotypes. David Hartman asked, "How would you compare your goals, your style, your approach to that of say, just to name three, Jerry Falwell, Jimmy Swaggart and Jim Bakker?" Robertson replied: "One of them is a pastor of a local church, the others are evangelists and I'm neither of those right now. I'm essentially a professional broadcaster."[38]

Robertson's self-definition remained a bone of contention in the months ahead, but slowly reporters acknowledged that he did bring a different persona to the politicization of Christians. In his introduction of Robertson in 1985, Robert MacNeil labeled him a "Southern Baptist TV Evangelist" but also noted that "his father was a U.S. Senator from Virginia" and that he possessed a "resume many politicians would envy, degrees from Yale Law School, and the New York Theological Seminary . . . and a Marine in Korea."

By 1986, as Robertson forces worked feverishly to secure support for the Republican nomination, the media probed more deeply into his work and character. In July, *U.S. News & World Report* Editor-in-Chief Mortimer Zuckerman thanked Robertson for contributing a "quite interesting and informative" interview for the July 14 issue of the magazine. Picturing Robertson on the cover, the magazine reported that he was "off to a fast start in what appears to be a certain run for the Presidency."[39]

The Race

Robertson later looked back on a March 1985 article in *The Saturday Evening Post* as the launching pad of his presidential bid. The authors interviewed a range of Washington insiders, including Bert Lance, Paul Weyrich, and former White House aide Dee Jepsen, and concluded that there was a "pattern" of interest in a Robertson candidacy at the grassroots level and among "a significant number of influential leaders." The article included an extended look at Robertson's "Agenda for Public Action," a document that was essentially a campaign platform. Such old and established evangelical periodicals as *Christian Life, Christian Herald,* and *Christianity Today* published serious and generally favorable articles in support of a Robertson candidacy.[40]

Robertson told writer Pat Assimakopoulos in *Christian Life* that his explorations with Christian leaders had been overwhelmingly positive: "I have met with heads of denominations and heads of independent ministries. The response I'm getting is quite favorable from a broad segment." In 1985, he crafted a reply to be sent to the increasing numbers of supporters inquiring about his intentions: "I do not desire to be president, much less to run for the office. I am aware of the ordeal by fire that a person like me would have to endure. Many people — including those with political knowledge — in and out of government are urging me to stand tall as a leader for traditional moral values. Such a move by me would never happen unless it was the *clear, unmistakable, and oft confirmed will and leading of our Lord.*" Speaking at the annual convention of "Concerned Women for America," which boasted a membership of 600,000, Robertson's enthusiasm was palpable: "I'm so excited about what you're doing, because you represent a move of God's Spirit in today's world. . . . Various other organizations around the country, hundreds of thousands of Christians are concerned." Several of the leaders of the organized Christian right, most importantly Jerry Falwell, signaled approval of a Robertson candidacy. Falwell, who had already pledged his support to Vice-President George Bush in the upcoming election, told reporters that he was "encouraging the Rev. Pat Robertson to run for the presidency, if only to serve as a power broker at the 1988 Republican convention."[41]

Early Successes

Some insiders among the conservative Republican network in Washington warmed to a Robertson candidacy, unlikely as it seemed. Richard Viguerie supplied Robertson with a list of "conservatives with whom you should discuss a possible Presidential bid." The list included the names of Howard Phillips, Paul Weyrich, Terry Dolan, and Ron Godwin; Robertson confirmed that "we have been in touch with all of them, with the possible exception of Ron Godwin." For some time Robertson had been a part of Paul Weyrich's inner circle in Washington, frequently attending meetings at Weyrich's Free Congress Research and Education Foundation. By the end of 1986 Weyrich considered him "an outsider much in the mold of Ronald Reagan," whose election would seem to most in Washington "preposterous." But he had strength with the "little people" and he had the "moral high ground" on many issues. It would take an "extraordinary situation" for Robertson to win the presidency, Weyrich surmised, but "Robertson is perhaps the brightest of all the presidential candidates, in terms of intellect and in terms of sheer understanding of the national forces." "He has indicated to me," Weyrich revealed, "that the Lord has told him to run in the same way that he told him to found CBN." While he was "not privy to the good Lord's communications with Pat Robertson," Weyrich thought it would be a mistake to write him off. Weyrich suggested young Marc Nuttle to head Robertson's staff, and the "infusion of some Weyrich allies and protégés" into Robertson's exploration organization fed the Washington "suspicion that Weyrich is really the mastermind behind the Robertson pre-candidacy." Weyrich conceded that "many of my people I've trained have gone into that operation," but far from masterminding it, he sharply disagree with Robertson's strategy and predicted that Robertson could not "go all the way." Howard Phillips, head of the Conservative Caucus, confirmed that "Weyrich is heavily involved" in the Robertson campaign, but "Robertson's the power behind Robertson."[42]

Giving added credibility to Robertson's pre-candidacy campaign was the courteous and respectful notice he received from William F. Buckley Jr. Granting that Robertson "hasn't a prayer, to use that word recklessly, of winning," Buckley bristled at the flurry of condescending attacks on his Christian persona. By the time the race began, Buckley insisted that Republicans needed to take him seriously: "Robertson isn't just competing for a share of the Republican vote; he's also importing his own army of new voters, and he has an organization that teaches them the ropes and takes care of all the details. . . . He is running an unusual, intelligent, and methodical campaign."[43]

In spite of Robertson's strategic disentanglement from religious right organizations at the beginning of the decade, throughout the 1980s many of his Christian supporters and friends came to identify with his political views as a result of his political commentary on *The 700 Club* and through the activities of the Freedom Council. In 1981 Robertson established the Freedom Council as an independent organization to resist "attempts to destroy religious freedom in America." This "new ministry" was introduced to CBN department heads at a seminar entitled "Restore America." The Freedom Council was a formidable organization from the beginning, with a budget of more than $5 million a year. At its peak it had coordinators in all fifty states and tens of thousands of pastors had been enlisted in a "grassroots network." The Freedom Council was essentially the political wing of CBN until disbanded on October 1, 1986, when Robertson formally began to explore a run for the Republican nomination for the presidency. Announcing the Freedom Council's termination, Bob Slosser, the organization's last president, restated its self-proclaimed historic aims: "The mission of the Freedom Council has been to alert Christian people to infringement upon religious freedom affecting all faiths worldwide. The organization has dedicated itself to prayer, education, and action leading citizens to public involvement."[44]

During his presidential campaign, Robertson's critics questioned the legality of CBN's support for the political activities of the Freedom Council. After a pointed criticism aired on NBC Nightly News, CBN issued a press release clarifying and defending its financial support for the Freedom Council: "NBC News unfairly and inaccurately reported on CBN's legitimate efforts to educate and inform Christians about important moral issues facing our society. . . . The Freedom Council was organized to educate Christians and others about our country's political process. CBN partners were fully informed that CBN actively contributed to and solicited funds for the Freedom Council."[45]

In 1985 and 1986, before Robertson established an exploratory committee, critics repeatedly charged that the Freedom Council was, in fact, a Robertson campaign organization. Robertson and the Freedom Council may well have pushed the boundaries, but they were careful not to threaten the tax-exempt status of CBN. Both outside and inside CBN, observers began to question whether the Freedom Council had abandoned its "clearly legal political education work" and "started down the slippery slope of questionable political involvement."[46]

After a meeting with CBN's chief financial officer, in which insiders raised questions about the support of the Council's political agenda, Robertson wrote a long, confidential memo "to be on record to state clearly what the purposes of The Freedom Council were at its inception and what they were at its demise." He wrote: "The Freedom Council was established . . . for the purpose of resisting attempts to destroy religious freedom in America. Our goal was to be active in court cases, to be active in educating Christian people to the dangers involved, and to mobilize Christians as registered voters and as participants in the primary process. A very minimum activity was to inform legislatures and U.S. Congress about key issues affecting freedom of religion and the loss of our religious heritage in America." CBN made "substantial contributions" to the Freedom Council, but, Robertson insisted, "It is my contention that The Freedom Council acted entirely within its rights and provisions as a non profit charity and did not engage in 'politics' other than that which is clearly permissible. . . ." The organization was disbanded because some Freedom Council workers, and an increasingly inquisitive national press, had the "perception . . . that the Freedom Council was nothing more than a stalking-horse for me."[47]

Responding to a *Washington Post* editorial in April 1988, Robertson meticulously explained his understanding of the legality of the actions of the organization. He was distressed that the "inflammatory and inaccurate statements in the press" had sparked a two-year audit by the IRS. The agency had dispatched "14 agents who are determined to leave no stone unturned," and Robertson remained convinced that they would discover that the Council had operated within "fully legal and ethical guidelines."[48]

The Freedom Council activity most seriously questioned by critics was its "party building" tactics beginning in 1984. According to Robertson, the Council "determined that we should take three key states and attempt mobilizing in those states on a congressional district basis." The model states were Michigan, North Carolina, and Florida: "Michigan, because it is a northern industrial state, North Carolina, because it is considered a conservative Bible-belt state, Florida, because it is a swing state." The Freedom Council's "party building" operations were ultimately ruled to be legal by the Federal Election Commission, but they clearly became a springboard for a Robertson presidential race.[49]

Marc Nuttle, an experienced campaign strategist who had worked in the 1984 Reagan-Bush campaign, began forming a Robertson campaign staff in the fall of 1986. In October 1986, he added a second critical staff member, Herbert Ellingwood, who had worked in the Justice Department and was a good friend of Attorney General Edwin Meese. The most important staff member in the successful organizing effort in Michigan was Marlene Elwell, a Roman Catholic activist who had led pro-life lobbying in the state for several years. After a visit with Robertson in Virginia Beach, she launched a series of training sessions in Michigan teaching newly aroused Christians how to win seats as precinct delegates at the Republican Party state convention. Robertson had begun touring Michigan and other targeted states in 1985, particularly Iowa and South Carolina, urging Freedom Council members (who numbered around 500,000) to assert themselves in party activities at the precinct level. While Freedom Council events avoided advocating the candidacy of Robertson, and he continued to insist that he had not decided to run, a Robertson candidacy seemed more and more likely.

The impact of Freedom Council organizing in Michigan was dramatic. Party regulars were stunned by the results of the early filing of candidates for election as delegates to the state convention in May 1986. Of the 9,000 candidates filing to run, reported the *Washington Post,* around 4,000 "were recruited by the state chapter of the Freedom Council, a group founded to teach 'people with Judeo-Christian values' how to become involved in politics." "'Pat Robertson hit a home run today,'" the Wayne County clerk told reporters after the filing deadline. "Michigan was crucial to everybody," said a long-time Robertson advisor. After the 1986 filings, the Robertson bandwagon was underway.[50]

The Michigan Republican Convention took place in February 1987, and Robertson confidently predicted that he would have more supporters than any other candidate, assuring him a large share of the state's national convention delegates. The campaigns of Vice-President George Bush and Congressman Jack Kemp had been caught off guard, and the only question was how deeply Robertson delegates had penetrated the Michigan party. At the convention, Robertson delegates joined with Kemp supporters to assure a conservative takeover of the state party machinery. The importance of the Robertson victory was blunted when the Bush campaign shrewdly released voting reports to the press that grossly overestimated their strength, although the ploy was exposed by the *New York Times* a few days after the count was finished. Political maneuvering continued, but, wrote Detroit columnist Hugh McDiarmid, "Let's face it. The 'Get George Bush' fundamentalists won the Republicans' big . . . holy war in Lansing this weekend, making Pat Robertson the presidential front-runner in Michigan in 1988 . . . whether top party leaders like it or not. Most of them don't."[51]

The national media snapped to attention. In the *Washington Post* Rowland Evans and Robert Novak editorialized about the stunning development: "Reassurances from Bush spin doctors that the state convention will not affect national delegates do not reflect the dismay in Washington." No one was more impressed than Pat Robertson. Two days after the victory, he wrote to Jesse Helms: "I just wanted to drop you a brief note to let you know what is happening with me. Last Saturday delegates favorable to my candidacy won a majority of seats on the State Central Committee of the Republican Party in Michigan. . . . It was a wonderful win in a state where George Bush beat Ronald Reagan two-to-one in 1980. I want to get by and have a chance to discuss what is going on, if you can find some time from your hectic schedule in the Senate."[52]

Planning moved quickly in the wake of the Michigan success. In March Robertson organized a political action committee, the Committee for Freedom, that could legally assist his candidacy while training "people to get involved in precinct level politics." For the first time he was free to solicit support for purely political purposes. In a letter to CBN supporters, he wrote: "Remember the Committee for Freedom is a Political Action Committee and is not a part of CBN or CBN University. Any contribution to the Committee for Freedom should be in addition to your splendid contributions to CBN or CBN University." On September 17, Robertson announced that he would become a candidate if, during the next twelve months, 3 million voters signed petitions asking him to run. The Committee for Freedom was replaced in July by Americans for Robertson, an exploratory committee which later became Robertson's campaign organization.[53]

By the fall of 1986 the Robertson campaign organization was one of the largest in the Republican field. Although the organizational transition from Freedom Council to Americans for Robertson seemed seamless, insiders insisted that "the carry over was somewhat incidental." The exploratory campaign was formally launched on September 17, 1987, 199 years to the day after the meeting of the thirty-nine signers of the Constitution in Independence Hall in Philadelphia. Always keen on symbolic meanings, Robertson delivered his announcement address before 3,500 ecstatic backers in Constitution Hall in Washington. It was viewed on closed circuit television by an estimated 200,000 people in "216 halls across our fifty states." "The vision born on September 17 was of one nation — under God — with liberty and justice for all," Robertson announced. In spite of the intentions of the founding fathers, he continued, "during the past twenty-five years an assault on our faith and values" had been launched by "a small elite of lawyers, judges, and educators." In his speech, Robertson outlined a wide-ranging political platform that included "a new vision of lean, efficient government," a "partnership between the government, American business, and the American working men and women," and opposition to "Communist tyranny," including the Sandinistas in Nicaragua. In conclusion, he announced: "If by September 17th, 1987, one year from today, three million registered voters have signed petitions telling me that they will pray — that they will work — that they will give toward my election, then I will run as a candidate for the nomination of the Republican Party."[54]

The announcement triggered a series of moves at CBN. Vice President Joseph G. Gray assured employees that the event had been "sponsored entirely" by the recently formed Americans for Robertson political action group, and he issued a "policy statement intended to clarify for employees what is legally permissible . . . in terms of political activity for any candidate on the grounds of CBN." Employees were encouraged to participate in the political process, but no such activity could implicate the ministry in any way. "CBN equipment and facilities may not be used for political activity," Gray warned, and it should be clear that "CBN does not make contributions or expenditures in connection with any election to any political office."[55]

The well-funded Robertson campaign machinery moved swiftly after the success in Michigan, aiming to "duplicate the grass-roots organizing effort for the Iowa caucuses" in September 1987. Marlene Elwell, described by Robertson as his "Roman Catholic political genius," was the architect of the effective campaigns in both Michigan and Iowa — even though, Robertson boasted, in Iowa she was working with only six paid workers, compared to thirty in what was reputed to be a well-oiled Bush campaign organization. In a caucus held at Iowa State University, Bob Dole got the most votes, but the storyline that captured the notice of the press was that Robertson finished a strong second, soundly defeating Vice-President George Bush; it was "a straw poll whose results were noticed around the nation." "Iowa was textbook perfect," Robertson recalled, led "by fresh, eager people, organized to perfection, who were working their hearts out under the leadership of a highly spiritual, highly motivated professional." Robertson clearly got the attention of Lee Atwater, who was managing the Bush campaign. Two reporters who covered the campaign described the impact of Bush's loss to Robertson in Iowa: "It wasn't Bush's own pale performance that disturbed his men. It was instead the sheer foot-stomping, hand-clapping, praise-the-Lordly intensity of the Robertson crowd rocking the field house with their fervor." Suddenly, Robertson was triggering a "schizoid reaction . . . among old-time Republicans." George Bush was "particularly frustrated" by Robertson, wrote his biographers Peter and Rochelle Schweizer, because "talking about his faith openly . . . came awkwardly to him." Media professionals still did not give Robertson a serious chance to get the nomination, reported political writer E. J. Dionne in the *New York Times,* but it was time to take a serious look at what was going on, because his constituency was "sufficiently upset by what they see as the spread of 'secularism' that they have won Mr. Robertson some attention-grabbing, if not nomination-winning, victories." "He gained a lot of respect tonight," Bob Dole's state chairman told reporters after Robertson received 34 percent of the votes in the straw poll.[56]

With a sweeping victory in Hawaii preceding his strong showing in the Iowa straw poll, Robertson moved his official entry into the race up to September 15. He made his formal announcement at a warehouse at 2127 Smith Street in Chesapeake, Virginia, where volunteer workers in the Americans for Robertson organization had been coordinating the drive to secure signatures supporting his candidacy. Robertson held a brief press conference, answering questions from the assembled reporters almost modestly. His answers were calm and reasoned — no fanaticism or bombast. He was ready, and his answers had been well crafted. The challenge before him, he confessed, was to introduce this Pat Robertson to the American electorate. It would be no easy task.[57]

Like so many of the things he had started, and would start, Robertson's campaign rested on the shoulders of fellow Christians who saw him as one of their own. The walls were lined with letters and petitions from supporters; many of the letters began, "Dear Brother Pat." The Robertson campaign had a number of campaign positives, wrote Wayne King in the *New York Times,* including years of experience in television production, fundraising, and direct mail and telephone contacts with supporters. But his ace in the hole was the "volunteers recruited in large measure from the ranks of devout Christians." Polls indicated that around 15 percent of the voters in the early campaigns "fall into the fundamentalist-evangelical camp," and the Robertson strategists predicted that number would double. "There is growing evidence," wrote King, "that Mr. Robertson is re-cruiting new Republican voters who have never before taken an active role in politics, and who vote sporadically, if at all."[58]

By the end of 1987 the Robertson campaign was euphoric. After his appearance on an extended *Firing Line* debate hosted by William Buckley, a telephone poll ranked Robertson as the most serious challenger to Vice-President Bush. Campaign chairman Marc Nuttle boasted that the debate and its aftermath confirmed "Pat Robertson's appeal to mainstream voters and it clearly broadens his base as well as that of the Republican party." Writing in the *National Review*, Peter L. Berger portrayed Robertson as a marketable and orthodox Republican candidate: "His manner, at least as it appears on television, is relaxed, reasonable, hardly that of an aggressive dogmatist. His stated political views are barely to the right of what is generally deemed to be respectable conservative opinion." After its early successes, the Robertson campaign targeted the Super Tuesday primaries in the southern states. Counting heavily on their proven local organizing and a strong vote from evangelical Christians, the campaign staff dispatched an "Urgent Memorandum" to "Southern Conservative Leaders" warning that a Bush-Kemp alliance had been formed to slow Robertson's momentum, leaving him as "the only true conservative choice."[59]

Issues, Distractions, and Latin American Activism

In his long career as a talk show host Robertson had spoken often, and sometimes loosely, on a wide range of political issues, but by 1987 his campaign had codified a coherent body of Robertson positions on all major campaign issues. Generally, his policy statements were conventionally conservative. Robertson's platform had been pretty well sketched out in the *Saturday Evening Post* article that had jump-started his presidential ambitions in March 1985. In August 1985 the *Conservative Digest* succinctly summarized the candidate's views on a range of topics, including "budget cuts, communist adventurism, defense spending, education, federal spending, integration, judicial reform, tax reform, and welfare spending."[60]

Like all conservative Republicans, Robertson wrestled in the 1980s with "Voodoo economics and Reaganomics," seeing deficit spending as a threat to national security, but acknowledging that "I don't have solutions." "If we ever needed the grace of God it's right now," he declared in a 1982 speech. As late as 1986 he remained reluctant to offer specific alternatives to deficit spending and Reaganomics. In June he told a group of reporters:

"I wrote an economic newsletter for five years on a monthly basis, and I consider it as one of my hobbies, micro-economics. . . . I don't have any specific policies except that if it doesn't come under control, we'll have three trillion dollar debt in the next four years."[61]

By the time he announced his candidacy, however, Robertson had a fully developed platform. His economic recommendations included slashing budgets, reducing deficits (which he regarded as both "fiscally and morally wrong"), extending "free-market principles," and opposition to "any new taxes of any kind." He supported welfare reform, programs for energy independence, extending farm exports and "phasing out subsidies over a reasonable period," and the promotion of free and fair trade.[62]

Often, his campaign policy statements included direct appeals to his religious constituency. For instance, his education plank stated: "Pat Robertson favors the return of traditional Judeo-Christian moral values to the heart of our school curriculum, and supports voluntary prayer as a legitimate freedom guaranteed by the First Amendment. . . . Pat Robertson wants to abandon the failed 'values clarification,' 'cultural relativism,' and 'new age' curriculum of so-called progressive education."[63]

Of course, Robertson was most at home with his core constituency when he addressed the family-values issues that had become the staple of the religious right. The centerpiece of his social agenda was "reversal of the Supreme Court's decision in Roe v. Wade." As president, he would appoint "pro-life justices and judges only." Of course, on those issues Robertson's record had long been clear. He expressed his views repeatedly in 1986 in forums ranging from the National Right to Life Convention to the Yale University Law School. Speaking to a Right to Life audience, he minced no words: "According to my organization, abortion is murder." At his former law school, Robertson staunchly denounced the Warren Court for taking "power . . . which the Constitution never gave it."[64]

Less clearly related to his high-profile religious-right identity, but closely connected to his personal heritage and religious convictions, were Robertson's foreign policy statements. Like Reagan, Robertson saw the president "as the leader of the noncommunist world." An unwavering opponent of "Godless communism," Robertson saw no room for compromise with Marxists. As a candidate, he announced four principles undergirding all of his foreign policy beliefs: protecting the "interests of the nation"; acting "consistent with the philosophical and moral principles of our own national life"; supporting policies that would benefit our allies rather than our adversaries; and making choices "simple enough to explain in common sense terms to our own people."[65]

Robertson saw the Soviet Union as the provocateur of unrest and revolutionary cruelty in Europe, Africa, and Latin America. He distrusted arms-reduction negotiations with the Soviets, calling rather for tough measures to weaken their control of Eastern Europe. But Robertson's lifelong affinity for China stood in stark contrast to his distaste for the Soviet Union. He believed "that a close relationship between the U.S. and China is conducive to regional peace and to the overall interests of both countries. . . . Along with many Americans, Pat Robertson applauds the economic and social reforms undertaken by China since the late 1970s."[66]

In the Middle East, Robertson's support for Israel was unequivocal. He firmly supported Israel's right to retain the Golan Heights and the West Bank, deplored the sale of weapons to Arab countries, and urged support for Israel's war on terrorism. On this issue, Robertson was particularly proud of his expertise: "Pat Robertson has been a consistent and outspoken supporter of Israel's right to exist for many years. A frequent visitor to the country, he has met with many of the nation's top leaders and is thoroughly familiar with Israel's major security concerns." While Robertson did his best to secularize the rationale for his support for Israel during the campaign, it was deeply rooted in theological beliefs that he had often expressed in his writings and television comments.[67]

Robertson was thoroughly disenchanted with the United Nations. In a speech before the Council on Foreign Relations in January 1987 he urged a reduction of funding to the UN and using the resulting savings to seed a new "Community of Democratic Nations." He appealed for an innovative new approach to "the global struggle of freedom against totalitarian tyranny." The world must move "in its quest for lasting peace from an arena of failed idealism, the rhetoric of fantasy and bitter disappointment to a new realism."[68]

In a statement that implicated both his antipathy for the Soviet Union and his views about the underdeveloped nations of the world, Robertson strongly supported "assistance to the men and women willing to fight for their freedom in countries such as Angola, Afghanistan, and Nicaragua." In Africa, he thought that the United States should encourage "moderate black leaders" throughout the continent who would stop the spread of communism and urged direct aid for pro-western "freedom fighters" resisting the "incompetent and corrupt Leninist regimes in . . . Angola and Mozambique." But Robertson's anti-communist worldview was most clearly and controversially articulated when he spoke of Latin America, particularly Nicaragua. In Latin America, as in other developing nations, Robertson believed that the hope for the future was the development of an enlightened capitalism. He insisted that "U.S. policy should encourage, wherever possible, the growth of a property-owning middle class and healthy, pluralistic social institutions to protect society from both right-wing coups and left-wing insurgency." He endorsed "the establishment of a free and democratic government in Nicaragua and the overthrow, by Nicaraguan democratic forces, of the Soviet-backed Sandinista government." A strong supporter of Reagan's aid for anti-government forces in Nicaragua, Robertson argued that "continued U.S. military aid to the anti-Sandinista democratic resistance in Nicaragua (Contras) is essential if the Managua regime is ever going to respect the desire of its own people for freedom and the sovereign rights of its neighbors."[69]

Robertson's views of Latin America and the rest of the developing world were deeply rooted in personal and religious experiences. By the time he became embroiled in controversy over his support of the Contras in Nicaragua, Robertson had spent years working with the growing charismatic Christian churches of the region. The American press, and to a remarkable degree commentators on American religion, were slow to recognize the huge Pentecostal revival that had been going on in Latin America since the end of World War II. By 1987, when a reporter wrote in *The Progressive* that "faith-healing, Bible-thumping, devil-exorcising preachers fill soccer stadiums from Santiago to San Salvador," the religious transformation of the region had been going on for decades.[70]

Generally, the evangelical boom provided natural allies for conservative political forces in the region. An on-the-scenes liberal observer in 1989 described the symbiosis: "The close links between missionary zeal, anticommunism, and U.S. imperialism, present today in Central America" had created alliances between "Central American oligarchs, military officials, and evangelical organizations." While the burgeoning independent Pentecostal and charismatic churches were largely apolitical, stressing personal morality, soul-saving, and self-improvement, they became a natural bulwark against the Marxist-based revolutionaries competing for converts in the region. After a 1983 trip to the region, which included a visit with Contra soldiers, Robertson became convinced that the rebels were "God's army," and that the leftist Sandinistas were guilty of massacres and atrocities in the region.[71]

Symbolizing the growing political clout of the booming Pentecostal/charismatic subculture in Central America was the rise to power of General Efram Rios Montt, who became president of Guatemala after a military coup in 1982. Montt was a member of a California-based group called Gospel Outreach, an independent charismatic church. Robertson was elated when Montt became president. *The 700 Club* aired regularly in Gua-temala, as it did in most of Latin America, and Robertson interviewed Montt the week after he had been installed by the military junta. Montt pledged himself to "return democratic voting processes" while stopping corruption and political oppression. He told Robertson, "We are now di-recting a military effort which is to manifest to our people what moral eth-ics should be, and my foundation is the word of God." Robertson was deeply impressed by the new president. His responses to questions about his association with Montt were filled with personal assurances: "I know Rios Montt and he has not allowed his army to kill, rape, and torture over 4,000 men, women and children. . . . Rios Montt is a Christian. He is neither a Communist nor a butcher. The previous administration consisted of thieves and butchers. There are those in the media who would like to see them replaced by Communists. I prefer a Christian."[72]

Along with other political and religious conservatives, Robertson was soon deeply involved in aiding the Contras in Nicaragua, cooperating with several private organizations founded to send non-military assistance to Nicaraguan refugees in Honduras after Congress had stopped government-funded aid for the rebels. Efforts to overthrow the Sandinista government in Nicaragua — which had taken power in 1979 after ousting the authoritar-ian Anastasio Somoza dictatorship and immediately established friendly relations with Cuba and the Soviet Union — was a hot-button issue in American politics throughout the 1980s. Speaking to a group composed of Americans of Cuban, Caribbean, and Central and South American origin in 1987, Robertson demanded that the United States resume "assisting the brave and honorable soldiers of the Democratic Resistance." Otherwise the Sandinistas, supported by Cuba and the Soviet Union, would forcibly ex-port "Marxist-Leninism" to El Salvador, Honduras, Costa Rica, and Mexico. He denounced congressional measures blocking Reagan's efforts to sup-port the Contras: "Despite the valiant efforts of this Administration to speak out common sense to the American people about Central America, the forces of surrender and betrayal are still strident, even within the Con-gress." During the campaign Robertson's language was somewhat more subdued, but he vigorously supported breaking relations with the Sandinista government and doing more to aid the United Nicaraguan Op-position (the Contras) with open rather than covert aid. Charging the Ortega regime with numerous atrocities, Robertson deplored political lib-erals' unwillingness to "communicate the truth about dictators such as Ortega."[73]

Supporters of the Sandinista regime in Nicaragua were outraged by the aid being sent to the Contras by American evangelical organizations. CBN's Operation Blessing insisted that its aid was not being sent "for political reasons": "We're doing it out of Christian concern and compassion," said Operation Blessing national director Bob Warren in 1984, while acknowledging that "CBN is a very red, white, and blue organization." By 1988 CBN had been identified as one of the "biggest contributors, raising millions of dollars, for food, medicine, clothing, vehicles and other aid for so-called Nicaraguan refugees, who also happened to be contras." While denying any intention to directly aid the Contras, Robertson "never hid his feelings on the matter." "He frequently likened the contras to freedom fighters," reported an article in the *Christian Century,* "and when the U.S. Congress balked at providing more aid in 1985 he went on television to denounce the 'craven submission of our leaders and Congress to the demands of communism.'" Robertson was pictured in the magazine visiting a Contra camp, although he strenuously denied that he had "reviewed troops."[74]

Robertson's religious experiences continued to influence his stance on Latin America. When the Sandinista coalition was replaced in power by a coalition of former Contra elements, Robertson saw it as a part of a "spiritual revolution in Latin America." After the election of Jorge Serrano Elias, "a charismatic Christian," to the presidency of Guatemala in 1991, Robertson exulted: "Guatemala may be the first country in Latin America where Evangelicals make up 50 percent of the population." The "tremendous Evangelical revival" in the region, "especially through the Pentecostal or Charismatic churches," offered proof that "the Marxist liberation theology must of necessity fail." The reason was simple: "The Evangelical personal emphasis will be on honesty, hard work, strong family bonds, quality education, thrift, and moral self-restraint." He had never urged the blind exportation of American values, but it was precisely these moral values "which made the United States a great nation." By the 1990s Robertson's newly formed Christian Coalition was directly in contact with evangelical political leaders of Latin America.[75]

The Search for a Broader Christian Constituency

After Robertson's strong showings in Michigan and Iowa, his campaign staff was keenly conscious that their candidate's core support was the religious people who had been energized by his candidacy. In a "sample letter to pastors" Robertson's campaign organization reminded pastors that "your participation in this year's presidential election is crucial to our country." The letter outlined the rights of churches: "According to the Tax Code, I.R.S. Regulations, and advice of legal counsel, you and your church are free to do the following: 1. You may encourage the members of your congregation to be good citizens by registering to vote and by voting on election day.... 2. You can preach on the scriptural commands of our Lord ... regarding the role of the Christian in the state.... 3. You can distribute to your congregation in a nonpartisan fashion, a list of the major issues of this election and the stands of the candidates in regard to each issue. 4. You can — if state law permits — have a registrar come to your church and register members to vote. 5. On election day you can arrange car pools or even use church buses to take members to the polls so long as the effort is nonpartisan in support of citizenship."[76]

Americans for Robertson accumulated a list of nearly 100 "Christian leaders" who endorsed Robertson's presidential bid. The list was telling. It was a virtual roll call of the leaders of the independent charismatic movement, including such influential old friends as Demos Shakarian, Oral Roberts, Jimmy Swaggart, Rex Humbard Sr., Morris Cerullo, Vinson Synan, Bob Tilton, John Gimenez, Earl Paulk, and many lesser lights of the movement. They were joined by the leaders of the two largest Pentecostal denominations in the country, Thomas Zimmerman of the Assemblies of God and J. O. Patterson of the Church of God in Christ. The only other conspicuous endorsers were leaders in the conservative Southern Baptist church with whom Robertson had crafted a cordial relationship based on issues despite his charismatic identity, including Paige Patterson, Bailey E. Smith, and Jimmy Draper. Perhaps the most enthusiastic of his supporters was his friend Bishop Patterson, head of the largest African American religious body in the country: "My support is not given solely because you are a dear friend, but rather because of your untiring efforts to better conditions for all mankind. This concern, along with your knowledge and awareness of political worldwide affairs, your expertise in business and industry, the high moral standards that are exemplified by you and your tremendous sense of fairness for everyone are but a few of my reasons for supporting you."[77]

More portentous was the list of influential religious right leaders who declined to endorse Robertson's candidacy. Christian celebrity Pat Boone, who directed the effort to recruit endorsements from celebrities and religious leaders, received a stream of rejections. Most were friendly, or at least polite. Many were as supportive as they could be. Robertson's old friend Bill Bright informed Boone that he was a "great admirer" of Robertson and had "discussed this matter with him in depth," but any direct involvement in the campaign could jeopardize the tax-exempt status of Campus Crusade for Christ International. In a "Personal and Confidential" letter to Robertson he assured his good friend that he would use every opportunity to express his confidence in Robertson in private and public meetings. Billy Graham predictably informed Robertson that he would not become involved: "I do not feel at liberty in my heart to get personally involved in politics now, no matter how much I admire you and love you in Christ." Such activities in the past had only served to do "damage to my witness." In a 1986 interview Robertson commented on his discussion with Graham about the campaign: "I talked with Billy Graham and he was extraordinarily supportive. He and I are very, very good friends and he is extremely supportive, although he personally does not feel he should get involved pro or con in any political campaigns. He was burned, as you know, rather badly during the Nixon Administration." High-profile religious right leaders Jerry Falwell and James Robinson both turned down endorsement requests. Robertson explained that Falwell had endorsed George Bush "before he realized I would be involved" but that he had "indicated a great deal of interest and support." Robinson sent best wishes but no endorsement: "I certainly encourage and bless Pat but I am not ready to endorse any political candidate."[78]

Robertson's dream of attracting endorsements from conservative, and particularly charismatic, Roman Catholics, never had much of a chance. Mother M. Angelica of the Catholic Cable Network offered a word of advice along with her rejection: "I feel this is very poor timing for any minister to run for political office. I think it is difficult to be faithful to the gospel and politics." Canon Dennis Bennett, one of the leaders in the Catholic Charismatic Renewal movement and a good friend, replied that an endorsement could "alienate people who might otherwise be won to Christ," a risk he was unwilling to take. Still, he did offer encouragement: "As private citizens we certainly intend to support Pat and his candidacy. In fact, we have already made a contribution to his campaign."[79]

More troubling to Robertson was his failure to gain the backing of several highly visible leaders of conservative Christian ministries. James Dobson of Focus on the Family informed Boone that he "respects Pat Robertson and considers him a personal friend," but he could not make an endorsement because of his organization's tax-exempt status. In February 1988, Dobson sent a formal apology to Robertson for "an unfortunate indiscretion on our part" regarding Robertson's ordination as a minister in the Southern Baptist Church, which had taken place while Robertson worked at the Freemason Street Baptist Church almost four decades before. In an interview with Chuck Colson on his radio program, Dobson had discussed with Colson "the concerns many non-Christians have expressed over your candidacy for President. [Colson] also shared about the conversation between the two of you a few years back, and his recommendation that you resign your ordination if you indeed decided to run. Regrettably, some of our listeners perceived his comments to be an implication that your candidacy should not be supported. Needless to say, I was very distressed to realize this was the case." Dobson appealed to Robertson's long experience in interviewing people to understand the potential for misunderstanding. He asked for forgiveness and assured him that neither he nor Colson had intended any harm. The program had obviously caused a ripple, and Robertson's campaign organization believed that "a strong group of Southern Baptist Republican Conservatives" had been spooked by Colson's remarks. "Is there any way we can get an endorsement from Chuck or a statement to satisfy these people?" asked an internal memo.[80]

It was not to be. Colson had been both a personal friend and trusted advisor to Robertson, and Robertson had hoped to recruit him as an advisor to the campaign. But in a four-page letter at the end of June 1987, Colson explained his unwillingness to publicly make an endorsement. It was a warm letter that assured his good friend that he believed he had "all of the intelligence, character and courage to be . . . an outstanding President." Colson offered a number of reasons for his decision, including the jeopardy attached to linking Robertson's campaign with Colson's Watergate legacy. But the critical reason was the quintessential charismatic explanation: he had prayed about the matter, "laying it before the Lord," and "because of the clear leading I received during prayer, I must with great personal regret decline your invitation." That was language that Pat Robertson understood. He replied to Colson: "I completely respect His leading in your life and can only thank you for the time that you spent in prayer about it." While he never received the endorsement, he continued to solicit Colson's advice throughout the campaign.[81]

Robertson's testiest exchange with his religious friends came following Tim and Beverly LaHaye's endorsement of Jack Kemp in a press conference in Des Moines just before the Iowa caucus. Both of them wrote apologetic letters to Robertson after a *Washington Post* interviewer reported that they had recommended that all Christians vote for Kemp rather than Robertson. They assured Robertson that their remarks had been distorted by the reporter, reminding him that his own words had often been distorted. Given the fact that Beverly had spoken at his 1986 Constitution Hall rally, Robertson replied magnanimously: "Tim, in all candor, I believe that your switch from what seemed to be a strong endorsement of my candidacy to the support of Jack Kemp was ill-advised. . . . As I told Bev, after Jack's campaign folds all of us who share the same hopes and dreams for America must coalesce together again."[82]

The failure to rally and unify religious conservatives was the biggest disappointment of the Robertson campaign. After the election, he wrote to a supporter: "If the evangelical Christians of America had backed me with the same intensity as black people backed Jesse Jackson, I would have been the nominee of the Republican Party, very possibly the next president of the United States. However, in the primaries many Christian people either did not participate or they chose one of the three other candidates. . . . I received the majority of the evangelical vote, but that was not nearly enough. For example, in South Carolina, the so-called Fundamentalist vote was split among several candidates besides me. All over the South we had tremendous opportunity, but we didn't take it." Two of his Florida supporters sent a similar analysis: "We can't begin to express our disappointment over the poor showing of support by the 'so called' Christians in your bid for the presidential nomination. It would appear your support came largely from the 'born again Christians' while the Sunday or pseudo Christians supported the rest of the candidates. They missed the whole point that this country must have a moral and Godly leadership in the high offices if we are ever going to reverse this nation's decline." Outside observers believed that the divided religious vote indicated a growing sophistication among the evangelical leaders of the religious right who opted to back winning candidates in order to enhance their own political clout.[83]

If the support of Robertson's religious friends was disappointing, the attacks of his opponents, which included scores of liberal organizations and activists who viewed him as a threat to religious liberty in America and an often vitriolic press, were relentless and condescending. Reporting on Robertson's 1986 speech in Constitution Hall, Christopher Hitchens wrote: "There is something frightening about stupidity; more especially, about stupidity in the mass, organized form. . . . The man who drew the job of introducing Robertson to the throng was Harald Bredesen. . . . He is a self-defined 'evangelical-charismatic,' with alleged Pentecostal powers to speak in tongues." When meeting with Reagan, "the ghastly old thespian's arms 'shook and pulsated' with the Holy Spirit." While there seemed little real danger in "this flat-out, barking, foaming lunacy," it seemed "wise to pay more attention to the workings of the irrational in our political life." People for the American Way published a compendium of quotations by and about Robertson designed to prove that he was "an extremist whose views place him well outside the mainstream of both the Republican Party and the nation."[84]

Robertson was sometimes thin-skinned when reacting to attacks in the press, particularly if they seemed to be based in sloppy journalism or bias against religion. "It pained Robertson to be thought kooky or scary, or to caricatured as, in his word, some bluenose trying to impose his own straitened moral code on America," noted campaign reporters Peter Goldman and Tom Mathews. After an NBC broadcast which he considered "bigoted, biased, untruthful and irresponsible," filled with "extreme religious bias and bigotry against evangelical Christianity," Robertson wrote a scorching protest to Larry Grossman, President of NBC. Nothing got under Robertson's skin more than the reporting of the local Norfolk newspaper. Robertson became so angry with the reporter assigned to cover his campaign, April Witt, that in April 1989 the campaign's director of communications, Connie Snapp, informed the paper's executive editor: "From now on, I am declaring April Witt persona non grata with Americans for Robertson and the subsequent Robertson presidential campaign."[85]

More than his strongly conservative politics, Pat Robertson's religion baffled and troubled his detractors, and in the end probably doomed his candidacy. He could not escape it. Every media introduction was likely to begin: "Faith healer, Born Again Evangelist, TV talk show host. . . ." When asked about his core charismatic beliefs, he tried to be diplomatic but honest. Would he "speak in tongues in the White House?" He replied: "I might pray in tongues. I see nothing wrong with that. It is a form of prayer and I never denied that I would. American people want Christian values. They like the idea of somebody who believes in God, who prays, who is an upstanding person with integrity." Many of his appearances were prefaced by a clip from *The 700 Club* featuring Robertson exercising the "word of knowledge": "Praise the gum diseases being healed by the power of God, several people being healed of hemorrhoids and verrucose [sic] veins, the Lord is healing you of this." He explained to one interviewer: "George Gallup told me that there were 7,500,000 Americans who had experienced some kind of a healing in answer to prayer or through faith. It isn't anything that is terribly uncommon."[86]

On the *MacNeil/Lehrer News Hour* Robertson confessed that he knew he was going to face "ridicule of some of the deeply held religious beliefs that I have." Even though he expressed these beliefs as the co-host of *The 700 Club,* "I do feel these things are rather personal." Two reporters who covered the campaign described Robertson's angst: "It was chief executive he was running for, not chief pastor, he argued, and his beliefs, while proudly and deeply held, were a private matter between him and God." To some extent, Robertson had reckoned with the likelihood that his religion would be "on the front pages of newspapers all across the country." Still, he resented the fact that he and Jesse Jackson, both ministers, "were treated in a totally different fashion by the national media." Biographer David John Marley concluded: "Not since George Wallace ran for the Oval Office had a candidate been the subject of such angry opposition."[87]

Clearly, Robertson had not fully considered the degree to which his charismatic utterances were foreign to even most religious Americans. A pamphlet published by People for the American Way listed eight pages of Robertson's religious statements that seemed fair game to his political opponents, none more widely publicized than his statement on *The 700 Club* on June 11, 1986, detailing his prayer diverting the path of Hurricane Gloria as it headed toward Virginia Beach. During the campaign, Robertson explained that the miraculous answer to that prayer had lent encouragement to him and his political supporters: "I felt, interestingly enough, that if I couldn't move a hurricane, I could hardly move a nation. I know that's a strange thing for anybody to say, and there's hardly anyone else who would feel the same way, but it was very important to the faith of many people." After the campaign, Robertson insisted that he had understood the political dilemma the hurricane episode presented him: "In 1985, I was two people. One believed and taught the miracle power of God. . . . The other was being scrutinized by the secular public as a potential political leader. If I prayed the way I knew how to pray, the secular world would say I was a religious fanatic. If I didn't pray as was needed, the storm would hit us and the faith of millions would be damaged." Some of Robertson's advisors believed that the hurricane episode would vanish quickly and that his charismatic beliefs would not become major campaign issues, but that was not to be the case.[88]

Robertson eschewed the label "charismatic" during the campaign, as he had for years at CBN. Asked directly in a New Orleans press conference in 1986 if he was charismatic, Robertson replied: "I'm an Evangelical. The word 'charismatic' means something extra. And it's an undefinable term. I don't want to go into the Greek of it, but the word is a bit misunderstood. I believe in the New Testament experiences as provided in the Book of Acts." Some political observers pointed out that Robertson's rhetoric was not totally outside the boundaries of historic Christian language: "Pat Robertson is accused of holding superstitious beliefs. He evidently believes that prayer can cure illness and avert natural disasters. Jews and Christians have believed this ever since the Psalms were written."[89]

Extreme anti-religious attacks on Robertson elicited defenses in unexpected places. Mainline *Christian Century* editor James M. Wall was clearly
miffed by *National Review* columnist John McLaughlin's attacks on
"Preacher Pat's" "Wacko Factor" in an article about Robertson and hurricane Gloria. Wall wrote: "That brief exercise in religious bigotry will be repeated as commentators try to underscore the 'bizarre' nature of the fundamentalist Protestant belief in miracles, faith-healing and prayer." Wall
suggested that Robertson react with a "genial wave and a wide smile," appearing "only slightly 'hurt' by the slurs against his faith" — a good description of the strategy he followed. In the heat of the campaign Wall bristled
at a *Newsweek* article that implied "one shouldn't 'bring' one's religion into
any office." "That secular mindset is what is really behind the near panic
that is beginning to spread among Republicans as they watch Robertson's
movement through the caucuses and primaries." Wall continued: "Media
attacks on Robertson will not succeed. His religious followers regard the
ridicule as preacher-bashing, and the nonreligious voters who support
him dismiss discussion of the 'kook factor' as so much political warfare....
A presidential campaign is the place for political debate, not theological
argument. Our media leaders would do well to keep that in mind. By now
they should have realized that in a theological argument Pat Robertson
has the upper hand. He knows the language and they don't." Wall's even-
handed treatment of Robertson's religion no doubt riled some of the readers of the respected mainline Christian journal. One reader wrote to "protest James Wall's kind and sympathetic treatment of Robertson.... If he is
a Christian, I am an atheist."[90]

Robertson tried as adroitly as possible to separate himself from the
group of preachers who had been labeled "televangelists." He repeatedly
insisted that the term did not fit him. "Pat Robertson is not a television
evangelist," wrote a skeptic in *The Nation;* "I heard him say so. He's a successful broadcasting executive. . . . So don't go calling him a television
evangelist — not unless you want to make him mad enough to send a hurricane your way. Broadcasting executives can do that sort of thing."
Actually, the distinction was quite clear in Robertson's mind, and in that of
most of his Christian supporters. After the election, he crafted a detailed
letter explaining the distinction to be sent to donors inquiring about his
rejection of the title: "I have no objection to the title of evangelist, but God
did not call me to be an evangelist. Therefore, I did not want the title used
in describing my work. I am a religious broadcaster, an educator, a businessman, a minister, but never have I been called by God to be an evangelist. It is a wonderful calling, but this was not *my* calling."[91]

Partly to defuse the televangelist label, on September 28, 1987, Robertson resigned his ordination as a minister in the Southern Baptist Church. In his resignation letter he explained that "many citizens" might view "the election of an ordained clergyman of any faith" to be "tantamount to a preference of one religious denomination over all others." Because of that perception, and because he had not "served as a parish clergyman for the past quarter of a century," he thought it best to resign from the Christian ministry. The Deacons of the Freemason Street Baptist Church confirmed the "termination" of his ordination after a formal vote on October 11; "much to the surprise of most people," the congregational vote "was covered by local TV channels . . . and a reporter from the New York *Times*." Robertson drafted a letter to be sent to disgruntled CBN supporters who resented his resignation. He explained that "the call of God on my life for service has never diminished. It has shifted, however, from service within the church body to service to the nation."[92]

On the Defensive

Robertson only imperfectly controlled his penchant to shoot from the hip in impromptu settings. In common with all candidates for the presidency, Robertson found himself constantly explaining remarks he had made that had little to do with his religion. Citing several egregious examples, Editor James M. Wall in the *Christian Century* surmised that it was "politics, not religion" that most threatened the Robertson campaign. For instance, Robertson turned heads with unsubstantiated charges that the Soviet Union still had missiles in Cuba, that the Bush campaign was somehow behind the Jimmy Swaggart scandal, and that CBN had known the location of American hostages held in Lebanon. Too often, Wall wrote, Robertson's responses to questions on these topics were those of a "talk show host," leaving him "a battered candidate with weakened credibility."[93]

From a personal point of view, the cruelest of the campaign controversies for the Robertson family during the campaign was the revelation that Pat and Dede's first son, Tim, had been conceived out of wedlock. The Robertson family tradition had always been to celebrate the couple's marriage in March, whereas the marriage had taken place in August. Robertson tried to evade the story when it surfaced during the campaign, but it quickly turned into a personal nightmare. The story was featured on *Nightline* and other television shows night after night. The exposé of Dede's pregnancy before wedlock came as a cruel shock to the couple's children. "There were suspicions, but I didn't know," recalled Gordon Robertson. "Mom and Dad's wedding date was always unknown." His father's memories of politics dated from "a kinder and gentler day," Gordon observed, but the jarring marriage revelation made clear that "those days are gone." Tim Robertson recalled that the story made him "extremely uncomfortable." "Personally, I was hurt — more for my mother than anybody else because that part of her life became public. She has sacrificed for me and for our family all her life. And I hurt for my father because he is a man who 33 years ago made a mistake — both of them made a mistake — but then he did what was right." When Tim heard the breaking news, he telephoned his father and encouraged him to use it as a platform "to proclaim the gospel to them" because "there is not a person in America who isn't going to sympathize with you."[94]

Less embarrassing but more serious was a Federal Election Commission investigation into charges that the Freedom Council had violated campaign rules in Michigan and elsewhere. Robertson submitted an affidavit to the FEC defending his personal conduct and the activities of the Americans for Robertson, Inc., "exploratory committee" between July 1986 and the formal announcement of his candidacy in September 1987. It was proper, he insisted, for him to continue as head of CBN and related companies until he made a final decision to run. In the meantime, Americans for Robertson, Inc., obeyed the rules for activities of exploratory committees.[95]

Robertson was most incensed by the charges included in a letter from former Republican congressman Paul N. McCloskey of California to Representative Andrew Jacobs Jr. of Indiana, charging that while on the same boat to Korea in 1951 as young Marine officers Pat had boasted that his father had assured him on the telephone that he would intervene to keep him out of combat. Robertson believed the charge was "mean and untrue"; "it somehow got to me." McCloskey's accusation undercut two of Pat Robertson's most prized personal self-images and memories. He was immensely proud of his achievement in becoming a Marine officer, and he believed that he had served with honor in Korea. He was no coward; a Robertson biographer pointed out the obvious — if "Robertson wanted to avoid combat, joining the Marine Corps was an odd decision." In addition, the accusation smeared the name of his revered father, whose long career in the Senate bore no hint of scandal. It is true that the senator's correspondence regarding his sons was constantly solicitous, even managerial, and that his recommendations held great weight in the military chain of command, but he would never have consciously acted unethically on his son's behalf.[96]

McCloskey first made the charge against Robertson in 1981 when he had come under attack from the California branch of the Moral Majority, but Robertson ignored the charge because "no one of any consequence paid any attention to the story." But in 1986, when the story resurfaced, one of his political advisors urged that "you have no choice but to sue to prove the falsity of the charge." In October 1986 Robertson filed a libel suit against Jacobs and McCloskey, charging they had made false statements with malice and reckless disregard for the truth.[97]

While some of his political advisors urged him to sue McCloskey, others, including his lawyer son, thought the suit was a mistake. As it turned out, the suit resulted in an avalanche of adverse coverage by the media. The case dragged on for months; in July 1987 a federal judge dismissed the suit against Jacobs, but refused to dismiss the suit against McCloskey because there was "sufficient" if not "overwhelming" evidence to permit a reasonable juror to find that he acted in malice. In the intervening months both sides accumulated hundreds of affidavit files, spent large sums of money, and fed the press with a continuing flow of information. Robertson ruefully told a reporter: "I have been humiliated. I have lost sleep. I have been the butt of jokes."[98]

"After a year-and-a-half of grueling, expensive work," Robertson believed that his lawyers "had enough evidence to win the case," but, in the end, he dropped the lawsuit, ostensibly because the trial date was set for March 8, 1988, the day of the "Super Tuesday" primaries. Robertson complained that U.S. District Judge Joyce Hens Green presented him with an unfair choice when she set the trial date. He felt that he was confronted with stopping campaigning two weeks ahead of the primaries, or dropping the suit and being forced to "listen to McCloskey . . . gloat publicly that I had 'chickened out.'" When Robertson dropped the suit, he was required to pay some of McCloskey's court costs, though not his legal fees. By the time the case ended, Robertson had already concluded that no good end would come from the trial. Some of his campaign workers subsequently speculated that the capitulation had been harmful to Robertson, implying that either he was weak or guilty as charged. In retrospect, Robertson described the affair as a "terrible ordeal," acknowledging that "I shouldn't have sued him."[99]

The controversy most damaging to Robertson during the campaign was the furor surrounding the scandals among televangelists that led to the collapse of Jim Bakker's PTL network and was fed by Oral Roberts's extreme appeals for money to build the City of Faith medical complex in Tulsa. Robertson campaigned through a deluge of press stories about the televangelist scandals. He quickly moved to distance himself from the unraveling PTL scandal in the spring of 1987, telling the *New York Times* that "the fallout from the infighting among television evangelists over the PTL turmoil in no way affects him," but few analysts believed that the scandals would not have a negative impact on his campaign. Particularly galling to Robertson were stories linking him to Jim Bakker, whom he had in fact regarded with disdain for years.[100]

From a political point of view, the most devastating revelation in the unraveling of the electronic church involved sordid sexual charges that devastated the huge ministry of Jimmy Swaggart. In 1986, Robertson had skillfully maneuvered to gain the support of Swaggart and other important televangelists. He visited Heritage USA to repair relations with Jim Bakker. Bakker did not formally endorse Robertson, and his support soon became a liability rather than an asset. But it was Swaggart's support that Robertson needed most. By the mid-1980s Swaggart was the nation's most popular television evangelist; his program was aired on more than 250 stations each week. Swaggart flirted with the idea of endorsing George Bush. He wrote to supporter Robert Hartley: "A few days ago I met with Vice-President George Bush concerning the upcoming election year, and his possible candidacy for President. He assured me that, if elected, the present Reagan policies would continue. He certainly is a man who stands for Christian principles." Hartley dashed off a concerned note to Robertson, enclosing a copy of Swaggart's letter: "I was disappointed to see included in it a paragraph that, in essence, endorsed George Bush! With the endorsement of Jerry Falwell several months ago and now Jimmy Swaggart, George Bush is strategically lining up ministries that should be in *our* camp for support." Robertson urged Hartley to "tell Jimmy Swaggart not to be misled by pious words. . . . George Bush can't have it both ways. He can't campaign against Christians in Michigan and then go down to Lynchburg and tell Jerry Falwell how born again he is." A worst-case campaign scenario seemed to loom on the horizon when the September issue of Swaggart's magazine, *The Evangelist,* charged that Robertson had accepted the "Kingdom Age" doctrine that anticipated a Christian America emerging through human effort, a concept considered heretical by most evangelical premillennialists.[101]

Supporters of Robertson and Swaggart urged the two men to meet. In a letter to Swaggart, Robert Hartley wrote: "Jimmy, I believe you are a Godly man and that you want to know the truth. That is why I ask you as a

spirit-filled brother in Christ to please contact Pat Robertson and personally discuss with him what he really believes. . . . Attached is a flyer used
by George Bush's people in Michigan to attack Pat Robertson. You also
need to be aware that one of Bush's largest contributors from Minnesota
is very active in the Pro-Abortion and Feminist Movement. TIME Magazine called what George Bush's people in Michigan were doing as 'Christian bashing.'" By September 10, a meeting between Robertson and
Swaggart had been held, and Swaggart was enthusiastically on board the
Robertson bandwagon, assuring him that he was "pulling for you with all
our strength and believing for victory." In a press conference held at the
Regency Hyatt Hotel in New Orleans, Swaggart gave his formal endorsement, taking care not to compromise his narrow religious convictions:
"Pat Robertson is one of us. And that doesn't necessarily mean the right
church, the right particular persuasion, but it does mean the same purpose and the same cause. He and I today were discussing this very thing. I
believe he is a man who will bend over backwards should God place him
in the position of which we speak, that he would try to be leader of all the
people. . . . Honesty, integrity, character. That's what America needs." A
pleased Robertson reacted to reporters the next day, delighted by
Swaggart's "apparent reversal." It was not an entirely comfortable alliance
for either man. "I didn't know Jimmy very well," Robertson recalled, and
he had been "hypercritical of me" in the past, but it was a badly needed
political endorsement at the time.[102]

Swaggart urged close cooperation between the two of them because of
his large numbers of requests for media interviews, and he offered Robertson wide-ranging advice about campaign strategy. Beginning with the caveat that he understood that "you are not attempting to make this into a
Christian nation," a point obviously settled in the private meeting,
Swaggart advised the candidate to play up his identity as a "religious
broadcaster." In the future his son Donnie would serve as a liaison with
Robertson's campaign committee to assure that in their press interviews
"specifics are addressed as they should be."[103]

Then, in February 1988, the Swaggart scandal erupted. On February 21,
1988, without giving the details of his transgressions, Swaggart tearfully
said to his family, his congregation, and a huge television audience, "I have
sinned against you, my Lord, and I would ask that your precious blood
would wash and cleanse every stain until it is in the seas of God's forgiveness." CBN President Tim Robertson informed Swaggart that his program
would no longer be aired on CBN after April 29 unless the fallen evangelist
would agree to submit to the period of forced leave from his ministry that

had been ordered by the General Presbytery of the Assemblies of God. Tim "applauded your actions of repentance and open submission" to his denominational board, "in vivid contrast to the debacle of PTL," but Swaggart's refusal to accept the church's demand that he take a leave of absence from the pulpit made CBN unwilling to continue airing his program. The wounded Swaggart wrote long letters to Pat Robertson in April and May, urging him not to "believe all the garbage" that was being published about him and imploring him to allow his continued presence on CBN network. In the end, he reluctantly but gracefully accepted the decision to drop his program from the CBN network.[104]

Robertson's relationship with Swaggart reached a tattered end in 1989, when Robertson responded to a caller on the Larry King show asking about similarities between Jim Bakker and Jimmy Swaggart. In what was intended as a defense of Swaggart, whom he believed "sincerely felt a call of God" in his life, Robertson affirmed that his moral failure could be attributed to a visit to a "bawdy house in New Orleans" at a very early age that "marred him psychologically." He needed "help and forgiveness." The response brought an immediate demand for a retraction from Swaggart's lawyer, insisting that the charges were "absolutely false." When Turner Broadcasting requested "support for these statements from you," Robertson insisted that the remarks were accurate, based on a "very confidential meeting" with the "very highest levels of his denomination." In the week that followed the remarks, Swaggart wrote to Robertson expressing his hurt because of the "very derogatory statements" and denying the factual basis of Robertson's account. After a "most amicable" telephone conversation with Swaggart, Robertson wrote again to the legal counsel at Turner Broadcasting Network, acknowledging that he may have been mistaken in a part of his statement. Swaggart's "moral failure," the evangelist insisted, had not been caused by "childhood psychological fixations," as Robertson had surmised, but by "demonic influence." Because of the "broad publicity" surrounding Swaggart's problems, Robertson did not believe it would serve anyone's interest to make a public retraction of what he had said, and he was convinced that there was "absolutely no legal liability." However, he did offer to make further "clarification" on *The 700 Club* if Swaggart's legal counsel demanded.[105]

The timing of the Swaggart scandal could not have been worse for Robertson; it broke days before the South Carolina primary. In a news conference in Columbia, South Carolina, "Mr. Robertson argued that to think that the timing of the disclosures about Mr. Swaggart had not been by design 'would stretch the credulity of almost anybody.' He said that he had no knowledge of who was behind that design, but he went on to make a broad and bitter attack on Vice President Bush's campaign." In later years, Robertson remained convinced that the "brutal" revelation came "almost like it was timed." Occasionally he went even further: In October 1987, he alerted the chairman of the board of the Associated Press and "a couple of senators" that he had credible information that a unit of the CIA "had been assigned to discredit me." "If units of the CIA are running amok in the United States contrary to law," he protested, "we need to do something about it." Robertson's critics saw his suspicions as bordering on paranoia, but he remained convinced in later years that the "dirty tricks" orchestrated by Bush campaign manager Lee Atwater played an important part in the campaign.[106]

In later years, with his perspective tempered somewhat by the passing of time, Robertson ruefully accepted that if "you play with the big boys, they play rough." "Lee played dirty," he recalled, but the two became friends before Atwater died. During the final months of his life, Atwater publicly apologized to a number of political figures, including Michael Dukakis. Robertson recalled a visit with Atwater in the hospital shortly before his death in 1991 during which his election nemesis "apologized for some of the dirty tricks during the campaign."[107]

The Collapse

Robertson's campaign intensified in the months after his strong showings in Michigan, Iowa, and Hawaii. His wife advised him to skip New Hampshire, where he had little base, and spend his time and money in the South, but he insisted on campaigning in New Hampshire, only to be routed, along with Bob Dole, by Vice-President Bush. Belatedly the campaign headed south, with high hopes of a strong showing in the South Carolina primary on March 5 and the first southern Super Tuesday on March 8, when the states of Florida, Texas, Tennessee, Louisiana, Oklahoma, Mississippi, Kentucky, Alabama, and Georgia voted. Robertson issued a challenge after his poor showing in New Hampshire: "Today we played in George Bush's backyard. Now we are going to the South which is my backyard. I throw down the gauntlet to George Bush in South Carolina." But strapped for money and facing a formidable Bush machine led by South Carolinian Lee Atwater, the Robertson campaign gravely miscalculated its strength in South Carolina. Bush won the state and Bob Dole finished just ahead of Robertson. On Super Tuesday, 1,308 delegates to the convention,

31.6 percent of the total number, were chosen. George Bush won 16 out of 17 of the 1988 Super Tuesday primaries and caucuses. In all, Bush received 50 percent of the vote, Senator Bob Dole 21 percent, and Robertson a disappointing 14 percent. Headlines after Super Tuesday proclaimed that Pat Robertson's invisible army of Christian voters had failed to materialize.[108]

Most of the scholarly studies of the campaign gave Robertson more credit than the press coverage at the time. In her detailed study of the primaries, Barbara Norrander found that religious conservatives did not participate at an "unduly high rate," in the Super Tuesday primaries, but since their socioeconomic group was generally "underrepresented" in elections, Robertson's candidacy "mobilized them enough so that they were no longer underrepresented." Robertson "received support from the most unique group of Republican voters," according to Norrander, but he failed because he simply did not reach beyond "religiously oriented" voters who "were predominately fundamentalist and frequent church attenders." Robertson's supporters were overwhelmingly native southerners "with lower incomes than other Republican voters."[109]

The best of the spate of scholarly articles that explored the causes of Robertson's failure in the Super Tuesday primaries correctly pointed out that Robertson's invisible army of Christian supporters could not be described by such broader words as "evangelicals," "born-again," or "fundamentalist" Christians. Rather, his support came overwhelmingly from the "Pentecostal/charismatic" religious subculture. Robertson's support among African Americans was based almost entirely on his charismatic religious image. His support had been strongest among upwardly mobile charismatics, people with "modern sensibilities and traditional values" who had the financial ability "to supply adequate resources for a presidential nominating campaign." Overall, however, "Robertson gained support from only a minority of the people his campaign was meant to attract."[110]

Influencing the Republican Party

Robertson's stinging defeats in the southern primaries deflated his dream. He later wrote, "After 'Super Tuesday,' I learned first-hand what the prophet meant when he wrote, 'It pleased the Lord to bruise Him.' I knew vividly what the Apostle Paul meant when he wrote, 'We are counted as sheep for the slaughter.'"[111]

Deeply disappointed by his showing in the Super Tuesday primaries in the South, Robertson appointed Allan R. Sutherlin as his new campaign manager to oversee the "wind-down stage" that would concentrate on paying campaign debts. Though it was clear that George Bush would be the nominee, Robertson stayed in the race for more than two months to solidify his position within the party and to influence the platform. In a late March rally Robertson told a crowd of supporters: "What we stand for is not just one candidate, it's principles." "When I go to the convention," Robertson vowed, "we're going to be talking about things like abortion . . . the selection of judges . . . what our relationship with the Soviet Union will be." Eight Robertson delegates were appointed to the platform committee.[112]

On May 16 Robertson announced that he was suspending his campaign. In marking the end of his campaign, Robertson reflected on both the accomplishment and the costs. He promised to take his delegates to the convention in New Orleans and to continue to press the causes that had rallied and united his supporters. He noted that he had "met cordially . . . in the White House" with the vice-president and that he "endorsed George Bush wholeheartedly and pledged my support to assist him in his race for the White House." He discussed the platform with the vice-president and expected it to be "a document that all Republicans can enthusiastically support." He considered it "an honor" to be the last competitor to contest the Republican nomination and encouraged his backers to continue their efforts to "win elections for school boards, city councils, state legislatures, and the United States Congress."[113]

From the beginning of his campaign for the Republican nomination Robertson recognized that he was not an "insider who had spent a lifetime cultivating the party loyalists," but he now made it clear that he was fully committed to the Republican Party and its platform. Frank J. Fahrenkopf Jr., chairman of the Republican National Committee, congratulated Robertson "on a job well done," noting that his "impact on the 1988 presidential election and the Republican Party have been most impressive." Americans for Robertson provided its list of approximately three million names and addresses to the Republican National Committee in return for pledged assistance in retiring the Americans for Robertson campaign debt. In June, at the instigation of Robertson, key Americans for Robertson staff members met with Vice-President Bush at his home, "where he was most complimentary and cordial," and with the Bush staff to coordinate future cooperation.[114]

The success of Robertson supporters in gaining influence in state Republican organizations still riled many party regulars. When Republican Congressman Bill Green attacked Robertson on that account, Robertson's campaign manager, Allan Sutherlin, wrote to Lee Atwater warning that the congressman had gotten some "stupid advice" and that the party should publicly acknowledge Robertson's contributions to the Bush campaign: "Pat Robertson led a unified effort of the major conservative evangelists and religious leaders of this nation including Jerry Falwell, Billy Graham and others in a 'National Citizenship Day' designed to motivate conservative Christians to register and vote. The public service announcements and the materials for this effort were distributed at the expense of Pat Robertson's PAC as a legal, independent expenditure.... Pat Robertson has supported Unity 88, Victory 88, and will continue to appear in support of the Vice President whenever possible through Election Day." Robertson wrote a letter of his own, this one to Green: "Some jackass has sent a letter out over your signature that I think you should be aware of." Robertson chided Green for trying "to split the Bush coalition seven weeks before the election."[115]

In retrospect, Robertson listed the accomplishments of his race: "I campaigned exhaustively in 34 states, mobilized a veritable army of supporters, raised 19 million dollars, won or am winning 7 states, and am now seeing my supporters elected to positions of responsibility in the Republican parties of 20 states." Of the eight Republican candidates, he had finished with the third most votes. He promised to attend the convention with his delegates, work to influence the party's platform, and "work for the election of Conservative Republicans to City Councils, School Boards, Legislatures, the House of Representatives, and the Senate."[116]

The Republican convention in New Orleans in the summer of 1988 was a "bittersweet" experience for Pat Robertson. According to the count of Americans for Robertson, he was joined in New Orleans by 128 delegates and 143 alternate delegates, along with "well over 100 other strong Robertson supporters who are bound to the other candidates by law." Like the campaign, the frenetic schedule in New Orleans was crammed with activities, beginning with a rally with "Robertson supporters" at the Robertson Hospitality Center located on St. Charles Avenue not far from the family's hotel. After being escorted to their suite at the Inter-Continental Hotel, Pat and Dede were joined by their children and spouses before a frantic schedule of press briefings, meetings, and celebrations. His Tuesday schedule began with a meeting with his staff at 5:20 a.m. before a morning appearance on *CBS This Morning,* followed by a private lunch with Jerry Falwell in his hotel suite. In the afternoon he held a caucus meeting with Robertson delegates and then proceeded for a rehearsal on the Superdome dais in the early afternoon. After dinner with the family, he proceeded to the "Conservative Victory Committee Reception and Dinner" hosted by such Republican luminaries as Bunker Hunt, Senator Charles Grassley, and Governor Pierre DuPont. Then he made his way with Dede to the Superdome to deliver his speech. Departing the convention at 11 p.m., the two of them went to the Robertson Hospitality Center for a "New Orleans Style Reception" celebrating with his team and supporters, before leaving to return to their hotel at 12:35 a.m. Campaign director Allan Sutherlin had correctly predicted, "You will be a principal focus of the media at an otherwise very bland convention."[117]

Assigned a major seventeen-minute speaking slot on Tuesday evening, August 16, after the keynote address, Robertson's speech (like that of others) "had been reviewed, timed, and edited by a panel of experts." After a meeting with Fred Malek, Convention Director for the Bush campaign, Allan Sutherlin reported that the Bush advisors wanted Robertson to address "Family Values," a seemingly natural topic. Robertson's speech touched on most of the themes of the campaign, ending with the warning that "the breakup of the American family is the number one social problem in our nation today." The speech was an unstinting endorsement of the candidacy of George Bush. Thanking the "millions of voters, volunteers, and supporters across America who committed themselves to my campaign," he released his delegates to vote for George Bush, "a man that I have come to respect and admire." It was a heady moment, a lasting family memory for the entire Robertson clan.[118]

After the convention Robertson made appearances for the Bush campaign in half a dozen states. "It was easy work," he recalled, because of the weaknesses of his Democratic opponent, Michael Dukakis, a "card carrying member of the A.C.L.U." Robertson's relationship with Bush became warmer in the final stages of the campaign. In August, Robertson wrote to him: "You are doing a wonderful job and I honestly feel you are going to make a great president. Let's win together!" On election evening, he called George Bush in Houston to congratulate him on his victory. The two had formed a cordial and respectful relationship; "As usual, Bush was most gracious." After speaking to the president-elect, "to my relief, it was over."[119]

For Robertson and his family, the campaign was "like a big blur." He later reflected on the downside: "The price was brutal. There was physical exhaustion. My faith was ridiculed. My motives and my words were distorted. Lies were spread about my war record, my education, and my resume. My family was savagely wounded. My media consultant in South Carolina said that in all of his experience, he had never seen a candidate for public office so mistreated in the press. Perhaps worst of all, some of my supporters began to believe the liberal press and, in the last days, abandoned me." "I never imagined it would cost so much personally," wrote Dede Robertson. Pat believed that he had made critically wrong decisions during the campaign because of the incredibly exhausting schedule. In the months after the election, his restless mind was filled with resentment and anger against his critics — "McCloskey, the press, and religious leaders who had let me down."[120]

But there were many positive memories as well. The group of candidates who went through the ordeal together developed a camaraderie born of hardship. Robertson sent a warm note to Bob Dole after hitching a ride on Dole's airplane to a party rally: "I continue to watch your great leadership, and I truly hope that you will be considered as our Vice Presidential nominee." Early in the campaign, after being a "friendly hitchhiker" on Robertson's airplane on a trip from South Carolina to Iowa, Jack Kemp wrote, "I truly enjoyed talking with you. I look forward to spending more time together as the two of us continue to work for the cause we believe in." Shortly before the Republican convention in New Orleans, Kemp dashed off a note to Robertson: "Greetings & I'm glad to hear you're on 'tap' for the Convention. . . . I hope you would be of help to advancing a pro-growth, pro tax cut agenda for the Party & the country." Shortly after the convention in New Orleans, George Bush wrote, "Before the great memories of New Orleans get overtaken by the next big event, I wanted to pause a moment to let you know how grateful I am for your contribution to the 1988 Convention program. The entire Bush family appreciates more than we can ever say the tremendous job you did for us. With friends like you by our side, I know we will win in November!"[121]

Finally, Robertson was compelled to reflect on the meaning of his defeat. His "third place finish was respectable," but he and his supporters keenly felt that "God had called me to win, not run third." In the months that followed he found layers of meaning in the race: "I have learned that the first time around is not always successful, but if we are going to do what God tells us we must start somewhere. I believe that I was obedient to Him. He told me to run, and I did so. The results of that race are in His hands. All He asks of us is obedience." Robertson's executive assistant, Barbara Johnson, crafted an explanation to answer an inquirer in 1997: "A lot of folks did not understand why Mr. Robertson ran for president. It was what he believed the Lord wanted him to do, and his *only* reason was in obedience to the Lord. He said many, many times that nothing else mattered, but that he was obedient to *whatever* the Lord asked. It was a tremendous price for him to pay, yet hundreds of thousands of Christians across America became involved in our fight for religious freedom."[122]

In the weeks after George Bush's election, Robertson pondered the meaning of his campaign, which he believed had "changed the course of American history" by activating so many committed Christians in the Republican Party machinery. Ralph Reed believed that Robertson's defeat was one of three losing campaigns since World War II (along with Barry Goldwater's in 1964 and George McGovern's in 1972) that carried the "seeds of ultimate victory" for their parties. Robertson confided to Reed: "Look, I ran against the incumbent vice president of the United States, against Lee Atwater. I went eighteen rounds with the best in the business, and I got a Ph.D. in politics as it's practiced at the presidential level." In his invitation to the presidential inaugural celebration in January 1989, the Bush team paid Robertson high honor: "In your capacity as a spiritual leader, you represent the faith of millions of families across our land. . . . As special guest of the Committee, you will be the representative of those millions of like faith who will be unable to be in Washington that day."[123]

This didn't seem like an end. It seemed like a beginning. As he thought about everything he had been through, Robertson began to sense that his greatest impact on the American political process still lay ahead.

time to play "hard ball" and begin organizing "like-minded people to insure that Evangelicals are elected to policy making positions in political parties, on school boards, on city councils, in state legislatures, and in the Congress." Ralph Reed recalled a White House meeting in November 1989 attended by Pat Robertson and other evangelical leaders in which the newly elected president explained the difficulty of identifying qualified evangelicals to appoint. Robertson evoked an explosion of laughter when he replied, "You have no difficulty identifying evangelicals and their allies during the campaign, but you cannot find them after the election?"[2]

Robertson was brimming with confidence about what he had accomplished. He had vivid memories of the grassroots conservative support he had awakened after campaigning in thirty-five states; he believed that his organization had been responsible for training 300,000 volunteers. Nonetheless, in November of 1988, after his campaign finally came to an end, Robertson was "physically and emotionally exhausted"; he felt as if he were "convalescing from a serious illness." In that frame of mind, he thought he might be finished with serious political involvement. Then his telephone rang. On the line was Reverend Billy McCormack, a Baptist pastor and former Washington lobbyist who had been the southern states director of the Freedom Council and headed the Louisiana state organization of Americans for Robertson. McCormack spoke earnestly and bluntly. "Pat," he said, "if you get out now, all of the work and money that went into your campaign will be wasted. You have to form a new organization to carry on." Robertson thanked his friend and promised to pray about it. In the days ahead, he pondered the advice and "decided that Billy McCormack was right. There was more to be done by Christians in American politics. He had raised an army and they were looking to him for leadership."[3]

A plan matured in his mind in the early months of 1989. Robertson was sure that, "given the political apathy of the nation, a small group of dedicated people — sometimes no more than four or five — could control many of the 175,000 neighborhood precincts in the United States. From there they could build a county organization, then a congressional district organization, then a state organization." He was convinced that "the Moral Majority had been politically ineffective because it was essentially a direct mail fundraising machine." What would succeed, he believed, was "a trained and dedicated grassroots organization focusing on a significant void in party politics and built on majorities in the precincts." As he pondered his options, he took stock of his political assets: "a list of 134,000 dedicated donors, an organizational framework, and a spirited and engaged Christian electorate that had been aroused by his campaign."[4]

In the summer of 1989, Pat and Dede flew to Vienna and drove into the Alps for a vacation. One evening, they dined at a quaint inn with a view of the beautiful mountain called the Zugspitze. His assistant later described their conversation that evening: "To the melody of a little mountain brook flowing beside their outdoor restaurant, they each threw out potential names for a proposed political organization. Finally, Pat hit on the name — The Christian Coalition." He and Dede "agreed that they would not deny the name of Christ by hiding behind one of the many secular names they had considered." In September 1989 Robertson filed for a Virginia non-profit, non-stock corporation to be named "The Christian Coalition." The initial board of directors was small: Pat Robertson, Billy McCormack, and Roberta Combs, who had headed the South Carolina chapter of Americans for Robertson. (In later years Robertson believed that "the decision to have such a small board proved to be a serious blunder.")[5]

While attending events in Washington surrounding the inauguration of George Bush in 1989, Robertson spoke at a banquet sponsored by a group called Students for America, which had honored him with its Man of the Year award. Sitting next to him, Robertson recalled, "was a very young-looking, slightly-built fellow who seemed to have a remarkable knowledge of politics and political strategy." His intuitive instincts took over and he "sensed that this young man might be a perfect fit for the new political organization he was planning to form."[6]

Robertson's fortuitous encounter with Ralph Reed had historic consequences. Reed was a former executive director of the College Republican National Committee who had worked in Reagan's campaign in 1984 and had supported Jack Kemp in 1988. Reed had vivid memories of the two men's spirited conversation before Robertson's speech. "With all respect," the cherubic-looking Reed boldly told Robertson, "the Robertson organizers had made a lot of mistakes" in his home state of Georgia during the campaign. Robertson's organization in Georgia had been too narrow in focus, he continued, showing little appreciation for the fact that "you have to build a coalition." The party regulars had reacted to the efforts to take over the state party "with all the horror of a country club invaded by yahoos."[7]

During Robertson's speech Reed wondered if he had spoken too candidly, but after the banquet ended and most of the crowd had dispersed, Robertson waved Reed over to where he was standing with Dede and a security guard. "I'm going to start an organization," he told the surprised young Emory University Ph.D. history student, and "I'd like for you to come and work for me." It was one of those impetuous acts that struck awe and fear in the hearts of those close to Robertson. This time it proved to be a stroke of political genius. Reed explained to Robertson that he was in the final stages of writing his dissertation and that he would need to finish before accepting a job. Robertson told Reed to send him a memo summarizing his ideas. Reed asked where to send it; Robertson replied, "You know where to find me." The next day, Reed discussed the offer with his friend and mentor Paul Weyrich. "Paul was pretty influential in my decision to go," recalled Reed; Weyrich told his young friend without reservation to take the job. He quickly wrote a memo outlining his ideas on how to make Robertson's concept work and "really got excited in the process." He waited anxiously for a reply, but nothing happened. Months dragged by. Reed finished the first draft of his dissertation and began applying for teaching positions.[8]

Finally, in late summer, Robertson was ready to move. He wrote to Reed offering him a job and inviting him to a planning meeting. On September 26, Robertson met with Reed and a group of supporters in Atlanta to brainstorm about the shape and agenda of the new organization. Two basic plans of action were discussed at the meeting; some urged a series of high visibility conferences, while others urged building a grassroots organization. In early October Robertson and Reed met again to discuss a series of proposals Reed had submitted after the Atlanta meeting. Reed's carefully crafted memo suggested that the new organization, chartered on October 1, 1989, immediately go into a "fundraising/organizational mode" looking for major donors "who will give $10,000 and up." The first steps would be a direct mail solicitation to the 1.8 million Americans for Robertson list and a meeting in Washington of fifty or more conservative leaders to officially "launch the organization."[9]

After making brief suggestions about his salary and authority in his memo, Reed addressed the issue of what to call the new organization. On that important issue he had firm ideas: "The name of the organization should appeal to non-Christians as well as evangelicals." He did not want to disguise the character of the organization, but the name would be important in marketing the group. The name, Reed argued, should be inclusive rather than exclusive: "Jews, Catholics, Mormons, agnostics, even non-believers would be welcome if they shared our political agenda. We must let the public and the press know that this is not a Christian agenda, it is an American agenda." On the name issue, and to a degree on the broader definition of the organization, Reed capitulated to Robertson, who had long before settled those questions in his mind. "Pat had this attitude after his presidential campaign," Reed recalled: "'We are who we are and I am not going to apologize for it.' There was a bit of a chip on the shoulder." Robertson informed Reed that the new organization would be called the Christian Coalition, and its objective would be to "mobilize and train Christians for effective political action." Robertson wanted to build an effective precinct field force. In retrospect, Reed conceded that Robertson was right, because "it gave us a market niche."[10]

By the end of October, Reed had drafted and submitted to Robertson "A Plan of Action" for launching the organization. He proposed a 1990 budget of $1,268,029 to be raised through "direct mail solicitation, major donors, conference fees, and membership dues." The rationale for the organization included the departure of Ronald Reagan, which meant that "grassroots Christian activists cannot depend on the White House to set our agenda." The "folding of the Moral Majority . . . left a tremendous vacuum," and since "the Robertson campaign mobilized more Christians at the grassroots than any similar undertaking in American political history," they must not allow "the activists and donor base developed during the campaign . . . to wither away." The mission of the organization would be to "draw Christians into a permanent campaign" by building an organization modeled on the National Rifle Association, the Chamber of Commerce, and the AFL-CIO. Its "strength will be its state affiliates and local chapters. Its capstone will be a national headquarters boasting a staff of technically proficient, dedicated professionals." In sum: "The mission of the Christian Coalition is to lead a permanent campaign to give Christians a voice in their government again."[11]

The first order of business was raising funds to launch the Christian Coalition. The key proved to be the list of 134,000 donors who had been "the core support base" of Americans for Robertson. The first solicitation for support went out in October. Reed began working in the ramshackle former office of Americans for Robertson in Virginia Beach. Some seed money had been raised during the Atlanta session in September, but the first mailing was made possible by a personal donation from Pat Robertson. When Robertson visited Reed's cluttered office, he told him that his surroundings looked even less promising than his early television enterprises and then wrote a personal check for $20,000 to the Christian Coalition to cover the expenses for a fundraising letter. In these unpromising surroundings, Robertson brimmed with confidence: "There was a dream. There was a faith. There was a vision for the future." That confidence proved justified: the result of the first mailing over Robertson's signature to his core donors was overwhelming. "It was like a waterfall," recalled Reed; "money just poured out." The Christian Coalition was on its way.[12]

Robertson's entry into the crowded field of religious right political action groups received a mixed reception from other Christian conservatives, as had his candidacy for the Republican nomination. Most of them were leery of another organization "that would compete for dollars," recalled Reed; to say the least, the reception to Robertson's proposal among movement leaders was less than "overwhelming." Beverly LaHaye, President of Concerned Women for America, protested the use of her picture in an early Christian Coalition brochure because the new organization appeared to "duplicate" her own group. A clearly irked Robertson apologized if Ralph Reed had overstepped by using her picture and offered a guarantee: "I also want to assure you that, absent a divine sex change, I have no intention of starting a women's organization to compete with Concerned Women for America." In February 1990 the Christian Coalition convened an impressive array of conservative religious leaders at the Mayflower Hotel in Washington during the meeting of the National Religious Broadcasters, including Tim and Beverly LaHaye, Jerry Falwell, Chuck Colson, Charles Stanley, D. James Kennedy, and several prominent Catholics. They hoped to gain allies for the Coalition's efforts to begin grassroots organizing. "Everybody was real nice at the meeting," recalled Reed, "but they wouldn't do anything."[13]

The meeting sparked a testy exchange between Robertson and Tom Minnery, vice-president of public policy at Focus on the Family. Two representatives of Focus on the Family attended the Christian Coalition organizational conference in Washington, and several weeks later Minnery wrote to Robertson stating that James Dobson wanted to know "what you hope to accomplish through this new movement personally." It was possible that the Christian Coalition could fill a "niche that is not now being filled by any other organizations, but I want to be sure . . . as we build our own coalition network." Obviously miffed by the inquiry from a Focus on the Family executive instead of Dobson, Robertson replied, "I will welcome the opportunity to meet with your employer, Dr. James Dobson, whenever he is on the East Coast." The difference between the two organizations, he explained, was that Christian Coalition was a 501(c)(4) political organization authorized to engage in political activities, as opposed to Focus on the Family, a 501(c)(3) organization which was "severely limited by tax laws from any political activity." A few months later Reed had his own encounter with a group from Focus on the Family while on an organizing tour in California. Encouraged when he was asked to meet with the group, he was taken aback when the discussion "turned into an interrogation." "I was a 28-year-old kid," he recalled, and he left the meeting wondering "why nobody likes us." Later, he conceded that it was understandable that other organizations would feel threatened.[14]

The most cooperative religious right organization was the Moral Majority. Mark DeMoss, Jerry Falwell's administrative assistant, informed Robertson that Falwell had personally written to eighteen conservative religious leaders, including such influential conservative Southern Baptist preachers as Jerry Vines, Bailey Smith, and Adrian Rogers, urging them to attend the February meeting in Washington. He wrote: "I feel very good about the Christian Coalition."[15]

Falwell had begun winding down the Moral Majority in 1986; it was disbanded in 1989. The Moral Majority had been founded in May 1979 at a meeting at Jerry Falwell's headquarters that included the leading "architects of the New Right," Paul Weyrich, Richard Viguerie, and Howard Phillips. Ralph Reed thought of them as "battled tested generals in search of an army." In Falwell, they found an uncompromising social conservative with a television audience of 12 million. Under the leadership of Jerry Falwell, by 1979 the Moral Majority had emerged as the nation's premier religious right organization.[16]

Pat Robertson had kept his distance from the Moral Majority. Liberals, he believed, "found an easy target in 1980 because the conservative Evangelicals involved in politics — Christian Voice, Moral Majority, and Religious Roundtable — have been, at times, unsophisticated, simplistic, and inept." CBN files included a dismissive paragraph to be sent to supporters asking questions about the Moral Majority: "The Moral Majority is doing what it feels best to help correct ills which it perceives in America today. Although The Christian Broadcasting Network, founded more than 20 years ago, is not associated with Moral Majority, founded in 1980, we support its right to speak and act." Robertson's dissatisfaction with the heavy-handed tactics of these early organizations led to a studied decision to "disassociate himself from the religious New Right, dropping politics entirely to work exclusively in the spiritual arena." "Barely containing his disdain," in 1992 Pat Robertson told a reporter: "The Moral Majority was just a huge mailing list that spewed out letters to 4 million people asking for money."[17]

After an initial period of high visibility and real political impact in the early 1980s, the Moral Majority steadily declined in influence. Its demise coincided with the rise of Robertson's political ambition and influence. Insiders blamed the collapse of the Moral Majority on its negative treatment by the press, but it also had serious ideological and structural flaws. Ideologically, Falwell's fundamentalist roots precluded the Moral Majority becoming a genuinely "ecumenical" collection of Christian social conservatives. The Moral Majority never effectively formed bonds with Catholics, and the organization awkwardly embraced the network of charismatic Christians in traditional Pentecostal denominations and independent megachurches. Falwell tried to bridge these theological divides — sometimes testing the tolerance of his fellow fundamentalists in the process — but with limited success. Nowhere was the chasm more evident than during Falwell's ill-fated effort to manage Jim Bakker's charismatic PTL Network in 1987.[18]

The Moral Majority also had serious structural flaws. It was "a preacher-led organization," observed Ralph Reed in 1994, never effectively organizing at the grassroots level. University of Virginia political analyst Larry Sabato told reporters that "Falwell lacked the political savvy to get involved in the mechanics of politics and his high negative ratings hurt candidates Falwell publicly supported." In his 1996 book, *Active Faith,* Ralph Reed summarized the weaknesses of the "old religious right." The Moral Majority and other early organizations "never truly developed a coherent and broad-based legislative agenda." "When it did address broader issues," Reed surmised, "the religious right was often artless." The "clergy-based leadership" too often betrayed "an attitude of arrogance and triumphalism." Reed believed that the heated rhetoric of those days was helpful in raising money, but not in winning political victories. Under his leadership the Christian Coalition consciously eschewed "military metaphors."[19]

"The exit of Falwell," *Time* magazine noted in 1987, "ends the initial era of the Religious Right and quickens speculation on its prospects in the next phase." Falwell believed that the mantle of the Moral Majority would be shared by the "hundreds of other organizations like Concerned Women for America and the Rutherford Institute" which "had spun off from the Moral Majority." But it soon became apparent that it was the Christian Coalition that would succeed and surpass the Moral Majority in size and influence.[20]

Triggered by the publication of negative comments about the Moral Majority "attributed to" Reed in 1995, R. Mark DeMoss, Falwell's close advisor and friend, sent to Reed, Robertson, and Falwell a perceptive and conciliatory assessment of the respective contributions of the Moral Majority and the Christian Coalition:

> Let me tell you how Jerry and I view the role that Moral Majority played and the role which the Christian Coalition is playing. Jerry started Moral Majority in 1979 expressly to *awaken* and *inform* reli-

gious people about the political process and to encourage full and active participation in it. This, as you know, was during a period when religious involvement in the political process was a less accepted idea than it is today. Consequently, Jerry was a "lightning rod" during most of the years that Moral Majority was in existence.

I think you would agree that Moral Majority did accomplish several things during its 10-years, perhaps the most important of which was encouraging tens of thousands of pastors across the country who had previously been uninvolved in the political process to become actively involved. Secondly, millions of voters registered in and through churches all across the country. Furthermore, I believe that a number of moral and social issues were elevated to the forefront of national debate and I believe that has been a good thing. Finally, dozens of groups and organizations which share the same values and principles upon which the Moral Majority was founded have been organized and flourished since then.

We would not deny that the Christian Coalition is more sophisticated and better organized than the Moral Majority and in fact, it should be more sophisticated because 15 years have passed since Moral Majority was founded. . . . But I do believe that Moral Majority played a role in breaking new ground and paving the way for religious conservatives to get involved politically and to do so with more success and less antagonism. . . .

We believe groups like Christian Coalition have advanced the movement to the next level, but the "first phase" was necessary in order for the "second phase" to begin and succeed. In other words, many, many people have participated in and contributed to the progress of this movement and you and others are likely paving the way for even greater progress and success in future years.

While I would never ask or expect you to eulogize the Moral Majority, I would hope that you would recognize the role that it played. Jerry and I certainly use every opportunity we have to compliment what you are doing and we will continue to do so.[21]

By the late 1990s both Pat Robertson and Ralph Reed had become more appreciative of the contributions of Falwell and the Moral Majority, and their friendship with Falwell was strong and respectful. Both Robertson and Reed were conspicuously present at Jerry Falwell's funeral in 2007, and CBN posted on its website a tribute from Robertson: "Jerry has been a tower of strength on many of the moral issues which have confronted our nation. . . . Jerry's courage and strength of convictions will be sadly missed in this time of increasing moral relativism."[22]

The Bush Years

By 1990 the Christian Coalition was off to a brilliant start. As the election of 1992 approached, the Christian Coalition claimed 250,000 members in more than 1,000 chapters in all 50 states. By 1992 the yearly budget had risen to more than $8.5 million, and a permanent staff of 30 worked out of offices in Chesapeake, Virginia.[23]

Ralph Reed was a dynamo of activity and a superlative organizer. While the growth of the Christian Coalition owed much to circumstances, it was clear to outside observers that its success in grassroots organizing was a product of "the well-conceived strategy and tactics developed by its leaders." In a 1994 letter to a young correspondent who felt "called of God to run for political office," Robertson offered a four-step plan that summarized the practical strategy the Christian Coalition had used throughout the country: "1. Get involved with the Christian Coalition, and learn about grassroots politics. 2. Volunteer to help someone who is already a candidate. . . . 3. Start out with something like running for your local school board, or city council. 4. Most of all, pray and seek the Lord to be sure what His will is for you." Training and encouraging novice candidates to run for office and participate in Republican Party activities at local levels, Reed and Robertson began "ferociously organizing their supporters in churches and related Christian groups." Coalition activists soon became a visible presence in the Republican Party structure in many states, often to the discomfort of old party regulars. In addition to training candidates and party activists, the Coalition began distributing "voter guides" to be passed out in local churches. The voter guides rated candidates' records on issues of interest to conservative Christians. In 1992 the Coalition printed 40 million guides, which were distributed to nearly 250,000 churches. Although many of the millions of voter guides were never used, many were, and Pat Robertson believed that the 1992 distribution was "the most comprehensive effort in the history of the country." An Illinois Assembly of God pastor wrote to Robertson, "Just a brief note to express our sincere appreciation for the Candidate Scorecard. Both the tabloids and bulletin inserts were used here and were received very positively. . . . We appreciate your leadership and involvement in these strategic arenas."[24]

By 1992 the Christian Coalition and Pat Robertson were sufficiently visible to elicit the respect and attention of Republican Party leaders, including President George H.W. Bush. Robertson held George Bush in high esteem. Even though he was openly critical when Bush "broke his word" in 1990 on raising taxes and when he moved toward "unilateral disarmament" in 1991, personally he felt closer to the courtly Bush than to any other president. In January 1991 President Bush invited Robertson to the White House "for the purpose of encouraging him and praying for him with regards to the Persian Gulf Crisis." The next day the president penned a poignant personal note of thanks: "There is a little lull here at this minute in the Oval Office. I am thinking of yesterday's visit, of your supportive words, and most of all of that special moment of prayer. Thank you for coming my way." Robertson received a number of personal notes from the president in the months that followed, as the Bush team geared up for the election of 1992, and as the power and presence of the Christian Coalition became more and more apparent. After an "enjoyable meeting" in the White House in March 1992, the president thanked Robertson for his "honesty and perspective," assuring him that he would "look forward to continuing to receive the benefit of your counsel during the months ahead."[25]

Many of the early supporters of the Christian Coalition viewed Pat Robertson as a potential presidential candidate in 1992, and some Coalition stalwarts were upset when Robertson endorsed Bush for a second term. Ralph Reed defended Robertson's decision to support Bush. He pointed out that Bush had been a "100% pro-life President" and that the Supreme Court was "now poised to overturn *Roe vs. Wade.*" The bottom line, Reed insisted, was that a Bush victory "would be eminently more advantageous to our agenda than Bill Clinton." Reed shared with a disenchanted Christian Coalition member the answer Robertson had given him about not running: "He asked me to convey to you that he was in prayer in late December in 1990, and the Lord instructed him to not oppose George Bush in 1992." Both he and Robertson knew, Reed continued, that "the reason Bush's re-election effort is in such deep trouble is because he has wandered from the strongly conservative principles that he articulated in his general election campaign of 1988." However, the Christian Coalition was "not prepared at this time as an organization to take on a sitting President of the United States. ... We believe that the time for us to take on an individual of Bush's stature is later in the decade, and not at this time."[26]

Robertson's growing stature in the Republican Party and his loyal support of the president earned him an invitation to speak at the Republican convention in Houston. Robertson's appearance on Wednesday evening seemed fairly inconspicuous in a convention that featured Ronald Rea-

The Clinton Era

Bill Clinton was a persona made to infuriate conservative Christians. Robertson's one-word description of Clinton's acceptance speech at the Democratic convention was "unbelievable": "In my opinion, atheism and its companion, secular humanism, are bad, but creating for political purposes a pseudo-Christianity to mask practices described by the Bible as 'abominations' is nothing short of blasphemy." Robertson was outraged that Christians who had opposed Clinton were "hooted down as 'bigots,' 'religious extremists,' and 'ignorant right wing fanatics.'" Bill Clinton's election was a sudden and unexpected end to the Reagan Revolution.[30]

As distasteful as Robertson found the character of Bill Clinton, he was unexpectedly balanced in his early assessments of the Clinton administration. He was encouraged by the new president's mildly pro-business economic pronouncements and was "very pleased to hear President Clinton say he's serious about reforming America's failed welfare system." Robertson liked some of Clinton's appointments, particularly Lloyd Bentsen at Treasury, Warren Christopher at State, and Les Aspin at Defense: "So far I give him an A+ for political shrewdness." Robertson quickly perceived that the new president would be a formidable political adversary; he never lost respect for Clinton in that regard. After Ralph Reed told a reporter in early 1993 that Clinton's was "the most radical, pro-abortion administration in American history," Robertson wrote a pointed rebuke to his young friend: "You are absolutely fantastic and anointed by the Lord for the work at hand, however, the old . . . College Republican still hangs around. . . . Bill Clinton is more popular than we are with the general public. In a contest between smiling Bill and the 'Religious Right' he will win. . . . If he can divert public attention from the foolishness of his proposals, to the perceived 'bigotry and harshness' of the 'fundamentalists,' his proposals will be given new life. . . . I am a target as big as a barn. It is hardly appropriate for you without my knowledge to send small arms fire at a well armed enemy in order to provoke him to open up with heavy artillery on me. . . . Please, Please. No press releases or public statements attacking Bill Clinton. . . . The time to war against Clinton directly and openly will come."[31]

The time to fight came soon. By 1993 both Robertson and Reed relished the Christian Coalition's "role in taking on Clinton." In his book *The Turning Tide*, published in 1993, Robertson believed that he could see "a return to common sense in this nation" which gave conservatives "every right to be optimistic." Indeed, the zenith of the Coalition's influence came during the Clinton years. An exhilarated Robertson wrote to his friend Dan Quayle in early 1994, "The Christian Coalition continues to grow by leaps and bounds. We currently have 950,000 members and supporters in 872 local chapters in all 50 states." By the fall of 1995 the group claimed 1.6 million members in 1,600 local affiliates and was widely recognized as one of "the most powerful grass-roots forces in American politics." In 1996 the Coalition reached its financial peak, with contributions of nearly $25 million.[32]

Robertson and other Christian Coalition leaders were euphoric about Reed's performance. After the board met at the end of 1995, Robertson sent a note of thanks to Reed: "We are all deeply appreciative of the super job you have done and continue to do at the Coalition. We are delighted at the team you have developed, and the good things that are happening to bring righteous initiatives to our government. . . . In recognition for the great job you have done in 1995, we are pleased to give you a bonus at this year-end of $50,000." "The person who deserved the credit is Bill Clinton," quipped Reed a decade later; the Christian Coalition "exploded" during his first term.[33]

Reed's success as a grassroots organizer was impressive. By 1995 political analysts estimated that as many as thirty state Republican Party organizations had been substantially influenced by the religious right. Reed downplayed such estimates but agreed that "our movement is now in many ways thoroughly integrated and enmeshed into the machinery of the Republican Party." The Christian Coalition "plan," exquisitely executed by Reed, was to encourage members to infiltrate local Republican committees and work their way up the organizational structure. A fifty-seven-page "county action plan" distributed by the Pennsylvania Christian Coalition gave step-by-step instructions about how to gain influence in the party at the local level, advising members to "never mention the name 'Christian Coalition.'" The potential was clear: "If we have as few as 75-150 people in each county we could become the most powerful political influence in the state." Responding to a young college graduate with political ambitions, Robertson concluded his own step-by-step instructions with a practical recommendation: "I would advise also that you get involved in Republican Party activities. There is always a shortage of good people to carry on the many tasks at hand. I'm sure the Christian Coalition in Michigan would also welcome your help, and you could learn a great deal from them."[34]

The strength of the Christian Coalition was its grassroots organization, but it also became a powerful lobbying presence in Washington. Beginning in 1990, the Coalition staged annual "Road to Victory" rallies that became virtual beauty contests for hopeful Republican candidates. The conferences attracted thousands of activists from all over the country who were treated to speeches from political figures ranging from President George Bush and Vice-President Dan Quayle to every aspiring presidential candidate in the decade of the nineties. The highlight of every rally was a marching-orders speech by Pat Robertson.

During his long and influential life, Pat Robertson made many impulsive appointments. Some were miserable failures, but Ralph Reed was a spectacular success. In 1990 Washington political strategist Paul Weyrich wrote to Robertson, "You made a brilliant move in hiring Ralph Reed, who has real credibility here." Robertson remained the visible image of the Christian Coalition, and frequently spoke at organizing events, but Reed was the on-the-ground presence guiding the dramatic growth of the organization. The partnership between the two was seamless. "Once his confidence in me developed," recalled Reed, "he was a very hands-off manager." Robertson was always important behind the scenes, Reed acknowledged: "Strategically, he and I were on the phone every day. . . . It was a lot like a junior and senior partner in a law firm. . . . He was a lot older and wiser than me." But Robertson was fully occupied with the daunting task of rebuilding CBN, and after a few months "he was no longer involved in the day to day decisions." Robertson was a crucial fundraiser, particularly in recruiting large donors for the 500-member President's Council, whose annual dues were $1,000 a year. Many felt that Robertson was at his best in the company of "a few select people" gathered at "my house on the Hot Springs Mountain." A 1994 invitation to one such gathering read: "I would like you to be my guest not only for the meeting on Friday, but to spend the night on Thursday night as well. Perhaps you could enjoy some of the recreation up there which includes golf, tennis, skeet, hiking, and some wonderful fresh air."[35]

In the public mind, and among conservative Christians, Robertson remained the guiding genius of the Christian Coalition. In a poll taken in the fall of 1996, only 18 percent of evangelical Christians recognized Ralph Reed's name, but three out of four knew Pat Robertson. As the "senior partner" in the Reed-Robertson team, and as the chairman of the board of the Christian Coalition, Robertson occasionally brought the energetic Reed to heel. Irritated by a 1993 fundraising letter targeting inactive members, Robertson jotted a message on the draft to be returned to Reed: "Ralph — This is dreadful — full of falsehood — hucksterish. Clean it up. We can accomplish the same thing without lying." After a harsh reprimand from his mentor about a comment that had appeared in the press, a chastened Reed wrote: "I think you know that I would never intentionally do anything to cause you harm. I am truly sorry that you felt this statement might do so. . . . Pat, working for you has been the greatest professional joy of my life. I appreciate you so very much."[36]

By 1994, Reed recalled, "we were hitting stride." The success of the Christian Coalition dramatically expanded the personal political reach of Pat Robertson. Scores of Washington offices were open to him; Secretary of Education Lamar Alexander sent an appreciative note after a visit with Robertson in which the two agreed "to work together in reforming our nation's schools." A parade of political leaders journeyed to Virginia Beach to seek Robertson's views and support. After spending a day visiting CBN, Georgia gubernatorial candidate Guy Milner wrote to Robertson, "Ginny and I both feel that what we are doing is the Lord's will for our lives, and discussions such as we had on Wednesday continue to give me a sense that this campaign is not really in our hands at all. If we win in November, it will be the Lord's victory and not ours." Robertson campaigned personally for some candidates, including appearances during the gubernatorial election of George Allen in Virginia in 1993. Allen was profusely grateful: "Your support and counsel, as you know, is very important to me. And your public commendation has further bolstered our winning campaign. I look forward to seeing you and working with you on the trail to victory." Robertson regularly wrote congratulatory notes to successful Republican candidates after congressional elections, and his files bulged with letters of thanks: "God willing, I do intend to make a difference in Congress"; "I promise to stay in touch. . . . God bless you in your many important projects. My prayers and thoughts are with you"; "Thank you for your friendship — Please let me know how I can help you"; "I certainly look forward to working with you . . . to address the important issues of concern to our community and nation." During these years Robertson formed enduring political friendships. After his election to the Senate in 1994, John Ashcroft of Missouri wrote, "Now that the campaign is over, I look forward to working with you over the next six years in the U.S. Senate. . . . Thanks again for all you did to make this victory possible." Robertson's rising political stature was captured in a note written by Texas congressman Dick Armey to a friend who had hosted a party rally in 1992: "Sharing the podium with Tom DeLay and Pat Robertson is pretty heady stuff and I am still on cloud nine over that experience." Haley Barbour, chairman of the Republican National Committee, solicited Robertson's advice about the best locale for the 1996 convention. Chicago was his choice, Robertson replied, offering a telling summary of his prejudices for rejecting New York City: "I have seen the incredible venom of the radical left in New York. If we hold a convention in

New York City you can make book that every night on the evening news there will be pictures of homosexual and lesbian radicals, joined with those of the feminist left."[37]

The rising influence of Pat Robertson and the Christian Coalition in the Republican Party was not uniformly welcome. The Coalition "sparks love from some Republicans, fear from others," reported the *Washington Post,* but "none can ignore it." By the mid-1990s Reed estimated that state affiliates of the Coalition dominated the party apparatus in at least a dozen states, including Florida and Texas. Robertson's stature within the Republican Party compelled the pro-choice element of the party to try to build bridges. Senator Arlen Specter of Pennsylvania, often at odds with the opponents of abortion within the party, solicited Robertson's participation in a Washington meeting seeking "ways to broaden the base of the national Republican Party." Unable to attend because he was in the midst of CBN's annual telethon, Robertson warned Specter that "if the pro-family issues such as prayer in the schools, choice in education, opposition to special homosexual rights, and pro-life were taken out of the Republican platform . . . 57.9% of Republican voters would no longer wish to be Republicans."[38]

The rise of the Christian Coalition vaulted Pat Robertson into an extended period of notoriety and scrutiny that was at least equal to the attention he received during his run for the Republican nomination in 1988. After the stunning Republican victory in the congressional elections in 1994, many traditional conservative leaders embraced the Christian Coalition as an important ally. William F. Buckley Jr. endorsed the Christian Coalition's campaign to pass a prayer amendment: "The Christian Coalition speaks for the majority of Americans whose patience has worn thin and who are not disposed to let a half-century go by before reinstating some recognition of religion in those schools where it is wanted." Robertson appeared on the cover of *U.S. News & World Report* in April 1995. When Congress returned to Washington, the magazine reported, it would find a new religious right "with charismatic leaders, millions of foot soldiers, full collection plates and a Republican Congress. . . . Robertson provides the theology and the finances, while Reed is the master political strategist and salesman." The message for Washington insiders was simple: "Christian conservatives believe their time has come."[39]

At the same time, as the Christian Coalition and Robertson increased in influence, they also became the chief target of those who believed the religious right was wrong at best and dangerous at worst. Before 1994, critics were often condescending and dismissive. An article in the *New Repub-*

lic just before the Congressional elections in 1994 predicted that "Christian conservatives" lacked the skills to be a significant political force: "Perhaps because the theological liberals scooped up the best divinity schools and richest congregations in the great schism of the early twentieth century, or perhaps because contemporary evangelicalism puts so much emphasis on emotions rather than doctrine, the evangelical church is a decapitated institution. . . . Which is why, by the end of the '94 electoral cycle, we're going to cease to read so much about the Christian right." Even after the 1994 election, an article in the *Humanist* judged that the Christian Coalition was "not particularly Christian and it's not a coalition."[40]

Expanding the Base and the Message

Pat Robertson and Ralph Reed built a powerful organization in the mid-1990s on two foundations: a relatively broad religious ecumenism and a flexible and pragmatic political agenda. Robertson was the chief architect of the Christian Coalition's efforts to cross denominational lines and unite Christian conservatives, a dream he had failed to achieve during his presidential race. By 1993 Reed publicly fleshed out a plan to expand the Christian Coalition's political agenda into a broad platform of action.

Bright, animated, and congenial, Reed alarmed opponents on the left, but charmed them at the same time. "The face of the new Christian conservative movement belongs to Ralph Reed, and it is a face any mother could love," reported the *Washington Post* in 1994. After the Republican victories in that year, Arthur J. Kropp, president of People for the American Way, told a reporter, "I would say he is on the front line of putting together what is probably the best political organization in the country." Some critics on the left believed that Reed did little more than put a friendly face on Robertson's sinister political plans, and some critics on the right feared that Reed's insider political rhetoric betrayed Robertson's political legacy, but almost without exception the two men were of one mind about expanding the reach and message of the Christian Coalition.[41]

As opposed to many narrower religious right political organizations, the Christian Coalition self-consciously tried to draw diverse Christians into united political action. The religious broadmindedness of Reed and Robertson surprised both critics and some supporters of the Christian Coalition. Speaking to the Anti-Defamation League in 1995, Reed acknowledged that "religious conservatives have at times been insensitive, particularly in their call for a 'Christian nation.'" The Christian Coalition's political goals were non-sectarian, Reed insisted; he believed that "America is not officially Christian, Jewish, or Muslim." In the United States the principle of "the separation of church and state is complete and inviolable." Recognizing that his remarks would inflame some conservatives, Reed faxed a draft of his speech to Robertson, who "approved both the tone and the content."[42]

In an effort to expand the religious diversity of the Christian Coalition, Robertson focused his efforts on uniting evangelicals and politically conservative Catholics. As one of the early leaders in the charismatic movement in the 1960s and 1970s, Robertson participated in scores of ecumenical conclaves where evangelicals mingled with Catholics, sharing the gifts of the Holy Spirit. Even more unifying was the pro-life movement, described by Keith Fournier, the leader of the Christian Coalition's Catholic outreach, as the "great ecumenical movement of modern times." Robertson had seen the unifying potential of such social issues very early in his political awakening. He wrote in 1979, "Leaders of the so-called 'New Right' have realized that issues such as abortion will bring evangelicals and urban Catholics together at the polls." In 1994 Robertson explained to a supporter why he had reached out to Catholics from the beginning of the Christian Coalition: "My vision of the Christian Coalition has always been a Christian organization that would include evangelical Christians, pro-family Roman Catholics, Greek Orthodox, and other people of faith who share our desire to return America to greatness through moral strength." "The outreach should not be interpreted as an endorsement of theological stands with which we disagree," he explained, but "when Catholics or Jews agree with us on the need to stop abortion, ban hardcore pornography, and allow voluntary school prayer, I believe it would be unwise for us not to work with those who share our views." In 1994 Reed estimated that the religious composition of the Coalition was roughly 40 percent Baptist, 20 percent Pentecostal/charismatic, 20 percent mainstream Protestants, and 20 percent Catholics or members of one of the booming "nondenominational churches now flourishing in America's middle-class white suburbs."[43]

Newsweek noted that Robertson's "movement managed a significant breakthrough" in May 1993 when Cardinal John O'Connor and the Christian Coalition joined forces to give conservatives a clear victory in New York City's local school board elections. An elated Robertson thanked the cardinal for distributing Coalition voter guides in New York City churches: "I wanted to take this opportunity to personally thank you for agreeing to distribute our nonpartisan, educational voter guides during the recent school board elections in New York City. Due in no small measure to your help, 70 pro-family school board candidates, more than half of all those who ran, were elected. . . . Thank you again for your stand on behalf of our shared moral concerns."[44]

Robertson carefully placed Roman Catholics in visible leadership positions in his family of organizations. In 1991 he hired Keith Fournier, a lawyer and conservative activist, as executive director of the American Center for Law and Justice. For nearly a decade Fournier was the most important liaison between Robertson and Catholics. Fournier was recommended to Robertson by Reverend Michael Scanlan, the President of Franciscan University of Steubenville, a pioneer in the Catholic charismatic renewal, and an early supporter of the Christian Coalition. In 1993 Reed thanked Scanlan for "being a part of our efforts and supporting our campaign to give Christians a voice in government again" and informed him that "I am working closely with Keith Fournier and Marlene Elwell on a Catholic outreach project to increase the relationships between evangelicals and Catholics on shared public policy issues. I have asked Marlene and Keith to contact you regarding this very important project." In 1995 those plans resulted in the formation of the Catholic Alliance, an "auxiliary" of the Coalition, which it was hoped would boost the membership of Catholics from 250,000 to more than a million. By the end of the year the Christian Coalition reported that 16 percent of its 1.5 million members were Catholics and set a goal of 30 percent. Fournier explained to the press that the new venture was "a sign of respecting differences, not an action to divide followers of Christ."[45]

The launching of the Catholic Alliance was intended to make it less awkward for the Catholic hierarchy to cooperate with Coalition projects. But the specter of Catholic churches distributing Christian Coalition voter guides riled the liberal Catholic intelligentsia. "All components factored in," observed the editor of *Commonweal*, "the archdiocese made a large mistake. The Christian Coalition is organized under the auspices of Pat Robertson, who holds a distinct ideological position in one political party. He and his coalition have political links to groups and ideas that are at odds with much of Catholic social teaching and certainly with parts of its theology." On the other hand, the *National Review* observed that the Christian Coalition was beginning to look much more like a "real rainbow coalition" than any other religious/political alliance. In hindsight, Ralph Reed believed that the Coalition had "a lot of success" in working with Catholics, but ultimately it was difficult for "an organization that was essentially run by Protestants" to gain much influence with Catholic bishops. Still, Reed believed that during the mid-1990s the Coalition "built a strong relationship with the Catholic community," giving Fournier much of the credit. Fournier was less sanguine. While the Catholic Alliance was "well intended," he thought it ended "an abysmal failure."[46]

During the Christian Coalition's courtship of Roman Catholics, Robertson had his most moving personal encounter with Catholicism. In 1995 he was invited to a private audience with visiting Pope John Paul II and attended a papal mass. Like many conservative Protestants, Robertson was an unabashed admirer of John Paul II, writing in his 1993 book *The Turning Tide* that "Pope John Paul II stands like a rock against all opposition in his clear enunciation of the foundational principles of the Christian faith." After the October meeting he told a reporter, "We're laying the foundation for some very significant harmony, socially and spiritually." But the alliance between the Christian Coalition and Catholics never got far beyond its early successes.[47]

More surprising to outsiders than the Christian Coalition's effort to build a wide-ranging religious coalition was Ralph Reed's public embrace of a broad and pragmatic political agenda. In its early years the Christian Coalition's public agenda featured the same pro-life and pro-family issues that had united the religious right for more than a decade. By 1995, when the Coalition published its "Contract with the American Family," a summary of the organization's positions with an introduction by Reed, the range of issues addressed was much broader. Coalition insiders saw the Contract as important because of a perceived neglect of family issues in Newt Gingrich's Contract with America. Reed claimed major responsibility for the inclusion of a tax credit for families earning less than $200,000 and tougher restrictions on Internet pornography in the Republican Contract with America in 1994, but the pro-family agenda went largely unaddressed. The Christian Coalition's contract was itself very broad. In the Coalition's Contract with the American Family, some of the planks were religious-right standards, such as the passage of a Religious Equality Act "that will legalize organized prayer in public places, including schools," but it also included an education agenda backing school vouchers and planks on the defunding of the National Endowments for the Arts and Humanities and tax breaks for families. Because of its breadth, the Contract with the American Family did little to allay concerns among some insiders that Reed's vision for the Coalition had become too broad.[48]

Those who viewed the Coalition as a conventional religious-right organization were taken by surprise by a series of interviews and articles by Reed beginning in 1993. In an article entitled "A Wider Net," published in *Policy Review*, Reed commented candidly about the past weaknesses of Christian conservatives and outlined his plan for the future. In spite of "talented leadership, strong grassroots support, and enormous financial resources," he wrote, the "pro-family movement still has limited appeal even among the 40 million voters who attend church frequently, identify themselves as evangelicals or orthodox Roman Catholics, and consider themselves traditionalist on cultural issues." Values alone were not enough, he insisted: "the successful candidate or movement must promote policies that personally benefit voters — such as tax cuts, education vouchers, higher wages, or retirement benefits." Reed concluded: "The key to success for the pro-family movement is to discuss a broader issues agenda in the language of the target audience — churchgoers and families with children. In doing so, a social movement until now composed largely of white evangelicals can win natural allies among Catholics and ethnic minorities. The Apostle Paul said that he had become 'all things to all people that I may by all means win some.'" Reed assured reporters that "the mainstream has nothing to fear from today's religious conservative." Religious conservatives must learn from the example of Martin Luther King Jr., wrote the young historian, that a high moral message must not be delivered in "harsh language" but through ennobling principles.[49]

By the fall of 1993 Reed was under increasingly heavy fire from religious conservatives. "To the disbelief of many," wrote a pro-life activist in the *Washington Post*, Reed had suggested in an opinion editorial published in the *New York Times* that "abortion was a key issue to only 12 percent of the voting public in the last election." After Reed's article appeared, a disgruntled senator Jesse Helms fired off a note to Pat Robertson: "I have nothing whatsoever against Ralph Reed . . . but I am obliged to say that I strongly disagree with what he said in recent articles and public comments. . . . If he is going to be in charge of 'Christianizing' the Republican Party, he can count me out. And, frankly, I suspect he will do you more harm than good. If he wants to try to secularize the Republican Party, that's his business — but he ought to leave the word *Christian* out of his sales pitch. . . . If I were not your friend, I would not have written this letter. I pray that my candor does not offend you." Robertson forwarded the protest to Reed, and the young activist wrote a polite answer to try to reassure the senator. Press reports of his recent comments were "simply inaccurate," he told Helms, and he assured him that they were on the same team: "Your advice and leadership mean a great deal to me. . . . Pat and I appreciate so much your courageous stand in the U.S. Senate on behalf of our shared values. God bless you for standing tall for faith and family."[50]

If Reed's openness offended the most rigid conservatives, his willingness to bargain and compromise made him the icon of a more reasonable and approachable religious right. He was pictured on the cover of *Time* on May 15, 1995, with the caption "The Right Hand of God: Ralph Reed and the Christian Coalition." Reed's plan to "cast a wider net" was fleshed out in a book, *Active Faith,* published in 1996. In his book, Reed stated the Coalition's aims in conciliatory language: "Religious conservatives do not claim to have all the answers, but we do think we have identified many of the problems. . . . For the vast majority of our supporters there has never been an understanding that God is a Republican or even a member of the Christian Coalition. We are people of faith struggling to do what is right, nothing more. We are sometimes wrong."[51]

Active Faith set off a firestorm among religious conservatives, who were offended by its tone and by Reed's perceived waffling on such key issues as the demand that the Republican Party platform include a constitutional amendment banning abortion. After reading a preview of the book in *Newsweek,* Congressman Robert K. Dornan wrote to Robertson: "What in heaven and hell is going on? . . . Honestly, Pat, if conservatives won't raise the issues of abortion, homosexuality, and Bill Clinton's character . . . then we'll be stuck with him for another four years. . . . Ralph's continued use of 'big tent' rhetoric will not bring anyone closer to truth or goodness or decency. . . . This type of misjudgment seems to be addictive with Ralph." After a series of television appearances in which Reed seemed to diminish the importance of abortion as a political issue, James Dobson sent Robertson a dense five-page "personal and confidential" letter expressing his outrage about Reed's positions and his demeanor. In a seven-page answer Reed replied respectfully, believing that Dobson's letter "mischaracterized my views on the issues." Reed acknowledged that there probably was "a tactical and stylistic difference" between the two of them, "but not a strategic disagreement about where we want to go." In particular, Dobson objected to Reed's implication that the 1996 Republican platform should substitute "morally compelling" language for a demand for a "Human Life Amendment"; such equivocation seemed to Dobson like a thinly veiled effort to help presumptive nominee Bob Dole unite the party. Only after a conversation with Robertson did Dobson feel reassured that the Coalition would not compromise on the abortion issue. On May 9, Robertson wrote to Dobson: "In following up our discussion and correspondence, I have been in touch in Washington today with the person who will undoubtedly have the key voice on the platform. I was assured that absolutely no change is contemplated in the abortion language from that contained in the 1992 draft. If others would wish a watered-down statement, they are free to draft a non-platform statement that they can hold out to their supporters, but, as I understand it, this will not be the official language of the Republican Party." Yet Robertson, like Reed, did not want to headline abortion in the coming election: "We must be careful not to allow ourselves to be diverted by what is intended to be a non-issue at this convention. The key is party unity, and I believe the leadership is going to do everything possible to assure unity so the Republican Party is able to win this most crucial election."[52]

In the midst of the furor over Ralph Reed's inclusive rhetoric, Pat Robertson told a reporter that he was "taking an elder statesman role."[131] But Robertson was never very detached from Reed's actions. He read and critiqued *Active Faith* before its publication. After reading the first draft of the 1996 book, Robertson warned, "I am afraid that you have written things here in haste about whose consequences you have not considered." Reed agreed that an editorial session with Robertson in Virginia Beach improved the book. In the foreword to *Active Faith,* Reed wrote: "I am indebted to Pat Robertson. He read every word, offered unique insights, and encouraged me during the editing process. I shall never forget our phone conversations from Switzerland in which he helped me revise the last several chapters. Furthermore, this book is about a vision and a social movement that Pat helped to birth and build. . . . I thank him for his kindness and generosity to me and to my family." In short, the events of these defining months saw Robertson cast as cheerleader, advisor, and referee between Reed and disgruntled conservative critics.[53]

The synergy between Ralph Reed and Pat Robertson was virtually complete, even though critics often pictured Robertson as a heavy-handed bigot and Reed as an enigmatic moderating influence. Unlike many of the leaders of the religious right, both Reed and Robertson had deep roots in politics before their religious conversions. Reed was a veteran party activist before he "came to Christ" at age twenty-two, and he knew that "if you were constantly making demands . . . and you were never delivering the vote, they would tune you out." Robertson's political education had been life-long, and he understood well the art of compromise. He and Reed differed from "most of the rest" of the religious political activists of the period, Robertson mused in later years, because the two of them "cut our teeth on politics. . . . We sort of knew how the game was played." Reed believed that the two "never had a disagreement in philosophy."[54]

Reed was not alone in being rebuked by rigid conservatives. In May 1995, conservative writer Lawrence Auster chided Robertson: "I am concerned that both you and Ralph Reed . . . are bending yourselves out of shape to try to appease liberals." As early as 1993 the *Christian Century* noted that many leaders in the "New Christian Right now say Robertson is too moderate." His support for the GATT agreement, and free trade in general, offended one of his closest allies in the Senate, Strom Thurmond of South Carolina, but Robertson resisted heavy lobbying from his father's old friend. When he questioned the practicality of a constitutional amendment banning abortion on *Evans & Novak* on CNN, the response was heated. "The purists thought that was horrible," he recalled. "They can get very irate over things that they don't understand." Writing to a supporter in 1994, Robertson explained the fundamentals of practical politics: "Regrettably, elections in the United States are never between perfection and less than perfection, but between two fallible human beings. The question is, in the primary or the general election which candidate's views come closer to what would be considered the perfect ideal." The point of politics, Robertson told a group of Missouri supporters in 1997, was being "a winner," and that demanded building political alliances.[55]

In keeping with this bigger-tent philosophy, the Christian Coalition was positioned to back any Republican candidate as the election of 1996 approached. Robertson told supporters that the Coalition planned to distribute more than "60 million Voter Guides and 17 million Congressional Scorecards to churches and Christian voters around the nation. These two programs will be the driving forces behind what I hope will be a brilliant ballot-box victory for Bible-believing Christians in 1996." Most of the Republican candidates made their pitches at the "Road to Victory" conference in 1995, including front-runner Bob Dole, a moderate often uncomfortable with the religious right. But Dole "delivered a speech blasting Hollywood values" that brought a rousing cheer from Reed. By 1996 Robertson and the Christian Coalition were solidly behind Dole, urging the faithful not to support third-party candidates who "would only siphon off key conservative votes from a Republican candidate" and assure the re-election of Bill Clinton. In later years, after a tiff with Dole, Robertson reminded him of the risks he had taken: "Bob, I fought like a tiger for your election in 1996. I have been severely criticized by some conservatives who felt that my help was crucial in your . . . win over Pat Buchanan in Iowa and your significant primary victory in South Carolina. . . . I was with you all the way during the campaign in which you fought so bravely." But after the election, Robertson attributed the Republican loss to Dole's suspect social conservatism. He told *The 700 Club*'s audience, "Despite the fact that Bob Dole is a fine and decent man, this election marks the second consecutive time when a Republican candidate for president lost the election because he muted social issues in favor of money issues.... Religious conservatives and the United States of America deserve better."[56]

New Directions

In the spring of 1997 Ralph Reed resigned as president of the Christian Coalition. The *Washington Post* speculated that "there were limits to what more Reed could achieve inside the Christian Coalition," where he found it "more and more difficult to balance the demands of a social movement filled with true believers with the pragmatic requirements of winning elections in a secular society." Reed, however, insisted that he left with the sense that his mission had been accomplished. When the coalition began, evangelicals "were marginalized by a larger culture"; by 1997 they had gained a place at the table of power, "widely acknowledged to be one of the most potent and effective forces in American politics." He wanted to become a lobbyist more directly involved in working for candidates, and was a part of the successful George W. Bush campaigns in 2000 and 2004. In that role, he believed, he would be able "to speak to more voters and more people."[57]

The parting of Reed and Robertson was cordial. In February, the Christian Coalition board had once again voted Reed a "bonus of $25,000, net of income taxes, ... in recognition of a job well done." Reed deeply admired Robertson, and the two remained close friends and confidants without interruption.[58]

Reed's departure came at the peak of the Christian Coalition's power and prestige, but also at a time when it had critical internal weaknesses. In his resignation announcement, Reed summarized the organization's achievements: "Last year the Christian Coalition's 1.9 million members and supporters in 2,000 local chapters distributed 45 million non-partisan voter guides in 125,000 churches. Its budget has grown from $200,000 in 1989 to $27 million in 1996. Religious conservatives have played a decisive role in the election of the first pro-family, conservative Congress in generations." In all, Reed judged, the movement had accomplished its goals: "We now have what we have always sought: a place at the table, a voice in the conversation we call democracy, a vital and vibrant role in the future of our nation." As for his friend Pat Robertson, Reed closed: "He is one of the towering evangelical figures of the 20th century, a pioneer of cable TV, a religious broadcasting entrepreneur, one of the most significant political leaders in the country, a philanthropist, author and a friend." In response to Reed's resignation, Robertson heaped praise on the "loyal, dedicated and bright young man who worked to meet the goal I had set for the organization at the start — to make the Christian Coalition one of the most effective grassroots organizations in the nation." The two of them had "worked in wonderful harmony together," and Reed agreed to continue to serve as a member of the board of directors of the Christian Coalition.[59]

In retrospect, Reed offered some thoughtful reflections on his years heading the Christian Coalition. He had tried to be "respectful" to his conservative critics, and in later years he became more understanding of their misgivings about his desire to position the Coalition at the center of the Republican Party. Partly, his clashes with James Dobson, Jerry Falwell, and other religious right leaders were predictable side effects of organizational "rivalry," but there were also real differences between Reed and the others. Reed wanted to "shave off some of the rough edges to our rhetorical approach," to speak in a less "harsh way," so that the Christian right message would not be "marginalized as a brand."[60]

Outsiders understood his contribution quite well. In an article entitled "Why Liberals Secretly Love James Dobson," Paul A. Gigot of the *Wall Street Journal* contrasted the styles of religious-right leaders Gary Bauer and James Dobson to the conciliatory tactics of Reed: "The Reed-Dobson split is over strategy more than philosophy. They often endorse the same candidates. But Mr. Dobson puts social issues like abortion and gay rights first. Mr. Reed tries to blend those subjects with taxes and other issues that broaden his candidates' appeal. Mr. Dobson broadcasts his message on TV and radio in a way which often makes him the issue. Mr. Reed narrowcasts different messages to different audiences to make the issues the issue. Mr. Dobson threatens to leave the party when he loses a debate. Mr. Reed tries to change the party from within." In later years, after he was no longer a competitor, Reed was magnanimous to his former critics: "We had different roles to play and we had different styles. We were both partially right."[61]

The Beginning of the End of the Christian Coalition

As president of the Christian Coalition, Pat Robertson announced that the organization would immediately launch "a vigorous, nationwide search for an executive director. . . . I am confident that the Lord who brought

[Ralph Reed] to us will also bring a capable successor. I expect the transition to be an orderly one which will position the Christian Coalition for continued growth and even greater success in the years ahead." Despite its successes, the organization was in financial straits that required the reduction of staff and the restructuring of some of its programs. Some observers believed that the Christian Coalition "imploded with Ralph Reed's 1997 departure," but the decline of the organization and its influence was not quite so abrupt. The Coalition remained strong; it still had an annual budget of more than $20 million. A spokesman told the press that the departure of Reed was "not the end of the Christian Coalition. It's not even the beginning of the end."[62]

The organization Reed left behind, built on a "strategy of working with the party establishment," was solidly aligned with the Republican Party. The annual "Road to Victory Conference and Strategy Briefing" in the capitol continued to attract a parade of political figures and potential candidates. Among the speakers in 1998 were Trent Lott, Newt Gingrich, Dick Armey, J. C. Watts, Dan Quayle, Tom DeLay, John Kasich, Mitch McConnell, Alan Keyes, Steve Forbes, Gary Bauer, Bob Smith, and John Ashcroft. The 1999 roster included Henry Hyde, Pat Buchanan, George W. Bush, Elizabeth Dole, and Orrin Hatch. Top Congressional leaders listed among the sponsors for a gala 70th birthday celebration for Robertson in March 2000 included his closest friends in Washington: from the Senate, John Ashcroft, Jesse Helms, Strom Thurmond, and Trent Lott; from the House of Representatives, Dennis Hastert, Dick Armey, and Tom DeLay.[63]

In June 1997 Robertson announced that Don Hodel would be the new president of the Christian Coalition and Randy Tate would be the organization's executive director. Robertson continued to serve as chairman of the board. The sixty-one-year-old Hodel had a long record as a conservative activist and had served the Reagan administration as Secretary of Energy and Secretary of the Interior. Hodel, who was a member of the board of Focus on the Family, had been a friend of both Robertson and conservative causes for years, and his appointment brought an aura of Washington-insider respectability to the Christian Coalition. Some observers speculated that Hodel would be "more skillful than Robertson at moving between the secular and religious worlds." "There's a grace and trustworthy manner about him that enables him to take very tough stands without it becoming polarizing or personal bitterness being engendered," observed one of his friends. The thirty-one-year-old Tate had been an alternate Robertson delegate at the 1988 Republican Convention and had gone on to serve in the Washington State House of Representatives from 1988 to 1994 before being elected to a single term in the House of Representatives as a part of the 1994 "Republican Revolution." The appointments, Robertson told reporters, would "link the Reagan Revolution with the rising influence of active people of faith."[64]

The new appointees inherited a formidable organization. A *Fortune* magazine list of the nation's "leading lobbying firms" ranked the Christian Coalition seventh in 1996 and 1997, ahead of such powerhouse groups as the American Medical Association, the American Education Association, and the Chamber of Commerce. Under the leadership of Don Hodel, the Coalition continued to be viewed as a team player within the Republican Party. The press had come to recognize that the Coalition had an identity distinct from such organizations as Gary Bauer's Family Research Council and Dobson's Focus on the Family. In 1998 a *National Journal* reporter wrote: "The Christian Coalition . . . is seen as a group that works within the system." Hodel sent copies of the article to the board of directors along with the caveat, "it reflects a lot of hard work on our parts."[65]

The new leaders of the Christian Coalition, Ralph Reed told reporters, needed to "make permanent what otherwise might be transitory." But to do so the Coalition would face difficult challenges. In the last half of the 1990s the Coalition fought two costly court battles with the Federal Election Commission and the Internal Revenue Service. These lawsuits, according to Robertson, could "effectively muzzle Christians before the 1998 elections." "I do not mean to sound so bleak," he warned supporters, "but this is perhaps the lowest time for the Christian Coalition."[66]

Both suits had been triggered by complaints from liberal advocacy groups in Washington. In 1996 the FEC sued the Christian Coalition, charging that the Coalition's voter guides and other activities constituted "express advocacy" on behalf of the Republican Party. Reed assured supporters that the charges were "a completely baseless and legally threadbare attempt to suppress and silence people of faith." But the suit sent tremors through the entire religious right. Jerry Falwell warned that the suit was a part of a general intimidation campaign that included a widely circulated message written by a special counsel of the National Council of Churches of Christ warning churches that they could lose their tax-exempt status for supporting "all forms of participation or intervention in any political campaign." In a widely distributed letter, Barry Lynn, Robertson's nemesis at Americans United for Separation of Church and State, informed "religious leaders" that "after carefully studying Coalition voter guides from previous years, I am convinced that they are in fact partisan campaign literature that advocate the election of certain candidates."

"Federal tax law strictly forbids non-profit organizations, including churches, from intervening in political campaigns," Lynn warned, and "the penalty of violating the IRS Code may include loss of tax-exempt status. The bottom line is that houses of worship that distribute Christian Coalition voter's guides run the risk of having their tax-exempt status challenged and possibly revoked."[67]

The Coalition immediately put together what it called "the finest election law legal team ever assembled" to fight the "totally baseless" and "frivolous" lawsuit. In August 1999 the Coalition won a major victory when U.S. District Judge Joyce Green ruled that the Coalition's distribution of voter guides did not violate federal elections laws. "It is one of the worst defeats for the FEC in the history of the agency," an elated Ralph Reed told the press. Barry Lynn found the decision "disappointing but not surprising" because "the courts have been lax in enforcing federal election law."[68]

The IRS posed a more difficult challenge. In 1998 the agency dealt a "major setback" to the Christian Coalition when it rejected the Coalition's ten-year struggle to win tax-exempt status. "This is the last piece of a puzzle," observed John Whitehead, president of the Rutherford Institute. "The Christian right has been potent for a while, but now it's going away." Once again, the action was taken in response to complaints by two powerful liberal public interest groups, People for the American Way and Americans United for Separation of Church and State. "The Christian Coalition has committed clear-cut, serious violations of law ... by coordinating its political activity with federal Republican candidates and party organizations," said Carole Shields, President of People for the American Way. Barry Lynn added: "The idea that they don't endorse candidates just flies in the face of all available evidence." The Coalition immediately announced plans for a "sweeping reorganization" that would allow direct political action. The Christian Coalition of Texas, which was a 501(c)(4) organization authorized to endorse candidates and make financial contributions to campaigns, was renamed the Christian Coalition of America and became the "principal vehicle for the operation of the Christian Coalition."[69]

Meanwhile, Robertson lost patience with the internal jitters caused by the IRS decision. Chief Counsel Jay Sekulow warned that some of the actions of the Coalition allowed the IRS to "make a forceful argument that the organization acted outside of the constraints of (c)(4)." Advising a restrained response, Sekulow wrote: "Litigation always has significant risks. Potentially adverse publicity also would not be helpful to the Christian Coalition at a time when it needs to be reinvigorated for the upcoming elections." But Robertson was ready for a fight. He wrote a feisty memo to his legal staff:

The Federal Election Commission sued the Christian Coalition over an eight-year period with tens of thousands of documents and exhaustive depositions. When it was all over, a Federal Judge . . . granted the Christian Coalition summary judgment and threw out the principal case of the FEC. . . . I do not want us spending a lot of time trying to finagle various companies to avoid illusory problems with the IRS. I don't care what Barry Lynn and his bunch of left-wingers try to do. Until the Christian Coalition of America does something, the IRS has absolutely no way that they can move against us. If they audit us, tough luck . . . they will lose. Let's stop wasting time and energy fighting dragons that don't exist. I will be only too delighted if the time ever comes to take on the IRS in court when they will have to come against us to eliminate a valid tax-exempt status of the organization. I don't even believe they are bold enough to try it. In the meantime, it's business as usual for the Co-alition. I don't want legerdemain between organizations, nor do I want any kind of phony 501(c)(3) tax exempt organization to muddy the picture. Fellows, the First Amendment still stands! The laws of the US Congress still stand! The rules of the Supreme Court still stand! If the IRS disagrees with these, they *will* lose in court!

Robertson had already taken his cause to Washington, asking conservative Senate leaders in June 1999 to initiate an inquiry into the Internal Revenue Service's "selective enforcement" in granting tax-exempt status.[70]

True to his word, in February 2000 Robertson sued the IRS in Federal Court and won a stunning victory that granted the Coalition tax-exempt status for 1990 and 1991, and, in effect, for the organization's entire existence. "This is a clear and concise victory for the Christian Coalition," exulted Jay Sekulow. An elated Pat Robertson sent a "Praise Report" to the members of the CBN board of directors: "So far, the Christian Coalition has won a stunning victory against the Federal Election Commission and now this victory against the IRS. Praise God for His goodness in this crucial matter just prior to what may be one of the most important elections in the nation's history. Unless we fight for freedom, federal regulators seem determined to try to take our freedoms away from us."[71]

In the midst of these legal distractions, the Christian Coalition continued with business as usual. By 1997 the business at hand was the personality and conduct of Bill Clinton. Robertson had been slow to publicly join the Clinton bashing early in his administration; in July 1993 he wrote to a supporter: "Although I certainly don't like some of President Clinton's initiatives, I have no interest in initiating impeachment proceedings against him. II Timothy 2:1-2 tells us to pray for those who are in authority over us." But it wasn't long before Robertson changed his mind about impeachment. In a July 1997 airing of *The 700 Club* Robertson offhandedly remarked that the philandering president might "slip out the back alley by himself" where "some gunman will assassinate him." The quip drew laughter from the audience, but the press and Clinton supporters were outraged. CBN drafted a reply letter to be sent to those offended by Robertson's increasingly vitriolic anti-Clinton remarks: "I am in receipt of your correspondence concerning my comments relative to President Clinton. I apologize if the way I delivered my remarks has offended you. One of the reasons that 'The 700 Club' has achieved the enormous popularity it has is because people know that I express my views quite candidly, without regard to the person or any man. . . . I realize that good people will differ with my strategic concepts, and I appreciate your willingness to let me know how you feel."[72]

By the time Robertson delivered his address at the 1998 Road to Victory Conference, the gloves were off. He told the cheering crowd, "For nearly nine months we have seen one man wreak political havoc on our most noble office. For nearly nine months we have been mocked, demeaned, belittled, and lied to. We have been forced to endure an account so lurid and so patently offensive that were it a movie it would be X-rated. We have been forced to stand by and watch helplessly as the office of Washington, Adams, and Lincoln has become the playpen for the poster child of the 60s sexual revolution. All the while we are told it is not our place to express outrage and demand better. *We will be silent no longer!*" While Clinton the man should be forgiven, Robertson believed, he should not be allowed to resign the office he had disgraced; it was inexcusable not to proceed with impeachment immediately. Robertson's remarks were seconded by other speakers who decried the lack of moral outrage in Congress about the president's conduct.[73]

Yet after the impeachment process began, Robertson became disgusted by what he regarded as strategic mistakes on the part of the Republicans, particularly their failure to block Clinton's State of the Union address to the joint houses of Congress. In a January 1999 airing of *The 700 Club* an irate Robertson blurted, "From a public relations standpoint, [Clinton] won. . . . They might as well dismiss this impeachment hearing and get on with something else, because it's over as far as I'm concerned." The remark was widely quoted; Christian Coalition president Don Hodel was taken aback. "I said what was obvious," Robertson later recalled. "Bill

Clinton had made a smash speech . . . and the impeachment was all over."
Nonetheless, he was forced to go into a defensive mode. He quickly faxed
an explanation to his friend Henry Hyde: "I wanted to tell you from the bottom of my heart how much I admire what you have been doing in the impeachment proceedings. You have shown grace under fire, incredible courage, extraordinary wisdom, and a wonderful sense of humor. I have
applauded the courageous decision that the Judiciary Committee made to
bring forth articles of impeachment against the President, and I have been
cheering on your very brilliant presentation before them." But he was
"stunned that the leadership of the House undercut your courageous stand
by offering the President the opportunity to address the nation for the
State of the Union. . . . I had hoped there were some Democrats who would
realize the truthfulness of your position. . . . Unfortunately, after that
speech it was plain to me that we were dealing with a hung jury. . . . Regrettably, my remarks were taken out of context and used against you. Nothing
could be further from the truth or my heart." Explaining his remarks to an
offended supporter, Robertson outlined his thinking:

1. The Congress turned over to an impeached man the opportunity
of a lifetime to address the nation. 2. The impeached man used the
opportunity with consummate skill to manipulate public opinion.
3. During the address it was obvious from the shouts of approval on
the Democratic side of the Chamber that the Democratic Senators
had no intention of voting to impeach a man they considered enormously popular. 4. Given the fact that the Constitution requires a
two-thirds vote in the US senate to convict an official in an impeachment trial, it was plain on its face that there was a hung
jury. . . . 5. All I said in an unprepared, ad-lib remark was what
seemed to be obvious. The Senate is not going to convict Bill
Clinton because the Democrats in the Senate will not let it happen.
Prior to that speech there was a real possibility that the brilliant
presentation of the House Managers would have prevailed. By allowing the President this incredible media opportunity, the leadership of the House of Representatives totally undercut the position
of their Judiciary Committee members.[74]

Undaunted by the failed impeachment, the new Christian Coalition
leadership moved with confidence on a number of issues. "Supercharged" by
the Monica Lewinsky scandal, the Coalition continued to sponsor huge rallies in Washington and distribute millions of voter guides throughout the

country. The new leaders shrugged off suggestions that the organization was in decline, and a spokesman for People for the American Way agreed that the Coalition remained "the powerhouse of religious conservatives."[75]

The leading legislative issue for the Coalition in 1998 was the passage of a "Religious Freedom Amendment" introduced by Congressman Ernest Istook. The fight for passage of the amendment was bitter, made difficult because of internal bickering among supporters about the proposed wording. Robertson unhesitatingly supported the amendment, and in May he instructed Hodel and Tate: "I want to emphasize how extremely important is the Religious Freedom Amendment.... I have been fighting . . . for this for some time. This is probably the most important single thing to change the culture of anti-Christian bigotry which has emanated from Supreme Court . . . decisions over the past 30 years. It is vital that the Coalition use all of its resources to get this amendment through.... We need mail, faxes, telephone calls, and an all-out push to our membership to contact their representatives. . . . I am counting on you guys to get it done. I'll give you all the support I can on-air." Clearly chagrined by the infighting among conservative groups, Robertson wrote, "I don't care a whit what Gary Bauer and Jim Dobson do about it. What I do want to see is that the amendment gets through." Hodel and Tate worked hard to stop defections among congressional supporters, particularly after Judge Roy S. Moore attempted to "derail" the amendment and substitute one of his own. Hodel asked Robertson and Jay Sekulow for legal opinions to bolster the Coalition case: "My first effort (successful, so far) is to try to hold people like Bauer and Dobson from publicly opposing RFA. Ultimately I am trying to get them to support RFA openly. I am concerned that the Moore letter might cause them to publicly question or oppose" it. Robertson's response concluded, "As much as I appreciate Judge Moore's courage in posting the Ten Commandments in his courtroom, his current effort to derail the Istook Amendment is regrettably not based on sound constitutional law." The amendment failed after a 224-203 vote in the House of Representatives, 61 votes short of the two-thirds required to pass a constitutional amendment.[76]

The new leadership team's work was hobbled by an accumulating debt of several million dollars. In 1998 Robertson reported that Hodel was making progress on that front: "I am pleased to report that under Don Hodel's leadership" past due accounts "are being worked down in a satisfactory manner, although there is still a struggle with the allocation of meager resources." The budgetary crisis lingered to the end of Hodel's term of office. In January 1999, in his resignation note to Robertson, he wrote: "*I pray that you will hear me when I tell you that the immediate financial situation is very, very serious."*[77]

But money was not the only problem. The Coalition was also beginning to see a deterioration in its "field operation" in counties and precincts all over the country. Perturbed by the dwindling grassroots effectiveness of the organization, Robertson wrote to a New Hampshire officer: "I won't go into details, but suffice it to say those involved at the headquarters had just not been doing the job that was necessary to organize counties and precincts." In March 1999 Robertson commissioned a survey of Coalition field operations and received a scathing review: "The overall strength is but a shadow of the media perspective of our organization." Less than one-quarter of the counties of the nation had a chapter. The report laid the responsibility squarely at the feet of the Washington office: "The lack of a sense of urgency is so stark, a blind person couldn't miss it. The leadership here does miss this fact though, because they stay behind closed doors." Nowhere was the skill and energy of Ralph Reed more sorely missed than in the organization's field work.[78]

Still, Don Hodel's resignation in January 1999 was more personal than programmatic. He was increasingly uncomfortable with Robertson's role as the spokesman for the Christian Coalition. When Hodel and Tate were appointed, Barry Lynn's assessment was snide but insightful: "You could put Jesus, Moses and Mohammed on the board and [Robertson would] still be the one calling the shots." Strains between the new president and the founder and chairman of the board of directors appeared early; in a 1998 memo Robertson speculated that Hodel was too enamored by the Washington think-tank establishment headed by Paul Weyrich, a circle Robertson had become dismissive of. On the other hand, Hodel often cringed at Robertson's public statements, particularly his endorsements of particular candidates, a practice he had the right to do as an individual but not as a spokesman for the Christian Coalition. Sometimes Robertson's views seemed to disagree with the publicly announced position of the Coalition. When Robertson supported Most Favored Nation trade status for China, Hodel sent a detailed memo to Coalition state leaders making it clear that Robertson was not the voice of the Coalition, reminding them that the Christian Coalition had in the past "strongly opposed MFN status for China." He began his memo with a conciliatory caveat: "First and most important, let us never forget that Pat Robertson is a great leader who has had and continues to have a profoundly beneficial effect upon our country." Obviously, "Pat will continue to speak his mind honestly on matters of national and international importance." However, in the matter of China's trade status, "Pat was stating his personal views as a private citizen and as CEO of CBN," not as the voice of the Christian Coalition. Hodel concluded: "We realize that any public positions taken by Pat, as founder and chairman of CC, may be interpreted as synonymous with the views of CC, however, he reserves the right to speak publicly on an issue or candidate without that becoming official CC policy. Certainly this is true with regard to candidate endorsements since CC does not and cannot endorse candidates."[79]

For Hodel, the irresolvable issue was Pat Robertson. The *Washington Times* reported that the last straw was Robertson's remarks about the botching of the Clinton impeachment, at the moment when the Christian Coalition was lobbying hard to win a conviction. The paper reported the obvious: Hodel for some time had believed "that Mr. Robertson was making frequent blunders on his '700 Club' TV program." In a last-minute effort to break the impasse, Hodel proposed that Robertson take a "step up" and assume a title such as "Chairman Emeritus" so that "when you speak as an analyst it does not necessarily reflect the policies or programs of Christian Coalition." Hodel insisted that he continued to have great respect for Robertson, and recognized that he was a "TV commentator/ analyst whom people are attentive to precisely because you are honest about what you see and think on current affairs," but he would remain only "if some version of [this plan] seems acceptable to you."[80]

Robertson expressed appreciation for Hodel's "very gracious message relayed to me by my secretary," which he had discussed with "a couple of the Christian Coalition board members." Unfortunately, Robertson continued, "It is my understanding that you have shared with the key staff your feeling that you were unable to work with me and, therefore, there remain to you only two options. The first was for me to withdraw from any official position under which either you would continue as President, or, in the alternative, if I stayed on you would resign." Robertson expressed "perplexity" about Hodel's feelings, but he assured him that his own resignation would critically wound the organization. He had no alternative but to accept Hodel's resignation. The proposal might have sounded reasonable in some internal conversations, but the notion that Robertson would casually abandon his political brainchild was a bizarre thought. Hodel was gracious, but he repeated his belief that Robertson should "separate yourself in some fashion from Christian Coalition for it to have any chance of achieving the success we both envisioned and still maintain your freedom to comment on anything you want." In retrospect, Robertson believed that Hodel was too much of a "hard core movement conservative": "With them there is no gray." Some outside observers agreed that the Christian Coalition became "more strident" during Hodel's tenure.[81]

Hodel's departure came as a shock to the press and to conservative activists. He had been the face of a dignified Washington insider. Phyllis Schlafly told reporters: "Hodel had a lot of stature and principled dedication and political smarts. . . . He had stature and the ability to work with a lot of people. I'm sorry he's gone."[82]

Randy Tate remained and attempted to smooth the transition. He commended Hodel, but assured the public that Robertson had always been the heart of the organization: "He's always been very engaged in the activities of the coalition. He lays out the vision. He is indeed the commander-in-chief of the organization, and that role has never changed." Robertson assumed the office of president of the Coalition, and the board dispatched Randy Tate to oversee the Washington office as vice president for government relations. Roberta Combs, who had been a successful state director in South Carolina, was named executive vice-president of field operations. Working out of the Chesapeake office, Combs assumed more and more responsibility for the day-to-day activities of the organization.[83]

The 2000 Election

Robertson brought a renewed energy to the Coalition after his return as president. He wrote to one of the state leaders: "I want to repeat that the Christian Coalition for the next twenty-one months is going into high gear. . . . Stakes in the United States in the year 2000 are enormous . . . the Presidency, control of the US House and Senate, three Supreme Court Justices, about 188 federal Circuit and District Court Judges. . . . Those involved in our field organization are going to be given quotas and be held accountable for verifiable results based on extremely high standards. It may be hard, but if all of us do what is possible, we will be able to play a key role in giving the American people an early Christmas present in November of the year 2000." When the Coalition's director of government relations resigned in the spring of 2000 because the organization had become "only a shell of what we used to be," Robertson expressed his regret but disagreed with his assessment of the Coalition's overall prognosis. He agreed that "the organization . . . was disintegrating during the last three years or so." But, he insisted, "We are now rebuilding our fund raising capability and our grassroots field support." On the other hand, he added, "I can't see how we could have been more involved in the campaign between George

Bush and John McCain. I have literally been besieged by the media for interviews and my comments. My words have been carried on national TV as never before." Indeed, in January 1999, at the peak of the impeachment proceedings, Robertson's views were sought by every major network news program. Ironically, observed Barry Lynn, "Robertson's power in Congress and in national political circles has reached new heights even though his Christian Coalition has waned in influence."[84]

The influence of Pat Robertson within the Republican Party was obvious as the election of 2000 approached. In 1999, at the urging of party activist Lew Eisenberg, Robertson and Republican National Committee chairman Jim Nicholson explored a meeting between him and Governor Christie Whitman of New Jersey to "further unity in the Republican Party as we go into the next election cycle." Robertson agreed to a meeting, but after reading Whitman's opinion piece in the *New York Times,* which he viewed as a blatant attack on the "conservative wing of the Republican Party," he reconsidered. He asked Nicholson to cancel the scheduled meeting: "Jim, as you know, I believe very much in party harmony and in working together with disparate groups. As I mentioned to Lew when we had lunch at the Jefferson Hotel some months ago, I am more than willing to accommodate most of his group's views. I also made clear that in the interest of comity, they should acknowledge the sincere concerns of religious conservatives, as well." He did not see that flexibility in Governor Whitman.[85]

Robertson thrust the Christian Coalition into the Republican primary in 1999 with great fervor, personally embracing the candidacy of George W. Bush. The organization's fundraising appeals announced a campaign "unprecedented in size and scope" to elect "pro-family" candidates. He set a goal to raise $21 million to support the effort. Robertson believed that the stakes in the election were high, and he authorized a mailing to the Coalition's "very best friends and supporters" asking them to make a gift three times larger than their largest previous gift. In June 1999 the invigorated Robertson requested a meeting with conservative senators in Washington, telling them that "if the Christian Coalition isn't in the game, the Republicans are going to lose" in 2000. Nearly all of the presidential hopefuls, including frontrunner George W. Bush, appeared at the Coalition's "Road to Victory" rally in October 1999, speaking to more than 3,000 assembled activists. Only John McCain, citing a schedule conflict, did not attend to speak to the delegates.[86]

It was clear that Bush was the favorite of the Coalition leadership. Ralph Reed told reporters that "he doesn't need to change his message for this audience one bit." Robertson seemingly gave Bush a pass on abortion, saying, "I personally am not interested in pushing him so far to the right that he will not be electable." He came close to openly endorsing Bush: "We had lunch together and talked about issues. I think he's a solid guy. I think he'd make a good president." By early 2000 Robertson was fully committed to Bush, chiding single-issue religious conservatives for their lack of political savvy. On *The 700 Club* he explained again the rules of pragmatic politics: "The people have got to get more sophisticated in this Christian . . . movement . . . to understand that you have to get people elected. If they're not elected they're not going to do you any good."[87]

Robertson aggressively supported Bush in the Republican primaries. In a mailing to Christian Coalition supporters in South Carolina, where the organization remained strong, Robertson told Coalition members that Republicans were faced with a clear-cut choice between Bush and McCain. On the one hand was a candidate "who has promised the voters (and me personally) that he will appoint judges to the Supreme Court like Clarence Thomas and Antonin Scalia," a man who opposed abortion, would cut taxes, and would reduce the size of government. Bush was a proven governor who could beat Al Gore in the general election. On the other hand, Robertson warned, John McCain was a Washington insider whose fight for campaign finance reform threatened the rights of citizens groups, and whose promise to appoint former New Hampshire senator Warren Rudman to the Supreme Court would place another liberal on the court. Armed with information supplied by Bush supporters, in February Robertson berated Rudman for attacks on the "Christian right" in which the senator allegedly charged that groups such as the Christian Coalition had brought into the Republican Party "enough anti-abortion zealots, would-be censors, homophobes, bigots and latter-day Elmer Gantrys to discredit any party." Before the Michigan primary, Robertson recorded a telephone call critical of McCain, using Rudman's comments, which infuriated the McCain camp. A McCain spokesman complained, "This is exactly the kind of politics that we had hoped we left behind in South Carolina. Pat Robertson and . . . Ralph Reed hand delivered Governor Bush's victory to him in South Carolina. . . . The people of Michigan have an opportunity to repudiate these kinds of negative smears."[88]

John McCain did his best to neutralize the opposition of the religious right. He wrote a courteous note to Robertson in reply to questions about his support for campaign finance reform. After answering the objections Robertson raised, he expressed hope that they could work together: "I accept the fact that we may not agree on every aspect of campaign finance reform. But I do believe that we can work together constructively to do what is best for the American people. We both have established track records doing exactly that. It would be a pleasure to work with you on this issue at your convenience."[89]

But the McCain-Robertson relationship became more and more caustic as the campaign continued. Speaking in Virginia Beach, McCain charged that Robertson represented the "outer reaches of American politics" and that he and Jerry Falwell were "agents of intolerance" who would destroy the Republican Party. Robertson relished the fight. He wrote to Roberta Combs: "John McCain handed George Bush something that money cannot buy. He insulted evangelical Christians — got them enraged — and mobilized them as a force for Bush.... I believe that the media is going to spur a tremendous flood of revenue to enable us to do the task at hand."[90]

After McCain's withdrawal from the race in May 2000, Robertson wrote a conciliatory letter to the senator: "I would like to congratulate you on your statesmanlike endorsement of George Bush this morning. Republicans throughout the country were delighted at this move to bring our Party together in harmony.... During the Primary Season and subsequently, we have exchanged harsh words. However, at this time, I ask that you would please forgive me for anything that I have said against you, even as I forgive you for that which has been said against me. I know that you indeed are a loyal Republican, and although I (for fifty-five years) was a member of the Democratic Party, I now consider myself not only a Jeffersonian Democrat, but a Reagan Republican, even as you are. Despite certain differing opinions on policy issues, may we work together to preserve the freedom of this great Nation." In a personal postscript Robertson noted that "your daughter-in-law attends my daughter-in-law's Bible study in Virginia Beach, and our granddaughters are good friends in Norfolk Academy."[91]

The Collapse of the Coalition

At the "Faith and Freedom Celebration" sponsored by the Christian Coalition during the 2000 Republican convention, Robertson chided the press: "I'm so amused when I read these articles that say that the Christian Coalition is dead.... They ought to put out the story to the fire department here that the largest ballroom in the Marriott Hotel is jam-packed with corpses." But the organization was facing major structural and financial challenges. New Executive Vice President Roberta Combs denied that the Coalition was "in decline," but acknowledged "we are in a rebuilding stage." Robertson reported to one of the leaders of the Coalition in Louisiana in January 2000 that "Roberta and I are extremely optimistic." He saw a rosy future: "There is nobody in the field at the present moment, nor will there be, who can match the effectiveness of the Christian Coalition as soon as we shake off the dust from the past and move boldly forward toward the 2000 Election."

But the Coalition had struggled with declining income and nagging debt for years, and by 2000 the financial situation was critical. In the spring of 1999 Robertson received a dire report from the Coalition's chief financial officer. The stark reality was that "net revenues" were 49 percent behind budget, representing a "significant shortfall per day of $35,570." Robertson grew increasingly perturbed that he could not get adequate financial reporting from the Coalition's executive secretary. After reading Jay Sekulow's detailed and encouraging financial report from the American Center for Law and Justice, Robertson scribbled a note on the cover before faxing it to Combs: "Roberta — This is good news from Jay. I need very much to receive orderly reports from the Coalition as we have here. I am not getting anything. Flying blind is dangerous!!!"[92]

Equally perplexing was the continued organizational deterioration of the Coalition. The causes were complicated, but Roberta Combs bore the brunt of the criticism. Combs had built "the most successful state organization we had," recalled Ralph Reed, and he and Robertson were always reluctant to place blame on her. The internal turmoil was due partly to the inherited financial exigency, but there were also growing strategy differences and structural weaknesses. A number of former Coalition leaders, including Reed, questioned the new fundraising tactics introduced by Combs such as expensive rallies, believing that they detracted from the focus on grassroots organizing. Reed told a reporter that he had never been an advocate of the rally strategy, which he believed had contributed to the decline of the Moral Majority: "They'd fly Dr. Falwell in on a Lear jet. They raised a little money and got people exited, but there was nothing permanent."[93]

Rebuilding was made difficult as well because Robertson more or less mandated staff reductions. He wrote to a state leader: "Roberta has reduced the overhead to an absolute minimum by letting go unproductive staff and eliminating some of the outrageous charges from secular fundraising groups who were both expensive and ineffective." Some of the departing staff, even those who remained loyal to Robertson, were bitter toward Combs. The organization in 2000, wrote one high official who left of his own accord, was now headed by "a sycophant who, while skilled at staging large-scale events, does not possess the abilities to identify, motivate, and lead a team of individuals capable of reestablishing Christian Coalition as the preeminent pro-family political organization in America." Several of the disgruntled senior executives received generous severance packages (a Robertson managerial hallmark) that included a stipulation that the departing "employee agrees, if he communicates publicly or for publication, about Employer, then in all such communications Employee will portray Employer, its officers, directors and employees in a positive manner favorable to Employer." Several were warned that they could face lawsuits after making derogatory remarks to the press.[94]

Reviving the dying organization was a nightmare for Combs. One of her defenders protested that the internal "ambushery" was brutal, reporting to Robertson that "many former staff members turned on her with a vengeance so unbecoming of Christians." In October 2001 Combs wrote frantically to Robertson: "As you can see, deposits have declined steadily over the past several months and I am very concerned. . . . I am working to cut overhead at the national office. . . . We need to schedule another board meeting at your earliest convenience to develop a strategy for the upcoming year."[95]

Robertson had finally had enough. On December 6, 2001, in a surprise to insiders, including Combs, he resigned as president of the Christian Coalition and from the board. In a public announcement he emphasized his other interests: "With the few years left to me of active service, I must focus on those things that will bring forth the greatest spiritual benefit." He had decided to concentrate his efforts on building CBN and Regent University. "Pat's resignation very well could be the death knell for the Christian Coalition," Barry Lynn told reporters. "Pat was the only real reason the group existed, and it can't exist without him."[96]

Robertson slowly detached himself from the Christian Coalition, occasionally offering advice and admonitions but no longer willing to expend much effort on a lost cause. As the financial morass deepened, Robertson became more and more exasperated. In 2002, a year after he had resigned from the board, Robertson wrote to a board member: "You must also be aware that, at the present moment, the Christian Coalition owes approximately $1.8 million and, to the best of my knowledge, is not paying their bills when they come due. We've had at CBN at least five telephone calls from the limousine owner who had not been paid for his work at the Road to Victory conference. A Virginia Beach police officer called with the news that his fellow officers were going to the *Washington Post* if they did not get paid the money promised them . . . and this is just the tip of the iceberg!!!" Similar complaints had come to him from creditors. Robertson wrote to Billy McCormack: "As a fiduciary of this organization, you have an absolute right to demand an accounting to find out what is going on." He fretted that perhaps Roberta was ill and "not able to continue" and concluded, "We owe it to her, to the organization, to the country, and to the Lord to get this matter straightened out. . . . I will do everything I can to help, but as a director of the organization, I'm afraid on this one, you're the man." Robertson outlined the only scenario for survival for Combs and the Coalition: "If the Coalition could meet its bills as they are due, and if it could begin to pay down the current debts, and if it could achieve some type of settlement with the plaintiff . . . in the current lawsuit, then it may well go forward. But talking about happier days ahead and acting as if there is no problem is not the way to go." Two months later Robertson wrote a frenetic memo to Combs: "My office received an anguished call from Andre Crouch about an honorarium . . . owed him. . . . The terrible thing is that not only are you not paying him, but you are not answering his telephone calls. . . . Even though I resigned some time ago from the Coalition, people still identify me with it. This kind of conduct is ruining all of our reputations. Please do something. If you can't pay them, talk to them. . . . Either the organization has got to find some way to pay its bills or it should close its doors."[97]

From 2002 until the collapse of the national organization in 2006, the Coalition drifted toward an ignominious end. After a series of scathing articles appeared describing the decline of the Coalition in 2005 and 2006, Robertson "contemplated coming into the organization to try to clean up the back bills and, with a new board, give it a fresh start." But when some of the board balked at that proposal, he concluded that it was the "Lord's will that I not personally become re-engaged with the Coalition." He gave some thought to establishing a "new organization" that would be free of debt and carry "none of the negative publicity that has been swirling around the Christian Coalition in the last several years." He wrote to Combs: "As my dear and trusted friend, you might be interested in playing a role in a new organization. . . . I thank you from the bottom of my heart for your sacrifice and struggle over the last few years to ensure conservative values in this nation." But the impulse for a new political initiative did not last, and, as the damaging attacks on the Coalition continued, Robertson made a final appeal to Combs in April 2006 to bring closure: "Several months ago, there was a vicious piece about the Christian Coalition in the Virginian-Pilot which was widely distributed.... I believe the most merciful thing for you and all involved would be to put the thing to death. Otherwise, I fear there will be unremitting pain in your life for years to come. The Christian Coalition of America is a Texas corporation. I advise filing for Chapter 7 bankruptcy in a bankruptcy court in Texas with as little publicity and fan fare as possible. It is a pity it has to end this way. You have worked very hard and sacrificed, but there comes a time to let it go.... I regret deeply that I personally could not come in and do a rescue operation, but as I explained in my past letter, at 76 I am just not up to a rebuilding effort of that nature."[98]

The decline and collapse of the Christian Coalition defied simple explanations. Some of the pioneering supporters who had helped build the organization felt betrayed by Robertson. One of the board members wrote to him in 2002: "My greatest regret is that you resigned and left us to sink or swim. I know you felt called to give it up and devote yourself to evangelism, but I had hoped you could have done both." Neither Robertson nor Reed blamed Roberta Combs for the collapse; both professed loyalty and respect for her to the end. By the time she assumed leadership, Ralph Reed believed, conditions in the country and in the organization had changed so much that the decline was probably irreversible. "Organizational declines are hard to stop," observed the veteran organizer. An American historian by training, Reed was a student of the "long and celebrated history of religiously inspired political activism in America," and he believed that the religious right movement was a part of that noble tradition. Like such earlier reforms as abolition and prohibition, the conservative political pro-family surge of the 1990s came to an end, Reed believed, mainly because it had succeeded. By the time he departed in 1997, "a Wheaton College grad was speaker of the House" and "committed evangelicals" were conspicuous in "the offices of Capitol Hill." "We wanted to change the direction of the government," and he believed they had succeeded. The numbers of "qualified evangelicals in the White House" had risen dramatically from the administration of George Bush to that of his son George W. Bush.[99]

Post-Coalition Politics

Pat Robertson remained as committed to political action as ever even in the wake of the collapse of the Christian Coalition. He wrote to an aspiring gubernatorial candidate in Virginia in 2002: "As Christians, I believe we have a responsibility to get involved in the political arena because, after all, that is where the bulk of the decisions affecting our lives are made. . . . If Christian people work together, they can succeed in winning back control of the institutions that have been taken from them over the past seventy years." In 2004 Robertson again vigorously supported George W. Bush. After the election, he estimated that evangelicals had delivered four million voters, assuring the president's victory. Once again, Robertson felt that conservatives had earned respect and a place at the table: "The Republicans are in power because the evangelicals and social conservatives voted them into power. . . . If the Republicans falter, they will lose big-time down the road."[100]

Robertson's relations with the administration deteriorated during Bush's time in office. Along with other evangelical leaders, Robertson was slow to embrace Bush's faith-based initiative, to the surprise of the administration. Within months an open war seemed about to erupt between John DiIulio, who headed the new agency, and evangelicals opposed to the initiative. DiIulio believed Robertson was a radical who needed to be marginalized by the administration. Karl Rove had to step in; at a meeting in the White House he reassured evangelical leaders that the program would work to their advantage and that DiIulio's disdain was not shared by others in the administration. Robertson's opposition to the initiative abated after Operation Blessing and other evangelical organizations received generous grants. Things seemed to go better for religious conservatives in the Justice Department, headed by Robertson's friend, Attorney General John Ashcroft, where many observers felt that the influence of the religious right was most obvious. The full extent of that influence became apparent in the investigation surrounding the dismissal of Regent University law school graduate Monica Goodling in 2008, which revealed that 150 Regent University law school graduates had been employed in the Bush administration.[101]

Nonetheless, George W. Bush ultimately did little to endear himself to the leaders of the religious right, including Pat Robertson. In his biography of Robertson, David John Marley observed that the president had little need for their intercession with the electorate because "he spoke the coded language of evangelicalism." Robertson, like most political operatives, never felt he received the respect and attention he deserved. In 2001 he complained to Karl Rove: "It has come to me that the White House is not interested in having the help of the Coalition in grassroots organizing. . . . Is this rumor, in fact, true?" After the election in 2004, he again complained to Rove that his recommendations seemed to carry little weight in the White House. Ralph Reed, who had become George W. Bush's chief link with evangelicals in 2000 and 2004, thought the strained relationship was more personal than programmatic, but the Bush administration clearly continued to distance itself from Robertson. By the middle of Bush's second term, Robertson declared the administration "chaotic and mismanaged," leaving evangelicals with "no coherent voice."[102]

In early 2007 Robertson and Ralph Reed began to privately explore a plan to "re-energize the Christian Coalition." Both men believed that the humiliating congressional defeats in 2006 laid bare a leaderless conservative movement; conservative activism at the "grass roots had more or less atrophied." The two agreed that Reed should explore conservative options and draft a proposal. In a seven-page document Reed suggested that "re-energizing" the Christian Coalition would be preferable to establishing a new advocacy group or doing nothing. Reed believed that would be the best alternative, "if it is achievable," because that name "remains the gold-standard in pro-family brands." As always, Reed's proposal was professional and filled with historical context, and he once again emphasized the need to "broaden the agenda" so that opponents could not "ghettoize the movement." To succeed, the organization needed the financial capability and client base that only Robertson could supply. Reed flew to Virginia Beach and the two discussed the proposal. Robertson was intrigued; "there is a terrible vacuum," he observed in December 2007. But in the end, recalled Reed, "Pat felt that with the time he had left" he had other things he wanted to do.[103]

Nonetheless, Robertson remained somewhat engaged as the election of 2008 approached. He was still "a force among conservative Christians, who carry major clout in Republican primary races," noted Larry J. Sabato of the Center for Politics at the University of Virginia. In January 2007 he met with Mitt Romney, and in March he invited the Mormon candidate to deliver the commencement address at Regent University. The move ruffled feathers at the university. In a memo to the faculty that reflected Robertson's feelings about the abuse regarding religion that he experienced in his 1988 race, he wrote, "Gov. Romney is running for the post of Chief Executive Officer, not Chief Theologian, and is not expected to mention the fact that he is a Mormon or to discuss his Mormon beliefs."[104]

Robertson also invited Rudy Giuliani to Regent University to deliver a major address in June 2007. That invitation triggered a similar explanation: "Mayor Giuliani is not expected to speak about his personal life or the fact that he is a Roman Catholic." Robertson and Giuliani were old friends, and Robertson's introduction before Giuliani's rousing speech foreshadowed an endorsement: "He cut taxes. He cleaned up crime. . . . His finest hour came on Sept. 11 when he rallied the cities of New York and the country together." When Robertson's official endorsement of Giuliani came in November 2007, it was a surprise to many — columnist Kathleen Parker suggested that it "just shifted 'strange bedfellows' into 'the weird turn pro' category." But as *Newsweek* correspondent Michael Gerson pointed out, "It should not have been a surprise." After all, wrote E. J. Dionne, "The 2008 Republican presidential field was hardly made to order for evangelical conservatives." The two men had long been friends, and Robertson had shown a willingness to settle for the best available candidate, not a perfect one. "I was a realist on that subject," Robertson observed; "he was not near as extreme on abortion as everyone thought he was," and he was a "true fiscal conservative." But the bottom line was that "he is very, very pro-Israel," which for Robertson came close to being a litmus test.[105]

When John McCain became the presumptive Republican nominee after his victory in Florida, Robertson was open to offering support to his old political nemesis. McCain made an effort to repair relations with the religious right by delivering the commencement address at Jerry Falwell's Liberty University in May 2006, but he repeatedly rejected offers from Robertson to appear on *The 700 Club*. Robertson was miffed, but he backed the Republican candidate, hoping to preserve the gains made by conservative activists during the Bush presidency. But for the first time in more than two decades, he watched the proceedings in 2008 from the sidelines as an observer and commentator rather than as a player.[106]

Like most Americans, Robertson was intrigued by the political skills of Barack Obama; he privately predicted that Obama would defeat Hillary Clinton for the Democratic nomination. As he did when Bill Clinton was elected, Robertson welcomed Obama as his new president, appearing to genuinely reserve judgment about his policies. Commenting on Rush Limbaugh's reported wish that the new president would fail, Robertson said, "That was a terrible thing to say. I mean, he's the president of all the country. If he succeeds, the country succeeds. And if he doesn't, it hurts us all. Anybody who would pull against our president is not exactly thinking rationally." More than at any time in many years, he was almost as disillusioned with the Republican Party as with the Democrats. He embraced the new president as a talented man who throughout the campaign had "behaved with grace and wisdom." Robertson greeted some of President Obama's early appointments and actions positively, and he was especially pleased that the president seemed poised to embrace proposals to aid small businesses. But the honeymoon was short-lived, and Robertson was soon offering sharp critiques of the president's legislative agenda and the huge budget deficit. By the middle of March 2009, he gave up hope for moderation and declared the new president "a left-wing radical."[107]

International Encounters

Pat Robertson's foray into American politics piqued the interest of evangelicals around the world. Reed recalled that the Christian Coalition "never made much of an effort" toward internationalization, in spite of many inquiries. Robertson and Reed discovered that there was not a solidly devout Christian base to sustain a movement in most European countries. Elsewhere, particularly in Latin America, conservative activists made serious attempts to establish organizations modeled on the Christian Coalition. In 1992, Robertson was approached by one of the presidential candidates in El Salvador seeking financial assistance. Reed informed the candidate that the Coalition could not legally make such contributions, but he offered a different kind of assistance: "I will be working very closely with Dean Titus and the rest of the team at Regent University to help put together training programs to be of assistance in turning out Christian voters to the polls. As you are probably aware, we are making plans to turn out approximately 30 million Christian voters in America in 1992, and this technology is being perfected in a way that can be applied to any democratic society around the world. . . . May God richly bless you as you seek to lift high the banner of faith and freedom in El Salvador." Robertson continued to look for ways to help conservative political movements in Latin America; after a meeting with fifteen Latin American Christian politicians in 1992, he funded a number of scholarships at Regent University for "emerging leaders." By 1994 ten such leaders had been "mentored," and José L. Gonzalez, head of an organization called SEMILLA, informed Robertson that he was "recruiting the cream of the rising Christian leadership of Latin America for this program." In 1999 Guatemalan presidential candidate Francisco Bianchi visited Robertson, sharing his vision of a "political party based on the Principles and Values that come from the Word of God." He invited Robertson to be the featured speaker at a conference of "pastors and leaders" to launch his plan, but Robertson declined the invitation.[108]

Throughout the decade of the nineties, Robertson received a stream of inquiries, invitations, and requests for support from Christian leaders who had established or hoped to establish Christian Coalitions in their countries, including South Africa, Zambia, Kenya, Zimbabwe, Australia, and New Zealand. Pastor Jan-Aage Torp wrote from Norway in 1993: "I am writing on behalf of thirteen Bible-believing Christian leaders in Norway that are concerned about the spiritual and moral development of our country. . . . Our honest perception is that this group has the stature and the power to influence Norway in a decisive manner. . . . Would you be willing to meet with Finn-Jarle Saele and myself during our visit to the USA? . . . Our objective is to seek your advice in the building of this new spiritual and moral endeavor. . . . Would you kindly consider an invitation to visit Norway during the latter stages of our parliamentary election campaign?" Barbara Johnson, Robertson's executive secretary, faxed a copy of the message to Reed with the note: "Pat said he would like to meet with them. . . . Pat wants you in the meeting." During a major reorganization in 1999, Christian Coalition International was established as a distinct tax-exempt organization to "respond to the dozens of requests that have come to the organization from activists from all over the world seeking help in organizing Christian Coalition chapters in their respective countries." But no substantial international connections were ever established.[109]

Postmortem

By the time he left the Christian Coalition, Robertson agreed with Ralph Reed that the Coalition had "fulfilled its purpose": "evangelicals have a seat at the table and evangelical issues are now on the agenda." Robertson believed the organization was still a potent force when he resigned as president in 2001. He told reporters: "Without us, I do not believe that George Bush would be sitting in the White House or that Republicans would be in control of the U.S. House."[110]

The anticlimactic decline of the Christian Coalition obscured the historic impact it had on American politics and on the legacy and reputation of Pat Robertson. In the words of a group of Georgetown University professors, the Christian Right movement had been "one of the few conservative social movements to achieve significant political influence in the postwar period." The movement had "repeatedly defied conventional wisdom," winning victories through the second term of George W. Bush. Staunch religious-right critic Robert Boston agreed that Robertson "largely achieved [his] goals."[111]

Robertson savored the accomplishments of the Christian Coalition. In 2002 he wrote to one of his comrades in the founding of the organization: "We have all accomplished a great deal in the political life of our nation. There are few, if any, people in our nation who truly appreciate all that we've done; but, nevertheless, we were not doing it for ourselves, but for our children and grandchildren." In a 1998 letter to an Illinois political leader, he wrote, "When I realize the tremendous impact of the Christian Coalition, and what people like you are doing to bring this country to the principles of its founders, I see the wisdom of my decision to enter into the political arena."[112]

In a 1990 address at the National Prayer Breakfast, Jerry Falwell succinctly described the fate of his and other religious reform movements: "One thing I have learned about Christians, having organized them for years. When they lose, they quit. And when they win, they quit. We are just quitters." Sociologist Robert Wuthnow agreed that religion-based reforms in the past had been imperiled by success, as in the case of the prohibition movement in the early twentieth century, and by failure, as in the unsuccessful anti-evolution campaign that drove fundamentalists to retreat into a period of rebuilding in the 1920s. It is a pattern similar to that of religious revivals: political reform movements cool when the issues that spawn them are replaced by new concerns.[113]

Pat Robertson was disgusted by a rash of negative critiques of the religious right written by conservative lobbyists beginning in 1999. In a widely circulated letter, Paul Weyrich, president of the Free Congress Foundation, asserted that the conservative political gains of the preceding two decades had "not achieved policies that have stemmed the tide of cultural collapse." "Real cultural victories," he concluded, would have to be won outside politics. Robertson strongly disagreed. He was irritated by a "puff piece" on "60 Minutes" about Weyrich's negative assessment of the accomplishments of the religious right. Robertson felt that correspondent Lesley Stahl misused quotations from an hour-long interview with him on the subject. He insisted that Stahl ignored the real accomplishments of religious conservatives in the 1990s: "I enumerated conservative accomplishments of which I was quite proud — child tax credits, reform of the IRS, a balanced budget, welfare reform, strong votes on partial-birth abortion, and blocking socialized medicine. These are just a few of the accomplishments that the naysayers would not acknowledge." Stahl "made it sound as if the absence of a vote on a Constitutional Amendment banning abortion was a huge defeat. Important as it is, abortion is only one part of the conservative agenda, which my work indicates is now embraced by a vast majority of the American people."[114]

Robertson was even more indignant after the publication of a book by syndicated columnist Cal Thomas, who had worked with Jerry Falwell in the formative years of the Moral Majority, and Ed Dobson, *Blinded by*

Might: Can the Religious Right Save America? Robertson bristled at Thomas's claim that the moral atmosphere of America was made worse, rather than better, by the political intervention of the religious right. He fired off a sharp note to Thomas: "I am sure you must understand that I look with some disfavor on someone like you taking pot shots at God's servants who are attempting to serve Him in this world. Supercilious hypocrites have never been in favor with me. . . . If I were you, I would reserve my barbs for the enemies of the Lord." Robertson called Thomas's attention to a *Wall Street Journal* article written by Fred Barnes that questioned the spate of negative assessments. Barnes wrote: "Messrs. Thomas, Dobson and Weyrich are serious people. But they're wrong on both counts against religious conservatives. The truth is that the Religious Right has had an enormous influence on politics and even some on the culture. And, judging by the churches I'm familiar with, political involvement hasn't corrupted many Christians." Robert Wuthnow agreed: "The religious right did succeed in placing a number of its issues squarely on the public agenda, a feat worthy of note in itself, Weyrich notwithstanding. If it failed to pass specific legislation, it at least made the public more conscious of a wide range of religious, moral, and social issues." Author Walter H. Capps wrote in 1990: "Though it has suffered numerous misadventures . . . and has invited scorn and ridicule, the movement has indeed had an impact. Moreover, the objectives that brought the movement into being are deemed to be as challenging today as they were in the beginning. The leadership of the movement will always be dedicated toward achieving an effective working relationship between national piety and national patriotism so that the two might function as harmonizing collaborative teammates in the pursuit of the common good."[115]

The rise of the religious political right in the last quarter of the twentieth century generated a virtual publishing industry among its many opponents as well as among friends and disinterested observers. Partly, these assessments reflected reasoned political differences, but they often became partisan and hysterical. Shrill rhetoric and reckless charges were not introduced to American political discourse by the culture wars of the late twentieth century, but the mudslinging of the era added a lusty chapter to that body of American lore. As in all political debate, the clarity of what happened was obscured by radical claims on all sides. Georgetown University political scientist Clyde Wilcox succinctly described the "two radically divergent visions of the Christian Right": "In the first it is an intolerant, uncompromising movement that would deprive women, gays and lesbians, and others of their rights, in the second it is a defensive movement that would protect conservative Christians from a hostile society and government." Whether the religious right was good or bad, Wilcox concluded, depended on an "individual's reactions to the agenda." It could hardly be denied, however, that the movement had compelled Americans to "consider basic moral and religious values" in crafting public policy.[116]

The most judicious and balanced scholarly accounts of Pat Robertson's political candidacy and the subsequent influence of the Christian Coalition offer relatively simple explanations for the rise and decline of the movement. Robertson's success as a candidate placed him squarely in a long line of "populist outsider" leaders. Such leaders, notes Professor Allen D. Hertzke, appeal to self-conscious groups "who often perceive themselves to be on the periphery of economic and cultural life," and who "feel ignored by elites with power to determine the destiny of the nation." In that context, Hertzke believes that Robertson's campaign was a movement "airing legitimate grievances, taking advantage of favorable opportunities and resources, and embodying a measure of cognitive liberation in the ecstatic dedication of their followers."[117]

In his balanced account of the Christian Coalition up to 1997, historian Justin Watson notes that the driving force behind the movement was a genuine sense of "victimization and demands for the recognition of the rights of evangelicals." Whether conservative Christians were indeed "victims" is less important than that they thought of themselves as victims. They reacted as threatened interest groups have always reacted in American political history, trying to gain recognition — or, as they termed it, a place at the table. Pat Robertson was a model populist leader for the discontented Christians of the late twentieth century: an eloquent fellow Christian who felt, along with millions of others, that he had been ridiculed and discriminated against by intellectual elites. John B. Donovan, Robertson's campaign biographer in 1988, saw him precisely in these populist terms: "In him we see the representative of the vast cultural underclass that seeks to overthrow the hegemony of the entrenched elite." Robertson harbored anti-elitist prejudices as deeply as any of the God-fearing new middle class that filled the teeming Pentecostal and conservative evangelical churches of the post–World War II years. He was, indeed, among their best and brightest. In that role, he became a leader of the kind of "revitalization movement" described by Anthony F. C. Wallace, creating new institutions and new social constructs that equipped a generation of alienated Americans to adapt to new social circumstances.[118]

If the Christian Coalition was, as some scholars have judged, a dogmatic and narrow movement intent on "Christianizing" American life and politics, it was doomed to failure in a modern world defined by cultural pluralism. Viewed as a monolithic resistance to modernity, the religious right movement of the late twentieth century could not succeed. It was that intransigence, the mindset of Christian Reconstructionism, that fired the fears of Barry Lynn and other critics on the left. However the Christian right worded its views on separation of church and state, it seemed to Lynn that the result was the same: "Does this mean the Religious Right wants theocracy in America? Its leaders bristle at the term and accuse me of being an alarmist when I suggest such a thing. In reply I can only recommend taking an honest look at the Religious Right's social goals for this country." Lynn believed that "Pat Robertson would dramatically alter the relationship between religious ideas and the secular ideas that ought to govern a secular country." In his melancholy assessment of the religious right and the destructive effect it had had on historic evangelical self-understanding, historian Randall Balmer saw the movement as just such a rigid appeal to anti-modernism: "The leaders of the Religious Right, just like their Puritan and Congregationalist forebears, are frightened by pluralism. That's understandable, especially for a movement that propagates the ideology that America is — and always has been — a *Christian* nation. Pluralism is messy. . . . The Puritans hated pluralism."[119]

On the other hand, Catholic theologian George Weigel argued, along with Richard John Neuhaus, that it was secularism that threatened pluralism in modern America, and that the religious right crusade was an effort to restore equilibrium: "The New Christian Right 'kicked a tripwire' in our national consciousness, alerting otherwise somnambulant people to the fact that the United States in the late 1970s was on the verge of all but establishing secularism as *the* legally protected form of philosophical and moral self-understanding in the American republic. The New Christian Right recognized this and challenged it — with the salutary result of reopening a national church-state (or better, religion-and-society) debate." Justin Watson asserts in his study of the Christian Coalition that Ralph Reed's embrace of cultural pluralism was unequivocal and rooted in his study of reform in American history. Though Robertson spoke in more sweeping terms about the nature of their political reform, his basic aim was defensive: he wanted to "make anti-Christian bigotry as unacceptable to American life as racism and anti-Semitism." Watson concludes: "Robertson and Reed are not pursuing a state-imposed religious establishment or a totalitarian theocratic order but a renewal of the cultural influence and prestige that evangelicalism once enjoyed in American society."[120]

In the end, Pat Robertson's Christian Coalition was successful because

Pat Robertson as a student at McCallie School, a prestigious college preparatory school in Chattanooga, Tennessee.

Near the front during the Korean War, Pat Robertson poses with his Washington and Lee University friends. Left to right: Pat Robertson, John Warner, and Edwin Gaines.

Lieutenant Pat Robertson reviews his Marine platoon.

Senator A. Willis Robertson acknowledges the warm reception he received while
speaking at the announcement of CBN's new headquarters building in 1966.

Pat and Dede with Tim, Gordon, and Elizabeth
just before leaving Bedford-Stuyvesant in 1959.

During the early years at CBN, Pat Robertson worked on camera and off.

Robertson spent many hours on the air during the early years of CBN. Evangelical leaders who visited the dilapidated facilities often commented about Robertson's erudite discussions of the "Deep Things of God" speaking to a single camera.

Robertson at the controls at radio station WXRI with disk jockey Gordon Churchill.

Family portrait about 1967.
Left to right: Anne, Tim, Elizabeth, Dede, Pat, and Gordon.

Pat surveys groundbreaking for the first building at Regent University
in Virginia Beach in 1976. With him are the first three employees at the university:
David Clark, Frances Burkihiser, and David Gyertson.

The board of directors through the booming years of the 1970s and 1980s.
Left to right: Bob Slosser, Pat Robertson, Dede Robertson,
Harald Bredesen, and Tucker Yates.

Pat Robertson with President Ronald Reagan. Though he was never close
to President Reagan, Robertson did have access to him and
interviewed him three times for broadcast on CBN.

Pat and Dede Robertson during Pat's campaign
for the Republican nomination for the presidency in 1988.

Pat Robertson chatting with President George H. W. Bush in the Oval Office. James Baker is seated in the background. Robertson visited the elder President Bush on a number of occasions and always felt comfortable with him.

Robertson with President George W. Bush during a Christian Coalition meeting. Robertson backed Bush's campaigns in 2000 and 2004, but he was never as comfortable with the younger Bush as he had been with his father.

President Bush spoke at the dedication of the "Flying Hospital" in 1996. This highly visible but extremely expensive humanitarian venture by Robertson's Operation Blessing brought much positive publicity before being discontinued in 2000.

Completed in 2002 at a cost of $5.2 million, the CBN Indonesia WorldReach Center is located in East Jakarta. More than 300 people are employed in its state-of-the-art television production studios and its large Operation Blessing humanitarian program.

Pat Robertson signing a partnership agreement with the China Charity Federation (CCF) with Yan Mingfu, then president of the CCF, in 2001.

Pat Robertson greets a student before a flag football game on campus at Regent University. Robertson has enjoyed mingling with the students during his years at the university.

Pat Robertson at an Operation Blessing relief site. Bill Horan greatly increased the reach of Operation Blessing when he became president in 2002. The organization was critically positioned to provide headline relief during the Indonesian tsunami and Hurricane Katrina.

The core team of The 700 Club: Gordon Robertson, Terry Meeuwsen, and
Pat Robertson. Meeuwsen joined the program as co-host in 1993, and
Gordon Robertson has been a regular since 1999 and CEO of CBN since 2008.

Pat Robertson introduces Mitt Romney as the commencement speaker at
Regent University in 2007. Romney's presence on campus miffed religious
conservatives and mystified political liberals, but it was consistent with
Robertson's pragmatic political behavior.

CHAPTER 6

Rebuilding the
Christian Broadcasting Network

—⟨ῶῶ⟩—

Nadir

The gloom of the economic crisis that gripped CBN in the summer of 1987 still lingers in the memories of many veteran employees in Virginia Beach. A "Special Communication to All CBN Employees," sent on June 5, 1987, delivered the opening salvo:

> After weeks of prayer and careful consideration, some difficult decisions have been reached to reduce the overall budget of CBN. Regretfully, these actions include a 22.3% reduction in overall staff worldwide or a total of 500 employees. Those employees affected represent 11% of full-time staff; 54% of part-time; and 22% of on-call workers. . . .
>
> The reason for this cutback is the significant drop in income to the ministry during this year. During the May telethon funds pledged were 66% below May 1986 totals. . . . As stewards of God's resources we must bring expenditures into line with reduced income. . . . We have cut air time, projects, and other non-labor items; however, personnel reductions still are required to achieve a $25 million budget decrease. . . .
>
> We understand that these budget reductions will be extremely difficult for those personnel affected, and we emphasize once again that everything will be done to lessen the impact. . . . God bless you.

Pat Robertson announced that he was "heartsick when I consider the consequences to these Godly, dedicated people and their families." CBN tried to cushion the blow, offering training, severance, and insurance benefits. In addition to reducing staff, CBN cancelled its toll-free telephone numbers and reduced the funds allotted to purchase airtime for *The 700 Club*.[1]

The financial crisis deepened in the months that followed, stretching into 1990. Contributions continued to lag far behind the amounts received in the mid-1980s — and well below budget. By September 1987 contributions had reached the lowest levels in five years. A second budget reduction of $9 million required the dismissal of another 145 employees, salary freezes, and delays in planned construction. The only bright spot in the financial crisis at the end of the 1980s was the growing profitability of the CBN Cable Network, which in 1988 changed its name to The Family Channel.[2]

A confluence of events and circumstances, some of them beyond the control of Pat Robertson or CBN, combined to cause the financial disaster of the late 1980s. It was, in Gordon Robertson's words, "the perfect storm." Heading the list of causes, at least in the mind of Pat Robertson, was the financial and sexual scandal at PTL that gripped the attention of the national media for months. In a June 1987 CBN press release, Robertson pointed the finger of blame at "the spill over effect of guilt by association" with his old employee Jim Bakker: "The shock of the Jim and Tammy scandals has hit the evangelical world like a bombshell. We probably have the best financial controls and forecasters in the evangelical world, but how could we have planned for this?" Robertson tried desperately to distance himself from the PTL scandal. Campaigning in Michigan when the story of Bakker's sexual tryst broke, Robertson told reporters that he had only seen Bakker "three or four times over 16 or 17 years."[3]

Over and over, Robertson stressed that CBN "emphasizes integrity and quality," and most of the loyal employees at CBN who survived the downsizing shared Robertson's outrage over the PTL scandal. Robertson's executive assistant Barbara Johnson informed a Regent University student that CBN would not be able to fund a summer mission trip, as it had done in the past: "Our Missions funds are very low because of the shortfall in contributions. This whole business to the south of us has seriously affected our contributions." A CBN form letter drafted to be sent to those turned down for aid laid the blame for rejections squarely on PTL: "Over the last three years CBN's income has dropped by tens of thousands of dollars because of publicity surrounding Jim Bakker and Heritage USA. We are struggling to meet the obligations we have." The resentment was hardly misdirected; the *Christian Century* named the "televangelist fiasco" and the financial collapse of the electronic church its "top religious story" of 1987.[4]

Putting the bravest face on the debacle, Pat Robertson told a *New York Times* reporter in March 1987 that he believed that a "great revival" would follow the scandals. He persisted in giving upbeat predictions. In 1989 he wrote, "The 'televangelist' scandals were really not an end to spiritual revival but a needed period of cleansing prior to a further visitation from God to His people." He applauded the efforts among evangelicals to bring financial transparency and responsibility to the independent ministries.[5]

The financial "perfect storm" at CBN at the end of the 1980s was not simply a product of the misconduct of Bakker and other televangelists. Robertson's political campaign tested the loyalties of CBN supporters in a variety of ways. The clear articulation of his political agenda during the campaign alienated some supporters. To a donor who objected to his position on free trade, Robertson wrote: "I am very sorry that you feel you can no longer support the worldwide ministry of CBN because of my personal view on an issue. . . . I hope you will ask the Lord what *He* would have you do." More important, the disappearance of Pat Robertson as the icon of CBN was a serious blow to the ministry. "Any time you take away your chairman of the board and founder, who has been host for 25 years," said a CBN spokesman in late 1987, "you are going to have a drop." Tim Robertson candidly acknowledged that some donors simply lost interest in *The 700 Club* and the ministry because of Pat Robertson's absence.[6]

More immediate was the threat that Robertson's political campaign would drain funds from the ministry. CBN struggled to keep donors informed about the needs of the ministry even as the Robertson campaign aggressively solicited funds. By 1989 the Christian Coalition offered similar fundraising competition. In 1989 Ralph Reed alerted the Coalition's telephone soliciting company that "approximately 40 percent of the persons they call are donors to CBN." It was imperative, he instructed, that there be no "confusion among our supporters about the relationship between CBN and the Christian Coalition." Nonetheless, a significant percentage of CBN donations probably diverted to Robertson's political activities before and after his presidential race. "Big donors were falling like flies," recalled CBN chaplain David Gyertson.[7]

Reorganizing and Rethinking CBN

Robertson's political foray demanded a major reorganization at CBN. In October 1987 Robertson's old friend Bob Slosser assumed the titles chairman of the board and chief executive officer, providing seasoned support for Tim Robertson, who had become president a year earlier. A ministry publication bravely announced that the ministry was ready for the tough challenges facing it: "With new leaders in place, CBN stands prayerful and ready to follow God's direction — and to proclaim the Good News of Jesus Christ to the world." While Slosser provided maturity and balance, the responsibility for presiding over the downsizing of the ministry fell mostly on the shoulders of young Tim Robertson, Pat and Dede's older son.[8]

In his eighteen-month tenure as the leader of CBN Tim Robertson guided a reshaping of the organization that was partly dictated by financial circumstances and partly by his own philosophical convictions. Tim was a gifted, and in some ways well prepared, replacement for his father as president of CBN. Upbeat, garrulous, and savvy with the media, he knew CBN well when he inherited the presidency in 1986. He was a traditional Robertson, schooled at McCallie School in Chattanooga, as his father had been, before becoming a fun-loving undergraduate at the University of Virginia. A bit of a playboy who sometimes worried that his lifestyle might embarrass his father, Tim settled down after marriage, worked for a year at CBN, and then enrolled at Gordon-Conwell Theological Seminary. He earned a Master of Divinity degree, joined an Episcopal church with his wife, and worked for three years as a youth leader in a Boston church while serving as manager of CBN's Boston TV station. Tim returned to Virginia Beach in 1982 to oversee CBN's Middle East Television, a formidable challenge considering the threatening environment in Lebanon in the early 1980s. Tim had worked at CBN off and on since he was fifteen years old — as a cameraman, a producer, a salesman, and a vice-president before assuming the presidency. He brought unquestioned skills to the job. Within the cable industry he was admired for his intelligence, innovative programming, and good business sense. When Pat Robertson resigned to campaign, explained Barbara Johnson, "the Board felt he was God's choice."[9]

In hindsight, many insiders, including Pat and Tim Robertson, agreed that the drastic retrenchment at the end of the 1980s forced CBN to trim fat and become more efficient. Painful as it was at the time, the downsizing streamlined the organization; Tim Robertson believed that CBN should have "reorganized and streamlined the ministry a lot sooner." Many of the layoffs were in the counseling centers, where full-time workers were re-placed by volunteers. Even in the best light, however, the decline in income was a "heavy hit" that both reduced the staff and throttled Tim Robertson's aspirations to "develop new programming." Nonetheless, he faced the crisis determined not to be a figurehead leader. In some ways, the environment was more open to experimentation in the absence of the hovering presence of Pat Robertson, and within the narrowing financial parameters he inher-ited, Tim moved aggressively to bring fresh ideas to the ministry.[10]

Tim was better prepared to assume the administrative leadership of CBN than he was to take over as co-host of *The 700 Club*. In August 1987 he was thrown into the program with little on-camera experience. Typically, he was self-effacing in his estimates of his early performances. Asked by a reporter to grade himself in early 1988, he gave himself a "C-plus so far," but insisted that he was becoming more and more comfortable. Tim was "im-mediately compared with his father," observed his mother; "everybody felt they could do a better job than him." Many veterans on the program found it difficult to be "subservient to Tim." Tim's good friend Scott Ross candidly told him, "I feel like you have the steering wheel but I have the license." In his father's judgment, Tim was an effective and creative host, but was never "comfortable raising money on the air."[11]

In addition to Tim's difficult adjustment to his new job, *The 700 Club* suffered other serious dislocations during these volatile months. Danuta Soderman, who had been Pat Robertson's popular co-host since 1983, abruptly left the show in May 1987. Though the parting was amicable at the time, in later years Soderman revealed that she objected to having to walk in lockstep with Robertson's political agenda. According to Tim Robert-son, she was disappointed that CBN was unable to "work out a special in-terview program for Danuta as we had hoped" because they could not find the necessary "advertiser support . . . to get it off the ground." Susan Howard, an actress who had appeared on the television show "Dallas," joined Tim and Ben Kinchlow to co-host *The 700 Club* in September 1987, but she left the show in November. A permanent female co-host for *The 700 Club* was not secured until Sheila Walsh joined the program as Pat Robertson's co-host in September 1988.[12]

The most serious blow to the show and to CBN management during Pat Robertson's absence was the departure of Ben Kinchlow in March 1988. Kinchlow had won respect as the executive vice president for ministry and development with "overall responsibility for 'Operation Blessing,' a world-wide humanitarian outreach, and CBN's international counseling centers." More important, he had been Pat Robertson's co-host on *The 700 Club* since 1975. Bob Slosser informed the staff of his departure: "Ben will be missed. He is loved and admired by all of us here at CBN. God has used this wonderful man in accomplishing His work through the Christian Broadcasting Network ministries. This is Ben's decision to go and we respect and support him in what he believes is God's present call on his life." Kinchlow felt burned out. Loosed from his fierce personal loyalty to Pat Robertson, he believed that "the Lord was leading him to take some extended time off to seek Him about the direction for his life." "Ben is very gifted and talented, and none of us wanted him to leave," Tim Robertson wrote to a distraught partner. "All of us would like very much for him to return, and pray that he will. However, we respect him for his decision. He felt the Lord had other things for him to do."[13]

In the midst of this instability, Tim introduced significant changes to *The 700 Club*. Pat Robertson's departure from the show, Tim surmised, demanded creative adjustments. His father could offer expertise on a wide variety of topics; neither Tim nor any of the other co-hosts could do so to the same degree. Tim believed that *The 700 Club* format that had evolved was the "logical outgrowth of my father's interests," but without Pat's presence on the set, Tim thought that it was time to downplay the "Christian talk show" image in favor of a broader program of social commentary. The revamped show highlighted "new sets, new music, and a new 700 Club logo." Tim enlisted a panel of "contributing editors" who appeared regularly in "special features," including Chuck Colson, James Dobson, Jack Hayford, and Gary Smalley. The program featured larger doses of Scott Ross's controversial "Taking It to the Streets" segments and his frequent "talks to high-profile celebrities and opinion leaders," which were intended to attract younger viewers but ended up offending many of the show's longtime fans.[14]

During these months, CBN explored a variety of other programming innovations. A thirty-minute "interactive talk show" called "Straight Talk," hosted by Ben Kinchlow and Scott Ross, was aired following *The 700 Club*. It featured discussions of such topics as "AIDS, women in the workplace, the condition of the church, interracial marriage and sexual abuse." "Straight Talk," boasted ministry literature, was a "no-nonsense format of questions and answers" about controversial issues, interviewing guests as "diverse" as those who appeared on popular network talk shows.[15]

There was some good news in all the changes. With its new set and fresh format, the show began lowering the age of its audience, and ratings remained stable because of increased exposure on cable television outlets. Many in the television industry applauded the changes. In February 1988

CBN received an Award of Merit from the National Religious Broadcasters "for demonstrating the highest technical standards and creativity in talent, writing, directing, and concepts in producing the daily magazine talk show, the '700 Club.'" In 1987 *The 700 Club* was nominated for a Daytime Emmy Award by the Academy of Television Arts and Sciences for an episode on AIDS co-hosted by Kinchlow and Soderman that featured Surgeon General C. Everett Koop. CBN launched a number of other new ventures during Tim's tenure as president, including a satellite radio network featuring contemporary music, guest interviews, and a call-in talk show co-hosted by Ben Kinchlow and Scott Ross. Nonetheless, these new initiatives did little to shore up the CBN donor base.[16]

In the long run, Tim Robertson's most important service to CBN was his embrace of his father's lifelong goal to create a diverse and strong network that was not explicitly religious. By the end of the 1980s, observers agreed that the CBN Cable Network had "distinguished itself as an innovator," clearly separating itself from religious networks such as PTL and TBN. Pat Robertson had long understood the value of surrounding *The 700 Club* with secular programming, believing that the show would reach a much larger and more diverse audience if it was not sandwiched between preachers. After his father's return to CBN, Tim worked closely with him to bring that concept to fruition in the development of The Family Channel.[17]

The Return of Pat Robertson to *The 700 Club*

Whether Pat Robertson would return to CBN and *The 700 Club* when he withdrew from the presidential campaign was a question much on the minds of insiders and outsiders in the spring of 1988. Some people believed that even during the campaign Robertson continued to give orders at CBN, but Tim Robertson insisted otherwise. He told a reporter that on several occasions he "called for advice only to be told that his dad was too busy campaigning to talk." In an article published in May 1988, the month that Robertson returned to CBN, Tim Robertson offered a prediction: "I don't think he'll ever come back and host the '700 Club.' He's had 20 years of it, and I kind of think he wants a change of scenery."[18]

There was a genuine sense of uncertainty at CBN. In April 1988, Barbara Johnson wrote to a supporter: "What God will lead Pat to do beyond this, I don't know. But I am confident that just as God led him to Portsmouth to start CBN in 1959, He will also lead him in whatever He wants him to do next."[19]

Not everyone at CBN wanted him back. Immediately after the decision had been made to withdraw from the race in early May 1988, one of the executives of Americans for Robertson queried campaign manager Allan Sutherlin about how to respond when asked by the press whether Pat would return to CBN: "Does CBN really want Pat back? I think we need to sit down with the appropriate CBN people and review the pros & cons. . . . Are you aware of all the animosity that exists over at CBN toward Pat and the campaign? I'm not quite sure that Pat knows the honest extent of it."[20]

But the question was answered with typical Robertson finality when his campaign ended on May 16, 1988. His withdrawal announcement included the terse statement: "At the urging of the Board of Directors of CBN, I have agreed to resume the leadership of CBN tomorrow. I look forward to playing a more active role in CBN University as well."[21]

The statement heralded a critical turning point in the life of Pat Robertson and in the future of CBN. His run for the presidency had changed his life and career in many ways. It had brought a degree of scrutiny, celebrity, and notoriety that far exceeded anything he had experienced earlier in life. Before that time, he had been a successful television entrepreneur and a celebrity in the booming charismatic movement who was less controversial than most of the flamboyant revivalists with large ministries. During and after his presidential race, he became, in the eyes of many political enemies, "the most dangerous man in America." Speaking of Robertson's decision to seek the Republican nomination for the presidency, Ralph Reed observed, "You can divide Pat's career by that moment."[22]

Now, in spite of his continued political involvement in the Christian Coalition, Robertson focused more and more on rebuilding his life, his business, and the ministry he had founded. Asked in 1993 whether he would run again for the presidency, Robertson replied that other matters demanded his full attention: "When I ran in 1988, it cost my companies in excess of $100 million in lost revenue. I am too deeply involved in a number of business ventures to walk away and seek public office." In 1994 he answered the question again: "The Lord, in His goodness, has given me both hands full with this ministry, and I really think I'll leave it up to someone else to go through that experience. At this time, I simply do not feel the Lord is asking me to go through that again." Even during his most fervent public involvement in politics in the 1990s, Robertson's central focus was on the practical business of building a spiritual empire that would have a worldwide influence.[23]

Yet in 1988 Pat Robertson's return to CBN and *The 700 Club* was not a foregone conclusion. "It was a funny time" for his son Tim. He felt that he was "beginning to feel fairly comfortable before the camera," and he believed the innovative changes he had approved in the programming at CBN would ultimately prove to be a financial boon. At the same time, he knew that religious ministries were not "family businesses" and that the succession "mantle isn't always there." In fact, the financial crisis that enveloped CBN had made his father's return an absolute necessity. Tim retained the title of president and CEO of CBN, but after his replacement on *The 700 Club* he focused his attention squarely on the burgeoning growth of the cable network, which he managed with considerable success.[24]

Both before Pat Robertson's departure and after his return, a mood of spiritual soul-searching settled over CBN. Immediately after the "PTL affair sent a shock through the entire evangelical community," and before he resigned as CEO in 1987, Robertson sensed that a spiritual malaise had settled over CBN. He believed it was "urgently necessary that as a staff we meet together to invoke His blessings on these months and years to come." In a memo to "All Staff" calling for a general prayer session, he wrote, "Only 40 people showed up for the prayer meeting prior to the telethon. Attendance at this Friday's meeting will not be optional. I am going to ask that all supervisors take a count of who is there. I want all personnel — and I mean all, including paid counselors — to be in attendance." Concern about the ministry's spiritual health deepened after Tim was appointed president. In September 1987, David Gyertson, then CBN corporate chaplain, laid down a spiritual challenge: "Beginning today, and continuing until God's purposes are fully achieved, we must call our people to earnest fasting and prayer. In order to facilitate this commitment, employees are to be encouraged to set aside their normal lunch period at least one day per week for prayer in chapel. This should be a time of intense intercession for both personal and corporate holiness."[25]

The mood of spiritual uncertainty was partly triggered by the financial crisis of the late 1980s, but it also had to do with the changes taking place on the CBN television network. Some insiders believed that *The 700 Club* had lost its spiritual way. Tim was less overtly "Christian" in his on-the-air demeanor; he confessed that he was at first uncomfortable with the kind of public spiritual displays expected of him on the program. He had to convince himself that "when you go on television and tell people that God answers prayer it means you have to pray on television." In September 1987, CBN vice-president Rob Hartley wrote an impassioned memo to Tim about the diminishing spiritual aura of *The 700 Club:*

Brother, it's time for us to get enthusiastic about bringing people to Jesus through our ministry here at CBN. Jesus said, "If I be lifted up, I will draw all men unto me." I believe He will also draw donors. . . . For the month of August, we had 2,930 salvations versus 10,865 in 1986. . . . *The 700 Club* desperately needs to have more ministry and testimonies which lift Jesus up and bear fruit for The Kingdom. Thursday's program was meant to "warm" our audience up in preparation for Seven Days Ablaze. Instead, the program was so "lukewarm" that virtually no ministry was done outside of a few short minutes that Ben attempted to insert into the program. MY BROTHER, WE'RE MISSING IT! This wonderful ministry was built through the power of the Holy Spirit as each program lifted Jesus up. . . . I know that if we begin to lift Jesus up again on our program, the ratings will come naturally.

Respected charismatic minister David Wilkerson gave a withering interview to CBN writer Scotty Sawyer while making a guest appearance on *The 700 Club*. He blasted the new format of *The 700 Club* and the increased secularization of CBN Network. In a dressing room interview before his appearance on the program he delivered a jeremiad and prophecy: "Christian television is dead unless there's a return to righteousness. . . . I remember when Pat Robertson preached judgment stronger than I've ever preached it. This network was a network of righteousness. . . . There's a great curse on — and I'm prophesying to you now — there's a greater curse on this network than there is on PTL. . . . All these doors are gonna be shut within two years unless there's a return to righteousness and all this hype is finished. It's nothing but hype and I want to cry." Rob Hartley wrote a memo to Pat Robertson, enclosing Wilkerson's comments: "I'm concerned that there is a haze among the CBN employees and a dense fog setting in among our donor base as to the mission of CBN today. . . . Immediate measures need to be taken to STOP this erosion!"[26]

Upon his return in the summer of 1988, Pat Robertson summoned CBN employees back to their original commitment and mission: "We are going to be starting a very special new year at CBN this fall. A tremendous amount of things are happening and we must seek God's will in it." He issued a call to all employees to join him at CBN's Labor Day prayer meeting and communion service: "LABOR DAY PRAYER MEETING IS NOT OPTIONAL! . . . I plan to come back a day early from what will be a very short vacation. I have to be here, and I expect others to do the same."[27]

Pat Robertson's return to *The 700 Club* and as chairman of the board marked the beginning of a slow and steady rebuilding of the organization into a formidable worldwide empire fulfilling the spiritual vision of Pat Robertson. CBN president Michael Little recalled, "It was slogging it through. . . . It was hard. Just his coming back did not do it." There was much work to be done.[28]

The Family Channel

The most transformative steps in the history of CBN were the series of technical and business maneuvers that led to the creation and sale of The Family Channel, which provided a financial bonanza for CBN and Pat Robertson. They began on April 29, 1977, when CBN dedicated its satellite earth station (celebrated in ceremonies that included a live transmission from Jerusalem), giving CBN the capacity to transmit programming 24 hours a day by satellite to affiliate stations. It was, in the words of Tim Robertson, "the defining technological moment for CBN." Cable television was beginning to catch on across the nation, and CBN initially offered old video tapes four hours a day on the satellite to be received by cable companies. By 1982 CBN Cable was available in around 12 million homes. After Tim Robertson joined CBN in 1982 he and his father carefully coordinated the transformation of CBN Cable Network into a viable commercial venture. In 1986, CBN sold the four television stations it owned and concentrated on expanding the cable network.[29]

The CBN Cable Network began steady growth after Pat Robertson returned to CBN in mid-1988, moving Tim into the position of CEO of the network. The network had begun selling advertising in 1981, using the proceeds to purchase "family oriented filmed programs to get more sales." By 1982 the CBN Cable Network was reaching around 15 million homes and supporting itself wholly by paid advertising. In 1988, the cable channel reached more than 40 million subscribers, offering programming that was 75 percent non-religious.[30] Throughout the 1980s, the CBN Cable Network defined itself as a family entertainment enterprise, not a religious network, and in late 1988, after much internal discussion, the CBN board changed the network's name to The Family Channel. The name change intentionally distanced the successful commercial television enterprise from the overtly Christian organization that owned it. This new "branding" also gave the channel more "commercial clout."[31]

By 1988, the soaring profitability of the channel posed a possible threat to the tax-exempt status of CBN. Some members of the legal staff believed that pending legislation in Congress would place strict restrictions on the percentage of income that a nonprofit entity such as CBN could garner from commercial enterprises. Robertson believed that the problem would become more acute in the future because the network still had much potential for growth. The CBN board developed a plan to move The Family Channel "outside of CBN," while assuring that the mother organization would profit from any future growth. In a form letter sent to donors who inquired about the sale, Robertson described the decision and its motivations: "CBN's Board of Directors, its outside attorneys and outside auditors determined that in order to comply with the Internal Revenue Service regulations, CBN Cable (which became known as The Family Channel) must be sold under the following conditions: The Family Cannel must be divested (1) at appraised value, (2) to a Christian-led organization (3) with a contractual agreement to air *"The 700 Club"* in perpetuity on cable and (4) with an understanding which would give CBN the support of outside investors who could expect substantial 'upside' potential for future profits."[32]

In 1990, The Family Channel, which had an assessed value of $175 million, was offered for sale. Pat Robertson headed a company called NIC, capitalized at $250 million, which purchased The Family Channel. Robertson was installed as chairman of the board, and Tim Robertson was named president and CEO of the purchasing group. In 1992 the new company, renamed International Family Entertainment (IFE), became a publicly held stock company. CBN was a major stockholder, as were Pat and Tim Robertson. The public offering was a financial windfall for IFE, providing around $100 million to expand its operations.[33]

The worth of the cable network skyrocketed, and in 1997 IFE was sold to Fox Kids Worldwide for an estimated $1.9 billion. The exhilarated Robertson described the financial windfall: "The entire transaction was described by our Washington counsel as a 'dream deal.' Out of it Regent University now has a $305 million endowment which makes it the best funded evangelical education institution in the country. CBN has received at least $250 million which has enabled it to win well over 100 million people to faith in Jesus Christ around the world to date. CBN is the remainder beneficiary of a trust which I set up which hopefully will bring it as much money as it has already received. On top of that, CBN has retained in perpetuity 17.5 hours of extremely valuable air time each week on The Family Channel for its religious programs." "This transaction," Robertson told the press, "will position CBN on firm financial ground for the future."[34]

The transactions of the 1990s that culminated in the sale of The Family Channel in 1997 received much scrutiny in the press and sparked charges that Pat and Tim Robertson had unethically enriched themselves by selling property owned by CBN and built with the contributions of its religious supporters. An article in *Business Week* snidely charged that "as chairman of . . . IFE, Robertson apparently has little reverence for the golden rule of corporate governance," even though he should have been familiar with the "age-old admonitions not to kill, steal, or worship graven images." Robertson's defense, offered repeatedly to supporters and to the press, was multifaceted: (1) The sale of The Family Channel was dictated by the fear that its profitability would jeopardize the tax-exempt status of CBN; (2) The successful bid made by Robertson's company of $250 million was substantially higher than any other bidder; (3) The investments of the Robertsons in the venture were made with their own money, not with funds supplied by CBN, and a large portion of Pat Robertson's investment had been placed in a charitable trust to be given to CBN in 2010; (4) CBN's investment in the development of the cable network had been minimal in its early stages (insider estimates ranged from $1 to $2 million), and since 1982 the network had been a profit-making venture; (5) IFE was able to engage in a much more aggressive commercial approach to developing a cable network than would have been possible if The Family Channel had continued to be managed by CBN; and (6) CBN and Regent University had received hundreds of millions of dollars as a result of the aggressive management of IFE and the subsequent sale of The Family Channel.[35]

The escalating value of The Family Channel was the direct result of the programming changes put in place in the 1980s and early 1990s. After the establishment of IFE in 1990, Tim Robertson announced that "this move strategically places us in a position to become America's leader in family entertainment for the 1990s. We remain absolutely committed to maintaining the same type of program format and the same high program standards that our audiences have grown to expect from The Family Channel." IFE moved aggressively to make the programming of The Family Channel more marketable to cable outlets and to advertisers. In the early 1980s *Forbes* magazine took note that Tim Robertson had begun "easing dad's network into secular programming, producing some shows and buying others." The public stock offering in 1992 enabled IFE to purchase the Ice Capades and Mary Tyler Moore Entertainment (MTM), a huge Hollywood production and distribution company which owned a film library that included *Hill Street Blues, The Mary Tyler Moore Show, The Bob Newhart Show, Remington Steele, Lou Grant,* and other popular shows, as well as a library of movies and television specials. The purchase of MTM at a bargain price of around $43 million became the vehicle for making the network a major competitor in the cable television market.[36]

Despite appearances, the stunning commercialization of The Family Channel, triggered by its focus on popular reruns, was not a radical departure from Pat Robertson's earlier practices at CBN. Robertson had The Family Channel model in mind in the early 1980s when CBN began airing such shows as *Burns and Allen, Jack Benny, The Life of Riley,* and *My Little Margie.* In 1982 he told a *Christian Life* reporter, "There is a window of opportunity open now to launch a complete television network. If we who know Jesus do not take this opportunity, someone else who does not know Him will try to fill the void. . . . There is an incredible hunger for quality programs with moral values." This approach, Pat Robertson assured supporters in the early 1980s, enabled the network to provide "good, wholesome, family entertainment to the American public . . . something of which we can all be thankful." Robertson had to repeatedly remind supporters of the consistency in programming philosophy throughout CBN's history.[37]

The initial sale of The Family Channel had several peripheral advantages for CBN. For the first time, CBN had a degree of deniability when programming appeared on The Family Channel that offended the sensibilities of the ministry's Christian supporters. Slowly, the distinction between The Family Channel, CBN, and *The 700 Club* became clearer. Surveys commissioned by IFE in 1992 and 1995 reported among their findings that "CBN and Christian Broadcasting Network brands/nomenclature [are] not associated with The Family Channel" and that the Family Channel was no longer "seen as [an] 'inspirational' [network]." When a CBN donor protested that something aired by The Family Channel was "offensive" or "disgusting," Robertson would patiently explain that CBN and IFE were "separate and distinct organizations." "Although I am Chairman of the parent company, International Family Entertainment," he continued, "I'm sure you understand that I do not oversee the day to day operation. That is in the hands of the president and his staff. I am sorry you do not like all the programs offered. I will give your letter to those who are in charge of the day to day operation of The Family Channel." Robertson dismissed protests from people threatening to stop their support to CBN because of an objectionable program broadcast by The Family Channel, but he usually was respectful of viewers' tastes. Sometimes he strongly sided with the critics of the programming and let it be known internally.[38]

The Modern *700 Club*

After the sale of The Family Channel, the financial survival of CBN rested heavily on the success of *The 700 Club*. The significance of the program, in Pat Robertson's words, was monumental: "It has financed everything else we have done." Upon his return to CBN in 1989, Robertson assured the press that "something like *The 700 Club* will be on forever." As always, the challenge was to find ways to "make it more appealing so more people will watch." "There are always more exciting ways of doing things," he told reporters, and he was "playing around with some program concepts in my mind."[39]

Robertson quickly returned to his familiar role as centerpiece of the show. His experience as a candidate gave new reason for CBN to cover news at a level that would compete with established news sources. CBN surveys uniformly confirmed that *The 700 Club* viewers tuned in to "hear the news and commentary they are not getting anywhere else." The "news/ magazine format" of the program, which included interviews with an impressive array of guests from entertainment, sports, and public affairs, allowed Robertson to exhibit his formidable skills as an interviewer and his broad knowledge of national and world affairs. According to a ministry publication, the program featured "the enlightened news commentary of Pat Robertson. The program's seasoned host uses his lifetime of experience in ministry, business and politics to help viewers understand the significance of events as they unfold."[40]

The program continued to be co-hosted by Sheila Walsh until her departure after five years in 1992. The feisty Walsh, whom Robertson described as a "naughty daughter," left to pursue advanced religious studies and subsequently established a successful teaching ministry. The show also continued to produce feature stories, including the popular "Straight Talk" and other highly-rated and often controversial segments produced by Scott Ross. The program settled into a familiar routine when Robertson's old friend, Ben Kinchlow, returned as co-host in April 1992. The popular Kinchlow's return was a clear boost to the program. "Brother Ben Is Back!" headlined CBN's newsletter. For both Robertson and regular viewers it was the return of an "old friend." Once again, Kinchlow's "big Texas smile, his gregarious personality and friendly down-home humor" provided a popular counterpoint for Robertson.[41]

The addition of Terry Meeuwsen as a co-host in June 1993 brought a degree of stability to the program for the next fifteen years. A native of Wisconsin who won the Miss America crown in 1973, Meeuwsen for a time pursued a career as a professional singer, touring with the New Christy

Minstrels, before settling in Milwaukee, where she co-hosted a daily talk show for a local television station. A deeply committed Christian, Meeuwsen experienced several years of personal and professional disappointment while seeking a career as a singer and surviving a failed marriage. She was a frequent guest co-host on *The 700 Club* beginning in the early 1980s. After rejecting a number of offers to move to Virginia Beach because she did not want to uproot her children, in 1993 she agreed to relocate to host an early morning "wakeup show" called *USam,* a pioneering venture by CBN to produce a "purely secular" program. The show was sufficiently successful to trigger network copies but was unable to attract the financial support needed to survive. Eventually she was invited to fill the co-host chair on *The 700 Club* left vacant by the departure of Sheila Walsh.[42]

Meeuwsen's presence, as she surmised in an interview, added a needed woman's perspective to the show: "Pat and Ben are wonderful, but I think it's important to get a woman's point of view. To offer a softer, more sensitive view of the issues. And as a mother of four children, I will bring a 'mom's' perspective that I think many in our audience will appreciate." Her calm, confident, and reasoned comments became a staple on the program for the next fifteen years. Pat Robertson had immense respect for her. In a foreword written for her autobiographical book, *The God Adventure,* which focused on her unhappy early years as a celebrity, Robertson wrote: "In this remarkable book, Terry opens her heart to tell of a brutal rape and a failed marriage to an alcoholic husband. Out of this has come the radiant life of a loving, mature woman who has understanding, compassion, and great wisdom." When young Gordon Robertson joined the program as co-host, Meeuwsen nurtured him in the craft of television hosting. "Working with Terry is a dream," said Gordon.[43]

By the middle of the 1990s *The 700 Club* was produced in a one-hour format that remained unchanged in the years ahead. "For more than three decades," CBN announced, "*The 700 Club* has offered a distinctively different kind of program. With its insightful news broadcasts, dynamic features, up-close and personal celebrity interviews and engaging teaching segments . . . *The 700 Club* brings a positive message to millions of homes every day!" *The 700 Club* attracted a core audience with an intense loyalty to the show and the hosts. Executive producer Norm Mintle explained, "Our viewers are more like family members. They watch the show, call the Counseling Center, and we pray with them. . . . For some people, we are their only source of spiritual encouragement. From the news stories to the testimonies, it's the spiritual element that makes us unique." The appeal of the show was no surprise to those familiar with evangelical Christian culture, including a writer for *Christianity Today:* "On the air, Robertson's persona is that of a folksy, congenial, reassuring father figure. He often shakes his head, grins, and guffaws at the state of world affairs." Spiritual content was woven into a fabric that included hard news and interviews with celebrities. It was, in the words of the ministry publication, *Frontlines,* "a TV program that changes hearts. . . . Around the world, when people tune into *The 700 Club,* they discover its exciting format, conservative values and family-friendly features. Many appreciate the Christian perspective on the news and Pat Robertson's insightful financial analyses. Some find spiritual encouragement from the heart warming testimonies. And thousands call in to request the ministry materials we offer. But what makes *The 700 Club* different from the secular 'news/entertainment shows' is our focus on the power of God to make a difference in the world." Robertson never lost sight of the fact that his viewers "like prayer a lot."[44]

Another "cornerstone of the program" after the mid-1990s was newscaster Lee Webb. Webb became the news anchor in December 1994. He brought twenty-one years of broadcast experience to the program. A popular journalist at an NBC affiliate in Jacksonville for nearly ten years from 1985 to 1994, the politically conservative Webb sparked a "fire storm in Jacksonville" when he made a speech at a Christian Coalition meeting criticizing the local media coverage of a clash between Planned Parenthood and a local school board. The station first suspended Webb, then opted not to renew his contract at the end of the year. The local CBN board member who had invited Webb to speak at the Christian Coalition meeting urged CBN to hire him, and by the end of the year he was on his way to Virginia Beach. Webb became a respected presence on the show; he "brought a lot of credibility," according to Terry Meeuwsen.[45]

Other regulars on the show added diverse talents. The regular appearance of special features producer Kristi Watts as Pat Robertson's co-host on the "Skinny Wednesday" version of *The 700 Club* brought out a playful and light-hearted side of Robertson. Other regulars from the news bureau such as John Jessup and Wendy Griffith were household names to regular viewers.[46]

Gordon Perry Robertson

By far the most important talent addition to *The 700 Club* in recent years was the insertion of Gordon Robertson as a co-host in 1999. Gordon arrived in Virginia Beach after working for five years as the head of CBN Asia in Manila, where he co-hosted a Filipino version of *The 700 Club*. His father asked him to join the CBN staff as a producer for the program. When he arrived in Virginia Beach, still recovering from jetlag, he was told he would co-host on April Fools' Day. His five years "in the minor leagues" on Philippine television had prepared him well to be on camera, and he soon began co-hosting the program at least once a week, as well as assuming responsibility for producing and hosting the fundraising telethons. A lawyer by profession, Gordon was widely read and articulate, and he readily offered news commentary, as he had done in the Philippines. While he was "comfortable with bringing a Christian perspective to the news of the day," Gordon was more self-effacing in manner and more modest in expressing his views. He believed that his father had "earned the right" to be as "partisan" as he saw fit in making political pronouncements, but he was more reserved in his comments.[47]

Before the cameras Gordon Robertson was friendly and upbeat, but at the same time calm, thoughtful, and soft-spoken. Tranquil and quiet in person, he confessed in 2007 that "I don't think to this day that I am any good on television." But his persona on the program, while quite different from that of his father, won immediate respect from the professionals who produced the program. "He is comfortable in front of the camera," observed co-host Terry Meeuwsen, because "he knows who he is." Most important, he brought to the show a serene, brooding spirituality that moved *The 700 Club* perceptively toward its historic religious roots. "The Lord has really anointed and gifted him," said his proud father.[48]

As a youngster, Gordon Robertson, Pat and Dede's younger son, seemed to be on a predictable trajectory toward a successful professional career. He graduated from Yale in 1980, worked for a year as a reporter, and then earned a law degree from Washington and Lee University. Upon graduation he joined the prestigious Norfolk law firm of Vandeventer, Black, Meredith & Martin, and within five years he became a partner specializing in real estate law.[49]

But Gordon's life was not the unbroken upward spiral that it seemed to outsiders, and even to his wife and family. He began abusing alcohol while still a teenager, and then he graduated to marijuana and hard drugs during what he later called "my lost two decades." "You name it, I did it. No limits," he later recalled. His drug abuse was sporadic, and he was a "high functioning" addict who could maintain grades in school and hide his addiction from others, including his wife, Kathryn. When she finally learned he was using hard drugs, it "shattered her world." "Gordon was really in trouble," recalled Scott Ross.[50]

Gordon's experimentation with drugs was hardly an unusual story for a teenager growing up in the 1970s. But his struggle was severe. In the Robertson family, he surmised, "I've got the record for rebellion." Gordon's drug abuse was driven by personal anxieties as well as societal pressures: "I wanted to make money. I wanted to run away from God. . . . I had no idea what I was getting into. I was trying hard to prove that I wasn't Pat Robertson's son. . . . I thought I would be accepted." On several occasions Gordon visited rehabilitation facilities and received professional counseling. "It wasn't particularly effective for me," he recalled. "I had to be born again."

Gordon's drug addiction, which began in his teen years, ended in India. In the midst of his family crisis at the end of 1993, Gordon received a telephone call from old family friend and prominent Virginia Beach minister, John Gimenez, asking him to join his team in a crusade in India scheduled to depart the next week. He informed Gordon that he had called because "he had a dream" about him. Gordon consented, believing that it would be impossible for Gimenez to secure a visa for him so quickly. But the next week he found himself in India, arriving in Rajamundry to participate in a crusade. What followed was a life-changing three-week episode. Surprised when Gimenez asked him to speak, he preached a "simple sermon." Afterward, an audience member told him, "Your words have pierced my heart." Left behind by Gimenez, Gordon stayed in Rajamundry for three weeks. While there, he believed he had a "road to Damascus experience" in which "Jesus spoke to me." Late one evening, while witnessing a Hindu festival, he heard the words: "Gordon, if you were the only one to believe, I would have come for you." By the time he had completed his trip to India, he wrote to his wife: "I think God is calling me to be a missionary."

Returning to his job in Norfolk, Gordon mulled his future. After another dream in which "millions of Asians" implored him to come help them, he visited his father to seek advice. He told him about his experience in Rajamundry and blurted out, "I think God wants me to quit my job." He expected an extended counseling session, but instead his father replied, "Then why haven't you?" and promptly left the room. The next day Gordon resigned his position and began winding up ten years of law practice. At that point his father guided Gordon and his family to Manila, where CBN had offices and where *The 700 Club* had been broadcast since 1976.

Gordon still intended to become a missionary. He spent a few weeks in Hong Kong, acting as a "mule" smuggling Bibles into China, where he learned about the booming house church movement there. He began to see his location in the Philippines as a base of operations for broader missions efforts. Seeking to capitalize on the millions of overseas Filipino workers dispersed throughout Asia and the Middle East, he formulated a plan for training them to be missionaries, to penetrate areas where conventional missionaries could not work. In early 1995 he established the Asian Center for Missions in Manila.[51]

By 1999 the Asian Center for Missions had trained 277 missionaries and deployed 105 abroad. The center partnered with Filipino churches to dispatch missionaries, who then established churches and training schools in other Asian nations. The Center soon became the largest missions agency based in the Philippines, supporting evangelists in Cambodia, China, Thailand, India, Indonesia, Malaysia, Vietnam, and Burkina Faso. From its beginnings, Gordon entrusted leadership of the organization to Filipino natives and encouraged them to raise most of the funds to support the missionaries. In 2008 the Center sponsored twelve training centers in the Philippines and other Asian nations and supported about 150 missionaries in cooperation with Filipino churches. "They are doing incredible work from a poor nation," observed CBN writer Nena Benigno; "Gordon encouraged them to go because Filipinos had been driven out of their country by poverty."[52]

Soon after arriving in Manila, Gordon filed papers for the establishment of CBN Asia, and he slowly began to develop his vision for reproducing the Christian Broadcasting Network in Asia. Among the cryptic pieces of advice his father offered to him before he moved to Manila was a memorable line: "Gordon, many people are in the Bible just because they begat someone. Just go beget somebody." Gordon slowly came to believe that his mission was to "beget" CBN in Asia. "People at CBN didn't think it would work" — including his father, as he later recalled — but he persevered.

In 1995, Gordon drafted a charter for an Operation Blessing Foundation, and in 1996 CBN Asia began producing a Filipino version of *The 700 Club* called *The 700 Club Asia*. In the summer of 1999, CBN Asia opened a studio in Manila where the program was produced. Gordon proudly announced: "For the first time in CBN's history, we have a production facility broadcasting indigenous programming live to a nationwide audience." By 1999 CBN Asia, under Gordon's leadership, had become a flourishing replica of CBN in the United States, complete with locally produced television productions, a humanitarian outreach, a counseling center, and an extensive fundraising apparatus.[53]

In the long run, Gordon's five years as co-host on *The 700 Club Asia* was his most important learning experience in the Philippines. At first, recalled one co-worker, "he was like a lawyer," but as time passed he "got softer" and began to "exercise the gift of knowledge." By the time he arrived in Virginia Beach, he was ready for his next step.[54]

When Gordon began co-hosting *The 700 Club* in 1999 he joined a smoothly functioning team. Predictably, Pat Robertson was the most popular "talent" on *The Club;* his presence on the program was an important factor in the loyalty of nearly 90 percent of viewers in a 1998 poll. Other regulars, such as Terry Meeuwsen and Lee Webb, also received high ratings from viewers. Nonetheless, a survey in 1997 reported that *700 Club* donors "sense uncertainty when hosts change or Pat is absent." When Pat did not appear, it was important to give an "explanation of his whereabouts and reports on his activities."[55]

The question of how to keep the program consistent enough to retain loyal viewers yet fresh enough to reach new audiences remained the challenge of *The 700 Club* throughout the 1990s. From time to time CBN announced that the format had been revamped to make the program "more flexible and energetic." "Our goal," reported executive producer Andy Freeman in 1997, "is to make The 'New' 700 Club the most exciting, unpredictable, informative, entertaining, and inspiring program on television." But for the most part, the program remained the same. A 2001 report noted that *The 700 Club's* tested format of "breaking news, interviews with Christian leaders, and hard-hitting analysis of current events" was its "long-standing recipe for success" and "a big reason why CBN friends and partners tune in to *The 700 Club*."[56]

The CBN Media Vision: An Alternative News Source

The 700 Club remains CBN's "brand product," but the development of a news delivery system was long a part of Pat Robertson's dream for CBN, and it became a reality with the establishment of a news bureau in 1982. The operation became more and more expansive in the years after Robertson's return to Virginia Beach, including the launching of a daily program called *CBN NewsWatch* in 2002. The news bureau's charge was to provide "a refreshing alternative to today's mainstream news sources." The CBN bureau had a well-defined slant, according to executive producer Michael Patrick, only because "we are free to leave the 'media herd' and report on different events." In addition to the headline news, CBN covered stories about "what God is doing." For instance, CBN's presence in the Middle East often triggered inside reports from the region, including stories about "human rights violations" against Christians that received scant attention in other media newscasts. CBN's marketing experts judged that news stories about religion were the surest way to retain the loyalty of viewers who considered themselves religious.[57]

By 2008 the CBN news bureau employed around 60 people in an up-to-date Virginia Beach facility. "Most of us have to catch up with [Pat Robertson's] vision," acknowledged bureau chief Rob Allman. Robertson wanted a news service that would "break stories," not simply report them. CBN's Washington bureau had five reporters, headed by Senior National Correspondent David Brody, who held White House credentials. Two reporters were on the staff in the Philippines. Another worked in San Jose, Costa Rica, where a Spanish version of world news was also produced. The Jerusalem bureau, headed by Mideast Bureau Chief Chris Mitchell, gave CBN one of the most visible presences in the Middle East. The reach of CBN's news bureau was vastly expanded by the worldwide outposts of CBN. "I consider anybody who works at CBN to be a source," explained Rob Allman. The presence of the WorldReach Centers, with state-of-the-art television production studios and experienced field staffs, enabled CBN to cover breaking stories around the world. CBN film crews were often among the first on the scene when covering stories in such WorldReach strongholds as the Philippines, China, Indonesia, and the Ukraine.[58]

In 1992 Robertson toyed with the idea of buying the floundering United Press International news service out of the largess of funds garnered from the sale of The Family Channel. The purchase of UPI would have furthered an ambitious Robertson plan, called StandardNews, to establish a national radio news service that would compete with secular news services. StandardNews absorbed an earlier CBN radio news service that supplied news to around 300 religious stations and hoped to reach out to a much broader network (Robertson's goal was 2,000 stations) with "news reports tailored for both Christian and secular stations."[59]

By direction from Pat Robertson, the news bureau aspired to be "unbiased" in its coverage of stories, while acknowledging that its choice of stories reflected the interests of the CBN audience. CBN conceded that the bureau's news coverage placed an exaggerated emphasis on the Middle East in general and Israel in particular. But the stories from the region resonated with *The 700 Club*'s audience. Allman reported that donor feedback uniformly asked for more such coverage, because "we believe you are telling us what others will not."[60]

The news bureau prided itself on its professional standards. Allman explained the distinctions the bureau tried to maintain: "[Pat Robertson's] views show through in the commentary he does. . . . He encourages the news division to be an independent division to do the stories in an objective manner. . . . When we pass it back to Pat, it turns into commentary. . . . We have done stories he disagreed with." Lee Webb often ends his news report by asking Robertson what he thinks of the story; at that point, the broadcast turns from news to advocacy. Both Webb and Rob Allman believed that viewers instinctively understood the transition, and that Robertson's highly personal and often acerbic comments did not compromise the objectivity of the reporting staff. Gordon Robertson believed that Allman had done "a fantastic job" in changing the show's "editorial slant" and broadening the coverage beyond a predictable focus on "the culture war." CBN vice-president Patrick Roddy, a veteran of years on the production staff of *Good Morning America,* confidently boasted: "There is a talent pool here that is as good as it gets."[61]

Testimonies and Spirituality

The 700 Club has depended heavily on CBN's increasingly sophisticated news bureau, but an even "bigger reason" for the loyalty of its audience, judged producer Andy Freeman, was "the stories they tell." A stream of professionally produced vignettes about the evangelistic and benevolent outreach of CBN became the most distinctive feature of the program and the central focus of the fundraising telethons produced three times a year. According to a ministry magazine, these "heart-moving testimonies" made the program "one of the most influential Christian television shows in the world." Filming "stories about real people with real problems" became the trademark of *The 700 Club.* A survey in 1998 reported that 85 percent of *The 700 Club* viewers either "greatly" or "somewhat" liked the testimonial segments, about the same ratings as respondents gave the news reporting.[62]

A stream of testimonials and personal stories combined the longtime commitments of CBN to evangelism, humanitarianism, and professional television production. After 2000, the growing visibility of CBN's international evangelism department, WorldReach, and the rapid expansion of its humanitarian wing, Operation Blessing, moved testimonials closer and closer to the center of *The 700 Club's* self-definition. The program featured skillfully produced stories dramatizing conversions, healings, and rescues from disaster within the United States and around the world. The professionally produced segments, many of them filmed by trained technicians in the WorldReach television studios scattered around the world, highlighted the evangelistic and humanitarian outreach of CBN.[63]

The stream of testimonial vignettes tied the program to its roots in the post–World War II charismatic revival. *The 700 Club* had always been overtly charismatic, displayed most clearly in the co-hosts' prayers and exercising of the "word of knowledge" to proclaim healings and other miracles in the lives of viewers. "The Lord speaks to us. . . . I haven't backed up on that," Robertson proclaimed in 2008. At the same time, in comparison to much religious programming, Pat Robertson was decorous in exercising the gifts of the Spirit on *The 700 Club*. In a 2008 discussion on the program, he stated a long-standing rule at CBN: "We go into the gifts of the Spirit with much humility." But Robertson never turned his back on his religious roots, and guests on *The 700 Club* included some of the most visible celebrities in the worldwide charismatic revival. Among Robertson's featured guests in 2008 were evangelist and healer Benny Hinn and John and Carol Arnott, pastors of the Toronto Airport Christian Fellowship, a ministry that gained international attention for a revival that lasted fourteen years and featured a series of dramatic techniques and miracle claims. Pat Robertson's pragmatic test of such claims was a simple question phrased in traditional biblical language: "Is the fruit good?"[64]

Gordon Robertson was even more driven than his father to explore the radical moves of the Holy Spirit that he believed could re-ignite the fading charismatic revival in the United States. His spiritual searching and probing was reminiscent of his father's relentless search for the will of God during his student days in New York. "I know there is more than what I experience now," observed Gordon in 2009. "I learned how to preach in the villages of India," he recalled. "You name a manifestation [of the Holy Spirit] and it was happening." During his years in Manila he cast a deeply spiritual aura around the CBN ministry. He was "very particular when he was here to be sure everyone was baptized in the Spirit," recalled one ministry leader. "He was very into releasing power. . . . All the way down to the janitor he would be asking for sharing the spirit." Gordon's beliefs and language echoed the spirit of the early Pentecostal movement; "Gordon is practically a classical Pentecostal," observed Pentecostal historian Vinson Synan. Speaking to a group of CBN partners in 2000, Gordon embraced the early Pentecostal concept of xenoglossy: "I've seen people baptized marvelously in the Holy Spirit and get whole languages. People who have never spoken Mandarin, get full Mandarin, people who have never spoken Korean, get full Korean, and use it as missionaries." In several programs in the summer of 2008 he explored and taught on the "gifts of the Holy Spirit," interviewed leaders of a revival in Lakeland, Florida, who claimed to have witnessed thirty-five resurrections from the dead, and labored to put modern miracle claims in the context of his reading of Charles G. Finney and Jonathan Edwards. The criticisms of early Pentecostalism and its "manifestations of the Holy Spirit," Gordon believed, were "surprisingly similar to what we are seeing today." On a few occasions when Gordon co-hosted *The 700 Club,* the program became pervasively spiritual, highlighting the miraculous to an unusual extent. Although many viewers probably did not recognize the controversial nature of the "word of faith" theology taught by many of the more radical television teachers, Gordon's embrace of it on the program was a conspicuous and bold step.[65]

In June 2008 Gordon launched, and often led, a twice-a-week, two-hour Spiritual Life webcast program. The program featured spiritual teaching and worship, but Gordon, his frequent co-host Marguerite Evans, and other guest leaders used the unscripted, spontaneous meetings as laboratories to exercise the gifts of the Holy Spirit, including healing, and viewers sent real-time comments and requests online. The Spiritual Life program was launched on June 19, 2008, during a special *700 Club* broadcast that featured participants from sites around the world, including India and the Philippines, all exercising the charismatic word of knowledge. An early program originating in Manila featured "the flowing of the spirit," and other programs were aired from Canada and other remote sites. By the end of 2008 the program had become a fixture on CBN's website.[66]

Internet distribution opened doors that had long seemed frustratingly closed to overtly charismatic insiders at CBN, including Gordon Robertson. *The 700 Club* might appear pervasively religious to outsiders because of the exercising of the "word of knowledge" by the co-hosts, but the program has developed deference to the mixed sensibilities of its audience through many years on the air. If the charismatic message sometimes seemed muted, it was because the broadcast was intended to be "more friendly to those who are not already believers." In addition, the program's rigid one-hour time slot demands a carefully scripted schedule, with specific time slots assigned for news, testimonials, guest appearances, prayer, and other regular segments. "It is tough to keep the Holy Spirit to a clock," noted Gordon, but time restraints vanished in programs streamed online; that, he observed, was what was "liberating about Internet programs." Now it was possible to broadcast a spontaneous program that included participants from around the world, in which you "go with the moment" and "allow the flowing of the Spirit."[67]

In spite of its limitations, *The 700 Club* has endeavored to appeal to a broad audience, including the booming megachurches that often bridge the gap between Pentecostals, charismatics, and other evangelicals. A survey of the program's "most loyal supporters" in the late 1990s grouped them in "four key 'mega clusters'": "Affluent families & Couples," "Upscale Urban Families," "Midscale Families and Couples," and a "Rural Mix." About 65 percent of viewers were females, and about 35 percent were women over 55 years of age. The viewer/donor base was spread rather evenly around the country; a list of top ten "markets" in which viewers were significantly more likely to give to CBN was headed by Helena, Montana, and included Presque Isle, Maine, and Juneau, Alaska. Ever conscious that they "market to a lot of people," the show's producers sought to minister to a wide diversity of tastes and needs.[68]

Domestic Production and Distribution

After the sale of The Family Channel, distribution of its programs became the largest financial burden for CBN. By the twenty-first century *The 700 Club* was distributed "in 95% of the television markets in the United States" and claimed a daily audience of around a million viewers. Broadcast three times daily on the ABC Family Channel Network, the show was also aired on FamilyNet and Trinity Broadcasting Network, and it was in syndication on approximately 230 independent television stations nationwide. During the first decade of the century, daily viewership hovered around one million, with the largest block viewing the program on syndicated stations. By 2007, programming on syndicated stations produced 74 percent of the television-generated income at CBN. CBN marketing expert John Turver has constantly negotiated to try to expand and improve the distribution of *The 700 Club*. By 2007 *The 700 Club* was aired in all major markets, and could be seen on cable or syndication by 97 percent of the nation's households — larger coverage than such daytime staples as *Oprah* and *Dr. Phil.* An international version of *The 700 Club* was translated into more than 70 foreign languages, seen in more than 200 countries, and was "accessible throughout the year by more than 1.5 billion people around the world."[69]

CBN produced several other programs for domestic consumption at its Virginia Beach studios. *CBN NewsWatch* was the news bureau's headline program. Anchored by Lee Webb and Wendy Griffith, the program was a conventional thirty-minute news broadcast that aired on approximately twenty-five stations each weekday afternoon and streamed on the CBN website. The news bureau also produced a thirty-minute weekly program called *Christian World News.* Featuring "News for the Global Church," the program was "devoted to the work of the Holy Spirit around the globe." It was distributed by Trinity Broadcasting Network and ran on a small number of stations in the United States, in addition to being streamed on the ministry website.[70]

As a part of its WorldReach program to reach diverse cultures around the world, CBN has developed a broad array of original programming. In the United States, the ministry produced and aired scores of original programs, particularly in the 1980s, but by 2009, besides *The 700 Club* and the news, only two programs were being produced in CBN studios in Virginia Beach and Nashville. *Living the Life* was a "fast-paced magazine-style talk show specifically designed for today's active women" that began airing in 2001. Co-hosted by Terry Meeuwsen, Louise DuArt, and Carolyn Castleberry, the program featured "an eclectic mix of stimulating interviews, inspiring stories, and informative segments that focus on health, relationships, faith, parenting, home, gardening, cooking and other engaging topics." The show was aired regularly on the ABC Family Channel and on a sprinkling of independent, mostly religious, cable channels. The other main CBN production for domestic consumption was an upbeat show that featured contemporary Christian music. Produced in Nashville at CBN's NorthStar Studios, *One Cubed International* was "a worldwide music video show whose mission statement is to reach this generation to express the unconditional love and salvation that God freely offered to everyone in this world. In everything that is *One Cubed,* we want to bring glory to God, never compromising and never settling, and always striving to be used by Him to the best of our abilities." Aired weekly on the ABC Family Channel, the American version of *One Cubed,* or a foreign language show modeled on it, was distributed by CBN studios around the world and aired in thirty-five countries in North and South America, Africa, Asia, and Europe. Also produced in Virginia Beach studios was a Canadian edition of *The 700 Club,* hosted by David Gyertson, presently a distinguished professor at Regent University. The thirty-minute weekly program has aired in Canada for thirty years. Sponsored by Christian Broadcasting Associates, a Canadian organization modeled on CBN in the United States, the program features the worldwide work of CBN. Gyertson, a former president of Regent University, Asbury College, and Taylor University, brings to the program a sophisticated persona and biblical erudition.[71]

The cost of distribution limited the multifaceted production capabilities at CBN. The first budget priority was securing the widest possible distribution of *The 700 Club;* other domestic programs were necessarily lower-budget priorities. Pat Robertson and other leaders at CBN believe that solutions to the distribution problem loom on the technological horizon. CBN experts have constantly probed the distribution possibilities of the Internet.

Gordon Robertson, in particular, has been captivated by the worldwide potential of the Internet: "There is an incredible hunger for Christianity in developing countries. When you consider the explosive growth of the Internet, especially in areas like China, you can see the tremendous opportunity to reach those who are unable to seek information on Christianity openly. . . . CBN.com will leverage whatever technology exists to minister worldwide." The potential Internet audience is gigantic, with negligible cost. As opposed to the media model used by Paul Crouch at the Trinity Broadcasting Network, which emphasized a huge worldwide distribution system that was the "envy of lots of folks," the emphasis at CBN was on the production of high quality Christian programming, an area in which they clearly led all competitors. Both Pat and Gordon Robertson believed that in the future the Internet would be the needed vehicle to get their quality programs distributed. A 2001 survey commissioned to explore future means of distribution for *The 700 Club* pinpointed the huge group of "Streamies" between the ages of twelve and twenty-four who favored the Internet over television as their source of information. By 2001 *The 700 Club* and other CBN programming was accessible for computer viewing, and by 2007 CBN was the leading religious provider of video and text material. CNB's Digital Media Group employed twenty-five professionals who operated thirty websites in a variety of languages, offering a wide variety of searchable video content. CBN websites had about 12 million visitors in 2006. "We are creating a new distribution system," observed Gordon Robertson in 2008; the worldwide potential would be unlimited when "people get used to receiving television through the Internet."[72]

The CBN Lifeline: Counseling

The extraordinary longevity of CBN and *The 700 Club* owed much to the careful and skillful development of a system of direct contact with ministry supporters. Counseling centers in Virginia Beach and Nashville have been, in the words of CBN president Michael Little, CBN's "signature," the "lifeblood" of the ministry. More than 300 counselors in Virginia Beach and another 150 in Nashville, all fulltime employees trained to follow manuals providing answers for clinical and spiritual problems, were housed in advanced media laboratories. Each counselor's computer was loaded with answers to practical and theological questions and had the capability of storing personal information about the caller, making it possible to establish a personal and permanent contact with every person who called CBN's toll-free number. *The Christian Counselor's Handbook,* "a distillation of the experiences our counselors have had in ministering . . . on the telephone," was published for the first time in 1977. The most recent version includes scriptural and practical advice in fifteen categories: Abuse, Attitude, Bondage, Church, God's Commands, Emotional Problems, Family, Finances, God's Gifts, Healing, Life and Death, Prayer, God's Principles, Rebellion, and Sexual Sins. Directions for counselors range from practical instructions, such as "listen carefully to the counselee," "always be courteous and helpful," "do not argue, condemn, criticize, preach, 'talk down to,' or overreact and talk loudly," and "do not counsel someone to stop taking medicine or not see a doctor," to such spiritual instructions as "when counseling, quote biblical passages that speak to the problem," "act with all the authority Jesus gives," "do not proselyte (from one church to another) or counsel someone to leave their church (unless it is an occult or non-Christian group)," and "expect God to answer your prayers with signs accompanying the gifts of the Holy Spirit."[73]

The counseling centers, according to their director, Vice-President Joel Palser, were the "backend of the show," the place where a caller talked with a live person representing Pat Robertson. Since the days of the first telethon in 1963, Pat Robertson has grasped the power of establishing direct contact with potential donors, and by 1974 the ministry had established a 24-hour "Prayer Counseling Center." The technologically-advanced CBN counseling centers made *The 700 Club* the quintessential "interactive television." Most of CBN's call-response methodology has been used by other religious and charitable organizations, but none have been more thorough or successful. The cumulative statistics published by the centers are eye-catching. By 1982, the ministry reported 525,000 calls in the first three months of the year, including 10,000 "reported answers to prayer" and 3,700 who "called to accept Christ." In the year 2007, the number of telephone calls handled by the counseling centers in the United States passed four million. Since the beginning of the interactive telephone service in the 1960s, Palser estimated that counselors had engaged in around 75 million ministry-related conversations.[74]

Such statistics only scratch the surface of the complexity and humanity of the system. Most calls received by CBN have been requests for prayer. The prayer cards carefully filled out by counselors span the spectrum of human depravity, despair, and physical tragedy. Several counselors have received "training in crisis intervention" to handle potential suicide callers; other veteran workers, many of whom have been CBN employees for decades, are specialists in particular problems. At the same time, CBN counselors have avoided offering "therapeutic counseling," recognizing that most of their callers are people seeking spiritual nurture and support. During its busiest hours, the counseling center becomes a cacophony of prayers for the sick and needy.[75]

To insiders, the most critical count in the yearly reports of the counseling centers is the number of callers who "prayed for salvation" or who "rededicated" their lives while praying with a counselor. In 2007, the centers reported that 36,000 callers had "prayed with a counselor and for the first time received salvation and another 22,000 had said a prayer of rededication." In the early days of the ministry, callers were "referred to local churches," but in recent years legal concerns about privacy stopped the practice of giving names of callers to "strange pastors." Callers are still urged to join a local church, but now they are provided with only general guidelines about "how to choose a church."[76]

The CBN counseling centers are also effective and unashamed ministry builders and fundraisers. Every caller is profiled on the ministry computers, including his or her special needs and requests and such personal information as birthdays and anniversaries. Counselors regularly call *700 Club* members or others who have given to the ministry. In 2007 the centers made more than 600,000 "outbound calls." The outbound calling program begins with "Project Jumpstart," a call that contacts "every person who says the sinner's prayer" and every person who makes a pledge during a telethon. The contact is added to a computerized family, which Palser believes provides many lonely people a caring friend: "If there is a crisis in their life. . . . If they are having surgery next week, we make timely calls to them." The outgoing calls aim to serve and minister, but they also are sales calls, encouraging the fulfillment of pledges, soliciting new memberships, and informing supporters about the ongoing projects at CBN. The counseling centers are clearly hotbeds of spiritual fervor, filled with "prayer warriors" who would much rather be shouting hallelujahs on the telephone than working at a checkout counter at Wal-Mart. But they are also salespersons; as Palser put it, "we are not embarrassed to pass the hat."[77]

The counseling centers are intensely active during the telethons, receiving thousands of calls in response to on-the-air appeals. During these intensive drives to recruit new members, the daily call volume has soared to 22,000, sometimes surpassing 1,000 an hour. During these high-volume times, the regular counselors are joined on the telephones by volunteers from the CBN staff, sometimes including President Michael Little. More than 90 percent of incoming calls come into the centers while *The 700 Club* is being aired. CBN charts the rate of call-ins by location and minute-by-minute; the marketing department can immediately detect which television markets are most responsive and which segments on the program prompted the greatest response. The sophisticated charting of responses allows producers to "choose features that stimulate positive phone/ministry/pledge activity."[78]

Counseling centers are critical elements in all of the international efforts of CBN. The thirteen regional centers supported by CBN overseas are staffed with counselors trained by Joel Palser. The internationalization of CBN has linked together a language network that allows staffs around the world to respond immediately to calls. Spanish-speaking callers in North America are expeditiously routed to trained counselors in Costa Rica, and counselors in the United States speak a variety of languages.

The Christian Broadcasting Network at Fifty

The management of the vast Christian Broadcasting Network empire remained remarkably stable in the two decades after Pat Robertson's return as president and chief operating officer in 1989. The administrative core changed little until 2007, when Pat Robertson resigned as CEO, turning that title over to his son Gordon. An inner circle of trusted vice-presidents, most of them longtime executives in the ministry, provided day-to-day leadership and continuity. Ever present was the symbolic and real presence of Pat Robertson, the glue that held CBN and its auxiliary spin-off organizations together. His leadership was often remote and unobtrusive, but he did not hesitate to become more directly involved when he deemed it necessary.

The financial rebuilding of CBN was a slow but steady uphill slog in the two decades after the difficult downsizing that began in 1987. Following a successful year in 1991, the local press announced that the level of support at CBN had nearly risen to the "golden day level" where it had been before the televangelism scandals. But the overall income of CBN continued to grow very slowly in the 1990s and still lagged well behind its income during the peak years in the mid-1980s. CBN's income declined significantly in 2001 in the wake of the stock market crash of 2000, as did the incomes of other religious ministries, once again necessitating a retrenchment in spending. A pronounced escalation in contributions began in 2003. In 2002, CBN's income from contributions was $90.9 million; it jumped to $106.5 million in 2003 and $113.5 million in 2004. In 2005 contributions rose sharply to $147 million and by 2007 reached $151.3 million. Partly, the spike in contributions in 2005 and 2006 was triggered by donations of more than $9 million for relief of tsunami victims and in excess of $23 million for Hurricane Katrina relief. Taking out one-time gifts, giving income remained relatively level. However, the jump in 2007 represented a significant real increase in contributions.[79]

The continued growth of CBN, particularly the continuing health of its donor base, was clearly related to the growing sophistication of telethon technology and the expertise of the marketing department. But leaders at CBN, including Pat Robertson, uniformly gave a major share of credit for the growth to Gordon Robertson. When he returned to Virginia Beach, many veterans thought they would "never return to the peaks of '85." "I took it as a personal mission when I became an executive producer that we are going to exceed them," Gordon recalled. By 2007, CBN had reached the financial plateau of the 1980s, though it was arguably still short of that goal when contributions were adjusted for inflation.[80]

Telethons have long been the financial backbone of the entire CBN ministry. When Gordon became executive producer at CBN in 2001 he "reimagined" the telethons, making CBN's worldwide evangelistic program, WorldReach, the "prime focus" of the ministry's fundraising. The key to CBN's recent success, Gordon believed, was that "we have built our ability to tell the WorldReach story." He introduced into the telethon format a stream of reports from all over the world telling of miracles and other life-changing experiences. These vignettes were often moving stories about the work of CBN around the world and proved to be powerful stimuli in gathering pledges. "The whole idea is to help people see the vision," observed John Turver. "Hopefully, it makes them feel really good" to be a part of something that is "totally global." Beginning in January 2002, the revamped telethon format resulted in steady increases in revenues for CBN, a trend that has continued to the present.[81]

Beyond the initial response of counseling center personnel, CBN has a vast and sophisticated system for tracking its partners and keeping them informed. In 2008 CBN had "the highest donor base" in its history. In addition to the telephone and mail contacts with donors, the ministry gives away millions of slickly produced compact discs and inspirational literature. Partners are invited to seminars in Virginia Beach, and larger donors have been invited to join Pat and Dede Robertson on tours abroad.[82]

The Robertsons' youngest daughter, Anne LeBlanc, heads a special division that works with donors who are members of the "Thousand Club" and over. Leblanc supervises a group of fifty field representatives who "minister to our partners in homes." Pat Robertson considers LeBlanc's special division CBN's "secret weapon." The field representatives cultivate personal relationships with big donors and regularly share with them the "full story" of CBN's work, including its rarely mentioned and somewhat clandestine television outreaches to Muslims. The ministry's "top secret missions" have proven to be immensely popular among major donors. The personable Leblanc knows every partner by name, her mother observed, and "she mothers every one of them."[83]

In its first fifty years, CBN became an expansive and diverse empire that broke new ground in areas ranging from building a network to counseling individual callers. But Pat Robertson's restless imagination would not let him be content with television. In addition to his forays into politics, Robertson has guided the formation of a number of major organizations with formal or informal ties of varying strength to the Christian Broadcasting Network. Before he was finished, Robertson would found an international evangelism program, an independent humanitarian aid program, a university, and a center for legal advocacy. Together these institutions go beyond Robertson's television persona to paint a remarkable picture of the range of his interests and impact.

CHAPTER 7

New Frontiers: WorldReach
and Operation Blessing

—*ᴐ៸៸ᴐ⊨*—

Pat Robertson's spiritual vision of the role of the Christian Broadcasting Network grew in stages throughout his life, but from the earliest years he embraced the idea that the organization would have a significant evangelistic and humanitarian outreach. Evangelism and humanitarianism have served CBN as fundraising platforms, of course, but WorldReach and Operation Blessing have been deeply embedded in the fabric of the organization, and they worked seamlessly with the ministry's television production capabilities and direct response call centers. In the inner halls of Pat Robertson's empire, these programs have been regarded as the frontline troops, honored and prayed for by a support system that provided funds and expertise.

WorldReach and the Evangelistic Learning Curve

Pat Robertson first publicly expressed the idea that CBN would play a critical role in the evangelization of the world in 1968, when the financial stability of the television ministry had been more or less assured. While praying privately that God would supply the funds to pay for a building extension in that year, he later recalled, "The Lord Himself entered in and said I don't want you to pray for the money. I want you to pray for the world. . . . It was like open heart surgery." Through the years, that mission was reaffirmed repeatedly by Robertson and others associated with CBN. "Pat, ten years ago was saying the same things he is today," the ministry newsletter reminded its readers in 1986: "Our mission at CBN is that of John the Baptist, to prepare the way." In 1976 Robertson told a local reporter: "I hope this will be a center for the gospel of the Lord Jesus Christ, not only for the United States, but for the whole world." "God has a plan for the present world," Robertson wrote in a message to his supporters in 1978; its first requirement was "the evangelization of the world with the gospel of His Kingdom." In the minds of the core leaders at CBN, evangelism is "who we are now." Pat is a "Renaissance man," observed veteran employee Jay Comisky, but the layer of leadership beneath him at CBN, including CEO Gordon Robertson and President Michael Little, exhibit a "single focus on evangelism." In the minds of many ministry insiders, CBN's international evangelistic outreach, named WorldReach in 1995, has been "the best untold story in Christendom."[1]

Because of his extensive travels and personal friendship with a broad array of religious leaders, Pat Robertson was probably as conscious of the progress of the Christian revival that swept the world in the years after World War II as anyone alive. Over and over he touted the booming Christian revival in the developing world. Invited to be one of the featured speakers at Billy Graham's International Conference for Itinerant Evangelists in Amsterdam in 1983, Robertson predicted that "God is getting ready to send the greatest harvest of souls that the Church of Jesus Christ has ever known." More directly, Robertson was intimately acquainted with the booming Pentecostal/charismatic revival that changed the religious demography of the developing world in the last half of the twentieth century. Speaking to the Maranatha World Leadership Conference in 1984, Robertson rejoiced that an "unprecedented outpouring of the Holy Spirit of God" was sweeping the world. He predicted that the time was near when "we'll be given the power and the gifts of the Spirit as never before." In 1995, Robertson told a large charismatic audience in an Orlando conference, "I believe . . . that God is getting ready to send on the earth the greatest manifestation of His Holy Spirit power that has ever taken place in the history of mankind from the day of Pentecost until now. . . . We will see hundreds of millions of people come into the Kingdom of God in the next four or five years."[2]

Like other charismatic leaders in the late twentieth century, Robertson was chagrined that for years this huge worldwide revival went almost unnoticed by most Americans, including mainstream religious leaders and most scholars. There was substance to his conclusion. In an article entitled "Thinking Globally about Christianity" published in 2003, Harvard theologian Harvey Cox expressed dismay at the reaction of many of the mainstream leaders he interviewed while researching the worldwide charismatic revival: "I found that these leaders viewed the rise of Pentecostalism with a mix of bewilderment, fear, and condescension." A 1994 book entitled *Christian Missions in the Twentieth Century* made only passing reference to "Pentecostalism" and contained no notice of the massive revivals transforming the developing world. Although academics had begun to study the worldwide revival by the end of the twentieth century, and the press gave some attention to it, Robertson complained that the worldwide Pentecostal/charismatic revival was "still largely unreported."[3]

A Renewed Commitment

Pat Robertson returned to CBN in 1989 after his presidential run with a renewed commitment to international evangelism. Since the CBN board had voted in 1973 to contribute a tenth of the ministry's gross income to other ministries, the organization had distributed millions of dollars to traditional charities and hundreds of churches and evangelistic ministries. Robertson announced in 1989 that CBN was preparing to "harvest millions of souls in the 90's." Up to that point, through its international television programs, CBN had "recorded 1,500,000 decisions for Christ," all of whom had "been referred to local churches."[4]

CBN's evangelistic outreach during its early years was extensive but neither well-defined nor focused. During this early period, recalled CBN President Michael Little, allocations of evangelistic and humanitarian gifts followed "few rules, few quotas"; the only "priority would be on the inspiration of the Holy Spirit." In 1994, Barbara Johnson, Robertson's administrative assistant, sketched for a supporter the expanse of CBN's evangelistic and humanitarian contributions: "Over the years CBN has given financial assistance to hundreds of Christian organizations, missions, and ministries. For the most part, these have been one-time contributions to assist them in their outreach. . . . We do not support any ministries on a monthly basis. We believe it is best for them to have their own support base. . . . These missions requests range from familiar ministries that are well known through the world" to others "across America with outreaches to abandoned children, unwed mothers, youth in crisis, prison outreaches, food pantries, etc." Continuing to head the list of those who received substantial contributions from CBN were Pat Robertson's trusted favorites, including independent evangelists and television personalities Reinhard Bonnke, Oral Roberts, Marilyn Hickey, and D. G. S. Dhinakaran. But the list of recipients was strikingly ecumenical and diverse, and the amounts disbursed were sometimes startling. In 1998, following the sale of the Family Channel, the CBN board made the stunning decision to spend down the proceeds from the sale of CBN-owned stock amounting to $136.1 million, rather than to establish an endowment. Most of those funds were targeted for evangelism. In 1998 alone CBN wrote checks for more than $14 million to other ministries; several received unexpected gifts of a million dollars. The checks uniformly included the postscript: "We would appreciate it if you would not use CBN's name in publicizing this gift." CBN continues to make large contributions to favored ministries, as does Pat Robertson with his private funds, but beginning in 1989 a new internal strategy brought sharper focus to the organization's evangelistic vision.[5]

The Blitz Strategy

Since the 1970s CBN International had been an internal department; its responsibility was mostly "customizing and distributing the International 700 Club," a version adapted to foreign audiences and dubbed in Spanish and Mandarin. International airing of *The 700 Club* began in the Philippines in 1977, and by the end of the 1980s the international version of the program and some other ministry productions were aired in 35 countries. CBN International entered a new phase in late 1989 when it launched a "blitz" media campaign in three Central American countries — Guatemala, El Salvador, and Nicaragua — using a strategy that would be repeated in subsequent years. Pat Robertson was elated by the response to the first blitz, called "Projecto Luz"; some insiders believed that it stirred in him the "missionary heart" that had been muted during the political campaign. The project set a goal of "two million decisions for Christ" and at its conclusion reported that "the response of the churches was overwhelming."[6]

The "blitz" concept was based on the "four-wall-marketing" strategy used by Hollywood movie producers to introduce new films. The strategy was to monopolize the media in a targeted market to blanket it with one's message. "Using a powerful combination of television, radio, newspaper and billboard advertisements," explained CBN president Michael Little, "CBN focuses the attention of millions of people on a series of television prime-time specials." These "evangelistic specials" were aired on as many television stations as possible for a period of seven to ten days, "road blocking" as much competitive programming as possible in order to capture the entire television audience. The blitz concept also focused CBN's

International Section on "the distribution of more culturally relevant indigenous language programming," a technique that ultimately became the trademark of the WorldReach program.[7]

The Central American blitz was followed by a series of large and small campaigns around the world. Each blitz was a response to developing opportunities, and each had unique characteristics. A second blitz in Argentina was stalled when television outlets refused to cooperate. On the other hand, in 1991 and 1992 CBN International reacted swiftly to the opening of the Soviet Union, airing its animated *Superbook Party* for two weeks, followed by a specially produced program for teenagers and young adults and an adult special entitled *Road to Everlasting Love.* The third special explored "such hard-hitting issues as alcoholism, abortion and adultery." The target set for the Russian blitz was to reach 55 million viewers and to record 20 million "decisions for Christ." President Michael Little viewed the Russian blitz as a providential moment in the ministry's history. In the first week CBN received more than a million letters, and by the time the mail began to subside several years later, "we had received 13 million letters." CBN established a "ministry center" with 400 employees in Kiev to respond to the deluge of mail. Center director Steve Weber recalled days when truckloads of letters would be dumped at their offices. The Kiev center continued airing a dubbed version of *The 700 Club* and became a "real data base" documenting the mushrooming Christian curiosity in Russia and other areas of the former Soviet Union. The Kiev center evolved into one of the most important outposts in the mature WorldReach program.[8]

Buoyed by the Russian experience, Robertson was determined to exploit the blitz strategy elsewhere. "The doors are opening and we will go where there is interest," he told a reporter in early 1993. In 1994 the ministry sponsored a huge blitz in the Philippines that was inaugurated with a concert featuring "the most popular Filipino entertainers." The blitz also featured an Operation Blessing medical clinic with a team of more than 100 doctors, dentists, and nurses, and a vast campaign on "radio, TV, newspapers, billboards and door-to-door canvassing to attract national attention to its three evangelistic programs specifically geared to reach children, teenagers and adults." Elaborate preparations attempted to tie the blitz to local churches, with limited success. Nonetheless, hopes ran high at the CBN office in the Philippines: "We are believing that through our special and house visits, we will see 20 million souls won for Christ!"[9]

Other blitzes followed on a regular basis in the late 1990s. A 1997 blitz in Nigeria "reached 70 percent of the nation's 100 million residents," and a huge campaign in India in 1998 featured a rally in Hyderabad in which Pat Robertson spoke to an audience of 350,000 in partnership with Indian evangelist D. G. S. Dhinakaran. The India blitz included a major medical mission sponsored by Operation Blessing that included a 175-member medical team treating 22,484 patients. During the Indian blitz CBN produced "five new CBN original productions in six languages" that were viewed by as many as 100 million people. Pat Robertson returned home from his Indian crusade filled with enthusiasm; for him, it had been "unbelievably profitable." In the euphoric aftermath of the Indian blitz, he wrote in a memo to the CBN staff: "I would say that the crusade was the greatest I have ever experienced in my life."[10]

Despite the variations by country, by the mid-1990s the blitz technique was more or less standardized. A country, or network of countries, was inundated with prime-time programming for eight to ten days. The programs featured specials that focused on such "global issues" as "family relationships, alcoholism, spousal abuse, AIDS." All of the programs included teaching that gave an "opportunity to learn about the Gospel." Most of the programs were produced "on-location in the blitz country by the production team of CBN International." "Pat really pushed the idea of doing more in-country," recalled Director of Operations Kim Mitchell.[11]

The blitz campaigns were intended to be only the first step. But it proved difficult to devise a follow-up procedure that would "demonstrate the power of Christ and the presence of the Holy Spirit." The intent of the blitzes was to create "cells" where new converts would establish a "vital relationship with Jesus and other believers," but the blitz teams learned by experience the complexity of working in different cultures.[12]

By the 1990s the international blitzes and the growing activities of Operation Blessing overseas were mainstays in justifying the ministry to CBN partners. But the blitzes did not simply supply the most important fundraising rationale for the ministry; they also refocused the ministry itself. The campaigns were expensive, but Robertson and other CBN leaders were genuinely intrigued by the ministry's evangelistic accomplishments. "It takes a bold heart to do what CBN does around the world," observed CBN Indonesia director Mark McClendon, whose center in Jakarta received more than five million dollars to build an impressive production center. "There is nothing in it for them," he marveled. "The only thing that was in it for them was just the people."[13]

CBN struggled to measure the effectiveness of the massive media blitzes, and there was some internal disagreement about the lasting impact of the blitzes. Insiders grappled with how to measure the results. "Salvations" are hard to measure, as Gordon Robertson noted. After a 1998 "hallway meeting" with Pat Robertson in which Robertson raised questions about the "accuracy" of blitz reports, CBN International Director of Operations Kim Mitchell informed him that "for all projects we hire professional, independent market survey companies to project results over the coverage area using generally accepted scientific sampling methodology." "Projected salvation results" were based on "a scientific sample of the questionnaires gathered from TV households." Preparation was the key to follow-up, Mitchell believed. In the 1997 Nigerian blitz, extensive precampaign preparations included soliciting the support and backing of churches and other religious organizations. In the aftermath, the organizers felt that they had received outstanding cooperation both before and after the blitz. Mitchell was particularly impressed by the thorough follow-up reviews of blitzes in Nigeria and Benin, but acknowledged in later years that the effectiveness of campaigns varied widely from country to country. Gordon Robertson believed that the blitzes had powerful, lasting influences in Latin America and the Ukraine, but in other places the results seemed superficial.[14]

Gordon Robertson reached the Philippines at the close of the huge blitz in that country in 1995, and his first assignment from CBN was to track the results of the campaign. He was disappointed by the lack of coordination and cooperation with churches following the blitz. Gordon concluded that the blitz strategy had limited impact unless there was a continuing CBN presence to sustain the interest. The conviction grew among CBN administrators that, in the words of Ron Oates, media blitzes were "a limited success" because "we were not staying the course."[15]

CBN Centers

Prior to the mid-1990s, CBN's presence abroad depended on a large network of "centers" that were funded beginning in the 1970s. A few of the centers were offices staffed by paid employees, but a majority were no more than loose affiliations with existing ministries and churches. The centers received irregular contributions in return for coordinating CBN activities. By the end of the 1980s CBN listed an extensive network of centers in more than 60 countries.[16]

After the inauguration of the blitz strategy in 1989, these international centers were viewed as critical links in follow-up operations. A 1998 report pointed out that this informal network was inadequate to follow up on the blitzes: "Responses to our media blitzes and relief initiatives have over-whelmed national leaders," and "many times the harvest has not been gleaned nor the fruit maintained." CBN International crafted a guide to give detailed follow-up instructions to its representatives at the centers. They should attempt to establish "a cooperative ministry venture with existing 'ground troops' (missionaries, national leaders) in the field. CBN will equip the leaders of each center with training material, video duplicating equipment, literature and seed money.... The partnering organization/lay leader provides the facility (office, apartment, home, etc.) and lay personnel to be trained. In sum, CBN provides the capital to formalize and launch the center partnering with national leadership to sustain the miracle of massive scale harvest events like the Gospel Media Blitz." Still, establishing centers remained a work in progress. In 1998, after the influx of money from the sale of The Family Channel, CBN had 97 centers in 59 countries and another 144 had been funded, bringing the total to 241. Kim Mitchell projected further additions that would bring the number to 300.[17]

Although CBN's international outreach took somewhat different directions in the late 1990s, the ministry still maintains nearly 200 centers throughout the world, even though leaders in Virginia Beach agreed that the strategy was not universally productive. In India, for instance, supporting well-established Christian ministries as CBN's "representatives" cost "huge amounts of money" but proved to be so flawed that all of the original centers were closed and replaced by others more directly identified with CBN. In other areas, especially Latin America and Africa, where the concept of affiliated centers was older, many of the outposts offered valuable voluntary assistance that expanded the reach of CBN's evangelistic and humanitarian work. In Nigeria, four remote centers in relatively inaccessible regions of the country were staffed by two salaried workers who made weekly visits into villages, equipped with projectors, to show the native-language programs produced at the regional center in Abuja. In the process, they explored the remotest villages in the nation, identifying locations where humanitarian relief was needed and aiding in the establishment of new churches.[18]

By the end of the 1990s, CBN's evangelistic program had become more structured and focused. After his return from India in November 1994, Pat Robertson announced to the CBN staff his "vision for WorldReach." In 1995, CBN International was formally renamed WorldReach during a large "RevivalFest" tent meeting on the CBN campus. Introduced by a televised message from Billy Graham, the tent revival attracted crowds from a variety of denominations and featured some of the legendary Pentecostal/

charismatic preachers of the post–World War II era. Oral Roberts launched the meeting on Monday evening; he was followed by T. L. Osborn, Benny Hinn, T. D. Jakes, and James Robinson. Among the other speakers were well-known evangelical figures Robert Schuller and Bill Bright. During the week's healing services, witnesses reported scores of miracles. In a characteristic symbolic act, an "Eternal Gospel Flame Lighting Ceremony" closed the meeting. An eternal flame was ignited at the CBN entrance, transported by a torch lit at the Cape Henry site where Robert Hunt, "a minister and ancestor of Pat Robertson," had "declared that the light of the Gospel would go forth from these shores to not only the New World but the entire world." RevivalFest was an "internal spiritual event, exhilarating to the staff and core supporters." In the charged atmosphere of the revival, Pat Robertson formally gave the WorldReach department a charge to bring "500 million souls to Jesus Christ by the new millennium."[19]

Operationally, WorldReach evolved in significant ways after 1995, crystallizing an innovative strategy that gave a unique character to CBN's international work and influence. Pat Robertson's international outlook had always been culturally aware, the product of a lifetime of exposure to national leaders around the world. But the vision of creating and supporting a worldwide network of media production centers staffed by skilled indigenous professionals owed much to his son Gordon. Gordon Robertson's deep commitment to building an indigenous, non-colonial worldwide network of "regional centers" that resembled CBN, complete with television production capabilities, humanitarian programs, and twenty-four-hour call-in response centers, transformed the way CBN worked outside the United States.

Gordon Robertson and the Shaping of WorldReach

Partly, the new WorldReach focus at the end of the 1990s simply sharpened CBN's aim to produce culturally relevant programming. During the trip to India that resulted in his own personal religious awakening, Gordon was overwhelmed by the deeply engrained, profoundly Hindu culture surrounding him. He experienced a particularly poignant moment of illumination while witnessing a Hindu holy man performing extraordinary physical feats during a broadcast on Indian television. Somehow, he thought, American Christians must find a relevant way to communicate in a culture so profoundly different. While the concept of broadcasting Christian programming in indigenous languages was not new at CBN, and Gordon was well aware of the cultural sensitivity of his father, he began to focus single-mindedly on the idea after settling in Manila, launching almost immediately a Philippine version of *The 700 Club*. He became increasingly convinced that Asians needed to produce their own programs, in their own way. "A key part of our history," observed career employee Ben Edwards, "is Gordon going to the Philippines. . . . Our strategy began to come together at that time." Gordon's desire to produce "recurring programming in the indigenous languages" became the mantra of WorldReach.[20]

Gordon's cultural sensitivity had many sources, but he often credited his reading of, and admiration for, T. L. Osborn of Tulsa, Oklahoma, one of the lesser-known giants of the post–World War II Pentecostal revival. Osborn was a part of a loose collection of independent healing ministers who had large followings in the United States in the 1950s and around the world in subsequent decades. These men ignited the worldwide Pentecostal revival and introduced a new epoch of missions because they respected indigenous cultures and had no colonial interest in controlling those responding to their message. Their huge independent ministries had no denominational loyalties, and they openly encouraged and aided the establishment of indigenous churches. The most responsible of the Pentecostal evangelists, including Osborn and Oral Roberts, labored to bring divine healing and the power of the Holy Spirit to the lost, but they also trained a generation of evangelists in the developing world to follow their example. Gordon Robertson devoured Osborn's writings and was profoundly influenced by the evangelist's cultural sensitivity and evangelistic fervor. During his transformative search for meaning in India and the Philippines, he listened for hours to tapes of Osborn. More than anything else, Gordon confessed, Osborn's message of training those in other cultures to craft their own indigenous revival of the Holy Spirit was "what turned me from being a lawyer."[21]

The question at CBN in the 1990s was whether it was possible to transfer the CBN model to other countries and other cultures. From its beginnings, CBN had been a self-conscious part of the post–World War II Pentecostal/charismatic revival, and Pat Robertson was one of its foremost celebrities. *The 700 Club* was the most sophisticated and technologically advanced expression of the central motif of the revival — the testimonial presentation of the miraculous working of God through the Holy Spirit. In the tens of thousands of tent meetings, conferences, and television broadcasts sponsored by these independent organizations, the ideological cutting edge of the revival was personal testimonials given by those who had been saved and healed by the power of the Holy Spirit. *The 700 Club* and

CBN instinctively and intentionally embraced testimonies, learning through the years to tell such stories effectively.

CBN's embrace of the concept of training indigenous workers to duplicate their media expertise in diverse cultural contexts was a bold and expensive step, but it was a logical one. As Osborn and other American healing revivalists laid hands on thousands of talented evangelists in Asia, Africa, and Latin America in the 1950s and 1960s, telling them that they could go and do mighty works on their own, at the end of the twentieth century WorldReach embraced the idea that indigenous Christians around the world could be trained to produce inspirational testimonial programming appropriate for their culture.

The WorldReach effort to recreate CBN abroad focused on television production, but it embraced far more. Gordon Robertson summed up the issue: "How can we transfer what we know about testimony . . . and a follow up mechanism. . . ? We want a transfer of ideas." During his years in Manila, Gordon set out to recreate the entire CBN ministry package in the Philippines. In quick succession beginning in 1995, using his legal expertise, Gordon secured tax-exempt charters for the Asian Center for Missions, CBN Asia, and Operation Blessing Asia. The CBN Asia Center in Manila came to include television production capabilities, a twenty-four-hour counseling center, and an active humanitarian operation, furnishing a model for future CBN regional centers. When some CBN ministry leaders in Virginia Beach protested that such a project would be prohibitively expensive, Gordon insisted that the vision of self-sufficient, indigenous CBN replicas abroad was financially feasible, and that the international centers would be CBN's logical contribution to worldwide revival.[22]

Regional Centers

WorldReach, observed CBN president Michael Little, made "quantum leaps" beginning in 1998 when the ministry diverted $24 million from the sale of The Family Channel to missions, most of it going to WorldReach. New regional centers in Kiev, Jakarta, and Hyderabad were the major original beneficiaries. By 1999 ground had been broken for the construction of television studios and ministry facilities at those three sites. In each of the pioneering centers, CBN worked with American directors with years of experience abroad.[23]

The Kiev regional center evolved out of the massive mail response following the blitz in the Soviet Union. The response center was organized by

Steve Weber, an experienced missionary in Russia and acquaintance of CBN president Michael Little. Accommodating hundreds of people in its mail-response center, the two-story studio and outreach facility constructed in Kiev was equipped with state-of-the-art television production and telephone equipment. By 2009 CBN's CIS (Commonwealth of Independent States) Regional Center was a beehive of activity, with branch offices in Moscow and in Almaty, Kazakhstan. The center's television studio produced indigenous programs viewed on more than 100 television stations. The center also maintained two facilities to respond to calls from eleven time zones. It directed a humanitarian operation that included a free medical clinic in Kiev and a number of other programs, including a Christian FM radio station and a concert department that staged performances in churches and halls throughout Ukraine.[24]

In Indonesia, Mark McClendon was an experienced missionary and television producer before joining CBN as a WorldReach director. McClendon joined CBN just as the major expansion of WorldReach began. In the wake of the political unrest in Indonesia following the removal of President Suharto in 1998, McClendon approached Gordon Robertson, who had just become director of WorldReach Asia, proposing the establishment of a CBN presence in Indonesia. Within a week, Gordon arrived in Jakarta with a party of CBN administrators, and within a few months a newly formed CBN Indonesia had been given a grant of $2 million to build a facility in Jakarta. Before it was finished in 2002, the completed complex in Jakarta cost $5.2 million; nearly a million dollars was raised in Indonesia after a visit by Pat Robertson. McClendon was the son of the former head of the innovative Communication Arts Department at Oral Roberts University, and the CBN Indonesia campus included a replica of the Prayer Tower constructed by Oral Roberts in Tulsa. By 2009, the facility located in East Jakarta employed around 300 people engaged in television production and viewer follow-up, along with a large contingent of humanitarian relief workers employed by Operation Blessing. McClendon marveled at the freedom he was given to develop the Jakarta center as a uniquely Indonesian enterprise simply because Gordon "was so confident that God would speak to me."[25]

The third of the new regional centers constructed with Family Channel money in the late 1990s was in Hyderabad, India. The Hyderabad facility produced programs in two South Indian languages, Telugu and Tamil, and housed a large Operation Blessing International humanitarian program. By 2005, a second center in New Delhi employed more than sixty people to produce Hindi-language programming and housed a call center servicing northern India. By 2007 the Hyderabad regional center employed around 150 people in its humanitarian, production, and counseling activities, and a small counseling center serving Tamil-language callers had been established in Chennai.[26]

By 2000, eleven of the 205 WorldReach centers had been designated "Regional Headquarters" or "Regional Centers," and by 2009, the number had grown to nineteen. Step by step, CBN organizations were legally chartered around the world. In Nigeria, for instance, where highly respected minister Ina Omakwu was the director of operations, *The 700 Club* was first aired in 1993 and a media blitz was conducted in 1997, but CBN Africa was not chartered until 2003. By 2008, Felix Oisamoje, who succeeded Omakwu as director, had drafted plans for a five-story CBN office and production facility which he hoped would be constructed in Abuja. The Abuja center was the West African English-language outpost for CBN; smaller regional centers in Africa were located in Johannesburg, South Africa, and in Benin, where French-language programming was produced.[27]

In addition to the large regional centers in Manila and Jakarta, WorldReach supported other Asian regional centers in Beijing and Hong Kong, as well as in Cambodia, Laos, and Thailand. All of the regional centers had some television production capability, and in some places the program production was extensive; CBN Siam, for instance, employed more than fifty people at its headquarters in Chiangmai to support television production, a call center, and an active humanitarian program. In addition to Kiev in Europe, WorldReach maintained a small regional center in Hereford, England, to oversee the distribution of programming throughout the continent and oversee call centers in France, Germany, Italy, Netherlands, Albania, Romania, and Hungary. In North America, a large regional center was maintained in Costa Rica, where CBN had been present for thirty-five years, as well as in Ontario, Canada. The Latin American regional center supervised forty Spanish-language counseling centers in Latin America that serviced callers from all over the region, as well as Spanish-speaking callers in the United States. "The empowerment of the WorldReach Centers to go do it," observed CBN veteran Jay Comisky, stirred a cauldron of activity around the world: "There is so much going on that nobody can keep up with it."[28]

"A Phone Number for Jesus"

Cumulatively, by 2009 CBN had aired television programs in eighty-nine languages reaching more than 230 countries and territories. CBN produces thirty-one different programs for distribution outside the United States, including an international version of *The 700 Club* that is aired in many countries with subtitles. In keeping with the WorldReach vision, the regional centers produce a variety of indigenous versions of *The 700 Club*, each using a culturally adjusted magazine format. In 2009, such programs were being produced and aired in Spanish, Tagalog, German, Thai, Portuguese, Italian, Hindi, Cantonese, French, Telugu, Bahasa Indonesia, Javanese, and Sudanese Arabic. English-language versions of *The 700 Club* were produced for airing in Canada and Africa. The African version, *Turning Point*, targeted both English-speaking audiences in Africa and also the large African diaspora in Europe. That program was produced in Nashville at CBN's NorthStar Studios and was hosted by British-born Nigerian Victor Oladokun and American co-host Kathy Edwards.[29]

Many of the native-language programs produced by CBN have large audiences. The Spanish-language *700 Club Hoy*, produced in Costa Rica and co-hosted by Osvaldo Carnival and Veronica Marcias, reaches a large Spanish-speaking audience in North America and in fifteen Latin American countries. *The 700 Club Asia*, produced in Manila in Tagalog, is hosted by Gordon Robertson's protégé, Peter Kairuz. It closely resembles the American version, opening with a news segment before turning to interviews and testimonials. Many of the programs are targeted in specific ways to local and regional audiences. The popular *Solsui Life*, produced in Jakarta, has been a remarkable broadcasting success in Indonesia. According to the producer, the program aimed to be "positive and inspiring without preaching," targeting "young urbanites who live in a secular culture." The magazine format program is hosted by "young and energetic" actor Choky Sitohang and Miss Indonesia 2005 Imelda Francisca. The program highlights "such topics as financial success and healthy relationships as well as featuring life-changing testimonies." The Hindi version of *The 700 Club, Ek Nayee Zindagi* ("A New Life"), produced in New Delhi, has deliberately made the program "younger" to reach the half of India's booming population under age 25.[30]

In spite of their cultural diversity, all of the magazine-format programs produced and distributed by the regional centers remain focused on testimonies. "We're on the hunt for testimonies constantly," observed Steve Weber in Kiev. The regional centers sometimes use testimonies from neighboring nations, but generally testimonies are most relevant when based in a familiar cultural milieu. In New Delhi, producer Priti Choudary sometimes adapts an "Asian testimony" for the Hindi version of *The 700 Club*, but an Indian audience is not likely to respond positively to a "WASP testimonial."[31]

CBN's overseas television productions of *700 Club*-style programs have been supplemented by indigenous versions of the popular *One Cubed* musical program aimed at younger audiences. In 2009 WorldReach produced and aired musical programs in twelve languages. Another dozen native-language programs produced in WorldReach centers have been story-based productions designed for specific cultures.

The other major WorldReach broadcasting strategy abroad has been the airing of the growing library of children's animation programs produced by CBN. These feature presentations of Bible stories often provided entry into foreign television markets that were not open to overtly Christian broadcasting. The popular *Superbook,* produced in 1981 and aired first in Japan, had by 2009 been dubbed in thirty languages and viewed by hundreds of millions of people around the world. When the first showing of *Superbook* was aired in China in 2001, an elated Gordon Robertson sent an email to his father's private secretary: "Please let my father know that the breakthrough has started." In Russia, the animation programs proved to be enormously popular — and the source of a flood of testimonies. An eight-year-old wrote in 2005, "I learned to love Jesus due to the *SuperBook Club,*" and added a request: "Do you happen to know a phone number for Jesus?" By 2007 WorldReach had aired CBN Animation Division products in 60 languages reaching audiences in around 200 nations. In 2009 CBN began a two-year, $6 million project to update its animated series using the latest technology.[32]

Different Regions, Different Models

Production professionals from Virginia Beach have provided training for WorldReach personnel all over the world, but many were already trained experts. Even in Beijing, where CBN has not been allowed to produce television programs, the private company of indigenous professionals who film episodes for WorldReach and Operation Blessing are "all Christians trained by CBN" equipped with "cutting-edge high-definition cameras." Priti Choudary, production manager of the CBN studio in New Delhi, was a television veteran when she joined CBN, having worked for CNN and the BBC. She was impressed by the "commitment to professionalism" at CBN and, as a Christian, was overjoyed that "God can use me without compromises." While CBN trained the staffs in the foreign centers, observed Michael Little, they also "teach us."[33]

In the 1990s WorldReach managers drafted a complex "flow chart" for the regional centers that made clear the profoundly evangelistic, and Pentecostal, aims of the ministry. After the "harvest" of responders during mass rallies and CBN's "global media blitzes," those who answered altar calls were to be sorted into "productive believers" and "insincere seekers." Those judged to be "sincere believers" were to be invited to a "Pentecost Rally" where they could experience a "Holy Spirit encounter." That step was followed by sessions in "Pentecost Training" that would equip the respondents for "spiritual warfare." Promising leaders were then to be given further training that would aid them in "building a congregation."[34]

A rigid model for evangelizing never fit the WorldReach model well, however, and the regional centers are as different in evangelistic approaches as the indigenous television programs are unique. But each of the centers, in its own culturally adjusted way, has been profoundly missionary. At one end of the spectrum, such as in China, the evangelistic message has been disguised or muted; at the other end, as in the Ukraine, Africa, and Latin America, WorldReach has worked hand-in-hand with churches.

Even in China, where overt evangelistic activities are illegal and CBN China was chartered solely as a humanitarian organization, evangelistic undertones permeate the Beijing center. CBN China can neither produce nor distribute religious programming, but the large and active humanitarian staff is made up of committed Christians; it is, noted the center's director, "very natural for them to share their faith" while carrying out their humanitarian missions. CBN China has often established humanitarian linkages with churches (mostly the legal Three-Self Churches), and its staff believes it is their mission to "train the church." CBN has informally funded a Chinese production company made up of Christians, training the personnel and using the company to produce testimonial segments for the American *700 Club*. It also supported the production of three programs that were not "overtly evangelistic" to be aired in the Chinese heartland. While Christian programming opportunities in mainland China remain limited, the WorldReach center in Hong Kong produces *The Hong Kong 700 Club*, which can be viewed in Hong Kong, Macau, and Guangdong, reaching a huge Cantonese-speaking audience.[35]

The Indonesian regional center has used a remarkably creative approach to Christian evangelism in a Muslim country. Director McClendon believes that the ultimate WorldReach mission in Indonesia has been the "transformation of the nation." Keenly conscious that the "core of CBN is media," McClendon believes that ten years of indigenous programming in Indonesia has had a "collective impact" on the "soul of the nation." The Jakarta center has "tried to include a local church in everything we do," particularly in its humanitarian work, but its programming has been intentionally non-confrontational. McClendon is well acquainted with the Christian missionaries in Indonesia, and often cooperates with them, but the mission of the substantial media presence of CBN Indonesia has been less overtly evangelistic: "We are the air force. . . . We are softening them up. . . . You have to be patient." While CBN Indonesia is not "totally free" in its broadcasting, noted WorldReach president Ben Edwards, McClendon's approach has won great "favor in getting programs on."[36]

Other Asian centers in predominately non-Christian settings have worked out evangelistic strategies appropriate to their culture. In Thailand, where the audience is primarily Buddhist and Muslim, the indigenously produced *700 Club* at first depended almost entirely on testimonials, but recently felt free to become more overtly Christian. "We pray on our program," reported host Niran Pattaranukool, and "Christians and non-Christians respond to us." In India, where no formal restraints have been placed on Christian broadcasting, the Christian message, particularly in the heavily Hindu north, has been presented through the exploration of "problems that people are troubled with and that are relevant to them."[37]

By far the most openly evangelistic WorldReach outpost in Asia has been the Manila regional center. The long and unique development of CBN in the Philippines has created a "CBN Asia Family of Ministries" that not only links it quite directly with churches and missionary organizations in the Philippines but reaches into other Asian nations as well. Aided by a very strong Operation Blessing ally, CBN Asia has built strong ties with both Protestants and Catholics. The Filipino version of *The 700 Club* is strongly charismatic, featuring CBN Asia president Peter Kairuz exercising the "word of knowledge." The call center receives thousands of calls and text messages from viewers giving "testimonies that they were healed instantly."[38]

In Africa, Europe, and Latin America, the regional centers have been openly and aggressively evangelistic. Churches were closely integrated into CBN's Nigerian blitz in 1997. "We were doing it for the churches," recalled Director Felix Oisamoje, and during the campaign they established scores of "umbrella organizations." The present broadcasts aired in Nigeria are strongly evangelistic and their extensive humanitarian efforts always had "the goal to establish a church." The Nigerian center has been particularly aggressive in church establishment in the northern, Hausa-speaking area of the country, which is predominantly Muslim.[39]

The most distinctly evangelistic of the regional centers is Kiev. There

Steve Weber conceived of a bold plan to use its huge database of names of correspondents to encourage the establishment of 40,000 cell churches in the Ukraine, Russia, and other nations of the former Soviet Union. The center developed training materials and conducted seminars in more than 100 cities instructing potential leaders "in the concepts of personal evangelism," teaching them how to establish "cell churches," and supplying them with the names of those who responded to WorldReach television programming. By 2003, the Kiev center reported that it had records of more than 40,000 cell churches that had been established; some had become large congregations, such as the Good News Church in Kharkov, Ukraine, which claimed 1,600 members. By 2009, the number of cell churches in the regional center database had surpassed 80,000, and the center had a working relationship with 14,000 other evangelical churches, offering them support and sending them contacts developed through their programming. "We have incredible favor with the churches," even the Orthodox churches outside of Russia, remarked director Weber. Kiev's program, noted WorldReach vice president Ben Edwards, "created a unity with local churches that doesn't exist anywhere else in the world." The cell church strategy had been a "phenomenal" success, according to Gordon Robertson, fulfilling the WorldReach aim "to find ways for people to get churched."[40]

The heart of the Kiev regional center has been an intensive follow-up counseling center staffed by workers trained by CBN vice-president Joel Palser. The international version of *The 700 Club* continues to generate thousands of calls from a vast geographic area. "We quite often receive testimonies," reported Tanya Danilova, coordinator of the Kiev call center, from those who were "healed after the word of knowledge by Gordon Robertson or Pat Robertson." "Many Russian people started sending money in response to our program," she observed, because "they trust this program." "You can't capture . . . how the word of knowledge gets translated months or years later," mused Steve Weber. "It is every day. . . . They call and say I am calling to tell you my illness is gone."[41]

WorldReach is a significant item in the CBN annual budget; after the large investments in regional centers funded by The Family Channel sale revenues, the international evangelism budget of WorldReach settled at approximately 10 percent of CBN gift receipts. In 2007 the budget allocation, including special "designated contributions" given for particular activities, WorldReach was allocated around $20 million. The CBN annual budget reported another $40 million in its foreign evangelism line based on the value of "bartered air time" negotiated by its regional centers.[42]

CBN has encouraged all of the regional centers to raise funds locally, but total financial independence seems neither likely nor practical. Aside from the high costs involved in television production, the symbiotic relationship between CBN and the international centers has made permanent ties inevitable. CBN Indonesia has been the most successful indigenous fundraising outpost. By 2008, an estimated 35 percent of the Jakarta regional center's budget came from inside Indonesia; director McClendon projected that the figure could reach 65 percent. The regional center in Manila has high hopes of becoming a stronger financial partner. Telethons based on the American model proved to be successful in the Philippines; office manager Robert John Tan reported that donations in recent years had "broken records." He hoped the Manila center would become sufficiently financially successful to become a source of funds for other offices, such as China and Thailand, where fundraising is not permitted (though the Beijing office has had some success in raising funds from foreign companies in China for humanitarian work). But elsewhere, many challenges to local fundraising remain. In India, many of those who have responded to the programming have been "secret believers" who do not want to receive mail or be identified as CBN supporters. In Kiev, some leaders fear visible fundraising could attract the attention of the Mafia. Some have helped pay their way in other ways. In both Nigeria and the Ukraine, where local financial support remains less than ten percent of the regional center budgets, the centers have been successful in securing millions of dollars of bartered airtime. Of the 110 stations airing programs distributed by the Kiev center, 80 have done so for free. In Nigeria much of the airtime has been provided by local stations in exchange for training provided for their staffs by the media professionals at CBN Nigeria.[43]

Throughout his life, Pat Robertson's personal and prophetic interest in the Middle East has placed that region at the center of his field of vision. Beginning with the opening of CBN's Middle East Television (METV) station in Lebanon in 1984, Robertson has persistently explored ways to spread the Christian message throughout the Middle East. METV was a highly visible presence in both Israel and the surrounding Arab nations in the early 1990s. During a 1995 visit to Israel, Pat Robertson was granted an interview with Israeli Prime Minister Benjamin Netanyahu and also was invited to the headquarters of PLO Chief Yasser Arafat, where he conducted an exclusive interview with the Palestinian leader. The expansion of satellite television transmission into the area opened new opportunities, and in 1997 METV began transmissions that beamed CBN programming, including *The 700 Club*, into Israel and other areas of the Middle East.[44]

In the late 1990s, Robertson and others at CBN worried about the future of METV as the political situation in Lebanon deteriorated. In 1998, Robertson explored moving the station to Ariel, Israel. Three of his best friends in the Senate, Sam Brownback, Jesse Helms, and John Ashcroft, wrote letters to Israeli Prime Minister Netanyahu urging him to approve the move. When that plan failed, in 1999 Robertson asked Ashcroft to seek assistance from the State Department to protect the employees at METV, who had been accused by the Lebanese government of "collaborating with Israel." The withdrawal of Israeli forces from southern Lebanon in 2000 forced CBN to evacuate the station. In 2001, after a temporary disruption, CBN sold its METV station and began concentrating its efforts on the production of programming that could be distributed by satellite.[45]

Pat Robertson and the CBN leadership began to focus more and more on reaching Muslims. In 2000 the ministry announced that its videos were "very popular in Turkey, Egypt and Algeria," and that its "music-oriented youth program, *One Cubed,* is reaching an Arabic audience as well." At that time CBN was "producing 13 half-hour programs in Arabic on end-time prophecy — a topic of great interest to many Muslims." The Muslim world, Robertson believed, remained the greatest "unreached" mission region of the world. The focus on satellite programming began to pay off as increased satellite coverage in the area opened broad new opportunities for beaming religious programming into Islamic countries. By 2009 WorldReach was producing programs in Arabic, Berber, Farsi, and Turkish that were being beamed into fifteen countries in North Africa and the Middle East, capable of reaching as many as 200 million viewers.[46]

The dramatic growth of WorldReach programming in the Middle East is both one of the ministry's proudest achievements and its most closely guarded secret. At present, live programming is beamed to the region continuously in both Arabic and Farsi from remote facilities in locations that are kept secret by CBN. "All kinds of Christian programming" is beamed into the region, including entertainment shows and evangelical programs. While revealing none of the mechanics of its follow-up system in the Middle East, CBN's website in 2010 reported: In response to its broadcasts and websites, CBN handles hundreds of phone calls and emails every month from all over the world. In partnership with Operation Blessing, CBN WorldReach also continues to respond to disasters, humanitarian needs, and the plight of the poor in the region.[47]

At CBN, few things have attracted the attention of Pat Robertson more than the WorldReach programming in the Muslim world. "I am vitally interested in it," he observed in 2008. "It is a thrill to me to know it is going on." And few things have caused more excitement among the major donors to the ministry than being given special reports about the secretive program. But the details of the operation remained closely guarded secrets. After decades of broadcasting in the Middle East, CBN's leaders had genuine concerns about the safety of those involved in producing and distributing programming in the region.[48]

The WorldReach Legacy

WorldReach is an important agency within CBN, employing more people in its overseas branches than all other CBN enterprises combined. In the expanse of Pat Robertson's institutional legacy, surmised Gordon Robertson, "WorldReach is the untold story." The concept of training indigenous Christians all over the world to produce high-quality television programming appropriate to their cultures combined with an ability to respond and offer counseling was innovative and unique. Gordon Robertson's vision to reproduce CBN in centers around the world, complete with production studios, humanitarian programs, and counseling centers, seems particularly relevant in a world increasingly linked by media.[49]

In centers around the world, CBN has created "stand-alone units, doing their own thing," noted Michael Little, and "in that sense they are out of our control." All around the world, in the words of Kiev director Steve Weber, "The legacy of CBN is incredible." You "can't capture it," he reflected, "it is every day. . . . The testimonies continue to pour in from villages on the Tundra and the cities of the Ukraine and Russia." The non-colonial transfer of expertise to the regional centers also reinforced the sense that these centers really were "doing their own thing," making room for indigenous reinterpretations of models originally developed in the United States.[50]

Finally, WorldReach had a rejuvenating effect on CBN itself. Evangelism has always been important at CBN both as a Christian imperative and as a fundraising technique. The development of the regional centers greatly increased the ability of CBN to tell the story of its contribution to Christian missions and of its expansive Operation Blessing humanitarian work. Sending production teams from Virginia Beach to film testimonies and stories abroad is expensive; the WorldReach network of media specialists abroad has provided skilled workers on location around the world. The only support the regional centers are required to provide CBN comes in the form of three testimony stories per center each month, to be edited and used on the telethons and *The 700 Club* in Virginia Beach, where they raise the profile of the international ministry in the United States. The effective telling of the WorldReach story, done relentlessly on the American *700 Club* and on the telethons, has raised morale within the organization and markedly improved the fundraising abilities of the ministry on the home front.[51]

The Blossoming of Operation Blessing

Operation Blessing International, the humanitarian wing of the CBN empire, had grown into one of the 100 largest humanitarian organizations in the United States by 2008, reporting annual revenues of $279,576,384. Of that amount, slightly more than $20 million was donated by supporters and more than $258 million was "gifts in kind," which included foods, medicines, and other goods donated by businesses for distribution in the United States and abroad by the Operation Blessing network. Since its founding in 1968 as a department of the Christian Broadcasting Network, Operation Blessing calculated that it had "helped more than 202 million people in more than 105 countries and all 50 states, providing goods and services valued at more than $1.5 billion."[52]

Operation Blessing International was officially incorporated as a 501(c)(3) nonprofit organization in 1986 but continued to function more or less as a department of CBN well into the first decade of the twenty-first century. OBI continued to be included in the financial accounting of CBN as an "affiliated organization." Despite the organizational separation, in 1995 CBN still supplied $20 million of Operation Blessing's $36 million budget. The reorganization of OBI was intended to facilitate fundraising and to alleviate its dependence on CBN for funds. However, the organizations remain tied together in many ways. CBN has continued to support OBI with a substantial subsidy amounting to around six percent of the network's annual budget. In addition, OBI's offices are housed on the premises of CBN. In 2009 the eight-person OBI board of directors included Pat Robertson, Dede Robertson, Gordon Robertson, and CBN president Michael Little.[53]

The mission of Operation Blessing changed markedly after 1990, when the organization began "moving from individual assistance to helping fund outreach centers across the U.S. These centers "provide broad, community impact through their partnerships with local ministries, food pantries, shelters and more." In the early 1990s, OBI worked largely through grants to CBN ministry centers abroad and by supporting established humanitarian groups such as Billy Graham's Samaritan's Purse Ministry and the AmeriCares Foundation. A 1991 internal report listed projects that had received donations in the United States, the Philippines, Chile, Cyprus, Vietnam, Ghana, Kenya, Panama, China, Ethiopia, Romania, and Poland. Foreshadowing core OBI programs of the future, by 1992 Operation Blessing had acquired a fleet of trucks "to transport food to the needy" and to respond to natural disasters. In that year, the organization helped "thousands recover from Hurricane Hugo, the San Francisco earthquake and the eruption of Mt. Pinatubo in the Philippines." Responding to disasters was seen as a way to open "doors to share the Gospel so that others might come to know Jesus as their personal Lord and Savior." In 1995 Operation Blessing "rushed emergency assistance to . . . Japan, the Virgin Islands, Mexico, Zaire, Ecuador, Ukraine and Colombia." The ministry's distribution capability also facilitated programs to respond to "God's urban call," bringing "hope to the inner city," a longtime humanitarian priority of Pat Robertson. During these years OBI began transporting food and medicines to inner-city churches and other community-based relief organizations. A second humanitarian program in place by the middle of the 1990s sent "waves of medical teams and medicines" in areas where "emergency relief" was needed.[54]

The Flying Hospital

By 1994 the vision of sending medical teams into needy areas matured into the most visible and expensive of Operation Blessing's projects of the 1990s: the Flying Hospital. In 1994 Robertson purchased an L-1011 jumbo-jet airliner, which was modified at a cost of around $25 million to include three operating stations, two dental stations, a pharmacy, a post-operative recovery area for twelve patients, and space for X-ray machines and other laboratory equipment. By May 1996 the airplane had been refitted and was ready to "bring health care, medical training and the Good News to those suffering around the world — people who need to know that God really cares." In his speech commissioning the airplane in a ceremony at Washington Dulles International Airport, former President George H. W. Bush said: "I can hardly think of a more worthwhile [project]. . . . It has this underpinning of faith that our country is crying out for."[55]

The Flying Hospital project attracted much positive publicity for OBI,

CBN, and Pat Robertson. The team of seventy volunteer medical professionals who spent two weeks in El Salvador in June and July of 1996 working in cooperation with around 100 Salvadoran medical professionals spoke glowingly of their trip. They reported that "7000 people were served and 187 surgeries were performed." The initial trip was followed in 1996 by similar trips to Panama and the Ukraine. Operation Blessing announced plans to conduct twelve medical mission trips each year, but only four were scheduled in 1997 because estimated costs ranged from $350,000 to $800,000 for each trip.[56]

The Flying Hospital was a formidable public relations success, but by 2000, "ground down by four years of oppressive maintenance costs," the ministry decided to sell the airplane. In its 2000 tax return CBN reported spending $8.3 million on the airplane during the year. According to Ron Oates, who coordinated the airplane's trips, in the end it was much more cost-effective to deliver medical help in underdeveloped areas by supporting and working with local clinics.[57]

The Bill Horan Era

The modern shape of Operation Blessing dates from the appointment of Bill Horan as chief operating officer in March 2002. By November, Horan was given the title of president. Horan was another of those impetuous Robertson appointments that could have been either a bane or a blessing. The two men met when Robertson was on vacation in the Cayman Islands. Robertson was impressed by the retired businessman who had founded a large international family-run business called Michigan Aggregate Machinery. An avid fisherman and president of the Cayman Island Angling Club, Horan fished with Robertson, and he and his wife socialized with Pat and Dede. Shortly after his return home, Robertson invited Horan, who had never watched *The 700 Club,* to Virginia Beach, hired him as chief operating officer, and gave him the charge to "grow Operation Blessing."[58]

"Bill learned quickly," observed Gordon Robertson; as soon as he got his feet on the ground and was appointed president of the organization, he began "doing great stuff." Under Horan's leadership, noted OBI Vice-President for Media and Development Deborah Benson, the organization "grew exponentially": "We went from 37 million a year in gifts in kind from corporations to over 200 million in two years." OBI quickly was transformed "from a small organization attached to a large organization" into a "significant player at the national and international level" of humanitarian organizations.[59]

The strategy he used to grow OBI, Horan told donors, was to "multiply the dollars you give by using the principle of leverage." Leverage meant increasing the value of the "gifts in kind" donated to OBI by corporations. Horan "lasered in" on gifts in kind, according to Deborah Benson; by 2007 OBI had received gifts from 240 corporate donors contributing medical supplies, foodstuffs, building supplies, and other surplus goods. OBI warehoused the goods in the United States in 220,000 square feet of storage space and in facilities around the world. In the United States, OBI maintained a fleet of twenty trucks and around sixty trailers, many of them refrigerated, at distribution centers. The fleet was capable of delivering donated goods to chronically needy areas and to move swiftly in cases of disaster.[60]

OBI's reputation within the community of humanitarian organizations, as well as in the public eye, soared as a result of its prominent participation in two of the most publicized disaster relief efforts in the first decade of the twenty-first century: Hurricane Katrina on the Gulf Coast and the Indonesian tsunami. In both cases OBI was among the most important "first responders" because it was strategically present in the distressed area. During the Katrina disaster, OBI's storage facilities and fleet of trucks were near the Gulf Coast devastation, and the organization immediately made available fifteen trucks to dispatch food and mobile kitchen equipment to Salvation Army staging areas in Mississippi, Louisiana, and Florida, making possible "the provision of up to 310,000 meals a day." The Federal Emergency Management Agency (FEMA) placed OBI on its website, along with the Red Cross, as one of three relief agencies recommended most highly to receive cash contributions. Critics of CBN were outraged that FEMA was "passing the plate for Pat Robertson," but the prominence of OBI in the relief effort was widely praised and had a dramatic impact on the contributions to the ministry and to CBN.[61]

OBI remained in New Orleans until the end of 2007. The organization reported in February 2007 that "since Katrina, OBI has helped provide nearly 900,000 meals, supplied thousands of roof tarps, purchased two mobile cranes to remove trees, fought mosquito infestation, and given nearly $5 million in cash grants to over 200 small faith-based organizations." Its most significant long-term project was a medical clinic in East New Orleans; before it closed at the end of 2007, the clinic "helped almost 35,000 patients and dispensed more than 83,000 free medications."[62]

The second natural disaster in which Operation Blessing found itself strategically placed to respond was the 2005 tsunami that caused devastation and death through Southeast Asia. CBN centers in Indonesia, India, Thailand, the Philippines, and Singapore "immediately mobilized massive relief efforts to provide emergency aid and medical care to tens of thousands of victims." Critical to OBI reaction was the response of the robust Operation Blessing office in Jakarta, whose energetic director, Non Rawung, was widely known and respected throughout the country. When the disastrous tsunami hit the Achay area of Sumatra, the Operation Blessing office in Jakarta had a medical team ready to assist. The director of the CBN WorldReach regional center in Jakarta secured government permission to send a team into the devastated area. Within forty-eight hours OBI had a team of ten workers in the region with cash to distribute, and within a week, OBI had a team of forty-five people working in the area, including doctors and nurses. The government would not allow overtly religious organizations into the area, but OBI was so respected by the government that the Indonesian Air Force began transporting OBI's personnel. OBI's response was extraordinary, and as the story was documented on *The 700 Club*, contributions flooded in to support the relief.[63]

Operation Blessing's high-profile responses to Katrina and the tsunami benefited OBI in more than financial terms. The disaster response efforts integrated the organization fully into the network of humanitarian organizations that regularly cooperated with one another. In a sense, the organization's success in the two disasters inevitably strengthened OBI's identification with the broader community of humanitarian organizations and weakened its identification as a wing of CBN.

Another development that contributed to OBI's growing sense of independence was George W. Bush's faith-based initiative. When the program was announced, Robertson warned that federal funding of religious groups was a "real Pandora's box" that would be "like a narcotic." But Robertson's criticism faded when Operation Blessing received $500,000 in the first wave of grants in 2002. According to press reports, OBI in 2006 received more than $14 million in government grants.[64]

Still, not everyone at CBN was convinced. "We shouldn't do this," warned Gordon Robertson, because inevitably "strings get attached." He believed that if OBI identified with the "elite NGOs in America," inevitably the organization's "evangelical witness becomes an issue." Gordon preferred the model of the Samaritan's Purse, the respected humanitarian outreach of the Billy Graham Evangelistic Association.[65]

By 2008 Operation Blessing International was working in a number of well-defined areas. Working closely with other humanitarian organizations, including FEMA and the United Nations High Commissioner of Refugees, OBI "responded to a record 20 disasters in 14 countries, helping more than 191,000 people in need." The organization provided free medical and dental care in 2,476 international medical and dental missions staffed mostly by volunteer healthcare specialists and dispensed free medicines to millions of people through its clinics. Other major outreaches abroad included a program for providing clean water in rural communities in China, India, Nigeria, and Thailand by building cisterns and digging wells; supporting orphans in existing institutions in Somaliland, Colombia, Guatemala, the Philippines, and Ukraine; and the support of a "micro-enterprise" program that trained and funded men and women in developing countries to build self-sustaining businesses. In addition, the organization focused on the delivery of foodstuffs around the world. In the United States OBI reported that in 2008 its "fleet of Hunger Strike Force tractor-trailers traveled more than 2 million miles and distributed more than 87.6 million pounds of donated food and other relief to those in need." OBI maintained 120 "points of distribution" around the country from which it distributed goods to around 5,000 relief groups.[66]

In the distribution of disaster relief OBI has become widely recognized as the "logistical arm" of such large organizations as the International Red Cross, FEMA, UNICEF, the Salvation Army, the United Nations World Food Program, and World Vision. On a regular schedule OBI has made deliveries to hundreds of local charities; among the 120 regular "drop sites" are scores of churches, government agencies, and other community service organizations. OBI has collaborated with governments to identify distribution points, both in the United States and abroad, but more often than not the local contacts are faith-based enterprises.[67]

Internationally, the work of OBI has been historically associated with the WorldReach centers and, consequently, with churches and religious organizations. In the Philippines, OBI director Kim Pascual established strong ties with the Philippine government and worked closely with the army in disaster relief (OBI was named NGO of the year by the army); still, "churches are the ones in the front lines" of relieving suffering, and the projects of OBI aim to "empower" them. The clean water projects in countries like India and Nigeria have almost always been carried out in cooperation with local churches. In places such as Indonesia and Ukraine, where WorldReach has had a strong presence, OBI's humanitarian projects have almost "always partnered with a church."[68]

Nonetheless, Bill Horan's vision for OBI has done much to broaden the self-definition and reach of the organization. Horan acknowledged that OBI was the "humanitarian arm of the ministry," but that description no longer adequately described the organization's total mission. Before his arrival, Horan thought, OBI's outlook had been "quite insular," exhibiting little desire to "find common ground with other organizations." Convinced that this narrow view was "not coming from Pat," Horan, whose religious background was Roman Catholic, reached out to Catholic charities and in Thailand cooperated with Buddhist groups. Acknowledging that OBI operatives around the world might pray with a recipient of aid, he insisted: "That is not what we are about." Horan frankly told WorldReach leaders that he did not think "spiritual counseling" was a part of the work of OBI employees. While they were in some ways still the "humanitarian arm of the ministry," CBN and OBI were different organizations, and their "missions are separate." The leaders of OBI saw themselves as an independent extension of Pat Robertson's "passion for helping . . . those that are hurting. . . . His heart is that we continue to grow so that we can bless people."[69]

Predictably, the independent spirit at OBI and its seeming diminution of evangelistic fervor did not sit well with some leaders at CBN. Most CBN administrators believed that it was "not desirable for us to have OB independent." As opposed to Regent University and the American Center for Law and Justice, which were never intended to exist under the CBN umbrella, OBI was created to be a part of "the CBN family of ministries." "The spirit of separateness got into OB in the early 1990s," observed Gordon Robertson. Bill Horan did not invent the idea, but "rightly or wrongly," he had "seized on the lack of strength in Africa" on the part of WorldReach to establish an independent chain of command.[70]

The relationship between CBN and OBI remained somewhat uncertain by 2009. "Operation Blessing and CBN are two organizations that vitally need one another," observed Gordon Robertson in 2007: "We have put a lot into these organizations." OBI continued to receive a 6.5 percent allocation in CBN's annual budget, and OBI continued to supply *The 700 Club* with fundraising stories to use during telethons. "We are very connected as sister organizations," insisted Deborah Benson. Nonetheless, many insiders believed (to mix family metaphors) that "in the last year or two they have been getting a divorce."[71]

Of course, the central question is where Pat Robertson stands in the internal organizational discussion. In the end, observed Michael Little, everyone will "do what they are told to do by Pat." For his part, Bill Horan was convinced that his efforts to broaden the reach of OBI had "Pat Robertson's blessing." Robertson no doubt heard the grumblings, but he insisted

CHAPTER 8

Home Front: Regent University and the American Center for Law and Justice

―∘∕∕∘―

The Christian Broadcasting Network at fifty years of age was a streamlined television ministry using cutting-edge technology to spread its message around the world. The ministry's mission outreach had been refined through the years into the WorldReach department, an international evangelistic network that was thoroughly integrated into the CBN managerial structure. CBN's historic humanitarian ministry outreach, Operation Blessing International, was an independent organization that remained closely related to CBN both financially and programmatically. Two other creations of Pat Robertson's restless imagination, Regent University and the American Center for Law and Justice, though independent from CBN, worked closely with other components of the Robertson family of organizations. In 2009 Pat Robertson remained chancellor and president of Regent University, and he served as president of the ACLJ board as well as one of its most enthusiastic boosters.

The Flowering of Regent University

CBN University was ten years old when Pat Robertson returned to Virginia Beach after his race for the Republican nomination for the presidency. At the time, the university was still tied closely to CBN and was dependent on the ministry for financial support. The downturn in contributions in the late 1980s forced retrenchments at the university, as it did in the operations of CBN. In 1989 CBN University was still a small school; fewer than

800 students were enrolled in five accredited graduate colleges and a law school, which had opened in 1986 and applied to the American Bar Association for accreditation.[1]

Pat Robertson arrived back in Virginia Beach after his political excursion with new aspirations and plans for his educational venture. He was anxious, thought David Gyertson, who served for a time as the university's president, "to leverage his influence quickly." On January 1, 1990, serving notice that the school intended to redefine itself, the board of trustees changed its name to Regent University.[2]

Broadening the Vision

The name change was intended to signal that the university's mission would expand. A carefully crafted letter explained the change to inquirers: "The name change was the result of several years of considerable research. . . . The research revealed strong support for a name change given the fact that we have grown considerably and now have programs in many areas outside of Communication. 'CBN University' made much more sense when the only college was a College of Communication. . . . The definition of a regent created considerable support among a Board of Trustees that was admittedly divided on the issue of even changing the name." Keith Fournier, executive director of the American Center for Law and Justice, explained the significance of the term "regent": "A regent is one who represents a king in his absence. . . . He is an agent of the king. At Regent University, this king is, of course, the King of kings, our Lord and Savior Jesus Christ. As a regent of Jesus, the graduate of Regent University should be well prepared to represent Christ in whatever vocation he or she may be called to serve the Lord."[3]

The name change also reflected the reality of the changing relationship between CBN and the university. As the school's graduates began entering a variety of professional careers, it became clear that a degree bearing the name of CBN was sometimes a liability rather than an asset, particularly in fields unrelated to communications and broadcasting. The leadership of CBN had long felt that the university was not "our core mission." Regent was, in the words of CBN president Michael Little, "a child we wanted to grow up." Still, in many ways the ties between Regent and CBN have remained strong. The two institutions have, in the words of Jay Sekulow, a strong "mutual respect," symbolized by the loyalty of each to Pat Robertson.[4]

Operationally and financially, by 2009 CBN and Regent were totally independent of one another. The two entities shared expenses for campus maintenance and security, but they do not share budgets. CBN ceded to Regent University the original land on which the first university buildings were built, and in July 2000 CBN sold to Regent University for $21 million the adjacent Founders Inn and Conference Center and an additional 78 acres of land.[5]

The motto of the newly named university captured its oft-repeated mission: "Christian Leadership to Change the World." In his book *The Scandal of the Evangelical Mind,* historian Mark Noll bemoaned the proliferation of evangelical educational institutions, including Regent, because each new institution implied "that no previously existing educational enterprise is capable of meeting the demands of the hour." "Despite the absence of formal education credentials" on the part of their founders, Noll noted, scores of evangelical leaders presumed "to establish a Christian university." The result "often appears naïve, inept, and tendentious." Yet in some ways, Regent stands as an exception to Noll's observation. Regent's founder and chancellor holds two advanced degrees and is broadly knowledgeable about the nation's system of higher education, and Regent University's pragmatically targeted mission has been innovative, if not totally unique, with a focus on training Christians in state-of-the-art facilities to be skilled journalists, media specialists, lawyers, religious leaders, and business leaders, among a growing list of specialties. After thirty years, the stated "divine mission" of Regent remained the same: "The university was founded for the specific purpose of preparing leaders who would not only succeed in their professions, but also advance as Christians equipped to effectively impact their world."[6]

Early faculty members enthusiastically embraced this mission. "I saw Regent as kind of being in the gap for the next generation of Christian leaders that would change the world," said one of the early professors in the divinity school. "In a way, [Pat Robertson] was an elitist," observed Divinity School dean Vinson Synan, because "he wanted to train leaders." The university's website in 2009 reasserted, in global terms, this statement of purpose: "Our students, faculty and administrators share a calling, founded on biblical principles, to make a significant difference in our communities, our cities, our nation and our world."[7]

Pat Robertson's plan to produce leaders who would influence the disciplines that were most influential in shaping the country fit with, and in some ways augmented, what was happening throughout Christian higher education. Christopher Hayes, Washington editor of *The Nation,* reported that "Regent's central insight — one that's come to dominate Christian higher education — is that in order to create Christian lawyers or journalists or film editors, the school would need to do more than simply augment its professional education with Bible study and group prayer. Students would be given a road map of what sort of life and career a Christian lawyer or journalist or film editor might have. They would, in the fashionable argot of evangelical pedagogy, be given a 'worldview.'"[8]

The expansion of Regent University in the two decades after 1990 was steady and sometimes spectacular. By 2001 Regent's enrollment had reached 2,450 students; during the 2008-2009 school year that figure reached 4,563, slightly more than half of whom were registered as part-time students. Undergraduates numbered 1,461, and the remainder were postgraduate, professional, and non-degree students. The student body was extraordinarily diverse, including students from all fifty states and forty-six countries; 34 percent of the student body was classified as "ethnic minorities." The average age of the student body was thirty-five — a figure made markedly higher by the percentage of part-time students enrolled in online programs.

The demographics of the university have been strongly influenced by its history and its religious commitment. "We are trying to open educational opportunities for the nations," said Vice-President for Student Services Jeff Pittman. Robertson is proud of the student body diversity. In 2007 he told an interviewer: "Without any overt effort on our part we have probably the best racial mix of any university in the country. Twenty-two percent of our students are African-American. We as well have a large number of Hispanics. From overseas at least 130 students attend Regent setting a foundation for a very rich cultural experience. Joining Regent . . . is like joining the United Nations; we have students from Egypt, Indonesia, China, India, Poland, Russia, Czech [Republic], the Ukraine, and Romania." By 2009 the university claimed more than 12,000 alumni.[9]

Within the bounds of Protestant Christianity, and to a limited extent the Catholic world as well, Regent has also been religiously diverse. Thirty-six denominations have been represented in the student body, though the university still draws heavily from the Pentecostal/charismatic subculture in the United States and abroad. "The faith factor" is the number one reason for the booming student growth at Regent. As Pat Robertson had long been the symbol of achievement and respectability in the charismatic movement, Regent University has been the upscale educational option for upwardly mobile charismatics around the world.[10]

The basic graduate programs at Regent were in place by 1990, when the university offered accredited programs in communications and the arts, education, business, religion, government, and psychology and counseling. The major graduate addition in later years was a School of Leadership Studies created in 1997, which combined with the School of Business in 2006 as the School of Global Leadership and Entrepreneurship. By 2009 the university offered thirty graduate and undergraduate degrees accredited by appropriate credentialing bodies.[11]

In each of the schools Robertson carefully picked deans who would implement his vision of educating students to be Christian leaders. The School of Communication and the Arts, the university's first degree-granting program, was for many years "the flagship school." Communications was, of course, a logical area of focus in the early days of CBN University. From the inception of the university, Pat Robertson believed it could supply Christian influence in all areas of communications with the help of the skilled professionals at CBN. The school remains one of the largest and most visible of Regent's programs. In 2002 it moved into a $35 million Communication and Performing Arts building that included an 800-seat theater and two film and television production studios. Dean Michael Patrick believed that Regent graduates, educated "in an environment where they are free to express their faith," had already had "a significant impact" in the artistic and journalistic worlds. An advocate of "redemptive filmmaking," Patrick insisted that Regent graduates could succeed in a Hollywood environment where a "growing number of actors, artists, producers and directors . . . have decided to choose a better way."[12]

The divinity school has also been central to Pat Robertson's plan to train Christian leaders to influence society. Through the years, the leaders of the divinity school remained self-consciously committed to the "original vision of the founder." While Robertson never attempted to outline a systematic theology in his writings, the divinity school reflected his openness and tolerance within a framework of biblical conservatism and a charismatic emphasis. In 2006, Robertson told Dean Vinson Synan: "I believe that it is absolutely important for the Regent University School of Divinity to be laying out the foundations of the faith for future generations. . . . I don't know of many [other schools of religion] that have maintained their original distinctive and mission. . . . We need to be major players and either charismatic or evangelical in religious thinking so that we will set the course for others to follow." Regent became a prestigious degree-granting institution for large numbers of "independent Pentecostal and charismatic" Christians, both in the United States and abroad. When he became dean in 1994, Synan correctly predicted that Regent would become "a seminary for Third World countries that cannot afford their own seminaries." While the school aimed to "serve as a dynamic center of spiritual renewal and church revitalization in the major traditional churches of Christendom," Synan believed that its most important contribution had been "to serve as a center of graduate training for the younger churches of the world, especially those created through the Pentecostal and charismatic movements of this century." By 2007 "the School of Divinity ranked among the top 15 ATS-accredited seminaries in active student enrollment" and according to Synan "was poised to become one of the premier seminaries in the United States."[13]

The Struggle to Build a Law School

By 2007, the law school was "the number one thing in Pat's mind," observed Vinson Synan: "It is his pride and joy right now." But the journey to respectability passed through a bitter and factious period that seriously disrupted the university. Not until 1996 did the School of Law receive accreditation from the American Bar Association. Prior to that time, operating under provisional accreditation, the school had graduated 700 lawyers. Before gaining accreditation, the Regent board of trustees fired the law school's highly visible dean, Herbert Titus, and weathered a series of lawsuits filed by terminated law professors contesting the school's tenure policies.[14]

Robertson's clash with Titus was, in his words, "one of the worst periods of my life." A Harvard Law School graduate, Titus was by all accounts a brilliant lawyer. At the end of his spiritual journey, Titus studied with and was influenced by Christian philosopher Francis Schaeffer. Titus was considered an articulate advocate of "Dominion" theology, believing that America's founders intended to establish "a new nation and civil government in accordance with God's law." "If a nation's legal and political structure does not reflect the law of God," he wrote, "it is bound to fail." "Herb was very appealing," observed Pat Robertson in retrospect, and many of his outspoken views found ready disciples on the Regent campus. In the early 1990s, as the health of Regent president Bob Slosser faltered, the influence of Titus grew, to the point where David Gyertson, who considered Titus one of "the brightest guys I have ever met," believed that Titus assumed he would become Regent's next president — only to watch the board choose Gyertson instead in 1993.[15]

Increasingly, Robertson, Gyertson, and the board of trustees felt that

Titus's religious views embraced "a world view that was more exclusive" than that of the university. As Titus attracted more and more supporters within the law school and the university, Gyertson and others feared the institution was losing its "broad umbrella" that made it open to diverse ideas and people of different Christian traditions, including Roman Catholics. In Robertson's mind the dean had become "essentially a cultist" who had surrounded himself with a coterie of supporters intent on controlling the university. Robertson thought Titus's "cult" was based on his "extraordinarily narrow view of Christianity." Dean Titus had broad support both in the law school and among Regent alumni. When the law school erupted in turmoil and faculty dismissals in 1993, the Alumni Association of Regent University issued a statement expressing "shock" at the firings, fearing they signaled a desire to "conform to the rest of academia."[16]

Yet the immediate issue that triggered the firing of Herb Titus in July 1993 was not theological, but instead the dean's ongoing clash with the American Bar Association and Regent's failure to secure accreditation for the law school. The school had been denied accreditation in 1987 for a variety of reasons, including the fact that it applied a religious test to all faculty hirings. As dean, Titus pursued the accreditation issue confrontationally: "He wanted to fight all the time," complained Robertson. According to Robertson, when he returned to CBN in 1988, Titus wanted to "fight the ABA" in a $600 million lawsuit. After more than seven years of frustration, Robertson concluded that the main obstacle to accreditation was Titus, and that the dean had to go. In September 1993, in a speech introducing J. Nelson Happy as the new dean of the law school, Robertson chastised the law students and professors who had stoked the fight with the ABA: "I can't think of anything in the world more counterproductive than the students and faculty of this school writing letters to a secular organization to try to take away the accreditation of the school and hurt yourselves. . . . God can forgive sin, but stupid is forever. And for people to act contrary to their own self-interest is stupid." "We would never have gotten ABA approval" had Titus remained dean, Robertson surmised years later. Dean Titus was offered "a golden parachute" that included his appointment to the John Marshall Chair in Constitutional Law at Regent with a lucrative salary and annual expense account, but he rejected the offer and threatened to sue.[17]

The firing of "a dean beloved by many students, faculty, and law alumni sparked confusion and anger," as *Christianity Today* put it. In the months that followed, eight of the law school's fourteen professors who had resigned or were fired filed a complaint with the American Bar Association. They were branded by Robertson as "cultists after the order of Jim Jones or the Branch Davidians." The fallout continued for two years, as five of the departing professors sued Regent University and Pat Robertson for defamation and violations of academic freedom and tenure rights. But in the end, the university won a court battle upholding their dismissal.[18]

There can be little doubt that the Robertson-Titus confrontation, while triggered by frustrations about the accreditation of the law school, raised broader questions about the basic identity of Regent University. Even critics who regarded Pat Robertson as a radical recognized that the turmoil seemed to signal a desire to clean out "extremist fanatics." According to a report filed by "ABA fact finders," Titus's "religious viewpoint is outside, or much narrower than that advocated or tolerated by Regent University generally." The stakes had been high; in the words of newly installed president Terry Lindvall, the confrontation had been "a battle for the soul of the university." In the end, Titus's "vision of a Christ-centered educational institution," said David Gyertson, "was different from the original vision of the institution."[19]

The board named J. Nelson Happy, Robertson's private attorney, to succeed Titus. The personable Happy took over a rebellious faculty and a seriously divided law school and skillfully moved it toward accreditation. At the time of the accreditation in 1996, Dean Happy acknowledged that "our school's reputation among academics is zero." In the *U.S. News & World Report* ranking of 178 American law schools, Regent placed last. But an ebullient Robertson told the press: "What we want here is a law school that will someday rival Harvard, Yale, Stanford, Michigan, University of Virginia, whatever the big five or big 10 are. Hopefully, our graduates will work into the Justice Department. They'll become U.S. attorneys and maybe one day, a Supreme Court justice." "Those were weird times," recalled Keith Fournier, but "Happy turned it into a real law school."[20]

Building the university's law school was arduous and costly, but Robertson and the board of trustees never wavered in their commitment. In 2000 only 39 percent of Regent graduates passed the Virginia bar exam on their first try, compared to a statewide average of 73 percent. By 2001, Dean Jeffrey Brauch had added a team of fulltime instructors in "legal research and writing," and the percentage of students passing bar exams in all states rose to 69 percent. By 2007, Dean Brauch outlined the progress of the school: "We tried to grow too big too fast. We have become much more selective in our admissions process. . . . Out bar passage is much higher. . . . We are smaller, but we are better." Regent has won a number of distinguished competitions during its brief history; in 2007 two Regent students won the ABA Law Student Division Negotiation Competition, succeeding the previous year's winners from Harvard University.[21]

The law school continued to struggle to raise its ratings; Jay Sekulow judged that the school remained ranked in the fourth tier of law schools because of "bias" and "because we are new." However, by 2007 the faculty had grown to thirty professors, including former Attorney General John Ashcroft. Perhaps even more important was the presence of Jay Sekulow on the faculty and as a member of the school's board of trustees. The highly successful chief counsel of the American Center for Law and Justice taught a popular course in the history of the Supreme Court, and employed thirty Regent law students as law clerks. Sekulow was not given to the kind of rapturous language often used by Pat Robertson in describing Regent, but he was extremely optimistic about the future of the law school: "I think we are the coming Harvard."[22]

In 2007, the law school received a mixed bag of attention with the resignation of Monica Goodling from her job in the U.S. Attorney General's office. Goodling, a 1999 Regent law school graduate who served as a top aide of Attorney General Alberto Gonzales, found herself at the center of the storm over the firing of United States attorneys. Goodling's involvement in the firings, her subsequent assertion of Fifth Amendment rights in her Congressional testimony, and her resignation focused attention on the school. Reporters covering the case were shocked to discover more than 150 graduates of the Regent law school serving in the Bush administration. The impact of the story, said Dean Jeff Brauch, was "at first extremely negative." The stories uniformly chronicled the school's long struggle for accreditation, the poor record of student passage of the bar exam, and the bitter fight with Titus. But the attention also provided Brauch and other Regent spokespersons opportunities to show the press the accomplishments and rising status of the law school. The school's success in placing students in government jobs was not lost on prospective students.[23]

Years of Expansion

The most far-reaching expansion of Regent University came in 2000 with the decision to introduce an undergraduate program. Initially, the undergraduate program offered only upper-division courses leading to a bachelor's degree in leadership and management, but by 2005 full-scale undergraduate programs were offered in five areas of study. The reason for the undergraduate addition was simple, Robertson told an interviewer in 2007: "I wanted to reach out to a much broader number of people not only in America but around the world. This undergraduate program is slated over the next years to bring at least 250,000 students into the Regent family. Regent has a destiny to be a major intellectual influence throughout the world."[24]

The numbers Robertson had in mind seemed possible because of the potential of online education. Robertson felt that the technologically-advanced environment in Virginia Beach gave Regent University the ability to become a leader in distance education. He thought Regent had "pioneered some online techniques" that would only "get more sophisticated as the years go on. We offer educational possibilities by having complete interactive education programs online with the most sophisticated kind of tools. We're on the cutting edge of it all." While the online education program has not yet attracted the tens of thousands of students some insiders predicted, the program received some acclaim, ranking second in the Online College OEDB rankings in 2009. Given its access to broadcast and Internet technology, Pat Robertson believed that in the future Regent would "reach out to campuses all around the world."[25]

The decision to introduce an undergraduate program had profound economic implications. As the expense of providing graduate education increasingly cut into Regent's endowment in the early years of the twenty-first century, a degree of financial gloom settled over the campus. The board finally "saw the handwriting on the wall," observed Vinson Synan, and looked to undergraduate studies as a way to expand tuition revenue. Because the undergraduate program was intended to focus largely on distance education, Regent was unprepared for an influx of freshman students on its Virginia Beach campus. The university scrambled to accommodate the needs of these on-campus students, a majority of whom were adults enrolled in evening classes. Although the board resisted the idea of turning Regent into a residential campus, a complex of graduate student apartments was completed in 2007. Dede was the most persistent advocate of new buildings, lobbying on the board for the construction of buildings for the booming schools of divinity and psychology and counseling.[26]

Celebrating its twenty-fifth anniversary in 2003, the university initiated a debate series called "The Clash of the Titans." The series brought an array of political and cultural figures to the campus to speak, including Ehud Barak, Bob Dole, Al Gore, Newt Gingrich, Geraldine Ferraro, Mike Huckabee, and Oliver North. The collection of distinguished participants in "The Clash of the Titans" was intended to highlight the intellectual openness of the campus. Barry Lynn participated in the 2003 debate as part of a team that included Harvard Law School professor Alan Dershowitz and ACLU president Nadine Strossen opposing a team composed of Jay Sekulow, David Limbaugh (Rush Limbaugh's brother), and Ann Coulter. Lynn described the debate as "a near apocalyptic two-hour showdown between competing teams in America's culture wars." Other campus programs, such as the Ronald Reagan Symposium hosted by the Robertson School of Government, featured visiting scholars from Harvard, Yale, Princeton, and Oxford discussing hot-button public issues. The appearances on campus of Mitt Romney and Rudy Giuliani in 2007 continued the pattern of welcoming controversial speakers to Regent.[27]

The expansion of Regent University, like the expansion of CBN, was accelerated by the financial fallout from the sale of the Family Channel. The sale of IFE stock in 1997 fed $147.5 million into the university's endowment, bringing its total to $276.5 million. The endowment increase vaulted Regent into the top 100 colleges and universities in total endowment assets, and into the top twenty-five colleges and universities ranked according to endowment assets per fulltime-equivalent student. "This is a tremendous opportunity for Regent University," Robertson exulted in a public statement. "This development places Regent on the same level as some of the most prestigious universities in the nation. The endowment will only enhance and strengthen the school as it moves forward to become one of the most preeminent universities in the country today."[28]

For a few years, the endowment showed healthy increases and helped fund the lavish expansion of the university and its highly visible special professorships and programs. But by 2006 "deficit spending and heavy withdrawals from its endowment" raised concerns from credit rating agencies, increasing the importance of expanding the undergraduate population. The board addressed the problem and, after running significant deficits for several years, Regent projected a balanced budget by 2010. Following the stock market crash in 2008, the endowment at Regent, like those of other universities, shrank dramatically — Robertson estimated the loss at more than $50 million. The university slashed budgets across the board, cutting more than $10 million and reducing staffs that had swelled during flush economic times.[29]

The control of Regent University is vested in a twenty-four-member board of trustees. The Robertson presence stands out; the board includes Pat Robertson, Dede Robertson, and their son Tim, as well as insiders Michael D. Little, president of CBN, and Jay Sekulow. The entire board is appointed by the directors of the Christian Broadcasting Network. "Regent could be independent" from CBN, observed Dede Robertson, "except that we keep control of the trustees." Michael Little agreed: "We select the members of the board very carefully."[30]

Universities are not docile institutions. But even during the law school controversy, only the foolhardy would have imagined that Pat Robertson's will would not prevail. By 2009 the university founder was well pleased with the mood on campus. "He likes the way it is now," observed Michael Little, "and that is why it is the way it is." While Pat Robertson's vision dominates the management of the university, the board is not intended to be a figurehead group. It is filled with successful business people, albeit all strong Robertson supporters. Indeed, the most independent voice may be that of Dede Robertson. "You can't talk about the university without talking about the influence of Dede," observed David Gyertson. Regent is not just Pat's legacy; it is "the Robertsons' legacy." Dede has recognized that she is "usually the voice of dissent"; more than anyone else on the board, she has been both willing and able to contest her husband. Still, observed David Gyertson, only after the departure of Pat Robertson would the board be compelled to assume a "governing function."[31]

The Presidential Cycle

Pat Robertson has held the title of chancellor throughout the history of Regent University, but many matters at CBN and the Christian Coalition have demanded his attention over the years, and the day-to-day management of the university passed through the hands of a series of presidents in the 1990s. College and university presidents typically have short lifespans, but presidential terms at Regent during the turbulent decade of the nineties were shorter than the national average. The turnover was partly the result of Robertson's managerial style: when leaders strayed too far from his vision, they got Pat Robertson's attention, and clarifications followed.

Pat Robertson's longtime friend Bob Slosser was forced to resign the presidency of Regent because of deteriorating health in 1990. He was replaced by David Gyertson, a former CBN chaplain who earned a Ph.D. from Michigan State University. Gyertson resigned his presidency in 1993, accepting a position as president of Asbury College. In 2000 he became president of Taylor University where he remained until returning to Regent in 2005 as Distinguished Professor in Leadership Management and Renewal. Gyertson, a mild-mannered and thoughtful man, resigned as Regent's president in the midst of the bitter clash between Herbert Titus and the Regent board of trustees. He later surmised that "the institution was outgrowing my ability to lead it. . . . The very soul of the institution was being challenged." Pat Robertson, who continued to hold Gyertson in high esteem, tersely explained his friend's departure: "Gyertson couldn't handle Herb."[32]

In a surprise appointment, David Gyertson was succeeded by faculty member Terrence R. Lindvall, who was "best known for serving as executive producer of many Regent award-winning films." Robertson announced that the new president was "a man of tremendous vision who is highly respected by both faculty and students. He will take Regent to its next level of excellence." An exuberant and popular teacher who had been "a founding member of Regent's faculty," Lindvall had Robertson's confidence as someone who could restore order: "He is a very bright guy, and I thought things would settle down under his leadership."[33]

Lindvall was stunned by the appointment; he later wrote that he was "coerced into the Regent Presidency . . . during riots at the Law School." Lindvall brought a new face of moderation and reason to Regent that elicited applause from outside observers, including a tribute from Harvard theologian Harvey Cox published in *The Atlantic Monthly*. In 1998 Lindvall was described in an article in the *American Journalism Review* as "a boyish 49-year-old with an infectious giggle and just enough of a love of the bawdy to disarm any visitor expecting Robertsonian pretense." Lindvall's appointment, reported the *Washington Times*, brought a "breath of fresh air" to the campus "because of his youth, reputation for zaniness, membership in the Democratic Party and willingness to break with tradition." "I'm seen as a secular liberal," Lindvall said to reporters.[34]

The air of moderation and openness that Lindvall brought to Regent was Robertson's antidote to the narrow religious agenda of the Christian Reconstructionists on the campus. Robertson biographer David John Marley observes that "Lindvall was brought in specifically to make Regent University less sectarian and more accepting of other Christian beliefs" — a fair description of what Robertson thought was his own original intent. Lindvall's contributions were considerable. The departure of Titus and the installation of Lindvall, writes Alec Foege, "were perceived as the beginning of the school's reach to the mainstream." Much had been accomplished in a short time: the law school had been accredited and the university's public image had improved. "Toppled" from the presidency in 1997, Lindvall "returned jubilantly to teaching," accepting an endowed chair in the communications department.[35]

Lindvall's departure was generally attributed on campus to his prankster personality. It is true that his refreshingly quirky behavior sometimes wore thin; "Lindvall was like Peck's bad boy," observed Robertson years later. But Robertson insisted that Lindvall's termination had to do with discontent among the board of trustees because he would not follow the board's instructions, insisting that "I didn't have anything to do with it until the very end." It is clear that the change was motivated by intellectual, rather than personal, issues. David John Marley, clearly a Lindvall admirer, portrays the removal from the presidency as a betrayal: "As soon as this openness threatened other parts of Robertson's empire, heads began to roll. Robertson used people to make the university appear mainstream, and then removed those same people once they were no longer needed." But the real explanation is probably less sinister: the transition appeared to be simply another course correction bringing the university back into line with the founding vision of Pat Robertson. If the Titus rebellion had threatened to pull the university too far to the right, Lindvall's probing probably veered too far to the left. Lindvall understood the Robertson vision, and probably agreed with it, surmised David Gyertson, but he "wanted to push the envelope."[36]

Lindvall's presidency was followed by a three-year term by Lt. Gen. Paul G. Cerjan, who retired from the Army in 1994 after thirty-four years of service. Having served in a variety of educational positions in the Army, including Commandant of the Army War College, Cerjan was well qualified for the position. He never established a strong rapport with Robertson, but he proved to be an efficient manager, although Robertson considered him a little too bureaucratic: "Generals are generals, and soon we had lots of colonels over there as well." An engineer by training, Cerjan oversaw the building of several buildings during his tenure. He resigned abruptly in September 2000 with little explanation, and soon after became president and CEO of the National Defense University Foundation. Robertson insisted that he and the general were on "very good terms," but he and the board felt that Cerjan was "not totally fulfilling the mission of the school." The general likely felt that he was not totally in command.[37]

Campus observers thought that each of the 1990's presidents at Regent had fatal deficiencies. Gyertson was too gentle to handle the harsh confrontation with Herb Titus; Lindvall's lighthearted openness pushed the school too far from the founder's conservative Christian vision; the military temperament of General Cerjan was tested by Robertson's loose and decentralized managerial style. So in the summer of 2001, Robertson himself became president, a position that he announced he would relinquish in 2010. After the instability of the 1990s, Robertson thought it was time to assure that his educational vision was clearly imprinted on Regent University: "The university didn't need another shock of bringing somebody in who was strange to it. I am the founder. I have been president twice before. So I'm not unfamiliar with it."[38]

Robertson served for nearly ten years as President of Regent University. He managed the university, as he did other institutions under his control, by appointing subordinates who understood and agreed with his vision, giving them latitude. Still, managing the university proved to be a difficult challenge. "It's one of a kind," observed Bob Andringa, president of the Council of Christian Colleges and Universities: "You had a visionary founder who's overseen phenomenal growth. It is one of the best-funded Christian universities in the world." In Robertson's mind, the transition was smooth; after he took active control, "the next thing you know we've got it in order." Robertson's accession to the presidency was "sort of accidental," he reminisced, but soon things were "going so well that I didn't want to rock the boat." During his presidency, Robertson felt that he was directly involved in major decisions at the university, including budgetary allocations, but as a "great delegator" he entrusted power to the academic deans of the seven schools once he found them trustworthy. By and large, the university functioned as a loose collection of competing schools; Dede Robertson observed that her husband "kind of lets them do what they want to do."[39]

The School of Communications proved to be the most challenging of the schools during Robertson's presidency. Like Terry Lindvall, many students and professors in the school felt compelled to explore the boundaries of creative Christian artistry. Angered by a student-sponsored film festival in 2002 that included movies Robertson considered inappropriate, the school imposed guidelines on future events that they would not "glorify degradation." Robertson thought it was time to reaffirm the school's Christian identity; David John Marley asserted that "it was the Communications Department that bore the brunt of his anger."[40]

In 2001 President Robertson had vested considerable powers in the hands of a newly appointed vice-president for academic affairs, Barry Ryan. Ryan held degrees from Fuller Theological Seminary, the University of California, Santa Barbara, and Berkeley, and he had taught in two small evangelical colleges in Southern California before serving as a Supreme Court Judicial Fellow in the office of Chief Justice William H. Rehnquist. Most people on campus perceived him as Robertson's surrogate commissioned to bring the campus back to its original Christian vision. The communications department was a chief focus of Ryan's discipline; several professors were either not renewed or fired. In 2004, Terry Lindvall departed, asserting that he felt uncomfortable with the "changing vision" of the university.[41]

Then, in an abrupt turn of events, Ryan himself was terminated in August 2006. No formal explanation was given, but rumors of "moral shortcomings" were rife on campus. When he left, Robertson praised his contributions to Regent, but privately acknowledged that Ryan "got in some trouble."[42]

While Robertson had clear ideas about the intellectual boundaries of Christian higher education, he insisted that students should be free to express their political opinions. When he was informed that a professor had "forbidden any students from displaying literature in support of candidates who are running for public office" in 1994, Robertson wrote a memo to President Terry Lindvall informing him that such restrictions were a violation of students' First Amendment rights, and that it was "counterproductive to an educational experience to not allow young men and women to get involved in citizenship." "Obviously Regent University as an institution should not take sides in a partisan battle," he advised, but "students and professors should feel free to advocate whatever party or candidate that they feel would be beneficial to the city, the state, or the nation. . . . Such activity is a very significant part of the experience of developing citizenship, and should never be discouraged in an educational institution." Law school dean Jeff Brauch insisted that the campus was broadly open to the exchange of ideas, while at the same time "there is no question who we are. . . . Every faculty member signs a statement of faith," and every student understands that "we are going to integrate faith into the classroom."[43]

The Regent University Legacy

Many seasoned insiders in the Pat Robertson network of institutions share the assessment of CBN president Michael Little that "Regent might have the most enduring legacy" of all of Pat Robertson's visionary creations. Pat Robertson's own estimate was that the university would come to rival not only Harvard and Yale as a center of learning but would in the future be compared to the great universities of Europe such as Oxford University and the Sorbonne.[44]

Hyperbole aside, Regent University was a stunning personal accomplishment for Pat Robertson. "How many people alive," asks Alec Foege in his book on the expansive Robertson empire, "can honestly say they've met someone who has conceived of and subsequently built an accredited private university?" It was a venture that tied Robertson to the past and to the future in powerful ways: "an accredited institution of higher learning designed to train Christians to infiltrate society with godly principles would irrefutably yoke Robertson to the United States' pre-Constitutional heritage. The esteemed Harvard College, after all, began in 1636 as a training ground for Puritan ministers. Besides, a successful academic institution would bring along with it an intellectual and organizational heft that a prosperous company or ministry alone could not."[45]

Probably the most widely read positive assessment of Regent University written by an outsider was Harvey Cox's 1995 article in *The Atlantic Monthly*. After lecturing at the university, Cox wrote a guarded, but glowing, description of the school. Cox was impressed by the university's "energetic young president," Terry Lindvall, and by the religious and political diversity on the campus. He praised Robertson's stand against dominion theology in the Titus affair, and for "cuddling up to the pope" by embracing evangelical-Catholic ecumenism. When viewed up close, Cox reported, Regent simply did not conform to "fundamentalist" stereotypes. Alec Foege agreed: "Regent, more than any other arm of Robertson's empire, seemed to interface most convincingly with the world around it."[46]

Even in the post-Lindvall era, Regent's quality continued to impress some outside visitors, including Pat Robertson's nemesis, Barry Lynn. A repeated visitor to the campus (at the invitation of Jay Sekulow), Lynn reported that at Regent's law school Robertson hired "people with good professional credentials" because he wanted Regent "graduates to be advocates in every institution you find in America." Lynn "came to our defense when the Monica Goodling story broke," said Dean Jeff Brauch. Lynn assured inquiring reporters that the students he met at Regent were "eager to debate issues," and added, "If someone walks into a courtroom and says 'Oh, the lawyer on the other side graduated from Regent, I don't have to prepare,' they're likely to have his or her head handed to them on a platter."[47]

The American Center for Law and Justice

Given his training in law at Yale University and his political pedigree, it would have been odd for Pat Robertson not to be involved in the evangelical efforts to redress the court decisions of the 1960s and 1970s that addressed the separation of church and state. Speaking before the Senate Judiciary Committee in 1982 at the invitation of Senator Strom Thurmond, Robertson supported a constitutional amendment to allow voluntary prayer in public schools and other institutions. He told the committee: "By 1982, under the incessant hammering of groups such as the American Civil Liberties Union, a group formed 62 years ago to defend Bolsheviks, religious freedom is no longer considered a paramount freedom but has become restricted and proscribed by successive court decisions." Robertson reminded the committee members: "When my father, A. Willis Robertson, was a member of this distinguished body, he met with various colleagues every Wednesday morning in the Senate Dining Room to read the Bible and pray. This to him was the highlight of his week. . . . I want to assure this committee, that if the recent Supreme Court decisions are constitutionally sound, then the Senate prayer breakfasts are unconstitutional." The public, he believed, overwhelmingly wanted "a reversal of the anti-religious court rulings." By the 1980s Robertson's attacks on the courts had begun to catch the attention of the press.[48]

Robertson gave both moral and financial support to the bevy of conservative legal advocacy groups that appeared in the 1980s. "He was advocating doing legal advocacy before it was cool," recalled Jay Sekulow. "He saw the potential before anyone else." In 1984 he contributed generously to the Creation Science Legal Defense Fund in its unsuccessful defense of a Louisiana law authorizing teaching of creationism in public schools. He was one of the original supporters of the Rutherford Institute, a conservative advocacy organization founded in 1982 by John Whitehead which was for many years the largest and best known of conservative legal groups. "He was giving money to everybody in those early days," recalled Sekulow, even though "most of them were not too grateful."[49]

Early Legal Explorations

For all his generosity, Robertson thought that many of the early legal efforts of conservatives were clumsy and ineffective. Given his legal background, it was understandable that he wanted his own organization. In his first attempt to enter the field, in 1981, he established the National Legal Foundation, which first functioned as a division of the Freedom Council. When the group hired Robert Skolrood in 1984, Robertson heralded it as "the start of a campaign to actively defend religious freedom in the court room." After the Freedom Council was abolished in 1986, CBN severed its relationship with the National Legal Foundation, though Robertson continued to support the group financially. In 1990, the National Legal Foundation won a major Supreme Court victory in the case of *Board of Education of Westside Community Schools v. Mergens.* In an 8-1 decision the Supreme Court overruled Omaha school officials who had barred student prayer groups from using school facilities after classes.[50]

Robertson received due credit for the *Mergens* victory as the founder of the National Legal Foundation, but the hero of the Omaha decision was the rising young attorney who argued the case before the Supreme Court, Jay Alan Sekulow. Sekulow first won public attention when he won the case of *Board of Airport Commissioners v. Jews for Jesus* in 1988, which allowed Jews for Jesus, an organization of which Sekulow was a member, to distribute materials in the Los Angeles airport. Sekulow subsequently established an advocacy group called Christian Advocates Serving Evangelism (C.A.S.E). Robertson was one of his "key supporters."

Sekulow was a Jewish convert to Christianity who embraced the charismatic movement in the 1970s and befriended many of the movement's most influential leaders. His work in the Los Angeles case caught the attention of TBN founder Paul Crouch, and he soon became a regular guest on that network, hosting a show named *Call to Action: Legal Issues Facing Christians Today.* His Los Angeles experience showed Sekulow the power of television to attract financial supporters; after he began appearing on TBN, financial contributions to C.A.S.E. spiraled upward. Crouch urged Pat Robertson to invite Sekulow to appear on *The 700 Club,* and by 1990 Sekulow and Robertson had begun a warm friendship based on respect for one another's legal expertise and objectives. "Pat wanted a bulldog litigator" to support, and it became more and more apparent that Sekulow was his man. After Sekulow's victory in the *Mergens* case, he received two congratulatory telephone calls, one from Kenneth Starr and the other from Pat Robertson.[51]

Discontented with the records of the established conservative legal groups, by 1990 Robertson was poised to move ahead and form his own advocacy group. For a short time, the Christian Coalition coordinated Robertson's efforts. Approached in April 1990 by the superintendent of Chesapeake Public Schools, who had been notified by the ACLU that it might take legal action against the school's program promoting "sexual abstinence," Ralph Reed replied: "Should the ACLU take legal action against the Chesapeake school system, the Christian Coalition Legal Defense fund is prepared to provide the finances to recruit the finest constitutional attorneys in the nation to defend this outstanding program. We are in a position to commit significant funds and legal talent to this effort should that become necessary." But by the summer, Reed was referring legal matters to the American Center for Law and Justice. He informed inquirers that he was passing requests along to "Pat, Herb Titus, . . . and Jay Sekulow, who serves as General Counsel to the ACLJ." In the fall of 1991, Robertson informed a California attorney that "the ACLJ should be staffed and ready to take action this fall. Up until this time we were unable to take on situations like the one you wrote about. I believe now, the ACLJ can help."[52]

The Origins of the American Center for Law and Justice

The ACLJ was incorporated on May 30, 1990; Robertson announced that he was preparing to launch a full-scale legal group that "will be our answer to the destruction of our values by the humanists, the leftists and the infamous ACLU." The American Center for Law and Justice, "born in prayer," would be a "joint effort of CBN, Regent University Law School, The Christian Coalition, C.A.S.E., and Free Speech Advocates." While the structure of the new organization was still in its formative stage, in a fundraising letter Robertson assured donors that the ACLJ would assemble "a staff of seasoned, tough litigators — skilled in Constitutional Law." It was still unclear how the ACLJ would coordinate the activities of the listed organizations; one supporter of C.A.S.E. felt that Robertson had inappropriately claimed credit for Sekulow's triumph in the *Mergens* case. Robertson replied: "CBN has worked closely with Jay Sekulow and his work at C.A.S.E. in several instances. However, CBN did not give funds directly to Jay for the Equal Access Case, which he so brilliantly argued. We had already invested substantial funds in this case through another group involved."[53]

Slowly, in the summer of 1990, the ACLJ began to take shape. Fundraiser Norm Berman was hired and given the title of vice-president for development; Robertson believed that his presence would "add further financial stability to the ongoing operation of the Center." Next, Robertson tried to lure Alan E. Sears, a former member of Edwin Meese's Justice Department staff and a noted litigator, to join the center as its executive director. In a June letter to Sears, Robertson wrote: "As I mentioned on the phone, we will make an initial commitment of $500,000 to get rolling, and I am sure we can see an annual income of up to $10 million within the next five years." Robertson assured Sears that he had "no problem paying good salaries to the key people" in the new organization, but his recruitment of Sears was not successful.[54]

Not until May 1991 did Robertson find a suitable executive director. In a meeting in Virginia Beach he offered the position to Keith Fournier, a practicing attorney in Steubenville, Ohio, and a former administrator at Franciscan University of Steubenville. Fournier was a Roman Catholic charismatic who had been an early supporter of the Christian Coalition. Before attending a meeting arranged by Ralph Reed in early 1990, Fournier wrote to Robertson: "I know another mutual friend, Harald Bredesen, has told you about me. We have much in common, including being lawyers. Most importantly, we serve the same Savior and are compelled to action by the same Spirit. I have long admired your work and particularly appreciate your humility and integrity. It's an honor to stand with you." But Fournier had had little direct contact with Robertson when he visited the Regent campus in the spring of 1991 while on a vacation trip with his family. He talked with law school dean Herb Titus, and the two of them then visited with Pat Robertson in his office. They discussed the ACLJ, which Fournier had heard about for the first time in his conversation with Dean Titus. Fournier was stunned when Robertson asked, "Keith, what would it take to get you here?" "But Pat," the surprised Fournier responded, "I am a Catholic." Robertson knew that quite well; he had a copy of Fournier's book on evangelical Catholics on his desk. He assured Fournier that he would be welcome in the ecumenical environment of CBN and Regent. Fournier accepted and for several years in the early 1990s became a bridge to Roman Catholics for Robertson and the Christian Coalition.[55]

Robertson was elated that the ACLJ was off the ground. As Fournier prepared to move to Virginia Beach, Robertson wrote to him: "Fear not, the Lord is going to take care of you and the American Center For Law and Justice. With the upcoming Rhode Island graduation case . . . I think we are going to have a very fertile field for legal action in the next several years under the umbrella of what seems to be a very conservative Court." Fournier immediately set four objectives: to build "the General Motors of Christian public-interest advocacy"; to "engage in litigation where rights and liberties are at stake"; "to develop and effectively execute a strategy of exposing and opposing the American Civil Liberties Union and its anti-family, anti-life, and anti-liberty pursuits"; and "to establish a network of attorneys who will provide counsel, assistance, and services to clients on a referral basis."[56]

The arrival of an executive director set the stage to begin serious fund-raising. In May 1991 Norm Berman informed Robertson that the ACLJ had approximately 6,000 donors and that he was preparing a mailing announcing the hiring of Fournier. The letter read: "It is a pleasure to an-nounce that Keith Fournier, an outstanding Christian, a superb lawyer, and a much beloved American is joining The American Center For Law and Justice as its Executive Director. Keith comes at just the right time. . . . The American Center For Law and Justice is going into court on your behalf. We will be expanding our legal staff. Coordinating closely with others in the field. Standing against the ACLU in every state." On the draft, Robertson jotted a note to Berman, along with instructions to "rush the letter": "Norm, Now that Keith is on board we are going to get aggressive. I will show you the strategy to raise the funds we need. Up to now we have been playing." At the end of January 1992, Fournier reported to Robertson that the ACLJ had raised more than $400,000 during the month, "a fourfold increase from our previous best month." The number of donors had risen to 20,619 and the organization had a mailing list of 27,221, "a six-fold increase from June, 1991."[57]

For the next seven years, Fournier skillfully administered the ACLJ and was the organization's chief cheerleader. He was a prolific writer who turned out a steady stream of position papers boosting the ACLJ and defending a variety of conservative causes. But Robertson still badly wanted to get Jay Sekulow directly involved in the ACLJ. In a February 1991 meeting of the board of directors, the minutes reported: "Board explored selection of General Counsel. Jay Sekulow was mentioned." Robertson wrote to Sekulow: "The Center For Law and Justice is finally rolling into gear with the appointment of an executive director. I sincerely hope that we can all participate together in bringing down this unholy liberal collusion which has done so much damage to the cause of Christ." Fournier also believed that Sekulow was "the lawyer who clearly had done the most for our movement," and he joined Robertson in courting him.[58]

Robertson's interest in Sekulow had been common knowledge ever since the founding of the ACLJ in the summer of 1990. The rumor prompted a letter from an executive at the Rutherford Foundation warning Robertson against the perils of establishing an "on-going relationship" with a relative unknown like Sekulow and urging Robertson instead to explore stronger linkages between CBN and Rutherford, since the two were the "leading institutions in their respective fields." But Robertson knew that Sekulow was the litigator he wanted, and for two years he continued to court him.[59]

For months Sekulow remained wary of abandoning his highly successful C.A.S.E., but in the summer of 1992 he finally agreed to become the chief counsel of the American Center for Law and Justice. In November, Robertson proudly announced the appointment: "I am extremely pleased to an-nounce that Jay Alan Sekulow has become the Center's Chief Counsel. Over the last year, we have been working together as a team, and Jay's acceptance of this position formalizes a working relationship that will thrust the Center into an even more pivotal role in the battle to restore our religious and civil liberties.... With Jay Sekulow now serving as Chief Counsel, we can pursue the ACLU even more actively than before. Jay knows how to beat the ACLU. He knows how to argue cases before the United States Supreme Court." After Sekulow agreed to join the Center as chief counsel, Robertson launched a fundraising campaign based on his involvement in "50 cases nation-wide in defense of your rights as a Christian." In a letter soliciting funds from "the top 15,000 donors," Robertson exulted: "It has finally happened! A viable public interest law firm with the God-given brains and muscle to force the ACLU and their allies on school boards across the country to stop stealing the rights of Christians."[60]

Sekulow's arrival initiated years of frenetic activity at the ACLJ, years filled with Supreme Court victories and remarkable institutional growth. On the surface, Sekulow, Fournier, and Robertson were a smoothly functioning team. Robertson provided the fundraising expertise, contacts, and mature legal counsel; Sekulow was the virtuoso litigator; and Fournier took care of the administrative minutiae that neither of the others cared to address. In 1993, Sekulow dedicated a brief instruction booklet he authored for Christian plaintiffs to Fournier: "Keith's superb management of the American Center has allowed me and our litigation team to do what we are best at — going to court." Fournier was justly proud of the accomplishments of the ACLJ before his departure at the end of 1997. He wrote in 1994: "The American Center currently has twenty-six full-time lawyers and fifty staff in five offices nationwide. Among the lawyers, there are Protestants, Catholics, Messianic Jews, and Eastern Orthodox believers." In addition, the Center was working with more than 450 "affiliate attorneys" throughout the United States.[61]

But Robertson's ecumenism, which led him to hire the Catholic Fournier and describe him as "an outstanding Christian," ironically played a role in Fournier's departure. Robertson dismissed him abruptly at the end of 1997 because Fournier, who had been ordained a deacon in his church, declined to participate in an ecumenical communion service at CBN. "I think it deeply offended him," Fournier later recalled. That was an understatement. It was an act of conscientious exclusiveness that Robertson was unwilling to tolerate: "This is nonsense. We are interdenominational." The two men continued to respect one another, and the ACLJ provided grants to a "cultural, policy and apologetics institute" established by

Fournier — Liberty, Life and Family — through March 2000. But Robertson wasn't interested in divisive doctrinal lines between Christians, and Fournier's rejection of ecumenical communion appeared to emphasize those lines.[62]

But there were other disagreements as well, and the communion episode may have been simply the last straw. Robertson was increasingly perturbed by Fournier's penchant for writing "position papers" and editorial pieces. "Keith and I had a good relationship," recalled Sekulow, but it appeared that Fournier "wanted to turn this into a think tank" along the lines of the Heritage Foundation. Fournier continued to be a prolific writer, and after leaving ACLJ he published his legally grounded conservative Catholic viewpoint on a website called Catholic Way. But Pat Robertson was not interested in supporting another think tank — he wanted "a champion to do battle." In Robertson's mind, Fournier's intellectual excursions had become too expensive: "The think tank was costing us enormous sums of money. Hundreds of thousands of dollars. . . . It was clear we had to shake the thing up and stop the losses."[63]

Victories in the 1990s

The 1990s were years of rapid growth for the ACLJ. The Center began "mobilizing a force of Christian attorneys from across the country" and conducting conferences to better equip them to launch lawsuits. The ACLJ also established branch offices throughout the country, and in 1992 construction began on the Law and Justice Center on the campus of Regent University. By 1993 the ACLJ was in the foreground of Pat Robertson's fundraising vision. As the construction of the $13.7 million Virginia Beach "strategic command center" neared completion, donors were urged to "take the next step in fulfilling the overall vision that Pat Robertson received almost two decades ago" to change the world through Christian leadership. The completion of the Center would provide Regent law school students "unique opportunities to intern" with the ACLJ. In the meantime, the ACLJ had in place more than 100 attorneys nationwide who were ready to "mobilize legal SWAT teams," was building a "legal defense fund to respond wherever Christian freedoms are challenged by schools, police, courts and other institutions," and had already gone on the offensive in launching lawsuits.[64]

The breadth of cases contested by the ACLJ in the 1990s spanned the field of conservative Christian social issues, including student activated prayer and other Christian concerns involving public schools, support for abortion protesters, opposition to same-sex marriage legislation, and an array of appeals for help from individuals, education officials, and state politicians. By 1993 the ACLJ had eleven full-time lawyers in four regional offices and was on the screen of outside observers. The ACLU warned its supporters that, "having seen first-hand the damage to civil liberties wrought by the far-less sophisticated Moral Majority a decade ago, now is the time to challenge Robertson's group." Delivering the Landon Lecture at Kansas State University in 1993, Robertson boasted: "The organization I work with has helped people whose free speech of their faith has been challenged. . . . We have not lost one case in two years." By 1993 the young ACLJ was already one of the largest among conservative advocacy organizations, though the Rutherford Institute, with a budget of $11 million and a staff of nine attorneys and fifty-five employees, remained larger.[65]

More than anything else, as Pat Robertson had predicted, the ACLJ gained increased visibility and support in cadence with Jay Sekulow's increasing fame. In 1993, Sekulow won two important Supreme Court victories that received broad media coverage. As opposed to the Rutherford Institute, which boasted that it responded to every one of its roughly 2,000 monthly requests for help, "ACLJ's specialty is the Big Case." Sekulow's eye for publicity and Robertson's fundraising expertise clearly were riling some of the ACLJ's competitors.[66]

The ACLJ's two victories in 1993 came in the cases of *Bray v. Alexandria Women's Health Clinic* and *Lamb's Chapel v. Center Moriches School*. Both decisions were handed down on June 1. On that day, observed an article in the American Bar Association student magazine, "Robertson looks like he's David slaying Goliath." In the *Bray* case Sekulow won a 5-4 decision upholding the rights of anti-abortion protesters in Washington, D.C., who obstructed the entrance to abortion clinics, holding that they had not violated the rights of clinic clients by conspiring to deprive them of the right to abortions and to interstate travel. In the *Lamb's Chapel* case Sekulow argued that the free speech rights of Christians were being proscribed because the Center Moriches School District, acting under a New York law prohibiting the use of school property for any religious use, denied Lamb's Chapel's request to show a religious-oriented film on family values after school hours. Under grilling from Justice Scalia, the school attorney admitted that communists and other groups were free to use school facilities. That led to a noted Sekulow response: "The way I see it is the communists are in, the atheists are in, but religion isn't in." The court ruled unanimously that the school district had violated the First Amendment rights of the petitioner. In 1997 Sekulow argued and won by a 6-3 vote the case of *Schenck v. Pro-Choice Network,* a case that ruled that buffer zones around abortion clinics were constitutional but that the creation of "floating buffer zones" was not.[67]

The ACLJ in the Sekulow Era

After the departure of Fournier, the ACLJ was reorganized along the lines of a law firm under the leadership of Jay Sekulow. In 1999 Sekulow joined Robertson and Regent law school dean J. Nelson Happy on the ACLJ Board of Directors. The board authorized Sekulow to "continue in his role as Chief Counsel and . . . continue to manage the daily operations of the organization." From the beginning, Robertson had wanted to "run it like a law firm," and under Sekulow's leadership "complete departments were eliminated." By 1999, in addition to the national office on the campus of Regent University in Virginia Beach, the ACLJ had offices in fourteen other American cities operating out of eight regional offices, which were awarded "grants" to support litigation in their regions.[68]

The reach of the Center had grown remarkably. In 1999 Pat Robertson informed Senator John Ashcroft: "Last year our American Center For Law And Justice received an absolutely astounding 102,000 requests for legal help springing from various forms of religious discrimination." In his report on the first quarter activities of ACLJ in 2000, Sekulow reeled off a litany of positives: "Revenues from Donations increased by over 52% from last year. Operating expenses increased by only 1%. Net Operating income increased by $1,575,000 from last year."[69]

Over the next decade Sekulow presided over an extraordinary period of triumphs and celebrity for both the ACLJ and himself. ACLJ lawyers adjudicated hundreds of cases at all levels of the judiciary. The organization listed four main areas in which it contested cases during these years: "Protecting the free speech rights of pro-life demonstrators," "Safeguarding the constitutional rights of religious groups to have equal access to public facilities," "Ensuring that public school students could form and participate in religious organizations . . . on campus," and "guaranteeing that minors could participate in the political process by protecting their free speech right in the political setting." The visibility of the ACLJ during these years continued to be closely tied to Sekulow's advocacy of highly visible and sometimes precedent-setting Supreme Court cases. In addition to cases argued by Sekulow, the ACLJ regularly filed amicus briefs supporting conservative causes, including support for the FCC regulation of "indecent" broadcasting, Federal legislation banning the promotion of child pornography, the rights of gun owners in Washington D.C., a ban on partial-birth abortion, efforts to protect the posting of Ten Commandments on public property, and a Justice Department case arguing that the detainees in Guantanamo Bay were being lawfully detained.[70]

The most significant achievement of Jay Sekulow and the ACLJ came in a series of Supreme Court victories expanding the rights of public expression of religion based on the First Amendment protection of speech. In 2003, in *Locke v. Davey,* Sekulow unsuccessfully argued that the free speech of students who were refused scholarships to major in pastoral studies had been denied, but in the case of *McConnell v. SEC* Sekulow presented oral arguments in a unanimous decision protecting the First Amendment rights of minors. In the 2007 case of *Morse v. Frederick* Sekulow surprised many observers by siding with the ACLU, filing an amicus brief in support of an Alaskan student who was disciplined for displaying a banner deemed by the school to be "pro-drug." While "strongly disagreeing with the student's message," the ACLJ urged the court to "uphold the free speech rights of the student arguing that a decision in favor of the school district would empower school districts across the country to ban future student speech they considered offensive — including speech advocating Christian beliefs." Public schools, warned Sekulow, "face a constant temptation to impose a suffocating blanket of political correctness upon the educational atmosphere." In a case that attracted considerable media attention in 2008 and 2009, Sekulow won a unanimous decision upholding the right of the city of Pleasant Grove, Utah, to display a monument of the Ten Commandments in a city park while refusing to allow a monument of "Seven Aphorisms" to be erected by a small sect called Summum. In his argument before the court in *Pleasant Grove City v. Summum,* Sekulow argued monuments were "government speech" which was protected by the First Amendment. The Supreme Court agreed that "the government has to be neutral toward private speech, but it does not have to be neutral in its own speech."[71]

In effect, in the years after his victory in the *Lamb's Chapel* case in 1993, Sekulow moved the focus of the constitutional debate about religious rights from arguments about the First Amendment's Establishment Clause to its Free Speech Clause. Increasingly, courts emphasized the distinction between government sponsorship of religious activities, which were consistently judged to be violations of the Establishment Clause, and religious speech by private citizens, which is protected by the Free Speech

Clause. It was this distinction, noted the National Education Association, that paved the way for the return of some school prayer.[72]

Ironically, Sekulow's embrace of First Amendment arguments sometimes led him into further cooperation with the ACLU. When the ACLU supported the ACLJ in a case upholding the use of school facilities by religious student groups after class hours, Sekulow welcomed the support: "They are not always wrong. I've enjoyed their support on a number of cases, but when we disagree, we disagree broadly, and what's different is that now there is someone to answer them. They're not used to that." Barry Lynn summarized the seismic shift: "Jay is a very bright person and he is very clever to have discovered this I think completely wrongheaded theory that all of these issues about access and speech ought to be dealt with as freedom of speech issues.... More and more courts have moved to that position.... He is not just a good craftsman of legal briefs; he is a good architect as well, because he really did design this theory that has made everything into a free speech case."[73]

In spite of this change in argument strategy, both Jay Sekulow and Pat Robertson continued to have well-defined views on the proper interpretation of the "separation between church and state," and both men wrote and spoke profusely on the subject. While there are nuances in what both Sekulow and Robertson believe, both have basically argued that the framers of the constitution intended no high wall of separation of church and state. Rather, Robertson wrote to an inquirer, the establishment clause was intended simply to assure that "the federal government could not have the power to prefer one sect over another as was the case in Europe." In his heavily documented discussion of the subject, *Witnessing Their Faith*, Sekulow wrote: "The Establishment Clause was designed to draw a line of demarcation in the relationship between church and state by prohibiting the creation of a national religion such as existed in England under the Anglican Church and in the European monarchies under the Roman Catholic Church."[74]

Robertson bristled at the charge that he did not believe in separation of church and state. Perturbed by a 1995 statement by Senator Arlen Specter challenging his stance, Robertson wrote to his law school classmate: "I believe that the institutional church should be separated from the institution of government. I would, however, suggest that neither the Constitution of the United States nor the time-honored tradition of this great land dictates that God should be separated from the government or from those who hold public office." "In the future," he urged the senator, "I would ask that your comments about me reflect truth and knowledge." Both Sekulow and Robertson believed that the courts had slowly eroded the Christian heritage of the nation by building an artificial wall that was not intended by the nation's founders, and both wrote books defending their views.[75]

By 2009, Sekulow was heralded widely as the "nation's top legal advocate for all causes Christian," and *Business Week* called the ACLJ "the leading advocacy group for religious freedom." Barry Lynn summed up the common view in Washington: "He is certainly the best legal mind on the Religious Right." By 2007, the ACLJ employed forty-four lawyers full-time, and its annual budget was approaching that of the ACLU. In addition to prosecuting numerous cases, Sekulow became a popular and respected spokesman for conservative causes, and the ACLJ sponsored a daily radio program with an audience of 1.5 million listeners and a weekly television broadcast. Sekulow continued to be a frequent guest on *The 700 Club*, but the financial and programmatic independence of ACLJ was physically emphasized by the move of its national headquarters to a location near the Supreme Court in 2003. The 6,000-square-foot building was valued at $5 million, and its renovation reportedly cost another $1 million. Sekulow informed Robertson that the gift came from an anonymous donor. Always careful to keep his mentor informed, Sekulow wrote: "We are thrilled that the Lord has provided this resource for our work at the American Center for Law and Justice, and pleased that the organization that you began more than ten years ago will now have a strong and lasting presence in Washington, D.C. Thank you for your prayers and support."[76]

Jay Sekulow's visibility in Washington made him an important counselor to the George W. Bush administration, particularly in the appointment of Supreme Court justices. Robertson was thrilled that his ACLJ protégé had the ear of the Bush administration. Robertson had long issued statements about the appointment of Supreme Court justices; he was generally disappointed by the decisions rendered by the appointees of Ronald Reagan and George H. W. Bush. Angered by two critical decisions on schools and abortion in 1992, he wrote: "It is my firmly considered opinion that those with an eye to see will look back on that week as the time when the Supreme Court of the United States of America . . . guaranteed that the wrath of Almighty God will fall upon the United States of America." In 2003, Robertson launched "Operation Supreme Court Freedom," asking his supporters to engage in a "prayer offensive" seeking the retirement of three liberal justices so that George W. Bush would be able to appoint conservative replacements. Robertson was delighted with the appointments of Chief Justice John Roberts in 2005 and Justice Samuel Alito in 2006. Both appointments were "grand slam" victories for Jay Sekulow, who was one of a three-person team of strategists chosen to steer Bush's Supreme Court appointees through the Senate.[77]

Sekulow's rise to stardom attracted critics on both the left and the right. The meteoric rise of the ACLJ and Sekulow rankled some older legal groups who competed with them for clients and donors. On occasion, the relations between the ACLJ and the Rutherford Institute turned testy. In a 1994 issue of the Rutherford Institute magazine, staff writers claimed the high moral ground for Rutherford and targeted the ACLJ as little more than a fundraising juggernaut. Others criticized ACLJ's dependence on its "star" litigator, Jay Sekulow, and on its selectivity in the cases it accepted. Rutherford historian R. Jonathan Moore writes: "Baldly naming names, [legal coordinator Alexis Crowe] cited another magazine's claim that the ACLJ took on only those cases with ideal, precedent setting, headline-generating legal potential. . . . And TRI staff did not hog the publicity if cases made it to the Supreme Court, readers learned, unlike the ACLJ, whose 'star,' Jay Sekulow, dedicated himself solely to high-profile arguments before the nation's highest court." Sekulow probably would readily agree that he reveled in headline-capturing victories, but the ACLJ did not uniformly turn its back on lost causes. Writing to Executive Director Fournier about a case involving a school principal who had distributed Bibles to students called to his office for discipline, Sekulow advised: "From a legal perspective, under the current status of the law, it would be difficult to defend what the ACLU is alleging the principal has done here. The Seventh Circuit has ruled that the distribution of Bibles in schools by the Gideons violated the Establishment Clause. Although I believe that the ruling is incorrect, the current make up of the Supreme Court does not provide us with sufficient basis for a successful legal challenge. However, I think it would be important to continue to offer our services . . . and not let the ACLU bully this principal, who is trying to do his job."[78]

An extended article published in *Legal Times* in 2005 pictured Sekulow as a jet-set, high-living legal superstar. Sekulow shrugged off the charges, offering no apologies for paying himself and his staff well. Were he in private practice, he insisted, he would be making more. Copies of the article moved quickly from the news department at CBN up to the desk of Pat Robertson with the caveat: "Hopefully, this won't spur any media attention!" Predictably, the article was highlighted by Americans United for Separation of Church and State, but the attention was short-lived.[79]

In 1999, the ACLJ board approved the incorporation of an "International Centre for Law and Justice," authorizing Sekulow "to do all things reasonable and necessary to establish the centre." By 2009, the ACLJ had two "affiliated centers," the European Centre for Law and Justice and the Slavic Centre for Law and Justice. In 1998, the European Centre opened headquarters in Strasbourg, France, and the Slavic Centre was established in Moscow. Both were staffed with "renowned international human rights attorneys" prosecuting religious persecution cases throughout Europe and the Middle East. The European centres had branches in Jerusalem and Slovakia and, according to Sekulow, were "doing a lot on Christian persecution issues."[80]

Both Pat and Gordon Robertson were enthusiastic supporters of the internationalization of the ACLJ. Pat Robertson "has a tremendous knowledge of the Middle East," observed Sekulow, and his mentor frequently urged him: "We have to protect the Christian minorities in the Middle East." The Christian Coalition's foreign explorations failed to produce results, Robertson thought, because by the time opportunities arose the "American branch was coming apart at the seams," but by 2009 the ACLJ had become a respected force abroad. Gordon Robertson believed that the ACLJ should "expand even more abroad," supporting Christians in India, and in other Asian and the Middle Eastern countries that had constitutional provisions supporting "freedom of religion."[81]

By 2009 the ACLJ was the most independent organization in the Robertson family, partly because of Sekulow's skills as a litigator and a fundraiser. Even though the ACLJ was still referred to by Americans United for Separation of Church and State as "TV preacher Pat Robertson's American Center for Law and Justice," and Sekulow was identified as "a confederate of TV preacher Pat Robertson," both Sekulow and the ACLJ clearly had identities of their own. Nonetheless, the ties between the ACLJ and the Robertson family of organizations have remained strong. Jay Sekulow is a conspicuous presence at Regent University, where he is a professor and a member of the university board of trustees. He has continued to be a frequent guest on *The 700 Club*, a "very important" connection for both the ACLJ and CBN. "There is still a very close working relationship," explained Sekulow: "The ACLJ would not have existed without Pat Robertson." Replying to a reporter in 2005, Robertson affirmed: "I meet regularly with Jay Sekulow to discuss the activities, programs, accomplishments and general operations of the ACLJ and affiliated organizations." Through the years, Sekulow has continued to send reports to Robertson, who still serves as president of the ACLJ.[82]

Despite such involvement, Robertson has seen the ACLJ succeed without his direct day-to-day involvement — and he has been happy to do so.

CHAPTER 9

Multiple Incarnations:
Entrepreneur, Author, Controversialist

—⊲ø/ø⊳—

During his campaign for the presidency, Pat Robertson was not being du-
plicitous when he insisted that he was a businessman, not an evangelist.
He was, in fact, never an evangelist, and he was, in fact, always a businessman. The crowning achievement of his business life was his savvy reading
of the potential of the cable television industry that provided a financial
endowment for all of his other accomplishments, including CBN and Regent University. On the other hand, his high-risk entrepreneurial spirit and
a series of business misadventures cost him dearly and exposed him to a
frustrating torrent of media investigation and criticism.

Of course, Pat Robertson was never *simply* a businessman. He was the
bestselling author of a series of sometimes controversial books, and he
was a television personality whose commentary was monitored meticulously by his detractors, particularly by those seeking to weaken his political influence. For many Americans, it was his personality as controversial-
ist that came to define the man and his legacy. To be sure, some of the
controversy surrounding Pat Robertson's writings and his comments on
the air was the result of skillful campaigns on the part of his opponents to
marginalize his influence, but it was also a part of who he was. "He is a lion
made to roar," observed his co-host on *The 700 Club*, Terry Meeuwsen, who
often found herself trying to tactfully tone down that roar.[1]

Entrepreneur

From his youth, Pat Robertson imagined that he would be a successful businessman. His Lexington friend Matt Paxton remembered him best as a young man determined "to do big things," to make a million dollars fast. Even during the depths of his religious search in New York City, business remained much on his mind. From the failure of his audio speaker venture in New York City through the floundering beginning of CBN and his television station, Robertson remained committed to building a successful business. His reluctance to seek ordination after graduating from seminary and to accept a regular position in the ministry — a recalcitrance that perplexed and annoyed his father — was basically a business decision. In the early days of his television venture, he preached to support his business habit.[2]

His self-definition as an innovative businessman became more and more marked through the years. Explaining changes in the format of radio station WXRI-FM to CBN's staff in 1980, Robertson wrote: "I am basically a pioneer who tries out things that have not always been tried out before. I do not claim infallibility, and there is always a possibility that what is done may fail. I hope and pray that this format will be the answer to the Christian radio problem that I have been struggling with for the past 18 years." Fourteen years later he explained to a supporter: "Since 1960, I have followed the call of God in Christian broadcasting, and in the process have started in addition to The Christian Broadcasting Network, several other business enterprises plus a university. Therefore, as one who organizes, manages, and assumes the risks of a business or enterprise, I am more an entrepreneur than a pastor. . . . God has not called me to the ministry. He has called me to be a Christian broadcaster."[3]

Robertson believes that he has a "God-given talent" as an "entrepreneur." By the 1990s, with the completion of the complicated IFE negotiations that enriched CBN, Regent University, and Pat and Tim Robertson, it was hard to gainsay his skills. "I like to create things," he told a reporter in 1992. "I'm a financial architect, and I'm good at it." In 1994, Jeff Sine of Morgan Stanley's media group wrote in the *Washington Post* that Robertson "is viewed as a very smart businessman, along with his son Tim. . . . The results speak for themselves." After all, observed Barry Lynn, Robertson was "the guy who took a tiny radio station and turned it into a huge international broadcasting empire. And you don't do that if your thinking is the thinking of a crazed man."[4]

Pat Robertson's reputation as a "very smart businessman" rested largely on his development of The Family Channel. In the media business, Alec Foege wrote, he had great skills: "As a broadcaster alone, Pat Robertson was one of the medium's greatest innovators." From the early 1970s Robertson saw the potential of cable television and satellite transmission and dreamed of putting together "a fourth commercial network for America." Few people had a better grasp of the rapidly changing technology driving television in the 1970s and 1980s. While the dream of a "fourth network" never fully materialized, the growth of The Family Channel became the financial anchor of all CBN activities by the late 1980s. In later years, Robertson still savored the days of running a public company whose stock was skyrocketing: "I hated to sell it. . . . You feel a sense of loss."[5]

Based on his undeniable success in the television industry, Pat Robertson is regarded by his supporters as a fount of financial wisdom. He scrupulously avoids giving specific tips, but he calls on his study of corporate economics at Yale and his lifelong fascination with finance and business to offer sweeping commentary and general economic predictions on "Money Monday" each week on *The 700 Club*. Robertson's business life has been marked by extravagant daring and risk-taking, but he generally advises viewers to "stick to what you know" and not "take risks." Pat Robertson could have saved himself a good deal of grief had he followed his own advice: "Stay in your line and stay close to shore."[6]

Robertson has managed the Pat Robertson Charitable Remainder Trust of $109 million resulting from the sale of IFE. He hoped to build that nest egg into a major endowment for CBN and embarked on a number of high-risk ventures — with disastrous results. In a detailed article published in *Fortune* in 2002, business writer Daniel Roth estimated that Robertson's losses had reached $78 million as a result of a series of "big, risky bets."[7]

Those close to Robertson have accepted his business misadventures with resignation. Her husband is an entrepreneur at heart, observed Dede Robertson; inevitably, some of his ventures "have been good and some have been very, very poor." He "likes the upside," observed his longtime friend Michael Little. While some of his ventures were disastrous, "his lifetime average was good."[8]

An Expensive Battle with California Environmentalists

Robertson's biggest financial setback came with the purchase of a rusting oil refinery in Santa Fe Springs, California. The purchase was recommended by his personal attorney and dean of the Regent University School of Law, J. Nelson Happy. According to press reports, Happy estimated that an initial investment of $20 million would be sufficient to restart the plant, with potential profits of $70 to $100 million a year. The plant was renamed Cenco Refining, and the new owners began remodeling the refinery to produce an advanced gasoline product known as CARBOB, or California Reformulated Gasoline Blendstock for Oxygenate Blending.

It soon became clear that the Robertson and Happy had underestimated community resistance in the town where the refinery had been a major pollution producer. Robertson knew from the beginning that other investors "thought the permitting would be extremely difficult to get," but he and his investment advisors believed that the risks had been adequately covered. Soon the venture was mired in lawsuits filed by environmental groups, by the California Department of Labor on behalf of former employees of the refinery, by both the state and the city for hazardous-waste violations, and by the Environmental Protection Agency over air pollution concerns. By the end of 2001, operating costs passed $300,000 a month and the interest on loans was more than $400,000.[9]

In November 2001 Robertson replaced Happy as chief executive and appointed a former trustee at Regent University, Lowell W. Morse, to try to bring the venture to completion. "We got forty-three different permits and it was going to be the cleanest refinery in America," Robertson insisted. But in 2002 "a small group of local environmentalists persuaded a judge to halt the refinery's operation," placing in jeopardy Cenco's ability to secure the bank funding needed to complete the project. "Mr. Robertson really wanted to do this," Morse told reporters, "but there comes a time when you say, 'How much longer can you keep up this battle?'" Robertson put the property up for sale. The Pat Robertson Charitable Remainder Trust had lost approximately $60 million.[10]

Gold and Diamonds in Africa

Less expensive, but probably more damaging to Pat Robertson's reputation, were two business misadventures in Africa. In 1998 Robertson's old friend John Gimenez alerted him to an opportunity to secure a lease on a gold-mining region in Liberia. Gimenez had done extensive evangelistic work in the country and believed that after seven years of civil war, Liberia was poised for economic development. Approached by Christian friends in Liberia with a proposal, Gimenez turned to Robertson. "In something like this," Gimenez told an investigative reporter, "Pat has a real heart to help people."[11]

In December 1998 Robertson created a company in the Cayman Islands called Freedom Gold, and in May 1999 he announced that "Dr. Charles G. Taylor, President of the Republic of Liberia, today signed a Mineral Development Agreement approving the grant of rights for a scientific exploration program and subsequent mining rights in the Bukon Jedeh area to Freedom Gold Limited. The Republic of Liberia considers its mineral resources to be an important element in jump-starting and sustaining the nation's economic growth.... In a statement to the President, Dr. Robertson, who signed the Agreement for Freedom Gold, said, 'I pray that this investment may become a wonderful blessing to the people of Liberia and will be one of many significant investments that will be made under your administration in the Nation of Liberia." The original agreement stipulated that the Liberian government would receive a 10 percent equity interest in the venture and that "Liberian citizens" would be offered the opportunity to purchase 15 percent of the shares "after the exploration period."[12]

By the fall Robertson reported that "scientific exploration in the Bukon Jedeh concession of Liberia" had begun and was "already providing much-needed employment and public services in this third-world country." By 2002 Freedom Gold had done extensive exploration, and Robertson confidently predicted that his investment was "the best means of helping the people through productive and profitable enterprises." The company's vice-president, Joseph Mathews, wrote to an American critic: "Freedom Gold has employed some 200 Liberians, has build a road of some 40 miles in the interior, has established a clinic to help needy people and has provided water pumps for clean drinking water to the residents in its area. In addition it is financing a school, and has seen 4 churches built in this remote southeastern part of the country."[13]

But Freedom Gold was soon deeply mired in a quagmire of Liberian politics. In November 2001 *Washington Post* reporter Colbert J. King wrote two blistering articles condemning Robertson's relations with Charles Taylor. He asked: "Now why is a freedom-loving, God-fearing man such as Pat Robertson signing on the dotted line with Taylor, a U.S. prison escapee, Libyan terrorist training camp graduate, human rights violator, and pillager of his own country and his neighbor, Sierra Leone?" In August 2003 *Fortune* reported that the company had "spent $8.4 million with little return, a necessary drill is stuck on the docks of Monrovia, and he's axed his Liberian workers." At the heart of the company's difficulties was the impending overthrow of President Taylor. Taylor was elected president in

1997, polling more than 75 percent of the vote, but he had long been an actor in the turbulent and bloody history of the nation. In 2003 President George W. Bush called on him to step down to end a civil war between his forces and those of Prince Johnson. Taylor resigned his presidency in August 2003, accepting asylum in Nigeria. Subsequently charged with eleven "crimes against humanity," Taylor went on trial in a UN-sponsored international court in the Hague, Netherlands, that began in 2007 and continued into 2009.[14]

Although he insisted that he had never met Taylor and had no intention of acting as his public defender, Robertson expressed indignation over President Bush's actions. "How dare the president of the United States say to the duly elected president of another country, 'You've got to step down,'" Robertson asked on *The 700 Club*. Admitting that Taylor had become such a "lightning rod" that his departure was inevitable, Robertson feared that the country would "lapse into chaos" if Taylor left abruptly. Worse yet, the United States was "undermining a Christian, Baptist president to bring in Muslim rebels to take over the country."[15]

Robertson sharply contested another *Washington Post* article about his Liberian venture that included rebukes from several leading evangelicals protesting his association with "the likes of Charles Taylor." CBN issued a news release in an attempt to get Robertson's side of the story before the public. Like other sub-Saharan African countries, Liberia was contentiously divided by a Christian/Muslim rift. Robertson believed that Taylor, who had early received support from Muslim backers, had experienced a genuine conversion during a "Liberia for Jesus" rally organized by Gimenez in 2002. The president reportedly prostrated himself on the stage and declared "I am not your president, Jesus is!" "He definitely has Christian sentiments," Robertson reported on *The 700 Club*. Undermining the Taylor government would have grave religious as well as political consequences, Robertson argued: "The Christian nations of Africa are right now under assault by Muslims funded either by Saudi Arabia or Libya. This fact is well known to the CIA. Regrettably, the State Department seems to be indifferent to this emerging tragedy." "Chaos is not a good thing in Africa or anywhere," observed Robertson in hindsight. He believed that sometimes stability and progress could come at the cost of supporting less-than-ideal dictators. Still, he had never intended to give "unqualified support" to Taylor in his public pronouncements, Robertson insisted, since he was "a man who I have never met, and about whose actions . . . I have no firsthand knowledge."[16]

After the political furor subsided, and as gold prices soared, Freedom

Gold once again ramped up exploration in 2006. The newly elected president, Ellen Johnson-Sirleaf, a Harvard-trained economist, welcomed foreign investment, and the venture, now freed from its association with Taylor, still had faint hopes of success. On the other hand, Robertson was not optimistic: "They stole it away from me. And I don't know if we can get it back." While costly in financial and public-relations terms, the Liberian venture was still not quite dead in 2009.[17]

Pat Robertson's interest in Africa preceded his Liberian venture. There was, first of all, a religious dimension. In 2002, the *New York Times* took note of the fact that "Christianity is growing faster in sub-Saharan Africa than in any other place on earth" and that most of the new converts were pouring into "Pentecostal churches . . . led by men influenced by American evangelists . . . who preach a message that success comes to those who pray." Robertson was well aware of the charismatic revival sweeping Africa, having long supported such celebrated mass evangelists as Reinhard Bonnke in his campaigns in Africa and having established scores of CBN centers throughout the continent. CBN carefully tracked the rising number of "people being won to the Lord" on the continent.[18]

But Robertson's interest in Africa had a political component as well. While he believed that the Christian revival in Africa, which often included highly publicized conversions of autocratic leaders, was an adequate justification for American Christian engagement, he had also for many years followed the Cold War political struggle on the continent. "The pot is boiling in Africa," he wrote in 1977. "Africans want no part of Communism, but they are no match for organized communist troops. . . . One wonders what U.S. Ambassador Andrew Young meant when he said that the Cuban troops were a 'stabilizing force' in Angola." Robertson recognized the perils of backing authoritarian regimes in Africa, but, like the American government, he often subsumed his reservations to larger concerns about the spread of communism. He wrote in 1980: "The United States obviously cannot be the guarantor of every petty dictator who is pro-western. Nevertheless, we must be aware that the spread of Marxist dictatorships means unspeakable repression to millions of people plus the rise of implacable foes of our society."[19]

He expressed his mix of religious and free-market beliefs regarding Africa succinctly in 2007: "I took the view of David Livingstone, who was a missionary pioneer. He said 'My task is to bring Christianity, civilization, and commerce to Africa, in that order.' It seemed that if people were going to improve their lot in life, they were going to have to get in business." Some African religious leaders agreed. The noted charismatic leader of the

Church of God Mission International in Nigeria, Archbishop Idahosa, wrote: "Africa doesn't need God, it needs money."[20]

It was in this ideological context that Robertson met and formed a personal relationship with President Mobutu Sese Seko, who seized power in Zaire in 1965 and remained president until 1997. Mobutu was initially seen by the CIA as a bastion against the expansion of Soviet influence in central Africa, and throughout the Cold War western nations backed him because of his support of anti-communist economic and military initiatives. But Mobutu also crushed political opposition and amassed an enormous personal fortune. In the 1990s, as the Cold War came to an end, Mobutu lost most of his support in the West, including foreign aid from the United States. In 1996 he left the country to seek treatment for prostate cancer in France, and during his absence a revolution led by guerrilla fighter Laurent-Desire Kabila forced him to relinquish power. He died in September 1997 in exile in Morocco.

By the early 1990s Robertson had befriended Mobutu, decrying the Clinton administration's sharp departure from Cold War policies in cutting ties with him. In 1995, reacting to the Clinton administration's refusal to grant a visa to Mobutu to visit the United States, Robertson told reporters: "I think he cannot understand why the United States has turned against him, and neither can I." The *Times* of London reported that Robertson had approached Newt Gingrich, Bob Dole, and Jesse Helms, asking them to support a Mobutu visit. On a visit to Kinshasa in 1995 Robertson told the local press, "The attitude of the State Department toward Zaire is outrageous, and has been for years."[21]

Robertson's first encounter with Mobutu came as a result of efforts to launch several Operation Blessing projects in Zaire in 1992. President George H. W. Bush gave him some pointed advice about the dangers of getting involved in Zaire: "Concerning your interests in Zaire, as you know, the political situation is quite volatile. The level of violence has increased in recent weeks. . . . Your Operation Blessing International Relief and Development could come under pressure to directly or indirectly support any number of political agendas. As you well know, remaining faithful to non-political humanitarian relief work provides for the most effective operation." Robertson reported that his first visit to the country had indeed been completely non-political: "We worked with the pastors to give seed to the people to plant, plus urgently needed medical supplies." But Robertson and Mobutu were soon on close personal terms. The president treated Robertson to a trip on the presidential yacht up the Congo River to his presidential estate. "Pat Robertson and Mobutu get along extremely well," reported one of the people accompanying him on an early trip. Mobutu agreed to air *The 700 Club* and *Superbook* on the national television network; Robertson surmised that the reason was his desire to have "a counterbalance to the Catholics." After several years, Robertson believed that "we have seen hundreds of thousands come to the Lord through our television programs in Zaire." On a subsequent trip, Robertson took with him several bankers who "presented a plan to Mobutu to stop the runaway inflation in his country and to relieve the human suffering of the people of Zaire." He also "spent several hours with Mobutu's Cabinet to teach them the principles of God's kingdom to govern a nation."[22]

In 1992 Robertson secured a timber concession covering 2.2 million acres near the Congo River in the heart of Zaire. This concession was later cancelled following the coup by the Marxist revolutionary Laurent Kabila. Robertson also shared with a local church a diamond concession on a half-mile stretch of the river. He crafted an agreement with the local pastor providing that 30 percent of the profit from the venture (if there was any) would go to humanitarian activity in Zaire. In Robertson's words, the company "endeavored to provide humanitarian assistance to the people, and provided medical supplies to a clinic in the village of Kamonia near the border of Angola." His workers scratched out a 3,000-foot airstrip to support the effort. Plagued by equipment failures, the need to provide security for workers, and the growing "political chaos" and corruption in the country, Robertson pumped several million dollars into the venture with virtually no return. In the fall of 1995, after "months of struggling in a dangerous and remote nation 6,000 miles from home," Robertson called it quits "because of equipment problems and the internal chaos in Zaire." The African Development Company was never profitable. In a form letter crafted to answer inquiries that came in for years, the ministry description of the business disaster was graphic: "Dr. Robertson had a concession in Africa to put a small pontoon dredge in a muddy, snake-infested river. There were no diamonds, but certainly a lot of river gravel. He does not, nor ever did, own a diamond mine, although he certainly wishes he had one!"[23]

More important in the long run than the loss of his investment was a series of charges leveled by the Norfolk newspaper, *The Virginian-Pilot*, that questioned the ethics and legality of the African Development Company business dealings, particularly the use of airplanes owned by Operation Blessing. The paper published several articles beginning in the fall of 1996 that triggered scrutiny by the national press. The articles were followed by stories in the *New York Times* and the *Washington Post*. Media investigation of the Zaire venture lasted for several years and included an investigation by the Virginia Office of Consumer Affairs into charges that Robertson had made "deceptive appeals" on *The 700 Club* in behalf of Operation Blessing operations in Zaire that were intended to benefit the African Development Company. Robertson felt vindicated after the Virginia attorney-general "conducted an exhaustive investigation of the charges, and concluded that there had been no improprieties or violation of law. The only charge was that the books and records of the African Development Company and the airplane company were not as precise as he would have hoped." Nonetheless, the Zaire project continued to draw criticism.[24]

The Robertson organization vehemently denied any misdeeds in Zaire. In a detailed letter to the editor published in the *Virginian-Pilot,* Robert W. Fanning, the chief operating officer of Operation Blessing, asserted that Operation Blessing had spent $ 1.7 million in humanitarian assistance in Zaire and that Robertson himself had made a "large, personal contribution" of around $500,000 "to cover all of Operation Blessing's expenses in Zaire." The entire Zaire operation, Fanning insisted, had been "a perfectly ethical and legal arrangement." Robertson readily acknowledged that his interest in Zaire and other African ventures was motivated partly by his desire to make a profit that would endow his ministry. On the other hand, he insisted that his investment in Zaire was also intended to help the poverty-stricken nation; it was a project consistent with his other initiatives to "support humanitarian efforts through economic development projects in African countries."[25]

Robertson's tactics in Africa rankled older, more established religious establishments, including both Roman Catholic and traditional Protestant missions, as did the free-wheeling, success-preaching, indigenous Pentecostal/charismatic churches. The Pentecostal/charismatic revival in the developing world was driven not only by the economic hope it offered to the poor, but also by the empowerment it gave to the indigenous religious entrepreneurs who challenged the authority and the religious control of the older Christian establishment. The "essential thrust" of Pentecostal theology in the developing world, suggests historian David Martin, "is the free and democratic availability of the gifts of the Spirit. . . . What [Pentecostals] define themselves *against* is . . . the priestly and the formulaic."[26]

These wildly successful African Pentecostal preachers built some of the largest churches in the world. As the *New York Times* noted in 2002, most of these preachers "either studied in the United States or learned from men who had." Indeed, many had been trained at Regent University. The *Times* report continued: "The Pentecostal churches, their critics say, willfully ignore Africa's problems, especially if they entail confronting corrupt regimes." But Robertson and other charismatics believed that they were attacking the problem at its motivational roots. Robertson insisted: "There is a sociological uplift in the gospel. The gospel is liberating." An economically successful Christian "wants to get in politics, he wants to get in business, he wants to improve the environment around him." David Martin agreed that the appeal of charismatic movement at the individual level was a gospel of self-help for the poor, offering hope that they could alter their lives, "beginning with themselves, their families and congregations."[27]

Robertson and other independent charismatics who worked easily with African dictators were often embarrassed by the behavior of their benefactors. Evangelical leader Joel Carpenter, director of the Nagel Institute for the Study of World Christianity at Calvin College, insisted that Robertson's "expressions of support for brutal and corrupt regimes in Liberia, the Congo, South Africa and Nigeria go beyond outrageous." Still, a potent combination of religious sympathies and political ideology seemed to shape choices for all American Christians who became involved in Cold War Africa, as well as Latin America, and those on the religious and political left met with difficulties of their own.[28]

Although Robertson defended both Mobutu and Charles Taylor when they first came under attack, like most charismatics, Robertson insisted that he was totally apolitical in his religious and economic interests in Africa. "Mr. Robertson is not involved in the internal politics of Zaire," declared a ministry release in 1995, "but he is committed to helping those who cannot help themselves." Partly, he insisted, his motives were pragmatic: "I found in the past that in order to function successfully in a foreign country, it helps enormously to have the favor of the government." In the end, however, he acknowledged that "I personally expended a great deal of effort and finances in an effort to help the people of Zaire without success." The final result of his "African adventures," he ruefully acknowledged in 2007, was that "I lost my shirt." It was just "too difficult to do business there."[29]

Other Business Misadventures and Near-Misses

Several other business misadventures gave ammunition to Robertson's critics and further damaged his hopes of building a largesse for CBN's future. In 1990 CBN founded American Benefits Plus to sell a Bible study course. When that venture "did not prove fruitful," in 1991 Robertson was approached by one of his employees, "a former public school superinten- dent," who persuaded him and the CBN board that "multi-level selling was simple, inexpensive to start, and fast-growing," and that it would be the perfect scheme for selling the Bible study course. Impressed by the success of such direct selling giants as Amway, CBN launched a multilevel market- ing scheme that during its first year marketed discount coupons on a wide variety of products and recruited 20,000 distributors.

But the company was soon in serious financial difficulty; according to ministry accounts, the company's "mild-mannered educator turned presi- dent was totally overwhelmed, the company was poorly managed, and he was dismissed." In early 1992, the CBN board, with Pat and Dede Robertson abstaining, voted unanimously to discontinue funding but granted per- mission to Pat Robertson to invest his own money in the venture to try to rescue it and to protect against potential legal actions by distributors. A new line of vitamins was added to the product list to be sold by American Sales. Robertson eventually recompensed CBN for its total investment and continued to fund the company's losses. In 1994 the company was re- named KaloVita, Inc., and the ministry reported that Robertson "put in place a highly professional management, a drastically reduced over- head, . . . and introduced new products." At the same time, Robertson sought a buyer for the company, finally selling it to Royal BodyCare, a Texas company, for $1.00 on November 1, 1994. In the end, the venture cost Robertson an estimated $6.8 million, including refunds to distributors and reimbursements, with interest, to CBN. Several years later, Robertson re- sponded to an inquirer: "I understand that the distributors who continued on with Royal BodyCare are doing quite well."[30]

Still, well before its demise, KaloVita had become an embarrassment to Robertson and CBN. The Norfolk newspaper first published exposés of the venture, followed by a wide-ranging *Newsweek* magazine review and a highly critical *ABC Primetime Live* segment that was aired on October 27, 1994. While not accusing CBN or Robertson of anything illegal, the cover- age cast serious doubts on the products marketed and asserted that Rob- ertson and his family members would have been the chief financial benefi- ciaries had the venture been successful.[31]

Another business venture that reaped bad publicity and legal trouble for Robertson was a commercial protein shake marketed by Basic Organics and for a time by General Nutrition Corporation, a health-food chain. Of course, Robertson had long been a self-taught health food and diet advisor who regularly gave tips on *The 700 Club* and in his writings.

The show tapped into the "enormous interest in losing weight" in the country, and Robertson believed that featuring health tips on *The 700 Club* met a real need. Among the diet aids he regularly touted on the broadcast was "Pat's Shake," a protein-rich breakfast substitute. An estimated 750,000 copies of the shake recipe were distributed to viewers, and the formula was posted on the CBN website, along with other health and diet tips. When a *New York Times* leveled the charge that the shake had been promoted "over the donor-based air time," CBN sprang to Robertson's defense. In a letter to the *Times*, Robertson's attorney stated categorically that "CBN refused to allow any advertising on the show. . . . It was never advertised on the show, period." The *Virginian-Pilot* probed the matter further in an article in March 2007 based on information revealed in a lawsuit involving the commercial product, raising questions about whether tax violations had occurred. Robertson and his attorneys continued to insist that "Pat's Shake," so often discussed on the show and distributed free to all, and the commercial product referred to in the articles, were "two very different ventures." In a deposition, Robertson stated that the GNC shake product was a totally different product "that we did not have anything to do with." The suit was dismissed, but, like other such legal actions, Robertson recalled, "it was an annoyance and it cost money."[32]

Among the most promising business ventures undertaken by Robertson in the wake of the IFE financial windfall were his effort to get in on "the stampede of American cable and TV interests to get overseas." In this area Robertson was dealing with technologies that he understood very well, but he still had to maneuver in the treacherous waters of international risk. By 1995 Robertson was "in the middle" of the opening for new technologies in Asia and Russia. Through Asia Pacific Media Corporation, Robertson explored a variety of options for getting into the communications market in Asia. He had high hopes for the China Internet Company, "a startup portal that was the number one lifestyle portal on the Internet in China" launched in 1999. But just as he was preparing to float a stock issue, the "dot-com" bubble burst in the United States, and the venture, which he believed would ultimately be worth billions of dollars, was scrapped. "It kills me to think about what I had in China," Robertson reflected years later. A similarly promising license to set up a satellite broadcast system in Russia was secured just before a dramatic collapse of the Russian economy cut that venture short. Robertson came very close to closing deals in Vietnam and Russia for cable television distribution systems, only to be thwarted by events over which he had no control.[33]

Pat Robertson's financial misadventures were the most frustrating and humbling experiences of his life. Those who knew him best insisted that his business escapades were motivated by a genuine religious intent. Even in the case of the African investments that seemed to his critics to skirt the boundaries of ethical guidelines, Barry Lynn conceded that "he believes it's all to the glory of God" because he intended to plow the profits "back into ministry . . . for the glory of God." Undeniably, Robertson enjoyed the thrill of the chase. "It lights him up. He likes doing deals," observed his son Gordon. Still, Gordon insisted, "Dad views it as a source of income for the kingdom. And he has used his business profits for that." "If it hadn't been for his business acumen," Gordon added, the present shape of CBN and Regent University would have been very different. His son Tim agreed. His father had made mistakes, particularly in bad personnel choices, but mostly he made "good decisions," and "the one really great one [the Family Channel sale] outweighs all the bombs."[34]

Nonetheless, Robertson felt remorse about his business losses. He reflected in 2008: "I wanted to generate another billion dollars for CBN and also have a little fun." He was taken by surprise by his setbacks: "I expected the Lord to bless what I would do," but in the end "he just literally blocked me to get into some things that would be very lucrative." In effect, "the Lord was saying, 'Not now.'" As he neared the age of eighty, he was reconciled and at peace with the results: "I think He wanted me to focus on world evangelization."[35]

Author

Pat Robertson is a prolific author; in 2009 he was listed as author or coauthor of twenty books in the Library of Congress catalog, including his single work of fiction, *The End of the Age,* published in 1995. His bestselling autobiography, *Shout It from the Housetops,* co-authored with Jamie Buckingham, was first published in 1972 and republished in a revised edition in 1995. Robertson's first major publishing triumph, *The Secret Kingdom,* was published in 1982 and rose to number three on *Time* magazine's list of America's bestselling nonfiction books. *The New World Order,* published in 1991, reached number four on the *New York Times* list of nonfiction bestsellers. These two titles, along with *Answers to 200 of Life's Most Probing Questions,* published in 1984, were the bestselling religious titles in their respective years of publication.

Robertson is a "dream author," reported a *Publishers Weekly* editor in 2005, because of his visibility on *The 700 Club* and his skills as a book promoter. One of his publishers described his particular gift: "His gift and his ability is to make the complexities of the world not simple, but understandable, and I think that's why, for us, he was and is a very successful author." Millions of copies of Robertson's books have been in circulation; in the first decade of the twenty-first century new titles appeared on a more or less annual schedule.[36]

Robertson's writings were often practical, common-sense applications of Biblical principles, and they all had some spiritual base, but they ranged over a wide variety of topics. Answering an interviewer about the sweep of his commentary, he replied: "I read voraciously. I read all kinds of publications and newsletters. I talk to people and try to get a good sense of what's going on in the political world and the financial world particularly. It takes a tremendous amount of reading, studying and more than anything — prayer. But most important, I talk to the Lord and read the Bible to try to bring it all together and gain an understanding of how the issues relate." "He really does have an open mind," observed his son Tim. "He has an inquiring mind." Barry Lynn agreed that the breadth of Robertson's curiosity and reading and his international experience exposed his readers to information they would not likely encounter elsewhere.[37]

Like most celebrity authors, ranging from Billy Graham to entertainment and political figures, Pat Robertson's books were products of his thinking, and were usually sketched out in his longhand scrawl after spurts of inspiration, but were fleshed out with the aid of research assistants provided by publishers. The amount of his direct input into the text has varied from book to book. Robertson has a strong proprietary pride in his books, and he has often minimized the role played by his "researchers." He has had to respond to inquiries through the years on the subject: "Concerning using ghostwriters for my books, I hope the following will be helpful in responding to your inquiry. As with most books, the publisher assigns a writer to work with me simply because people with full schedules, such as mine, do not have time to do all the research needed. The assigned writer . . . provides the research material from which I wrote the book. This was the case with 'The New World Order,' 'The New Millennium,' and one or two others. In the case of my autobiography, 'Shout It from the Housetops,' the publisher assigned Jamie Buckingham to work with me. We would get together to work — I would talk and Jamie would write. After he finished his writing, I read the material and if it wasn't exactly right, I would rewrite it — and it ended up that I had to personally rewrite quite a bit of it."[38]

Robertson was shocked when ghostwriter Mel White publicly announced that he had written every word of *America's Dates with Destiny,* a book released under Robertson's name during his presidential campaign. Robertson later recalled, "During the presidential campaign of 1988, Sam Moore, president of Word Books, insisted that I write another book. I pled time constraints, but Sam Moore said that he would arrange for a skilled writer to craft a manuscript. The writer chosen was Mel White, who had written books for other evangelical leaders. What I didn't know was that White was a closet homosexual who 'came out of the closet' after . . . *America's Dates with Destiny* was published. When Dede saw the manuscript, she said, 'I don't like it.' Her reaction was prophetic. *America's Dates with Destiny* was a complete bomb, and, without question, the most disappointing book with which I had been associated."[39]

Robertson's most original, important, and influential book was *The Secret Kingdom,* written in collaboration with his good friend Bob Slosser. In the book he outlined "the fundamental principles of human life," principles "given to me by God." Inspired by Robertson's reflections on the early Cape Henry settlers' appeal to the invisible world for help in their time of need, the "thoughts accruing from many months of reading and meditation poured in upon me" as he looked out on the Atlantic Ocean one evening. The first chapter of the book outlined the bleak condition of "the visible world." Then Robertson outlined eight "laws" of the invisible world designed to sustain those who entered "the secret kingdom." Each law received a chapter: "the Law of Reciprocity" (one must give in order to receive), "the Law of Use" (one must either use or lose talents), "the Law of Perseverance" (effort is required for success, as opposed to merely "claiming it"), "the Law of Responsibility" (kingdom laws must be obeyed to receive blessings), "the Law of Greatness" (greatness follows service), "the Law of Unity" (kingdom citizens work in unity), "the Law of Miracles" (kingdom citizens grasp the possibilities of God's power), and "the Law of Dominion" (God granted humanity dominion over the earth).[40]

Commending the book to a correspondent, Robertson summarized his view of its significance: "I regard my book, 'The Secret Kingdom,' the best book I have ever written. I recommend it, not because I am the author but because it sets forth the keys to a stable, prosperous, and satisfying life. These timeless principles of God's eternal kingdom will help the reader to face the problems of life." A sympathetic reviewer described the book as "an important, original work, sure to attract the attention of theologians everywhere." In fact, Robertson's "laws" highlighted his ability to synthesize and organize ideas that had been boiling in the creative caldron of

Pentecostal/charismatic thinking for three decades. He codified and simplified the concept of "seed faith," and moderated the most exaggerated claims of the "word of faith" teaching. The most controversial element in the book was the chapter on "dominion"; in later years he repeatedly offered clarifications denying that he held postmillennial end-times views identified with "dominion theology." The widely circulated book became a virtual catechism for millions of charismatic Christians around the world. In 1982 a study guide entitled *The Secret Kingdom Leaders Guide* provided a manual for class use in churches and schools.[41]

Israel, The New World Order, *and* The New Millennium

Robertson's two other bestselling books, written after he had become a political lightning rod in the 1990s, were provocative and controversial. *The New Millennium,* published in 1990, and *The New World Order,* published in 1991, explored themes of world crisis, conspiratorial forces, and prophetic speculation that had long appeared in *Pat Robertson's Perspective* but were given much broader expression and much wider circulation in the two books. *The New Millennium* was a detailed analysis of the modern "trilateral" world which divided power between the United States, the European Union, and an Eastern power locus comprised of Japan and China. The book was filled with prophecies, and, in Rob Boston's words, "vintage Robertson musing about the end of time." After a sweeping analysis of recent world history, *The New Millennium* ended with a description of the divine earthly millennium in which there would be "a one world government, headed by Jesus Christ, and there will be one system of laws for all of the inhabitants of the earth based on righteousness, justice, and fairness. The hard cases will be settled by the Lord Himself with absolute wisdom." Before that kingdom is established, Robertson warned, human efforts to impose a "one world government which tried to be a counterfeit of the millennial government that Christ will establish will become the most hellish nightmare this world has ever known."[42]

The dire predictions of *The New Millennium* were fleshed out in *The New World Order.* Robertson explained: "When I was writing *The New Millennium,* I came across so much information about a new world order that I felt I must do another book so that Christians might be aware of what was happening." He disdained President George H. W. Bush's appropriation of the term: "The rhapsodic gushing coming out of the White House announcing the emergence of a 'New World Order' is, I believe, naïve and dangerous. At its core the concept of a 'New World Order' based on a one-world government has been the darling of the powerful Council of Foreign Relations ever since its founding in the late 1920s. To those of us who are weary of a world divided and hanging over the brink of a nuclear precipice, the concept of a world at peace regulated by a fair-minded international authority has a certain appeal." But the result of such a plan would be catastrophic; one had only to observe the United Nations to see the "incredible disaster . . . this would bring upon the world." In the wake of the collapse of the Soviet Union, the world faced a new kind of threat: "We are no longer threatened from without by a group of balding hard-line Communists. We are now threatened from within by a group of intelligent, well-dressed liberals who over the next few years intend to convince the nations of the world that the only way to lasting peace is the establishment of a new world order." When the book came under heavy fire after being labeled anti-Semitic in the mid-1990s, Robertson repeatedly asserted that the book was nothing more complicated that a straightforward protest against "one-world government."[43]

The New World Order mined and cited a wide variety of conspiratorial literature that traced purported efforts by the wealthy and powerful to manipulate the modern world for their own benefit, beginning with the formation of the Order of the Illuminati, going through the Freemasons, a cabal of international bankers led by the Rothschild family, the rise of modern communism, the founding of the Federal Reserve banking system, and ending with a collection of modern elitist organizations headed by the Council on Foreign Relations. Robertson was included in a sweeping attack on the religious right by the Anti-Defamation League in 1994, but *The New World Order* was only noted in passing. But in February 1995, the book was blasted in a long review written by Michael Lind in the *New York Review of Books*. Lind, a former conservative stalwart, charged Robertson with blatant "anti-Semitism." The charge took Robertson totally by surprise. He later explained: "One of my trusted researchers had come up with what I thought were objective writings dealing with the eighteenth century. Unfortunately, these writers were known anti-Semites. The book, which clearly identified Scottish and English international bankers, suddenly changed under Lind's withering gaze to 'Jewish' bankers." Lind's review set off a firestorm of responses supporting and challenging his anti-Semitism charges.[44]

Robertson was particularly riled by two articles supporting Lind's charge written by *New York Times* columnist Frank Rich. On copies of the articles sent to his office, Robertson scrawled: "Outrageous. . . . This man is filled with vitriol." He wrote to Arthur Ochs Sulzberger, chairman of the board of the New York Times Company: "Dear Punch: Today I was astounded to read the attached column by your staff writer, Frank Rich, quoting one of your book reviewers, Michael Lind. I also attach my letter to the editor answering Rich. . . . After twenty-one years of fighting in every forum conceivable to defend the rights of Israel and the Jewish people, I will not tolerate . . . being called anti-Semitic." In his letter to the editor, Robertson vehemently denied the charge: "For over three decades I have consistently been one of the most reliable allies of the Jewish people and the state of Israel in the American evangelical community. As I state in my book, 'Rest assured that the next objection of the presently constituted new world order, under the present United Nations, will be to make Israel its target.' (p. 256) If that is anti-Semitism, then it is the most bizarre and self-defeating anti-Semitism ever uttered."[45]

A number of journalists came to Robertson's defense; perhaps the most effective was Norman Podhoretz, a neoconservative editor of the influential Jewish magazine *Commentary*. Podhoretz agreed that "knowingly or unknowingly" Robertson "subscribed to and purveyed ideas that have an old and well-established anti-Semitic pedigree," but the charge of anti-Semitism just did not make sense, given his "fervent political support of Israel" and the fact that he has "donated large sums of money to Jewish causes and organizations." While Podhoretz disapproved of Robertson's use of conspiratorial sources, he concluded that "I would still maintain that the contamination represented by those passages, when set within the context of Robertson's record as a whole," should absolve him from criticism on that count.[46]

The anti-Semitism charge was personally hurtful to Robertson, but it had relatively limited staying power. On the other hand, the conspiracy theme of *The New World Order* raised larger questions about the interpretative framework of the book (and of Robertson's earlier writings) and highlighted his flirtation with conspiratorial thinking. In the eyes of his critics, *The New World Order* embraced "conspiracy theories of history so bizarre they would make Oliver Stone blush." Even some more friendly readers, such as the reviewer for *Christianity Today*, described the book as "conspiracy-laden." Robertson denied it: "I do not believe . . . in a 'conspiracy theory of world history.'" Despite his denials, and the pass Robertson gave in his book to many politicians as innocent tools of forces they did not understand, the text followed a path through hundreds of years of elites seeking to impose a new world order: "How can we account for the fact that for over two hundred years a small group, their spiritual successors, and their converts have labored ceaselessly to bring us what we thought we already had — a renewed world order? Can it be that the phrase *the new world order* means something entirely different to the inner circle of a secret society than it does to the ordinary person? . . . Indeed, it may well be that men of goodwill like Woodrow Wilson, Jimmy Carter, and George Bush . . . are unwittingly carrying out the mission and mouthing the phrases of a tightly knit cabal whose goal is nothing less than a new order for the human race under the domination of Lucifer and his followers." The book traced the path of a hidden, elitist "establishment" that manipulated politics for its own self-interest: "In truth, the real power to choose presidents and prime ministers is not in public view — it is behind the scenes. Such men generally prefer to operate in great secrecy. . . . Invariably, however, they control such enormous wealth that their collective voices can cause rulers to tremble and governments . . . to fall." The "visible home of the Establishment" in the United States was the address of the Council on Foreign Relations in New York City, and from there it reached out to a list of government agencies, foundations, banks, universities, media sources, and international corporations.[47]

The ideas fleshed out in *The New World Order* had been incubating in Robertson's mind since the late 1970s. In November 1976 Robertson wrote to a supporter who had inquired about the "Trilateral Commission": "I have read some of the reports about plots by the Rockefellers to seize power, etc. Even if some of these things were true, which they probably aren't, I believe that we as Christians will worry ourselves to death looking for plots instead of spending our time shining the light of God's love into the darkness of this world. I do believe that we must accord a measure of trust to our leaders, and that includes trust in their motives. Otherwise we find ourselves always suspicious and always confused." But Robertson's fears of an internal threat to the country grew in rhythm with his growing disappointment with the presidency of Jimmy Carter and his growing drift toward political involvement. By 1977 he was focusing on the power of the "Trilateral Commission" and the Rockefeller family: "It is doubtful that some monstrous plot is in operation. It does make me wonder why there can't be someone other than a single enormously wealthy family who picks our officials for us, regardless of which party wins the elections." In 1980, in *Pat Robertson's Perspective*, he warned that the Council on Foreign Relations "has been the source of United States fiscal and foreign policy direction since World War II. Its membership is drawn from the elite world of international banking, major corporations, New York law firms, major broadcasting and publishing firms, Ivy-type universities and major foundations.... Some have alleged that these groups represent a sinister plot to gain control of the world for monopoly capitalism.... The major thrust of CFR and the Trilateral Commission is to destroy nationalism in favor of an interdependent one world government."[48]

The book was a smash hit, surpassing 500,000 copies in circulation; in later years Robertson still regarded it as "a compelling assessment of the imminent dangers looming on the world's horizon." Appearing on *Evans & Novak* in April 1995, Robertson was unapologetic, noting that the book was a "runaway best seller" that did not become the target of politically motivated criticism until four years after its release. He believed that the attacks on the book were an ill-concealed effort to undermine the Christian Coalition: "They're grasping at straws to try to discredit what we're doing."[49]

In retrospect, Robertson regretted the use of the suspect anti-Semitic sources by his researchers, though he insisted that they had nothing to do with the book's central argument. In his letter to the *New York Times* Robertson maintained that his fundamental premise, that there was a strong connection between "the world of high finance and the U.S. foreign policy establishment," was based largely on "the pioneering work of Carroll Quigley, who was Bill Clinton's professor and mentor at Georgetown." It was somewhat ironic that Robertson's distrust of the "the establishment," in his general formation of the book's argument, sounded much like the anti-Vietnam War rhetoric of leftist intellectuals such as Quigley and New Left diplomatic historian William Appleton Williams. In general, his conspiracy thinking fit with President Dwight Eisenhower's concerns about the military-industrial complex and the theoretical formulations of such New Left books as C. Wright Mills's *The Power Elite.* In common with anti-war activists, Robertson was convinced that elites "kept alive the Cold War" to promote their economic interests.[50]

In later years Robertson defended both the theme of the book and its sensationalist search for conspiracy: "I'm a writer and not a bad writer.... If you are going to write it so people want to read it, you have to set a little sense of drama in it.... I felt that this whole concept of the new world order had been proposed over and over again by psychics and mystics to prepare the world for a satanic rule.... It has been the plan." "I am not interested in conspiracies," Robertson continued to avow, but "one would have to be blind" to ignore the "good old boy network" that for many years dominated American policy.[51]

The Sweep of Robertson's Authorship

The breadth of Robertson's bibliography reflects his own broad interests. Some of his books are practical, inspirational, and folksy. Others, such as *The Plan,* which Robertson recalled was "very painful when I wrote it" in the wake of his failed presidential campaign, are basically autobiographical. Almost all of his books contain personal stories that became permanent fixtures in Robertson lore. A few are based on serious research and argue substantial historical and legal questions. Most of the books are to some extent collaborative; Robertson has generally acknowledged the contributions of others while taking full responsibility for the contents.[52]

Courting Disaster: How the Supreme Court Is Usurping the Power of Congress and the People, published in 2004, is the best example of a carefully researched and critically argued book. Basically a description of the activist drift of the Supreme Court in the twentieth century — and, in Robertson's mind, the court's flaunting of "the original intent" of the Constitution — the book is documented by references to 167 Supreme Court cases. Robertson's own legal expertise no doubt informed the book, as did his long involvement in support of litigation challenging the drift of the court, but he also acknowledged the obvious contributions of Jay Sekulow, the general counsel of the American Center for Law and Justice, as well as senior counsel Stuart Roth and a half-dozen law clerks. He acknowledged that "this work has been a cooperative effort."[53]

Another popular genre of Robertson writing is collections of his common-sense answers to practical, and sometimes technical and theological, questions. His popular *Answers to 200 of Life's Most Probing Questions,* published in 1984, offered brief answers to questions including a "top ten" determined by a Gallup poll to be the questions most people would like to ask God, such as "Why is there suffering in the world?" and "What is heaven like?" Robertson thanked three CBN University professors, J. Rodman Williams, Herbert W. Titus, and Peter Prosser, "for their verification of theological concepts," but his question-and-answer books have probably been his most single-handed authorial productions.[54]

Fifty Years in the Limelight:
Candor, Gaffes, and Attackers

Pat Robertson has been one of the most controversial personalities of his time. Scores of bloggers regularly catalog his doings and sayings, generally nurturing the "wacko" image that was first widely fleshed out with the rise of Robertson's political ambitions in the last half of the 1980s. Negative information about Robertson on the Internet is profuse. One researcher reported: "No matter how technologically adroit he might be, out here on the gloriously infinite Infobahn, Pat Robertson can hardly muster up a respectable level of control. The first 50 entries I pull up are mostly reprinted magazine articles attacking (and mocking) Robertson."[55]

Robertson has supplied his critics with ample ammunition. When Paul Weyrich decided that Pat Robertson was not a viable candidate for the presidency, he candidly observed: "I did not take into account one factor, and that is that he had been doing a television show where nobody challenged what he said for many years. . . . He used to get on his program and make statements about things he had heard, maybe they were true, maybe they weren't, but nobody challenged him." It is open to question as to whether Pat Robertson has been more apt to speak loosely than many other national figures; he has certainly logged more time, and said more, in front of a television audience than any other figure in American politics. His comments on the air and in print, particularly after his political incarnation in the 1980s, have been carefully monitored and reported by his adversaries. His comments sometimes demanded explanation and sometimes apology, and they were occasionally the source of serious embarrassment for him and others at CBN.[56]

Nothing could strike fear inside the CBN empire more than Pat Robertson's words when he became heated and unrestrained in his impromptu comments about the news, his critics, and his prejudices. "There is nothing like being on national television live," reflected Gordon Robertson in 2009, particularly when every word is targeted and taped by those who will "spin it in a negative" way if possible. "He has given them plenty of ammunition," Gordon observed, but much of the criticism distorts his intended meaning, and his detractors are not interested in explanations or apologies. All in all, Gordon said in defense of his father, "When you look at the overall history, when you consider fourteen to fifteen thousand hours of live television commentary . . . you have a handful of comments that you have apologized for. . . . He is quotable, but I think he is careful."[57]

Robertson has not always been careful. But his gaffes can often be easily explained, if not explained away. Partly, his most unguarded comments have come at his most comfortable times on *The 700 Club*, in conversation with his loyal and sympathetic family of supporters. "He feels so comfortable with his audience," remarked Terry Meeuwsen, that he sometimes forgets that other people are listening. More than once "he has been surprised" that anyone would disagree with his statements. It is much like a person talking "back to your television at home," remarked Barry Lynn; you "reach a point of frustration" where you say what you think. "He has reached a point where he doesn't feel like he has to bite his tongue," and in fact often "he just says what a lot of people at home think."[58]

It is not as if Robertson does not understand the potential that some of his statements have to cause controversy and offense. In a form letter drafted to respond to those who had been offended by some remark, Robertson offered an explanation: "Please understand that my intent is not to offend people, but to bring insight and present a clear perspective on the issues we all face today. One of the reasons that 'The 700 Club' has achieved the enormous popularity it has is because people know that I express my views quite candidly without regard to the person of any man. That carries the risk of offending some. However, it must be clearly understood by all that boldly speaking the truth always offends some people. Nevertheless, that risk of offense is far outweighed by the need of the people to be informed."[59]

Robertson's critics consider him a "Teflon televangelist" who "gets passes" from the media; they seem always willing to "forget the last silly thing" he said and continue to take him seriously, as Barry Lynn put it. Robertson, on the other hand, bristles at the monitoring of his program by Americans United for Separation of Church and State, People for the American Way, and Media Matters, charging that they often "change the sense" of his statements and feed misinformation to the press. Rob Boston of Americans United vehemently denied the charge: "His outbursts are frequently so wacky we couldn't improve on them even if we wanted to."[60]

The glaring spotlight on him by the end of the twentieth century made his friends more and more reluctant to defend some of his statements. Tim Robertson candidly observed, "When my dad issues one of his famous faux pas, many are less likely to rise to his defense." Biographer David John Marley ascribed the diminishing number of Robertson defenders to the waning of his clout during the second Bush administration: "During the George W. Bush administration Robertson took more heat for his controversial comments than he had in his entire career. This was in part due to his lack of power, which brought out attacks from the Left, but he was also criticized by the Right and the White House."[61]

Most insiders at CBN, and Robertson himself, felt that he was unfairly targeted by a politically motivated liberal media. Through the years, Robertson has had a few friends in the press, but generally his relations with the media have been adversarial. "It hurts us when we see some of the things that are said about him," said WorldReach executive Ron Oates; "he has become a whipping boy." His friend Ralph Reed wrote in reaction to a 1992 attack in the *Boston Globe:* "In all my years in politics, I have never seen a man of Pat Robertson's reputation smeared in such a vicious and bigoted manner.... It is unfortunate that a religious leader with his record of serving his fellow man has been subject to such anti-Christian bigotry as evidenced by your column." Robertson firmly believed that the press was dominated by people with deep prejudices against Christians: "With few notable exceptions, the press in the United States and Europe display virulent hostility toward conservative evangelical Christianity. With the advent of political correctness, most groups in our society, except evangelical Christians, are protected from verbal abuse. Evangelical Christians are fair game for ongoing slander and ridicule."[62]

"You have to have thick skin" to deal with the media, Robertson observed on *The 700 Club* in 2008; one's only guideline should be, "Are you pleasing God?" His ability to slough off criticism sometimes won him admiration. During a 1996 roast in Los Angeles, emcee Larry King wisecracked: "Pat, we've always admired how cool and calm you are under fire from the press.... Ronald Reagan may have been our Teflon president, but you are 100 percent asbestos."[63]

But Robertson could also be thin-skinned. After a particularly offensive article in the *Miami Herald* in 1990, an irate Robertson wrote to the editor: "Your writer ... reeks with the stench of Fascism. Your editorial writers are the spiritual heirs of Joseph Goebbels.... You are not going to get away with it. This is America, not Nazi Germany. Christians are Americans too. We no longer intend to allow ourselves to be made the punching bag of the liberal media in America. We will not stand idly by while you rip our First Amendment freedoms from us by lies, innuendo, slander, and intimidation." CBN on occasion refused to cooperate with specific reporters, but Robertson was particularly irritated by the local *Virginian-Pilot*. After the paper's publication of the series of articles in 1999 implying that Operation Blessing airplanes may have been illegally used to further Robertson's business venture in Zaire, Robertson wrote a letter to the president of the paper's parent company: "Knowing your mother, father and brother as well as I did, and realizing your work with Tim on the Cable Board, I have always believed that there was an underlying strain of honor and decency in you. Has my belief in you been in error?"[64]

No critic has gotten under Robertson's skin more than Barry Lynn of Americans United for Separation of Church and State. Robertson believes that Lynn systematically takes "out of context remarks that are made" to further causes that could only be described as "evil." "If they find anything slightly controversial," Robertson wrote, "they take it out of context, add or subtract words or phrases from my speech, then insert their own editorial explanation that alters what was said. This material is then sent to an individual at the Associated Press office in Washington who, in turn, feeds the doctored statement around the world to my discredit and embarrassment." In the decade after 1997 Robertson described Lynn as "off the wall," "an intolerant jerk," and "lower than a child molester," because of Lynn's harassment and because Robertson regarded many of the causes embraced by Americans United as extremist. Responding to a correspondent who questioned his "intolerant jerk" remark, Robertson wrote: "The word jerk means an annoyingly stupid or foolish person. Foolish means lacking in sense, judgment, or discretion. . . . Apparently you have not read some of the material Mr. Lynn writes. If you had, you would understand what I am talking about. I don't suppose it helped John the Baptist's ministry either that he called the Pharisees and Sadducees a generation of snakes, but he spoke the truth."[65]

Lynn responded that tracking Robertson is his business. In 1997 he told reporters: "We are clearly getting under Robertson's skin. . . . That's what his name-calling is about. All I can say to Pat Robertson is this: Get used to us." Americans United regularly cataloged Robertson's "more provocative opinions" on issues large and small in its publication, *Church and State*. Lynn's pursuit of Robertson has been relentless, culminating in the publication of the book *Piety and Politics* in 2006. Lynn believed that Robertson intended to undermine the separation of church and state, but he also characterized him as a "reckless buffoon" in an effort to marginalize him. Of course, it was in Lynn's own self-interest to remind his readers that Robertson "is genuinely important, even if frightening, because he is the 'Christian voice' to the world." He warned that "moderate evangelicals" and political liberals who believed that the "Religious Right was on the way to political irrelevance" were badly mistaken.[66]

Deeply committed to his version of separation of church and state, Lynn played hardball for the cause, but he sometimes seemed surprised that Robertson had a "particular distaste for me personally." Lynn "got along very well" with Robertson's American Center for Law and Justice colleague Jay Sekulow, but Robertson's resentment toward Lynn ran deep. A 1999 encounter between the two men illustrated the depth of his personal distaste. Lynn greeted Robertson at a Washington restaurant in 1999 while attending the Christian Coalition's "Road to Victory" conference. Ever cordial in public, Robertson rose to greet Lynn and thank him for attending the meeting. In a moment of small talk Lynn informed him that his mother was a fan of *The 700 Club,* but she could not understand "why Pat Robertson says those nasty things about me." In response, Lynn reported, "he chortled that maybe she could come and visit him, and they'd straighten things out." But a few days after the encounter Robertson wrote a letter to Lynn, noting that Lynn had mischaracterized Robertson's speech at the conference, as usual, and offering an explanation to Lynn's mother: "Barry, what you need to tell your mother is that, unfortunately, when you were a little boy, she didn't teach you to tell the truth, and this is the reason Pat Robertson says unkind things about you from time-to-time."[67]

Gaffes, Religious Conviction, Political Absolutes, and Hyperbole

Most of the "gaffes" highlighted by Robertson's religious and political critics were little more than candid expressions of his religious and political convictions. And more often than not, they endeared him to his supporters. For instance, Robertson knew that many people thought it "absurd to talk to a hurricane," but "that is what the Holy Spirit led me to do." Such open expressions as diverting hurricanes and praying for divine healings while undergoing surgery for prostate cancer might seem bizarre to secularists and many conventional Christians, but they are commonplace experiences for charismatic Christians. After Robertson prayed (successfully, he believed) that Hurricane Felix would miss Virginia Beach, a local friend wrote to him: "First, let me thank you for interceding and having the threatening hurricane turned out to sea. I did not board up any windows or doors, even though I am living right on the ocean front. It all goes to show that I have more faith in you than your son, Tim." A delighted Robertson replied, "Your comments about Hurricane Felix were marvelous. I am sharing a copy with Lisa and Tim."[68]

Probably the biggest furor caused by Robertson's candid expression of his religious convictions came in the wake of 9/11. An appearance by Jerry Falwell on *The 700 Club* the week after the tragedy triggered a deluge of stories in the national press. Robertson concurred when Falwell charged that "the pagans and the abortionists and the feminists and the gays and the lesbians" were responsible for the disaster. The comments were immediately repudiated, even by such conservatives as William F. Buckley and Rush Limbaugh. Both Robertson and Falwell offered clarifications and apologies for the insensitivity of the remarks, but Robertson insisted that his consciousness of the nation's cultural sinfulness was no different from

Abraham Lincoln's belief that divine wrath had brought the horror of the Civil War. Indeed, such moral understandings of national judgment were very much a part of American political rhetoric from the days of Native American attacks on Puritan settlements. At one level the statement was not exceptional; ministers on the left and the right agreed that God might wreak punishment on a nation for its wickedness. The judgment of Falwell and Robertson was ill-timed, to be sure, but they were hardly the first Americans to attribute national disaster to moral decay. The whole episode was offensive not so much because it was a self-conscious confession of national culpability, but rather because it located the fault on one side of the raging culture war. The remarks were an example of the "politics of desert" that "links American tolerance of lesbians and gay men, feminists, atheists, and others with God's punishment on the polity."[69]

The 9/11 episode was not Robertson's first highly publicized encounter with gay-rights supporters. In 1999 Robertson's comments about homosexuality in Scotland led to his resignation from the board of the Laura Ashley Company and the scuttling of a telebanking deal with the Bank of Scotland. The British press pounced on comments made by Robertson on *The 700 Club:* "In Europe, the big word is tolerance. You tolerate everything. Homosexuals are riding high in the media. . . . And in Scotland you can't believe how strong the homosexuals are." Robertson was "dumbfounded" by the furor caused by his remarks in the United Kingdom, but when he characterized Scotland as a "dark land" that had betrayed its Christian history to accommodate gays and lesbians, a resolution was introduced in the Scottish Parliament demanding that the Bank of Scotland withdraw from the deal because of Robertson's "vitriolic attack on Scotland and its people." In a hasty meeting in Boston in June 1999 the bank bought out Robertson's interest in the venture; seemingly surprised by the storm of outrage about his remarks in the United Kingdom, Robertson "expressed regret that media comments about him had made it impossible to proceed." In the case of Laura Ashley and the Bank of Scotland, Robertson was liberally compensated when the deals collapsed, but the outcry blistered his image once again.[70]

The most embarrassing of Robertson's spontaneous comments on *The 700 Club* was a 2006 remark about Israeli prime minister Ariel Sharon following Sharon's debilitating stroke in January. Robertson remembered Sharon as "a very likable person, and I am sad to see him in this condition." But, like other conservatives in Israel and the United States, he was adamantly opposed to Sharon's plan to cede land for peace and his withdrawal from the Gaza Strip two years earlier. He observed: "Ariel Sharon, who was

. . . a delightful person to be with, I prayed with him personally, but here, he's at the point of death. He was dividing God's land. And I would say woe unto any prime minister of Israel who takes a similar course to appease the EU, the United Nations or the United States of America. God says, 'This land belongs to Me. You better leave it alone.'" Robertson protested years later: "People for the American Way took this statement and editorialized it, asserting that I had stated that God had caused Ariel Sharon's illness — something that I never said. The erroneous statement was carried by the Associated Press throughout the world." The media reaction was immediate. CBN's Public Relations department issued a clarification on the day of the comments: "Pat Robertson expresses his deep sadness over Ariel Sharon's life threatening stroke and concern for Israel's future security. . . . Robertson is simply reminding his viewers what the Bible has to say about efforts made to divide the land of Israel."[71]

In the days that followed, media criticism was relentless. A *Washington Post* article a day after the broadcast linked Robertson with Iranian president Mahmoud Ahmadinejad, who had stated that Sharon's "severe illness . . . was deserved." In an editorial a few days later, the paper continued to link Robertson with the Iranian president: "There is little reason to believe that either will cease his disgraceful behavior. . . . They share a self-righteousness that blinds them to the distance that they have placed between themselves and the majority of people who find their remarks repulsive." *Media Matters for America* reported that the story triggered "an international uproar" that threatened CBN's participation in the development of a Christian theme park in Galilee.[72]

Robertson was soon in full defense mode, appearing on a number of national television programs. Throughout the affair, Robertson insisted that he was misquoted and misrepresented. He saw the furor as another unfair attack by his enemies. He wrote to a supporter, "The Associated Press and People for the American Way grossly distorted my remarks. . . . It is unfortunate that my remarks are often taken out of context, amplified, and interpreted by reporters who do not know the Bible."[73]

But within a week, Robertson felt compelled to apologize. In 2008, he wrote: "To quell the storm, I was forced to make a humble public apology to Sharon's son and to the Israeli people on international television — for something I did not say!" In a letter marked for "hand delivery" to Omri Sharon, the son of the stricken prime minister, Robertson expressed his warm personal regard for the prime minister, who had hosted him at a luncheon, and for "the privilege of meeting with him in his office and praying with him about a year ago." He still felt that his remarks had been distorted by the press, but he also was ready to apologize: "I ask your forgiveness and the forgiveness of the people of Israel for remarks I made at the time concerning the writing of the holy prophet Joel and his view of the inviolate nature of the land of Israel. I personally feel very passionate about the safety of your country and the divine claim of the Jewish people to Eretz Israel and what has been called Judea and Samaria. My zeal, my love of Israel, and my concern for the future safety of your nation led me to make remarks which I can now view in retrospect as inappropriate and insensitive in light of a national grief experienced because of your father's illness. I ask your forgiveness and the forgiveness of the people of Israel for saying what was clearly insensitive at the time." The affair settled down in a matter of days, and by the end of the month the Israeli government reconsidered its decision to block CBN's participation in the Christian theme park venture.[74]

Robertson frequently has voiced his political views with unguarded candor. Perhaps the most famous example was an offhanded, frustrated assertion regarding Venezuelan president Hugo Chavez: "We have the ability to take him out." "If he thinks we're trying to assassinate him, I think that we really ought to go ahead and do it," Robertson observed on *The 700 Club*. Venezuela immediately registered protests, religious leaders issued a deluge of condemnations, and U.S. government sources repudiated Robertson's statements. A State Department spokesman called the comment "inappropriate," and Defense Secretary Donald Rumsfeld observed that such an act would be "against the law," while noting that Robertson was a "private citizen" and "private citizens say all kinds of things all the time."[75]

Robertson once again insisted that his remarks had been "misinterpreted by the news media," but after reviewing his comments, he issued an apology: "Is it right to call for assassination? No, and I apologize for that statement. I spoke in frustration that we should accommodate the man who thinks the U.S. is out to kill him." In his defense he quoted theologian Dietrich Bonhoeffer, who was executed by the Nazis for supporting a plot to kill Adolf Hitler, an example Robertson thought "deserves our respect and consideration today."[76]

A few people offered a degree of support for Robertson's candid remarks. William F. Buckley Jr., while strongly condemning the comment, noted that "presidential complicity in assassination plots" was not a novelty in recent American history, pointing to the high-level discussions plotting the assassination of Fidel Castro. Others pointed out that Richard Nixon and Ronald Reagan had been accused of complicity in the assassination of Salvador Allende of Chile and an attempt on the life of Libya's

Muammar Gadhafi. Robertson's mistake in the Chavez affair, according to Buckley, was his candor and his vulnerability as a religious commentator. Insiders understood "how passionate he was about [this] particular issue," but, said Terry Meeuwsen, if you are a "spiritual leader," there are "things you cannot say."[77]

Islam and the Politics of 9/11

Pat Robertson's often-repeated assessment of Islam has been frank and confrontational: "Islam is a wicked religion. . . . It kills people. . . . It is clear what they want to do. . . . They say they want to conquer the world in the name of Islam. . . . I think Allah is the devil." After a news report on Islamic radicalism in Britain in 2006, Robertson vented his wrath about radical Islamic terrorism and its origins: "Ladies and gentlemen . . . these people are crazed fanatics and I want to say it now — I believe it is motivated by demonic power. . . . And by the way, Islam is not a religion of peace." In a follow-up statement hurriedly issued by CBN, Robertson emphasized that his comments referred "specifically to the radicals and terrorists who want to bomb innocent people. I believe that they are motivated by demonic power and are satanic." Disclaimers aside, an independent study of *The 700 Club* published in 2004 found a consistent pattern: "Radical or militant Islam is represented as a clear, terrifying, deadly, and invisible threat that knows no boundaries."[78]

Robertson was not oblivious to the nuances within the Islamic community. He was well aware of the tensions between moderate and militant Muslims in the Middle East and regularly commented about the political complexities of the region. But the rising tide of Islamic terrorism placed him squarely in opposition to any compromise with radical Islam or to excusing moderates who tolerated terrorists. His candid and unflinching critiques of radical Islam were regularly followed by sharp criticism from Islamic sources, the media, and liberal religious leaders. For instance, in 1997, after Robertson observed that the phenomenon of Americans converting to Islam was "nothing short of insanity," the Council on American-Islamic Relations demanded an apology for his "hate-filled remarks." Such remarks, the Council spokesman insisted, were a part of a "pattern of demonization of Islam and Muslims we see growing in strength in this country."[79]

The 9/11 attack unleashed an extended period of public confrontation between a number of conservative evangelicals, including Pat Robertson, and their critics, sometimes exposing a fault line in the alliance between President Bush and his supporters in the religious right on how to approach Islam. Commenting on the growing Muslim population in the United States in February 2002, Robertson observed: "Ladies and gentlemen, I have taken issue with our esteemed president in regard to his stand in saying Islam is a peaceful religion. It just is not. And the Koran makes it clear, if you see an infidel, you are to kill him. . . . They want to coexist until they can control, dominate and then if need be, destroy." Questioned by reporters about Robertson's comments and similar statements made by Franklin Graham, Bush press secretary Ari Fleischer replied: "I think . . . virtually all Americans agree with the president on that position. Anybody who doesn't is stating an unfortunate view." Robertson immediately faxed to Fleischer a detailed listing of Muslim acts of violence and atrocities, including the destruction of his Middle East Television station in Lebanon, the Jihad against Christians in Sudan, and the actions of repressive Islamic regimes in Iraq, Iran, Libya, Syria, Sudan, and Somalia. He concluded: "The hatred that inspires the terrorists did not arise in a vacuum. They have been taught these things since childhood by mullahs in Muslim mosques who take a literal view of the words of Muhammad and the Koran."[80]

Robertson's spat with the White House lasted for months. In November the president offered a general disclaimer of the anti-Muslim rhetoric coming from Robertson and other evangelicals in a conversation with UN Secretary-General Kofi Annan: "Some of the comments that have been uttered about Islam do not reflect the sentiments of my government or the sentiments of the American people. Islam, as practiced by the vast majority of people, is a peaceful religion, a religion that respects others." CBN director of public relations Angell Watts promptly dispatched another letter to Ari Fleischer, noting that CBN had received "considerable backlash from criticism coming from the White House." Watts documented Robertson's recent charge that "depicting Jews — and sometimes also Zionists — as 'the descendants of apes and pigs' is extremely widespread today in public discourse in the Arab and Islamic worlds." As for the president, Robertson minimized differences with him: "I want everybody to understand that one disagreement, a minor disagreement among friends, does not end a friendship; and so I'm not one throwing rocks at the President. I appreciate the President, appreciate what he's doing; and I want everybody to know that something like this does not sever the support that I have given to him over the years." However, he reminded a reporter, "He is not elected as chief theologian."[81]

Robertson's critics argued that his insensitive anti-Islamic rhetoric was a form of religious extremism that supplied Muslim radicals with ammunition. "Falwell, Robertson and Graham's hate-filled campaign," observed *Newsweek,* "is lighting fires that could grow into a terrible conflagration." The magazine *Sojourners* offered a similar critique: "These kinds of verbal assaults on Islam and the prophet of Islam do far more damage than most Americans realize. They feed extremism among Muslims who want to frame conflict as being between Christians and Muslims." Barry Lynn was more direct: "His characterizations of Islam and Hinduism are crude and marked by an appalling form of ignorance, coming as they do from a man who claims to have studied religion as an academic subject."[82]

On the other hand, Robertson and his views obviously had many supporters. Responding to a generally non-confrontational interview with Robertson in the *Washington Times,* one reader wrote: "Thanks for the candid interview with Pat Robertson, which finally put into print some politically incorrect, but nonetheless true, statements about Islam." Many of his Israeli friends stood firmly with him, and nothing brought stronger support from CBN donors than CBN's programs targeted at the Muslim world.[83]

Robertson continued to insist that the problem of Islamic radicalism was neither a fantasy nor simply the violent behavior of a small minority, but rather it was based on the core teachings of Muhammad. He repeatedly urged his critics to read the Koran: "In terms of Islam, I don't think the issues have been ventilated at all in the press because no one has read the Koran." Robertson told *The 700 Club* audience in 2002: "Jews in Germany did not want to read *Mein Kampf* and did not want to believe it. They said it is not possible that anybody could be as monstrous as this person, and in today's world people say it is not possible for us to believe that a religious system could teach what the Koran clearly teaches. It's the religion that's the problem, not necessarily the adherents to it. But read the man who has considered himself the spokesman of God Almighty and what his statements are." "The media will not listen," Robertson insisted, because they did not want to confront the radicals. That same year, he noted that "an Iranian mullah" had preached a sermon calling "for the deaths of Jerry Falwell, Franklin Graham and Pat Robertson." Such threats, Robertson asserted, showed that Muslim leaders did not believe that "one shouldn't be condemned to be killed just because one criticizes their religion."[84]

Robertson and his critics agree that his hostility to Islam, like his hostility to other non-Judeo-Christian religions, reflects his clear-cut vision of truth and error. His antipathy to Islam is the result of the "dualism" in his thought process, observed one scholar. Such a mindset poses radical choices: "Within an orientation of exclusivity, there can be only one right position, and all else must stand in opposition; Islam competes with Christianity for souls, and claims about Mohammed pose a challenge to the divinity of Christ." Robertson agreed that the issue was one of truth. He told Bill O'Reilly: "I do think, obviously, the best test of truth is in the marketplace. We need to get the truth out. I don't think truth is served by glossing over the beliefs of the founders of these people. We need to understand what's motivating them, then to say to millions of Muslims, Look, you're nice guys, you don't really believe what Mohammed taught.... We disagree [with his teachings]."[85]

A Legacy Stained?

Many insiders have been openly concerned about the apparent increase in the number of candid and controversial Robertson statements. Every such assertion on *The 700 Club* triggers a public recitation of real and supposed gaffes by his vigilant critics: "a very small nuke thrown off on Foggy Bottom [the State Department] to shake things up" (intended as humor); praying for vacancies on the Supreme Court; predicting disaster following "gay days" at Disney World; claims that he had done a 2,000 pound leg-press (a statement that required a ministry clarification on the "incline leg press machine" used for the exercise). Some of his friends fear that Robertson's reputation is being trivialized by a crescendo of controversial remarks, many calling for public explanations and some for apologies. Many supporters fear that the repeated controversies have marginalized Robertson. Calls for President Bush to repudiate Robertson's Chavez assassination remark were overkill, observed William F. Buckley Jr.: "In fact, lesser voices than the president's have done all the disavowing that needs to be done. For the president to throw yet another spear into the infidel suggests that another spear is needed, even though those who have eyes to see, and minds to use, know that Mr. Robertson is quite dead, needing no supplementary toxin."[86]

While he has been impulsive at times on the air, in part the so-called "wacko factor" in Robertson's persona is dictated by the language he speaks. "We have a tendency to use the language of Zion," explained his friend Ben Kinchlow: "We say things that we know are biblically based.... Non-charismatics do not understand and secularists think it is crazy." The regular viewers of *The 700 Club* rarely object to anything he says. It is the eavesdroppers who are shocked by his remarks, sometimes because they so sharply disagree with his views and sometimes because they have difficulty translating or even contextualizing "the language of Zion."[87]

Through the years, Robertson has acquiesced to pleas that he bridle his most reckless public comments. His speech became more measured in the late 1980s as he came to see himself as a viable political candidate. But his public pronouncements on a variety of subjects became once again more candid, and more widely monitored, after 1990. Chastised after his unguarded comment about Prime Minister Ariel Sharon, Robertson told reporters that "I have seen an intensity of attack against me that is unparalleled in the 40-some years of the broadcast. . . . I've just got to be careful." Patrick Roddy, a former news producer on *Good Morning America,* began briefing Robertson each morning before the show, and for a time Robertson worked the program with an earpiece, on occasion correcting statements he had made while still on the air. Some of Robertson's closest friends bristle at the suggestion that he should somehow be bridled, but all of those close to him share the sentiment expressed by his old friend Ben Kinchlow in 2008: "I hope his legacy is not stained by something that has no lasting significance."[88]

CHAPTER 10

Religious Life:
A Charismatic Middle Way

—◈—

At the height of his business explorations, Robertson insisted that "business is sort of like a hobby for me. I kind of enjoy it, but it's more of a sideline than a main cause." Robertson's self-definition was singular and simple: "I consider myself a servant. My life belongs to Jesus. . . . The big things I have accomplished were not me, they were him." Those closest to Robertson agree that there is a surety about his decisions when "he honestly believes he has heard from the Lord." David Gyertson expressed a common confidence shared by those close to him: "In thirty-eight years I have never had a moment when I questioned that Pat ultimately wanted to know the purpose of God. . . . We have seen his mistakes, . . . but we know that he wants to hear." Scott Ross agreed: "I have seen the man on the floor on his knees. . . . That is why he is still standing. He is just a man of God." Wherever his adventurous mind led him, Dede Robertson believed, "the Lord has always been faithful in bringing Pat back to where he wants him to be." Even those who know Robertson well readily acknowledged that he has "serious weaknesses," but they believe that he is a "genuine spirit" with little capacity for "Machiavellianism."[1]

A Wide Net

During his race for the presidency in 1988, when Robertson intentionally downplayed his religious image, some critics charged that he was concealing his core Christian mindset. Democratic congressman and religion

scholar Walter H. Capps wrote: "The truth is that the real Pat Robertson —
unlike the vast majority of citizens — is a sectarian Christian. The real Pat
Robertson speaks in tongues and receives prophecies. The real Pat Robertson is quick to acknowledge that the most significant event in his life was
his baptism in the Holy Spirit. The real Pat Robertson is a Pentecostal
evangelist, who wishes all persons . . . to come to a saving knowledge of Jesus Christ."[2]

Capps's description of Robertson's core religious persona was mostly
correct, though Robertson has resisted being defined as a "Pentecostal
evangelist," and his theology has never been narrowly "sectarian." His religious beliefs have not been tightly defined or systematic; they have rather
been quite eclectic. At the base of his belief system, always mitigating his
most deeply held "Pentecostal leadings," is a literalistic, somewhat fundamentalist, way of reading and interpreting Scripture. He regards himself as
an orthodox Reformation Christian: "We must read the Bible, study the Bible, understand the Bible and live the Bible. Our faith and doctrine must be
that of the Reformation." He has retained a lifelong confidence in the "Inductive Bible Study" methods of Wilbert Webster White that he learned
during his years at New York Seminary, and he has insisted that all theological truth can be grasped through a disciplined reading of the Scriptures. In his internally famous memo to Regent University leaders warning
against the perceived radicalism of the shepherding movement, Robertson defined his theology, and that of Regent, in traditional terms: "I believe
that our theology should be inductively derived from the Bible. This means
that what we do and teach is Biblical. Martin Luther said, 'Unless I am persuaded by scriptural and sound reason, here I stand.'" Biblical discussions
with Robertson were likely to end with a disarming exhortation to "read
the Bible." He told the dean of Regent's divinity school: "Exegesis is something that comes out of the Bible. We read the Bible and from a careful,
honest study of the Bible we draw forth theological truths." Robertson was
never a student of, nor indeed much interested in, systematic theology.
When asked by Robert Walker of Christian Life Publications to submit a
list of "the seven books he feels the most important for a Christian to read,"
Robertson gave five titles, all revivalist accounts, including two books by
Charles G. Finney and one by John Wesley.[3]

Like all who depend on such common-sense hermeneutical approaches, Robertson could seem more simplistic and dismissive than he
intended. Participating as a part of a distinguished panel discussion on
fundamentalism in 1990, sponsored by the Center for Jewish-Christian
Learning, Robertson began one of his comments with, for him, a rather

typical caveat: "Well, to those of us who do believe that the Bible is an inspired book. . . ." One of his fellow participants, Sister Mary Christine Athans, replied: "I believe that the scripture is inspired, and I don't quite hold your position." "I stand corrected, Sister," replied Robertson, whose commitment to inductive Bible reading was not intended to set narrow limits on the faith of others.[4]

After his sharp and long opposition to the shepherding leaders beginning in the mid-1970s, Robertson embraced the descriptive term "evangelical," distancing himself from those whom he regarded as extremists among both fundamentalists and charismatics. He did not like religious "labels" at all, but in a memo to ministry leaders he insisted that "if labels are forced on us, the only one with which I am comfortable is *Evangelical,* for that places us in the mainstream of God's move today." For decades, Robertson's answer to inquiries about how he described himself was cryptic: "I consider myself an evangelical Christian, rather than a Fundamentalist or a Charismatic."[5]

Yet by the end of the twentieth century, Robertson was less enamored with the label "evangelical." The growing visibility of a vocal evangelical intelligentsia intent on distancing "evangelicalism" from Robertson and other cultural conservatives made him despair in his hopes for unity among evangelicals. In 2006, he told the dean of Regent University School of Religion, "The National Association of Evangelicals went on hard times and was taken over . . . by a tiny group of people who claimed to represent all the evangelical people, which they didn't." By the early twenty-first century, Robertson was convinced that "charismatic . . . is becoming more of an umbrella of what God is doing as opposed to evangelical."[6]

Terminology aside, Pat Robertson cast a wide net to gather diverse religious supporters, but he distanced himself from those whom he considered extremists among fundamentalists and Pentecostals. There were pragmatic reasons for separating from extremists: "The Christians who supported the Christian Broadcasting Network . . . would defect in droves if we started teaching heresy so it is extremely important [to maintain] a Biblical standard." He knew he could not satisfy the narrow moral restrictions of right-wing Pentecostals. Criticized by a viewer who believed his "views are liberal" because he wore a wedding ring, Robertson replied that such remarks were "interesting" since he was generally regarded as "far right." He never tolerated frauds or fools among Pentecostal extremists: "I am totally and unalterably opposed to religious falsehood and those Christian cults which manipulate and abuse sincere and eager Christians believers." He shied away from many ministers on the fringes of the booming healing revival: "Some of these spiritual charlatans say things that are simply nonsense. They've been doing it for years — since biblical times, really — and they will continue doing it until Jesus comes." Robertson often felt helpless to openly expose the suspects: "Gullible Christians will not permit Christian leaders like me, who know the truth, to speak out for fear of being labeled 'not loving.'"[7]

Neither did Robertson cater to the narrow demands of separatist fundamentalism. He concluded early in his religious journey that "Fundamentalists were known as obscurantist, mean-spirited, narrow-minded, all those things that we didn't desire to be." Robertson's early courtship of mainstream denominational leaders in the Norfolk area offended his fundamentalist friend George Lauderdale, causing him to resign from the original board of CBN and for a time become a critic of the ministry. Lauderdale later regretted his actions. "Pat was gracious," he recalled, "but it hurt him."[8]

It was in this centrist context that Robertson publicly, though not in an adversarial way, distanced himself from the Christian Reconstructionist movement. In the 1970s he interviewed the leading spokesman of the teaching, Rousas John Rushdoony, on *The 700 Club*. Robertson was always a sympathetic interviewer, and he agreed with much that Rushdoony said about reclaiming the Puritan vision of a Christian nation, but he was careful to distance himself from extreme expressions of dominionism and from Rushdoony's association with postmillennialism. In a ministry reply crafted to answer those asking if he supported the movement, Robertson wrote: "I can assure you I do not concur with the extremes of the Dominion Theology movement in this country. . . . We do not expect some kind of restructured Utopia here on earth, but join those in Revelation who say, 'even so come Lord Jesus.' I am firmly committed to the concept that we should 'occupy until he comes.' That means we do everything we can to change this world now." In a long letter to Gary North, the director of the Institute for Christian Economics and son-in-law of Rushdoony, Robertson explained his objections to dominionism, insisting that "I did not want my silence in the matter to be taken as concurrence." He agreed that Christians should "take dominion over satanic forces," but he did not "believe that we are going to see heaven on earth short of the coming of Jesus Christ." When a second edition of Robertson's popular book, *The Secret Kingdom*, was published in 1992, he included a clarification of the "Law of Dominion," which many had regarded as a Christian Reconstructionist principle: "The Law of Dominion should not be confused with the teaching of what is sometimes called 'dominion theology' or 'Reconstructionism.'"[9]

On the other end of the spectrum, Robertson was an adamant and outspoken critic of liberal Christian denominations, which combined theological liberalism with cultural causes abhorred by Robertson. His distrust of liberal denominations was deeply rooted in his experiences. In 1974, he wrote to a Methodist minister: "I have worked in the Methodist Church, the Southern Baptist Church, and the Dutch Reformed Church. In each one I find a predominate preponderance of people who have not experienced a born again relationship with the Lord Jesus Christ, who go to church on Sunday because it is the thing to do, and who are led by and large by elders, deacons and ministers who really do not have a saving vital relationship with Jesus Christ. The big main line denominational churches are filled with social reformers and master planners who are as cold as fish." In a 1984 speech he outlined his objections: "Coming into the twentieth century . . . you find a liberal Christianity that does not pay a great deal of attention to the Bible. They do not believe in Israel . . . and they have tended, as in the World Council of Churches, to be pro-Marxists . . . because they do not embrace the Bible as such." "The churches are breaking apart, sadly," Robertson observed in 2006: "Most of the Presbyterians, American Baptists, Methodists have . . . departed from the faith," opening the way for the "emergence of serious heresies."[10]

Robertson has always believed that he represents the center, not the fringe, of modern Protestant thought. From the beginning of his ministry Robertson imagined that he had "served as a bridge between some of the more traditional denominations and the Pentecostal-charismatic groups, and I think that I have helped to bring what would be called credibility in the eyes of people like Baptists and others as to what God was doing."[11]

Charismatic Core

While Pat Robertson has thought of himself as an evangelical centrist, committed to building bridges between churches and Christians whose histories, traditions, and beliefs were substantially different, his core religious persona has been rooted deep in the twentieth-century charismatic movement. Robertson's charismatic language has sometimes been muted by his practicality and common sense, as well as by his desire to build a broad television ministry, but he has never shied away from expressing his faith in the language of the movement.

During the early years of CBN, the identity of the ministry was quite clearly charismatic, as were CBN's supporters. While the gifts of the Spirit were exercised less frequently on *The 700 Club* over time, Robertson continued to speak frankly and frequently about his belief in the gifts of the Holy Spirit. On *The 700 Club* in March 1979 Robertson explained in some detail his practice of praying in tongues and urged viewers: "As you begin to speak, just begin to speak a language. Just say, 'I thank you, Lord,' and just walk out into what He's giving you. It's marvelous. You'll enjoy it. . . . You don't have to worry about what other people think." He then prayed: "Father, one more time we pray for those people. Fill them with the Holy Spirit and power. Let them know the power that was yours when you started your church on the day of Pentecost."[12]

In 1990, Robertson reviewed for a correspondent the depth of his acquaintance with the movement he had joined in the 1950s: "I have incidentally observed from afar A. A. Allen, Jack Coe, William Branham, and the Voice of Healing evangelists. I have known well and ministered beside Oral Roberts and Kathryn Kuhlman. 'Mr. Pentecost,' David DuPlessis, who ministered with the great Smith Wigglesworth, was a close friend. I am an expert on revivals from John Wesley to Charles Finney. . . . I have known personally those who have raised the dead, performed great miracles, witnessed visitations of God, and have been the spiritual leaders of our time." Speaking at Christ for the Nations in 1994, Robertson recalled that he had visited Gordon Lindsay's Voice of Healing offices in 1959 when he was a neophyte in the charismatic movement, and that he always considered Lindsay a "giant."[13]

Some of Robertson's closest religious friends throughout his life were the leading figures in the charismatic movement. When correspondents criticized popular independent evangelists, Robertson often quickly came to their defense. In a 1976 reply to a letter which was "rather critical of a number of God's servants," Robertson offered a defense of Rex Humbard: "Rex Humbard has gone through an absolutely devastating experience in which he was unjustly treated on a national level of government. I learned of this from an impeccable source. God has brought him forth as gold and is now using him to win many to the Lord." Two decades later, Robertson's executive secretary answered similarly: "You obviously have a problem with Oral Roberts, Benny Hinn, and Marilyn Hickey. Yet, all of these have been used by God to bring hundreds of thousands to Jesus. You know, we may not always agree with everything particular ministers do, but that does not mean God is not using these ministers." Robertson saw independent evangelists such as Benny Hinn, Reinhart Bonnke, and D. G. S. Dhinakaran as "people who push the kingdom of heaven forward." Robertson's religious litmus test was pragmatic: is a minister bringing people to Christ?[14]

Robertson's friendships, cultivated in hundreds of conferences and personal encounters, have included hundreds of well-known and little-known leaders in the amorphous charismatic movement. Demos Shakarian, founder of the influential Full Gospel Business Men's Fellowship International, was a "dear friend." In Virginia Beach, Robertson's good friend John Gimenez, whose Rock Church ministry was acclaimed among charismatics, was a loyal lifetime companion who changed Gordon Robertson's life by taking him to India. Many other charismatic ministers who were not well known to Robertson received his friendly encouragement and aid. He admired at a distance the worldwide mission work of Morris Cerullo and his son, David Cerullo, and traveled to Charlotte, North Carolina, in 2006 where he joined Rex Humbard and Rod Parsley in inaugurating a new religious television enterprise, the Inspiration Network.[15]

Of all the first-generation leaders of the American healing revival, Oral Roberts was closest to Pat Robertson. When Roberts came under criticism in 1987 for his extreme fundraising pleas, Robertson defended his friend and mentor at his own political risk. He wrote to one of Roberts's critics: "I am a great supporter of Oral. He and I have been friends for years and . . . I have been supportive of his teaching concerning 'Seed Faith.'" He backhandedly defended his friend's assertion that God would kill him if he did not receive sufficient funds to complete the City of Faith: "I believe that my dear friend, Oral, may have had a bad day when he made his statement that God would take his life unless $4.5 million came in by the end of March." Two decades later, when Oral Roberts University faced a dire financial crisis, Robertson sent a team of investigators to see if CBN could help rescue the university, and he also sent a generous financial gift to Richard Roberts to help stabilize the university.[16]

Robertson's ties to independent charismatic ministers served him well during his political campaign. They were more loyal to him during his campaign than any other category of American religious leaders. In a "historic meeting" in Dallas, twenty-seven "founding trustees" of an organization called "Charismatic Bible Ministries," which included virtually every major independent ministry in the country, sent a greeting to Robertson: "We believe you are a very special man of God and we are praying for you to know God's decision, also for your family and ministry. We believe God will guide you!"[17]

"Before he ran for president," observed his friend Michael Little, Robertson "enjoyed some of the guys who were far out there," but "after the grinding of the political campaign," he became somewhat more guarded. Nonetheless, Robertson continued to believe in and support some of the more controversial television evangelists, including Benny Hinn. Often criticized for preaching an extreme version of the "word of faith" teaching, his theatrical healing techniques, and his flamboyant lifestyle, in the 1990s Hinn was assailed by critics, including evangelical author Hank Hanegraaff. After Hanegraaff appeared on *The 700 Club,* Robertson aroused criticism by inviting the evangelist to defend himself on the program. He explained Hinn's appearance: "Many Christians have had concerns about Benny Hinn's teachings. During the summer several leading Bible scholars met privately with Benny Hinn to discuss those concerns. Benny was receptive to their instruction and admonitions, and admitted that he has been wrong about some things. Since there has been so much controversy surrounding some of Benny Hinn's theology, his lifestyle and his healing claims, we felt we owed it to our television viewers to let them hear firsthand Benny's response, and then make their own determination about his ministry." Robertson urged inquirers to read a long Hinn interview published in *Charisma* magazine. Robertson continued to defend Hinn in later years, insisting in a ministry response letter that Hinn had "realized changes needed to be made in his ministry, and he said he was making them." After a critical television special about Hinn in 2003, Robertson simply repeated his consistent pragmatic test: "We have had Benny on *The 700 Club* from time to time to share with us about his ministry throughout the world. . . . He is bearing good fruit by bringing the lost into the Kingdom of God." Acknowledging a Christmas gift from Hinn in 2007, Robertson wrote: "I am always thrilled when I see your crusades on television and realize the tremendous outreach that God is giving to you overseas. This is indeed the day of harvest beyond anything that any generation has ever seen in the history of mankind. We both should be very grateful to be part of it." Interviewing Hinn on *The 700 Club* in 2008, Robertson commended him to the audience as "a man of God that God is using all around the world."[18]

Robertson also endorsed the controversial "Toronto Blessing," which erupted in 1995 in the Airport Vineyard Church in Toronto. Encouraged by the church's pastor, John Arnott, those "drunk in the spirit" received the gift of holy laughter, as well as other spiritual gifts. Robertson became one of the most visible defenders of the "Laughing Revival." He wrote to an inquirer in 1997: "Over the past forty years, I have encountered many spiritual expressions in the church. Some are harmless, some are not. Some definitely are of God, some may be questionable. . . . The Bible says, *'In Thy presence there is fullness of joy.'* Just because you or I have never experienced the overflowing joy that the Bible describes is no reason for us to dispute its existence. . . . I have stood many times against error and false teaching, but happy Christians laughing in the presence of the Lord is hardly wrong or something to be condemned on national television." Robertson's test of the movement, as always, was pragmatic: "The main question is whether or not the hearts of those participating . . . are drawn closer to Jesus in humble faith." Robertson remained supportive of the ministry of John and Carol Arnott, as did his son Gordon, commending the "great revival" still taking place at the church in 2008.[19]

Pat Robertson's clearest identification with the independent charismatic ministries has been his thoroughgoing embrace of the "Seed Faith" teaching made popular in the 1950s by Oral Roberts and Kenneth Hagin. The word of faith message was controversial, particularly as used by some extreme advocates such as Robert Tilton, and Robertson distanced himself from the most radical expressions of the idea. Responding to an inquirer, he wrote: "I assume when you say 'Faith Movement' that you are referring to what is known as 'name it and claim it.' I don't believe it is that simple. . . . Is someone handicapped because they have little faith? Not necessarily. . . . This is a very complex subject. . . . I recommend that you read the promises that God has given in His Word, and seek the Lord to give you guidance." "I believe in faith, miracles, and in the power of the Holy Spirit with signs following," he wrote to another inquirer. "However, some of the things going on within the 'faith' movement simply are not biblical." In the mid-1980s, when the doctrine came under fire from many within the charismatic movement, a memo regarding "the 'Faith and Word Message'" was sent to all of the ministry department heads and all CBN station managers. The directive stated unequivocally that "Pat is a positive confession teacher. He believes strongly in 'what you say you get.' He does not teach glibly or without judging what he says in light of Scripture, nor is he blind to the actualities of diversity, suffering, sin, etc.," but "CBN has no real problem with the teachers and teachings on the subject." CBN would not "come down" on employees in the organization who disagreed, but the "Biblical principles" upon which the teaching was based had been an important part of Robertson's book, *The Secret Kingdom,* and were incorporated in the CBN Counselor's Handbook. In his 1985 book, *Beyond Reason,* Robertson stated the "five steps to receiving a miracle" in the language of the faith teaching: "*1. Ask for it. . . . 2. Be prepared to obey the Holy Spirit. . . . 3. Offer your body to God. . . . 4. Receive by faith. 5. Act your faith.*"[20]

Robertson's embrace of the word of faith teaching has been moderated by his common-sense mindset, as well as his beliefs in Biblical authority and inductive investigation. He confronted often and with some clarity the central dilemma of Pentecostal and charismatic theology: to what extent can Christians place absolute confidence in the miraculous intervention of the Holy Spirit? How does one account for failure without diminishing faith? In a question-and-answer book he published in 2003, Robertson wrote: "Can God heal our bodies? Yes, He can. Does He heal everyone, every time we ask Him? Apparently not." Are Christians compelled to abandon their belief in miracles if they do not receive their requests? What if one's leg was cut off? Could it be healed? Robertson replied: "No amount of healing can bring that leg back. But God can do the miraculous. I'm aware of a case involving T. L. Osborn at a meeting he held in Ghana. A man whose leg had been cut off at the knee was standing at the periphery of the crown of 200,000 listening to the message. The power of Jesus Christ touched him, the word of God brought faith in his heart, and miraculously, spontaneously his leg began to grow, his foot and toes grew, his entire leg was restored like new! Now, that is a miracle! . . . Does He do miracles today? Yes, He does, all around the world."[21]

Robertson readily acknowledged mystery and inscrutability in the working of God's miraculous intervention, but, like all Pentecostals and charismatics, he often worded his personal leadings and prophecies with a certainty and finality that fueled consternation among his critics. A former CBN employee wrote in 1988: "Robertson . . . reached such a deluded state that he had begun to confuse his own thoughts, desires, and emotions with the so-called 'inspiration of the Holy Spirit.'" But in fact Robertson was usually quite careful about his use of what he believed was his gift of prophecy. He generally prefaced his prophetic statements with disclaimers. In his book *The New Millennium,* which was filled with predictions, Robertson wrote: "We approach these subjects with humility, recognizing that we are fallible human beings." The world is filled with "volatile forces" that make the work of predicting an inexact enterprise. "In some cases," he acknowledged, "things may in fact turn out quite differently than we had anticipated."[22]

The dichotomy between confidence in the leading of the Holy Spirit and failed expectations was a problem that Robertson tried to confront honestly. He wrote to CBN partners in 1996: "We know God answers prayer and gives us direction in life. That's why each year leading up to our annual CBN staff New Year's day prayer meeting, I take time apart to pray, seeking God for His wisdom and direction for the coming year. This year as I sought the Lord, several things became clear." Still, twice he inserted the caveat: "If I am hearing Him correctly." In a letter attempting to explain his friend Oral Roberts's "bad day" when he predicted God would take his life in 1987, Robertson wrote: "All of us who work in God's service know the truth of the Apostle Paul's writing when he said, 'We see through a glass darkly.' No one has a direct pipeline to God to have precise information day after day after day. God leads us, God speaks to us, God directs us, but the chance to be mistaken is always present. This in no wise diminishes the call of a man of God, it merely indicates that we are all vessels made of clay and in time of stress or sickness can make mistakes."[23]

Most charismatics try to guard against missing the true leading of the Holy Spirit. In 1985 Robertson sent a memo to the CBN staff: "At last Friday's prayer meeting, the Lord gave a message in tongues. There followed a lengthy message which did not seem to be the interpretation of the brief message in tongues. Carl Witten sent me a letter to the effect that he felt his was the interpretation. I send it to you for your interest and edification." After a similar memo in 1995 in which Robertson questioned the prophetic utterances of some "gifted people," longtime CBN employee Jay Comisky thought it demonstrated that Robertson was "sensitive to saying, 'What is the Holy Spirit saying today?'"[24]

Speaking Charismatic Language

With his education, his training in inductive Bible interpretation, and his innate rationalism to go along with his belief in the power of the Holy Spirit, Robertson has been more driven than most charismatics to explore the anomalies of divine guidance and mistaken predictions. In 1974, speaking to a theological class at Oral Roberts University entitled "The Holy Spirit in the Now," Robertson probed the question of "how" the Spirit leads. Critical of the "wild fire" that plagued the early Pentecostal and charismatic movements in which "a great deal of what passes for prophecy is just foolishness," Robertson offered two rules for testing: "You can't get revelation from God apart from the Bible," and "Inside of the depths of your being, there is a deep, settled peace." While "peace of mind" seemed to Robertson a reliable standard, further quantification was elusive.[25]

Through the years Robertson has offered a variety of ways to test the leading of the Spirit. Always in the forefront was the primacy of the Scriptures. In a form letter prepared for questioners on the subject, he wrote: "So while we thank God for revelations, we do not allow them to take us away from the continual study of the Bible." "God's primary means for giving us His guidance is the Holy Bible. The Bible is our rule book of faith and practice," Robertson wrote in 1996. But Bible study was enriched for those "filled with His Holy Spirit": "He guides by means of specific scriptures that suddenly come alive for you. He guides by bringing people to you providentially to give you advice and counsel. He guides through circumstances."[26]

The most consistent advice Robertson has offered is to verify one's leadings by receiving confirmation from others and by testing outcomes. Robertson repeatedly asserted that his race for the presidency came only after "the clear, unmistakable, and oft confirmed will and leading of our Lord." One should always seek verification from "two or three witnesses" to "confirm what God is saying." At every step in receiving a prophecy, one must test: "As you go along, test every step. Be willing to go forward, but also be willing to stop the project in the event God has not led you." His ultimate check was totally practical: "The Bible says that we can tell if someone is a prophet by seeing if what he has said comes to pass. That's a very pragmatic test, and it works." In 2003 he wrote: "The best way to discern whether one who claims to speak for the Lord is real or not is to look at his or her track record. If a person glorifies Jesus Christ and is true to the Bible, and if the so-called prophetic words come to pass, that person should be heeded in the future." While Robertson believes that "The Lord speaks to us," one must be careful to avoid "the nutty stuff."[27]

In 2000, Robertson was re-ordained to the ministry in an elaborate ceremony at Regent University. The "Ordination Council" of six ministers included some of the most visible leaders of the charismatic revival. Vinson Synan, dean of the School of Divinity at Regent, was one of the most respected leaders of the American charismatic movement; Dr. D. G. S. Dhinakaran from Chennai, India, was one of the most celebrated leaders of the revival outside the United States. Other members of the Ordination Council were Thomas E. Trask, the General Superintendent of the Assemblies of God, and Jack W. Hayford, the founding pastor of The Church on the Way and leader of the Foursquare Gospel Church. Bishop John W. Howe from the Episcopal Diocese of Central Florida and Pastor Emeritus Frank Hughes of the South Norfolk Baptist Church represented mainline and evangelical churches.[28]

Some observers portrayed the ceremony as a crass attempt to "prove to his faithful viewers that he was more interested in religion than politics." But in Robertson's mind the ceremony clearly had a more spiritual intent. It returned Robertson to his charismatic roots and affirmed his excitement about CBN's role in the progress of charismatic Christianity around the world. "American politics are irrelevant at this point," Robertson observed in 2007, "because the great plan of God is starting to unfold." "In the last days people's heart will open to the gospel": this was a drama, Robertson believed, that was being played out in the revivals of Benny Hinn and Reinhart Bonnke and through CBN's WorldReach programming that had "led almost 500 million people to the Lord." The present was a transformative Christian moment, Robertson exulted, and "I am part of it."[29]

Prophecy and the Millennium

Nowhere was Pat Robertson's charismatic language more evident, and more apt to be misunderstood, than in his prophetic interpretations and personal prophetic predictions. Robertson embraced the role of prophet. He wrote in *Religious Broadcasting* in 1981: "To know what is happening in the world, and to know what God is doing through these events is a high calling for a Christian communicator. Do this, and in a real sense, you are a prophet." Robertson always hedged his forays into prophecy. Disclaimers abounded in his writings: "If I am reading the signs of the time correctly"; "I may be exaggerating"; "I may be far too pessimistic." Pat Robertson's penchant for prophesying found its most dogmatic expressions in *Pat Robertson's Perspective,* a newsletter that began publication in the late 1970s and by the early 1980s was mailed regularly to the ministry's 200,000 partners. There Robertson offered observations that were a mixture of common sense, erudition, and "prophecies relevant to these times." In a 1980 issue of *Perspective* that focused on "Prophetic Insights," he described the limits of his gift: "I approach this subject with humility, recognizing that other men of good will may differ. I underscore emphatically that some of the tentative hypotheses are intended to provoke thought. They are put forth for reflection, prayer, and study — not as something set in stone brought down from the mountain." He repeatedly pointed out that *Perspective* "only goes to our partners," and that the views he expressed were solely his and not those of the Christian Broadcasting Network. A paragraph drafted for inclusion in letters to "our special 700 CLUB friends" explained the confidential nature of some of the writing: "It may cause confusion if it were reprinted in various newspapers who were speaking to a secular audience who did not know the Lord." Still, Robertson felt that he wrote with "God's anointing" in the publication and that "it helped to clarify complicated issues, as well as point out God's hand in troubling situations."[30]

In his interpretations of prophecy, Robertson has been more cautious than most of the noted premillennialists. Asked to identify the "Antichrist" by an inquirer, Robertson replied: "I'm reluctant to be specific about such matters, because many Bible teachers have made mistakes, misinterpreted prophecy, ascribed fulfillments where there were none, and basically missed it! . . . The truth is, we just don't know who the Antichrist will be or where he will come from. . . . Again, I caution against jumping to false conclusions when the Bible is silent or not clearly understood. Dogmatic statements about the veiled prophetic references in Scripture lead to confusion among believers and ridicule from non-believers." Robertson's views on end-time prophecy strayed in significant ways from the conventional millennial formula that had been the standard of premillennialists since the late nineteenth century. In general, he was less dogmatic than most about the particulars of the end-time scenario. "I avoid like a plague the apocalyptic problems," he wrote to an inquirer in 1981.[31]

From his days as a student at New York Seminary, Robertson was a premillennialist, in common with other evangelicals, but he disagreed with the dominant premillennialist theory that there would be a "pre-tribulation" rapture, or "catching away" of the saved, before the millennium could begin, a theory first widely publicized in the Scofield Bible and taught in many evangelical and fundamentalist schools. Robertson explained his view in a form letter dispatched by CBN to inquirers in the 1970s: "You would probably be interested to know that the Scofield Bible took their cue from John Nelson Darby, who was a member of the Plymouth Church of England in 1830. Up until that time no one had heard of the rapture and there was to be one second coming of Jesus, and that it would be a resurrection and rapture. . . . Darby went to a meeting of the Irvinites who were a Pentecostal sect in England. A girl at that meeting brought what was supposed to be a prophecy that dealt in some measure with rapture prior to the tribulation. Darby became inspired with the idea and began to write on it. Scofield and a number of the present day fundamentalist churches have taken up the idea."[32]

Robertson has never wavered in his judgment that modern millennial theorizing about a pre-tribulation rapture was "speculative nonsense." The issue had been settled for him during his studies in New York: "There is no way from inductive Bible study, which is what we did in seminary, that you can come out with this pre-tribulation rapture. . . . It just isn't in the Bible." While still a student, "independently of anybody else," he concluded that the concept of "the pre-tribulation rapture" was "totally wrong." On the other hand, he has emphasized repeatedly that "I do not think it should be a point of division among the Body of Christ." "I am open," Robertson confided in 2008; "I am very indulgent in knowing my own capacity for fallacy. I am willing to give others the benefit of the doubt."[33]

While Robertson was often lumped together with Hal Lindsey, Tim LaHaye, and other popular end-times writers, particularly because of his novel about a catastrophic asteroid bringing a dramatic end to life on earth, he was never supportive of that popular prophetic genre that sold millions of books. He was irate when Hal Lindsey criticized him on TBN. He fired off a protest to Paul Crouch: "I disagreed with some of the things that appeared in The Late Great Planet Earth, even though it did sell 6 million copies. But for him to make a statement that I don't believe in the Bible or the second coming of the Lord, or any of the other essential truths of the word is frankly slanderous." Robertson was particularly incensed that Lindsey reportedly "insinuated that I believed in what is known as Replacement Theology where the church is favored over Israel. I believe no such thing and have taught vehemently against Replacement Theology."[34]

Robertson's views of Biblical prophecy, particularly his interpretation of Ezekiel and Daniel, have differed little from other premillennialist interpretations in predicting the "twilight of the times of the Gentiles" and the restoration of Israel. He has repeatedly made specific prophetic applications to events in the Middle East, sometimes with great clarity. In 1980 he wrote: "If the approximate dating of events is even close and if Anti-Christ is yet to come, then we must conclude that there is a man alive today, approximately 27 years old, who is now being groomed to be the Satanic messiah." Nonetheless, he has usually been more tentative and less dogmatic than most popular proponents of premillennialism. His projections were almost always sprinkled with "ifs." Before one interpretative segment in *The New Millennium,* he wrote: "I would like also to engage in some speculation about future events which these biblical certainties may have foretold. If you happen to be one who dislikes a bit of intrigue and speculation, this section of this chapter is not for you. For others I hope you enjoy this section but please feel free to judge carefully and critically."[35]

Because Robertson never entered wholeheartedly into the prevailing premillennialist excitement, and because during his political campaign he made clear his commitment to improving society through the political process, he was sometimes accused of embracing postmillennialism. One study of how his millennial views influenced his political campaign suggested that he constructed an "idiosyncratic synthesis of the premillennial and postmillennial visions" which shifted his emphasis from visions of end-time cataclysm to "revival and repentance." The authors argued that the synthesis appeared to "work for him" but caused trouble with "his original audience of premillennialist believers," citing Robertson's clash with Jimmy Swaggart on the subject in 1986. But Robertson quickly settled his spat with Swaggart, assuring him that he embraced a premillennialist end-time scenario, and the two agreed to disagree amiably about the pre-tribulation rapture. While some students of the religious right insisted that premillennialist beliefs necessarily restricted a sense of political activism, that never was the case. Evangelical premillennialists embraced political reform as a response to Jesus' command to "Occupy, until I come." While some historians have described the accommodation as a "crashing contradiction," Joel Carpenter, in his seminal study of fundamentalism, *Revive Us Again,* writes, "The record is clear: repeatedly, and with growing intensity fundamentalists called for and looked longingly toward a spiritual quickening in the churches and a great religious awakening in their land. Fundamentalist leaders held out both hopes — for rapture and revival with little sense of contradiction." This evangelical settlement, explained Robertson, "means we do everything we can to change this world now. If for no other reason, we do it to prepare the way for the coming of the Lord."[36]

Most inscrutable to his adversaries are Robertson's personal annual prophetic projections. Each year Robertson returns from a December vacation retreat to deliver prophecies about the coming year, an event much anticipated by his closest followers. A recent student of such prophecies by religious leaders described them as defenses of evangelical beliefs that identified "hidden sources of evil in their midst." Robertson's predictions have often focused on doom and gloom. One critic charged that "Robertson has been predicting worldwide cataclysm for years. In 1980, he claimed that God told him the Soviet Union would invade the Middle East to seize oil reserves, sparking the collapse of Western Europe and global economic instability.... Some evangelicals have grown weary of Robertson's attempt to play global fortune-teller."[37]

In spite of his ever-present disclaimers, Robertson's projections have often had an air of finality and confidence. Nothing frustrates his critics more than the ease with which he reverses opinions about the leadings he has received through prayer. Yet within the context of his charismatic Christianity, there is nothing particularly extraordinary about Robertson's annual predictions. His modus operandi, noted historian Vinson Synan, "originates in his theology" and is well understood by his community of supporters. For a charismatic, the gift of prophecy is simple and straightforward; in Gordon Robertson's words, "You hear from God, and you repeat it." Like his interpretations of Biblical prophecy, Pat Robertson's wide-ranging predictions have generally been surrounded by disclaimers. In December 2006 Robertson candidly explained his understanding of his yearly prophetic utterances: "For the past decades, I have enjoyed the opportunity to spend several days between Christmas and New Year's Day in a special time of prayer and Bible study. During these periods, I have earnestly asked the Lord for any insight or direction He wishes to give me for the year ahead. At some times, His word to me has been remarkably precise and the subsequent fulfillment amazing. At other times, either my spiritual perception was lacking or else subsequent prayer or actions by others caused a different result than what I anticipated. Therefore, I must speak with great humility recognizing that I 'see through a glass darkly.'"[38]

The test of his prophetic gift, like the test of charismatic leading, is entirely pragmatic. When he offered his predictions for 2007, he told his co-host on *The 700 Club,* Terry Meeuwsen, "I've put these things out with humility, but nevertheless, I have a relatively good track record. Sometimes I've missed." All charismatics, agreed Ben Kinchlow, know that "prophecy is a very 'iffy' proposition," but most insiders listen when Robertson speaks. "I have heard Pat come back and say, 'I missed it. I was wrong.' But it is hard for him to do that, and he will sure let you know when he is right," said Scott Ross. Nonetheless, "He has a pretty good score." In 2009, Steven Vegh, writing in the *Virginian-Pilot,* conceded that "Robertson's predictions last year for the economy were pretty much on target.... His prophecy of a stock market crash for 2009 came true, a tad early in the fall. His forecast of a recession proved true."[39]

Israel

Pat Robertson has generally been flexible and tolerant about differences in prophetic interpretation, but he has been absolutely unbending on "two scriptural keys [that] unlock the riddle of the second coming." He wrote in 1975: "The first is that the gospel is to be preached to the whole world.... That is being accomplished on TV.... The second key to the end of this age . . . concerns the Jewish people." Robertson strongly believed that WorldReach was contributing to the accomplishment of the first prophetic precursor to the second coming, but throughout his life, he has also been wedded to the prophetic significance of events in Israel. "Israel is God's time clock," he said in 2007.[40]

In a 1996 letter Robertson summarized his long-held belief: "The regathering of the Jews to the nation of Israel is a fulfillment of God's promise. The Bible teaches that the Jews are and remain and shall ever be the apple of God's eye — His chosen people — and nobody will ever be able to change this. The reference of the promise of the restoration of the Jews into the nation of Israel is found in hundreds of prophetic references. The times of the Gentiles came to a close in 1948, when Israel was once again recognized as a nation. The apostle Paul in the book of Romans wrote about the Gentiles being 'grafted into the tree.' They did not 're-place' Israel. . . . The covenant was with Israel, not the Gentiles." Robertson remained tolerant of those who "see the scripture differently and disagree," willing to "keep the unity in Christ and love one another," but he would never compromise his support for the nation of Israel. In answer to a correspondent who objected to his strong support of Israel, he wrote: "If my remarks on television have offended you I am sorry. What I have said is the truth and it accords with Bible prophecy. A long time ago, I learned that it is best to live in the world as God has made it and not to fight either His principles or His plans. Whether we agree or not, His plan is to bring back the Jewish people to a homeland in the Middle East and to bless them there." The promise that God would "bless them" who blessed Israel was inviolate, and for decades his retort to those who disliked his pro-Israeli rhetoric was, "Personally, I would rather be among those that God blesses rather than those whom God curses, wouldn't you?" But Robertson also insisted that "I love the Palestinian people, especially those who are Christians." When CBN began broadcasting in the Middle East in 1969 Robertson announced that their programming aimed to speak to everyone in the region: "We may help stop the killing if we tell the Arabs, Jews and Russians of the love of God." Everything that happened in the region was the fulfillment of prophecy leading to the return of Christ to "rule from Jerusalem."[41]

Robertson was happy to be part of a booming evangelical-Israeli alliance that by the 1980s had gained public recognition in both the U.S. and Israel. In a 1994 speech to the Christians' Israel Public Action Campaign Robertson said: "It has been my firm belief that evangelical Christians should link hands with our friends in Israel in a bond of friendship which transcends political consideration or mere human emotion. I have reaffirmed time and time again my personal commitment to stand shoulder-to-shoulder with the nation of Israel." Citing Billy Graham as an example, in a 1984 speech, Robertson appealed to evangelicals to support the cause: "The evangelicals hold a great affinity for the Jewish people who are alive today, whether they are found in America or whether they are found in Israel. Therefore, there is tremendous support among evangelical Christians for the State of Israel and for Jewish rights." Generally, evangelical support for Israel was anchored in the belief, expressed often by Robertson, that "at the climax of history, the Israelis will turn to God, and the nation will once again become a center of God's revelation to all mankind. . . . Some people think that a certain sign of the return of Jesus Christ to earth will be the restoration of the Jewish people to an understanding of God's full revelation in Christ." In the absence of a temple, a priesthood, and the offering of Levitical sacrifices for the forgiveness of sins, "the only thing that is available to them or any of us is the one true High Priest who offered a permanent sacrifice for the sins of all the world."[42]

Robertson has fully supported the Messianic Jewish organizations that targeted the conversion of Jews, and he has shared the sense of many such organizations that Messianic Jews are still fully Jewish. Responding to a question from a rabbi in 1997, Robertson wrote: "CBN, of course, is very supportive of the Messianic Jews. Where some people become confused is with the theory that a Jew has to stop being a Jew in order to accept Jesus Christ as Messiah. That is, of course, incorrect. In fact, the completion of the Jewish religion is Jesus. A Jew certainly does not have to forsake the glorious heritage of centuries in order to receive the One who was foretold throughout all of the Jewish history. Both Jew and Gentile will be judged by the same standard. God will judge us all in the light of what we do with what we know. . . . Obviously, all of us need to come to Jesus, and in Jesus we are neither Jews nor Gentiles." The solidarity of CBN with Jewish believers has been displayed in annual celebrations of Jewish feasts and holidays on the CBN campus. A celebration of Rosh Hashanah each year in September has drawn large crowds to ceremonies presided over by Pat and Gordon Robertson; in the words of one observer, such celebrations have engendered "a strong psychological link between Christians and Jews by acculturating . . . the audience to Jewish customs through staging and taking part in [Pat Robertson's] own Rosh Hashanah celebration."[43]

Robertson's most solemn political commitment to Israel has been to the preservation of Israeli land, particularly Jerusalem. In 1977 he warned: "There is a terrible judgment pronounced in the Bible against the nations that have 'divided my land.' . . . Many Bible scholars feel that the downfall of mighty Britain came about because Britain presumed to 'divide His land.'" Robertson vehemently objected to any political settlement that demanded that Israel relinquish territory. In a speech in Jerusalem that attracted widespread attention in the Israeli press, Robertson objected to George

Bush's "road map for peace," which included land concessions, and to Israeli prime minister Ariel Sharon's plan to withdraw from the Gaza Strip: "I
shudder to think of any politician who would dare to stand in front of
God's prophecies. . . . I want to say here tonight, the prophecies of God will
stand. . . . God will bring wrath on those who frustrate His plan, even if they
claim to be born again Christians. . . . I say to you tonight, God will not allow the United Nations or the French or the Germans or the Russians or
the Arabs or the United States to take from the Jews this city or His land
that He has given to His chosen people." He was "heart sick" over remarks
made by his "old friend" Prime Minister Ehud Olmert in 2008 favoring re-
linquishing most of Israel's West Bank land holdings to the Palestinians:
"He is a lame duck and he ought to keep his mouth shut. . . . This shocks
me." Robertson has long allied himself with the most ardent Christian supporters of an undivided Jewish Jerusalem; in 1997 he joined nine other sig-
natories, including John Hagee, Jerry Falwell, Ralph Reed, Oral Roberts,
and E. V. Hill, in a *New York Times* advertisement that stated: "We, the un-
dersigned Christian leaders, communicating weekly to more than 100 million Christian Americans, are proud to join together in supporting the
continued sovereignty of the State of Israel over the holy city of Jerusalem.
We support Israel's efforts to reach reconciliation with its Arab neighbors,
but we believe that Jerusalem or any portion of it shall not be negotiable in
any peace process. Jerusalem must remain undivided as the eternal capital
of the Jewish people."[44]

In addition to his devout religious beliefs about Israel, Robertson has
also voiced a practical political rationale for his strong support for Israel,
one that frequently came to the forefront during his political years. "I'm
one of the nation's most vociferous supporters of the nation of Israel," he
told the National Press Club in a 1985 speech. "There are some who accuse
me of having the Star of David on my shirts. I believe in supporting Israel
because of its significance to us as an ally. I believe in supporting Israel because of its significance in the Middle East as a bastion of the West in what
is otherwise a sea of confusion."[45]

Pat Robertson's passion for Israel was not distant and impersonal; his
personal knowledge of Israeli politics and political leaders was as deep as
that of any American religious leader. He met and interviewed prime ministers Ariel Sharon, Ehud Barak, Benjamin Netanyahu, Shimon Peres,
Menachem Begin, and Yitzhak Rabin. His degree of support for Israeli
leaders depended on their political postures. In addition to his vehement
opposition to anyone who would compromise Israel's land claims, Robertson despised socialism anywhere in the world, including in Israel. During

his campaign for the presidency, he told the National Press Club: "I told one of my very good Jewish friends in Washington that I did not think the United States taxpayers should underwrite socialist operations in Israel which were failing in many respects."[46]

Robertson's favorite Israeli politician has been Benjamin Netanyahu. He was elated when Netanyahu became prime minister in 1996, and the two formed a strong personal bond. When Netanyahu left office in 1999 he sent Robertson a copy of his "Farewell Address" with a handwritten note: "Many thanks for your unflagging support." Robertson replied: "You are absolutely right, my support for you was unflagging, and I was very distressed at the outcome of the election. However, I know that you have a great future ahead for service to the people of Israel and the people of the world. One brief setback is merely a milestone on the way to greater victories." A few days later Netanyahu sent a fuller note to his friend "Pat": "Before stepping down, I would like to tell you how much I appreciate your personal friendship and dedication to Israel's cause. Few possess your courage, eloquence and deep understanding, and I know that those of us who are aware of your activities are deeply grateful. It is, of course, a disappointment for me to have to quit in mid-course. But I believe some of the principles we introduced will remain in place. . . . I intend to devote my time now mostly to writing and lecturing, but I am not going to leave the political scene. Too much is at stake." Robertson was elated when Netanyahu once again was named prime minister in 2009, revealing on *The 700 Club* that the two had recently discussed their shared opposition to the division of Jerusalem.[47]

Ecumenism

The independent charismatic revival which Pat Robertson embraced was in some ways the most extraordinary twentieth-century manifestation of Christian ecumenism. Robertson warmly supported the charismatic movement's most noted ecumenical advocate, David DuPlessis, who championed the spread of the gifts of the Spirit in the mainline Protestant denominations and the Roman Catholic Church. After DuPlessis was interviewed by Robertson on *The 700 Club* in 1978, CBN issued a news release endorsing his view that "the world wants to see unity among Christians. No matter what our different theologies, organizations, cultures or expressions of worship are, we must demonstrate that unity." Almost two decades later, speaking at a massive charismatic celebration called "Orlando '95

Congress on the Holy Spirit," Pat Robertson spoke rhapsodically about the cooperation among charismatic Christians: "It is so wonderful to see our Catholic brethren here tonight. . . . Lutherans believe in something else, Catholics believe in something different, Pentecostal Holiness, they believe a little different. That doesn't make any difference. We go in unity of the Spirit, we've got that. One day God will give us unity of faith. We need to hold on to what we've got. And we build on that. And we move like a mighty army."[48]

As a matter of both business necessity and religious tolerance, Pat Robertson has never believed that Christians should be separated by narrow creedal differences. In the earliest days of WYAH-TV, the station offered a weekly "Ministers Forum" that was self-consciously ecumenical: "The five panelists and moderator comprise a diversification of liberal, conservative, and fundamental views. The result of such debate is complete dissection of every topic and leaves no proverbial stones unturned." Through the 1970s Robertson's theological openness was resisted most notably by mainstream churches that still regarded as heretical the beliefs of "Spirit-filled" Pentecostals. Robertson replied patiently and at length to a local Methodist minister in 1974 who objected to his television station's programming, expressing his willingness to "correct a few things." In the first place, he insisted, "we have never given the impression that if somebody does not have the baptism in the Holy Spirit he is not a Christian. I have specifically denied that allegation time and time again, and to the best of my knowledge nobody who has ever been associated with CBN has ever made such a claim. . . . Nevertheless I will make sure that such a statement is never either expressed or implied on any of our broadcasts." It was more difficult to bridle "the teaching concerning the speaking in tongues and the baptism of the Holy Spirit," he continued: "It is hard for me to muzzle everyone who appears on a station which operates as long as ours does. . . . I can teach certain things, but I can't enforce thought control on all of our staff or guests." Several years later, when a Baptist minister informed Robertson that "Bible-believing people are sick to death of having the gift of tongues crammed down their throats," Robertson's reply was irenic: "Brother, God is doing such marvelous things today. Why not step back and look at the grandeur of His plan instead of dwelling on the differences which arise over supposed divergences from church dogma."[49]

Not surprisingly, Robertson has had difficulty finding any perfect church. In 1976 he wrote to an inquirer asking about how to choose a "church home": "In our own home community there is an incredible dearth of satisfactory churches. The denominational churches do not believe in the fullness of the Spirit, the Pentecostal churches have their little doctrinal and customary quirks; some of the independent churches have error in their teaching or various excesses. It is extremely difficult for so-called charismatic believers to find a church home."[50]

Robertson's ecumenism often came as a disappointment to orthodox Pentecostals. The ecumenical church recommendations made on *The 700 Club* and by CBN counselors often offended them. A viewer asked in 1976: "As Bible-believing, God-fearing, Spirit-baptized Christians, we'ld [sic] like to know how you can compromise your stand in Christ Jesus as you are? How in the name of all that's righteous, just, and holy, can Spirit baptized believers send babes-in-Christ into the organized structure? These structures do not believe that God's gifts are for today." The CBN director of counseling replied: "It is our desire that those churches with whom we work and use for follow-up be spirit-filled churches that have recognized the Lordship of Jesus Christ and who worship and teach this truth freely. However, those who do not recognize the Pentecostal experience but who have a genuine love for the Lord Jesus should certainly be more qualified to handle a new babe in Christ rather than let this person go without any fellowship whatever. Therefore, in working with these churches not only are we providing a basis of fellowship in Christ for new converts but we are also promoting the unity in the body of Christ that Jesus so yearned for."[51]

When the CBN Center was dedicated in 1979, Robertson and his colleagues celebrated the event as a symbol of a new spirit of unity among evangelicals. Billy Graham's appearance on the program, and his embrace of Robertson and others leaders from the Pentecostal/charismatic movement, gave a "glimpse . . . of the spiritual unity that Jesus had asked His Father to send upon His Church." It was a moment of acceptance and welcome that charismatics had awaited for years. CBN vice-president Bob Slosser complained that "news people" covering the event "failed to understand the significance of the harmony experienced during that weekend by evangelicals and charismatics, Pentecostals and mainline churchmen, Catholics and Protestants, laymen and clergymen." CBN, Regent, and other Robertson enterprises have been heavily populated by charismatics, but other non-charismatic evangelicals have been sprinkled throughout the organizations, often in positions of influence and authority.[52]

The most remarkable boundary that Robertson and other charismatics crossed in the 1970s was the Protestant-Catholic divide. Robertson was enamored of John Paul II. In 1979 he commended the pope in *Pat Robertson's Perspective:* "We thank God for a man of strong intellect and per-

sonal charisma who is not ashamed to stand for Jesus Christ and to call
the world to follow the way of personal morality — and the way of the
cross." By the 1990s he was an unabashed admirer of the pope: "I have some
theological differences with the Catholic Church. But this pope is a tremendous historic figure. He did as much as anyone to bring down communism. Frankly, I feel I have a lot more in common with this pope than with
liberal Protestants. The real battle is not between Protestants and Catholics anymore, it's between conservative Christians fighting for the fundamentals of the faith, and liberals who deny the central truths of Christianity." Robertson's papal audience in 1995 was one of the highlights of his life.
His Catholic friend Keith Fournier wrote to him on the eve of the meeting:
"I believe that your visit with him on Saturday is part of a very big spiritual
work that is happening in our time. . . . You, along with others, are playing a
significant historic role in bringing peace to God's people. I admire what
you are doing and I stand with you as your brother in Jesus Christ." Robertson delivered a three-page letter to the pope pledging himself to "work for
Christian unity and world evangelization." Acknowledging "there are doctrinal differences that separate us," Robertson observed that "the moral
crisis facing society today and the obvious social breakdown mandates a
closer cooperation."[53]

Robertson had taken a bold ecumenical step earlier in 1995 when he
signed a statement entitled "Evangelicals and Catholics Together," which
had been crafted by Charles Colson and Richard John Neuhaus. The document was signed by twenty Protestant leaders and twenty Catholic leaders. It was "a brave thing for him to do," observed Fournier. The irenic statement, published in *First Things* in May 1994, ended with the declaration:
"We do know that this is a time of opportunity — and, if of opportunity,
then of responsibility — for Evangelicals and Catholics to be Christians together in a way that helps prepare the world for the coming of him to
whom belongs the kingdom, the power, and the glory forever." The statement sparked "no small amount of controversy" among evangelicals who
feared that it failed to make clear their "distinctly Protestant views."
Colson convened a second conference in early 1995 that drafted clarifying
statements. Robertson's support never wavered, though he informed
Colson that "we have received quite a few letters concerning the . . . statement" and expressed appreciation for the "clarification." Robertson's letter
to those protesting his signature was uncompromising: "People of faith are
under attack as never before in the history of the United States of America
by forces which wish to destroy all religious values, all worship, and all
freedoms for Christians like you and me. We obviously have differences

within the Christian faith, and between Jews and Christians. The document is not about theology. Neither Catholics nor Evangelicals have yielded or compromised anything in the realm of doctrine or theology. *The primary issues addressed in the document are missions, evangelism, societal concerns, and religious liberty. . . .* I am sorry you do not agree with this assessment, but believe me, it rests on very solid evidence of what is happening in our country."[54]

Robertson's friendly relations with Roman Catholics drew fire from both the left and the right. Following his papal audience, *Christianity Today* reported that "some liberal Catholics were downright incensed that Robertson would be included among the limited number of papal guests." The *National Catholic Reporter* observed: "Robertson's brand of religion should be soundly discredited and rebuked, not rewarded with a papal audience." Criticism of Robertson by liberal Catholics was predictable, but the reaction of right-wing fundamentalists was even more strident. Robertson's choice of Keith Fournier as executive director of the American Center for Law and Justice sparked a brief and candid exchange with Bob Jones III, the president of Bob Jones University. Jones informed Robertson that he was "surprised and embarrassed" that he would place in such a responsible position someone representing a "false religion." Robertson defended Fournier as "a dedicated believer in the Lord Jesus Christ" who was also a skilled advocate for Christianity, and noted that Jones had used a Catholic attorney, Bill Ball, to "represent your university." He advised Jones: "When I go to a doctor for surgery, I am reminded of the famous words of the great Martin Luther, 'I would rather be attended by a Turkish physician than a Christian butcher.'"[55]

Robertson's spat with Jones highlighted real and substantive differences between those who were willing to overlook historically important theological issues for the sake of Christian unity and those with narrower consciences. The "unifying factor" of Christianity "is a belief in Jesus Christ," Robertson repeatedly affirmed, and "it is time we focus on the similarities between evangelicals and Catholics": "That is the heart of Christianity, no matter what the denomination." He was unwilling to answer Jones's starkly divisive question: "Is Catholicism a false religion or isn't it?" In *The Secret Kingdom* Robertson wrote that diversity often characterized Christians' efforts in their quest for the "common good." In the mid-1990s he reaffirmed that the "unity springing from the truth of the kingdom of God does not insist on, or even desire, uniformity." It was perfectly proper to continue to advocate narrow views of Christian truth, but often the greater good demanded that believers subjugate private convictions for the sake of unity. In a form letter responding to inquiries on the subject, Robertson explained: "I have made clear time and time again, that as a Baptist my theological views differ on a number of key points with Roman Catholicism. However, I also recognize that a million and a half babies are being slaughtered in America every year, pornography is rampant, and promiscuity is out of control. . . . It is my belief that, given the secular tide of political correctness which is seeking to eradicate any mention of God in our society, those who believe in God should join together to support those things upon which they can agree. . . . Please join with me and Christians everywhere to pray for worldwide evangelization."[56]

CHAPTER 11

The Man, the Empire, the Legacy

—◦◦◦◦—

Pat Robertson's self-image is deeply rooted in the soil of Virginia. His descent from families steeped in the history of the Old Dominion and the nation, his privileged adolescence as the son of a courtly and influential senator and an accomplished and genteel mother, and his educational pedigree did much to define his character. Throughout his life, in private and public, Robertson told audiences and questioners that "his proud Virginia family heritage gave him an advantage." In a ministry form letter Robertson detailed his lineage: "I was born in a family that descended directly or collaterally from a member of the Jamestown Colony, a signer of the Declaration of Independence, two U.S. Presidents, plus the Churchill family in England. My father was a popular and powerful U.S. Senator." Robertson's upbringing has served him well in political, business, or religious discourse; he has never been reluctant to throw the weight of his pedigree behind his cause. There is nothing feigned about his fierce loyalty to his personal heritage — and to the heroes of his youth in Lexington, Robert E. Lee and Thomas J. "Stonewall" Jackson, and beyond them, to the legends of Virginia, George Washington, James Madison, and Thomas Jefferson.[1]

By the late 1970s, Robertson's identification with his Virginia roots was wrapped in prophetic meaning. Like most Virginians, Robertson was proudly aware that it was in Virginia, not in New England, that the history of Anglo-America began. The first outpost of permanent English settlement in the New World was at Jamestown, not at Plymouth. The Virginia Company settlers who established Jamestown came ashore first at Cape

Henry, not far from the CBN headquarters in Virginia Beach. The April 29, 1607, landing of this group became a defining prophetic moment for Pat Robertson and CBN. Robertson came to believe that "in an inexplicable way" CBN was "indeed the fulfillment of the prayers of those settlers." Robertson reminded listeners on *The 700 Club* on April 29, 2009: "Today is a historic day. . . . America was first conceived at Cape Henry. . . . The country's Godly foundation was laid in Virginia."[2]

Privileged Populist

Pat Robertson has always believed that honor required that he should live a life of privileged responsibility. His parents expected him to "keep pace with what they considered extraordinary ability." If he did not, his mother "would be disappointed and her feelings would be hurt." He drank deeply at the fount of *noblesse oblige*: "When I was an undergraduate at Washington and Lee University right after World War II, I learned one simple concept that has remained with me for almost fifty years — *noblesse oblige* — nobility obligates. Every privilege — whether of educational opportunity, social status, riches, intellectual achievement, corporate or political power — is accompanied by a commensurate responsibility." His is the code of the Old South; his outward manner, unless seriously provoked, is steadfastly courteous and courtly. Asked by a reporter about his manners, Robertson replied: "Well, I was born in Stonewall Jackson's home, which had been turned into a hospital. I grew up with pictures of Robert E. Lee all over the house and was told that he was the prime example of a Southern gentleman that I should emulate. . . . I have a heritage that goes back to the founding of this nation. My people got here during the seventeenth century." Among other things, Robertson believes, his affection for Virginia and the Old South deepened his respect for "family values" and his "love of Christianity."[3]

Like many southern young men of his generation, Pat Robertson was a man's man. His father was proud of his son's impressive physical development as well as his intellectual prowess. In 1945, writing to a friend about Pat's upcoming summer employment as a "fire patrolman" in Montana, an appointment he had "arranged with the United States Forest Service," Senator Robertson noted with pride: "While Pat is only fifteen years old he is six feet two inches tall, plays football and made his letter in boxing at the McCallie school in Chattanooga this spring. Although he is the youngest boy in the junior class he has, so far, made the highest scholastic average of anyone in the class." Among his several notable early achievements, Pat Robertson valued none more highly than earning a commission as a Marine officer upon his graduation from Washington and Lee and his subsequent service in Korea. "Once a Marine, always a Marine," Robertson commented on *The 700 Club* on Veterans Day 2008. Of the many criticisms leveled at him during his long life, few have been more personally hurtful to him than the charges made during his presidential campaign that impugned his service record. He has jealously guarded his manhood. Editing a Christian Coalition direct mail solicitation in 1993, Robertson struck through the phrase "upsets me so much," scribbling in the margin: "'Upsets me so much' is feminine. Ex-Marine officers don't talk that way." "He is not a hugger," observed CBN vice-president Joel Palser; "when he expresses something personal, I am always surprised."[4]

Robertson's privileged background has made him a formidable interviewer on television for fifty years. He differs from "the flamboyant style of some TV performers," noted Associated Press religion writer George W. Cornell, because of his "relaxed, Ivy-League manner, with an easy smile, his accent softened by his upbringing in an old Virginia family." His life experiences were wide-ranging and his social skills well honed. A Lexington friend who had known him in high school recalled: "Pat has always had beautiful manners. He's never been pushy; he's always been smooth talking, not glib. He's disarming." Describing his receiving-line experience during a visit to the Reagan White House for a dinner honoring the president of France, Robertson told a reporter: "I went through with Roger Mudd, who was a classmate of mine at Washington and Lee. We talked about how to cook and slice Virginia ham. . . . Roger said that he intended to greet Mitterrand with 'Howdy.' I scared up a little college French. *'Enchante.'*" "I have never met a man who can be more diplomatic," observed a CBN representative in China who witnessed his meetings with Chinese government officials. A young business associate who accompanied him for a meeting with the chairman of Goldman Sachs was amazed by Robertson's poise: "He was totally comfortable. He totally orchestrated the interview."[5]

Robertson's charm can also be disarming to those who dislike his views. In 1995, at an audience with Pope John Paul II, Robertson met for the first time the general secretary of the National Council of Churches, Joan Brown Campbell. The *Christian Century* described the meeting: "Robertson and Campbell had never met before, although they had been media adversaries for some time. 'We have said some not-too-attractive things about each other,' Campbell said. According to Campbell, Robertson told her, 'Now that we've met, I'll have more trouble saying those things.' Campbell reported that she now understands Robertson a little bit better. The two have agreed to a future meeting." Writer Andrew Sullivan had a similar reaction after attending Robertson's seventieth birthday celebration at Regent University, where he "discovered a shocking truth about the religious right: they're really quite nice."[6]

In predictable ways, Robertson's pedigree thrust him to the forefront in the early Pentecostal/charismatic revival. When he first broached his television plans with Gordon Lindsay, the foremost publicist among a coterie of early independent healing ministers, Lindsay told him: "Pat, I believe you are the one who can do it. You are young, you are a fine Christian. You have a splendid education. You come from a family that is well-respected. Your father is a Senator and I understand that you have a praying mother. I believe you are the man to do it."[7]

Despite his privileged background, Pat Robertson also frequently draws on his brief encounters with poverty. He well remembers a long summer toiling on the farm of a "distant relative," working in the fields from "sun up" to dusk. "In retrospect," he later wrote, "some of the most valuable lifetime experiences came when I was 13 and was doing exhausting work for $15 a month on the farm in Virginia." He repeatedly harks back to the lessons he learned during his spiritual quest living in the run-down Bedford-Stuyvesant neighborhood in New York. During his political campaign he insisted he was not "some 'limousine liberal' or 'country club Republican'" but rather one who has "felt the pain of the people over the years and has actually lived among them for a short time." Nor has he ever forgotten the early struggles he and his young family experienced in Virginia Beach; he has remained intensely loyal to those who shared in the sacrifices of the fragile early years of CBN. On October 1, 1993, William Garthwaite, one of the original employees, wrote to Robertson: "October 1, 1961 was an exciting day. I remember it well! I also remember . . . the hard times of a meager beginning. Many only see the results and are not aware of the cost of your obedience." Robertson replied: "Every anniversary brings back memories of that first day! I marvel at God's faithfulness and how far He has brought us." "Pat never forgets the old days," observed Terry Meeuwsen; "there is nothing we do traditionally that he takes lightly. . . . They are real to him."[8]

The combination of a sophisticated yet traditional, and secure yet not wealthy, upbringing with critical years of personal economic struggle fed in Pat Robertson a lifelong aversion to elites — "the very rich," "the trilateral world," "humanistic elites." The self-interest of elites, Robertson concluded in 1978, "could border on the threshold of conspiracy," a theme that would surface in his writing. In response to a "senior economist" at the Federal Reserve Bank who suggested that Robertson often ventured into areas where he had little expertise, he wrote: "You are probably right that I don't have the expertise in some of the fields that I have been expressing opinions in, but I honestly feel that my opinions are probably as valid as a great deal of the other material which comes out from the economic indicators of our government and the self serving instruments of stock brokers." The issue between them, he insisted, was whether the common people must "abdicate our roles as citizens in favor of the pronouncements of some 'super educated' elite who are able to tell us what is best for us."[9]

His family and friends uniformly praise his high IQ. "Pat is a brilliant man," proclaimed his friend Vinson Synan. "He has tremendous recall." Even some of his adversaries agree; Skipp Porteous, cofounder of the anti-Robertson Institute for First Amendment Studies, told a reporter: "I greatly admire the man for what he's accomplished. . . . He's simply brilliant. He's been able to translate his faith into something tangible and find ways through modern technology to reach the world with what he believes." Robertson's erudition is deep in some areas, including religion, politics, the law, and economics, but he has a conversational knowledge of an astonishing array of topics. In 1968, Robertson acknowledged to a reporter that he did not "read widely or study enough," but through the years, and after hundreds of interviews with celebrities and writers, he had scanned thousands of books and engaged in casual conversations with their authors. "He has a lifelong curiosity," observed his friend Michael Little. Tens of thousands of viewers have trusted implicitly his commentary and advice. Biographer Neil Eskelin reported the remarks of a regular viewer from Chicago: "I've learned more about world events watching Pat than I ever imagined. He makes it so clear and down to earth."[10]

Robertson has also impressed those around him by his "visionary role." Ken Auletta, the media critic of the *New Yorker,* lauded Robertson as "both a visionary and a smart businessman." "He is constantly spinning off ideas," observed his longtime nemesis Barry Lynn. The visionary side of Robertson's mindset is apparent in the plethora of evangelical, humanitarian, legal, political, and educational organizations he fathered through the years and also in his wide-ranging business ventures, his management style, and in the methodology and content of his writings. "My thrust in life is to cast the vision," he surmised late in life. "I am like an architect. I can create corporations and entities and get them going."[11]

The personal characteristic of Pat Robertson most often overlooked in the heated rhetoric of partisan politics and in his frequent resort to the supernatural language of his charismatic faith is his pragmatism. "I am a businessman," he insisted; "I don't live in gaga land." He can be a "polarizing figure," acknowledged his friend David Gyertson, but he also "has an irenic side" and has exhibited over and over a "willingness to engage differing ideas." His readiness to compromise to gain the attainable was the hallmark of his political campaign and his vision for the Christian Coalition, and it also has made him a thoroughgoing ecumenist. Robertson's pragmatic actions often catch the public by surprise because he has been so successfully portrayed in the media as an inflexible zealot. His critics — and even his allies — were taken aback when Robertson announced his willingness to accept "a strategic, incremental" approach to limiting abortion, announced in a "60 Minutes" interview in 1999; and by his willingness to excuse the moral and political shortcomings of China; and by his defense of an "escape valve for mercy" to make the death penalty less rigid; and his endorsement of Rudy Giuliani in the 2008 presidential campaign; and his appearance in 2008 with Al Sharpton in a television ad for environmentalism; and his joining with Bono and George Clooney to promote a campaign to end world poverty. Some of his friends and critics believe that his flexible attitude was born of the need to compromise his more strident pronouncements during his political campaign, but he has always shown a remarkable readiness to engage in civil dialog with those with whom he disagreed. Replying to a supporter who questioned an appearance on "Larry King Live," Robertson wrote: "Larry King has always been nice to me, and although I may not agree with all of his philosophies, as a Christian I believe I should treat him with courtesy. In interviews with him I do not hesitate to speak the truth on issues. I do, however, try to speak with kindness." His "practical mindset" has served Robertson well in personal contacts with celebrities, observed Jay Sekulow: "He understands the give and take. . . . He knows them all."[12]

Managing the Empire

Forty years after the journey of the bedraggled Robertson family to Virginia Beach, he stood atop a vast, sprawling international empire of television production and broadcast, a worldwide evangelistic outreach, a major humanitarian organization, a flourishing university, and one of the most successful legal advocacy groups in the country. In his extensively researched study of the Robertson empire published in 1996, Alec Foege concluded that "Pat Robertson's empire resists summation." The level of Robertson's control and active management of these institutions varied, but all were products of his fertile imagination and restless energy. "Time is the enemy of this guy," observed Grant Babre, director of CBN's NorthStar Studios in Nashville; "there are always new goals on his horizon." It has always been so. In 1968, a reporter for *Christian Life* magazine observed: "Robertson has a restless streak which may be his greatest human motivation. He admits that 'often I'm likely to be a step or two ahead of the Lord.'" His great strength, in the eyes of David Gyertson, was his "never being satisfied." As in his business ventures, not all of his ministry ideas bore fruit. Like Walt Disney, observed Gyertson, Robertson failed more often than he succeeded, but the successes were large.[13]

During the first two decades of CBN's existence, when Robertson worked tirelessly to build his television and radio businesses, he was deeply involved in the day-to-day operations of the stations. "I used to be 'hands-on,'" he told his biographer in 1988, "because we were a small group and we all had to roll up our sleeves." He issued memos with titles ranging from "How to Turn a Problem Into an Opportunity" to a "Policy Clarifications" reminder that "the use of alcoholic beverages or narcotics by staff members is ground for immediate dismissal." He carefully scrutinized budgets trying to prune waste. In a 1978 directive he wrote: "Every division head and every manager, and for that matter every employee, will be asked to begin careful planning of his or her area of responsibility. From planning the use of the telephone, to travel, to eliminating personal secretaries in favor of secretarial pools, to changing the way we light TV shows, to analysis of freight bills and routing, to the elimination of unnecessary or inefficient personnel, to long range corporate planning, *everybody* will be involved." Perusing the budget in 1984, Robertson came across "an interesting item labeled 'Various' in the amount of nine million dollars." Shocked by such vagueness, which reminded him of "our friends in Foggy Bottom across the Potomac," Robertson slashed away at the budget: "I'm still Scottish enough to think that saving two or three million dollars is significant. As the late Senator Dirksen said: 'A billion here and a billion there, and before long, you're talking about real money.'"[14]

In the early years at CBN, and to some extent even in the twenty-first century, Robertson knew by name most of the people working in the organization. "I have had a janitor come here and read me out," Robertson recalled: "If I have somebody who has a word from the Lord, I don't care who they are. I am open to anything that seems to come from the Lord."

He thanks CBN workers when things go well. After a successful telethon in 1979, he wrote to the counselors who had manned the telephones: "I am writing this letter to you at 1:15 in the morning on February 3rd. . . . Words fail me to express to you how much I thank you for the part you played in the greatest victory we have ever known at CBN. You are a part of me and a part of CBN. May God bless you beyond measure for your sacrificial participation in this telethon." And he upbraided them when he sensed disloyalty or a lapse of spiritual commitment. In 1984 he wrote: "It has been our policy to make available one-half hour of paid time to each employee to attend prayer meeting. . . . More and more staff, office workers, and executives are skipping prayer on the one hand, and stretching the lunch hour 30 minutes more. . . . The word is this: People are being paid to pray because it is good for the spiritual life of CBN. If they don't pray, they need to work in their jobs." Extended and obvious laxity on the part of the staff would invariably draw a memo addressed to "All Staff" reminding that *"LABOR DAY PRAYER MEETING IS NOT OPTIONAL!"* After a particularly disappointing telethon in 1983 in which "two entire rows of phones" were not manned by volunteers, Robertson wrote to the staff: "I don't mean to sound overdramatic, but we will not hesitate to dismiss employees who do not support this very important activity to the spiritual and financial life of CBN."[15]

Even in later years, as Robertson's attention darted from politics to education to business to CBN, Michael Little recalled that Robertson remained "markedly concerned about every aspect of CBN and Regent." "He knows every piece of equipment on the premises and when it was installed," said Little, and his recall of detail was remarkable: "He is very hands-on about certain things, and you never know which things they are." After touring the grounds with Robertson in 1989, supervisor Jay Comisky, one of the oldest and most respected employees at CBN, wrote a memo confirming "the priorities we discussed" for additional spraying for weeds and edging curbs. Comisky wondered whether the crew chief whose work Robertson had criticized should be charged with a "Class A" offense, which according to "Grounds Services Law" was "punishable by firing squad." Comisky asked Robertson to inform him whether to "pardon" the crew chief, remembering that "he has a wife and kids to support," or proceed with execution by "firing squad." At the bottom of the memo, Robertson penned his response: "Pardon — Then shoot him."[16]

By the 1990s, Robertson's empire had become so diverse and vast that his managerial methods necessarily changed. Increasingly, his style was, in the words of Jay Sekulow, "jurisdictional." "I don't micromanage," Robertson insisted in 2008. "I keep setting the standard. . . . If you've got somebody good running it, you let them alone." "I have been in charge at CBN," Robertson observed, but the organization "runs like a machine" because of the "wonderful vice presidents" and other loyal employees with whom "we have worked for so long." At Regent University and Operation Blessing, Robertson believes that leadership is the key to their institutional ups and downs. "The way Dad structures organizations," surmised Gordon Robertson, "each one of those departments takes on a life of its own." As a result, there are "always tensions" in the system caused by internal competition and leaders who might not share completely the Robertson vision. Retired Marine Colonel Ron Oates confessed that for someone who "comes out of a very structured background" Robertson's decentralized style calls for adjustments, but "it works."[17]

In this loose organizational environment, in which subordinates were often given great independence, Robertson's spontaneous, seat-of-the-pants selection of lieutenants often caused fear and trepidation. Ralph Reed, one of Robertson's most successful spontaneous hires, acknowledged that his mentor had picked some "doozies," adding, "That's one of his flaws." Robertson has often been slow to admit mistakes, though he certainly admits he is capable of them, like everyone else: "Even the Lord messed up with Judas."[18]

Many insiders feel that Robertson has tolerated some of his bad appointments longer than was healthy, to the detriment of the organization. When he does remove people, he often offers golden parachutes. "We don't hurt people," Robertson insisted. When Robertson terminated Keith Fournier, for more than three years the ACLJ continued to give grants to his new organization "to fund your work and the work of your organization and its mission." Jay Sekulow insisted that Robertson was "the most caring person" he had ever known. On the other hand, others who have been terminated by Pat Robertson feel that he is arbitrary and brutal in his personnel decisions. "Strife and controversy is something we don't like," Robertson insisted, but "there is nobody who is indispensable." "Pat can be really mean," an unnamed Regent University professor told an interviewer: "He has a habit of using people and then getting rid of them." Vinson Synan saw the internal power struggles at Regent in a different light: "If you cross him, he will fire you. . . . But usually it is for incompetence." Robertson summed up his rule in dealing with subordinates: "If they don't perform, you replace them."[19]

Robertson recognizes that he has been surrounded at CBN by a circle of intensely loyal "good people," including CEO Gordon Robertson and

President Michael Little and a stable panel of competent vice-presidents. Regent University has been a more difficult challenge, but by 2009, when he decided to give up the presidency, Robertson believed that the panel of deans was exemplary. Even in universities, Robertson insisted, "If you get good people in place, an organization will run itself."[20]

The loyal core of leaders throughout the Robertson empire have had a deep and personal commitment "to support Pat." Uniformly, observed David Gyertson, they wanted to help "ensure that he finished strong and finished well." "He inspires people quickly," observed Michael Little. "People say, 'I want to connect.'" "I watched Pat," recalled one of the early employees at CBN; "he had something I didn't have. And I wanted it." "There are a few who are here because of their jobs," observed an acerbic Dede Robertson, but most worked for Robertson because "they see the anointing of the Lord on him."[21]

While Robertson "has a penchant for longtime loyalty," observed Joel Palser, "he does not like wannabes." Most of Robertson's loyal supporters have not had close personal relationships with him. Michael Little "gets the faithfulness award" for being "supportive of the general," observed Terry Meeuwsen, but the two rarely converse. His longtime maverick friend, Scott Ross, has probably spoken more irreverently to Robertson than anyone else in Virginia Beach. Ross is a genuine family friend, having been something of a mentor to both Tim and Gordon. Other leaders in the ministry might go for years without a personal encounter with Robertson. A few of the more devout longtime employees have had special trusting relationships with Robertson. Ben Edwards, elevated to the position of vice-president of WorldReach in 2008, has felt free to speak to him personally, and Robertson has treated Edwards like a son. Other longtime ministry employees, including Jay Comisky and Joel Palser, have the ear of Robertson when needed. He listens to his family most, Michael Little thought, "because he trusts their motives." Everyone agreed that heading his list of confidants was Dede: "He listens to his wife more than anyone else."[22]

Loyalty runs in both directions. Robertson holds himself aloof from those surrounding him, but he respects everyone who shares his vision. "He was a real encouraging guy," recalled Jay Sekulow of his early days with the American Center for Law and Justice. "When you are getting clobbered, the guy has a gift of getting you through it." It was not unusual for Robertson to send financial assistance to a former employee who needed help, even when CBN was facing financial difficulties of its own. When he faced a personal life crisis, Joel Palser recalled, Pat and Dede "ministered to me." If he is not a "buddy," most agree with Lee Webb that "he is a kind and gentle man."[23]

Those closest to him acknowledge that Robertson is "opinionated" and "very strong willed," and his reactions to ministry developments have sometimes been volatile and noisy. His son Gordon often seemed an island of calm in the midst of his father's sometimes stormy world. "You have to let the shock and awe pass over you," reflected Gordon. "With me," he mused, it is best "to deliver my opinion and state my case. Do it succinctly. . . . He'll think about it." Sometimes, after thought, his father would tell him: "OK, Gordon, we'll do it your way." But at other times, Gordon, like everyone else at CBN, listened and took directions. "I may not always like the way my father tells me decisions," he said, "but he has an uncanny ability to be right."[24]

Pat Robertson remains at the center of everything that exists in the Robertson empire — "The atomic reactor in this is Pat," said David Gyertson. Robertson agreed that "every organization must have a head, some final source of authority." He has been that source. Across the vast expanse of the Robertson empire, only Pat Robertson's word carries final authority, and there has been a constant jockeying for positions close to the dynamo.[25]

Life at Home

Pat Robertson's personal life once again settled down and became more stable once he returned to CBN and *The 700 Club* in 1988. During the 1990s, he was a frequent speaker at Christian Coalition functions and he and Dede traveled with the Flying Hospital. He has always loved to travel, and has continued to make occasional trips combining religious and business matters. By 2000 his responsibilities as president of Regent University and his regular schedule on *The 700 Club* more and more demanded his presence in Virginia Beach. After resigning from the Christian Coalition in 2002, and the steady downscaling of his political activities, Robertson established a routine of reading, prayer, business conferences, writing, and preparing for his appearances on *The 700 Club*.[26]

Robertson's personal financial circumstances improved markedly in the 1980s. He began taking a modest regular salary from CBN in the early 1970s, and by the end of the 1980s his salary was pegged at $57,000 a year. After 1990 Robertson went off the CBN payroll because of the profitability of the Family Channel, subsequently drawing his annual salary from IFE.

After the sale of IFE, Robertson emerged a relatively wealthy man. In addition, by the 1990s Robertson's books had yielded hundreds of thousands of dollars in royalties.[27]

Robertson has often struggled with his conscience, and with the accountability he feels to CBN supporters, regarding his income and lifestyle. He wrestled particularly with the propriety of the board's decision to build a house on the CBN campus in 1983. In a memo to "All Staff" he recalled the "magnificent provision of the Lord in my life 19 years ago when He took me from a rather unpleasant near slum ... in Portsmouth and gave me free of charge a lovely country place in Suffolk with trees, and songbirds, and fields and a stable of horses." But the construction of a "gigantic sewer treatment plant on the property" necessitated a move. The board requested that the Robertson family move to the campus, and CBN constructed a chancellor's house that was "finished very beautifully and at a reasonable price." But Robertson brooded that "this residence may upset the saints and may ... 'give occasion for the enemies of the Lord to blaspheme.'" He told the staff: "I have decided after much prayer against moving into the newly constructed 'Chancellor's Residence.'" He asked for prayers for a "miracle" that could resolve this dilemma. A week later, Robertson informed the staff that God had given him the answer: "Here is God's clear answer. He showed me that I should personally pay for the Chancellor's residence and donate it to CBN!" At first, it did not appear that he had adequate personal funds to make such an offer, but "Then the Lord showed me that 'The Secret Kingdom' was His answer. It is a national best seller. . . . God gave the royalty rights . . . to me as His provision so that I would have something to give to Him so that He could give me a place to live in a time of need 'blameless and beyond reproach.'" Robertson's donation of approximately $300,000 toward the construction of the house impressed his supporters and provided an answer to those who questioned the grandeur of the residence. Harald Bredesen recalled that "it was a very happy moment for me when he built his home on royalties."[28]

By the 1990s the Robertson family was living well. Pat and Dede enjoyed visits to a home on Hot Springs Mountain in western Virginia, completed in 1993, where Pat relished getting "away from time to time to the peace of the mountains." Described in the press as an 11,000-square-foot, $1.5 million mansion, the mountain home drew fire from critics and an official rejoinder from CBN. Robertson's reply to inquiries explained: "Concerning my home in the western part of Virginia, I can only assume that the information on the Internet was picked up from an article that appeared in *The National Enquirer,* which was strewn with misinformation. I built the home to accommodate my family's needs. . . . I paid for this home with income received from personal business ventures . . . not from funds given by CBN. I do not receive any income from CBN. . . . I also make this house available to CBN and Regent University for conferences, etc."[29]

Harald Bredesen believed that the Robertsons had lived "a very sacrificial life," but that is a matter of perspective. Robertson is surrounded by accoutrements that reflect his heritage and prosperity. He travels first class. When traveling, he explained to a supporter, he does not seek out a "Motel 6" to stay in because "that would not be an efficient use of my time or of my staff."[30]

But Robertson has also been generous with his personal wealth. He wrote to a supporter: "You will also be interested to know that I personally am the largest supporter to CBN, Operation Blessing, and to other organizations that are carrying on the Lord's service." In 1993 Robertson wrote a personal check for $52,000 to CBN "to defray the cost of the work done . . . for the personal security measures recommended by . . . CBN Security." In 1999, when he had high hopes for his business prospects, Robertson wrote a check for $2 million as a gift to WorldReach. A memo attached to the check revealed his deep personal commitment to CBN's evangelistic outreach: "I want this money to be used for WorldReach in addition to those funds that have already been allocated by the Board of CBN. In other words, I would like you to put this money into a separate account that could be authorized by Gordon and by Ben Edwards working together for a new series of projects to win people to the Lord, and to produce follow-up for those who have already been so won. I repeat, do not mingle this money in with other CBN funds or use it to deduct from authorized funds that are in the budget for WorldReach." Through the years, Robertson made hundreds of anonymous contributions to a wide variety of people and causes.[31]

For most of his adult life, Pat Robertson's chief recreational passion has been riding horses. He still keeps a few horses stabled at his home, including a "thoroughbred jumper" that he regularly puts through his paces. In the late 1980s, Robertson toyed with the idea of making a major investment in Arabian horses but was unable to finance the venture. In 1997 Robertson bought several racing thoroughbreds, described as "modestly talented horses," that recorded moderate winnings at several smaller tracks. Five years later the *New York Times* broke a story about Robertson's horse-racing venture. By that time, Robertson's stable included several promising horses, including "Mr. Pat," a two-year-old he purchased for $520,000 that showed enough promise to be nominated for the Triple Crown. Robertson told the *Times* reporter that "it's an enormous thrill to be involved in something that is so invigorating." "It's as exciting as can be," he exulted. "I love Saratoga. I go there for the breakfasts in the morning and to watch the horses train. . . . There is a certain mystique to horse racing." At the same time, Robertson expressed regret about the connection of horseracing to gambling and insisted that he did not gamble and had consistently urged Christians to avoid the practice. But Robertson clearly underestimated the critical fallout that would come. The article itself included biting criticisms from prominent Christian leaders. Martin Marty observed: "This is like saying you're investing in a bordello but aren't in favor of prostitution."[32]

Alarmed by the reaction, Robertson immediately disbanded his racing venture. In a letter drafted to be sent to a reported 200 supporters who reacted negatively to the story, Robertson wrote: "I am sorry that my fondness for the performance of equine athletes has caused you an offense. Therefore, for your sake and the sake of others like you, I have set in motion the necessary plans to dispose of all my thoroughbred racing and breeding stock between now and the breeding sale in Kentucky in November." Robertson explained that his love of horses reached far back into his childhood and that "very frankly, none of this brought any sense of embarrassment to me because I felt . . . there is nothing wrong with contests of skill, either between human athletes or equine athletes." "As a Virginian," he continued, "I am proud of the fact that the number one athlete born in Virginia was not a human being, but a horse named Secretariat."[33]

Personally, the price was high. G. G. Conklin, Robertson's personal assistant, explained that "most of us understand the biblical reason he's taking this direction, but have such a sense of loss for him that he will no longer have this enjoyment in his life." For Robertson the episode highlighted the disconnect that appeared from time to time between his upbringing and the sensibilities of the community of faith he had adopted. Clearly, he was somewhat naïve, or at least unguarded, about the impact of the story on his core supporters. But both pragmatism and concern for the conscience of his audience made his reaction predictable.[34]

Some friends thought that Pat Robertson had a warmer and more intimate relationship with his horses than he did with people. He has always been a loner. Even as a young man, recalled his Lexington friend Matt Paxton, "Pat always kept his own counsel, played his cards a little close. . . . He gives the impression of being a great extrovert, very gracious and very friendly with a ready smile, but when it's all said and done, I think he's always been a private person." Of course, the Robertsons have had many friends, and both Pat and Dede enjoy public functions hosted by the ministry or by Regent University. But he has had few social friends on the campus. One insider observed: "He spent a lot of time with the Bible instead of socializing." They have been friends with such political and religious figures as Dan and Marilyn Quayle and Bill and Vonette Bright but rarely have had occasions to socialize with them. Robertson has enjoyed mingling with Regent University students through the years. On Thanksgivings he sometimes hosted Dean Vinson Synan and the students from the School of Religion: "He just loves to be around the students," according to Synan.[35]

Mostly, in the years after the run for office, Pat and Dede Robertson have stayed home and stayed busy. Pat wrote to a viewer in 1997: "Dede and I have been happily married for forty-three years. She is staying busy being a homemaker, teaching in a women's Bible study, serving on several boards, and [keeping up] with our four grown children and twelve grandchildren." In their later years, the bond between Pat and Dede has deepened. "Often Dede has been more discerning about people's hearts than Pat has," observed David Gyertson. Dede "is perfect for him," surmised Scott Ross: "You don't walk on Dede," and "there are times when [Pat] has been sorry he didn't listen to her." Robertson knows that he is opinionated and hard to turn when he makes up his mind, and Dede is more likely to succeed in persuading him than anyone else. Asked by a reporter in 1986 if he struggled with the three temptations that vexed political and religious leaders — "women, money and pride," Robertson replied that he had no problems with the first two, but pride he had to "address on a day-to-day basis." In 2003 he acknowledged that Dede had been the stable balance in his life. She had taught him "the greatest virtue," humility: "In my case, it is not only humility but common sense to recognize the unique wisdom and ability that God has given to my wife. We are life partners, and both of us need to be in agreement on important issues. She is a very accomplished interior decorator and designer, and she has an uncanny ability to read people. Not only that, she knows how to hear from the Lord. So we pray together about important and not-so-important issues." It has been a perfect match, observed the Robertsons' daughter Anne; her father is "spontaneous" and creative, and her mother is "the voice of reason."[36]

Every other year at Christmas the entire Robertson clan, including the four children and their spouses and fourteen grandchildren, gather at the mountain house. They are "terrific people," boasts the clan patriarch. Pat Robertson's children adore and admire him. "They have been through a lot of things together," observed Scott Ross. In many ways, his relationship with his daughters has mirrored the loving and tender relationship he had with his mother. He dotes on his daughters. Elizabeth, he mused, "looks just like my mother," filled with grace and "ebullience." His younger daughter, Anne, has been a lively and capable presence at CBN, pampered by her father and a warm friend of her mother. Robertson's relationship with his two sons has been much like the formal but deeply attentive bond with his father. Senator Robertson was ever concerned and solicitous about the needs of his son, but he was never his buddy; in the words of biographer John Donovan, "Robertson's father remained a somewhat distant presence throughout his life." Pat sounded very much like Senator Robertson when he said, "I don't dominate my kids. I just try to set them up." Scott Ross recalled that Pat once told him about a memo he had sent to his son Tim: "I told him, 'That is nuts. He is your son and you write him a *memo?*'" But it was the paternal child-rearing style he had inherited, and it had served him well. He was there to offer advice, and to provide a safety net, but beyond that, his sons were on their own.[37]

Succession

"You will never let go of this place," Scott Ross once told Pat Robertson. "You will be pulling strings from your grave." Some of the subsidiaries in the Robertson empire are only loosely tied to CBN or Pat Robertson. ACLJ is Jay Sekulow's organization, although it is still regularly identified with the name of its founder. Operation Blessing's separatist sensibilities by 2009 were the source of some internal tensions, though it seemed to be inseparably joined with CBN. But the organizational core of Pat Robertson's empire is the Christian Broadcasting Network and Regent University. In both of those institutions, mused Dede Robertson in 2007, succession issues were "weighing on him a little bit. . . . Not that anything weighs on him very much."[38]

The succession issue at CBN was solved in 2007 when the board first named Gordon Robertson as "successor" to his father, and a few months later, in December, officially appointed him chief executive officer and vice-chairman of the CBN board. "People began to wonder," remarked Pat Robertson, so "It seemed appropriate." "I am still going to be watching what he is doing," Pat added, but Gordon brought undeniable skills to the job, including an avaricious interest in modern technology. Some critics questioned Gordon's ability to replace his father. Barry Lynn observed that he had met Gordon Robertson and went away feeling that he was "not exactly a burning bush of enthusiasm." But almost uniformly insiders wel-comed the appointment, because Gordon has an intimate knowledge of the complex network that makes up the CBN empire. In addition, in spite of his calm, soft-spoken outward demeanor, he is widely informed about public events and capable of offering the same kind of commentary his fa-ther has given for years on *The 700 Club*. All in all, the appointment of Gordon was welcomed, Terry Meeuwsen thought, because it was a sign that "there is a continuity building here" and that "the wagon isn't just tied to one person."[39]

In many ways Gordon is a more nuanced presence on *The 700 Club* than his father. Deeply committed to igniting religious revival, Gordon is also conservative politically, though less tied to party politics or a specific agenda than his father. Longtime CBN observer Steven G. Vegh of the *Virginian-Pilot* noted the differences: "While Gordon Robertson looks much like his father, he is a mild, non-confrontational personality lacking the acidity that suffused Pat's calls to 'gut' the State Department or assassi-nate Venezuela's socialist leader." For instance, Gordon showed a more nuanced openness to understanding moderate Islam. As opposed to her more volatile father, said Gordon's sister, Anne LeBlanc, Gordon is "so gen-tle and sincere and honest" that he inspires in his own way. Like their mother, she observed, Gordon "is the voice of reason."[40]

Into the summer of 2009 speculation swirled in Virginia Beach about who would succeed Pat Robertson as president of Regent University. In October, the board selected Dr. Carlos Campo, who had been serving as provost since 2007, as president-elect. He was scheduled to take office in the summer of 2010 when Robertson, who retains the title of chancellor, steps down. In Campo, Robertson believed that he had found a man who understood Regent's founding mission. In a statement released at the time of his appointment, the president-elect accepted the challenge to fulfill Robertson's vision: "Many of the greatest universities of all time were es-tablished on Christian values but have since drifted from their missions. Regent has not lost its focus as a center for Christian thought and action, and that's a vision I'm excited to advance and communicate."[41]

Legacy

Pat Robertson has been "a larger than life personality" who has always re-mained "true in his inner life," according to his friend Ralph Reed. Keith Fournier agreed: "He is a man who has changed history because he has allowed his faith to inform his life." The evidence of his lifetime of accomplishments conspicuously covers the paneled walls of his office in Virginia Beach. There hang scores of "Man of the Year" plaques, author's awards, "Distinguished Service" awards, and perhaps most conspicuously, awards from Israeli organizations given "with respect, admiration, and honor [to] acknowledge the longstanding friendship of Dr. Robertson with the State of Israel." The list of honors drones on seemingly endlessly, as does the list of authors, celebrities, and world leaders who have conversed with him. Ironically, the man who has so often spoken disdainfully of elites was even selected in 1992 by *Newsweek* magazine as "one of America's 100 Cultural Elite."[42]

While Robertson's lifetime influence will no doubt be measured partly by the impact he had on American politics for two decades beginning in the mid-1980s, his more important legacy almost surely resides in the network of institutions he created and nurtured. Barry Lynn surmised: "He has created an empire that will live far beyond the end of his days." A recent study of American parachurch organizations commented on the power and breadth of such organizations in modern society: "It is difficult to overstate the importance of parachurch organizations in contemporary American evangelicalism, as they structure and direct billions of evangelical dollars toward humanitarianism, political advocacy, and evangelism." Pat Robertson's empire spanned the gamut of parachurch concerns. Robertson believes that his "legacy consists of everyone who has ever been touched by his multiple 'ministries,' such as Regent, 'The 700 Club' and overseas relief efforts." After being recognized by a stranger during a trip to Europe, Ben Kinchlow mused, "People don't realize the scope of CBN." The reach is almost beyond description or cataloging.[43]

It seems likely that the enduring imprint of Pat Robertson will be most permanently etched in the United States and abroad by the Christian Broadcasting Network and Regent University. The Christian Broadcasting Network, anchored by *The 700 Club* program that seems destined to survive in perpetuity, bears a deep imprint of its founder. The core leadership at CBN is as deeply steeped in the spiritual vision of Pat Robertson as it is in the technology of the twenty-first century. The WorldReach evangelistic outreach around the world, using advanced technology and production methods in vastly different cultural settings, may in the long run be Pat Robertson's most important contribution to the molding of Christianity around the world. Others believe that Regent University, which has trained thousands of Christians to excel in their chosen fields, will be Robertson's most lasting contribution. But more remarkable than any one institution is the sheer breadth of Robertson's legacy. In his long life, Pat Robertson has accomplished much.

It is perhaps inevitable that in the minds of many people Pat Robertson will always be defined by his mistakes rather than by his accomplishments. His sometimes intemperate remarks and his business misadventures, carefully monitored and expeditiously reported, have supplied ample material for caricaturists. Others dismiss Robertson as an extremist, a bigot far outside the rational mainstream of American religion and politics. That, of course, is a matter of perspective. If Pentecostals and charismatics constitute a lunatic religious fringe, lunacy has become a worldwide epidemic. Knowledgeable observers know that charismatic Christianity is a very diverse community of believers, and within that community Robertson has long been recognized as a voice of moderation and tolerance. He brought to the movement an ecumenical sensibility and reasonableness, as well as a sense of empowerment because of his background and education. Robertson speaks the language of charismatics, and is often misunderstood by those not tutored in the language, but his theology is fundamentally conservative and pragmatic.

Politically, in the 1990s Pat Robertson and the Christian Coalition were at the center of the religious right. In that movement Robertson, and his young friend Ralph Reed, sought change based on their vision of American history and values. But they did not seek theocratic revolution; they were pragmatic politicians who wanted to be significant actors in the American political drama. And they succeeded: they influenced elections, legislation, and Supreme Court appointments.

It would be a serious mistake to dismiss the contributions of perhaps the foremost conservative religious visionary in modern American history because his religious and political views were controversial. Pat Robertson has spoken persuasively to a portion of his generation, in the United States and around the world. And through the institutional empire he will leave behind, it seems that he will speak for many years to come.

Bibliographical Note

—◦◦◦—

The literature about Pat Robertson and the religious and political movements he has influenced is vast. This book is extensively documented
with endnotes that make clear the secondary and primary sources I have
relied on. In addition to the hundreds of documents copied from the files
in Pat Robertson's office, the book is enriched by the many hours of interviews I have personally taped with individuals around the world. Those
interviews are listed below.

Interviews (tapes in the possession of the author)

Allman, Rob, Virginia Beach, VA, September 25, 2007
Audam, Mali, Abuja, Nigeria, April 22, 2008
Babre, Grant, Nashville, TN, March 30, 2007
Baratha, Ir. Sandi, Jakarta, Indonesia, April 3, 2008
Benigno, Nena, Manila, Philippines, March 31, 2008
Bredesen, Harald, Virginia Beach, Va., Jan. 8, 1987
Buchanan, John, Washington DC, December 2, 1986
Carter, Michael, Virginia Beach, VA, October 24, 2007
Cepeda-Lara, Grace, Manila, Philippines, March 31, 2008
Choudary, Priti, New Delhi, India, April 14, 2008
Comisky, Jay, Virginia Beach, VA, April 30, 2007
Danilova, Tanya, Kiev, Ukraine, April 16, 2008
Edwards, Ben, Virginia Beach, VA, October 18, 2007

————, Virginia Beach, VA, December 5, 2007

Foresman, Bob, December 13, 1983

Gammill, Christopher R., Virginia Beach, VA, October 16, 2007

Gimenez, John, Virginia Beach, VA, November 10, 1981

Goodwin, Ron, Washington, DC, December 1, 1986

Gornitsky, Vitaly, Kiev, Ukraine, April 16, 2008

Gyertson, David, Virginia Beach, VA, October 17, 2007

Hotono, Nely, Jakarta, Indonesia, April 3, 2008

Ibanez, Malou R., Manila, Philippines, March 31, 2006

Kairuz, Peter, Manila, Philippines, March 31, 2008

Kalma, John, Abuja, Nigeria, April 22, 2008

Kinchlow, Ben, Virginia Beach, VA, March 19, 2008

Lauderdale, George, Atlanta, GA, January 12, 1987

LeBlanc, Anne Willis, Virginia Beach, VA, November 19, 2007

Little, Michael, Virginia Beach, VA, March 4, 2007

————, Virginia Beach, VA, April 10, 2007

————, Virginia Beach, VA, October 16, 2007

Lumpkin, William, Norfolk, VA, December 10, 1986

Lynn, Barry, Washington, DC, January 3, 2008

McClendon, Mark, Jakarta, Indonesia, April 2, 2008

————, Jakarta, Indonesia, April 3, 2008

Meeuwsen, Terry, Virginia Beach, VA, September 25, 2007

Miller, Benson, Virginia Beach, VA, December 18, 1986

Mitchell, Kim, Abuja, Nigeria, April 23, 2008

————, Abuja, Nigeria, April 24, 2008

Oates, Ron, Virginia Beach, VA, October 16, 2007

Oisamoje, Felix, Abuja, Nigeria, April 23, 2008

————, Abuja, Nigeria, April 24, 2008

Osborn, T. L. and Daisy, Tulsa, Oklahoma, September 6, 1991

Palser, Joel, Virginia Beach, VA, April 11, 2007

————, Virginia Beach, VA, December 8, 2007

Pascual, Kim April C., Manila, Philippines, March 31, 2008

Pattaranukool, Niran, Virginia Beach, VA, September 22, 2007

Paxton, Jr., Matthew W., Lexington, VA, December 15, 1986

Periasamy, Kumar, Hyderabad, India, June 5, 2007

Rawung, Non, Jakarta, Indonesia, April 3, 2008

Reed, Ralph E., Jr., Atlanta, GA, May 23, 2007

————, Atlanta, GA, September 10, 2007

Robertson, Adelia, Virginia Beach, VA, October 25, 2007

Robertson, Gordon, Virginia Beach, VA, April 9, 2007

————, Virginia Beach, VA, October 15, 2007

————, Virginia Beach, VA, December 10, 2007

————, Telephone Interview, June 19, 2008

————, Virginia Beach, VA, October 10, 2008

————, Virginia Beach, VA, March 18, 2009

————, Virginia Beach, VA, March 19, 2009

Robertson, Pat, Virginia Beach, VA, January 14, 1987

————, Virginia Beach, VA, March 5, 2007

————, Virginia Beach, VA, October 17, 2007

————, Virginia Beach, VA, October 18, 2007

————, Virginia Beach, VA, October 23, 2007

————, Virginia Beach, VA, December 6, 2007

————, Virginia Beach, VA, March 18, 2008

————, Virginia Beach, VA, March 19, 2008

————, Virginia Beach, VA, October 6, 2008

Robertson, Timothy, Virginia Beach, VA, December 18, 1986

————, Virginia Beach, VA, April 10, 2007

————, Virginia Beach, VA, December 5, 2007

Robinson, Elizabeth, University Park, TX, August 13, 2008

Ross, Scott, Virginia Beach, VA, October 26, 2007

Shevenko, Yuliya, Kiev, Ukraine, April 16, 2008

Shakarian, Demos, Tulsa, OK, January 27, 1983

Slosser, Bob, Virginia Beach, VA, November 19, 1986

Synan, Vinson, Virginia Beach, VA, April 9, 2007

————, Virginia Beach, VA, July 13, 2007

————, Virginia Beach, VA, December 10, 2007

Tan, Robert John V., Manila, Philippines, March 31, 2008

Turver, John, Virginia Beach, VA, April 11, 2007

————, Virginia Beach, VA, December 8, 2007

Waddell, Kara, Beijing, China, March 28, 2008

Walker, Robert, West Palm Beach, FL, January 26, 1987

Webb, Lee, Virginia Beach, VA, November 16, 2007

Weber, Steve, Kiev, Ukraine, April 16, 2008

West, David, Virginia Beach, VA, December 8, 1986

Weyrich, Paul, Washington, DC, December 16, 1986

Weisenbach, William A., New York City, Nov. 6, 1986

Yates, S. Tucker, Virginia Beach, VA, December 9, 1986

Abbreviations

AL	Anne LeBlanc
AWR	A. Willis Robertson
AWRP	A. Willis Robertson Papers
BE	Ben Edwards
BJ	Barbara Johnson
BK	Ben Kinchlow
BS	Bob Slosser
DR	Adelia "Dede" Robertson
DS	Demos Shakarian
ER	Elizabeth Robinson
GCR	Gladys Churchill Robertson
GGC	G.G. Conklin
GL	George Lauderdale
GR	Gordon Robertson
HB	Harald Bredesen
JS	Jay Sekulow
JT	John Turver
LW	Lee Webb
ML	Michael Little
PR	M.G. "Pat" Robertson
ROA	Robertson Office Archives
RR	Ralph Reed
RUA	Regent University Archives
RW	Robert Walker
SR	Scott Ross
SW	Steve Weber
TM	Terry Meeuwsen
TR	Timothy Robertson
TY	Tucker Yates
VS	Vinson Synan

Endnotes

—≈∿∿≈—

Notes to Chapter 1

1. PR, "What Is Revival?," *The Flame*, Apr. 1980, 2; "God's Care Illuminated Virginia's Early Years," *The Flame*, May 1976, 3-4.

2. "Lexington Gains 30 Percent in 1930 Over 1920 Census," *Lexington Gazette*, May 6, 1930, 1; George Peck, "The American Way," *Lexington Gazette*, Oct. 5, 1949, 6.

3. *Lexington Gazette*, Mar. 25, 1930, 4, 7, 8.

4. Matthew W. Paxton Jr. int.

5. Virginius Dabney, "The Willis Robertson Story," *Virginia and the Virginia Record*, Aug. 1954, 8-42; AWR to D. S. Freeman, Mar. 13, 1947, photocopy in ROA.

6. See AWR to PR, Nov. 21, 1956, A. Willis Robertson Papers, Special Collections Research Center, Swem Library, College of William and Mary (AWRP). This large collection contains many personal letters from the senator to his son Pat. Restrictions on the papers forbid direct quotations if any of those mentioned are still living. I have tried to capture the essence of some of the letters written by the senator to Pat because they reveal much about his profound love for his son, his high hopes for his success, his deep disappointment when Pat floundered, and, finally, his acceptance of his son's choices. AWR to PR, Mar. 6, 1958, AWRP; TR int., Dec. 18, 1986; see also AL int. and ER int.

7. "Mrs. Robertson Dies at Home in Lexington," *The News-Gazette*, Lexington, Apr. 24, 1968, 10C; Margaret Wilkins, "Mrs. Robertson Remains Close to Constituents," *Richmond News Leader*, May 9, 1966, 16; John B. Donovan, *Pat Robertson: The Authorized Biography* (New York: Macmillan Publishing Company, 1988), 6.

8. PR int., Jan. 14, 1987; Wilkins, "Mrs. Robertson"; AWR to PR, Sept. 11, 1958, AWRP.

9. PR int., Jan. 14, 1987; GCR to Louise Lumpkin, Feb. 11, 1949, ROA; Wilkins, "Mrs. Robertson"; Neil Eskelin, *Pat Robertson: A Biography* (Shreveport: Huntington House, 1987), 48; GL int.; Paxton int.

10. Paxton int. For insight into the relationship of Senator Robertson with his el-

der son, see AWR to A. Willis Robertson, Jr., June 15, 1960; Nov. 10, 1960; Oct. 23, 1961, AWRP.

11. "Marion Gordon 'Pat' Robertson," typed manuscript labeled "Rough Draft," ROA, 1; PR to Marguerite Hall, Jan. 11, 1994, ROA.

12. Paxton int.; GL int.

13. The McCallie connection surfaces repeatedly in Robertson's biography; see AWR to Honorable Bill Brock, Oct. 2, 1963, AWRP; "Marion Gordon 'Pat' Robertson," 6; AWR to George B. Tullidge, May 3, 1945, AWRP.

14. For a good description of Washington and Lee during these years, see William C. Avirett, "Washington and Lee in Third Century," *New York Herald Tribune*, Sept. 25, 1949, Scrapbook, Special Collections, Washington and Lee University; *The Calyx of Washington and Lee University, 1949-1950*, 240. See *The Calyx* for general information about life at Washington and Lee. Also see *Come and Cheer Washington and Lee: The University at 250 Years* (Lexington: Washington and Lee University, 1998), 180.

15. "Marion Gordon 'Pat' Robertson," 7; *The Calyx of Washington and Lee University, 1949-1950*, 116; PR int., Mar. 18, 2009. Robertson was one of eleven undergraduate students inducted into Phi Beta Kappa in November 1949. "Phi Beta Kappa Picks Thirteen at W & L," *Roanoke Times*, Nov. 2, 1949 (Scrapbook, Special Collections, Washington and Lee University). Robertson is rarely pictured in the university yearbook, but he did show up for the Phi Beta Kappa picture: *The Calyx of Washington and Lee University, 1949-1950*, 101.

16. *Come and Cheer Washington and Lee*, 176.

17. "Marion Gordon 'Pat' Robertson," 7.

18. "2 Graduate from W & L as Lieutenants," *Washington Post*, June 9, 1950, 25; see "Marion Gordon 'Pat' Robertson," 7-8.

19. "Marion Gordon 'Pat' Robertson," 8.

20. AWR to PR, Mar. 17, 1952, Feb. 1, 1952, Apr. 24, 1952, July 5, 1952, AWRP.

21. AWR to PR, Oct. 1, 1952, Mar. 14, 1953, AWRP.

22. AWR to PR, Mar. 14, 1953, AWRP.

23. Donovan, *Pat Robertson*, 11. AWR to J. Peter Grace Jr., June 24, 1954, AWRP.

24. "Marion Gordon 'Pat' Robertson," ROA, 3; AWR to PR, June 2, 1955, June 13, 1955, AWRP.

25. DR int.

26. See "Marion Gordon 'Pat' Robertson," 9.

27. Eskelin, *Pat Robertson*, 60; PR int., Jan. 14, 1987.

28. PR to Mrs. Pieder Beeli, Mar. 10, 1995, ROA; April Witt, "Robertson's Wife Makes TV Confession," *Richmond Ledger Star*, Oct. 10, 1987, B1.

29. "Marion Gordon 'Pat' Robertson," 9; AWR to PR, Jan. 12, 1956, Apr. 16, 1956, Apr. 17, 1956, AWRP. "Marion Gordon 'Pat' Robertson," 10.

30. GGC to author, 23 June 2009, e-mail comments from PR.

31. GL int.

32. Mrs. Robertson regularly talked with local preachers about the spiritual condition of her husband and sons. David John Marley notes that Mrs. Robertson wrote to Kathryn Kuhlman asking for prayers for her sons. David John Marley, *Pat Robertson: An American Life* (Lanham, MD: Rowman & Littlefield Publishers, Inc., 2007), 4. Robertson recalled that his mother "did a lot of praying for her wayward son." While it "probably drove me away," he observed, "it worked with God." PR int., June 12, 2007; GGC to author,

June 23, 2009, e-mail comments from PR. Also see http://www.patrobertson.com/index.asp, Apr. 1, 2008. Donovan, *Pat Robertson,* 32, 33.

33. PR int., Jan. 14, 1987.

34. Wesley G. Pippert, "What Have We Got that No One Else Has? God" (Portsmouth, VA: Christian Broadcasting Network, Inc., n.d.), 2, reprint of article published in *Christian Life* magazine. This is one of Robertson's fuller descriptions of his encounter with Vanderbreggen. A good summary of the episode is in Eskelin, *Pat Robertson,* 63-67.

35. BS int. AWR to PR, Apr. 6, 1956 (framed letter in PR office). AWR to PR, June 6, 1956, AWRP.

37. PR with Jamie Buckingham, *Shout It from the Housetops* (Plainfield, NJ: Logos International, 1972), 27.

38. PR, "We Can All Be Directed of the Lord!" *Full Gospel Men's Voice,* Apr. 1962, 2.

39. PR int., Jan. 14, 1987.

40. PR int., Jan. 14, 1987; *Shout It from the Housetops,* 49-64.

41. RW int.

42. HB int.; *Shout It from the Housetops, 59-62.*

43. See Harald Bredesen, *Yes, Lord,* rev. ed. (Ventura, Calif.: Regal, 2007).

44. See Bredesen, *Yes, Lord.*

45. HB int.; *Shout It from the Housetops,* 63-64.

46. PR int., Jan. 14, 1987; HB int.

47. HB int.

48. PR int., Jan. 14, 1987.

49. Eskelin, *Pat Robertson,* 73-75.

50. Lisa Hogberg, "Wife Nearly Left Pat Robertson," *Richmond Ledger Star,* June 9, 1980, 1.

51. [GGC to author, June 23, 2009, e-mail comments from PR; AWR to Donald Grey Barnhouse, June 13, 1960, AWRP.

52. AWR to PR, June 14, 1960; AWR to Dr. L. Nelson Bell, July 9, 1959; AWR to PR, Apr. 20, 1959; AWR to PR, June 26, 1959, AWRP.

53. AWR to PR, Aug. 28, 1959, AWRP; GCR to Mrs. S. M. Heflin, undated handwritten letter, ROA.

54. GL int.

55. GL int.; PR int., Jan. 14, 1987.

56. GL int.

57. PR, *The Plan* (Nashville: Thomas Nelson, 1989), 41-43; "Marion Gordon 'Pat' Robertson," 12.

58. PR with Jamie Buckingham, *The Autobiography of Pat Robertson* (South Plainfield, N.J.: Bridge Publishing, 1995), 123-35; DR int.

59. *Autobiography of Pat Robertson,* 140; GL int.

Notes to Chapter 2

1. *Autobiography of Pat Robertson,* 137-47.

2. *Autobiography of Pat Robertson,* 146.

3. AWR to PR, Jan. 25, 1960; HB int.; AWR to PR, June 14, 1960; AWR to PR, Oct. 28, 1959, AWRP.

4. GL int.

5. AWR to Mrs. Charles B. Borland, June 19, 1961, AWRP; William Lumpkin int.

6. "CBN Statement of Faith," undated copy of CBN bylaws, ROA; GL int.

7. GL int., HB int., RW int., DS int.

8. HB int.; "Christian TV for Tidewater," *The Flame*, Oct.-Nov. 1974, 3.

9. Memo, PR to All Staff, Aug. 23, 1985, RUA; Nelson Martin, "Christian Broadcaster Tells Global Goal," *Christian Times*, Mar. 30, 1989, 3; Eskelin, *Pat Robertson*, 30. The hectic events leading to the opening of the television station are described in detail in *Autobiography of Pat Robertson*, 199-211.

10. RW int.; Eskelin, *Pat Robertson*, 122; "Decatrend 4," *Charisma*, Aug. 1985, 49.

11. "CBN Open House," *Radio Telegram*, Aug. 1968, 12.

12. *Autobiography of Pat Robertson*, 202.

13. Stanley W. Mooneyham, "Christian TV for Tidewater," *Adult Power*, 16 June 1963, 7.

14. Mooneyham, "Christian TV for Tidewater," 7. "How 'The 700 Club' Began," *The Flame*, Apr. 1978, 2.

15. Paul Williams, "Home Viewers Have Best Laugh as Critics Cringe," *Ledger-Star*, undated clipping, RUA; "Special to the Times Herald," CBN press release, n.d., RUA; "Jim and Tammy Show," *The Virginian-Pilot*, May 5, 1968, Supplement, 9; CBN press release, [1967], RUA; "For Release October 18, Friday," CBN press release, [1968], RUA. For information on the early contributions of Jim and Tammy Bakker, see Eskelin, *Pat Robertson*, 124-26.

16. Eskelin, *Pat Robertson*, 124-26; "Generosity Called God's Work," *The Virginian-Pilot*, Nov. 17, 1965, 21.

17. For Jim Bakker's account of his role in the 1965 telethon, see Jim Bakker with Robert Paul Lamb, *Move That Mountain!* (Plainfield, N.J.: Logos International, n.d.), 57-59; "The Telethon that Wouldn't End," *TouchPoint*, Oct., 1986, 4. For a description of the early telethons, see Pat Robertson and Jamie Buckingham, *Shout It from the Housetops* (Plainfield, N.J.: Logos International, 1972), 188-93; Nancy Scudder, "Pat Robertson," *Christian Contemporary* 3:3 (1977), repr. Christian Broadcasting Network.

18. "Christian Network Gleans $150,000," *Ledger-Star*, Nov. 29, 1966; "Religious Station to Open Telethon," *The Virginian-Pilot*, Nov. 18, 1967; "Christian Network Raises $360,000," *The Virginian-Pilot*, Nov. 29, 1969; "CBN Telethon Nears Goal," "Telethon Hailed As Success For CBN," undated CBN press releases, RUA.

19. For Jim Bakker's account of his hiring and his early vision of a talk show, see Bakker and Lamb, *Move That Mountain!*, 51-56. "How 'The 700 Club' Began," 7. The Bakkers, particularly Tammy Faye, felt that Robertson appropriated Jim's idea once he saw its potential to succeed. See Joe E. Barnhart with Steven Winzenburg, *Jim and Tammy* (Buffalo: Prometheus Books, 1988), 39-47. On the other hand, many of the leaders at CBN felt that Bakker unscrupulously copied *"The 700 Club"* when he founded the PTL network. See "Turning the Other Channel," *Forbes*, July 7, 1980, 123.

20. TR int., Apr. 10, 2007; Bakker and Lamb, *Move That Mountain!*, 69-72; "CNN Larry King Live," Oct. 24, 1996, transcript, ROA; SR, "Media in the Mass Age," *Vision*, Winter 1969, 15; "'It's a Little Hard to Believe,'" *TouchPoint*, Oct. 1986, 5; VS int., July 13, 2007.

21. Bakker and Lamb, *Move That Mountain!*, 60-62, 106-8; "Jim Bakker's Lost America," *Esquire*, Dec. 1987, 182; Jon D. Hall, "The Rise and Fall of 'Holy Joe,'" *Time*, Aug. 3, 1987, 55; Donovan, *Pat Robertson*, 105-7; PR to Jamie Buckingham, July 28, 1975, ROA; PR to P. Charlton, Sept. 15, 1977, ROA.

22. TR int., Apr. 10, 2007; "How *'The 700 Club'* Began," 8; PR to Eugene G. Ziobron, Mar. 26, 1992, ROA.

23. Art Harris and Michael Isakoff, "Robertson's Bakker Connection," *Washington Post,* Feb. 6, 1988; *The Flame,* Nov. 1976; PR to Berneice Morgan, Apr. 3, 1991; PR to Sally J. Wright, Feb. 12, 1990; PR to Wava Farley, May 18, 1994; "CNN Larry King Live," transcripts of Nov. 1, 1996, Oct. 24, 1996; BJ, e-mail, Aug. 22, 2007, ROA.

24. Untitled press release, [Nov. 1967]; "WYAH-TV Events Fact Sheet, Fall '67," press release, Oct. 2, 1967; untitled press release, [July 1967], RUA; Mal Vincent, "TV on a Prayer and $3," *The Virginian-Pilot,* Nov. 5, 1967; "News Release," [Sept. 1968], RUA.

25. "TV Studio Planned," *The Virginian-Pilot,* Mar. 23, 1966; "Channel 27 Breaks Ground for New TV Facility," press release, [March, 1967], RUA.

26. "Supplement," *The Virginian-Pilot,* May 5, 1968, 3. This twelve-page supplement is a broad description of the new building and provides much historical background.

27. PR, "As I View It," *The Flame,* July 1977, 2; HB int.; *Autobiography of Pat Robertson,* 302.

28. "Supplement," *The Virginian-Pilot,* May 5, 1968, 12.

29. "Supplement," *The Virginian-Pilot,* May 5, 1968, 5; see "Tidewater Aids Snow-Bound Indians," *The Ledger-Star,* Dec. 28, 1967.

30. "Christian Broadcasting's Radio-Telethon Center," *SESAC Music,* Autumn 1968, 6.

31. PR, "CBN Triples in 1974," *The Flame,* Mar. 1975, 2; "God's Plan to CBN for 1976," *The Flame,* special edition, 4; "It Is God's Time to Reach the World," *The Flame,* Sept.-Oct. 1975, 2; Donovan, *Pat Robertson,* 102 (see 99-107).

32. PR, "As I View It," *The Flame,* Sept. 1974, 3; "Doors Open Miraculously for Exclusive Interview with Prime Minister Rabin," *The Flame,* Feb. 1975, 5; see William Martin, "Heavenly Hosts," *Texas Monthly,* Mar. 1979, 123.

33. Martin, "Heavenly Hosts," 125; "New CBN Television Thrust," *The Flame,* Fall 1973, 2.

34. PR to Mrs. Robert L. Banks, 1 Nov. 1973, ROA; Scudder, "Pat Robertson."

35. "Decade of the Tube," *Christianity Today,* Mar. 17, 1972, 40, 41; Henry Harrison, "God's Revival Power," *The Flame,* July 1974, 4; C. Gerald Fraser, "Varieties of Religious Spokesmen Seeking More Out of TV Shows," *New York Times,* Sept. 23, 1974; Michael J. Connor, "On This Talk Show, the Talk Can Take a Miraculous Turn," *Wall Street Journal,* Jan. 14, 1976, 1, 22; Scudder, "Pat Robertson"; PR to Robert A. Woosley, Apr. 25, 1979, ROA.

36. PR to Darrel R. Young, Sept. 23, 1975; PR to Mary Hindle, Oct. 4, 1979, ROA; "New CBN Television Program Thrust," *The Flame,* Fall 1973, 2.

37. "God's Plan to CBN for 1976," 2, 5; see Ethel A. Steadman, "Christian TV Plans Project," *The Virginian-Pilot,* Jan. 5, 1976.

38. "America's First Prayer Meeting Held in Virginia Beach," *The Flame,* special edition [1976], 6; "Pat to Pray for Partners' Needs at Settlers' Historic Prayer Site," *The Flame,* Apr. 1976, 3; "CBN International Headquarters, a Bicentennial Gift to God, Fulfills First Colonists' Dream of World Evangelization," *The Flame,* Feb.-Mar. 1976, 4, 5; "Prophecy delivered by Pat Robertson September 25, 1976, at the start of Seven Days Ablaze on CBN's new site," typed manuscript, ROA.

39. For an overview of the groundbreaking, see *The Flame,* Nov. 1976; PR, "Phase Two of International Center Begins," *The Flame,* July 1977, 2.

40. "Graham Echoes Pope, 'Praise the Lord Jesus Christ,'" *The Flame,* Dec. 1979, 4.

41. PR to Grace C. Johnson, Sept. 23, 1980, ROA; PR to All Staff, Sept. 7, 1979, RUA; "CBN

International Headquarters Building Set for Summer 1979 Completion," undated CBN press release, ROA.

42. PR int., June 12, 2007; PR, "Are Satellites the Modern 'Angels' Who Will Proclaim Christ's Return?," *The Flame*, Dec. 1976, 2; "CBN Signs Global Satellite Deal," *The Virginian-Pilot*, Apr. 30, 1977; PR, "Let Me Share My Vision of a Fourth Network With You," *The Flame*, Oct. 1977, 2.

43. "1978 Opens with First Nationwide Telethon," *The Flame*, Dec. 1977, 7; "First Use of Earth Station Brings 1993 Souls to Christ," *The Flame*, Apr. 1977, 4, 5; TR int.; see "News From CBN," press release, Dec. 11, 1978, RUA; "CBN Satellite Services Continues Meteoric Rise with Recognition of Five Millionth Cable Household," Feb. 9, 1979; "New Report Cites Cable Industry Growth Through April," May 1, 1979, CBN press releases, RUA.

44. "God's Plan to CBN for 1976," 4, 5.

45. Memo, Fred W. Schwarz to BJ, Nov. 29, 1978, ROA.

46. TR int., Dec. 18, 1986.

47. William Martin, "The Birth of a Media Myth," *Atlantic*, June 1971, 10; see 9-13, 15; see also William F. Fore, "Religion and Television: Report on the Research," *Christian Century*, July 18, 1984, 710-13. Richard N. Ostling, "Power, Glory — and Politics," *Time*, Feb. 17, 1986, 63; PR to Donald L. Collins, Jan. 17, 1983, ROA. For an extended interview with Robertson on this subject, see "Dr. Pat Robertson," *View*, Dec. 1982, 42-46.

48. Undated [1978] copy of advertisement, RUA; PR to Mr. and Mrs. James Sirigotis, Nov. 19, 1986, ROA.

49. "Christian Television," *Charisma*, Nov. 1981, 18; "New 'Soap Opera' Tries to Achieve Moral Tone," *Christian Science Monitor*, June 29, 1981, 3.

50. "CBN Update News Debuts this Week in More than Four Million Households," Nov. 13, 1978, CBN press release, RUA. PR to Mr. P. D. Hill, July 7, 1981, ROA. Jean McNair, "Christian Network Plans Nightly News Broadcast," *Washington Post*, Dec. 20, 1985, E1.

51. "CBN Produced #4 Rated Show for ABC," Apr. 5, 1988, CBN press release, RUA.

52. See "Heaven Can Wait for Harry Erwin — But He Can't Wait for Heaven," Mar. 19, 1979, CBN news release, RUA.

53. "Friday Prayer Meeting, April 10, 1981," typed transcript, ROA; Terry L. Heaton to Mrs. Louise Forrester, Nov. 15, 1985, ROA; ML to Wayne Duncan, July 31, 1986, ROA; see also PR to J. Edward Pawlick, June 10, 1986, ROA.

54. Rex Humbard Jr. to PR, Mar. 24, 1983, ROA.

55. See Kinchlow's autobiography, *Plain Bread* (Waco: Word, 1985); a good sketch of Kinchlow is David M. Hazard, "Meet Ben!" *Christian Herald*, Oct. 1979, 34-35, 69, 72.

56. BK int.; "International Broadcast Co-Host Ben Kinchlow Warns 'Church is Becoming a White Elephant in the Black Community,'" CBN press release, Oct. 25, 1978, RUA.

57. See Julio Iglesias, "Danuta Soderman: On Camera and Off," *Saturday Evening Post*, Dec. 1985, 54, 57, 103.

58. Form letter entitled "Danuta's Absence," Nov. 30, 1987, ROA; see Marley, *Pat Robertson*, 122.

59. Frank M. Roberts, "CBN — the Fourth Network," *Logos Journal*, Sept./Oct. 1977, 10-12; "CBN Fulfills a Minister's Dream," *The Ledger-Star*, Aug. 13, 1980; "Statement of Stewardship for the Year Ended March 31, 1987," CBN brochure, RUA.

60. PR to Ralph George, Feb. 15, 1984; PR to Beverly Hughes, July 5, 1978, ROA.

61. PR to All Staff, May 23, 1983, RUA; see "God Doubles Response During Family Special," *The Flame*, July 1983, 1.

62. PW int.; TY int.; *Autobiography of Pat Robertson,* 363 (see 333-63); PR to Virgil Williams, Sept. 27, 1977, ROA.

63. Bryan Hatchett, "Brother Pat," *Hampton Roads Magazine,* May 1974, 32-35; PR to Bryan Hatchett, Apr. 30, 1974, ROA; Neil Hickey, "That Old-Time Religion Goes Big-time," *TV Guide,* Feb. 15, 1975, 4, see 2-6; PR to S. Ditchfield et al., Feb. 20, 1975, ROA. William F. Willoughby, "Gotta Get Some Distortion Glasses," *Washington Star,* Apr. 12, 1975, B4.

64. PR to Jack A. Crickard, Sept. 17, 1981, ROA; "Gospel TV," *Time,* Feb. 17, 1986.

65. PR to Mrs. J. R. Whitaker, Feb. 9, 1977, ROA.

66. See "Pastors, Church Members are the Real 'Network' of CBN," Mar. 27, 1979; "Two Weeks of Special Telecasts Greatest in CBN History," Jan. 16, 1979, CBN press release, RUA.

67. See *TouchPoint,* June 1982, 3-4.

68. See BK int.; "Operation Blessing: People Caring for People," June 8, 1979; "NYC Street Kids Find Refuge," Mar. 20, 1979, CBN press releases, RUA. *TouchPoint,* June 1982, 4. "Partners Give Nearly $700,000 for Starving Cambodians," *The Flame,* Feb. 1980, 8; "Operation Blessing Report," *TouchPoint,* June 1982, 2. For a good description of Operation Blessing cooperation with churches in Appalachia, see "Operation Blessing," *TouchPoint,* Nov. 1985, 1,2. For Operation Blessing growth during these years, see "First Quarter 1983 CBN Ministry Results," *TouchPoint,* June 1983, 5; PR to All Staff, Jan. 11, 1983; "Operation Blessing: 'This Is What We're Here For,'" *TouchPoint,* Nov. 1985, 1, 2; memo entitled "Year End Report on CBN Activities," G. Benton Miller Jr. to Diane A. Green, Aug. 22, 1988, ROA; CBN news releases, July 15, 1987, Dec. 12, 1987, RUA. PR to Bernard H. Rose, Sept. 7, 1990, ROA. PR int., March 5, 2007.

69. "CBN University Officially Open with Convocation Sept. 19," *The Flame,* Aug.-Sept., 1978, 3, 7; David W. Clark to Dr. Willard F. Day, Jan. 17, 1978, RUA. PR to Bob McElroy, Feb. 8, 1979, ROA; "CBN University Regents Meet as Opening Draws Nearer," CBN press release, June 16, 1978, RUA. Memo from Pat Robertson to "All CBN Tidewater Employees," Sept. 25, 1980, RUA; see also "CBN University Graduates Expected to Have an Impact on U.S. 'Media Establishment,'" CBN press release, Apr. 21, 1978, RUA.

70. "CBN University News," press release, May 25, 1983, RUA. See "CBN Highlights," *The Flame,* Oct. 1986, 11; "CBN University," undated information sheet, ROA; http://www.regent.edu/about_us/overview/history.cfm#Timeline, Mar. 9, 2009. "CBN University Graduation," CBN press release, May 15, 1987, RUA. See also "From All Over the World They Come — Why?" *TouchPoint,* Oct. 1985, 1, 2.

71. Int. of Richard Gottier by Vinson Synan, Feb. 7, 2007, typed transcript in the possession of the author; "Distinguished Educator Dr. Richard Gottier to Assume Presidency of CBN University," *The Flame,* June 1979, 3; Gottier int. transcript; Vinson Synan, *A Seminary to the Changing World* (Virginia Beach: Regent University School of Religion, 2002), 21.

72. "CBN News," press release, Feb. 13, 1984, RUA; BJ to Norman Edinger, May 15, 1985, ROA. CBN University news release, n.d., RUA.

73. Herbert W. Titus, *The Biblical Basis of Public Policy* (Chesapeake, Va.: National Perspectives Institute, 1986), 10. CBN news release, Dec. 10, 1987, RUA.

74. *Autobiography of Pat Robertson,* 365. PR, "CBN Outreach Triples in 1974," *The Flame,* Mar. 1975, 2. See mission files, ROA, which contain hundreds of folders documenting a surprising variety of recipients. See, for instance, a contribution to the SCLC, PR to Dr. Claude Young, May 8, 1985, and a $25,000 contribution to Russell Kaemmerling, editor of the conservative *Southern Baptist Advocate.* Robertson wrote to Kaemmerling: "You are doing a wonderful job with the Advocate. . . . I send this contribution along with my prayer that God will use it to bless many people and to bring a message of truth to a great denom-

ination" (PR to Russell Kaemmerling, Aug. 16, 1985). PR to Bernard Cardinal Law, Dec. 10, 1985; PR to Law, Dec. 11, 1984; Law to PR, Dec. 18, 1984; Law to PR, Jan. 15, 1986, mission files, ROA. PR to Edgar J. Fisher Jr., June 12, 1979, ROA.

75. PR, "It Is God's Time to Reach the World," *The Flame,* Sept.-Oct. 1975, 2. See mission files, ROA. Dhinakaran and Bonnke were among the most favored recipients of funds from CBN. They received particularly generous donations in the 1990s. Ron Steele, *Plundering Hell to Populate Heaven: The Reinhart Bonnke Story* (Tulsa: Albury Press, 1987), 11.

76. Undated CBN press releases: "For Immediate Release," "News Release," RUA. A discussion of CBN's early excursions abroad may be found in *Shout It from the Housetops* 209-25. "Year-End Report," *The Flame,* Dec. 1976, 6. "Prophecy Foretells 'A New Day' for CBN," *The Flame,* Apr. 1976, 5. "Pat Challenges Evangelists to Reap Harvest of Millions," *TouchPoint,* Sept. 1983, 6; "Address International Conference for Itinerant Evangelists Amsterdam, July 18, 1983," typed manuscript, ROA.

77. See "Interview: CBN's Pat Robertson," *Folio,* Nov. 8, 1983, 4, 5. "First African Nation Airs CBN Telecasts," CBN press release, Oct. 20, 1978, RUA. See "God's Message for CBN: 'Look on the Fields,'" *TouchPoint,* Apr. 1983, 1; "CBN: At Home and Abroad," CBN press release, June 1984, RUA. TR int., Dec. 18, 1986; "CBN WorldReach," *NRB,* Oct. 1998, 32-38.

78. PR, *The Plan* (Nashville: Thomas Nelson, 1989), 67. "CBN Requests Middle East Radio Station in Cyprus," *The Flame,* Fall 1973, 1. "CBN Makes History Broadcasting in Israel," CBN press release, July 6, 1979, RUA; "CBN Dream Fulfilled: Holy Land Broadcasts Start July 2!" *The Flame,* Special Jerusalem Edition, 1978, 4, 5; "Just 12 Short Years Ago," *The Flame,* Aug. 1979, 2. See *The Plan,* 67-72. "1982: The Year God Opened the Door to Israel and the Middle East," *TouchPoint,* Jan. 1983, 4. Untitled front page article, *TouchPoint,* June 1982, 1. "God Protects Middle East TV Staff As Terrorist Bomb Damages Station," *TouchPoint,* Apr. 1983, 3. "CBN: At Home and Abroad," CBN news release, June 1983, RUA. See "'Make No Mistakes Here,'" and "These are the People Who Watch Middle East Television," *TouchPoint,* Apr. 1987, 2-3, 6-7.

79. Kenneth R. Clark, "The $70 Miracle Named CBN," *Chicago Tribune,* July 26, 1985.

80. Memo from PR to CBN Vice Presidents, Apr. 20, 1984, RUA.

81. TR int., Dec. 18, 1986.

82. TR int., Dec. 18, 1986; BK int.; DR int.; TY int.; BS int.; HB int.

83. HB int.; BS int.; TY int.

84. HB int.; PR int., Jan. 14, 1987; BS int.

85. Phyllis Mather Rice, "Interview with Pat Robertson," *Your Church,* May/June, 1979, 12. DR int.; BS int., TY int., HB int., GL int., RW int.

86. RW int.

87. See "CBN Time Line," June 6, 2005, ROA.

Notes to Chapter 3

1. PR to Alfred C. Berglund, Oct. 9, 1985, ROA; Michael J. Connor, "On this Talk Show, the Talk Can Take a Miraculous Turn," *Wall Street Journal,* Jan. 14, 1976, 1, 22. Robertson did not receive any compensation from CBN for the first nine years of its existence; after that, he "received a modest" salary. In 1976, his salary from CBN was under $20,000. See Eskelin, *Pat Robertson,* 117-18. See "The Christian Broadcasting Network," pamphlet published by CBN, no date, 17.

2. See Rice, "Interview with Pat Robertson," 11-12; Cory SerVaas and Maynard Good Stoddard, "CBN's Pat Robertson: White House Next?" *The Saturday Evening Post,* Mar. 1985. TR int., Dec. 18, 1986.

3. AWR to PR, June 4, 1957, Dec. 1, 1960. For a sampling of the correspondence, see AWR to PR, June 6, 1955; July 23, 1959. AWR to PR, Feb. 24, 1959. Also see Untitled Speech "prepared for A. Willis Robertson for delivery to the Senate Breakfast Group, Jan. 4, 1961," Box 215, Folder 24, AWRP. "Lexington Native Honored by DAR Tuesday Evening," Oct. 4, 1961, and "Mr. Robertson Opens Session," Sept. 23, 1964, unidentified clippings in *Lexington News-Gazette* archives files.

4. "TV Station Planned," *The Virginian-Pilot,* Mar. 23, 1966, 21. GGC to author, e-mail containing comments from PR, June 23, 2009. David John Marley states that "Robertson allegedly told his staff that his coauthor Jamie Buckingham told him to put the section in the book back in 1972 and that the Lord had never told him to remain out of politics" (Marley, *Pat Robertson,* 117). Unidentified article, *Lexington News-Gazette* file on AWR. DR int.; TR int., Dec. 18, 1986; PR to Alexander G. Monroe, July 1, 1993, ROA.

5. GGC to author, e-mail containing comments from PR, June 23, 2009. "Speaking Engagements," *The Flame,* Apr. 1975, 2. "FGBMFI World Convention Speech," July 9, 1977, ROA. See, for instance, "Speech to Congressional Clearinghouse on the Future," typed manuscript, Mar. 17, 1982; "Yale University Law School," typed manuscript, Mar. 25, 1986, ROA. See "CBN President Dr. Robertson Receives Harmony Award," CBN news release, Sept. 20, 1978, RUA; "M. G. Robertson — Awards and Honors Received," typed list, ROA. The walls of Pat Robertson's office in Virginia Beach are lined with scores of award plaques from various organizations.

6. A good overview of Dede Robertson is Holly G. Miller, "First Lady of CBN," *Saturday Evening Post,* Sept. 1986, 60-67. DR int.; see "Biography of Dede Robertson," Americans for Robertson Papers, RUA.

7. BS int.

8. See AL int., Nov. 19, 2007; ER int., Aug. 13, 2008; TR int., Dec. 18, 1986; GR int., Apr. 9, 2007.

9. Jamie Buckingham, "M. G. 'Pat' Robertson," *Charisma,* Aug. 1985, 110-13. See *Time,* Feb. 17, 1986; "Tonight It's Hall of Fame Time for Pat!" *NoonNews* [A Daily Report to the CBN Family], Feb. 5, 1986, RUA. "Robertson as 1987's Religious Newsmaker," *Christian Century,* Jan. 6-13, 1988, 3, 4.

10. E. S. Caldwell, "Trend Toward Mega Churches," *Charisma,* Aug. 1985, 31.

11. "WorldWide Charismatic Revival," *Charisma,* Aug. 1985, 40; PR, "Transcript of Remarks at the National Religious Broadcasters, Feb. 5, 1986," typed manuscript, 11, ROA.

12. "Acceptance of Charismatics," *Charisma,* Aug. 1985, 99. See this entire issue of *Charisma* for the ten "Decatrends" articles. This issue was a celebratory embrace of the new status charismatics had attained by the mid-1980s.

13. Edward E. Plowman, "Decade of the Tube," *Christianity Today,* Mar. 17, 1972, 41. Kenneth F. Bunting, "Christian Movement Reaches Millions on Air Waves," *Los Angeles Times,* Jan. 7, 1979, B1. "Decatrend 4," *Charisma,* Aug. 1985, 49.

14. For examples of the attention received by religious television see Michael Doan, "The 'Electronic Church' Spreads the Word," *U.S. News & World Report,* Aug. 23, 1984, 69; Jonathan Alter and Rich Thomas, "TV Time: Eyes on the Prize?" *Newsweek,* June 8, 1987, 72; "Stars of the Cathode Church," *Time,* Feb. 4, 1980, 64-65; Kenneth A. Briggs, "The Electronic Church Is Turning More People On," *New York Times,* Feb. 10, 1980, 21; Russell Chan-

dler, "The Electronic Church — Big time Religion," *Los Angeles Times,* Feb. 25, 1980, 1, 3, 13. See Russell Chandler, "Christian Right Advancing, Scholar Says," *New York Times,* Nov. 2, 1985, part II, 21. Ostling, "Power, Glory — and Politics," 62-69. John W. Jenkins, "Toward the Anti-Humanist New Christian Nation," *The Humanist,* July/Aug. 1981, 20.

15. Bruce and Michele Buckingham, "Trend Toward Christians in Politics," *Charisma,* Aug. 1985, 89. Howard Means, "God Is Back," *The Washingtonian,* Dec. 1986, 162.

16. Nick Cavnar, "Trend Toward Mature Unity," *Charisma,* Aug. 1985, 56-62.

17. S. David Moore, "The Shepherding Movement in Historical Perspective," M.A. thesis, School of Theology and Missions, Oral Roberts University, 1996, 8. Moore's thesis is an excellent and balanced account of the controversy. See also VS int., Dec. 10, 2007.

18. Keith Fournier int.; Derek Prince int.

19. Juan Carlos Ortiz with Jamie Buckingham, *Call to Discipleship* (Logos, 1975), 100. "Interview," *Logos,* Jan./Feb. 1980, 39, 40.

20. See Harold B. Smith et al., "America's Pentecostals: Where They Are Going," *Christianity Today,* Oct. 16, 1987, 26-30. Moore, "Shepherding Movement," 47-48. On the FGBMFI position, see Don J. Locke to Full Gospel Business Men's Fellowship International, Sept. 25, 1975, typed copy of memo with handwritten note from Locke to PR, ROA. PR, "Holy Spirit in the Now IV," typed manuscript of lecture delivered at Oral Roberts University, Oct. 24, 1974, ROA.

21. See "Charismatic Movement Is Facing Internal Discord Over Teaching Called 'Discipling,'" *New York Times,* Sept. 16, 1975, C31; Russell Chandler, "Charismatics Close 'Shepherding' Gap," *Los Angeles Times,* Mar. 20, 1976, A26. PR, memo to CBN Area Directors & All CBN Staff, May 20, 1975, ROA.

22. PR to Jay Bramlitt, May 22, 1975, ROA. See memo from Jim Bramlett to All CBN Staff, May 23, 1975, ROA. PR to Don Hawkinson, May 22, 1975, ROA. PR to John Gilman and Eric Aucoin, May 22, 1975, ROA.

23. PR to Bob Mumford, June 27, 1975, ROA.

24. PR to John Gilman and Eric Aucoin, copy to Bob Johnson, Jerry Rose, Neal Hail, Jerry Horstmann, S. Ditchfield, D. Rehberg, July 29, 1975, ROA.

25. PR to Brick Bradford, Aug. 1, 1975; PR to Dan Malachuk, July 31, 1975, ROA.

26. Moore, "Shepherding Movement," 52-58. Brick Bradford to "Co-Laborers in Christ," Sept. 16, 1975, ROA.

27. VS int.; SR int.; PR to E. M. Fjorbak, Nov. 24, 1975, ROA.

28. Bob Mumford to PR, Sept. 9, 1975, ROA.

29. PR to Charles V. Simpson, Sept. 11, 1975; see Simpson to PR, Aug. 28, 1975, ROA. PR to Bob Mumford, Sept. 15, 1975, ROA. PR to Mrs. W. G. Prewitt, Oct. 28, 1975, ROA. PR to Mike Lynch, Oct. 17, 1975; see also PR to Donald Dawson, Oct. 27, 1975; PR to Mrs. T. R. Klay, Sept. 25, 1975; PR to Mrs. Nancy Richards, Apr. 1, 1977; PR to Thomas Opie, Feb. 16, 1976, ROA.

30. PR to Mrs. James Gilmore, Nov. 15, 1977, ROA.

31. *Charisma,* Sept. 1978, 8. Several other publishers were initially somewhat sympathetic with the new movement. See Dan Malachuk, "Publisher's Preface," *Logos Journal,* Sept./Oct. 1975, 5; PR to Dan Malachuk, Sept. 9, 1975; Pat Robertson to Robert Walker, June 24, 1975, ROA. Stephen Strang, "Five Years of Renewal," *Charisma,* Sept. 1980, 29. See Bert Ghezzi, "Bob Mumford," *Charisma,* Aug. 1987, 26. Doris Conrad to PR, Mar. 28, 1980, ROA.

32. Joseph C. McKinney to PR, Nov. 18, 1980, ROA. Derek Prince to "Dear Brother," Mar. 28, 1984, ROA.

33. Kilian McDonnell, OSB, to PR, Feb. 20, 1979, ROA. PR to McDonnell, Mar. 28, 1979; see also BJ to Doris Conrad, Apr. 14, 1980; PR to Warren Black, Feb. 15, 1990; PR to Mrs. Susan M. Merola, Sept. 26, 1991, ROA. PR to A. R. Hill, May 15, 1987, ROA.

34. PR to Dr. R. Gottier et al., Aug. 30, 1982, ROA. For Robertson's later assessment of this memo, see PR int. by VS, Dec. 18, 2006, typed transcript in possession of author.

35. "Memorandum" from Bob Mumford, Nov. 1, 1989, ROA. Bob Mumford to PR, Dec. 11, 1989, ROA. PR to Bob Mumford, Dec. 21, 1989, ROA. Jamie Buckingham, "The End of the Discipleship Era," *Ministries Today,* Jan./Feb. 1990, 46-51.

36. Bob Mumford to PR, July 7, 1993, ROA. PR to Bob Mumford, July 9, 1989, ROA.

37. VS int., Apr. 4, 2007.

Notes to Chapter 4

1. PR int., Mar. 5, 2007. See PR to The Honorable Strom Thurmond, Apr. 11, 1995, ROA. Wesley G. Pippert, "TV on a Prayer," *Christian Life,* Apr. 1968, 35, 72.

2. "Powertime Speech," June 6, 1968, manuscript copy, ROA.

3. CBN news release, July 1967, RUA. CBN news release, Sept. 1968, RUA.

4. PR to Mrs. G. Malcolm Doolittle, Nov. 27, 1972, ROA.

5. PR to Donovan A. Dunn, Sept. 20, 1974, ROA. PR to John F. Steinbruck, Sept. 28, 1974, ROA.

6. "Why I Broke Silence on the Watergate Issue," *The Flame,* July 1974, 2. "God's Plan of Revival for this Nation and Its Leaders," *The Flame,* July 1974, 3. PR to Mrs. H. M. Jackson, Feb. 24, 1976, ROA.

7. PR to Eugene Wall, Mar. 12, 1976, ROA. Ralph Reed, *Active Faith* (New York: Free Press, 1996), 106. See Donald Moore, "Robertson Sees Political Stalemate," *Ledger-Star,* Nov. 29, 1984, clipping file, RUA.

8. PR, *The New World Order* (Dallas: Word Publishing, 1991), 104-5. PR int., Oct., 17, 2007.

9. *Pat Robertson's Perspective,* Feb. 1977, 1. *Pat Robertson's Perspective,* Jan.-Feb. 1978, 1.

10. *Pat Robertson's Perspective,* Nov.-Dec. 1978, 2-4.

11. PR to Joyce Walters, Oct. 29, 1979; see Joyce Walters to PR, Oct. 9, 1979, ROA. PR int., Oct. 17, 2007.

12. *Pat Robertson's Perspective,* Nov.-Dec. 1978, 3; for a general discussion of Robertson's reversal on Jimmy Carter, see Marley, *Pat Robertson,* 39-53. *Pat Robertson's Perspective,* Apr. 1979, 1. Robertson used *Perspective* to offer wide-ranging commentary on the prophetic significance of the Middle East. His interest "in prophetical events in Israel" was a lifelong constant, but it was piqued by three visits he made to Israel in 1975. While there, he had the "privilege of interviewing Israeli Prime Minister Yizhak Rabin." By 1977, the newsletter was filled with tidbits about Middle Eastern politics: "Sadat is a responsible leader." "Assad of Syria has been surprisingly moderate lately." "As I see it, peace is inevitable in that area now, as war was inevitable in 1967." "Keep your eyes on Iran. . . . A coup is not probable, but it could happen. . . . The Bible predicts this exact outcome." See "Ambassador Abba Eban Shares Israel's Concerns," *The Flame,* Dec. 1975, 3; *Pat Robertson's Perspective,* Mar. 1977, 1.

13. "Grateful Viewers Praise CBN's Anti-Abortion Stand," *The Flame,* Mar. 1975, 5. *Pat Robertson's Perspective,* June 1977, 1.

14. *Pat Robertson's Perspective,* May-June 1978, 4. "Preachers in Politics," *U.S. News & World Report,* Sept. 24, 1979, 37-41.

15. PR, "It's Time to Pray, America, for a Tricentennial Revival," *The Flame,* July-Aug. 1976, 2; also see PR, "My Reply to a Disheartened Man of God," *The Flame,* Sept. 1976, 2.

16. PR to Reverend John Gimenez, Feb. 13, 1979, ROA. CBN's financial contribution to Gimenez in the run-up to the rally was $60,000. See "Washington for Jesus" file, ROA. See PR to Reverend John Gimenez and Reverend John Gilman, Feb. 27, 1980; Memo from Bruce Evensen to PR, Oct. 18, 1979, ROA.

17. John Gimenez to PR, Nov. 13, 1978, ROA. John G. Turner, *Bill Bright & Campus Crusade for Christ* (Chapel Hill: University of North Carolina Press, 2008), 191. John Gimenez int., Nov. 10, 1981.

18. PR to Bishop J. O. Patterson, June 26, 1979, ROA. Patterson to John Gimenez, copy to PR, Jan. 24, 1980, ROA.

19. John Gimenez int.; PR to Jerry Falwell, Mar. 25, 1980, ROA.

20. "A Christian Declaration," *The Flame,* Feb. 1980, 2, 3. "Petition to the President and the Congress of the United States," copy in ROA.

21. See Michael Hernandez, "The Greatest Christian Media Event in History," *Tidewater Chronicle,* May 1980, 6. See "Schedule of Activities, Main Rally 'Washington for Jesus,'" undated typed schedule, ROA. See James M. Wall, "God's Piece of Cheese," *Christian Century,* Feb. 27, 1980, 219-20. Marjorie Hyer, "Support for Christian Rally Here Drifting Away," *Washington Post,* Mar. 15, 1980, B5. For press coverage of the event, see Ben A. Franklin, "200,000 March and Pray at Christian Rally in Capital," *New York Times,* Apr. 30, 1980, A1, A20; Penny Girard and Sean Dunnahoo, "Christian Rally Draws 200,000," *Los Angeles Times,* Apr. 30, 1980, 1, 17. Hernandez, "The Greatest Christian Media Event in History," 6.

22. Jesse Helms to PR, May 6, 1980; PR to Helms, May 13, 1980, ROA. PR to Robert Maddox, May 1, 1980, ROA. Maddox to PR, May 5, 1980, ROA.

23. Rev. John Gimenez to PR, July 23, 1980, ROA. Gimenez habitually overestimated the extent of Robertson's offers of assistance. CBN did extend some financial aid, but Robertson's intent was to give mostly advice and counsel. Robertson int., Nov. 17, 2007; John Gimenez to PR, June 1, 1981, ROA.

24. PR to Bill Bright, May 1, 1980, ROA. Bright to PR, May 12, 1980, ROA. PR to William L. Armstrong, May 13, 1980, ROA.

25. PR to Frank Kazzerski, Feb. 5, 1988, ROA. See PR, *The New Millennium* (Dallas: Word Publishing, 1990), 93.

26. Contemporary press coverage of the event may be found in Kenneth A. Briggs, "Evangelicals Hear Plea: Politics Now," *New York Times,* Aug. 24, 1980, 33. "Robertson Remarks," National Affairs Briefing, Aug. 21-22, typed manuscript, ROA. James Robinson was delighted that Robertson agreed to participate and thanked him profusely; see Robinson to PR, Sept. 9, 1980, ROA.

27. *Pat Robertson's Perspective,* Apr. 1980, 3.

28. *Pat Robertson's Perspective,* Sept. 1981, 1.

29. Marley, *Pat Robertson,* 79; see 74-83. See "Reagan Names Pat Robertson to Crime Victims' Task Force," *His People,* Sept. 1982, 8; Ronald Reagan to PR, June 30, 1982, ROA. When Nancy Reagan's mother died in 1987, Robertson wrote: "Dede and I have had you in our prayers constantly since learning of your operation last week. Now with the passing of Nancy's mother we want you both to know that we are continuing to lift you up in prayer...." PR to President and Mrs. Ronald Reagan, Oct. 27, 1987, ROA.

30. "As I View It," *The Flame,* Jan. 1980, 2; PR int., Oct. 17, 2007. Allan J. Mayer et al., "A Tide of Born-Again Politics," *Newsweek,* Sept. 15, 1980, 29, 36.

31. *Pat Robertson's Perspective,* Aug. 1980, 4. James Breig, "TV Religion: The Price is Right," *U.S. Catholic,* Aug. 1981, 11.

32. Frederick Talbott, "Pat Robertson Backs Away from Politics," Norfolk *Ledger-Star,* Sept. 30, 1980, C1. Marley, *Pat Robertson,* 107.

33. PR int., Oct. 17, 2007. David West int., Dec. 8, 1986. See Dudley Clendinen, "Spurred by White House Parley, TV Evangelists Spread Political Word," *Washington Post,* Sept. 10, 1984, B8.

34. Wall, "God's Piece of Cheese," 219. PR to John R. Craig, Sept. 5, 1980, ROA.

35. PR, "Remarks in Support of Senate Joint Resolution 199," Aug. 18, 1982, typed manuscript, ROA. See George Vecsey, "Clerics Back a School-Prayer Bill," *New York Times,* Jan. 24, 1980, 12.

36. "Statement Released to the Press on Mar. 20, 1984," typed manuscript, ROA. Newt Gingrich to PR, Feb. 24, 1994, ROA.

37. PR to Pete Wilson, Mar. 21, 1984; Jesse Helms to PR, Mar. 27, 1984; Helms to PR, Apr. 2, 1994; Richard Lugar to PR, Apr. 3, 1984, ROA.

38. For typical early articles, see James Mann and Sarah A. Peterson, "Preachers in Politics: Decisive Force in '80?" *U.S. News & World Report,* Sept. 15, 1980, 24-26; David Nyhan, "Reaching and Preaching to 5 Million Viewers," *Star Television,* July 6-12, 6F. See "Pat Robertson — 'Good Morning America' int. with David Hartman," Oct. 9, 1985, typed transcript, ROA.

39. "Pat Robertson — MacNeil/Lehrer News Hour int.," typed transcript, ROA. For sample articles during this pre-announcement period, see Richard M. Ostling et al., "Standing Tall for Moral Principles," *Time,* Feb. 17, 1986, 66-69; Marjorie Hyer, "Robertson Issues a Call to Arms," *Washington Post,* Feb. 8, 1986, C14; Godfrey Sperling Jr., "Pat Robertson's Candidacy," *Christian Science Monitor,* June 17, 1986, 19; "Painful Scrutiny for Robertson," *Newsweek,* Sept. 13, 1986, 48. Mortimer B. Zuckerman to PR, July 18, 1986, ROA; John W. Mashek, "From Pulpit or Podium, a Forceful Presence," *U.S. News & World Report,* July 14, 1986, 24, 25.

40. SerVaas and Stoddard, "CBN's Pat Robertson: White House Next?"

41. "Pat Robertson and Politics," *Christian Leader,* Aug. 1986, 44, see 44-46. See also Terry Lindvall, "C.T. at Thirty," *Christianity Today,* Oct. 17, 1986, 19-20; PR, "The American Church at the Crossroads," *Christian Herald,* Mar. 1985, 22-24. PR to George C. Walsh, Oct. 30, 1985, ROA. "Speech by PR to Concerned Women for America Second National Convention," Sept. 27, 1985, typed manuscript, 2, ROA. Diane Winston, *Dallas Times Herald,* May 30, 1987, n.p., copy in RUA.

42. Richard A. Viguerie to PR, Dec. 30, 1985; PR to Viguerie, Jan. 8, 1986, ROA. Paul Weyrich int., Dec. 16, 1986. Jack W. Germond and Jules Witcover, "The Miracle Worker," *The Washingtonian,* Nov. 1986, 119, 120.

43. Wm. F. Buckley Jr. to PR, Mar. 31, 1987, ROA. "Christ-Hunting," *National Review,* Oct. 10, 1986, 62. "Robertson's Way," *National Review,* Jan. 22, 1988, 19.

44. PR to Division/Department Heads, Oct. 8, 1981, RUA. Reed, *Active Faith,* 107. Management News, Public Relations Division, Sept. 25, 1986, ROA.

45. Rob Boston, *The Most Dangerous Man in America? Pat Robertson and the Rise of the Christian Coalition* (Amherst, N.Y.: Prometheus, 1996), 29, 30. CBN news release, April 6, 1988, ROA.

46. Marley, *Pat Robertson,* 73; see 68-85. Grumblings of concern were whispered inside the organization by the mid-1980s, though CBN leaders vehemently denied the allegations that the Freedom Council ever violated its legal and ethical guidelines. The strongest section of Marley's biography is his chapters on the campaign. The section is based on extensive research in the Americans for Robertson files at Regent University and is generally judicious and balanced; see 107-79.

47. PR to Allen Rundle, Feb. 26, 1987, ROA.

48. PR, "Freedom Council: 'Fully Within Legal and Ethical Guidelines,'" *Washington Post,* Apr. 30, 1988, A21. A full discussion of the charges against the Freedom Council may be found in Matthew C. Moen, *The Transformation of the Christian Right* (Tuscaloosa: University of Alabama Press, 1992).

49. PR int., Oct. 6, 2008. See Marley's highly skeptical description of these actions by the Freedom Council. He concluded that "the council's training sessions were little more than a front for Robertson's campaign." *Pat Robertson,* 108-9. The *Virginian-Pilot* was relentless in its reporting on CBN in general and the Freedom Council in particular in the mid-1980s. Robertson never forgave the local newspaper for its probing stories on his political campaign.

50. Paul Taylor, "Robertson Shows Strength in Michigan GOP Precinct Delegate Contest," *Washington Post,* May 38, 1986, A3.

51. Remer Tyson, "Robertson Presidential Campaign Is in High Gear," *Detroit Free Press,* Feb. 10, 1987, 8A; see David Waymire, "Robertson, Kemp Sweep GOP Support," *The Flint Journal,* Feb. 22, 1987, A1, A22; Tim Jones, "Bush Loses in Big Realignment, State GOP Conservatives Contend," *Detroit Free Press,* Feb. 22, 1987, 1A, 15A. See Eskelin, *Pat Robertson,* 14-15. "Bush Foes Win Fight, but War's Not Over," *Detroit Free Press,* Feb. 22, 1987, A3.

52. "The Effect of the Evangelicals," Feb. 27, 1987, clipping file, ROA. PR to Jesse Helms, Feb. 24, 1987, Americans for Robertson Archives, Box 181, RUA.

53. PR to John Doe, Mar. 12, 1986, ROA.

54. David West int. PR, "A New Vision for America," manuscript copy, Americans for Robertson files, RUA. Robertson's reflections on the campaign are detailed in PR, *The Plan* (Nashville: Thomas Nelson Publishers, 1989).

55. See Joseph Gray, "Policy Statement on Employee Political Activity," Management News, Sept. 26, 1986, ROA.

56. Richard L. Berke, "Gain for Pat Robertson in Later Michigan Tally," *New York Times,* Feb. 15, 1987, 16. Memo from Marlene Elwell to PR et al., Sept. 28, 1987, Americans for Robertson (AFR) files, RUA. PR, *The Plan,* 17, 109. Peter Goldman and Tom Mathews, *The Quest for the Presidency 1988* (New York: Simon & Schuster, 1989), 230, 244; see 230-49. Peter and Rochelle Schweizer, *The Bushes: Portrait of a Dynasty* (New York: Doubleday, 2004), 357. "Religion and Politics," Sept. 15, 1987, 14; see also Bill Petersen, "Robertson's Iowa Victory Shocks Rivals," *Washington Post,* Sept. 14, 1987, A8. "Straw-poll Win in Iowa Boosts Robertson Bid," *Virginian-Pilot,* Sept. 14, 1987, A1, A4.

57. For a report on the Hawaii race, see "Pat Robertson Pineapples Dole," Americans for Robertson press release, Feb. 5, 1988, AFR file, RUA.

58. Personal notes by the author, Sept. 15, 1987. See T. R. Reid, "Exuberant Robertson Announces He'll Seek GOP Nod," *Washington Post,* Sept. 16, 1987, A9; Wayne King, "Robertson, Displaying Mail, Says He Will Join '88 Race," *New York Times,* Sept. 16, 1987, 12; Richard Benedetto, "Pat Robertson's Race Is On," *USA Today,* Sept. 16, 1987, 4A.

59. Americans for Robertson press release, Oct. 29, 1987, AFR files, Box 442, RUA.

change with Jim Wallis, the editor of *Sojourners* magazine, in 1985. Robertson had a brief exchange with Wallis in 1981, when the National Council of Churches urged a letter-writing campaign supporting the leftist Democratic Revolutionary Front in El Salvador and a halt to American military aid to the government. Wallis framed what he considered to be a more balanced petition, soliciting signatures from evangelical leaders to a resolution urging the cessation of American aid to El Salvador in the absence of land-reform measures. After receiving a copy of the petition, Robertson wrote to his friend Richard Lovelace at Gordon-Conwell Theological Seminary, "Is Wallis confused . . . or a dedicated Marxist?" In the past, he had "engaged in brief dialogue with Jim Wallis and [had] been supportive of a number of things that they *[Sojourners]* do," but Wallis's proposed resolution seemed to him "a bit strange." It was clear to Robertson that "if the United States fails to act in El Salvador there is a very real possibility that all of Central America will fall to Marxism." Robertson was baffled by Wallis's thinking: "I find it difficult to make common cause with those who promote atheism as a state doctrine and who torture and imprison the people of God" (PR to Richard Lovelace, Apr. 1, ROA). Lovelace replied that he had signed the statement "with some reluctance" to give assurance that in "the U.S. people . . . will not stand for anticommunism which is not also anti-poverty and anti-terrorism." He assured Robertson that Wallis was not a Marxist (Lovelace to PR, May 4, ROA). In the fall of 1985 Robertson and Wallis had a public and private dialogue that clarified their foreign policy disagreements. The Oct. issue of *Sojourners* included a detailed eight-page article alleging that CBN was misleading "millions of well-meaning U.S. Christians" who donated "money that is serving, directly or indirectly, to sustain Nicaraguan *contras* and to perpetuate the *contra* terrorism that has killed or injured more than 8,000 Nicaraguans since 1982, more than half of them civilians" (Vicki Kemper, "In the Name of Relief," *Sojourners,* Oct. 1985, 13, see 13-20). In an editorial introduction, Wallis expressed reluctance about publishing an article so critical of another Christian organization, but he felt he had no recourse since neither CBN nor Robertson had responded to requests for information from *Sojourners.* Robertson did reply by mail after the article had gone to press, and Wallis reproduced a part of his reply in his editorial (Wallis, "Christians and Contras," *Sojourners,* Oct. 1985, 4). Wallis, however, did not print several paragraphs in Robertson's reply that explained much about Robertson's motivations. After protesting that CBN's relief efforts in Central America, basically food and medicine, were being distributed by the Knights of Malta, "one of the oldest and most respected charitable organizations in the world," Robertson insisted that the article had presented a very unbalanced picture of the situation in Nicaragua. He enclosed a tape from *The 700 Club:* "On last Thursday's show our news department broke the story about the Sandinistas planting mines, called 'bouncing betty's,' along the border with Honduras. These are aimed at civilians who attempt to flee the country. Our reporter interviewed several victims whose genitals had been blown away while they were crossing the border from Nicaragua to freedom. The tape speaks for itself. I have no more to say on the matter." Finally, Robertson asserted, he and Wallis were coming from different philosophical perspectives: "I know you and your associates are sympathetic to Marxism and so-called 'Liberation Theology.' You basically dislike free enterprise and favor collectivism. May I suggest sometime a Sabbatical in which you travel, as I have, to Afghan refugee camps, the Berlin Wall, persecuted churches in East Germany, churches made stables in China, camps in Sudan where starving people have journeyed on foot for eight weeks to escape Ethiopian Marxist soldiers who steal their food, the refugee camps in Honduras which house the victims of Marxism from Nicaragua" (PR to Wallis, Aug. 18,

ROA). Wallis thanked Robertson for the "cordial and respectful" response and hoped that they could continue an "honest dialogue." He urged a more thorough response from CBN on the specifics included in the article and responded to Robertson's other charges. He assured Robertson that he would personally look into the accusations against the Sandinista government, insisting that he had never been hesitant to criticize wrongdoing on their part. However, he continued to believe that "the exaggerated and even hysterical charges made against the Nicaraguan government by the Reagan administration and the political right wing in this country simply do not square with the facts." He would be glad to continue a dialogue with Robertson on that topic, "either off or on the record." He insisted that he favored neither "Marxism nor collectivism" but that he believed the American economic system had been captured by "large corporations which are accountable to no one." In its "focus on the poor," Wallis believed that Liberation Theology had made useful contributions, but he disagreed with other facets of "its more academic formulation." Finally, he deplored the injustices perpetrated by communist regimes, but he decried "right-wing Christians" who "rail against the Eastern bloc while defending regimes in Latin America" (Wallis to PR, Sept. 24, ROA). Robertson ended his side of the discussion with the assertion that Wallis was the idealist and he the pragmatist. Unwilling to extend the discussion further, Robertson concluded, "I suppose that the problem we encounter in the real world is the undermining of oppressive right-wing regimes in the name of human rights, which has the effect in the long run of installing an even more oppressive totalitarian government on the left. So rather than be utopian, we make the best of a bad situation. We often work with those who are amenable to reason, instead of those who, at least in modern history, have been the consistent and systematic oppressors of church and family." Robertson thought Wallis was too much of a moral purist to accept a pragmatic compromise that assumed it was all right to back "right-wing dictators" who were friendly to the United States (PR to Wallis, Oct. 2, ROA). Wallis, for his part, thought those dictators were likely to be more repressive than the left-wing alternatives, and that, in the end, "Christians must refuse to simply choose between communism or fascism." Wallis urged Robertson to continue the exchange, believing that the publication of their differences would be a "real contribution to the Christian community" (Wallis to PR, Oct. 25, Apr. 18, ROA). But Robertson had never been very interested in extended theoretical conversations, and at any rate by the spring of 1986 his political trajectory had made his schedule a bedlam of activity. Still, in later years, Robertson remained convinced that his views on the Nicaraguan conflict had been correct and that Wallis was a "Marxist . . . who was masquerading as something he was not" (PR int., Mar. 18, 2008). And whatever Wallis may have thought of Robertson's views, Robertson was not alone in the 1990s in challenging liberation theology's romanticizing of Latin American leftist revolutionaries.

75. *Pat Robertson's Perspective*, Mar.-Apr. 1991, 1.

76. "Sample Letter to Pastors," undated letter, AFR, Box 108, RUA.

77. "Christian Leaders Who Have Endorsed PR for President," typed list, AFR Papers, Box 253, RUA. J. O. Patterson to PR, Sept. 22, 1987, AFR Papers, Box 442, RUA; see also Patterson to PR, Feb. 11, 1987, AFR Papers, Box 181, RUA.

78. See letter from Pat Boone, July 18, 1987, AFR file, Box 253, RUA. Boone also contacted Hollywood celebrities seeking endorsements. Among the responses was a note from Jane Russell: "I have read, & listened to Pat Robertson for many years & have yet to disagree with him. I like his style & think he would make an excellent President." July 6, 1987, AFR files, RUA. Bill Bright to Boone, July 13, 1987, AFR files, Box 181, RUA. Bright to PR,

July 14, 1987, AFR files, Box 181, RUA. Billy Graham to PR, Oct. 11, 1985, AFR files, Box 181, RUA. "Newsmaker Saturday," CNN int. of PR, Sept. 13, 1986 by Charles Bierbauer and Tom Mintier, typed transcript, ROA. James Robinson to Boone, July 31, 1987, AFR files, RUA.

79. Mother M. Angelica to Pat Boone, July 8, 1987, AFR files, RUA. Dennis Bennett to Boone, July 9, 1987, AFR files, Box 181, RUA.

80. Diane Passno to Pat Boone, July 21, 1987, AFR files, Box 181, RUA. James M. Dobson to PR, Feb. 5, 1988, AFR files, Box 181, RUA. A memo was attached to the letter, dated Feb. 11, 1988.

81. Charles Colson to PR, June 30, 1987, AFR files, Box 181, RUA. PR to Colson, July 27, 1987, AFR files, Box 181, RUA; see, in the same box, Colson to PR, Aug. 12, 1987.

82. Beverly LaHaye to PR, Dec. 7, 1987; Tim LaHaye to PR, Dec. 4, 1987; PR to Tim LaHaye, Dec. 18, 1987, AFR files, Box 181, RUA.

83. PR to Marilyn P. Kelly, Nov. 17, 1988, ROA. Clarence and Edna Wakefield to PR, Nov. 27, 1988, AFR files, Box 442, RUA. See Justin Watson, *The Christian Coalition: Dreams of Restoration, Demands for Recognition* (New York: St. Martin's Press, 1997), 35-37.

84. Christopher Hitchens, "Minority Report," *The Nation,* Oct. 4, 1986, 303. Jim Castelli, "Pat Robertson: Extremist," 26-page paper published by People for the American Way, Aug. 1986, 1.

85. Goldman and Mathews, *The Quest for the Presidency,* 246. PR to Larry Grossman, Dec. 22, 1987, AFR Papers, Box 182, RUA. Robertson was livid that the piece had featured the remarks of Gerald Straub, a former employee who wrote an extremely critical book about him. Robertson wrote: "This man was fired by our organization for multiple acts of adultery followed by blatant lying. He abandoned his . . . wife and children. Until a few weeks ago, his wife was continuously employed by CBN. . . . His publisher represents the humanist organization which is comprised of those who subscribe to atheism. There is nothing factual or objective in what this man has to say." Connie Snapp to Sanda Rowe, Apr. 20, 1987; PR to Frank Batten, Apr. 20, 1987; AFR Papers, Box 182, RUA. Robertson's disdain for the local newspaper never relented. He has refused to read the paper in the two decades after his political campaign.

86. A scholarly analysis of this issue is Stephen D. Johnson et al., "Pat Robertson: Who Supported His Candidacy for President?" *Journal for the Scientific Study of Religion* 1989, no. 4 (1989): 387-99. "Pat Robertson — MacNeil/Lehrer News Hour int.," Nov. 11, 1985, typed transcript, ROA. "Transcript," Face the Nation, Aug. 17, 1986, 4, 5, ROA. "Transcript," Face the Nation, Aug. 17, 1986, 1, ROA. "Pat Robertson — 'Good Morning America' int. with David Hartman," Oct. 9, 1985, typed transcript, ROA.

87. "Pat Robertson — MacNeil/Lehrer News Hour int." Goldman and Mathews, *The Quest for the Presidency,* 246. Marley, *Pat Robertson,* 128, 119. Sara Diamond wrote: "Throughout the campaign, the mainstream press seemed to have declared open season on Robertson. They had plenty of ammunition but the shots they fired were largely trivial." *Spiritual Warfare,* 76.

88. Castelli, "Pat Robertson: Extremist," 7; see 1-13. PR, *The Plan,* 62-64. David West int.

89. "Transcript of Remarks at the New Orleans Press Conference, Regency Hyatt House, September 1986," typed manuscript, ROA. Berger, "Who's Afraid of Uncle Pat?" 21.

90. James M. Wall, "Robertson Is Working on the 'Wacko Factor,'" *Christian Century,* July 16-23, 1986, 635, 636. Wall, "The Media Want Faith Checked at the Door," *Christian Century,* Mar. 2, 1988, 203, 204. Sam Washburn, "Letters," *Christian Century,* May 11, 1988, 484.

91. Calvin Trillin, "Uncivil Liberties," *The Nation,* Mar. 19, 1988, 366. PR to Ruth E. Hall, Nov. 23, 1988, ROA.

92. See "Robertson Quits Ministry for '88 Race," *Washington Post,* Sept. 30, 1987, A6. PR to Mrs. Dorothy Ferguson, Sept. 28, 1987, ROA. Donald J. Dunlap to PR, Oct. 12, 1987, AFR Archives, Box 442, RUA. "Ordination," form letter from PR dated Aug. 1988, ROA.

93. James M. Wall, "Politics, Not Religion, Trips Up Robertson," *Christian Century,* Apr. 6, 1988, 331, 332.

94. See John W. Anderson, "A Heavenly Home for TV Preachers," *The Nation,* Mar. 12, 1988, 338. GR int., Oct. 10, 2008. Stephen Strang, "CBN's New Boss," *Charisma & Christian Life,* Jan. 1988, 74.

95. "Before the Federal Election Commission," copy of "Affidavit of Mr. M. G. Robertson," AFR Papers, Box 182, RUA.

96. For Robertson's post-election assessment of the McCloskey affair, see Robertson, *The Plan,* 117-23. Marley, *Pat Robertson,* 6. Alec Foege cited letters from Senator Robertson which he believed proved that Pat received "preferential treatment." In one, the senator thanked General Lemuel Shepherd for "your encouraging message concerning Pat" which gave assurance that he would "get some more training before engaging in combat." See Alec Foege, *The Empire God Built* (New York: John Wiley & Sons, Inc., 1996), 220, 221.

97. For various accounts of the affair, see Eskelin, *Pat Robertson,* 20; Donovan, *Pat Robertson,* 21-24.

98. April Witt, "Robertson Fighting for Honor," *The Virginian Pilot and Ledger Star,* Apr. 22, 1987, A3. For a few examples of the local paper's coverage, see James Rowley, "Robertson Used Influence, Korea Vets Claim in Papers," A1; Ellen Whitford, "Robertson Challenges Immunity," June 20, 1987, A5; April Witt, "1 Robertson Suit Stands, 1 Dismissed," July 25, 1987, A5.

99. See copy of handwritten notes by Barbara Gattullo entitled "Analysis to Allan," May 3, 1988, AFR Papers, RUA. PR int., Oct. 17, 2007.

100. Wayne King, "Robertson Shifts Political Tack in Bid to Steer Clear of Evangelists' Battles," *New York Times,* Mar. 29, 1987, 19.

101. "Robertson's Bakker Connection," *Washington Post,* Feb. 6, 1988, G1, 4, 5; Jimmy Swaggart to Robert Hartley, Aug. 13, 1986; Hartley to PR, Aug. 18, 1986; PR to Hartley, Aug. 25, 1986, ROA. Jimmy Swaggart, "The Coming Kingdom," *The Evangelist,* Sept. 1986, 4-12.

102. Robert Hartley to Jimmy Swaggart Ministries, Attn. Bonnie Wiser, Sept. 5, 1986; see Hartley to Dr. PR, Sept. 10, 1986, ROA. "Transcript of Remarks at the New Orleans Press Conference, Regency Hyatt House, September 1986," typed manuscript, ROA. PR int., Mar. 19, 2008.

103. Jimmy Swaggart to PR, Sept. 10, 1986, ROA.

104. TR to Jimmy Swaggart, Apr. 15, 1988; Swaggart to PR, Apr. 19, 1988; Swaggart to PR, May 25, 1988, ROA.

105. See Col. Emile M. Weber to Mr. Larry King, Oct. 19, 1989; Benita S. Baird to PR, Oct. 30, 1989; PR to Baird, Oct. 31, 1989; Jimmy Swaggart to PR, Nov. 7, 1989; PR to Baird, Nov. 15, 1989, ROA.

106. Robin Toner, "Robertson Hints at Bush Link to Disclosures on Swaggart," *New York Times,* Feb. 24, 1988, A18. Robertson int., Oct. 17, 2007. PR to Frank Batten, Oct. 20, 1987, AFR files, Box 442, RUA. See Boston, *Most Dangerous Man,* 45.

107. Robertson int., Oct. 17, 2007.

108. See Robertson, *The Plan,* 108-17, 142, 144-46. For a broad scholarly assessment of

the 1988 Super Tuesday primaries, see Barbara Norrander, *Super Tuesday* (Lexington: University of Kentucky Press, 1992). Kim A. Lawton, "Pat's Big Surprise: The Army Is Still Invisible," *Christianity Today,* Apr. 8, 1988, 44.

109. Norrander, *Super Tuesday,* 133, 163.

110. Clyde Wilcox, "Religion and the Preacher Vote in the South: Sources of Support for Jackson and Robertson in Southern Primaries," *Sociological Analysis* 53:3 (1992): 323; see 323-31; Norrander, *Super Tuesday,* 131-33; John C. Green, "PR and the Latest Crusade: Religious Resources and the 1988 Presidential Campaign," *Social Science Quarterly,* Mar. 1993, 157-68; John C. Green and James L. Guth, "The Christian Right in the Republican Party: The Case of PR's Supporters," *The Journal of Politics* 30 (1988): 150-65; Corwin E. Smidt and James M. Penning, "Religious Self-Identifications and Support for Robertson: An Analysis of Delegates to the 1988 Michigan Republican State Convention," *Review of Religious Research,* June 1991, 321-36. Clyde Wilcox, "Blacks and the New Christian Right: Support for the Moral Majority and Pat Robertson Among Washington, D.C. Blacks," *Review of Religious Research,* Sept. 1990, 43-55. John C. Green, "Pat Robertson and the Latest Crusade: Religious Resources and the 1988 Presidential Campaign," *Social Science Quarterly,* Mar. 1993, 165. Johnson et al., "Pat Robertson: Who Supported His Candidacy for President?" 397.

111. PR to Carol J. Clemente, July 18, 1988, AFR Papers, RUA.

112. Press release, "Allan Sutherlin — Political Director/Campaign Manager," AFR Papers, RUA. Undated fundraising letter signed by Dede Robertson, RUA. James A. Barnes, "Blessing Bush," *National Journal,* Apr. 9, 1988, 939. "Republican National Convention Committee on Resolutions," undated typed list, AFR Papers, RUA.

113. "Pat Robertson — Statement Outline — Monday, May 16, 1988," typed copy, AFR Papers, RUA.

114. David West int.; Frank J. Fahrenkopf, Jr., to PR, May 23, 1988; see also PR to Fahrenkopf, May 31, 1988, AFR Papers, Box 181, RUA. "Agreement Between the Republican National Committee and Americans for Robertson, Inc.," typed manuscript dated June 29, 1988, AFR Papers, RUA. Allan Sutherlin to PR, June 24, 1988, AFR Papers, Box 442, RUA.

115. Allan R. Sutherlin to Lee Atwater, Sept. 27, 1988; PR to Bill Green, Sept. 23, 1988, AFR Papers, Box 442, RUA.

116. Press release, "PR Suspends Campaign," May 16, 1988, AFR Papers, RUA.

117. "Americans for Robertson Delegate Apportionment," Aug. 12, 1988; untitled form letter signed by PR, Aug. 5, 1988; "Robertson Travel Schedule, New Orleans, Louisiana, Republican National Convention," typed draft dated Aug. 11, 1988; Allan Sutherlin to PR, June 2, 1968, AFR Papers, Box 314, RUA.

118. Robertson, *The Plan,* 16. All of the speakers received detailed instructions from Convention Director Fred Malek about the themes to be included in their addresses. See Malek to PR, Aug. 4, 1988; Jack Burgess to PR, July 28, 1988; Allan Sutherlin to PR, June 2, 1968, AFR Papers, Box 314, RUA. Robertson, *The Plan,* 202; see 193-202.

119. PR to George Bush, Aug. 26, 1988, ROA. Robertson, *The Plan,* 167-68.

120. This is the most common description offered by all of the members of the family. Both Dede Robertson and Anne LeBlanc traveled extensively during the campaign. Dede thought the whole experience was "horrible" and felt that some of the leaders of the campaign staff were "very self-seeking" and "untrustworthy." See DR and AL int. PR to Margaret E. Armbrester, July 18, 1988, letter in possession of the author. Undated fundraising letter signed by Dede Robertson, RUA. See Robertson, *The Plan,* 143-47, 167-71.

121. PR to Bob Dole, June 30, 1988; Jack Kemp to PR, June 5, 1987, AFR Papers, Box 181,

RUA. Handwritten note on stationery of the Secretary of Housing and Urban Development signed "Jack" and addressed to "Pat," undated, ROA. George Bush to PR, Oct. 24, 1988, ROA.

122. Robertson, *The Plan*, 12. PR to Mrs. Kenneth Finch, Apr. 15, 1991, ROA. This question is the focus of Robertson's book, *The Plan*. BJ to Carl Zigenfuss, Jan. 9, 1997, ROA.

123. PR int., Mar. 5, 2007. Dan Gilgoff, *The Jesus Machine* (New York: St. Martin's Griffin, 2007), 91, 92.

Notes to Chapter 5

1. "Pat Robertson Suspends Campaign," AFR press release, May 16, 1988, AFR Papers, RUA.

2. *Pat Robertson's Perspective*, Mar. 1989, 4, 5; Sept. 1989, 6, 7. Reed, *Active Faith*, 16.

3. GGC to author, email with notes by PR, June 23, 2009.

4. GGC to author, email with notes by PR, June 23, 2009.

5. GGC to author, email with notes by PR, June 23, 2009.

6. GGC to author, email with notes by PR, June 23, 2009.

7. See Reed, *Active Faith*, 127-29; RR int., May 23, 2007.

8. RR int., May 23, 2007.

9. "National Political Organization," Memo from Ralph Reed to PR, Sept. 26, 1989, Christian Coalition file, ROA.

10. "National Political Organization"; RR int., May 23, 2007.

11. "The Christian Coalition: A Plan for Action," proposal submitted by Ralph Reed Oct. 24, 1989, Christian Coalition file, ROA.

12. RR int., May 23, 2007. PR, "Remarks to Road to Victory," Sept. 12, 1997, typed manuscript, ROA. RR int., May 23, 2007. For an extensive description of the early days of the Christian Coalition, see Reed, *Active Faith*, 104-50.

13. RR, *Active Faith*, 11-14. See Beverly LaHaye to PR, Apr. 19, 1990; PR to LaHaye, Apr. 24, 1990, ROA. See RR, *Active Faith*, 13-17.

14. Tom Minnery to PR, May 18, 1990, ROA. PR to Tom Minnery, May 22, 1990, ROA. RR int., May 23, 2007. A good discussion of the "sibling rivalries" encountered by Bill Bright in the early years of his Campus Crusade for Christ may be found in Turner, *Bill Bright and Campus Crusade for Christ*, 69-92.

15. Mark DeMoss to PR, Dec. 7, 1989, ROA.

16. Reed, *Active Faith*, 107; see Reed's description of the origins and tactics of the Moral Majority, 108-18.

17. *Pat Robertson's Perspective*, Fall 1980, 3. Memo from Roy Harrelson to BJ, Oct. 28, 1981, ROA. "Robertson Calls Moral Majority a 'Vastly Overrated' Group," Newsletter of the EP News Service, Mar. 20, 1982. Rick McKay, "Religious Right Reviving Gospel of Political Activism," *Atlanta Constitution*, Sept. 11, 1992, NewsBank NewsFile Collection.

18. Among the many examinations of the demise of the Moral Majority, see Jeffrey K. Hadden, Anson Shupe, James Hawdon, and Kenneth Martin, "Why Jerry Falwell Killed the Moral Majority," in Marshall W. Fishwick, *The God Pumpers: Religion in the Electronic Age* (Bowling Green, Ohio: Bowling Green State University Popular Press, 1987), 101-15; Ted G. Jelen and Clyde Wilcox, "The Effects of Religious Self-Identification on Support for the New Christian Right," *Social Science Journal* 2 (1992): 199-211; Peter Steinfels, "There's Nothing Monolithic about Evangelical Politics," *New York Times*, Mar. 28, 1988, A8.

19. David Von Drehle, "Life of the Grand Old Party," *Washington Post,* Aug. 14, 1994, A1. Drew Digby, "Falwell Political Output Limited," *The News and Daily Advance* (Lynchburg, Virginia), Sept. 6, 1987, A6. RR, *Active Faith,* 120-23. See Dan Gilgoff's description of the philosophical and tactical differences between the Moral Majority and the Christian Co-alition, *The Jesus Machine,* 95, 96.

20. Richard N. Ostling, "A Jerry Built Coalition Regroups," *Time,* Nov. 16, 1987, 68. Joe Maxwell, "Liberty U. Weathers Debt Crisis," *Christianity Today,* Feb. 10, 1992, 46.

21. R. Mark DeMoss to Dr. Ralph Reed, Aug. 19,1994, ROA.

22. "Statement from PR Regarding the Passing of Jerry Falwell," www.CBN.com, May 29, 2007.

23. Watson, *The Christian Coalition,* 53-55. Watson's book is the best general account of the glory years of the Christian Coalition.

24. PR to Jack Doussard, June 30, 1994, ROA. See James M. Penning, "Pat Robertson and the GOP: 1988 and Beyond," *Sociology of Religion* 3 (1994): 327-44; Howard Fineman, "God and the Grassroots," *Newsweek,* Nov. 8, 1993, 42-45; Kim A. Lawton, "The New Face(s) of the Religious Right," *Christianity Today,* July 20, 1992, 42-45. Sam Mayo to PR, Nov. 4, 1992, ROA.

25. See *Pat Robertson's Perspective,* Nov.-Dec. 1990; Oct.-Nov. 1991. George Bush to PR, Jan. 10, 1991; Bush to PR, Mar. 3, 1992, ROA. Handwritten notation: "Your letter to the voters was really great." Bush betrayed great personal warmth in brief notes, often handwritten, on stationery from Camp David, Air Force One, and Walker's Point in Kennebunkport. See George Bush to PR, Aug. 8, 1992; Bush to PR, Sept. 12, 1992, ROA.

26. RR to Peyton E. Pitts, Apr. 7, 1992; RR to Francis Chadwick, Dec. 9, 1991, ROA.

27. "Republicans Court Religious Right," *Christian Century,* Aug. 26-Sept. 2, 1992, 770. See www.PatRobertson.com, Sept. 2, 2008. David Kuo, *Tempting Faith* (New York: Free Press, 2006), 40.

28. "Religious Right Rallies," Associated Press News Release, News Bank NewsFile Collection, www.mhtml:file://E:politics.6.mht. Steve Ginsburg et al., eds., "NBC News Meet the Press," Sept. 27, 1992, edited transcript, ROA. Roy Beck, "Washington's Profamily Activists," *Christianity Today,* Nov. 9, 1992, 21.

29. *The Robertson Report,* Sept. 17, 1992; Sept. 23, 1992, ROA. "Building a Christian G.O.P.," *Harper's,* Jan. 1993, 26, 27.

30. *Pat Robertson's Perspective,* July-Aug. 1992, 1; Nov.-Dec. 1992, 3, 5.

31. *Pat Robertson's Perspective,* Nov.-Dec. 1992; *The Robertson Report,* Jan. 3, 1993; Dec. 23, 1992. PR to RR, Apr. 2, 1993, ROA.

32. RR int., Apr. 23, 2007. PR, *The Turning Tide* (Dallas: Word Publishing, 1993), 10, 11. PR to Dan Quayle, Jan. 26, 1994, ROA. Linda Feldmann, "The Kingdom and the Clout of Ralph Reed," *Christian Science Monitor,* Sept. 8, 1985, 10. See Watson, *Christian Coalition,* 53-55.

33. PR to RR, Dec. 19, 1995, ROA. RR int., Sept. 10, 2007.

34. Feldmann, "The Kingdom and the Clout of Ralph Reed," 10. "Building a Christian G.O.P.," 26. PR to Daniel Jay Bush, Dec. 5, 1995, ROA.

35. For Reed's background, see RR, *Active Faith,* 18-36. Paul Weyrich to PR, Apr. 2, 1990, RR int., Apr. 23, 2007 and Sept. 10, 2007. Undated fundraising letter signed by PR; Let-ter from PR to Christian Coalition contributors, June 23, 1994, ROA.

36. Michael Kagay, "Growth Area Seen for Religious Right," *New York Times,* Aug. 10, 1996, 9. Handwritten comments on Ben Hart to BJ, Apr. 5, 1993; RR to PR, Apr. 6, 1993, ROA.

37. RR int., Apr. 23, 2007. Lamar Alexander to PR, June 25, 1992; Guy Milner to PR, Feb.

21, 1994; George Allen to PR, Jan. 12, 1993, ROA. See John Dillin, "Role of Religion Grabs Spotlight in Heated Virginia Governor's Race," *Christian Science Monitor,* Oct. 29, 1993, 2. John Talent to PR, n.d. [1992]; Doug Wead to PR, Nov. 23, 1992; Ben McEwen to PR, Nov. 18, 1992; Bill Paxon to PR, Nov. 17, 1992; John Ashcroft to PR, Dec. 4, 1994, ROA. Robertson's files contain scores of letters from Republican politicians expressing their thanks and welcoming his advice. Along with Ashcroft, his favorite insider in the Republican Party was probably Dan Quayle. See PR to Dan Quayle, Oct. 1, 1992; Quayle to PR, Oct. 10, 1992; PR to Quayle, Jan. 26, 1994, ROA. Dick Armey to Dick Weinhold, copy to PR, June 4, 1992; Haley Barbour to PR, Apr. 5, 1996; PR to Barbour, Apr. 18, 1996, ROA.

38. Von Drehle, "Life of the Grand Old Party," A1. Arlen Specter to PR, Mar. 19, 1993; PR to Specter, Mar. 31, 1993, ROA. Robertson had a lifelong testy, but generally respectful, relationship with Specter. He bristled at Specter's remark in March 1995 that implied that Robertson in a 1991 Larry King interview had stated that he believed there was no constitutional doctrine of separation of church and state. On *The 700 Club* Robertson responded: "He was a year behind me at Yale Law School. He should have learned better. . . . 'I believe absolutely in the separation of church and state.' . . . Mr. Specter, if you're going to run for president, please tell the truth." "PR Responding to Sen. Arlen Specter's Comments, The 700 Club, Mar. 30, 1995," typed copy of Robertson comments, ROA; see PR to Lawrence Auster, May 18, 1995. In October 1995 Robertson again charged Specter with distorting his position on separation of church and state: "If you are not able to have the intellectual honesty to differentiate buzz words from constitutional reality, then you have no business holding a high public office. However, I think better of you, and therefore I am sure that in future discussions between us you will evidence the intellectual honesty which has been the hallmark of your distinguished public career." PR to Specter, Oct. 19, 1995, ROA. In spite of such testy exchanges, through the years the two remained friends. After Specter appeared on *The 700 Club* in 2001, CBN was forced to craft a response for "giving air time to a strong prodeath Senator." While acknowledging that Specter was "completely wrong" about abortion, a ministry representative defensively pointed out that Specter had often supported profamily initiatives "in keeping with our traditional values and the benefit of this nation." "Let's continue to make him a prayer focus on the life issue." Andy Freeman to John Scherer, CBN memo, Mar. 15, 2001, ROA.

39. "Onward, Christian Coalition Soldiers," Richmond *Times Dispatch,* May 17, 1995, 10. Steven V. Roberts et al., "Church Meets State," *U.S. News & World Report,* Apr. 24, 1995, 26.

40. David Frum, "Dead Wrong," *New Republic,* Sept. 12, 1994, 17-20. Edd Doerr, "Pat's Patsy Political Program," *Humanist,* Nov./Dec. 1995, 39.

41. Von Drehle, "Life of the Grand Old Party," A1. Gayle White, "The Might's Right," *Atlanta Journal-Constitution,* Jan. 15, 1995, A1.

42. RR, *Active Faith,* 211. Reed specifically repudiated Christian Reconstructionist theology: "Reconstructionism is an authoritarian ideology that threatens the most basic civil liberties of a free and democratic society," 261; see 260-62.

43. Keith Fournier int., Dec. 6, 2007. *Pat Robertson's Perspective,* Mid-July 1979, 3. PR to Cristina "Ting" Hernandez, Apr. 8, 1994; see PR to David L. Drye, Feb. 10, 1994, ROA. Von Drehle, "Life of the Grand Old Party," A1.

44. Kenneth L. Woodward and Patrick Rogers, "Allies in a Cultural War," *Newsweek,* Nov. 8, 1993, 45, 46. PR to John Cardinal O'Connor, June 10, 1993, ROA.

45. RR to Michael Scanlan, July 13, 1993, ROA. Deborah Kovach Caldwell, "Christian

Coalition Courts Conservative Catholics," *Dallas Morning News,* Jan. 13, 1996, 1G. See Esther Diskin, "Reed Seeks to Forge Alliance with Catholics," *The Virginian-Pilot,* Sept. 4, 1995, A1, A5.

46. "Alliance for Regress," *Commonweal,* May 21, 1993, 3. "The Real Rainbow Coalition," *National Review,* July 19, 1993, 18-20. Ralph Reed unsuccessfully attempted to recruit Cardinal O'Connor to address the "third annual Road to Victory Conference and Strategy Briefing" in Washington. He complimented the cardinal for his "leadership on behalf of our shared values." RR to O'Connor, Apr. 8, 1993, ROA. RR int., Sept. 9, 2007. RR, *Active Faith,* 216; see 214-24. Keith Fournier int., Dec. 6, 2007.

47. PR, *The Turning Tide,* 279. See Boston, *The Most Dangerous Man,* 158, 159.

48. *Contract with the American Family,* (Nashville: Moorings, 1995). For a brief summary of the issues embraced by the religious right, see Roberts et al., "Church Meets State," 31, 32. A sweeping summary of the early positions of the Christian Coalition may be found in "Questions for New York Times Editorial Board Meeting June 16, 1993," typed manuscript, ROA. This document gives PR's responses to fourteen questions posed by the *Times.* PR to Mel Cruz, May 11, 1995, ROA. Gilgoff, *The Jesus Machine,* 101.

49. RR, "A Wider Net," *Policy Review,* Summer 1993, 31-35. Von Drehle, "Life of the Grand Old Party," A1. RR int., Sept. 10, 2007.

50. Martin Mawyer, "God and the GOP," *Washington Post,* Sept. 26, 1993, C1, C4. Jesse Helms to PR, Sept. 28, 1993; RR to Jesse Helms, Nov. 1, 1993, ROA.

51. RR, *Active Faith,* 25, 26.

52. Robert K. Dornan to PR, May 16, 1996; RR to James Dobson, Oct. 11, 1995; Dobson to RR, Oct. 9, 1995, ROA. For a description of Dobson's reaction to Reed's book, see Kuo, *Tempting Faith,* 74-78. PR to Dobson, May 9, 1996; Dobson to PR, May 8, 1986; Dobson to PR, May 7, 1996; Paul Weyrich to PR, May 8, 1996, ROA. Robertson repeatedly assured supporters that the Christian Coalition remained orthodox on abortion. He wrote in 1994: "The Christian Coalition has *never* advocated that the Republican Party compromise its position on the protection of innocent life." PR to Donald W. Riche, Aug. 3, 1994, ROA.

53. Watson, *The Christian Coalition,* 77; see 76-80. PR to RR, Jan. 25, 1996, ROA. RR int., Apr. 23, 2007. RR, *Active Faith,* vii.

54. RR int., Sept. 10, 2008. PR int., Sept. 17, 2008. RR int., Sept. 10, 2008.

55. Lawrence Auster to PR, May 1, 1995. See also Auster to RR, Apr. 29, 1995, ROA. "Researching Religious Trends," *Christian Century,* Dec. 8, 1993, 1232. Strom Thurmond to PR, Sept. 21, 1994, ROA; this memo includes the senator's "talking points" against the GATT treaty. PR int., Sept. 17, 2007. See "Evans & Novak," transcript of int., Apr. 15, 1995, 5, copy in ROA. PR to Robert Weedy, May 10, 1994, ROA. Teresa Malcolm, "Robertson Wants 'a Winner,'" *National Catholic Reporter,* Oct. 3, 1997, 6.

56. Undated fundraising letter from PR, ROA. Linda Feldmann, "The Kingdom and the Clout of Ralph Reed," 10. PR to Tracy B. Hall, Oct. 1, 1996; PR to Bob Dole, June 3, 1999, ROA. Dole had been offended by several public statements by Robertson, particularly concerning his moderate position on abortion. See Dole to PR, May 26, 1999, ROA. In his response Robertson was apologetic to his respected friend: "Please forgive me if remarks that I have made have either been taken out of context or have not been carefully thought through." "PR Post-Election Analysis Broadcast on the 700 Club," CBN News Release, ROA.

57. Dan Balz, "Ralph Reed Wants to Take Movement to New Political Level," *Washington Post,* Apr. 25, 1997, A11. Esther Diskin, "Christian Coalition Chief Resigning," *The Virginian-Pilot,* Apr. 24, 1997, A1, A8. RR int., Sept. 10, 2007.

58. Dick Weinhold to PR, Feb. 3, 1997, ROA.

59. "Statement by Ralph Reed, Jr., Apr. 23, 1997," copy of fax to PR, ROA. "Statement by Pat Robertson, Gratitude and Support for Ralph Reed," Apr. 23, 1997, ROA.

60. RR int., Sept. 10, 2008.

61. June 5, 1998, A14. RR int., Sept. 10, 2008.

62. "Statement by Pat Robertson, Gratitude and Support for Ralph Reed." Gilgoff, *The Jesus Machine,* 107; see 106-37. Gilgoff's lucid description of the rise of "purists" such as James Dobson to leadership of the pro-family movement after the resignation of Reed more or less tells that story from Dobson's perspective. No doubt there was a steady transfer of clout from the Christian Coalition to Focus on the Family, but it did not happen overnight. The Coalition remained a respected presence in Washington through the election of 2004. Tony Wharton, "Coalition Ends Year with Layoffs," *The Virginian-Pilot,* Dec. 20, 1997, B3.

63. See Ramesh Ponnuru, "Fall from Grace," *National Review,* May 18, 1998, 40-42. See "Road to Victory '98, Agenda for Pat and Dede Robertson," printed schedule; Christian Coalition press release, Sept. 21, 1999, ROA. Robertson sustained a cozy personal relationship with many of the conservative Republican leaders in Washington and communicated with them both by telephone and by mail. See, for instance, PR to Tom DeLay, June 23, 2000, ROA. Probably Robertson's closest personal relationship was with Senator John Ashcroft. He was a strong supporter during Ashcroft's senate career. After Ashcroft's confirmation as attorney general, he wrote to Robertson: "You are a stalwart friend, and a powerful defender. Thank you for all your help in preparing the way to Senate confirmation!" Ashcroft to PR, Jan. 29, 2001, framed letter in office of PR. Robertson asked Ashcroft to join the Board of Trustees of Regent University in 1999, but because of his reelection campaign the senator declined. He did later join the faculty of the university's law school. See Ashcroft to PR, Aug. 2, 1999, ROA. Ashcroft's lifelong identification with the Assemblies of God, the moderate Pentecostal denomination that Robertson knew and respected, made their personal affinity complete.

64. Jean Torkelson, "Religious Group Picks Coloradan," *Rocky Mountain News,* June 12, 1997, 5A. Barbara A. Serrano, "What Shaped These NW Republicans?" *Seattle Times,* June 12, 1997, A2. See Tony Wharton, "Coalition's Leadership Will be a Team of 2," *The Virginian-Pilot,* June 13, 1997, A1, A14. Robertson had known Hodel for many years. Both campaigned for George Bush in South Carolina in 1988 after Robertson had dropped out of the race. Robertson wrote to Hodel: "The Bush campaign must realize you would make an exceptional Vice President. Your stand for the conservative issues that are so close to my heart was greatly evident in Charleston. It is a privilege to be in association with you." PR to Hodel, Aug. 9, 1988, ROA.

65. Copy of *Fortune* article from Netscape website, Nov. 17, 1998, ROA. Sent as memo from Don Hodel to PR, Nov. 19, 1998. Lisa Caruso, "Christian Groups Differ on Tactics," *National Journal,* July 7, 1998, 5, 6; Hodel note dated July 7, 1998, attached, ROA.

66. Ceci Connolly, "Political Machine Loses Wheel," *Washington Post,* Sept. 12, 1997, A4.

67. RR to Friends and Supporters of the Christian Coalition, July 30, 1996; Fax Transmittal Sheet, July 31, 1996, BJ to PR, July 31, 1996. Johnson wrote: "Today, Jerry Falwell called about the letter the National Council of Churches is circulating. He said this is being universally mailed. He sees this letter as a result of the FEC action against Christian Coalition, and plans to go public with a statement of his own. If you want to talk to Jerry, you can

reach him at [redacted] any time" (ROA). Barry W. Lynn to Dear Religious Leader, undated letter, copy dated Sept. 23, 1998, addressed to "Calvary Church," ROA. For a description of the IRS episode from the perspective of People for the American Way, see Robert Boston, *Close Encounters with the Religious Right* (Amherst, N.Y.: Prometheus Books, 2000), 68-75.

68. Christian Coalition news release, July 30, 1996, ROA. Bill Miller and Susan B. Glasser, "A Victory for Christian Coalition," *Washington Post,* Aug. 3, 1999, A1.

69. Warren Fiske, "Revoke Christian Coalition's Tax-Exempt Status, 2 Groups Say," *The Virginian-Pilot,* Sept. 18, 1998, A10. See Jay Sekulow to PR et al. [minutes of Mar. 30, 1999, Christian Coalition Directors Meeting]; "Christian Coalition Announces Sweeping Reorganization," Christian Coalition news release, June 10, 1999, ROA; Thomas B. Edsall, "Christian Coalition Denied Tax-Exempt Status, Will Reorganize," *Washington Post,* June 11, 1999, A4.

70. Jay Sekulow to PR, Mar. 11, 1999; PR to Steve Wolkomir and Marshall Staunton, copy to Alan Dye and Jay Sekulow, Coalition Memorandum, Oct. 7, 1999, ROA. Alan Fram, "Robertson Warns GOP of Gore Threat," Associated Press release, June 18, 1999, copy in ROA.

71. Marc Davis, "Christian Coalition Claims Victory Over IRS," *The Virginian-Pilot,* July 26, 2000, B2. PR to CBN Board of Directors, July 26, 2000, ROA.

72. See Ralph Reed's description of the Clinton years in *Active Faith,* 151-87. PR to Bob Kydd, July 22, 1993, ROA. Bill Sizemore, "PR Draws Fire for Assassination Remark," *The Virginian-Pilot,* July 21, 1998, A6. "Clinton Letter," undated typed response letter; see PR to Janet Winslow, Apr. 27, 1998, ROA.

73. PR, "Remarks to Road to Victory '98," Sept. 18, 1998, typed copy, ROA. Robertson's speech was immediately reported by the news media. Judy Woodruff of CNN reported that during the speech "Robertson heard some boo's from those in attendance when he suggested President Clinton does not deserve forgiveness." About two hours later she issued the following retraction: "Earlier on CNN we inadvertently misquoted the Reverend Pat Robertson. We said the Christian Coalition chairman suggested the president does not deserve forgiveness. That was wrong. He said just the opposite, that the president does deserve forgiveness. CNN regrets the error." Typed transcript of "CNN Breaking News" and "CNN Inside Politics," Sept. 18, 1998, ROA. Coverage of the conference can be found in Laurie Goodstein, "The Testing of a President," *New York Times,* Sept. 20, 1998, 34.

74. Andrew Phillips, "Comeback Kid — The Sequel," *Maclean's,* Feb. 1, 1999, 34-35. See Richard L. Berke, "Robertson, Praising Speech, Suggests G.O.P. Halt Trial," *New York Times,* Jan. 21, 1999, A1. PR int., Mar. 18, 2008. PR to Henry Hyde, Jan. 27, 1999; PR to Michael Ewing Shotwell, Jan. 27, 1999, ROA.

75. Jill Lawrence and Jim Drinkard, "Christian Coalition Gains Momentum," *USA Today,* Sept. 18, 1998, A6.

76. PR to Don Hodel and Randy Tate, May 8, 1998; Hodel to PR, May 21, 1998; PR to Hodel, May 21, 1998; see Roy S. Moore to Hodel, May 7, 1998; Hodel to Jay Sekulow, May 15, 1998, ROA.

77. PR to Gary L. Taylor, May 21, 1998; Don Hodel to PR, Jan. 27, 1999, ROA.

78. PR to Evelyn T. Reilly, Mar. 7, 1999; Bill Thomson to PR, Mar. 4, 1999, ROA.

79. Wharton, "Coalition's Leadership will be a Team of 2," A14. Don Hodel to PR, Mar. 24, 1998, ROA. When a wire service report noted that "Christian Coalition's Robertson" had given $10,000 to John Ashcroft's Senate campaign, Hodel politely asked Robertson

how he should "respond to inevitable questions." Undated handwritten note from Hodel to PR; Hodel to BJ, July 2, 1998, ROA.

80. Ralph Z. Hallow, "Christian Coalition President Resigns," *Washington Times*, Feb. 10, 1999, A1. Undated memo from Don Hodel to PR, received Jan. 27, 1999, ROA. See PR int., Mar. 18, 2008.

81. PR to Don Hodel, Jan. 27, 1999; Hodel to PR, Jan. 27, 1999, ROA. PR int., Mar. 18, 2008. See Marley, *Pat Robertson*, 233.

82. Hallow, "Christian Coalition President Resigns," A1.

83. Liz Szabo, "President of Christian Coalition Resigns," *The Virginian-Pilot*, Feb. 10, 1999, A4.

84. PR to Evelyn T. Reilly, Mar. 7, 1999; Jeffrey K. Taylor to PR, Apr. 9, 2000; PR to Taylor, Apr. 11, 2000, ROA. BJ to PR, Jan. 21, 1999, ROA; this fax transmission includes a list of fourteen interview requests. "Congressional Leaders Sponsor Birthday Gala for Pat Robertson," *Church and State*, May 2000, 17.

85. PR to Jim Nicholson, Feb. 16, 1999, ROA.

86. "Straw Poll House Mailing," copy of proposed Christian Coalition mail solicitation, Mar. 31, 1999, ROA. Paula Wells to PR, June 10, 1999, ROA. Fram, "Robertson Warns GOP of Gore Threat."

87. Judy Keen, "Christian Coalition Confab Draws Most GOP Hopefuls," *USA Today*, Oct. 1, 1999, 8A. Thomas B. Edsall, "Christian Coalition Leader Praises Bush," *Washington Post*, Oct. 2, 1999, A5. "Christian Coalition Head to Endorse George W. Bush," *Church and State*, Mar. 2000, 17.

88. "Dear South Carolina Friends," undated typed manuscript, ROA. See GGC to ML, Feb. 15, 2000; Mitch McConnell to PR, Feb. 23, 2000, ROA. "Interview with Pat Robertson," copy of transcript from Fox Special Report with Brit Hume, Feb. 22, 2000, ROA. "Robertson Attacks McCain Official," Associated Press release, Feb. 22, 2000, copy in ROA.

89. John McCain to PR, June 2, 1999, ROA.

90. Craig Timberg, "McCain Attacks Two Leaders of Christian Right," *Washington Post*, Feb. 29, 2000, A1. Memo from PR to Roberta Combs, Mar. 1, 2000, ROA.

91. PR to John McCain, May 9, 2000, ROA.

92. R. H. Melton, "Robertson Promises Voters Blitz by Right," *Washington Post*, Aug. 2, 2000, A18; Warren Fiske, "Christian Coalition Still a Force at Convention," *The Virginian-Pilot*, Aug. 2, 2000, A1, A10. PR to Billy McCormack, Jan. 3, 2000; Steve Wolkomir to PR, Mar. 12, 1999, ROA. Copy of "American Center for Law and Justice Combined Financial Results," First Quarter 2000. ROA.

93. RR int., Sept. 10, 2007. Mary Jacoby, "What Has She Done to the Christian Coalition?" *St. Petersburg Times*, Oct. 3, 1999, 1A.

94. PR to Billy McCormack, Jan. 3, 2000; Jeffrey K. Taylor to PR, Apr. 9, 2000; David N. Ventker to Chuck Cunningham, Aug. 6, 1999; Ventker to Dave Welch, Aug. 6, 1999, ROA.

95. Billy McCormack to PR, Nov. 11, 2002; Roberta Combs to PR, Oct. 10, 2001, ROA.

96. Thomas B. Edsall, "Robertson Quits Political Post," *Washington Post*, Dec. 6, 2001, A2. B. Drummond Ayers Jr., "Robertson Resigns from Christian Coalition," *New York Times*, Dec. 6, 2001, A24.

97. PR to Billy McCormack, Nov. 11, 2002; PR to McCormack, Nov. 7, 2002; PR to Roberta Combs, Dec. 23, 2002, ROA.

98. PR to Roberta Combs, Feb. 8, 2006; PR to Combs, Apr. 11, 2006, ROA. For a sampling of the press coverage of the final decline of the Christian Coalition, which included

the secession of several of the stronger state organizations, see Bill Sizemore, "Once-Powerful Group Teeters on Insolvency," *The Virginian-Pilot,* Oct. 8, 2005, A1, A4; Jim Galloway, "Christian Coalition Group Splits," *Atlanta Journal-Constitution,* Sept. 26, 2006, B3; Jeff Brumley, "Christian Coalition Struggles Nationally, But Not in Florida," *Florida Times-Union,* Apr. 14, 2006, A1.

99. Billy McCormack to PR, Nov. 11, 2002, ROA. RR int., Sept. 10, 2007; PR int., Oct. 7, 2008. Reed, *Active Faith,* 70. See Reed's chapter entitled "All God's Children," 27-69. RR int., Apr. 23, 2007.

100. PR to Nick Jesson, Feb. 27, 2002, ROA. Richard S. Dunham et al., "Can the GOP Get Down to Business?" *Business Week,* Nov. 22, 2004, 43.

101. Marley, *Pat Robertson,* 271, 272; see Marley's chapter "Robertson and W," 267-87.

102. Marley, *Pat Robertson,* 273. PR to Karl Rove, May 24, 2001; see PR to Karl Rove, Mar. 17, 2005, ROA. RR int., June 19, 2008. *The 700 Club,* June 19, 2008.

103. RR to PR, Dec. 1, 2006. See PR int., Dec. 6, 2007. RR int., Sept. 10, 2007; PR int., Dec. 6, 2007.

104. Stephen G. Vegh, "Regent Students Upset at Romney's Choice as Speaker," *Knight Ridder Tribune Business News,* Mar. 2, 2007, 1. PR to All Staff at Regent University, Feb. 23, 2007, ROA. Vegh, "Regent Students Upset at Romney's Choice as Speaker," 1; Thomas Burr, "Evangelical Students Protest Romney as Speaker," *Salt Lake Tribune,* Mar. 3, 2007, 1.

105. PR to All Staff at Regent University, Feb. 23, 2007, ROA. Kimball Payne, "Giuliani Reaches Out to Social Conservatives in Virginia," *Newport News Daily Press,* June 26, 2007, 1. Kathleen Parker, "In Politics Now, What's God Got to Do with It?" *The Birmingham News,* Nov. 12, 2007, 9A. Michael Gerson, "The Kingmaker's New Subject," *Newsweek,* Nov. 19, 2007, 33. E. J. Dionne, *Souled Out* (Princeton: Princeton University Press, 2008), 51. PR int., Mar. 18, 2009; Dec. 6, 2007; Mar. 18, 2009.

106. *The 700 Club,* June 18, 2008; RR int., May 23, 2007.

107. "That was a Terrible Thing to Say, Pat Robertson," *The Christian Century,* Mar. 24, 2009, 9. *The 700 Club,* Jan. 20, 2009. Gordon Robertson gave President Obama an even friendlier welcome. He was less involved in party politics and more open to dialogue with Democrats. Gordon was impressed by Barak Obama's "eloquence" and was slow to offer harsh judgments about his actions. See *The 700 Club,* Aug. 29, 2008. For PR denouncing Obama, see *The 700 Club,* Mar. 23, 2009; PR int., Mar. 18, 2009.

108. RR to Edgardo Rodriguez Engelhard, Mar. 16, 1992; José L. Gonzalez to PR, Oct. 6, 1994; José Garcia to PR, Aug. 12, 1999, ROA.

109. Jan-Aage Torp to PR, Apr. 19, 1993; see PR to Jack Stagman, May 8, 1997, ROA. "Christian Coalition Announces Sweeping Reorganization," Christian Coalition news release, June 10, 2007, ROA.

110. PR int., Nov. 17, 2007. Edsall, "Robertson Quits Political Post," A2.

111. John C. Green, Mark J. Rozell, and Clyde D. Wilcox, eds., *The Christian Right in American Politics* (Washington, D.C.: Georgetown University Press, 2003), 1. Robert Boston, *Why the Religious Right Is Wrong about Separation of Church and State,* 2nd ed. (Amherst, N.Y.: Prometheus Press, 2006), 13.

112. PR to Billy McCormack, Nov. 11, 2002; PR to Jill Jensen, Oct. 5, 1998, ROA.

113. Quoted in RR, *Active Faith,* 17. Robert Wuthnow, *Christianity in the Twenty-first Century* (New York: Oxford University Press, 1993), 164-65.

114. Paul M. Weyrich, "Political Activism is not Enough," *USA Today,* Feb. 23, 1999, 14A. PR to Lesley Stahl, May 17, 1999, ROA.

115. Cal Thomas and Ed Dobson, *Blinded by Might: Can the Religious Right Save America?* (Grand Rapids: Zondervan Publishing House, 1999). PR to Cal Thomas, Apr. 9, 1999, ROA. "Fight or Flight," Apr. 9, 1999. Wuthnow, *Christianity in the Twenty-first Century*, 173. Nonetheless, vitriolic insider conservative criticisms continued. Kevin Phillips's 2006 attack on the Bush administration insisted that Robertson, whom he consistently referred to as "Pentecostal Pat Robertson," was a "Christian Reconstructionist" whether he was willing to admit it or not. See Kevin Phillips, *American Theocracy: The Peril and Politics of Radical Religion, Oil, and Borrowed Money in the 21st Century* (New York: Viking, 2006), 215. Critics on the left such as Michelle Goldberg see all Christian conservatives as proponents of "Christian nationalism" which, despite their denials, was rooted in the teachings of Christian Reconstruction. *Kingdom Coming: The Rise of Christian Nationalism* (New York: W.W. Norton & Company, 2007), 13. Walter H. Capps, *The New Religious Right: Piety, Patriotism, and Politics* (Columbia: University of South Carolina Press, 1990), 3.

116. Clyde Wilcox, *Onward Christian Soldiers?* 2nd. ed. (Boulder: Westview Press, 2000), 155-56. Most observers would agree with Ruth Murray Brown's conclusion that "the Christian Right can take some satisfaction in substantive progress on their political agenda. The movement seems to have brought citizens who had previously shunned it into the political process." *For a Christian America* (Amherst, N.Y.: Prometheus Books, 2002), 276.

117. Allen D. Hertzke, *Echoes of Discontent: Jesse Jackson, Pat Robertson, and the Resurgence of Populism* (Washington, D.C.: CQ Press, 1993), xi-xiii.

118. Watson, *Christian Coalition*, 5; see Watson's chapter on "Demands for Recognition," 123-74. Donovan, *Pat Robertson*, viii. See Walter H. Capps's discussion of this model in *The New Religious Right*, 198-210.

119. See Steve Bruce, "The Inevitable Failure of the New Christian Right," *Sociology of Religion*, Fall 1994, 229-42; Steve Bruce, *The Rise and Fall of the Christian Right* (Oxford: Clarendon Press, 1990). Barry Lynn, *Piety and Politics: The Right-Wing Assault on Religious Freedom* (New York: Three Rivers, 2007), 250. Lynn simply does not accept the disclaimers of religious right leaders: "What they are really after is a type of theocratic state.... They want to run your life, mine, and everyone else's as much as they possibly can" (17). Barry Lynn int., Jan. 3, 2008. Randall Balmer, *Thy Kingdom Come: How the Religious Right Distorts the Faith and Threatens America* (New York: Basic Books, 2006), 183.

120. "Half Full or Half Empty," in Michael Cromartie, ed., *No Longer Exiles* (Washington, D.C.: Ethics and Public Policy Center, 1993), 126. Watson, *The Christian Coalition*, 161, 5.

121. See Matthew C. Moen, "From Revolution to Evolution: The Changing Nature of the Christian Right," *Sociology of Religion*," Fall 1994, 345-58.

Notes to Chapter 6

1. "Special Communication to All CBN Employees," *The News Paper* (Public Relations Division Newsletter), June 5, 1987. Defending the fairness of the massive layoff, Allen Rundle, Executive Vice President for Finance & Administration, wrote to an inquirer: "During our financial cuts earlier this month, we did lay off four vice presidents along with about 500 other CBN employees." Rundle to Donald K. Wales, June 29, 1987, ROA. CBN news release, June 5, 1987, RUA. See "CBN Faces Summer Crisis," *TouchPoint*, July 1987, 1, 2.

2. "CBN's Money Problems," *Christian Century*, June 8, 1988, 567. David Jackson to TR, Sept. 25, 1987, AFR Papers, Box 442, RUA; TR int., Apr. 10, 2007.

3. GR int., Oct. 9, 2008. CBN news release, June 5, 1987, RUA. The press documented the spread of economic distress throughout all of the older television ministries in the wake of the PTL scandal. See Laura Sessions Stepp, "TV Evangelists Have a Devil of a Year," *Washington Post*, Nov. 29, 1987, B3.

4. Hugh McCann, "Robertson on Bakker: 'Lord Cleaning House,'" *Detroit News*, Mar. 22, 1987, D8, D9. BJ to Margaret Jordan, June 4, 1987, ROA. Form letter dated Dec. 10, 1990, ROA. "The Television Fiasco: Top '87 Religion Story," *Christian Century*, Dec. 23-30, 1987, 1163.

5. Robin Toner, "Preachers' Battle Transfixing the South," *New York Times*, Mar. 26, 1987, A16. PR, "As I View It," *The Flame*, Sept. 1989, 2. See BJ to Marilyn Hayes, Nov. 5, 1987, ROA.

6. PR to Ellsworth Molter, Dec. 27, 1994, ROA. April Witt, "CBN Fund-Raising Telethon Got 58% Less than in 1986," *The Virginian-Pilot and the Ledger-Star*, Oct. 24, 1987, A1. TR int., Apr. 2007.

7. RR to Tim Twardowski, Jan. 26, 1989, copied to PR, ROA. David Gyertson int.

8. CBN news release, Oct. 7, 1987, RUA. "New Leadership at CBN," *TouchPoint*, Nov. 1987, 2.

9. A good sketch of Tim Robertson is Stephen Strang, "CBN's New Boss," *Charisma & Christian Life*, Jan. 1988, 18-23, 74, 75. BJ to Barbara Ezzolo, Apr. 15, 1988, ROA.

10. Sally Kirby Hartman, "What Pat Begat," *Virginia Business*, May 1988, 40. TR int., Dec. 5, 2007. See TR int., Dec. 18, 1986.

11. Strang, "CBN's New Boss," 23. DR int.; SR int.; PR int., Mar. 19, 2008.

12. See Marley, *Pat Robertson*, 122. TR to Harold Walker, Aug. 1, 1988, ROA. According to an interview published in 1995, Soderman indicated that she no longer considered herself a "born-again Christian." PR expressed disappointment about the statement, but he showed no ill feelings toward his former co-host. Robertson uniformly held his co-hosts in high esteem. See Karen McCowan, "Danuta Sparks Eugene Radio," *The Register-Guard*, Apr. 22, 1995, copy in ROA; PR to Bonnie Aarnes, June 7, 1995, PR to Mrs. C. H. Sandifer, Oct. 29, 1993, ROA. "Susan Howard," *TouchPoint*, Sept. 1987, 3.

13. Bob Slosser to All Staff, Jan. 26, 1988, RUA. BJ to Barbara Ezzolo, Apr. 15, 1988, ROA. See "On the '700 Club' Today," *The News Paper*, Feb. 29, 1988, 1. Ben Kinchlow int.; TR to Harold Walker, Aug. 1, 1988, ROA. Scott Ross believed that Kinchlow had become uncomfortable with his role as "a token" black man on the program, but his devotion to PR was unstinting. "He was never so comfortable with Tim." SR int.

14. "What's Happening to *The 700 Club*," *TouchPoint*, 2. From his early association with the ministry to the present, Scott Ross's maverick persona and his penchant for exploring the fringes of the Christian community sometimes made him a liability with the donor base and persona non grata within the organization. The ministry files included a paragraph written by PR to be sent to donors offended by a Ross production: "The other matter you wrote about concerning Scott Ross and his part in *'The 700 Club.'* My brother, I appreciate your concern, but I assure you that Scott is a truly born-again, Spirit-filled brother, and God is using him. You might not agree with some of the segments he produces, but I feel it would be much more effective if you would pray for him rather than judge him. . . . What Scott was in his past years before he came to the Lord is forgiven — and forgotten — by the Lord. Can we do less?" PR to Wayne E. Streat, Jan. 9, 1986, ROA. Robertson despised "rock and roll music," recalled Ross, but he was astonished by the pos-

Notes to Pages 184-190

itive impact that Ross's reporting had on ratings. See TR int., Apr. 10, 2007; SR int., Oct. 26, 2007.

15. CBN news releases, Aug. 31, 1987; Dec. 9, 1987; Mar. 31, 1988, RUA.

16. See "'700 Club' Rollout, Two Weeks Away Aug. 31," *The News Paper*, Aug. 17, 1987, 1. CBN news releases, May 12, 1987; Feb. 2, 1988; Feb. 29, 1988, RUA. The network also received an Emmy nomination in 1987 for a *700 Club* news segment on "sexaholics" and "two prestigious 'Telly Awards'" for excellence in the production of commercials in 1988. CBN news releases, Aug. 11, 1987; May 3, 1988, RUA. See "Have You Heard?" *TouchPoint*, Sept. 1987, 5; Strang, "CBN's New Boss," 18; SR int.; TR int., Dec. 5, 2007.

17. Hartman, "What Pat Begat," 37. TR int., Apr. 10, 2007.

18. Hartman, "What Pat Begat," 41.

19. BJ to Barbara Ezzolo, Apr. 15, 1988, ROA.

20. Barbara Gattullo to Allan Sutherlin, May 3, 1988, AFR Papers, RUA.

21. Americans for Robertson press release, May 16, 1988, AFC files, RUA.

22. Boston, *The Most Dangerous Man in America?* Boston's phrase was echoed in a spate of other book titles. RR int., Sept. 10, 2007.

23. "Questions for New York Times Editorial Board Meeting, June 16, 1993," ROA. PR to Robert Bohannon, Feb. 7, 1994, ROA.

24. TR int., Dec. 5, 2007; SR int.

25. PR to All Staff, May 19, 1987, RUA. David Gyertson to Chapel Worship & Prayer Leaders, June 15, 1987. See "An Urgent Calling — And an Unchanging Mission," *TouchPoint*, Nov. 1987, 1.

26. Strang, "CBN's New Boss," 23. Rob Hartley to TR, Sept. 25, 1987, RUA. Typed transcript of telephone int. with David Wilkerson, n.d., AFC files, Box 442, RUA. Hartley to PR, Sept. 29, 1987, RUA.

27. PR to All Staff, Aug. 23, 1988, RUA.

28. ML int., Apr. 10, 2007.

29. TR int., Apr. 10, 2007.

30. PR to Dave Lefurgey, Apr. 30, 1990, ROA. Robertson received many inquiries about the various reorganizations and sales of the cable network. In this reply, written shortly after the sale of the network, he maintained that the startup and expansion of the network had never been funded basically by money donated to CBN. In addition, he defended the sale of the cable network as an extraordinarily profitable coup for CBN: "After that we began selling time to broadcasters on this network, and with the proceeds of those sales we purchased family oriented filmed programs to get more sales. At no time did CBN startup investment in the Family Channel, to the best of my knowledge, ever exceed one million dollars. Because of the pressure from the Internal Revenue Service, CBN has now sold the cable network for $250 million. The reason it was so valuable was because of the commercials playing on it, not because of the donations from CBN partners. Nevertheless, a multiplication of 250 times over 13 years is about as dramatic an increase as could possibly be hoped for on any investment." See "Robertson Rejoins CBN," *Broadcasting*, May 23, 1988, 51.

31. TR int., Apr. 10, 2007. TR was proud of his role in fighting for the "Family Channel" label. See also Earl Weyrich, "Television and the Family," *Religious Broadcasting*, Oct. 1989, 12, 13.

32. "In hindsight, [the legislation] never happened," recalled Tim Robertson; TR int., Apr. 10, 2007. PR to DSave Lefurgey, Apr. 30, 1990.

33. Many articles in contemporary Christian and trade journals covered, and com-

387

mented on, the sale of The Family Channel. For a sampling, see John W. Kennedy, "Redeeming the Wasteland?" *Christianity Today,* Oct. 2, 1995, 92; "The Expanding CBN Empire," *The Christian Century,* July 27, 1994, 712; Gary Cohen, "On God's Green Earth," *U.S. News & World Report,* Apr. 24, 1995, 31, 32; "Robertson Bullish on Family Channel, UPI," *Christianity Today,* June 22, 1992, 51, 52. Sara Diamond states the case of those questioning the ethics of the transactions: "The deal was technically legal though ethically questionable. In brief, over the years, Robertson had used tax-free money to create a 'religious' ministry, which he then used as collateral to create a commercial cable network, the value of which mushroomed after the Robertsons became the controlling stockholders." Diamond, *Not by Politics Alone: The Enduring Influence of the Christian Right* (New York: The Guilford Press, 1998), 29.

34. PR to Jeffrey V. Sippel, Sept. 1, 1999, ROA. Chris Stone, "Robertson Shakes Up Empire," *Christianity Today,* Jan. 14, 1997, 60.

35. The complexity of the transactions of the 1990s necessitated a correction in the *New York Times* article on the 1997 sale of IFE. An article in its Business Day section stated that IFE owned CBN. "Corrections," *New York Times,* June 13, 1997, A2. The subsequent sale of the Fox Family Channel in 2001 to a new channel called ABC Family for about $5.3 billion placed The Family Channel in the hands of the Walt Disney Company, long a target of attacks on *The 700 Club.* Robertson sternly resisted efforts by ABC to rid itself of the "in perpetuity" obligation to air *The 700 Club.* A Florida newspaper editor called the marriage "a divine act of goofiness." Daryl Lease, "A Meteor Named Pat," *Sarasota Herald Tribune,* July 30, 2001, A11. Elizabeth Lesly, "The Divine Right of Moguls," *Business Week,* May 19, 1997, 118.

Two ministry documents, one written in 1992 commenting on the formation of International Family Entertainment and the second written in 1999, give the ministry defense of the sale of IFE to Rupert Murdoch's Fox Kids Worldwide.

Letter from Susan Norman to John M. Higgins, finance editor of Multichannel News, Mar. 19, 1992, ROA:

> We are a bit surprised at a media request to outline benefits of The Family Channel spin-off that accrued to CBN. It would seem the benefits are obvious. From the public offering, CBN will receive in excess of $100,000,000 in cash to add to the $23,000,000 in cash it received at the time of the spin-off. It will have marketable securities valued at approximately $240,500,000 remaining, for a total of $363,500,000 which constitutes approximately 16 times the book value of The Family Channel on Dec. 31, 1989. On top of that CBN has carriage of its "700 Club" at a nominal fee in virtual perpetuity, and it has been relieved of sizeable program obligations.
>
> In more complete answer to your Mar. 18 FAX concerning The Family Channel, please note the following:
>
> 2. Your statement "Pat and Tim Robertson's stake was obtained by their ability to borrow most of the acquisition cost from the ministry" is incorrect.
>
> Their stock was purchased with their own money at a price equal to or exceeding its fair market value determined by an appraisal specifically and in writing prepared by the leading appraiser in the nation. . . .
>
> 3. The spin-off transaction resulted in CBN receiving $23,000,000 or almost 100% of the book value of the Channel in cash, plus the assumption of liabilities of roughly twice that amount, not "80% paper" as you suggested.

$22,000,000 of preferred equity also came into the new company behind the secured notes received by CBN.

4. The benefits to CBN of this transaction are obvious: (a) the transaction was forced on it by the rules of the I.R.S. (b) the transaction fulfills I.R.S. guidelines, yet keeps this contract agreed to maintain the original intention of the channel as a wholesome outlet for family programs, (c) CBN maintains in virtual perpetuity the carriage of its "700 Club" program twice a day, something that no cash buyer would even consider, (d) CBN is able to participate fully in the upside potential of the future growth of the company. , . . (e) CBN gains liquidity for its charitable mission from selling from time to time parts of a rapidly enhancing and proven public commercial asset, (f) CBN as a charity was never able to engage in the massive investment for original family entertainment or national advertising that I.F.E. has undertaken. By the spin-off, I.F.E. in fact assumed substantial amounts of existing program obligations from CBN. . . .

6. Please note also that at this spin-off on Jan. 5, 1990 100% of the stock purchased by Tim Robertson was forfeitable by him unless he remained an employee of I.F.E. for 5 years, and unless the company met or exceeded stringent financial performance goals. . . .

8. Pat Robertson placed his "A" stock in a charitable trust shortly after the spin-off. The trust is irrevocable. . . .

Pat Robertson purchased "B" stock in I.F.E. along with other employees. . . .

9. Neither Pat Robertson nor any related party was able to vote on the spin-off of The Family Channel or any future transactions regarding the two companies. Oversight of activities between CBN and I.F.E. has been entrusted to a committee of outside directors of CBN's Board who are advised by CBN's outside legal counsel. . . .

Letter from Ruth Kastberg to Josephine Shanthi Catlin, Aug. 4, 1999, ROA:

The transaction, which occurred June 1997, between International Family Entertainment (IFE), the parent company of the Family Channel, and Fox Kids Worldwide, a global children's television entertainment company owned in part by Rupert Murdoch's News Corporation, benefited both CBN and Regent University.

Through the sale of IFE stock, CBN received more than $136 million, funds that are enabling us to move forward with CBN WorldReach, our worldwide evangelistic campaign to take the life-changing Gospel of Jesus Christ, a message of love, hope and compassion to 500 million people. At the same time, the sale will provide CBN in the year 2010 with another $109 million from a trust formed by Mr. Robertson for the ministry, funds that will help position the ministry for the future.

At Regent University, proceeds from the sale of IFE stock totaled $147.5 million, bringing the graduate school's total endowment to more than $276 million, and placing the university in the top 100 ranking of endowment assets at the nation's colleges and universities.

The conditions of the sale to Fox require that The Family Channel retain its family programming. . . . *"The 700 Club"* will retain its current broadcast schedule.

36. The Family Channel news release, Jan. 8, 1990, RUA. Christopher Palmer, "All in the Family," *Forbes,* Dec. 6, 1993, 258.

37. "Interview with Christian Life Magazine," manuscript dated Feb. 24, 1982, ROA. See Cathy Chisholm Justice, "Changes at CBN Draw New Viewers," *Memphis Press-Scimitar,* Dec. 22, 1981, copy in ROA. PR to Isabel Matheny, Feb. 28, 1995, ROA. See PR to Mr. and Mrs. Brad Knigga, Oct. 24, 1995; Janet Mosier, untitled and undated statement by Public Liaison Coordinator of The Family Channel; "Statement for CBN Supporters and Partners Regarding Globe Article," Mar. 30, 1993, ROA.

38. "Audience/Donor Research," CBN Research Plan — Discovery Phase (Part 1), Mar. 2001, document in possession of the author, 14. PR to Richard G. Johnson, Mar. 23, 1994; PR to Marguerite Farmer, Mar. 15, 1994, ROA.

39. PR int., Mar. 19, 2008. "Robertson Rejoins CBN," *Broadcasting,* May 23, 1988, 51.

40. "*The 700 Club* with Pat Robertson," undated CBN news release, RUA.

41. *The 700 Club* broadcast, Nov. 4, 2008; PR to Mrs. C. H. Sandifer, Oct. 29, 1993, ROA. Letter to Dear Friend from SR, July 19, 1990, RUA. "Brother Ben Is Back!" *Frontlines,* May 1992, 4, 5.

42. TM int.

43. "Welcome Terry," *Frontlines,* June 1993, 4, 5. TM, *The God Adventure* (Sisters, Oregon: Multnomah Publishers, 2004), 9. GR int., Nov. 15, 2007.

44. "Friends You Can Turn To," *Frontlines,* Feb. 1995, 2. John W. Kennedy, "Redeeming the Wasteland?" 92. "A TV Show That Changes Hearts," *Frontlines,* 4. PR int., Mar. 5, 2007.

45. GR int., Mar. 19, 2009. LW int., Nov. 16, 2007; CBN Biography, undated document from Public Relations Division, RUA. TM int.

46. See http://www.cbn.com/700club/showinfo/staff/kristiwatts.aspx, Nov. 6, 2008.

47. GR int., Apr. 9, 2007; Dec. 10, 2007.

48. GR int., Oct. 15, 2007. RM int.; PR int., Mar. 5, 2007.

49. Most of the information in this section on Gordon Robertson is based on interviews with him on Oct. 15, 2007, Dec. 10, 2007, and Oct. 10, 2008.

50. SR int.

51. "Philippines Missions Institute Started," *Frontlines,* May 1995, 3.

52. See Russell G. Shubin, "The Escalating Filipino Force for the Nations," *Mission Frontiers,* Sept.-Dec. 1998, 38-40. Nena Benigno int.

53. "CBN Asia Launches New Studio," *Frontlines,* June 1999, 3. For a summary of the activities of CBN Asia see, "CBN Asia, Inc. 1999 Performance Review," pamphlet in possession of the author.

54. Nena Benigno int.

55. "Former 700 Club Viewer Survey," presented Oct. 21, 1998, to CBN Marketing by Norman Berman & Associates, document in possession of the author. Meeuwsen's ratings among women viewers were only slightly behind those of Robertson. "Audience/Donor Research," CBN Research Plan — Discovery Phase (Part 1), 20.

56. "Club Hits Home with 'Real TV,'" *Frontlines,* Jan. 2001, 2.

57. "CBN NewsWatch," *Frontlines,* May 2003, 2. "News You Can Trust," *Frontlines,* Nov. 2000, 2. "Bringing Hidden Stories to Light," *Frontlines,* July 2007, 6. JT int., Apr. 11, 2007.

58. Rob Allman int., Sept. 25, 2007. See http://www.cbn.com/cbnnews/?WT.svl=menu, Nov. 24, 2008.

59. See "Robertson Bullish on Family Channel, UPI," *Christianity Today,* June 22, 1992,

51; "Earthly Inheritance," *Economist,* May 23, 1992, 28. "New Radio Network," *Frontlines,* Feb. 1993, 3.

60. Rob Allman int.

61. Rob Allman int.; GR int., Mar. 19, 2009; Patrick Roddy int.

62. "The *All New* 700 Club," *Frontlines,* Feb. 1997, 4, 5. "Former 700 Club Viewer Survey."

63. "Club Hits Home with 'Real TV,'" 2.

64. PR int., Mar. 5, 2007. *The 700 Club,* Sept. 10, 2009.; Sept. 22, 2008.

65. GR int., Mar. 18, 2009; Nena Benigno int.; VS int., Dec. 10, 2007. Transcript of remarks at "CBN Partner Ministry Weekend," Nov. 9-12, 2000, copy in ROA. GR int., Oct. 10, 2008; *The 700 Club,* Aug. 1, 1008; June 19, 2008; Nov. 28, 2008; Jan. 19, 2009.

66. *The 700 Club,* June 19, 2008; GR telephone int., June 19, 2008. http://event.cbn.com/spiritualgifts/ (Nov. 6, 2008).

67. GR int., Mar. 18, 2009; Oct. 10, 2008.

68. "CBN Audience Summit," Dec. 13, 1999, notebook in possession of the author. "Audience/Donor Research," CBN Research Plan — Discovery Phase (Part 1), 38, 39; "*The 700 Club* Audience Demographics Report by CBN Syndication Department," [1999], report in possession of the author. TR int., Apr. 10, 2007.

69. See http://www.cbn.com/700club/ShowInfo/About/about/700club.aspx, Dec. 3, 2008; "CBN Presents *The 700 Club,*" marketing pamphlet prepared by CBN, 2002, in possession of author. See GGC to Larry Walton, Jan. 20, 1998, ROA. "*The 700 Club* Dec. 2001 Audience Report," undated CBN report, RUA. "Syndication Revenue Track," charts prepared by the CBN Syndication Department in 2007, copy in possession of the author. See Tom Knox to ML, Sept. 3, 1998, RUA; CBN news release, Sept. 23, 1997, ROA. "*The 700 Club* US Penetration TV HH," and "*The 700 Club* Distribution," charts prepared by CBN Syndication Department, 2007, in possession of the author. http://www.cbn.com/700club/ShowInfo/About/about/700club.aspx, Nov. 24, 2008.

70. http://www.cbn.com/CBNnews/index.aspx?WT.svl=HomeLeftMenuHeader, Mar. 12, 2009.

71. http://www.cbn.com/CBNTelevision.aspx?WT.svl=menu, Nov. 24, 2008; "Living the Life," *Frontlines,* Sept. 2001, 2. http://www.canadianedition.com/index.php, Nov. 24, 2008.

72. "A Site to Behold," *Frontlines,* Sept. 2001, 3, 4. GR int., Apr. 9, 2007. "Audience/Donor Research," CBN Research Plan — Discovery Phase (Part 1), 10. George Winslow, "God Comes to the Internet," *Broadcasting and Cable,* Feb. 12, 2007, 34. GR int., Oct. 10, 2008.

73. ML int., Apr. 10, 2007. *The Christian Counselor's Handbook* (Wheaton, Ill.: Tyndale House Publishers, Inc., n.d.), 9.

74. See http://www.cbn.com/spirituallife/PrayerAndCounseling/index.aspx?WT.svl=BottomMenu, Dec. 9, 2008. *TouchPoint,* June 1982, 3. Joel Palser int., Apr. 11, 2007.

75. Joel Palser int., Dec. 8, 2008.

76. "Content for Dr. Robertson's Year End Partner Presentation," undated document prepared by Joel Palser, copy in possession of the author. Joel Palser int., Apr. 11, 2007; Dec. 8, 2007.

77. JT int., Apr. 11, 2007. Joel Palser int., Apr. 11, 2007.

78. JT int., Dec. 8, 2007; Joel Palser int., Dec. 8, 2007. K. Pollak, "MMDI Spectrogram," document dated Oct. 2002, in the possession of the author.

79. For a graphic display of the disastrous drop after 1985 in telethons pledges and the

slow progress in rebuilding, see Kathy Pollak, "January Telethon History 1982-2002," CBN report, document in possession of author. Majorie Mayfield, "Pledges Rise to Golden Day Level," *The Virginian-Pilot,* Feb. 8. 1991, D1. See "Robertson, Dobson Groups Suffer Donation Downturn," *Church and State,* July/Aug. 2001, 21; Kathy Pollak to Management Council, June 5, 2001, ROA. "CBN Audited Financial Statements," booklet prepared by Vice-President Michael Carter, in possession of author.

80. GR int., Dec. 10, 2007.

81. PR to Diane Dew, May 28, 1991, ROA. GR int., Dec. 10, 2007. JT int., Dec. 8, 2007. GR int., Dec. 10, 2007; Oct. 10, 2008.

82. DR int.

83. AL int.; DR int.

Notes to Chapter 7

1. PR int., Oct. 18, 2007. "The Future is Ours," *The Networker,* Jan. 1985, 5. See PR int., Mar. 18, 2008. Ethel A. Steadman, "Christian TV Plans Project," Norfolk *Virginian-Pilot,* Jan. 5, 1976, A1. *Pat Robertson's Perspective,* Jan.-Feb. 1978, 2. Jay Comisky int.; see also ML int., Oct. 16, 2007; Ron Oates int. It is remarkable that even the most recent Robertson biography, David John Marley's *Pat Robertson: An American Life,* makes no mention of WorldReach.

2. PR, "Multiplication Principles," *Decision,* Jan. 1985, 12. PR, "God's Master Plan for the Future," *People of Destiny,* Jan./Feb. 1985, 8. "Orlando '95 Congress on the Holy Spirit," manuscript of speech, ROA. For an example of Robertson's soaring confidence in the worldwide charismatic revival, see PR, *The New Millennium,* 95-97.

3. In Mark Juergensmeyer, ed., *Global Religions: An Introduction* (Oxford: Oxford University Press, 2003), 16. Timothy Yates, *Christian Missions in the Twentieth Century* (Cambridge: Cambridge University Press, 1994), 239. A few recent texts give passing recognition to the importance of mass revivals and charismatic evangelists in the globalization of Christianity in the last half of the twentieth century. See, for instance, Linda Woodhead et al., *Religions in the Modern World* (London and New York: Routledge, 2002). PR int., Oct. 23, 2007. In recent years, scholars from a variety of disciplines contributed useful insights into the spread of Pentecostal/charismatic religion around the world. For a few examples of recent studies of the worldwide charismatic revival, see Vinson Synan, ed., *The Century of the Holy Spirit* (Nashville: Thomas Nelson, 2001); David Martin, *Pentecostalism: The World Their Parish* (Oxford: Blackwell, 2002); Simon Coleman, *The Globalization of Charismatic Christianity: Spreading the Gospel of Prosperity* (Cambridge: Cambridge University Press, 2000); Andre Corten and Ruth Marshall-Fratani, eds., *Between Babel and Pentecost: Transnational Pentecostalism in Africa and Latin America* (London: Hurst & Company, 2001); John Michelethwait and Adrian Wooldridge, *God Is Back* (New York: The Penguin Press, 2008); Laurie Goodstein, "Pentecostal and Charismatic Groups Growing," *New York Times,* Oct. 6, 2006, A20.

4. PR, "As I View It," *The Flame,* Nov./Dec. 1989, 2.

5. ML int., Nov. 15, 2007; see also David Gyertson int.; BJ to Cathy Tsokris, Feb. 8, 1994, ROA. Reinhard Bonnke was a particular favorite of Robertson. The ministry calculated that as of June 2001 Bonnke had been given $1,487,921.90, including a $100,000 personal donation from Pat Robertson. See handwritten calculation attached to Bonnke to PR,

June 12, 2001, ROA. With his personal contribution, Robertson sent the note: "Thank you for your call today. I'm delighted to learn of the response in Nigeria, and agree with you that 'this is the time for harvest.' I'm enclosing my personal check to help in your crusade in Port Harcourt in December. God bless you." PR to Bonnke, Nov. 15, 1999, ROA. See the mission files in ROA. A sampling of the approximately 2,000 diverse ministries, individuals, and charitable organizations receiving contributions includes the Ansari Hospital for Afghan Refugees in Pakistan, American University in Haiti, The Bowery Ministry, Brooklyn Tabernacle (one of the million-dollar recipients), Jesus Calls (the Chennai, India, ministry of D. G. S. Dhinakaran who received multiple contributions amounting to more than $400,000), Gideons International, and scores of churches from a variety of denominations. CBN news release, "CBN to Further Worldwide Evangelism with Proceeds from IFE Stock Sale," June 11, 1997, RUA. ML int., Nov. 15, 2007; PR to Caroline Woods, Apr. 22, 1998; PR to Rory Alec, Oct. 28, 2003, ROA.

6. Ben Edwards int., Oct. 18, 2007. PR, *The New Millennium*, 95; "CBN to Focus on the International Scene," CBN news release, Feb. 14, 1993, RUA. ML int., Mar. 18, 2009.

7. PR int., Oct. 18, 2007. "CBN's Blitz Strategy Highlighted at International Evangelism Conference," *Frontlines*, July 1995, 3. Ben Edwards int., Oct. 18, 2007.

8. "CBN's *Superbook Party* Airs Across Entire Soviet Union!" *Frontlines*, Jan. 1992, 4. "Reaching 20 Million," *Frontlines*, Feb. 1994, 2. Steve Weber int.; ML int., Apr. 10, 2007; PR int., Mar. 5, 2007; "Special Follow-up Rallies Planned for 20 Soviet Cities," *Frontlines*, Jan. 1992, 4; Kim Mitchell int.

9. "CBN to Focus on the International Scene," CBN news release, Feb. 14, 1993, RUA. "Reaching 20 Million." "Targeting the World for Christ," *Frontlines*, June 1994, 4, 5.

10. "CBN WorldReach," CBN WorldReach news release, Dec. 22, 1998, RUA. PR to Ken Pelissero, Nov. 16, 1998, ROA. Robertson's missionary vision was often fired by visits abroad. After a trip to China where he had a "historic meeting" with Premier Zhu Rongji, he returned home excited about the "opportunities" he saw there. "Pat Robertson's Trip to China Reveals Ministry Opportunities," *Frontlines*, Nov. 1998, 3.

11. "CBN WorldReach," *NRB*, Oct. 1998, 32. Kim Mitchell int.

12. *CBN WorldReach*, Jan. 1998, 2,

13. "Partners Take the Gospel to the Lost and Needy Worldwide," *Frontlines*, Dec. 1994, 4, 5. Mark McClendon int.

14. GR int., Mar. 18, 2009. Kim Mitchell to PR, Feb. 3, 1998, ROA. Kim Mitchell int.; see Deborah Howse, CBN WorldReach memo, Mar. 26, 1999, ROA. GR int., Mar. 19, 2009.

15. Ron Oates int.

16. TR int., Dec. 18, 1986.

17. "WorldReach Centers," *CBN WorldReach*, Jan. 1998, 4. "Future WorldReach Centers," *CBN WorldReach*, Jan. 1998, Appendix, 1-4; Kim Mitchell to PR, Feb. 3, 1998, ROA; "Reaching Nations," *Frontlines*, Dec. 1997, 2; "97 CBN WorldReach Centers in 72 Countries," *Frontlines*, Oct. 1997, 4, 5.

18. Ron Oates int.; Felix Oisamoje int., Apr. 23, 2008.

19. "Background," undated CBN news release, ROA. For a detailed description of this event see the entire issue of *WorldReach*, Oct. 1995. Outside of the United States, the term WorldReach has limited usage. In most countries the term CBN International would still be more widely recognized. ML int., Mar. 18, 2009. "Help Us Pray for the Harvest," *Frontlines*, Aug. 1995, 4, 5; "CBN WorldReach," *NRB*, Oct. 1998, 30-31; ML int., Oct. 15, 2007.

20. See GR int., Oct. 15, 2007; Dec. 10, 2007. Ben Edwards int., Oct. 18, 2007.

21. For an introduction to T. L. Osborn's ministry, see David Edwin Harrell Jr., *All Things Are Possible* (Bloomington: Indiana University Press, 1975), 63-66, 169-72; Synan, *The Century of the Holy Spirit*, 325-48; David Edwin Harrell Jr., "India: Mass Healing Ministries and Revivalism," unpublished paper delivered at the American Society of Church History, 2002, in possession of the author; T. L. and Daisy Osborn int.; GR int., Apr. 9, 2007.

22. GR int., Apr. 9, 2007; Oct. 15, 2007; Ron Oates int. The only part of the Manila model that CBN did not try to reproduce was the Asian Center for Missions. That unique organization, which works in close cooperation with CBN Asia, was the product of Gordon Robertson's vision to establish training centers to cooperate with Filipino churches in sending and supporting more than 100 native preachers as missionaries in Asia. This mission program was a uniquely Filipino undertaking. In the Philippines, he observed, "every family has family members that have gone overseas." GR int., Oct. 10, 2008. The Center's historian explained: "Gordon encouraged them to go because Filipinos had been driven out of their country by poverty. . . . We are like the Jews — we are scattered too." Nena Benigno int.

23. ML int., Oct. 15, 2007. See "CBN WorldReach Second Quarter FY2000 Performance Report," CBN pamphlet in possession of the author.

24. ML int., Oct. 15, 2007; Mark McClendon int.; http://www.cbn.com/worldreach/ worldreach_regional_centers.aspx, Jan. 30, 2009.

25. Mark McClendon int.; "Reaching the Indonesian People with the Gospel," *Frontlines*, Mar. 2003, 4.

26. See Priti Choudary int.; http://www.cbn.com/worldreach/worldreach_regional _centers.aspx; Jan. 30, 2009; "Second Quarter FY2000 Performance Report"; Kumar Periasamy int.

27. "Combined Report of CBN WorldReach Highlights, Dec. 1999," CBN WorldReach report in possession of the author; http://www.cbn.com/worldreach/worldreach_regional _centers.aspx; Feb. 28, 2009; Felix Oisamoje int.; Kim Mitchell int., Apr. 24, 2008; "Update on CBN Africa's Promised Land," *Frontlines Africa*, Dec. 2007, 4.

28. See http://www.cbn.com/worldreach/worldreach_regional_centers.aspx, Feb. 28, 2009; Ben Edwards int.; Ron Oates int.; Kim Mitchell int., Apr. 23 and Apr. 24, 2008; Jay Comisky int. For insight into the slow and erratic expansion of regional centers see "Combined Report of CBN WorldReach Highlights Dec. 1999," "Second Quarter FY2000 Performance Report."

29. See http://www.cbn.com/worldreach/worldreach_about.aspx, Jan. 28, 2009. Felix Oisamoje int.; Ben Edwards int., Oct. 18, 2007; http://www.cbn.com/worldreach/ worldreach_tv_programs_turning_point.aspx, Feb. 9, 2009.

30. See http://www.cbn.com/worldreach/worldreach_tv_programs_700club_hoy .aspx, Feb. 9, 2009. See http://www.cbn.com/worldreach/worldreach_tv_programs _700club_asia.aspx, Feb. 9, 2009; Peter Kairuz int.; Nena Benigno int. See http:// www.cbn.com/worldreach/worldreach_tv_programs_solusi_life.aspx, Feb. 9, 2009; Priti Choudary int.

31. See Priti Choudary int.; Niran Pattaranukool int.; Steve Weber int.; Robert John Tan int.

32. For an overview of the current programming by WorldReach see http:// www.cbn.com/worldreach/worldreach_television_programs.aspx, Jan. 28, 2009. GR to

GGC, Jan. 12, 2001, ROA. "Animation for the Next Generation," *Frontlines,* June 2005, 2. See "CBN Animation," *Frontlines,* June 2007, 4, 5.

33. Kara Waddell int.; Priti Choudary int.; ML int., Apr. 10, 2007.

34. "World Reach Flow Chart," *CBN WorldReach,* Jan. 1998, Appendix 1.

35. Kara Waddell int.; Ron Oates int.; GR int., Oct. 10, 2008. Early plans to "develop church leaders in China" never fully materialized because of the continuing illegal status of the "house church" movement there. See "The China Project," *Frontlines,* Aug. 1997, 4-5; "Bringing Hope to China," *Frontlines,* June 2000, 4, 5. Kara Waddell int. "Touching Hearts in Asia," *Frontlines,* Aug. 2007, 5.

36. Mark McClendon int.; GR int., Oct. 10, 2008; Ben Edwards int., Dec. 5, 2007.

37. Niran Pattaranukool int.; Priti Choudary int.

38. See "CBN Asia Family of Ministries Ties Up with Asia Pay on Online Donation," *Frontlines Asia,* Mar.-May 2008, 6; *Asian Mission Times,* (n.d.) 9:2; Robert John Tan int.; Peter Kairuz int.

39. Felix Oisamoje int.; Kim Mitchell int., Apr. 23, 2008; Ben Edwards int., Oct. 18, 2007.

40. "CBN WorldReach Cell Churches: Setting Hearts on Fire for Jesus," *Frontlines,* Oct. 2003, 3. Steve Weber int.; see letter from Karekin II to PR, Nov. 23, 1999, ROA; Ben Edwards int., Oct. 18, 2007; GR int., Mar. 18, 2009.

41. Tanya Danilova int.; Steve Weber int.

42. GR int., Oct. 15, 2007; Ben Edwards int., Oct. 18, 2007; Ron Oates int. See "The Christian Broadcasting Network, Inc. and Affiliated Organizations Combined Financial Statements Mar. 31, 2007 and 2006," 3, report in possession of the author. The financial report for 2007 added an estimated $40 million worth of "bartered air time" to the CBN investment in international evangelism.

43. Mark McClendon int., Apr. 2, 2008; Robert John Tan int.; Malou Ibanez int.; Kumar Periasamy int.; GR int., Mar. 19, 2009; Steve Weber int.; Mali Audam int.; Felix Oisamoje int.; ML int., Apr. 15, 2007.

44. "Pat Robertson Has Rare Interview with PLO's Yasser Arafat," *Frontlines,* Nov. 1995, 3. "US Religious Station MET Starts on Israeli Satellite," *World Broadcast Information,* June 20, 1997; "METV Reaching 200 Million Via AMOS Satellite," *Frontlines,* Aug. 1997, 3.

45. Sam Brownback to Benjamin Netanyahu, May 5, 1998; Jesse Helms to Netanyahu, May 5, 1998; John Ashcroft to Netanyahu, May 6, 1998, copies in ROA. PR to Ashcroft, July 27, 1999, ROA. "METV Evacuates Station in Southern Lebanon," *Frontlines,* July 2000, 3.

46. "Beyond the Middle East," *Frontlines,* Oct. 2000, 3; "Be a Light Unto My People," *Frontlines,* Mar. 1998, 4, 5. Anita Wadhwani, "Network Plants Gospel Flag Deep in Non-Christian World," Nashville *Tennessean,* Mar. 25, 2007, 1A. See http://www.cbn.com/worldreach/worldreach_region_middle_east.aspx, Mar. 3, 2009.

47. ML int., Apr. 10, 2007. See "They Met God and He Isn't Allah," *Frontlines,* Apr. 2004, 1, 2. Ben Edwards int., Dec. 5, 2007; http://www.cbn.com/worldreach/worldreach_region_middle_east.aspx, March 1, 2010.

48. PR int., Mar. 18, 2008; Jay Comisky int.; Ben Edwards int., Oct. 18, 2007.

49. *The 700 Club,* Sept. 3, 2008; Sept. 11, 2008. GR int., Apr. 9, 2007; Oct. 15, 2007.

50. Steve Weber int.

51. Robert John Tan int.; GR int., Dec. 10, 2007; Kim Mitchell int.

52. See http://www.ob.org, June 22, 2009.

53. Foege, *The Empire God Built,* 52. "The Christian Broadcasting Network, Inc and Affiliated Organizations Combined Financial Statements, Mar. 31, 2007 and 2006." See http://www.ob.org/press_room/annual_report/FY08.pdf, June 22, 2009.

54. http://www.ob.org/_about/history.asp, June 22, 2009. Memo from Bob Warren to PR, Jan. 16, 1991. "The Many Faces of Operation Blessing," *Frontlines,* Nov. 1992, 4, 5; "'Convoy of Hope' Reaching 17 Cities," *Frontlines,* Oct. 1994, 2. "Opening Doors for the Gospel," *Blessings,* Jan. 1996, 1. See Paul B. Thompson, "City Reach: Responding to God's Urban Call," *Blessings,* Mar. 1996, 1, 2. For a sampling of articles about Operation Blessing's programs to aid the urban poor, see "Hope for the Inner City," *Blessings,* Oct. 1995, 1; "Hunger Strike Force Reaches Thousands Nationwide," *Blessings,* Sept. 1996, 1; "Homelessness: A Challenge and Opportunity," *Blessings,* Nov. 1995, 1; "10 Million Pounds," *Frontlines,* Dec. 1997, 3. "Operation Blessing Moves Forward," *Frontlines,* Oct. 1994, 2; Patrick K. Lackey, "Team that Aided Rwandans Says Efforts Saved Hundreds," *Virginian-Pilot and Ledger-Star,* Aug. 3, 1994, A6.

55. "Flying Hospital Inaugural Flight," *Blessings,* Special Issue, May 1996; "Flying Hospital Prepares for Inaugural Flight," *Blessings,* Dec. 1994, 1. For a slightly different description of the configuration of the airplane see Christopher Serb, "A New Hospital Takes Wing," *Hospitals & Health Networks,* Oct. 5, 1995, 88. Jennifer Pinkerton, "Operation Blessing Puts Care in Air," *Washington Times,* May 22, 1996, A1.

56. See Janet S. West, "Operation Blessing International's Flying Hospital Takes Flight to New Surgical Frontiers," *AORN Journal,* Nov. 1996, 704; Nancy Lewis, "'Flying Hospital' Returns to Beach," *Virginian-Pilot,* July 9, 1996, clipping file, RUA. See "Giving Compassion Wings," *Saturday Evening Post,* Mar.-Apr. 1997, 54; "Miracle of Healing the Nations," *Blessings,* Dec. 1996, 1, 2; Ron Oates int.

57. Ron Oates int.; Bill Sizemore, "After Five Years, $25 Million Hospital Plane Is a Financial Flop," *Virginian-Pilot,* Dec. 24, 2001, A1.

58. Bill Horan int.

59. GR int., Dec. 10, 2007; Deborah Benson int.

60. "A Message from the President," *Blessings,* Oct. 2007, 2; Deborah Benson int.

61. "A Message from the President," 2. "Compassion After the Storm," *Frontlines,* Nov. 2005, 1, 2. Typical of the negative response are "Another FEMA Failure," *Church and State,* Oct. 2005, 13; Rebecca Adams, "Blessing Mess," *CQ Weekly,* Sept. 5, 2005, 2275; but see also "Operation Blessing Stages Emergency Relief for Hurricane Katrina's Victims," *Pat Robertson Newswire,* Aug. 29, 2005, Gale Document A135588758, http://find.galegroup.com.

62. "CBN Is Still There," *Frontlines,* Feb. 2007, 2; Kate Morgan, "Free Health Clinic in Eastern New Orleans to Close," Associated Press State & Local Wire, Dec. 8, 2007, http://www.lexisnexis.com, Dec. 12, 2007; Sarah Pate, *Facing the Medical Crisis Post-Katrina,* 8 page pamphlet published by Operation Blessing in 2006.

63. "Love in Action," *Frontlines,* Feb. 2005, 2, 3. Non Rawung int.; Mark McClendon int., Apr. 2, 2008; Deborah Benson int.

64. See "Robertson Charity Wins 'Faith-Based' Grant," *Washington Post,* Oct. 3, 2002, A2; "Robertson Grant Irks Faith-Based Critics," *The Christian Century,* Oct. 23, 2002, 13; Barry W. Lynn, *Piety and Politics,* 137, 138. See "Critical Book by Ex-Staffer in Religion-Based Effort Is Out," *Washington Post,* Oct. 17, 2006, A19; Bill Sizemore, "Gaining Faith in Federal Money?" *Virginian-Pilot,* Jan. 17, 2006, A1.

65. GR int., Mar. 19, 2009. Both Gordon and Pat Robertson had long supported Billy Graham's humanitarian organization, Samaritan's Purse, which operated as a wing of the

Billy Graham Evangelistic Association. See Gene Kapp to Franklin Graham, Apr. 13, 1993, ROA.

66. For a first-hand account of the experiences of a volunteer nurse, see "Nurse to the Needy," *Today's Christian Woman,* Sept.-Oct. 2002, 34. http://www.ob.org, June 22, 2009.

67. http://www.ob.org/_about/history.asp, June 22, 2009. For typical articles, see "'Lighthouse Mission' Serves Hungry," *Blessings,* Mar. 2007, 1, 4; "Who's Hungry in America?" *Blessings,* July 2007, 1, 4. Deborah Benson int.

68. Kim Pascual int.; Peter Kairuz int.; Robert John Tan int.; "Raising a New Generation for the Bondoc Peninsula," *Blessings Asia* (n.d.) 5:3, 1, 2. See John Kalma int.; Kumar Periasamy int.; "Blessings Overflow Through 'Living Waters.'" *Frontlines,* Sept. 2006, 2; John Kalma, "Operation Blessing International Nigeria, Brief Presentation," undated report in possession of the author. Mark McClendon int., Apr. 2, 2008; Yuliya Shevenko int.

69. Bill Horan int.; ML int., Mar. 18, 2009; Deborah Benson int.

70. ML int., Mar. 18, 2009; GR int., Dec. 10, 2007; Mar. 19, 2009.

71. GR int., Oct. 3, 2007; Deborah Benson int.; ML int., Mar. 18, 2009; Michael Carter int.

72. ML int., Mar. 18, 2009; Bill Horan int.; PR int., Oct. 18, 2007; Mar. 19, 2008.

Notes to Chapter 8

1. See Bob Slosser to All Campus, Oct. 29, 1987, RUA.

2. David Gyertson int. A good summary of the transition period, and the name change, is Keith A. Fournier, "Regent University Christian Leadership to Change the World: A Wedding of Action and the Academy," manuscript of a speech delivered at Regent University, Sept. 5, 1996, ROA. Also see "A New Name," *The Flame,* Jan. 1990, 3, 15.

3. Butch Maltby to Rev. J. Murray Marshall, May 30, 1990, ROA. Fournier, "Regent University," 1.

4. ML int., Mar. 18, 2009. JS int.

5. Michael Carter int.

6. Mark A. Noll, *The Scandal of the Evangelical Mind* (Grand Rapids: Eerdmans, 1994), 16, 17. http://www.regent.edu/about_us/overview/history.cfm, June 2, 2009.

7. VS interview with Joseph Umidi, May 24, 2007, typed transcript in possession of the author. VS int., July 13, 2007. http://www.regent.edu/about_us/, June 2, 2009.

8. Christopher Hayes, "Student Body Right," *American Prospect,* Sept. 1, 2005. Accessed at http://vnweb.hwwilsonweb.com/hww/results/results_single_fulltext.jhtml, Dec. 8, 2007.

9. Jeff Pittman int.; Thomas River interview with PR, http://www.cbn.com, May 30, 2007. For current statistics on the university, see http://www.regent.edu/about_us/quick_facts.cfm.

10. Michael Patrick int.; Foege, *The Empire God Built,* 185.

11. See http://sss.regent.edu/about_us/overview/accreditation.cfm, June 2, 2009.

12. Michael Patrick int.; Bobbie Fisher, "Regent Hosts Candlelight Forum in Hollywood," *Christian Leader,* Fall/Winter 2007, 22; see 22-24.

13. VS int. with PR, Dec. 18, 2006, typed transcript in possession of the author. VS int., Apr. 9, 2007. Thomas Pear, "Regent's New Dean of Divinity Followed Unusual Path to Job," *The Virginian-Pilot and the Ledger-Star,* July 19, 1994, B3. Vinson Synan, "A Vision for Regent

University School of Divinity," undated document in possession of the author. See "Regent University School of Divinity," undated pamphlet in possession of the author; Vinson Synan, *A Seminary to Change the World* (Virginia Beach: Regent University School of Divinity, 2007), 30.

14. VS int., July 13, 2007.

15. Herbert W. Titus, *The Biblical Basis of Public Policy* (Chesapeake, Va.: National Perspectives Institute, 1986), 6, 10; David Gyertson int.

16. PR int., Mar. 18, 2008; David Gyertson int.; PR int., Mar. 18, 2008; Oct. 18, 2007. See Mark O'Keefe, "Holy Warriors," *Student Lawyer*, Dec. 1993, 14, 15.

17. See Marley, *Pat Robertson*, 257. Quoted in O'Keefe, "Holy Warriors," 14, 15. PR int., Oct. 18, 2007. See PR to Maude E. Steele, Jan. 18, 1999, ROA.

18. Mark O'Keefe, "Faculty Complaint Clouds Regent Law Accreditation," *Christianity Today*, Jan. 10, 1994, 40. "PR Calls Lawyers 'Inept,'" *The Christian Century*, Apr. 13, 1994, 378. For accounts of the legal wrangling after the Titus dismissal, see Jennifer Ferranti, "Regent University Wins Faculty Tenure Lawsuit," *Christianity Today*, Oct. 2, 1995, 104; Denise K. Magner, "Va. Judge Sides with Regent U. in Faculty-Contract Dispute," *The Chronicle of Higher Education*, Sept. 15, 1995, A21; Ken Myers, "Professors at Evangelist's School Sue Over Defamation, Contracts," *The National Law Journal*, Oct. 24, 1994, A17. Keith Fournier tried to act as peacemaker in 1995 in the lawsuit between Titus and Robertson, suggesting to his boss that while there was "no question of the rightness of your position" he believed it might be possible to resolve their dispute "without compromising the important issues." Keith A. Fournier to PR, Oct. 4, 1995, ROA.

19. Boston, *The Most Dangerous Man*, 231-33. Foege, *The Empire God Built*, 185. Marley, *Pat Robertson*, 258. See Marley's balanced treatment of the implications of the law school struggle, 257-59. David Gyertson int.

20. Julia Duin, "Regent Law School Small, Its Dreams Big," *Washington Times*, July 7, 1996, A1. Keith Fournier int.

21. Philip Walzer, "Watching Regent Grow," *Virginian-Pilot*, May 30, 2001, A1. Jeff Brauch int.; Kristi Lemoine, "Regent University School of Law Takes Negotiation Competition Prize," *Student Lawyer*, Sept. 2007, 38.

22. Jeff Brauch int.; JS int.

23. See Charlie Savage, "Scandal Puts Spotlight on Christian Law School Grads Influential in Justice Dept.," *Boston Globe*, Apr. 8, 2007, A1; Dahlia Lithwick, "Justice's Holy Hires," *Washington Post*, Apr. 8, 2007, B2; David Stout and David Johnston, "A Top Aide to Gonzales Resigns, Becoming Latest Fallout Casualty," *New York Times*, Apr. 7, 2007, A1. Jeff Brauch int.

24. Philip Walzer, "Regent University Plans Full Undergraduate Program," Norfolk *Virginian-Pilot*, Apr. 25, 2005, A1. Thomas River interview with PR, http://www.cbn.com, May 30, 2007.

25. Thomas River interview with PR; PR int., Mar. 19, 2008. http://oedb.org/rankings, June 2, 2009. *The 700 Club*, Sept. 12, 2007.

26. VS int., Apr. 9, 2007; DR int.; Fournier, "Regent University"; Tim Robertson int., Apr. 10, 2007; "Robertson's Regent Banking on Tuition to Stop Deficits," Associated Press State & Local Wire, Aug. 12, 2007. DR int.

27. Barry W. Lynn, "My Debate at Regent U," *Church and State*, Dec. 2003, 21. See Steven G. Vegh, "At Regent Scholars Discuss Religion in Democracy," *Virginian-Pilot*, Feb. 3, 2007, Gale Document Number CJ158783668. See BJ to Mrs. DeKonly, Mar. 23, 2007, ROA.

28. "Regent University Endowment to Top $276 Million," Regent University Press Release, June 11, 1997, RUA.

29. PR int., Mar. 19, 2008. Steven G. Vegh, "Regent University Banks on More Undergrads to Aid Finances," *Virginian-Pilot*, Aug. 7, 2007, 1A. The Regent endowment peaked in 2000 at around $366 million before falling to a low of $248 million in 2004-2005. It began increasing again, reaching $278 million in 2007. PR int., Mar. 18, 2009.

30. http://www.regent.edu/about_us/leadership/trustees.cfm, June 2, 2009. DR int.; ML int., Nov. 15, 2007.

31. ML int., Nov. 15, 2007; David Gyertson int.; DR int.

32. David Gyertson int.; see "Gyertson Accepts New Position," *Regent University Impact* 3:4 (1993), 5. PR int., Oct. 18, 2007.

33. Untitled announcement, *Regent University Impact* 3:4 (1993), 2.

34. See http://facultystaff.vwc.edu/~tlindvall/illustratedbio.htm, June 12, 2009. Harvey Cox, "The Warring Visions of the Religious Right," *The Atlantic Monthly*, Nov. 1995, 59-69. Marc Fisher, "Pat Robertson's J-School," *American Journalism Review*, Mar. 1998, 46. Julia Duin, "Regent's President Returns to Classroom," *Washington Times*, Sept. 6, 1997, A3.

35. Marley, *Pat Robertson*, 260. Marley's treatment of Lindvall reflects clear appreciation of the "young vibrant leader"; see 253-66. Foege, *The Empire God Built*, 186. http://facultystaff.vwc.edu/~tlindvall/illustratedbio.htm, June 12, 2009.

36. PR int., Oct. 18, 2007. Lindvall's pranks on campus are Regent legends. It is fitting that his current biographical page on the website of Virginia Wesleyan College, where he now teaches, is a series of cartoons. http://facultystaff.vwc.edu/~tlindvall/illustratedbio.htm, June 12, 2009. PR int., Oct. 6, 2008. Marley, *Pat Robertson*, 253. David Gyertson int.

37. PR int., Oct. 6, 2008.

38. See Ron Oates int.; VS int., Apr. 9, 2007. PR int., Oct. 18, 2007.

39. David John Marley correctly concludes that finding faculty and administrators who understood and could implement the delicate balance between excellence and openness was a more difficult challenge "than he could have imagined." Marley, *Pat Robertson*, 101. Philip Walzer, "Watching Regent Grow," *Virginian-Pilot*, May 30, 2001, A1. PR int., Oct. 18, 2007. Walzer, "Watching Regent Grow," A1; PR int., Mar. 19, 2008; DR int.

40. Steven Vegh, "Regent Film Students to be Asked to Follow Artistic Guidelines," *Virginian-Pilot*, Jan. 10, 2003, A1. Marley, *Pat Robertson*, 262.

41. For a biographical sketch of Ryan, see http://www.pr-inside.com/argosy-university-has-named-barry-t-r206496.htm, June 18, 2009. See Marley's scathing indictment of Ryan, *Pat Robertson*, 262-64. He notes that Ryan "reportedly had a reputation as someone who saw dissent as disloyalty and would remove anyone who challenged his authority. A university is not a great place for a person who dislikes dissent, but based on Robertson's choice, it was clear that he wanted to remove anyone whose actions on campus could threaten or even embarrass his greater empire" (262). It is certainly consistent with Robertson's managerial style to act swiftly to protect the institutions he founded to assure they did not veer from the mission he had set for them. Marley, *Pat Robertson*, 262, 263.

42. PR int., Mar. 18, 2009. Marley states that "Ryan allegedly had a history of sexual misconduct that caused him to leave both Westmont and Point Loma." *Pat Robertson*, 262.

43. PR to Terry Lindvall, Mar. 17, 1994, ROA. Jeff Brauch int.

44. ML int., Oct. 16, 2007. See SR int.; Keith Fournier int.; DR int. See PR, *The Greatest Virtue* (Virginia Beach: CBN, 2003), 56; http://www.regent.edu/about_us/, June 2, 2009; PR int., Mar. 5, 2007; JS int.; Tim Robertson int., Apr. 10, 2007.

45. Foege, *The Empire God Built,* 182.

46. Cox, "The Warring Visions of the Religious Right," 59-69. Foege, *The Empire God Built,* 178.

47. Barry Lynn int.; Jeff Brauch int.; Steven G. Vegh, "What Is the Real Face of Regent's Law School?" Norfolk *Virginian-Pilot,* June 18, 2007, A11.

48. PR, "Remarks in Support of Senate Joint Resolution 199 Before the Senate Judiciary Committee, Aug. 18, 1982," 4, 7, manuscript copy in ROA. PR, "A War on Religion in Name of Freedom," *Virginian-Pilot,* Feb. 13, 1983, C1, C2. See "Evangelist Blasts ACLU for Secular Emphasis," *Daily Press,* Dec. 14, 1981, press clipping, RUA; Diane Winston, Raleigh *News and Observer,* Feb. 17, 1985, press clipping, RUA.

49. JS int.; see Bill Keith, "Creation Science Legal Defense Fund Application for Grant," Feb. 24, 1984; Herbert Titus to PR and Ted Pantaleo, Mar. 6, 1984; Bill Keith to BJ, Jan. 21, 1987, ROA. CBN contributed more than $100,000 to defend the Louisiana law. At a press conference in New Orleans in 1987 during his presidential campaign, Robertson announced that he "was outraged by the Supreme Court decision declaring that the teaching of creation science is unconstitutional." "PR Responds to Supreme Court Decision Regarding Creation Science," Americans for Robertson press release, June 19, 1987, AFR Papers, RUA. See Tim Stafford, "Move Over, ACLU," *Christianity Today,* Oct. 25, 1993, 20-24. JS int.

50. Bob Partlow to CBN Vice Presidents, CBN University President, Vice Presidents and Deans, Oct. 2, 1984, RUA. See also JS int.; Majorie Mayfield, "Religious Clubs Get OK to Meet in Public Schools," *Virginian-Pilot,* June 5, 1990, A1, A5.

51. JS int.

52. In August Robertson informed a correspondent that "those of us forming the American Center For Law and Justice do not wish to become associated with the National Legal Foundation." PR to Meldarene Begley, Aug. 7, 1990. RR to C. Fred Bateman, Apr. 10, 1990, ROA. RR to John Marshall Meisburg Jr., Aug. 9, 1990, ROA. See RR int., May 23, 2007. BJ to John M. Gustafson, Aug. 9, 1990 *[sic]* (this letter seems to be a 1991 response to Gustafson to BJ, Aug. 27, 1990, ROA).

53. "The Rising Storm," *The Flame,* June/July 1990, 10, 11. Fundraising letter signed by PR, June 5, 1990, ROA. See "Articles of Incorporation of American Center for Law and Justice, Inc.," ROA. The original directors of the organization were Pat Robertson, Herb Titus, Ralph Reed, Jay Sekulow, and Alan E. Sears. PR to Marian R. Hardy, Jan. 16, 1991; see Hardy to PR, Aug. 1, 1990, ROA.

54. PR to Alan E. Sears, June 14, 1990, ROA. In 1994 Sears became president and CEO of the Alliance Defense Fund, a conservative legal firm established with the backing of several prominent evangelical leaders, including Bill Bright, James Dobson, and James Kennedy.

55. Keith A. Fournier to PR, Jan. 18, 1990, ROA. Fournier's other "mutual friend" was Chuck Colson. Keith Fournier int.

56. PR to Keith Fournier, May 29, 1991. See Fournier to PR, May 29, 1991; Keith Fournier int.; PR int., Oct. 17, 2007. Fournier, "Fighting for Law and Justice" (Virginia Beach: Liberty, Life and Family Publications, 1994), 6.

57. Norm Berman to PR, May 24, 1991, with PR handwritten notes, ROA. Keith Fournier to PR, Feb. 3, 1992, ROA.

58. RR, "Meeting of the Board of Directors American Center for Law and Justice, Virginia Beach, Virginia," Feb. 19, 1991, ROA. PR to JS, June 4, 1991; JS to PR, May 29, 1991, ROA. See Fournier's description of the courtship of Sekulow in "Fighting for Law and Justice," 12-15.

59. Michael Patrick to PR, May 16, 1990, ROA.

60. PR, "Opening Statement," *Law and Justice,* Nov. 1992, 2. PR to Rob Hartley, May 28, 1992, ROA.

61. JS, *Knowing Your Rights* (Virginia Beach: CBN, 1993), i. Fournier, "Fighting for Law and Justice," 17. See JS to PR, Feb. 11, 1999, ROA.

62. Keith Fournier int.; PR int., Oct. 17, 2007. JS to Keith Fournier, Sept. 20, 1999; JS to PR and J. Nelson Happy, Sept. 20, 1999, ROA.

63. For an example of Fournier's writings during these years see "Cal Thomas Fails to Understand the Papal Stance on Evolution," ACLJ memo, Nov. 1, 1996, ROA. JS int.; PR int., Oct. 17, 2007.

64. "It's Time to Fight for Our God-given Freedoms," *Frontlines,* Oct. 1992, 4, 5. "Fall Opening Slated for Legal Command Center," *Frontlines,* July 1993, 5. "But the War Rages On," *Frontlines,* Sept. 1993, 5.

65. See ROA for copies of bi-monthly reports by Regional Counsels to JS. Mark O'Keefe, "Holy Warriors," 15. See also "Robertson's Lawyers," *Christian Century,* Oct. 21, 1992, 930. PR, *The Turning Tide* (Manhattan, Kansas: Kansas State University, 1993), 9. See Tim Stafford, "Move Over, ACLU," 20-24.

66. Sara Diamond, "The Religious Right Goes to Court," *Humanist,* May/June 1994, 35-37.

67. O'Keefe, "Holy Warriors," 12, 19, 20. See JS, ACLJ memo, Feb. 25, 1997, ROA.

68. J. Nelson Happy, "Minutes of the 1999 Annual Meeting of American Center for Law and Justice, Inc.," ROA; JS int.

69. PR to John Ashcroft, Sept. 10, 1999, ROA. "American Center for Law and Justice, First Quarter 2000 Combined Financial Results," ROA.

70. http://www.aclj.org/About/Default.aspx?Section=10, Aug. 31, 2009. A listing of ACLJ Supreme Court cases may be found at http://www.aclj.org/Cases.

71. Linda Greenhouse, "Free-Speech Case Divides Bush and Religious Right," *New York Times,* Mar. 18, 2007, 1, 22. http://www.aclj.org/Cases/, Aug. 31, 2009. See Joan Biskupic, "High Court Tackles Utah Monument Rules," *USA Today,* Nov. 12, 2008, 4A; Richard W. Garnett, "We Must Guard Our Free Speech Fortress," *USA Today,* Mar. 30, 2009, 13A.

72. Michael D. Simpson, "School Prayer is Back," *NEA Today,* Sept. 1994, 19.

73. Nancy E. Roman, "Center Uses Free Speech to Defend Religious Rights," *Washington Times,* July 18, 1993, A1. Barry Lynn int.

74. PR to Cecelia Chapman, July 16, 1996, ROA. JS, *Witnessing Their Faith* (Oxford: Rowman & Littlefield Publishers, Inc., 2006), xii.

75. PR to Arlen Specter, Oct. 12, 1995, ROA. JS, *Witnessing Their Faith;* PR, *Courting Disaster* (Nashville: Integrity Publishers, 2004). The literature on separation of church and state is vast. In addition to differences over the "original intent" of the Establishment Clause, the discussion invariably includes explorations of the nation's cultural self-definition. Robertson is deeply committed to preserving the nation's religious heritage, believing that the vision of the founders was deeply rooted in the Christian religion. He

believes that America's challenge is "not to forget the religious nature of our nation's origins." *Courting Disaster,* 43. Opponents feared that those embracing the idea of a Christian nation would like to impose a religious and intellectual tyranny. William Martin writes: "We cannot separate religion and politics. The question is how they are to be related in such a way as to maintain the pluralism that has served us so well. The core of that pluralism is not the dogma that all opinions are equally valid but the conviction that civility and the public peace are important, that respect for minorities and their opinions is a crucial element of a democratic society, and that, however persuaded I am of the rightness of my position, I may still, after all, be wrong." *With God on Our Side* (New York: Broadway Books, 1996), 385. On the meaning of the nation's Christian heritage, Robertson's views often seemed narrower than those expressed by Sekulow. For instance, while Sekulow honored the nation's Christian heritage, he rejected outright the notion of returning to pre-1962 mandated prayers in public schools. "Mandatory school prayer does not fall within the protection of the First Amendment," Sekulow told reporters in 1993. "I could tolerate a 30 second [Muslim] prayer. In America we learn that the price of freedom is sometimes you hear things you don't like." Tim Stafford, "Move Over, ACLU," 24.

76. Barry Lynn int.; JS int.; http://www.aclj.org/About, Aug. 31, 2009. JS to PR, Sept. 4, 2001, ROA.

77. *Pat Robertson's Perspective,* July-Aug. 1992, 3. "Robertson Asks God to Oust Liberal Justices," *Christian Century,* Aug. 9, 2003, 13. See Pat Robertson National Public Radio Interview by Madeleine Brand, Feb. 23, 2005, NewsBank News File Collection, Jan. 21, 2008; Dale Eisman, "'Out-of-Control' Federal Judges Endanger U.S., Robertson Says," *Virginian-Pilot,* May 2, 2005, A1; "Federal Judges Worse than al-Qaeda Terrorists, Robertson Tells ABC," *Church and State,* June 2005, 17, 18. See http://www.aclj.org/news/Read.aspx?ID =1485, Aug. 31, 2009.

78. R. Jonathan Moore, *Suing for America's Soul* (Grand Rapids: Eerdmans, 2007), 127, 128. JS to Keith Fournier, Oct. 4, 1995, ROA.

79. See George Thomas to Rob Allman and Drew Parkhill; Drew Parkhill to GR; GR to GGC, Nov. 1, 2005. The first memo was sent at 10:49 a.m., the second at 10:52, and the third at 12:50 p.m. Gordon's memo was sent "for Dad." The attached article, written by Tony Mauro, was entitled "The Secrets of Jay Sekulow." "Pat Robertson Attorney Has High-Flying Lifestyle, Says Legal Newspaper," *Church and State,* Dec. 2005, 15.

80. Happy, "Minutes of the 1999 Annual Meeting of American Center for Law and Justice, Inc." See http://www.eclj.org/About/; http://www.sclj.org/, Aug. 30, 2009. JS int.

81. JS int.; PR int., Oct. 17, 2007; GR int., Dec. 10, 2007.

82. "Religious Right Groups File Briefs to Defend Colson Prison Program," *Church and State,* Nov. 2006, 20. JS int.; Foege, *The Empire God Built,* 189. JS int.; BJ to Tony Mauro, Oct. 28, 2005, ROA. For a sampling of Sekulow's reports to Robertson, see JS to PR, Apr. 17, 1997 ("Same-Sex Marriage Update"); JS to PR, May 17, 2001 ("Attorney General Ashcroft's Prayer Meeting"); JS to PR, July 19, 2002 *("Davey v. Locke"),* ROA.

83. PR int., Oct. 18, 2007. David John Marley notes: "The reason that Robertson and Sekulow got along so well was that they agreed on an important point: American politics was hostile to anyone with religious ideals and someone had to stand up for their rights." *Pat Robertson,* 213. Robertson and Sekulow have agreed about almost every issue. Sekulow has often sought Robertson's advice, but the two rarely disagree. JS int.

Notes to Chapter 9

1. TM int.
2. Matt Paxton int.
3. PR to All CBN Staff, Oct. 6, 1980, RUA. PR to Joseph Becker, Nov. 16, 1994, ROA.
4. PR int., Nov. 23, 2007. See http://www.patrobertson.com/index.asp, Dec. 10, 2008. Monci J. Williams, "The Power and the Glory," *Total,* July 31-Aug. 6, 1992, 11. Quoted in Foege, *The Empire God Built,* 15. Barry Lynn int.
5. Foege, *The Empire God Built,* 229, 230. See *Pat Robertson's Perspective,* Mar. 1977, 2; PR to Leslie Lutz, Mar. 25, 1994, ROA. PR int., Mar. 19, 2008.
6. PR int., Oct. 23, 2007. *The 700 Club,* June 3, 2008; July 21, 2008.
7. Daniel Roth, "Pat Robertson's Quest for Eternal Life," *Fortune,* June 10, 2002, 132-46. A "Correction" to Roth's article was published which acknowledged that at the time the article was written "no loss has been realized on those assets" and that Robertson's "uncanny ability to persuade ordinary folks to send him cash" had no bearing on his private investments since "no charitable donations have been used to fund CENCO or Freedom Gold." "Correction," *Fortune,* July 19, 2002, 30.
8. DR int.; ML int., Nov. 15, 2007.
9. See "Cenco Refining Company," undated document answering questions for investors, ROA.
10. Fiona Williams, "Evangelist Robertson Shifts Management at Santa Fe Springs, Calif., Refinery," *Long Beach Press-Telegram,* November 13, 2001, 12. PR int., Oct. 23, 2007. Greg Winter, "Grand Plan Haunts Pat Robertson," *New York Times,* Feb. 3, 2002, 24. See Roth, "Pat Robertson's Quest for Eternal Life," 132-46. Roth's description of the refinery debacle is detailed. See also "Miracle Never Came," *Oil Express,* Feb. 10, 2003, 7.
11. For a description of the origins of the Liberian venture, see Daniel Roth, "Pat Robertson's Quest for Eternal Life," *Fortune,* June 10, 2002, 132-41.
12. "Press Release," May 18, 1999. Unidentified document, ROA.
13. GGC to Mr. and Mrs. Robert Wetty, Sept. 15, 1999, ROA. Joseph Mathews to Sue H. Jones, Feb. 14, 2002, ROA.
14. Colbert I. King, "Pat Robertson and His Business Buddies," *Washington Post,* November 10, 2001, A27. See King, "Pat Robertson's Gold," *Washington Post,* September 22, 2001, A29; "TV Preacher Robertson Joins Liberian Dictator in Gold-Mining Venture," *Church and State,* November 2001, 19. Daniel Roth, "Pat Robertson: He's No Goldfinger," *Fortune,* August 11, 2003, 34.
15. Sonja Barisic, "Pat Robertson Defends Liberian President," AP Online, July 10, 2003, copy in ROA.
16. See Alan Cooperman, "Robertson Defends Liberia's President," *Washington Post,* July 10, 2003, A19; Cooperman to PR, July 10, 2003. "Notebook," *New Republic,* July 21, 2003, 8, 9. For a critical description of a 2002 rally in Monrovia led by John Gimenez, see "Liberian Dictator Says Country Under Rule of Jesus Christ," *Church and State,* April 2002, 17. PR int., Oct. 23, 2007. http//www.cbn.com/, Oct. 26, 2004; copy in ROA.
17. See Steven G. Vegh, "Robertson's Ready to Resume Gold Prospecting in Liberia," *Virginian-Pilot,* July 14, 2006. PR int., Oct. 23, 2007.
18. Norimitsu Onishi, "Africans Fill Churches that Celebrate Wealth," *New York Times,* Mar. 13, 2002, A1, A4. See, for example, PR to W. F. Ross, Apr. 26, 1996, ROA. Robertson often chided the press for ignoring the sweep of the charismatic revival in the southern hemi-

sphere. See "Media Missing Story of Christian Growth in 'Global South,'" *National Catholic Reporter,* Mar. 4, 2005, 3.

19. *Pat Robertson's Perspective,* Apr. 1977, 3; Jan. 1980, 2.

20. PR int., Oct. 23, 2007. Toby Lester, "Oh Gods!" *Atlantic Monthly,* Feb. 2002, 45.

21. See Rob Boston's account of Robertson's Zaire venture, *The Most Dangerous Man,* 195-207. Thomas Maier, "Robertson's Ties with Zaire Leader Questioned," *Newsday,* May 21, 1995, A43. James Adams, "Top TV Evangelist Trumpets a Tyrant," London *Sunday Times,* August 20, 1995. Jonathan C. Randal, "Robertson Aids Zaire," *Washington Post,* May 18, 1995, A21.

22. George Bush to PR, Mar. 3, 1992, ROA. PR to Jeffrey O'Rourke, Sept. 25, 1996, ROA. Andrew Purvis and Adam Zagorin, "Jewels for Jesus," *Time,* Feb. 27, 1995, 30. PR to Thomas M. Payne, Jan. 14, 1998, ROA. Years later, Robertson estimated that as a result of the television broadcasts in Zaire, "we had five million people won to the Lord." PR int., Mar. 18, 2009. See Robertson to O'Rourke; this letter, written as the collapse of the Mobutu regime drew near, acknowledged that the president had not "chosen to follow these principles and his nation is still in chaos."

23. Bill Sizemore, "With Pat Robertson's African Mining Operation Awash in Red Ink the Blame Game Has Begun," *Virginian-Pilot,* Mar. 4, 1997, A1, A4. GGC to author, Oct. 23, 2009; "The Facts About Pat Robertson and His Activities in Zaire," Operation Blessing press release, May 1997, 3. GGC to Loy K. Cash, Jan. 26, 2006, ROA.

24. Beginning in 1996, Virginia Beach reporter Bill Sizemore wrote a series of carefully researched and highly critical articles about the African Development Company and its relationship with Operation Blessing; the most detailed is "With Pat Robertson's African Mining Operation Awash in Red Ink the Blame Game Has Begun." See Sizemore, "Operation Blessing Planes Were Used Mostly for Mining, 2 Pilots Say," *Virginian-Pilot,* April 27, 1997, A4; "Charity Planes Served Mining Firm, Pilots Say," *Washington Post,* April 28, 1997, A6; "Pat Robertson's Aid Sent to Mines, Pilot Says," *New York Times,* April 28, 1997, 12. GGC to author, Oct. 23, 2009. See "Robertson Charity Misled Donors about Africa Work," *Church and State,* Sept. 1999, 20.

25. Robert W. Fanning to Editor, *Virginian-Pilot,* April 29, 1997, ROA. See "The Facts about Pat Robertson and His Activities in Zaire," Operation Blessing news release, May 1997, ROA. "Pat Robertson Returns from Medical Mission to Zaire," CBN news release, May 19, 1995, ROA.

26. The older Catholic and Protestant missionary establishment in Zaire and throughout Africa had been to some extent influenced by Liberation Theology, and sometimes by Marxist ideology, and they often found themselves at odds with authoritarian dictators. The charismatic/Pentecostal independents were less involved in politics but undiscriminating in their political associations. For a summary of the resentment of the older religious elements, see Boston, *The Most Dangerous Man,* 199, 200. David Martin, *Forbidden Revolutions: Pentecostalism in Latin America and Catholicism in Eastern Europe* (London: SPCK, 1996), 10, 11.

27. Onishi, "Africans Fill Churches that Celebrate Wealth," A4. PR int., Oct. 23, 2007. Martin, *Forbidden Revolutions,* 12.

28. Joel Carpenter, "Offshore Accounts," *Evangelical Studies Bulletin,* Spring 2007, 4. Martin, *Forbidden Revolutions,* 45-48.

29. "Zaire African Development Corporation Response," undated [1995] policy statement, ROA. PR to Thomas M. Payne, Jan. 14, 1998, ROA. Robertson was also criticized for

hosting Zairian rebel leader Laurent Desire Kabila on *The 700 Club* on Apr. 25, 1995. The former Marxist leader who unseated Mobutu in 1997 and ruled until his death in 2001 was an "unlikely ally," noted an article in the *Wall Street Journal,* "Will a Zairian Rebel Visit U.S. as a Guest of Pat Robertson?" Apr. 30, 1997, A1. PR to Pierre Ishienda Balonga, Dec. 7, 1999, ROA. PR int., Oct. 23, 2007.

30. For an official accounting of the history of the KaloVita venture, see "The Real Story Behind the ABC Primetime Live Report," Nov. 4, 1994, ROA. PR to Thomas M. Payne, Jan. 14, 1998, ROA.

31. See Michael Isikoff and Mark Hosenball, "With God There's No Cap," *Newsweek,* October 3, 1994,

32. See, for example, *Pat Robertson's Perspective,* Feb. 1990, 7. PR int., Oct. 23, 2007. See "Pat's Millennium Shake," http//www.cbn.org/living/health/patshake.asp, Nov. 10, 1999. See also "Pat's Age-Defying Protein Pancakes," undated CBN flyer; "Pat's Weight-Loss Challenge," undated CBN flyer. A full description of the shake, along with disclaimers, may be found in Pat Robertson, *Bring It On* (Nashville: W Publishing Group, 2003), 313-25. Maria Aspan, "Fitness May Be Next to Godliness, but It Won't Sell Protein Shakes," *New York Times,* June 5, 2006, C3. Angel Vasko to BJ, June 6, 2006, ROA. Bill Sizemore, "Shake Lawsuit Opens Rare Window on Pat Robertson's Media Empire," *Virginian-Pilot,* Mar. 18, 2007. PR int., Oct. 23, 2007.

33. See Paul Magnusson and Lorraine Woellert, "Business Is Not His Calling," *Business Week,* June 28, 1999, 42; Gary Cohen, "On God's Green Earth," *U.S. News & World Report,* April 24, 1995. PR int., Oct. 23, 2007. "Robertson Close to Deal on Vietnam Cable," *Broadcasting and Cable,* May 30, 1994, 32. See also PR int., Oct. 6, 2008.

34. Barry Lynn int.; GR int., Dec. 10, 2007; TR int., Dec. 5, 2007. See also BK int., Mar. 19, 2008; David Gyertson int.

35. PR int., Mar. 19, 2008.

36. Quoted in Steven G. Vegh, "Pat Robertson a Prominent Force in Publishing," *Virginian-Pilot,* April 11, 2005, A1.

37. "How Pat Gets Everything in *Perspective*," *Frontlines,* Nov. 1992, 3. TR int., Apr. 10, 2007. Barry Lynn int.

38. PR to Amy, file copy of letter dated June 6, 2002, ROA.

39. GGC to author, Oct. 23, 2009. White, at the time a professor at Fuller Theological Seminary who had ghostwritten copy for a number of evangelical leaders, asserted in 2006 that he wrote the campaign book with virtually no direction from Robertson, who was fully engaged in the campaign. See White's account in Mel White, *Religion Gone Bad* (New York: Jeremy P. Tarcher/Penguin, 2006), 61-64. Robertson insisted that he read the manuscript, in spite of his rigorous campaign schedule, and while he considered it a "weak book," he did not think it needed serious revision. PR int., Mar. 18, 2009. See David John Marley's description in *Pat Robertson,* 115-17.

40. PR int., Mar. 18, 2009; SR int. See Marley, *Pat Robertson,* 87-89; John B. Donovan, *Pat Robertson,* 128. PR with Bob Slosser, *The Secret Kingdom* (Nashville: Thomas Nelson, 1982).

41. PR to Rick Pettigrew, Nov. 29, 1994, ROA. Karen Hull, "The Secret Kingdom," *The Saturday Evening Post,* Apr. 1983, 112; see 46-47, 111-12. PR with Bob Slosser, prepared by Leslie H. Stobbe, *The Secret Kingdom Leader's Guide* (Nashville: Thomas Nelson, 1983).

42. Boston, *The Most Dangerous Man,* 145. PR, *The New Millennium* (Dallas: Word, 1990), 317, 318.

43. PR to Verna A. Hendricks, June 3, 1994; PR to Jan Mathews, Mar. 4, 1991; PR to Mr. and Mrs. Max Feingold, Apr. 16, 1991; PR to Marilyn P. Perreten, Sept. 6, 1995, ROA.

44. See Don Feder, "Anti-Defamation League Slanders Christian Right," *Human Events,* July 1, 1994, 15. GGC to author, Oct. 23, 2009. See Michael Lind, "On Pat Robertson," *New York Review of Books,* April 20, 1995, 67-68; Jacob Heilbrunn, "His Anti-Semitic Sources," *New York Review of Books,* April 20, 1995, 68-71.

45. Copies of Frank Rich articles of Mar. 2, 1995, and Sept. 22, 1994, with handwritten comments, ROA. PR to Arthur Ochs Sulzberger, Mar. 2, 1995, ROA. PR to *New York Times,* Mar. 2, 1995, ROA. Robertson's letter was written on Christian Coalition letterhead. The anti-Semitism exchange was aimed mostly at Robertson's political success with the Christian Coalition. Ralph Reed worked with Robertson in drafting the letter to the *Times.* He wrote: "I know Pat Robertson as well as anyone can on a professional basis. He is one of the dearest and most reliable friends of Israel and the Jewish people to emerge from the evangelical community in the United States in this century." RR, *Active Faith,* 209.

46. Norman Podhoretz, "In the Matter of Pat Robertson," *Commentary,* Aug. 1995, 27-32.

47. Boston, *The Most Dangerous Man,* 16. Timothy K. Jones, "Here's to You, Mr. Robertson," *Christianity Today,* July 20, 1992, 19. PR to *New York Times,* Mar. 2, 1995, ROA. PR, *The New World Order,* 37, 95, 96.

48. PR to Alice Jarvis, Nov. 5, 1976, ROA. *Pat Robertson's Perspective,* Feb. 1977, 1; May 1980, 3, 4; see Sept.-Oct. 1990, 1-3; May-June 1991, 1.

49. PR to E. G. Ruml, Oct. 22, 1996, ROA. *Evans & Novak* transcript, Apr. 15, 1995, ROA.

50. PR int., Oct. 23, 2007. PR to *New York Times,* Mar. 2, 1995, ROA. PR int., Oct. 23, 2007.

51. PR int., Oct. 23, 2007.

52. PR int., Mar. 5, 2007.

53. PR, *Courting Disaster* (Nashville: Integrity, 2004), vii.

54. PR, *Answers to 200 of Life's Most Probing Questions* (Nashville: Thomas Nelson, 1984).

55. Foege, *The Empire God Built,* 165.

56. Quoted in William Martin, *With God on Our Side: The Rise of the Religious Right in America* (New York: Broadway Books, 1996), 285.

57. TM int.; GR int., Mar. 19, 2009; Dec. 10, 2007.

58. TM int.; Barry Lynn int.

59. Form letter signed by PR, Aug. 25, 1995, ROA.

60. Barry Lynn int.; Boston quoted in *Church and State,* Sept. 2008.

61. TR int., Apr. 10, 2007. Marley, *Pat Robertson,* 173.

62. In the 1970s Robertson had a warm and friendly relationship with William Willoughby of the *Washington Star.* Ron Oates int. Robertson offered a surprisingly mild analysis of media bias in 1992: "I don't think the media believes it's biased. Since they rarely run into a conservative or a Republican in their line of work, they think their slanted news coverage is objective reporting of reality. That's what's so frustrating to me. We can't correct the bias if they don't think it's there." *The Robertson Report,* December 2, 1992. RR to Anthony Lewis, Nov. 24, 1992, ROA. PR, *The Greatest Virtue,* 60.

63. *The 700 Club,* September 12, 2008. Larry King quoted in Foege, *The Empire God Built,* 210.

64. PR to the editor, *Miami Herald,* July 13, 1990, ROA (letter written on Christian Coalition letterhead). PR to John O. Wynne, June 10, 1999, ROA. Interestingly, Robertson felt that "The *New York Times* along the way has treated me very well." PR int., Mar. 18, 2008.

65. PR int., Mar. 5, 2007. PR, *The Greatest Virtue*, 62. Barry Lynn to "Dear Friend," undated Americans United fundraising letter forwarded to PR by Don Hodel on Oct. 7, 1998, ROA. PR to Michael Green, Feb. 18, 1997, ROA.

66. "PR and Americans United: Nasty Name-Calling," *Church and State*, Mar. 1997, 7. "Robertson Redux: Pat's Provocative Patter," *Church and State*, Oct. 2005, 11. Lynn, *Piety and Politics*, 237, 258. In particular, Lynn objected to Jim Wallis's charge that Americans United attacked "anyone who has the audacity to be religious in public" (168).

67. See Mary Jacoby, "Watchdog, Televangelist Locked in Long War of Ideas," *St. Petersburg Times*, August 16, 1999, 1A. Jay Sekulow int.; "My Chat with Pat: Exchanging Views with Brother Robertson," *Church and State*, Nov. 1999, 23. PR to Barry W. Lynn, Oct. 4, 1999, ROA.

68. PR with William Procter, *Beyond Reason* (New York: William Morrow and Company, Inc., 1985), 103-4. See "TV Preacher Robertson Undergoes Surgery for Prostate Cancer," *Church and State*, Apr. 2003, 18. Hunter A. Hogan Jr. to PR, Sept. 1, 1995; PR to Hogan, Oct. 4, 1995, ROA.

69. See Tom Inflield, "Falwell's Finger-Pointing Draws Caution," *Philadelphia Inquirer*, September 17, 2001, A9. Dinesh D'Souza expanded on this theme in 2006 by linking 9/11 with "the cultural left." See Warren Bass, "In an Angry Polemic, Dinesh D'Sousa Blames American Liberals for the 2001 Terrorist Attacks," *Washington Post*, Jan. 14, 2007, T5. See Andrew R. Murphy, "'One Nation Under God,' Sept. 11 and the Chosen Nation: Moral Decline and Divine Punishment in American Public Discourse," *Political Theology* (London: Equinox Publishing Ltd., 2005), 9-30. See "Hall of Shame," *National Review*, November 15, 2002, 15-18. Cynthia Burack, "Getting What 'We' Deserve: Terrorism, Tolerance, Sexuality, and the Christian Right," *New Political Science*, Sept. 2003, 329; see 329-49. This article is a good summary of the reaction to the comments surrounding the 9/11 statements. Burack also sees the episode as a part of a broad religious-right assault on homosexuality in particular and tolerance in general.

70. Stephen Breen, "Bank Faces Shareholders on Robertson Deal," *The Scotsman*, June 9, 1999, 2. The course of the Laura Ashley and Bank of Scotland affairs were widely covered by the press in the United Kingdom. A sampling of the articles includes David Montgomery, "Union Quits Bank Deal in Protest Over TV Preacher," *The Scotsman*, June 8, 1999, 7; Andrew Marshall and Andrew Collier, "One Hell of a Deal," *The Independent* (London), Apr. 14, 1999, 3; Mary Braid, "Gay Jibe May Lead to Bank Boycott," *The Independent* (London), June 3, 1999, 7; Jill Treanor, "Bank of Scotland Faces New Blow," *The Guardian* (London), June 8, 1999, 23; James Buxton, "Bank of Scotland Apology," *The Financial Times* (U.K.), June 11, 1999, 24; Mairi Mallon, "Robertson Steps Down from Laura Ashley Board," *The Scotsman*, June 10, 1999, 6. "Bank of Scotland Pays Robertson," *The Irish Times*, June 7, 1999, 18; Quentin Sommerville and Ian Fraser, "Bank Pays 4 Million Pounds to Ditch Robertson," *The Sunday Herald* (London), June 6, 1999, 3.

71. Transcript of *The 700 Club*, Jan. 5, 2006, ROA. GGC to author, Oct. 23, 2009. CBN news release, Jan. 5, 2006, ROA.

72. "Iranian Leader, Evangelist Call Prime Minister's Illness Deserved," *Washington Post*, Jan. 6, 2006, A12. Editorial, "Robertson Loves Ahmadinejad," *Washington Post*, Jan. 8, 2006, B6. See also Steven G. Vegh, "Robertson Implies Land Transfer Prompted God to Punish Sharon," *Virginian-Pilot*, Jan. 6, 2006, A7. http://mediamatters.org, Aug. 11, 2006.

73. See http://mediamatters.org/, Aug. 11, 2006. PR to Glen W. Bocox, Feb. 15, 2006, ROA.

74. Robertson, *The Greatest Virtue*, 63. PR to Omri Sharon, Jan. 11, 2006, ROA. See "Israelis Reverse Stand on Robertson," *The Christian Century*, Feb. 7, 2006, 13.

75. Laurie Goodstein, "Robertson Suggests U.S. Kill Venezuela's Leader," *New York Times*, August 24, 2005, A10. In 1986, the Associated Press reported that Robertson had urged the assassination of Moammar Khadafy. See "Kill Khadafy to Stop Terror, Robertson Says," *Virginian Pilot*, April 12, 1986, clipping in RUA. Alan Cooperman, "Robertson Calls for Chavez Assassination," *Washington Post*, August 23, 2005, A2.

76. Alan Cooperman, "Robertson Apologizes for Calling for Assassination," *Washington Post*, August 25, 2005, A3.

77. See "Robertson's Death Wishes," *National Review*, September 26, 2005, 71. David John Marley asserts: "As a politician he had a sense of realpolitik that should make Henry Kissinger proud." *Pat Robertson*, 283. TM int.; Joel Palser int., Apr. 11, 2007.

78. PR int., Mar. 18, 2008. See *The 700 Club*, June 6, 2008; PR, *Bring It On*, 256-61. "Statement Made by Pat Robertson on *The 700 Club* (3/13/2006) After Dale Hurd's Story on Radical Muslims," undated copy of remarks, ROA. "Pat Robertson Comments on CBN News Story About Radical Islam in Europe on Today's Edition of *The 700 Club*," Public Relations Department memo issued Mar. 13, 2006, ROA. Eric Gormly, "Peering Beneath the Veil: An Ethnographic Content Analysis of Islam as Portrayed on *The 700 Club* Following the Sept. 11th Attacks," *Journal of Media and Religion* 3:4 (2004), 227. Gormly concludes that, as portrayed on *The 700 Club*, "there is no such thing as a moderate Muslim" (230).

79. See *Pat Robertson's Perspective*, Mar. 1977, 1; Apr. 1982, 1. Carlye Murphy, "Remarks by Pat Robertson Insult Islam, Muslims Say," *Washington Post*, November 8, 1997, A14.

80. Alan Cooperman, "Robertson calls Islam a Religion of Violence, Mayhem," *Washington Post*, Feb. 22, 2002, A2. "CNN Live Event/Special, 12:46," Feb. 25, 2002, transcript #022503CN.V54, copy in ROA. PR to Ari Fleischer, Feb. 26, 2002, ROA.

81. "Bush Rebukes Preachers for Slurs on Islam," *Christian Century*, November 20, 2002, 13. Angell Watts to Ari Fleischer, Nov. 22, 2002, ROA. "Today Pat Robertson on *The 700 Club* Program Made a Statement in Response to the Statement of President Bush Dealing with Islam," CBN press release, Nov. 14, 2002, ROA. Larry Witham, "Robertson Pleads for Scrutiny of Koran," *Washington Times*, November 26, 2002, A1.

82. Fareed Zakaria, "Time to Take on America's Haters," *Newsweek*, November 21, 2002, 40. See also press release from Religious Action Center of Reform Judaism, Nov. 15, 2002, copy in ROA; CBN press release, "Pat Robertson's Response to Rabbi Pelavin," Nov. 20, 2002, ROA. Charles Kimball, "Osama and Me," *Sojourners*, Jan./Feb. 2003, 17. Lynn, *Piety and Politics*, 43. For examples of criticism of Robertson's comments about Islam from more liberal evangelicals and Roman Catholics, see Mark Stricherz, "Evangelicals Advise on Muslim Dialogue," *Christianity Today*, July 2003, 42; "Anti-Islam Slurs Remind Catholics of the Past," *National Catholic Reporter*, Mar. 8, 2002, 28.

83. Vincent Davis, "Robertson Right on Islam," *Washington Times*, November 30, 2002, A11. See, for instance, Geneive Abdo, "Israeli Award for Pat Robertson Irks Muslims," *Chicago Tribune*, Feb. 12, 2004, 21; Ben Edwards int., Dec. 5, 2007; GR int., Mar. 19, 2009.

84. Larry Witham, "Robertson Pleads for Scrutiny of Koran," *Washington Times*, November 26, 2002, A1. *The 700 Club*, Nov. 14, 2002; June 6, 2008. This was the central issue in a Robertson interview on *The O'Reilly Factor* in Feb. 2002. See Fox News Network, *The O'Reilly Factor*, Feb. 27, 2002, transcript #022702cb.256, copy in ROA. Julia Duin, "Islam's 'Idealistic Version of Itself' Not Quite the Reality, Historian Says," *Washington Times*, Oct. 30, 2002, A14.

85. Eric Gormly, "Peering Beneath the Veil," 235. *The O'Reilly Factor,* Feb. 27, 2002, transcript.

86. See, for samples of the cumulative listing, John J. Miller, *National Review,* April 28, 2001, 28-30; Editorial, "Hits and Misses," *Virginian-Pilot,* April 27, 2006, A4; "Robertson Suggests Lobbing Nuclear Bomb at U.S. State Department," *Church and State,* Nov. 2003, 15-16; Goodstein, "Robertson Suggests U.S. Kill Venezuela's Leader"; Cooperman, "Robertson Calls for Chavez Assassination"; Steven G. Vegh, "Ton of Truth," *Virginian-Pilot,* June 8, 2006, A1. The ministry response to "e-mails concerning Pat's leg press" explained that the exercise was on an "inclined leg press machine" and concluded: "His doctor . . . has leg pressed 2700 pounds. It is not nearly as hard as the authors of these reports make it out to be. We have multiple witnesses to the 2000 pound leg press, plus video of the 10 reps of 1000 pounds." "Statement in Response to E-Mails Concerning Pat's Leg Press," undated document, ROA. Buckley, "Robertson's Death Wishes," 71.

87. BK int.

88. BK int.; see Steven G. Vegh, "Evangelist to Get Some In-ear Coaching on Air," *Virginian-Pilot,* Feb. 11, 2006, A1; Patrick Roddy int.; *The 700 Club,* Feb. 23, 2009.

Notes to Chapter 10

1. Paul Magnusson and Lorraine Woellert, "Business Is Not His Calling," *Business Week,* June 28, 1999, 42. PR int., Mar. 18, 2009. RR to Francis Chadwick, Dec. 9, 1991, ROA. David Gyertson int.; SR int.; DR int.; Patrick Roddy int.; Anton N. Marco to author, July 25, 1988. "Number one, he *is* an evangelist," observed Vinson Synan; "that is central to his being." Vinson Synan int., Apr. 9, 2007. "He is faithful in his time with the Lord," agreed Terry Meeuwsen. In his excellent study, Alex Foege makes a surprising, and fundamentally incorrect, assertion about Robertson's religion: "Virtually the only aspect of Robertson that I do not explore in detail is his religious convictions. Religion is merely the means by which Robertson has achieved his ends." *The Empire God Built,* 8.

2. Capps, *The New Religious Right,* 181.

3. See PR int., Dec. 6, 2007. PR, "The American Church at the Crossroads," *Christian Herald,* Mar. 1985, 22-24. Many fundamentalists in the late nineteenth and early twentieth century, eschewing the rise of theological modernism, put more and more emphasis on reading the Scriptures without commentary. Some of their conferences restricted the proceedings to Bible reading alone. Memo from PR to R. Gottier et al., Aug. 30, 1982, RUA. PR int. by VS, Dec. 18, 2006, typed copy in possession of author. BJ to RW, Jan. 5, 1983, ROA.

4. "Fundamentalism," *Proceedings of the Center for Jewish-Christian Learning,* Spring, 1990, 18.

5. Memo from PR to R. Gottier et al., Aug. 30, 1982, RUA. PR to Cathy Hicks, June 23, 1993, ROA. When the librarian of the Pentecostal section of the Oral Roberts University Library requested a file of *Pat Robertson's Perspective* for the collection, Barbara Johnson replied: "One correction, however. The *Perspective* should not be classified as a 'Pentecostal' periodical." BJ to Karen Robinson, Mar. 6, 1985, ROA.

6. PR int. by VS, Dec. 18, 2006, typed copy in possession of author.

7. PR int. by VS, Dec. 18, 2006, typed copy in possession of author. PR to Joanne M. Gleichauf, Feb. 17, 1997, ROA. PR to Harry Turner, Mar. 1, 1990, ROA. PR, *Bring It On,* 231. PR to Lori Ably, Jan. 17, 1992, ROA.

8. PR int. by VS, Dec. 18, 2006, typed copy in possession of author; GL int.

9. See Marley, *Pat Robertson,* 56-61. Marley points out that during the George W. Bush administration "critics of the Christian Right were quick to claim that almost every evangelical was a Reconstructionist" (56). Robertson's language, particularly in *The Secret Kingdom,* made him vulnerable. PR to Martina McDaniel, July 30, 1993, ROA. PR to Gary North, Aug. 18, 1986, ROA. For a good discussion of this subject see Justin Watson, *The Christian Coalition,* 115-19. Many of Robertson's political opponents on the left refused to accept any explanation that separated Robertson from "Dominionism or "Christian Reconstructionism." See Kevin Phillips, *American Theocracy,* 215; Simone Richmond, "The End of Civil Law," *Tikkun,* Sept./Oct. 2005, 11. On the other hand, Harvey Cox, after questioning faculty members at Regent University, wrote: "Regent, they insisted, is absolutely not a dominion-theology school, and Pat Robertson himself had demonstrated this recently by getting rid of the dean of the law school." "The Warring Visions of the Religious Right," 68.

10. PR to Wrightson S. Tongue, July 11, 1974, ROA. "A Heritage Roundtable: Anti-Semitism in the Modern World," *The Heritage Lectures,* no. 28, 1984, 20. PR int. by VS, Dec. 18, 2006, typed copy in possession of author.

11. PR int. by VS, Dec. 18, 2006, typed copy in possession of author.

12. See Henry Harrison, "God's Revival Power," *The Flame,* July 1974, 4; Edward E. Plowman, "Decade of the Tube," *Christianity Today,* Mar. 17, 1972, 40; VS int., Apr. 9, 2007. Typed transcript of *The 700 Club,* Mar. 8, 1979, copy in ROA.

13. PR to Harry Turner, Mar. 1, 1990, ROA. PR, "Lessons from History," speech at Christ for the Nations, June 26, 1994, audio tape, ROA.

14. PR to Mrs. Lester Shirey, Apr. 7, 1976, ROA. BJ to Bruce West, Feb. 26, 1999, ROA. Joel Palser int., Dec. 8, 2007.

15. See PR to Rose Shakarian, July 26, 1993; PR to Rock Church, Oct. 15, 1993; PR to Morris Cerullo, Sept. 23, 1993, ROA. Mark Washburn, "Biggest Names in Evangelical TV Join Groundbreaking for New HQ," *Charlotte Observer,* Nov. 6, 2006, 1A.

16. PR to John Parish, Feb. 13, 1987, ROA. PR int., Dec. 10, 2007; *The 700 Club,* Jan. 3, 2008.

17. Oral Roberts to PR, Feb. 12, 1986, ROA.

18. Michael Little int., Mar. 18, 2009. PR to Siegfried E. Rybak, Oct. 28, 1993, ROA. See Steven Strang, "Benny Hinn Speaks Out," *Charisma,* Aug. 1993, 24-29. Form letter signed by PR, dated Aug. 25, 1995, ROA. BJ to CBN Partner Rep Andrew, Mar. 29, 2005, ROA. PR to Benny Hinn, Jan. 18, 2007, ROA. *The 700 Club,* Aug. 4, 2008.

19. See Gayle White, "Holy Laughter," *Atlanta Journal-Constitution,* Oct. 7, 1995, G6. PR to Mr. and Mrs. Alexander A. Coviello, June 9, 1997, ROA. See also BJ to Ken James, June 18, 1997, ROA. *The 700 Club,* Feb. 21, 2008.

20. PR to Mr. and Mrs. William Stevens, Nov. 4, 1996; PR to Mrs. Patricia Finch, Oct. 29, 1993; Lyn Barnes to All Area Directors, Jan. 4, 1984, ROA. PR with William Proctor, *Beyond Reason,* 169; see 58-72, 166-75.

21. PR, *Bring It On,* 205.

22. Gerald Thomas Straub, *Salvation for Sale* (Updated ed.; Buffalo: Prometheus Books, 1988), 351. PR, *The New Millennium,* xii.

23. "1996: A Year of Boldness," *Pat Robertson's Commentary,* undated CBN Partner Newsletter, RUA. PR to John Parish, Feb. 13, 1987, ROA.

24. PR to All Staff, Mar. 19, 1985, RUA. Jay Comisky int.

25. PR, "Holy Spirit in the Now IV," Oct. 24, 1974, manuscript copy, ROA.

26. Form letter signed by PR, Aug. 25, 1995, ROA. "How Does God Guide People?" *Frontlines*, Jan. 1996, 6.

27. PR to George C. Walsh, Oct. 30, 1985, ROA. PR, *The Plan*, 92-93. PR to Mr. and Mrs. B. G. King Sr., Aug. 9, 1978, ROA. "How Do I Know I am Hearing a Word from God?" *Frontlines*, Feb. 1996, 6. PR, *Bring It On*, 231. PR int., Mar. 5, 2007.

28. "Reaffirmation of Ordination Vows by M. G. 'Pat' Robertson," Mar. 27, 2000, Program in possession of author.

29. Marley, *Pat Robertson*, 248. See also Liz Szabo, *Virginian-Pilot*, Mar. 23, 2000, clipping, ROA. PR int., Oct. 23, 2007. See also PR int., Mar. 5, 2007; *Pat Robertson's Perspective*, Apr.-May 1992, 4-5.

30. PR, "What Do You Tell the World?" *Religious Broadcasting*, Nov. 1981, 28. See PR, "Discerning the Signs of the Times," *The Flame*, Mar. 1979, 2; PR, "What Do You Tell the World?" 28. "Special Issue: Prophetic Insights for the 'Decade of Destiny,'" *Pat Robertson's Perspective*, Feb./Mar. 1980, 1. PR to Jack Hartman, Jan. 12, 1981; Jim Spencer, "CBN Head Advises on World Strife," *Ledger-Star*, Feb. 3, 1980, 6. "SAMPLE PARAGRAPH: Perspective," undated document, ROA. *Pat Robertson's Perspective*, Mar. 1989, note attached to this issue which was the first after a lapse of several years. Michael Little wrote to a supporter: "Concerning the Perspective, the intended audience is presumed to be Christians who are supporting the 700 Club with their finances and prayers. Pat wanted to be able to deal with current events in light of the Bible to help our partners prepare for the future and know of certain situations that need prayer." ML to Barbara Lindquist, July 5, 1979, ROA.

31. PR, *Bring It On*, 289, 290. PR to Jack Hartman, Jan. 12, 1981, ROA.

32. PR to Nobel Bowman, July 18, 1972, ROA.

33. PR int., Mar. 18, 2008; Oct. 23, 2007. PR to Tim M. Cowart, June 21, 1995, ROA. PR int., Mar. 18, 2008.

34. For a good survey of the apocalyptic book explosion, see Glenn W. Shuck, *Marks of the Beast* (New York: New York University Press, 2005). See also Nancy Gibbs, "Apocalypse Now," *Time*, July 1, 2002, 40-48. PR to Ruth Brown, Oct. 31, 2005, ROA. This memo is subtitled, "Paul Crouch from PR." A ministry policy statement on "Replacement Theology" read: "Replacement theology states that the church replaced Israel in salvation history. . . . Jews are therefore only another unreached people with no prophetic significance. This has been the traditional Catholic teach [sic] until recent years. Of course, Evangelicals and Pentecostals have rejected this theory because we believe that the Jews are God's chosen people, that God is still dealing with Israel, that 'Israel shall be saved,' and that Israel will play an important role in the end times." "Replacement Theology," undated statement, ROA.

35. "Special Issue: Prophetic Insights," *Pat Robertson's Perspective*, Feb./Mar. 1980, 7. Throughout its publication history, *Pat Robertson's Perspective* was filled with prophetic analysis and predictions that reflected conventional premillennial thinking. Robertson's premillennial beliefs are also scattered throughout his writings. See, for instance, PR, "World Experiences Twilight of 'Times of the Gentiles,'" *The Flame*, Dec. 1974, 2; PR, *The New Millennium*, 312-16; quote on 312.

36. Stephen O'Leary and Michael MacFarland, "The Political Use of Mythic Discourse," *Quarterly Journal of Speech*, Nov. 1989, 446, 447. See Jimmy Swaggart to PR, Aug. 26, 1986, ROA. See Shuck, *Marks of the Beast*, 60. PR, *Bring It On*, 291. Joel Carpenter, *Revive Us Again* (New York: Oxford University Press, 1997), 110, 111; see also George M. Marsden, *Fun-

damentalism and American Culture (New York: Oxford University Press, 1980), 43. PR to Gary North, Aug. 18, 1986, ROA.

37. Shuck, *Marks of the Beast,* 3. "Pat Robertson Predicts 'Mass Killing' Will Strike U. S. Later this Year," *Church and State,* Feb. 2007, 17.

38. See Steven G. Vegh, "Pat Robertson, A Prophet to His Believers," *Virginian-Pilot,* Jan. 13, 2006, A12. Spiritual Gifts Webcast, Mar. 16, 2009. "Forecast for 2007," undated document, ROA.

39. *The 700 Club,* Jan. 2, 2007. BK int., Mar. 19, 2008; SR int.; Vegh, "PR Sees Left Tilt, Rebound Under Obama," Jan. 3, 2009, http://web.ebscohost,com, Apr. 26, 2009.

40. PR, "Two Scriptural Keys Unlock Riddle of the Second Coming," *The Flame,* Feb. 1975, 2-4. PR int., Oct. 23, 2007.

41. PR to J. R. Niemela, Nov. 11, 1996; PR to Rosemary Faraj, Aug. 11, 1982; Pat Robertson to Edgar J. Fisher Jr., June 12, 1979; PR to Musil Shihadeh, Aug. 4, 1975, ROA. Larry Bonko, "He'll Ask Israel to Help Arabs," *Norfolk Ledger-Star,* Apr. 8, 1969, B1. "Ushering in the Second Coming in the Land of Jesus' Birth," *Frontlines,* Dec. 2004, 2.

42. See William Claiborne, "Israelis Look on U.S. Evangelical Christians as Potent Allies in Battle with Arab States," *Washington Post,* Mar. 23, 1980, A11. See PR, "Christians' Israel Public Action Campaign U.S. Solidarity Rally, Jan. 30, 1994," typed copy, ROA; *The 700 Club,* Sept. 24, 2008. "A Heritage Roundtable: Anti-Semitism in the Modern World," *The Heritage Lectures* 28 (1984), 20. PR, "Answers," *Frontlines,* Apr. 1994, 6. PR to Arnold Hardin, Apr. 6, 1994, ROA.

43. See Steve Gushee, "Christian's Israel Jubilee Vexes Some Jews," *Palm Beach Post,* Apr. 2, 1998, 1A. A good discussion of the various dimensions of the Jewish-evangelical alliance is Colin Shindler, "Likud and the Christian Dispensationalists: A Symbiotic Relationship," *Israel Studies* 5:1 (Mar. 31, 2000): 153-65. PR to Rabbi Joseph Hilbrant, June 11, 1997, ROA. Eric Gormly, "Evangelical Solidarity with the Jews: A Veiled Agenda?" *Review of Religious Research* 46:3, 261.

44. *Pat Robertson's Perspective,* July 1977, 1; see *Pat Robertson's Perspective,* Sept. 1980, 1. "Excerpt from Dr. Robertson's Address at the Feast of Tabernacles in Jesusalem — Oct. 2004 — Pertaining to the Dividing of Jerusalem," undated manuscript, ROA. See Edgar Lefkovits, "Robertson Warns Bush Against Dividing Jerusalem," *The Jerusalem Post,* Oct. 4, 2004, 23:51. *The 700 Club,* Oct. 11, 2008. "Christians Call for a United Jerusalem," *New York Times,* Apr. 18, 1997, A13.

45. "Transcript of Remarks at the National Press Club, Oct. 18, 1985," typed transcript, ROA.

46. "Transcript of Remarks at the National Press Club, Oct. 18, 1985," typed transcript, ROA. See *Pat Robertson's Perspective,* Nov. 1977.

47. Benjamin Netanyahu to PR, June 8, 1999; PR to Netanyahu, June 24, 1999; Netanyahu to PR, June 24, 1999, ROA. *The 700 Club,* Feb. 2, 2009.

48. "Churches on Verge of New Unity as 'Holy Spirit' Movement sweeps Denominations," CBN news release, May 24, 1978, RUA. "Orlando '95 Congress on the Holy Spirit," speech manuscript, ROA.

49. Undated Christian Broadcasting Network news release, RUA. PR to Wrightson S. Tongue, July 11, 1974; PR to Robert A. Woosley, Apr. 25, 1947, ROA.

50. PR to Ben Thomas, July 12, 1976, ROA.

51. Jerry and Karen Kool to PR, Apr. 13, 1976; James O. Murphy to Jerry Kool, June 23, 1976, ROA.

52. BS, "Graham Echoes Pope, 'Praise the Lord Jesus Christ,'" *The Flame,* Dec. 1979, 3, 4. See LW int.; ML int., Oct. 15, 2007.

53. *Pat Robertson's Perspective,* Nov. 1979, 4. *The Robertson Report,* Aug. 18, 1993, n.p. Keith Fournier to PR, Oct. 4, 1995, ROA. In the 1990s, mostly as a result of the political efforts of the Christian Coalition, Robertson befriended a number of Catholic leaders. At the death of Cardinal O'Connor, Robertson grieved that "tragic loss" of "a dear friend to me": "He was the kind of man that did more to bring together a feeling of harmony and love between Roman Catholics and Evangelicals than any man I know in the world, and I mourn his passing." Undated CBN news release, RUA. CBN news release, Oct. 7, 1995, ROA.

54. Keith Fournier int.; http://www.leaderu.com/ftissues/ft9405/articles/mission.html, Apr. 17, 2009. Chuck Colson to PR, Jan. 24, 1995; PR to Colson, Feb. 2, 1995, ROA. See the discussion of the charismatic flirtation with Roman Catholicism in *Charisma,* July 1995, 22-33. Robertson told one of the authors contributing to the issue: "While there may be differences between the two faith communities, it is time we focus on the similarities between evangelicals and Catholics. The unifying factor is a belief in Jesus Christ. That is the heart of Christianity, no matter what the denomination." Joe Maxwell, "Catholics and Protestants: Can We Walk Together?" *Charisma,* July 1995, 23. PR to Lucille Ayers, Aug. 30, 1994, ROA.

55. Heidi Schlumpf Kezmoh, "Top Evangelicals Confer with Pope," *Christianity Today,* Nov. 13, 1995, 88. "Robertson Should Be Exposed, Not Given Papal Invitation," *National Catholic Reporter,* Oct. 6, 1995, 24. Bob Jones III to PR, Mar. 30, 1993; PR to Jones, Apr. 5, 1993, ROA. Fournier was well aware of Robertson's exchange with Jones and long appreciated the price Robertson paid for befriending him. See Keith Fournier int.

56. Maxwell, "Catholics and Protestants: Can We Walk Together?" 23. Bob Jones III to PR, Apr. 26, 1993, ROA. PR, "Answers," *Frontlines,* Dec. 1994, 6. PR, form letter, Mar. 28, 1996, ROA.

Notes to Chapter 11

1. A listing of "Dr. Robertson's Favorites" compiled for his private files noted that he continued to maintain memberships in his undergraduate and law fraternities, S.A.E. and Phi Alpha Delta. Undated document, ROA. Neil Eskelin, the first full-time employee at the television station in Portsmouth and a biographer of Robertson, was particularly impressed by the imprint that Robertson's father and mother left on his character. See Eskelin, *Pat Robertson,* 10. Anna Batten Billingsley, "Robertson Says His Proud Virginia Family Heritage Gave Him an Advantage." *Richmond News Leader,* July 1986, 1. See PR, "We Can All be Directed of the Lord!" *Full Gospel Business Men's Voice,* Apr. 1962, 1-4. PR to John J. Capello, Mar. 20, 1997, ROA. See "Marion Gordon 'Pat' Robertson," undated "rough draft" manuscript, ROA; undated letter to "Dear Supporter" from PR, "paid for by Virginia Republican Party," Americans for Robertson files, RUA. See PR to Steve Yoken, June 23, 1993, ROA.

2. PR int., Dec. 6, 2007. PR, "PR's Personal Scrapbook of the Historic Consecration of the New CBN Site," *The Flame,* May 1976, 4, 5. For a fleshing out of this theme, see PR, *The New Millennium,* 312, 313. Neil Eskelin relates an interesting story about Pat's father delivering an address at Cape Henry in 1947 that highlighted the Christian vision of the early Virginia settlers: "But the philosophy of the Christian religion, upon which a new experi-

ment in self-government was to be founded, was symbolized by the cross erected on this spot by the first settlers — 'give thyself.'" Eskelin, *Pat Robertson,* 49. *The 700 Club,* Apr. 29, 2009.

3. Quoted in Donovan, *Pat Robertson,* 9. PR, "Nobility Obligates — the Responsibilities of the Media," undated document, ROA. "Partisan Conversation," *Southern Partisan,* Winter 1986, 42.

4. AWR to George B. Tullidge, May 3, 1945, ROA. *The 700 Club,* Nov. 11, 2008. A sample of Robertson's defense of his service record is PR to Thomas M. Payne, Jan. 14, 1998, ROA. Handwritten comments on Ben Hart to BJ, Apr. 5, 1993, ROA. Joel Palser int., Dec. 8, 2007.

5. "Religious-moral TV Network Competes with the Big Three," copy of unidentified newspaper clipping dated Apr. 1983, RUA. Quoted in Foege, *The Empire God Built,* 73. Larry Bonko, "Partaking of a Dinner Fit for Kings," *Richmond Ledger-Star,* Apr. 4, 1984, 9. Kara Waddell int.

6. "NCC head, Robertson Meet," *Christian Century,* Oct. 25, 1995, 982. Andrew Sullivan, "Enemies: A Love Story," *New York Times,* Apr. 16, 2000, 28.

7. R. J. Koland to PR, Nov. 26, 1997, ROA.

8. http://www.patrobertson.com/index.asp, Mar. 10, 2009. "Partisan Conversation," 40. Robertson's identification with the poor manifested itself in many ways. When a supporter objected to the appearance of Jimmy Carter on *The 700 Club* in 1997, Robertson replied: "It was our desire to have the former President interviewed so he could share how he has been helping the needy and to discuss his involvement in peace negotiations." PR to Evelyn Hutchinson, Feb. 12, 1997, ROA. William A. Garthwaite to PR, Oct. 1, 1993; PR to Garthwaite, Dec. 1, 1993, ROA. TM int.

9. For some examples from *Pat Robertson's Perspective,* see Nov./Dec. 1978, 1; June 1981, 2; July/Aug. 1990, 2. See also Robertson, *The New Millennium,* 103-5. *Pat Robertson's Perspective,* Nov./Dec. 1978, 1. PR to R. Alton Gilbert, June 11, 1979, ROA.

10. VS int., Apr. 9, 2007. Porteous quoted in Foege, *The Empire God Built,* 15. Wesley G. Pippert, "TV on a Prayer," *Christian Life,* Apr. 1968, 72. Most of the books that Robertson reviews on *The 700 Club* are light fare, and he is an expert at quickly scanning them to prepare for interviewing the author. However, he is exposed to a kaleidoscopic array of ideas in the process. ML int., Mar. 18, 2009. Eskelin, *Pat Robertson,* 176.

11. Auletta quoted in Foege, *The Empire God Built,* 16. See also ML int., Apr. 10, 2007. Barry Lynn int.; PR int., Oct. 18, 2007; Oct. 23, 2007.

12. PR int., Mar. 18, 2009. David Gyertson int.; see undated document entitled "Statement From Pat Robertson in Response to Comments Made on 60 Minutes Interview Regarding the Republican Party's Position on Abortion," ROA; PR, "Friendship with China Is a Moral Imperative," *Wall Street Journal,* June 30, 1998, 4; PR, "The Importance of an 'Escape Valve for Mercy,'" *Capitol University Law Review* 3 (2000): 580-83; "Al Sharpton and Pat Robertson Unite and Concur on Climate Change," NewsReleaseWire.com, Apr. 15, 2008; http://www.one.org/c/us/pressrelease/199/. PR to C. Bayhansen, Feb. 26, 1992, ROA. JS int.

13. Foege, *The Empire God Built,* 16. Grant Babre int.; Wesley G. Pippert, "TV on a Prayer," 72; David Gyertson int.

14. Donovan, *Pat Robertson,* 112. PR to All Division/Department Heads/Managers, May 23, 1978; PR to CBN Staff, CBNU Faculty, CBNU Students, May 11, 1983; PR to CBN Division Heads/Department Heads, June 7, 1978; PR to Vice Presidents, Department Heads, June 12, 1984, RUA.

15. PR int., Mar. 19, 2008. PR to Dear Counselor, Feb. 3, 1979, ROA. PR to Vice Presi-

dents, Department Heads, June 12, 1984; PR to All Staff, Aug. 23, 1988; PR to All Staff, May 17, 1983, RUA.

16. ML int., Apr. 10, 2007. Jay Comiskey to PR, July 20, 1989, ROA.

17. JS int.; PR int., Mar. 19, 2008; GR int., Mar. 19, 2009; Ron Oates int.

18. RR int.; PR int., Dec. 6, 2007.

19. SR int.; PR int., Dec. 6, 2007. JS to Keith Fournier, Sept. 20, 1999, ROA. Jay Sekulow int.; PR int., Oct. 18, 2007. David John Marley is probably correct in assuming that Robertson contributed toward an endowment for Terry Lindvall at Virginia Wesleyan College. *Pat Robertson,* 263. Anonymous quoted in Foege, *The Empire God Built,* 38. Vinson Synan int., Dec. 10, 2007; PR int., Oct. 18, 2007. John Donovan writes: "Those who know say Robertson is an iron ruler who replaces weak links in his chain without a moment's hesitation. . . . 'He has a strong temper and a commander temperament,' says one former staff member." *Pat Robertson,* 113.

20. PR int., Oct. 18, 2007.

21. David Gyertson int.; ML int., Oct. 15, 2007. Early employee quoted in Eskelin, *Pat Robertson,* 116. DR int.

22. Joel Palser int., Dec. 8, 2007; TM int.; David Gyertson int.; Joel Palser int., Dec. 8, 2007; ML int., Mar. 18, 2009.

23. Jay Sekulow int.; see BJ to Jeff Anderson, Apr. 17, 1987, ROA. Joel Palser int., Dec. 8, 2007; LW int.

24. GR int., Oct. 15, 2007; Oct. 10, 2008.

25. David Gyertson int.; PR, *The Greatest Virtue,* 96.

26. PR int., Mar. 18, 2009; ML int., Mar. 19, 2009.

27. See Michael J. Connor, "On This Talk Show, the Talk Can Take a Miraculous Turn," *Wall Street Journal,* January 14, 1976, 1, 22; Scott Sunde, "Revelations from TV Evangelists," *Dallas Times Herald,* Apr. 23, 1987, G3.

28. PR to All Staff, June 30, 1983; PR to All Staff, July 5, 1983, ROA. See BJ to Mrs. Willard Brooks, June 27, 1984; BJ to Raymond L. Williams, Mar. 1, 1984, ROA. HB int.

29. PR to Dan Quayle, Oct. 19, 1993; PR to Ileita C. Weikle, Aug. 19, 1993; PR to Mrs. Maude Steele, Jan. 18, 1999, ROA. See http://www.balaams-ass.com/journal/warnings/patrobsn.htm, Oct. 25, 1998.

30. HB int.; PR to Pat Tripp, Sept. 18, 1987, ROA.

31. PR to Pat Tripp, Sept. 18, 1987; PR to Bob Prigmore, Sept. 8, 1993; PR to Ken Pelissero, June 21, 1999, ROA. See, for example, BJ to Martha Tyree, Apr. 1, 1987; PR to W. Bogart Holland, Dec. 6, 1999, ROA.

32. PR int., Mar. 18, 2009. PR, *The Plan,* 138, 139. Robertson has frequently referred to his love of horses, and the lessons he learned from them, in his writings. See PR, *The Greatest Virtue,* 39-41. Bill Finley, "The Moralist Loves Racing," *New York Times,* Apr. 22, 2002, D1, D6. See Robertson's statement on gambling in PR, *Answers to 200 of Life's Most Probing Questions,* 225, 226. Finley, "The Moralist Loves Racing," D6.

33. http://www.patrobertson.com/index.asp, May 15, 2002. See "Robertson Race Horses Scratched After Critics Charge Hypocrisy," *Church and State,* June 2002, 16. Robertson acknowledged that gambling could be "addictive" and have a "pernicious effect" on people, but he refused to be stampeded on the subject: "I hesitate to say that gambling will keep someone out of heaven. . . . The Bible does not specifically condemn or condone gambling." *Bring It On,* 101, 102.

34. Bill Finley, "Robertson Selling His Horses in Response to Protests from His Followers," *New York Times,* May 9, 2002, D3.

35. Paxton quoted in Foege, *The Empire God Built,* 72. Insider quoted in Donovan, *Pat Robertson,* 108. VS int., Apr. 9, 2007; July 13, 2007.

36. PR to Joanne M. Gleichauf, Feb. 17, 1997, ROA. David Gyertson int.; SR int.; "Pat Robertson and Politics," *Christian Life,* Aug. 1986, 45. PR, *The Greatest Virtue,* 97. AL int.

37. DR int.; PR int., Mar. 18, 2008. SR int. See Robertson's description of his relationship with his mother, http://www.patrobertson.com/index.asp, May 20, 2009. Donovan, *Pat Robertson,* 13. PR int., Mar. 18, 2009; SR int.

38. SR int.; DR int.

39. PR int., Dec. 6, 2007; Oct. 18, 2007. "Passing the Right's Torch," *Church and State,* May 2006, 23. TM int.; see also Grant Babre int.; Ron Oates int.; David Gyertson int.

40. Vegh, "Robertson Hands Off CBN Operation to Son," *Virginian-Pilot,* Dec. 4, 2007, 1, 13. AL int.

41. PR int., Oct. 21, 2009. http://www.regent.edu/about_us/leadership/executive.cfm, Nov. 26, 2009.

42. RR int., Sept. 10, 2007; Keith Fournier int. Citation from Israel Ministry of Tourism, Ambassador's Award, 2004. "Pat Robertson: Founder and Chairman, The Christian Broadcasting Network," typed manuscript dated Aug. 13, 2003, ROA.

43. Barry Lynn int.; Turner, *Bill Bright and Campus Crusade for Christ,* 3. See Steven G. Vegh, "Building His Legacy on Religion, Politics," *Virginian-Pilot,* Mar. 22, 2005, A1; "Pat Robertson: Founder and Chairman, The Christian Broadcasting Network." Ben Kinchlow int., Mar. 19, 2008.

Index

—⟨∿∿⟩—

119, 373n.78; foreign policy statements, 100-104; and Freedom Council, 93-95, 96, 113, 370n.49; Iowa caucus, 97-98; issues and distractions, 99-104; and the label "charismatic," 110-11; and the label "televangelist," 111-12; Michigan Republican Convention, 95-96; personal attacks and Robertson family, 112-13, 122-23, 375n.96; and the press, 91, 96, 98-99, 108-12, 122-23, 370n.49, 374n.85, 374n.87; primary defeats, 118-20; Reed on, 124, 127, 186; and religious right leaders and celebrities, 92-93, 105-8, 314-15; and religious voters, 119; and Republican Convention in New Orleans, 120, 121-22, 123; and Republican Party platform, 120; and Robertson's charismatic/evangelical beliefs, 109-11, 308-9, 322-23; and *The 700 Club,* 48, 185; social agenda and family values platform, 100, 122; Super Tuesday primaries, 99, 114, 118-20; and the televangelist scandals, 114-18; and Weyrich, 91, 92; withdrawal, 186; reflections on, 119-24, 126, 176

Robertson, Pat [religious faith]: and the "Antichrist," 321, 322; Bedford-Stuyvesant ministry, 20-22, 24, 52, 337; charismatic beliefs and religious persona, 308-33, 409n.1; charismatic language, 318-24, 352; distancing himself from extremists, 310-12; distrust of theological liberalism, 312; and early charismatic movement, 16-20, 27, 312-13; ecumenism, 328-33; evangelical born-again experience, 12-20; and "evangelical" label, 310, 409n.5; and inductive Bible study, 15, 309-10, 409n.3; and Israel, 324-28, 367n.12, 411n.34; and the "leading of the Holy Spirit," 317-19; and miracles, 317; and Pentecostal/charismatic revival, 312-20, 328-33; and premillennialism, 311, 320-23, 411nn.34-35; and presidential campaign, 105, 308-9, 314-15; prophetic

interpretations and predictions, 19, 309, 317, 318-24; re-ordination (2000), 319-20; and Dede Robertson, 14, 308; and "Seed Faith," 289, 314, 316; at seminary, 15-20, 309, 321; and shepherding controversy, 75-77, 309, 310; and speaking in tongues, 16, 17-20; spiritual transformation and early ministry, 12-25, 337. *See also* Charismatic revival; Evangelicalism; Pentecostalism

Robertson, Timothy: on CBN as Christian organization, 59; and CBN cable programming, 43, 45, 189; as CBN president, 61, 116-17, 182-85, 187, 189; conception and birth, 10, 112-13; early life, 63, 65-66, 182; and The Family Channel/IFE, 190-91; on his grandfather Willis Robertson, 4, 64; and Regent University, 251; on Robertson and Jim Bakker, 33; on Robertson as father, 63; on Robertson's business ventures, 286; on Robertson's gaffes and controversial statements, 296; on Robertson's open mind and curiosity, 287; on Robertson's personality and presence, 59-60, 181; and Robertson's presidential campaign, 113; on Robertson's *700 Club* appearances, 181, 187; as *The 700 Club* co-host, 183, 187-88

Robertson Hospitality Center (New Orleans), 121, 122

Robinson, James, 86, 106, 220

Rock Church ministry (Virginia Beach), 82, 314

Rockefeller family and the "Trilateral Commission," 292

Roddy, Patrick, 201, 307

Roe v. Wade (1973), 68, 100

Rogers, Adrian, 131

Roman Catholics: and charismatic revival, 70, 75, 106, 143, 144, 330-33, 413nn.53-54; and Christian Coalition, 143-45, 380n.46, 413n.53; and Fournier at the ACLJ, 261, 263-64, 332; and Moral Majority, 132; Protestant-Catholic ecumenism,